The concept of "witness" is utterly important to Christian faith as a historic religion. It is essential to upon the people of God: to go and tell the story of God. To tell of Jesus, who came and lived among us. To announce that he is God's ultimate act of revelation, for in Jesus, God himself walked among humans. Ervin Budiselić's study touches on all the above and more. It is a thorough and competent exegetical analysis of Luke's use of the concept of "witness," framed by an informing background study of "witness" and its semantic connotations in both the Old and the New Testament. The study concludes with several pertinent pointers for the witness of the church today – a most needed hermeneutical step too often neglected. As such, this is a book that ought to be present in the classroom as well as the pulpit.

Marcel V. Măcelaru, PhD
Head of the Theology Department,
Director of the Ars Theologica Research Centre,
"Aurel Vlaicu" University of Arad, Romania

In this wide-ranging and insightful work, Ervin Budiselić explores an important theme in both parts of the Christian Bible: the practice of witness. This volume demonstrates in detail how the Hebrew Bible shifts the practice of witnessing in the court of law to the more explicitly theological environment of covenant-making and keeping. It then shows how that signal theological work undergirds developments in early Christianity as seen in the New Testament and especially Luke-Acts. For the first generations of Jesus followers, under the guidance of the divine Spirit, the content of the testimony becomes inextricably linked to the character of the witness. Budiselić methodically works through all the relevant biblical texts to show the profundity of Luke-Acts's thinking on the role of the witness in the life of the church. This study has sweeping implications for the contemporary church as it bears witness to its Lord in a religiously diverse society.

Mark W. Hamilton, PhD
Robert and Kay Onstead Professor of Biblical Studies,
Abilene Christian University, Texas, USA

Ervin Budiselić explores the important biblical, theological and hermeneutic concept of testimony. Giving special attention to that concept in Luke-Acts, the author presents the development of the theological theme of witnessing from the most convenient Old Testament texts through the younger deuterocanonical texts to the New Testament texts, showing the changes in the perception of the theological and anthropological perspective of the dynamics of witnessing. In comparing the Lukan concept of witness with the rest of the Bible, this book provides some new perspectives on the concept of witness but also reminds the church on her task of being a witness by faithfully emulating Jesus's life and ministry.

Maksimilijan Matjaž, PhD
Professor of New Testament,
University of Ljubljana, Slovenia

Uniqueness of the Concept of Witness in Lukan Writings within the Biblical Canon

Ervin Budiselić

Langham
ACADEMIC

Published 2024 by Langham Academic
An imprint of Langham Publishing
www.langhampublishing.org

Langham Publishing and its imprints are a ministry of Langham Partnership

Langham Partnership
PO Box 296, Carlisle, Cumbria, CA3 9WZ, UK
www.langham.org

ISBNs:
978-1-83973-791-6 Print
978-1-83973-990-3 ePub
978-1-83973-991-0 PDF

British Library Cataloguing-in-Publication Data
A catalogue record for this book is available from the British Library

ISBN: 978-1-83973-791-6

Cover & Book Design: projectluz.com

Contents

Acknowledgments

Above all, I am grateful to my Lord Jesus Christ for his calling to serve Him. I am not worthy of that heavenly calling. But no one is.

I am grateful to many people who made me who I am and because of whom I was able to finish my education. Well, I am not at the end of my journey, I have just started. I will not mention your names. God knows who you are, and you will get your acknowledgment on that Day.

I would also like to thank my mentors for their support in this work. Your advice and guidance were truly great.

Finally, special thanks to my wife, my kids, and my parents. I would not be able to finish my PhD without your sacrificial love and service. Thank you. I am in your debt.

Abbreviations

AB	Anchor Bible
AJPS	*Asian Journal of Pentecostal Studies*
AOTC	Apollos Old Testament Commentary
AYB	Anchor Yale Bible
BBR	*Bulletin for Biblical Research*
BCBC	Believers Church Bible Commentary
BCOTWP	Baker Commentary on the Old Testament Wisdom and Psalms
BDB	Brown-Driver-Briggs Hebrew Lexicon
BEB	*Baker Encyclopedia of the Bible*
BECNT	Baker Exegetical Commentary on the New Testament
BGNTL	Baker's Greek New Testament Library
BHS	*Biblia Hebraica Stuttgartensia*
BNTC	Black's New Testament Commentary
BSac	Bibliotheca Sacra
BST	Bible Speaks Today
BV	*Bogoslovni vestnik*
CBCOT	Cambridge Bible Commentaries on the Old Testament
CBQ	*Catholic Biblical Quarterly*
CCEB	Commentary Critical and Explanatory on the Whole Bible
CCGNT	Classic Commentaries on the Greek New Testament
CCS	Christocentric Commentary Series
CEV	Contemporary English Version

CHALOT	*Concise Hebrew and Aramaic Lexicon of the Old Testament*
COT	Commentary on the Old Testament
CPNIV	College Press NIV Commentary
DBLG	Dictionary of Biblical Languages with Semantic Domains: Greek
DBLH	Dictionary of Biblical Languages with Semantic Domains: Hebrew
DOTWPW	Dictionary of the Old Testament: Wisdom, Poetry and Writings
DSB	Daily Study Bible Series
ECC	Eerdmans Critical Commentary
EDB	Eerdmans Dictionary of the Bible
EDBT	Evangelical Dictionary of Biblical Theology
EDNT	Exegetical Dictionary of the New Testament
GHCLOT	*Gesenius' Hebrew-Chaldee Lexicon to the Old Testament*
GJCT	Global Journal of Classical Theology
HCOT	Historical Commentary on the Old Testament
HNTC	Holman New Testament Commentary
HT	Hebrew Text
IBC	Interpretation Bible Commentaries
IBCTP	Interpretation: A Bible Commentary for Teaching and Preaching
ICC	International Critical Commentary
IVPNTC	IVP New Testament Commentary Series
JBL	*Journal of Biblical Literature*
JETS	*Journal of the Evangelical Theological Society*
JRT	*Journal of Religious Thought*
JSS	*Journal of Semitic Studies*
KJV	King James Version
LES	Lexham English Septuagint
LTNB	Lexham Textual Notes on the Bible
LTW	Lexham Theological Wordbook
LXX	Septuagint

MT	Masoretic Text
NAC	New American Commentary
NASB	New American Standard Bible
NASB95	New American Standard Bible 1995
NET Bible	New English Translation
NICNT	New International Commentary on the New Testament
NICOT	New International Commentary on the Old Testament
NIGTC	New International Greek Testament Commentary
NIV	New International Version
NIVAC	NIV Application Commentary
NJPS	New Jewish Publication Society Translation
NKJV	New King James Version
NLT	New Living Translation
NovT	Novum Testamentum
NRSV	New Revised Standard Version
NT	New Testament
OT	Old Testament
OTL	Old Testament Library
OTS	Old Testament Survey Series
P	Peshitta
PCNT	Paideia Commentaries on the New Testament
PNTC	Pillar New Testament Commentary
REB	Revised English Bible
RQ	*Restoration Quarterly*
RSV	Revised Standard Version
T	Targum
TCBC	Tyndale Concise Bible Commentary
TDNT	*Theological Dictionary of the New Testament*
TDOT	*Theological Dictionary of the Old Testament*
TEV	Today's English Version (The Good News Bible)
TLNT	Theological Lexicon of the New Testament
TLOT	Theological Lexicon of the Old Testament
TPC	The Pulpit Commentary
TWOT	*Theological Wordbook of the Old Testament*
WBC	Word Biblical Commentary

WSNTDICT	*The Complete Word Study Dictionary: New Testament*
W&W	Word & World
YLT	Young's Literal Translation
ZAR	*Zeitschrift für Altorientalische und Biblische Rechtsgeschichte*

Introduction

In this research, we focus on the biblical concept of witness, and give special emphasis to the Lukan use of that concept. In this introductory part we will first introduce the importance of the concept of witness in the Bible and secondly, present the key question of our research. After that, we will present the *status quaestionis* regarding the topic of witness in Lukan writings and briefly present the outline of this research. Lastly, we will define and set limits for our treatment of the concept.

1. Importance of the concept of witness in the Bible

In the Bible, the concept of witness is present from Genesis to Revelation. Rare are biblical books where this concept is not found in *explicit* terms. Although the concept of witness in the OT is relevant and should inform the church's activity, the most relevant part of Scripture for the church to model its activity of witness on should be the NT. And while in his final speeches recorded in the NT, Jesus commanded his disciples to preach the good news (Mark 16:15), to make disciples (Matt 28:19) and to forgive or retain people's sins (John 20:23), in Lukan writings – Gospel and Acts, Jesus's final words to his disciples were specifically about their task to be his witnesses (Luke 24:48; Acts 1:8). Hence, we could say that the topic of witness in Lukan writings, especially in Acts, has a prominent place. Furthermore, the Lukan writings make up 25 percent of the NT thus making him the chief contributor to the NT. Taking these two factors together – the prominence of the topic of witness and the scope of Lukan writings – it seems reasonable to say that in studying the concept of witness in the NT, special attention or emphasis must be given to the Lukan writings.

In theological education we may learn that people often study history in order to reshape their present and pave the way for the future. In other words, to change or reform the present, we need to point out how "our present" has deviated from some particular ideal or norm of the past. Hence, people will go back to history, recover that past ideal, then expose this ideal to the present in order to claim the specific route that our present must be heading. In a sense, this dissertation has somewhat the same agenda. Through studying the concept of witness in Lukan writings within the wider biblical context, we want to recover the importance of the concept of witness for the life of the church: how the concept of witness in the Bible, especially as it is presented in Lukan writings, should inform, and shape the witnessing of the church today, and the life and work of the church in general.

2. The research question

In the past, there was a great tendency to read Luke's pneumatology through the eyes of Paul – particularly regarding whether the Spirit for Luke was merely a second grace distinct from the gift of salvation and granted subsequently from it, or a soteriological necessity. Furthermore, the charismatic theology of Luke is sometimes thought to have a dispensational limit, sometimes regarded as abnormal or secondary,[1] presumably because it comes from the genre of narrative and not from the didactic part of the NT.

The issue of Lukan pneumatology is important for the Lukan concept of witness because in the context of the Bible as a whole, Acts 1:8 offers unique requirements for being Jesus's witness: the reception of πνεῦμα ἅγιος "the Holy Spirit" and δύναμις "power." Acts 1:8 not only outlines the content of the book of Acts, but it is a crucial verse for understanding the Lukan concept of witness in general. These words of Jesus after his resurrection hold great significance because in the immediate context they are directed toward the eyewitnesses of his earthly ministry.[2] However, Acts describes several cases where people other than eyewitnesses receive the promised πνεῦμα

1. Stronstad, *Charismatic Theology*, 84.

2. Later in this work we will see that this point can be questioned. In other words, in the group that Jesus addresses in Acts 1, there might been those who were not the eyewitnesses of his entire ministry.

ἅγιος, which makes this relationship between Lukan pneumatology and the concept of witness interesting.

Based on this convergence, the primary question in this research is to explore the significance and impact of the πνεῦμα ἅγιος on the concept of witness in Luke's theology, that is, *why* Jesus makes reception of πνεῦμα ἅγιος a necessary condition for his disciples to be his witnesses in Acts 1:8, and *how* the πνεῦμα ἅγιος impacts their witness. Finding answers to these questions will eventually lead to a better understanding of the place and role that the πνεῦμα ἅγιος must have in the witnessing activity of the church and Christians today. The search for the answer to these questions requires several steps. The first step is to analyze the concept of witness and its aspects in its wider biblical context: the OT and NT. After establishing the wider context, the second step is to analyze the Lukan concept of witness: its aspects and characteristics. Through the comparison of Luke with the rest of the Bible, it will be possible to argue the degree to which the Lukan concept of witness in Luke/Acts is similar or different. Based on the results, it will be possible to take the third step, which is to argue for the theological implications of the Lukan concept of witness for the church today.

3. *Status quaestionis*

In Lukan scholarship, the concept of witness is treated in three different ways. First, some authors focus on Lukan pneumatology, and as part of that discussion refer to the Lukan concept of witness. This discussion about Lukan pneumatology and surrounding issues such as the background for Luke's understanding of the Spirit, the purpose of the Spirit in believers' lives, etc., has prevailed since the 1920s and in our time it is represented by James D. G. Dunn, Gonzalo Haya-Prats,[3] Robert P. Menzies, John M. Penney, Max Turner, James B. Shelton, Ju Hur[4] and others. Additionally, the Lukan concept

3. His dissertation was originally written in 1967, translated to French in 1975, and to English in 2011.

4. James D. G. Dunn, *Baptism in Holy Spirit and Jesus and Spirit*; Haya-Prats, *Empowered Believers*; Menzies, *Empowered for Witness;* Penney, *Lukan Pneumatology*; Turner, *Power from on High*; Shelton, *Mighty in Word*; Hur, *Dynamic Reading.*

of witness is analyzed as part of the wider study of Lukan theology which may or may not include his pneumatology.[5]

Second, a discussion of the Lukan concept of witness may appear as part of the general study of that concept in the NT. So, Allison A. Trites[6] offered a survey of the concept of witness in NT writings, focusing primarily on the legal aspect of witness and lawsuit motif which originates from the OT, especially from Isaiah 40–55. As part of his research, he discusses the concept of witness in the book of Acts but places the concept of witness in Luke alongside those in the other Synoptic Gospels. His work is primarily of a comparative nature, but in the framework of the NT. But more often the Lukan concept of witness is analyzed within the context of the Lukan writings alone[7] or authors have conducted theological and/or exegetical research strictly on Luke 24:48 and Acts 1:8.[8]

Third, some researchers are focused on a particular element of the witness in Acts. For example: Trites analyzes "two witness, motifs," Daniel R. Schwartz, Earle E. Ellis, Bertram L. Melbourne, Thomas S. Moore, and Frank Jabini[9] analyze the fulfilment of "to the end of the earth" phrase from Acts 1:8, etc., and David L. Tiede[10] wrote about "Theo-Political Claims of Christian Witness" based on Acts 1:6–8.

The dominant methodology in some of these studies (Dunn, Menzies, Haya-Prats, Turner, Stronstad) is historical-critical, but their emphasis is on tradition, source and/or redaction criticism. If the methodology is more literary-critical (giving more attention to the synchronic analysis of the text), attention is often focused predominantly on Luke/Acts without giving much attention to the wider biblical context of witnessing (Thayil, Kyaligonza, Shelton, O'Reilly). Even when the wider biblical concept is taken into

5. Stronstad, *Charismatic Theology*; O'Reilly, *Word and Sign in Acts*; Marshal and Peterson, "Spirit of Prophecy as Power"; Thompson, *Acts of Risen Jesus*; Johnson, *Challenge of Luke-Acts*.

6. Trites, *NT Concept of Witness*.

7. de Dietrich, "You Are My Witnesses"; Kelly, "Development of Witness"; Gaventa, "You Will Be My Witnesses"; Aletti, "Testimoni del Risorto"; etc.

8. Thayil, "Jesus in Luke 24,48 and Acts 1,8"; Kyaligonza, "You Will be My Witnesses"; etc.

9. Schwartz, "End of the ΓH"; Ellis, "End of Earth"; Melbourne, "Acts 1:8 Re-Examined"; Moore, "To the End of Earth"; Jabini, "Witness to the End of World"

10. Tiede, "Acts 1:6–8", W&W.

consideration (OT and/or NT), the dominant approach is diachronic (tradition, source, and redaction criticism).

Realizing that every approach has its own limitations, and one research project cannot employ all methodologies and approaches, in this work we will study the Lukan concept of witness within the wider biblical context. Concretely, in order to realize the importance and significance of πνεῦμα ἅγιος and δύναμις in Lukan writings for his concept of witness, we will first analyze different aspects of that concept within the wider biblical context, and then compare it to that of Luke. For this purpose, we will use some works that are particularly focused on the study of the concept of witness in the OT such as Wells, Czander, and Bovati.[11]

This survey of methodology furthermore demonstrates the topical/thematical challenge that is ahead of us. Namely, the *status quaestionis* on the Lukan concept of witness is predominantly, but not exclusively, connected with the book of Acts, especially Acts 1:8, and how the gift of the Spirit at Pentecost is connected to the task of witness. Max Turner offered an excellent summary of various understandings of Lukan pneumatology, pointing out areas of agreement and disagreement.[12] Turner notes that scholars appear to agree on five things. First, the essential background for Luke's pneumatological material is Jewish and deeply rooted in the OT. Second, the Spirit, for Luke, is the uniting motif and driving force within Lucan salvation history and legitimizes the mission to which this history leads. Third, the Spirit is the Spirit of Prophecy, and in Acts especially it is defined as an empowering for witness. Four, Luke has little interest in the Spirit as the power of spiritual, ethical and religious renewal of the individual.[13] Five, Luke's understanding of the Holy Spirit goes beyond Judaism by giving the Holy Spirit Christocentric functions in the sense that he makes the Spirit the chief witness to the Christ event, and also in presenting Jesus as the one who pours out this Spirit in God's place as his own executive power.

11. Wells, *Law of Testimony*; Czander, "You are my Witnesses"; Bovati, *Re-Establishing Justice*.

12. Turner, "Spirit of Prophecy as Power," 328–332.

13. However, this "little interest" had been differently interpreted: for Schweizer and Menzies this meant that Luke has virtually no interest in this regard; Haya-Prats concluded that the Spirit has some role in the life of an individual; and some like James D. G. Dunn have attempted to show that the focus of Luke's pneumatology was a new covenant life of sonship.

Turner also delineates the areas where scholars tend to disagree with each other. We can label these areas as *what*, *why* and *when*. Regarding *what*, the debate is over whether the Spirit in Acts is Joel's "Spirit of prophecy" alone, or is it a gift that comprises more than just a prophecy? Regarding *why*, there seem to be three possible views of the purpose of the baptism of the Spirit. The Spirit is given: a) exclusively for the mission; there is no connection with soteriology, miracles or the ethical renewal of an individual, b) primarily as empowering for mission, but also to benefit the church (guidance, different blessing, etc.), c) for all the benefits mentioned under b), but the Spirit also plays a soteriological and transforming role in the life of the individual believer and the church. Regarding *when* the baptism of the Spirit is received, the possible answers are that people receive the baptism of the Spirit: a) as *donum superadditum*, an additional gift received after salvation (usually through laying of hands), b) in water baptism (sacramentalistic position), c) in the process of repentance, faith and water baptism, or d) the book of Acts does not give us consistent answer regarding when people receive the Spirit.[14]

For the purpose of our research, we do not have to pursue all the details of this debate. We instead focus on the general impact of *πνεῦμα* and *δύναμις* on the concept of witness. The general frame of the debate is that *πνεῦμα* and *δύναμις* modify the concept of witness in Lukan writings by enabling witnesses to testify both in words and deeds. On one level, Jesus empowered by *πνεῦμα* and *δύναμις* is a model for the early church. Shepherd[15] observes that "[j]ust as Jesus in his earthly ministry was 'full of the Holy Spirit' (Luke 4:1), went 'in the power of the Spirit' (Luke 4:14) and was 'anointed' by the Spirit (Luke 4:18), so now Jesus continues to act in the Spirit." Stronstad points out that Jesus being anointed with the Spirit was a prophet powerful in both works and word (Luke 24:19), so his disciples baptized with the Spirit will also be prophets powerful in both works and word.[16] On that note, Russell also says that Acts 1:4–8 promises an anointing for a prophetic ministry of "forthtelling," continuing Jesus's prophetic proclamation of the eschatological jubilee."[17] On this basis we can conclude with Shelton that an "important

14. Turner, "Spirit of Prophecy as Power", 337–338, 340–347.
15. Shepherd, *Narrative Function*, 154.
16. Stronstad, *Prophethood of all Believers*, 64–65.
17. Russell, *Anointing with Holy Spirit*, 57.

aspect of Luke's pneumatology is that he sees the experience of Jesus with the Holy Spirit as archetypical for believers. Jesus, like his witnesses in the infancy narratives (Luke 1–2) and his subsequent followers, relied on the fullness of the Spirit to accomplish his ministry."[18]

On a second level, the debate is whether all church members participated in the same way in Jesus's paradigm of witnessing, or was this participation only for selected individuals in the early church? This question is closely connected with the purpose of the baptism in the Spirit in Lukan writings. Based on the answers one offers to these questions, one can find different applications for today. Scholars like Menzies and Menzies observe that Luke consistently portrays the Spirit as the source of power for service:

> Luke repeatedly portrays *dynamis* as the source of miracles of healing, exorcism, and marvellous deeds.[19] Most decisively, whenever Luke employs the collocation of *pneuma* (Spirit) and *dynamis*, he has a combination of prophetic phenomena (inspired speech and/or special revelation) and miraculous activity in view.[20] Since the promise of Pentecostal empowering is extended to all of God's servants (Acts 2:17–18), this text is of special significance for the contemporary Church.[21]

Menzies and Menzies argue that Luke never attributes soteriological functions to the Spirit[22] nor is the Spirit the source of moral transformation.[23] Conversely, Luke describes the gift of the Spirit exclusively in charismatic terms, as the source of power for effective witness.[24] If that is the case, then all believers who receive the baptism in the Spirit (whether apostles or lay believers back then, and clergy and laity in our day and time) have equal share in the Acts 1:4–8 mandate, and can manifest and expect the same results.

18. Shelton, *Mighty in Word,* 157.
19. Luke 4:36; 5:17; 6:19; 8:46; 9:1; Acts 4:7; 6:8.
20. Luke 1:17, 35; 4:14; 24:49; Acts 1:8; 10:38.
21. Menzies and Menzies, *Spirit and Power*, 146–147.
22. Menzies and Menzies, *Spirit and Power*, 70.
23. Menzies and Menzies, 89.
24. Menzies and Menzies, 70.

Haya-Prats follows Menzies and Menzies by arguing that Luke never ascribes miracles to the Holy Spirit.[25] Accordingly, the Spirit is the source of the message, the divine power that enables believers to proclaim the gospel, and it is δύναμις that produces extraordinary phenomena such as healing, exorcism or any other superhuman phenomena that can be perceived by the senses. However,

> [t]he consequences of this abiding fullness of the Spirit surpass the *strictly* prophetic manifestations: at times they will be manifested as power, other times as wisdom, as joy, as comfort, and as testimony . . . It is necessary to show the content of the gift of the Holy Spirit because the interpretation falls easily into one of the extremes: at times it is interpreted as the giving of the sanctifying Spirit, of which Paul speaks to us, while at other times it is reduced to a prophetic charisma, in the most restricted sense of phrase.[26]

Such a view enables him to conclude that the promise of Acts 1:8 concerning the power of the Spirit for testimony does not contain Jesus's entire understanding of the sending of the Spirit. On Pentecost, Peter promises that same gift of the Spirit to all who are baptized, even though they are not explicitly called to be witnesses. Finally, a gift of the Spirit equal to Pentecost is present at Cornelius's conversion, yet again this gift does not explicitly make him a witness. If all who receive the gift of the Spirit do not become witnesses, then this ministry is limited, and in Haya-Prats' case[27] the mission of testimony is limited to the apostles.

Like Haya-Prats, Max Turner points to the wideness of the Spirit's work outside the circle of people mentioned in Luke 24 and Acts 1.[28] On this basis, he concludes that

25. Haya-Prats, *Empowered Believers*, 33–34.

26. Haya-Prats, 53–54.

27. Haya-Prats, 65–66.

28. Turner, *Power from on High*, 345. "Even if we restrict ourselves to the circle of those addressed in Luke 24 and Acts 1, we find that the Spirit also gave them discernment and guidance in church matters (cf. e.g. 5.3, 9; 15.28). Beyond the circle of those disciples, we could multiply such instances, the Spirit giving wisdom, direction and encouragement to the church (6.3, 5; 9.31; 11.24, 28; 13:52; 15.28; 20.28), personal guidance (20.23; 21.4, 11) and so on" (Turner, *Power from on High*, 344).

> while empowering for mission is the aspect of the gift of the Spirit to the disciples that is most specifically focused in Luke 24.49 and Acts 1.8, we cannot say the Pentecostal gift to them was "empowering for witness" *alone*. And if the promised Spirit of prophecy is envisaged to enable activities other than empowerment for witness, we cannot guarantee that Luke thought all Christians received the Spirit primarily as such empowering.[29]

And on that basis, Turner further argues:

> But Luke does not in fact portray the whole church as actively involved in witness . . . and he was well aware that the same gifts could as readily fuel the preaching and teaching which built up and directed the Christian church in its walk with God (9.31; 11.24; 15:32 . . .). Thus the Spirit was either more than simply "empowering for mission", or this last must at least be taken sufficiently broadly to include the building up of God's people. Furthermore, Luke is aware of the church being served by the spiritual gifts of wisdom (e.g. 6.3, 5) and revelation (e.g. 5.1–10; 11.28; 15:28[?]; 20:28[?]), outside of the context of witness, preaching or teaching.[30]

The consequence of Menzies and Menzies's view is that all who receive baptism in the Spirit (can) participate in witnessing. Haya-Prats and Turner, on the other hand, via different routes conclude that baptism in the Spirit does not necessarily imply participation in the task of witnessing. These examples show that the debate is complex, and how, in essence, our understanding of the concept of witness in Luke/Acts depends on our view of Lukan pneumatology. Consequently, how we choose to apply whatever Luke writes, an additional dimension of this discussion, will be guided by these assumptions. Moreover, even if a particular view is argued, that does not mean that scholars will necessarily claim the Lukan concept of witness is applicable or mandatory in the same way for the church today.

When we combine methodological approaches with the different understandings of Lukan pneumatology and their impact on the concept of

29. Turner, *Power from on High*, 345 (emphasis original).

30. Turner, *Power from on High*, 432.

witness, we see that a) Luke presents a pattern according to which the oral proclamation of the gospel has been confirmed by signs and wonders, b) the Spirit himself provides the witness through signs and wonders, and c) the Spirit is a second witness (in conjunction with apostles and OT Scriptures), according to the pattern from Deuteronomy that requires that testimony must be based on two or three witnesses. However, we will approach this pneumatological debate from a different standpoint: by studying various aspects of the concept of witness in the Bible and comparing the results to that concept in Lukan writings. Based on research results we will make our limited contribution to this debate.

4. The outline of the research

Besides the introduction, conclusion and summary, this research has four major parts: study of the concept of witness in the OT, study of the concept of witness in the NT, unique aspects of the concept of witness in Lukan writings, and application.

Chapter 1 provides introductory analysis of Acts 1:8 and the usage of *πνεῦμα* and *δύναμις* in Luke/Acts. This sets the stage for analyzing the concept in the OT. Chapter 2 introduces the concept of witness in the OT through a study of the etymology and semantics of the Hebrew words for witness in the OT. Chapter 3 analyzes the concept of witness in the OT, and chapter 4 brings to bear the analysis of all these texts from chapter 3 in the LXX, noticing especially where LXX deviates or differs from MT. Based on the preceding analysis, chapter 5 will summarize the results by presenting major aspects of the concept of witness in the OT. Here we will offer a revision of the concept of witness by introducing two additional categories: the temporal aspects of witness, and the mode of witness. Since the concept of witness is not present only on a phenomenological level (where explicit Hebrew words for witness appear), in chapter 6 we will analyze the semantic range of the concept of witness based on selected parts of the OT. This dynamic aspect together with phenomenological level of witnessing will enable us to see how deeply the concept of witness is interwoven with other significant theological topics in the OT.

Part two of the study begins with chapter 7, which introduces the concept of witness in the NT through a study of the etymology and semantics of the Greek words for witness. Chapter 8 analyzes texts utilizing the concept of witness in the NT, and chapter 9 summarizes the results by presenting major aspects of the concept of witness in the NT. Here we will also group witnesses according to their categories and offer a revision of the concept of witness, based on categories of the temporal aspect of witness, and the mode of witness. Chapter 10 analyzes the semantic range of the concept of witness in the NT based on selected phenomena. Like in the OT, the dynamic aspect together with phenomenological level of witnessing will enable us to see how deeply the concept of witness is interwoven with other significant theological topics in the NT.

Part three of the study begins with chapter 11, which discusses unique aspects of the concept of witness in Lukan writings. First, we will repeat major views and issues connected with the debate about the Lukan concept of witness. Second, we will interpret the significance of the πνεῦμα ἅγιος for the concept of witness in Luke's theology. We will do this by analyzing the development of the concept of witness in Acts, evaluating the role of miracles as accompaniment to verbal proclamation, discussing why Luke portrays apostles as the predominant witnesses in Acts, and establishing the significance of the Old Testament for Luke's concept of witness. Based on that interpretation, we will be able to compare the concept of witness in the Lukan writings with the wider biblical context and see similarities and differences between the Lukan writings and the rest of Scripture.

Part four of the study (chapter 12) addresses applications drawn from the study. Here we will suggest in what ways the Lukan concept of witness, notably, the book of Acts, provides a prophetic vision for the church today.

In the study of this topic, we will be focused not so much on a *diachronic* (although this approach is not excluded), but on a *synchronic* approach. Hence, primarily we will use analysis, synthesis, comparison, and literary analysis of the texts. We will use analysis when we study the Bible to collect data, and synthesis when we draw conclusions, arguments or claims based on results of analysis. Comparison will be used when we discuss similarities and differences between the concepts of witness in various biblical books from both testaments, and literary analysis (etymology, semantic, syntax, structure, etc.) will be used in analysis of biblical texts, particularly in discussion about Acts 1:8.

5. Some preliminary remarks, definitions and delimitations

As part of this introduction, we set the following definitions and limits. First, when we talk about the biblical concept of witness, we are referring to the topic of witness that is present in the Bible. By studying this topic, our goal is to see how the Bible understands, develops, and defines that concept. While the concept of witness as it is presented and developed in the Bible remains the same, our understanding, interpretations, and definitions of it might change in time.

Second, when we use the word "witness," due to the complexity of its usage in English, this word sometimes signifies activity "the act of giving witness," or a person "who gives witness." Occasionally, witness can signify the content of the message that is given – testimony. Hence, the concept of witness includes "witness," "witnessing activity", and "testimony."

Third, although the topic of witness could be analyzed in various different ways, in this work we will limit ourselves to the study of this topic within the Protestant biblical canon. This approach has certain disadvantages,[31] but limitation to certain methodologies, approaches and scope of work is necessary. For translation of Hebrew and Greek texts into English, we will mostly use the NRSV and the NIV translations. The NIV was selected as highly used and respected translation in Protestant-evangelical Christianity, and the NRSV as highly used and respected translation in wider ecumenical circles.

Finally, a word about the work itself. Originally, the plan was to study the Lukan concept of witness primarily within the context of discussion about Lukan pneumatology, and to use the biblical context as a sort of appendix providing background information. Hence, this work would then have looked more like that of Menzies, Haya-Prats or Thayil and Kyaligonza. But, in agreement with my mentors, we decided to give the biblical context of witness a significant space in this research. In this way we can situate the Lukan concept of witness within the wider biblical canon. This will

31. "For example, an appeal to the canon, a carefully circumscribed body of literature, does not settle the question of sources for biblical history. The boundaries of the canon are not the boundaries of the source material for Israelite or primitive Christian history. Restrict yourself to the canon and you will not understand the canon. Extra-biblical literature is the basis of chronology, archaeology illuminates the daily life and cultic fixtures of ancient Israel, and inscriptions and Near Eastern annals give the course of world history in which Israelite history must be fitted" (Krentz, *Historical-Critical Method*, 48).

allow us to determine Luke's unique contributions to the concept of witness. Consequently, we are able to contribute to the discussion of Lukan pneumatology without being involved in that debate too extensively.

CHAPTER 1

Introductory Analysis of Acts 1:8

Since the primary question in this research is to explore the significance and impact of πνεῦμα ἅγιος on the concept of witness in Luke's theology, we should examine why Jesus makes reception of πνεῦμα ἅγιος a necessary condition for his disciples to be his witnesses in Acts 1:8, and how πνεῦμα ἅγιος impacts their witness. Here, then, we will first focus our attention on Acts 1:8, and then the usage of πνεῦμα and δύναμις in the context of witnessing in Luke/Acts.

1. The problem of Acts 1:8

Acts 1:8 is probably the most significant passage for the book of Acts. It provides the key for understanding the work,[1] by providing its outline – how the church was spread from Jerusalem, to Judea, to Samaria and to the end of the earth. But more significantly, this passage is the key text for understanding the specifics of the Lukan concept of witness in Acts, because it provides a crucial bridge between Jesus's ministry in Luke's gospel and continuation of his ministry through his disciples in the book of Acts:[2]

> ἀλλὰ λήμψεσθε δύναμιν ἐπελθόντος τοῦ ἁγίου πνεύματος ἐφ' ὑμᾶς, καὶ ἔσεσθέ μου μάρτυρες. "But you will receive power

1. Ash and Oster, *Djela Apostolska*, 26.

2. The book of Acts portrays what Jesus continues to do and teach, even though his earthly life is over – that Jesus is the real subject of the words and works recounted in Acts. "He continues to do and teach through his witnesses, and the Acts of the Apostles is the account of this witness to Jesus in word and deed on the part of Jesus's disciples" (O'Reilly, *Word and Sign in Acts*, 15).

when the Holy Spirit has come upon you; and you will be my witnesses" (NRSV).

A brief grammatical analysis of Acts 1:8 shows us that, first, the text has two main clauses: "you will receive power" and "you will be my witnesses." In the first main clause, the main verb is λήμψεσθε "will receive," and in the second main clause, the main verb is ἔσεσθέ "you will be" in connection with becoming *μάρτυρες* "witnesses." Acts 1:8 contains three verbs whose tenses and grammatical voices reveal the internal dynamic of the text: 1) λήμψεσθε "will receive" (future indicative middle, plural) in connection with *δύναμιν* "power;" 2) ἐπελθόντος "having come" (aorist active participle, singular) in connection with *τοῦ ἁγίου πνεύματος* "the Holy Spirit" and; 3) ἔσεσθέ "you will be" (future indicative middle, plural) in connection with disciples being *μου μάρτυρες* "my witnesses." On this basis we can conclude that the first and foundational action that precedes everything else is the "coming" of the Holy Spirit. As the result of his coming, the disciples will "receive" power when the Holy Spirit "comes" on them, and they "will be" his witnesses. Jesus here clearly emphasizes that it is not only important to receive *ὁ ἅγιος πνεῦμα* but also the *δύναμις* that he brings, and this reception qualifies disciples to be witnesses. Syntactically speaking, the connection between *δύναμις* and *μάρτυς* is closer than the connection between *ὁ ἅγιος πνεῦμα* and *μάρτυς*. For this reason, it is necessary to observe the concept of witness not only through the prism of the coming of "the Holy Spirit," but also through reception of the "power." Additional argument for this claim can be found in Luke 24:49, where Jesus speaks about "sending upon you what my Father promised" (obviously, the Holy Spirit), but also about "clothing with power from on high." The question: why does Luke on two occasions make such a careful distinction between the coming of "the Spirit" and "power" in connection to witnessing? Because of this distinction, we need to observe the concept of witness in the Lukan writings through the prism of both of these elements.

2. The usage of *πνεῦμα* and *δύναμις* in the context of witnessing in Luke-Acts

Discussing Luke's usage of *πνεῦμα* and *δύναμις* in the context of witnessing is part of a wider debate about Lukan pneumatology which has continued since the 1920s.[3] According to William H. Shepherd this debate includes two important questions: a) what (or who) is the Holy Spirit?, and b) what does the Holy Spirit do? Answering the second question, Shepherd says that "there is a broad agreement that for Luke, the Spirit is the Spirit of prophecy."[4] Although the scholarly consensus is such, there is no agreement on the issue of what exactly this Spirit does. Hence, our focus here will be on the usage of the πνεῦμα and δύναμις in the context of witnessing. First, we will observe in general Luke's usage of πνεῦμα and δύναμις in his writings. Second, we will identify texts where πνεῦμα and δύναμις appear together, especially in the context of witness.

2.1 Lukan usage of πνεῦμα and δύναμις

In his gospel, Luke uses the word πνεῦμα thirty-six times. Out of that number, seventeen times πνεῦμα refers to the Holy Spirit,[5] twelve times to demonic (evil, unclean) spirits,[6] four times to spirits of different people,[7] two times to a ghost (Luke 24:37, 39), and once to Jesus's spirit (Luke 23:46). Activities and effects of the Holy Spirit can be summarized in the following ways: a) three times filling with the Spirit results in speaking: εἶπον "said" (Luke 1:41 and 10:21) and ἐπροφήτευσεν λέγων "prophesied saying" (Luke 1:67); b) two times the Spirit is presented as the one who guides (Luke 2:27; 4:2); c) twice the Spirit is the one who gives revelation: χρηματίζω "make known a divine revelation" (Luke 2:25, 26); d) several things are mentioned only once: "baptism in the Holy Spirit" (Luke 3:16); the descent of the Spirit on Jesus (Luke 3:22); the Father's giving of the Spirit to those who seek him (Luke 11:13); blasphemy against the Spirit (Luke 12:10); the Spirit teaching the disciples what to say (Luke 12:12); the condition of being filled with the Holy Spirit (Luke 4:1), and once being filled with "the Spirit and power" (Luke 4:14).

---

3. Hur, *Dynamic Reading*, 13.

4. Shepherd, *Narrative Function*, 11.

5. Luke 1:15, 35, 41, 67; 2:25, 26, 27; 3:16, 22; 4:1, 2, 14, 18; 10:21; 11:13; 12:10, 12.

6. Luke 4:33, 36; 6:18; 7:21; 8:2, 29; 9:39, 42; 10:20; 11:24, 26; 13:11.

7. Luke 1:17 (Elijah); 1:47 (Mary); 1:80 (John); 8:55 (human spirit – dead girl). The meaning in Luke 1:80 is ambiguous because it can refer to the human spirit or divine Spirit. Also, "Elijah's spirit" can be understood as human spirit or divine Spirit (Luke 1:17).

In the Gospel of Luke δύναμις appears fifteen times, and we can divide these texts into three groups. In the first group δύναμις appears together with the word πνεῦμα: in Luke 1:17 as the description of the ministry of John the Baptist, in Luke 1:35 as an angel informing Mary that she will conceive the child, and in Luke 4:14 as the description of Jesus's ministry. In the second group, δύναμις is connected with miracles and exorcisms: in Luke 4:36 δύναμις in connection with ἐξουσία refers to exorcisms, and in Luke 9:1 the result of δύναμις and ἐξουσία are healings and exorcisms; in Luke 5:17; 6:19; 8:46 the result of δύναμις are healings, and in Luke 10:13 and Luke 19:37 δύναμις stands for miracles. In the third group δύναμις has different meanings: in Luke 10:19 it stands for the enemy's power;[8] in Luke 21:26 it stands for "the powers of the heavens;" in Luke 21:27 Jesus is coming with δύναμις and "glory," and in Luke 22:69 Jesus's future position is described as sitting ἐκ δεξιῶν τῆς δυνάμεως τοῦ θεοῦ "at the right hand of the power of God;" and finally, in Luke 24:49 Jesus's speech about ἐξ ὕψους δύναμιν "power from on high," undoubtedly which is connected with "the promise of the Father," the Holy Spirit.

In the book of Acts, Luke uses πνεῦμα seventy times. Out of that number, fifty-five times πνεῦμα refers to the Holy Spirit,[9] eight times to the evil spirits,[10] three times to the human spirit (Acts 7:59; 17:16, 18:25), twice to spiritual beings in general (Acts 23:8, 9), and twice either to the human spirit or the divine Spirit (Acts 19:21; 20:22). The Spirit's activity that is mentioned the most (twenty-three times) is the "coming of the Spirit," that is, baptism, filling, receiving, or anointing of the Spirit.[11] Another activity that is mostly attributed to the Spirit is speaking (fifteen times): eight times the Spirit directly speaks,[12] and seven times the Spirit speaks or will speak through people.[13] Furthermore, seven times people are described as being

8. Δύναμις again appears together with ἐξουσία, yet here ἐξουσία, which Jesus gave to his apostles, is victorious over δύναμις of the enemy.

9. It is debatable whether Acts 18:25; 19:21 and 20:22 refer to the Holy Spirit or human spirit. If 18:25 refers to human spirit and other two verses to the Holy Spirit, then the total number of references on the Holy Spirit in Acts is fifty-seven (Hur, *Dynamic Reading*, 132).

10. Acts 5:16; 8:7; 16:16, 18; 19:12, 13, 15, 16.

11. Acts 1:5, 8; 2:4, 17, 18, 33, 38; 4:31; 8:15, 17, 18, 19; 9:17; 10:38, 44, 45, 47; 11:15, 16; 15:8; 19:2 (two times), 6.

12. Acts 5:32; 8:29; 10:19; 11:12; 13:2; 20:23; 21:11; 28:25.

13. Acts 1:2, 16; 2:4; 4:8, 25; 11:28; 21:4.

filled with the Spirit.[14] Also, the presence of the Spirit often results in having a particular attribute or ability: wisdom (Acts 6:3, 10), faith (Acts 6:5; 11:24), joy (Acts 13:52). On one occasion, filling with the Spirit is connected with none of these things but with the recovery of sight (Acts 9:17). Three times the text mentions "lying," "resisting," or putting the Spirit to "a test,"[15] and seven times the Spirit is connected with different activities: carrying Philip away (Acts 8:39), bringing comfort (Acts 9:31), sending people (Acts 13:4), being involved in making decisions (Acts 15:28), forbidding something (Acts 16:6, 7), and appointing leaders in the church (Acts 20:28). From this short overview, it is noticeable that the most prominent activities of the Spirit in Acts are the coming and filling with the Spirit, and speaking. However, the activity of speaking is most prominent in Acts because sometimes coming and filling with the Spirit[16] and the condition of being filled with the Spirit,[17] result in some form of speaking.

In the book of Acts *δύναμις* appears ten times. Three times *δύναμις* refers to the miracles (2:22; 8:13; 19:11), three times from the context we can see that it refers to miracles (4:33; 6:8; 10:38), three times *δύναμις* is not clearly identified (1:8; 3:12; 4:7), although in Acts 3:12 and 4:7 *δύναμις* appears in the context of debates about miracles. In Acts 8:10 *δύναμις* appears as part of the description of Simon the Sorcerer, which again suggests the connection with the miraculous realm. Just as in Luke's gospel, we have examples where *πνεῦμα* and *δύναμις* appear together: in Acts 1:8 as a description of the future ministry of Jesus's disciples and Acts 10:38 as a description of Jesus's earthly ministry. The significance of this juxtaposition we will discuss next.

2.2 The joint usage of *πνεῦμα* and *δύναμις*

Occasionally, as we have already seen, Luke brings *πνεῦμα* and *δύναμις* together. He uses the terms together in his gospel when introducing major characters and their ministries into the story. So, John the Baptist will go

14. Acts 6:3, 5, 10; 7:55; 11:24; 13:9, 52.

15. Acts 5:3, 9; 7:51.

16. Acts 1:8 "witnessing" (*ἔσεσθέ μου μάρτυρες*); Acts 2:17, 18 "prophesying" (*προφητεύω*); Acts 4:31 and 10:45 (although 10:44, 47; 11:15, 16 and 15:8 refer to glossolalia mentioned in 10:45) "proclaiming," "speaking" (*λαλέω*); 19:6 "speaking" and "prophesying" (*λαλέω* + *προφητεύω*).

17. Acts 6:10 "speaking" (*λαλέω*); Acts 7:55 and 13:9 "said" (*εἶπον*).

before Jesus "with the spirit and power of Elijah" (Luke 1:17), and his ministry will be to return people back to God.[18] Mary will be impregnated as the result of the coming of the Holy Spirit and power (Luke 1:35), and she will give birth to the Messiah. After the temptation in the desert, Jesus begins his ministry *τῇ δυνάμει τοῦ πνεύματος* "in the power of the Spirit" (Luke 4:14). The immediate context establishes the meaning: Jesus is described in verse 15 as the one who *διδάσκω* "teaches," and in Luke 4:18–19 as the one who is *ἀποστέλλω* "sent" with a specific purpose, and that includes both *εὐαγγελίζω* "proclaim the good news" and *κηρύσσω* "proclaim." Based on the context of Luke 4, we can see that Jesus's ministry up to this point included both (verbal) proclamation of the kingdom of God, and miracles (Luke 4:18–27).

In Acts, Luke introduces another group – Jesus's disciples – who must follow the same pattern of reception of "the Spirit" and "power" (Acts 1:8). Finally, Acts 10:38 connects Jesus's anointing with *πνεῦμα* and *δύναμις* for the purpose of "doing good" and "healing all who were under the power of the devil" (NIV),[19] and offers another summary of Jesus's ministry similar to Luke 4:14.

Additionally, Luke 24:49 where Jesus mentions "promise of the Father" and "power from on high" can also be taken as a text that belongs in this category. Based on these texts, we can see that all major characters in the story are introduced with *πνεῦμα* and *δύναμις*. Yet two of them (John the Baptist and Mary) are not attributed any miracles (unless we consider Jesus's conception as Mary's miracle),[20] and all characters except Mary were involved in the ministry. All characters participated in the activity of testifying – even Mary (cf. Luke 1:46–55; 2:51).

In several examples we have an explicit connection between the concept of witness and *πνεῦμα* and/or *δύναμις*.[21] Luke 24:48–49 and Acts 1:8 describe

---

18. The ministry of John the Baptist announced in Luke 1:17 was marked with bold proclamation which includes the aspect of witnessing, yet his ministry, according to John 10:41, did not include the performance of miracles.

19. Interestingly, in verse 38 Peter mentions only that Jesus "did good" and "healed all who were oppressed by the devil." He does not mention Jesus's activity in terms of preaching/teaching, although in verse 36 Peter mentions that God *εὐαγγελίζω* the message of peace through Jesus Christ.

20. For example, (Shelton, *Mighty in Word*, 75) considers Jesus's conception (Luke 1:35), Simeon's identification of Jesus as Messiah (Luke 2:22–35), glossolalia at Pentecost (Acts 2:4), Stephen's vision (Acts 7:55), etc. as "miracles."

21. Luke 24:48–49; Acts 1:8; 4:33; 5:32; 6:3; 10:38–39; 15:8; 20:23.

the future ministry of the disciples. In Luke 24:48–49, Jesus identifies his disciples as witnesses because they were witnesses of his life and ministry, and instructs them to wait on πνεῦμα and δύναμις. Likewise, Acts 10:38–39 describes the disciples as witnesses of Jesus's life and ministry, but here πνεῦμα and δύναμις characterize Jesus's ministry, not theirs. In Acts 1:8 we read that πνεῦμα and δύναμις will modify and shape the disciples' future ministry. In Acts 4:33 Luke says that apostles gave witness with δυνάμει μεγάλῃ "great power" which can be viewed as power for working miracles, or power or strength of conviction with which the witness is given.[22] In the rest of examples, πνεῦμα is connected with the concept of witness: a) in Acts 5:32 the Holy Spirit is one of the μάρτυρες together with the disciples, b) in Acts 6:3 being full of the Spirit is the characteristic which can be viewed, observed and testified to by others, c) in Acts 15:8 the giving of the Spirit was a form of testimony given by God, and, d) in Acts 20:23 πνεῦμα testifies to Paul about future events in his life.

3. The preliminary conclusion

On this basis, we conclude that equal attention must be given to analysis of each term, "power" and "Spirit," and that we must avoid emphasizing one term over the other. Speaking of the Pentecost event, in Luke 24:48–49, Jesus mentions not only the coming of the Spirit or receiving power. Rather, the coming of the Spirit is described as sending "what my Father promised," and that will result in "clothing with power from on high." Although it is obvious that Luke hereby points out that the Holy Spirit is the source of the power behind Jesus's ministry[23] this does not mean that the πνεῦμα is identical with δύναμις or vice versa. What is emphasized is the fact that "the Holy Spirit" will bring "power," and both are needed for being Jesus's witnesses. According to Luke 24:48–49, the apostles are already Jesus's witnesses because they witnessed the main events from his life and ministry. However, in order to be his witnesses in the future, they must receive δύναμις, which πνεῦμα will bring (Acts 1:8).

22. Kelly, "Development of Witness," 58.

23. O'Reilly, Leo. *Word and Sign in Acts*, 33–34.

With this preliminary conclusion we turn now to the analysis of the concept of witness in the biblical context. We want to see how the concept of witness is defined and developed in the Bible. Then we will return to the Lukan writings and discuss the impact of *πνεῦμα ἅγιος* on the concept of witness in Luke's theology.

CHAPTER 2

Introduction to the Concept of Witness in the Old Testament

1. Etymology and semantics of the Hebrew words for witness in the Old Testament

The concept of witness in the OT utilizes several words that have in common the *'d* root (עד), to which various prefixes and suffixes are added. These words describe various entities as "witnesses," as well as referring to the act of "witnessing/testifying," or the content of that witnessing (i.e. "testimony"). Hence, a "witness" is someone who is defined as such, or due to performing activity that is explicitly or implicitly classified as "witnessing/testifying." We will look at the etymology and semantic range of words deriving from the root *'d*, identify major words that are used in the context of witness/testimony as antonyms to witness, and offer some preliminary remarks for this research.

1.1 Etymology

The most important term for analyzing witness or testimony in the OT is the noun *ʿēḏ* (עֵד) "a witness",[1] and its cognates: the noun *ʿēḏîm* (עֵדִים) "witnesses," a plural form of *ʿēḏ* (עֵד), fem. noun *ʿēḏāh* (עֵדָה) "a witness," an abstract noun *ʿēḏûṯ* (עֵדוּת) "testimony" and its plural form *ʿēḏôṯ* (עֵדְוֹת)[2] or

1. Wells, *Law of Testimony*, 16.

2. The noun *ʿēḏôṯ* (עֵדְוֹת) contains šwa which is usually not part of this word.

ʿēḏōṯ (עֵדֹת), fem. noun *tᵊʿûḏāh* (תְּעוּדָה) "testimony," and denominative verb *ʿûḏ* (עוּד) "to testify, cause to testify."

As the starting point for discussing the etymology of these words, Horacio Simian-Yofre[3] argues for their derivation from the root *ʿûḏ* (עוּד) since Hebrew words for witness have Semitic cognates in that root. To be specific, the verbal root *ʿd* is attested in several Semitic languages such as Ugaritic (perhaps), Arabic, Aramaic, Syriac, Phoenician, and Ethiopic. Arabic possesses this root which, in the G stem, means "to return, come back, revert," in the D stem, "to accustom, habituate, get used to," and in C stem "to cause to return, reiterate, repeat." Hence, the basic idea of this root is to repeat and to affirm something solemnly, and this sense comes to the fore in the Hiphil stem of the Hebrew verb *ʿûḏ* (עוּד). When used denominatively, the stem means "to call, invoke as witness for" (Josh 8:2; Jer 32:10, 25, 44), "against" (Deut 4:25; 30:16; 31:28), or "to bear witness for or against" (1 Kgs 21:10–13; Job 29:11; Lam 2:13; Mal 2:14).[4] Giovanna Raengo Czander claims that among scholars there is no agreement concerning the etymology of *ʿēḏ* (עֵד), but she is also in agreement that the word *ʿēḏ* (עֵד) derives from the root עוד whose primary meaning seems to be expressed by the verbs "go around, repeat, do again and again."[5] This etymology corresponds with the fact that witnessing involves the idea of return or repetition, since in some instances a witness who is present at some event or occasion, can later be called to testify, confirm, or repeat what happened. The best solution for this problem probably comes from John A. Thompson[6] who says that the final answer as to whether biliteral or triliteral verb phonemes were original in Semitic languages cannot be given, yet there is a good support for the claim that the expressions with meaning of witness such as *ʿēḏ* (עֵד), *ʿēḏûṯ* (עֵדוּת), *tᵊʿûḏāh* (תְּעוּדָה), derives from the biliteral root עד which had an original semantic value of "recurrence." This biliteral root was crucial for the development of other *ʿd* group of words whose semantic meanings we will look at next.

3. Simian-Yofre, *TDOT* 10:497.
4. Luke, "*Biblical Idea of Marturia*", 56–57.
5. Czander, *"You are my Witnesses"*, 61–62.
6. Thompson, "*Expansions of the* עד *Root*", *JSSR* 10 (1965): 240.

1.2 Semantic range

1.2.1 ʿûḏ (עוּד)

The verbal root *ʿd* is attested in several Semitic languages, and the basic idea of the root is "to repeat or reiterate something," and hence, "to affirm something solemnly." When used denominatively, the stem means "to call, invoke as witness for or against," or "to bear witness for or against."[7] Most frequently this word is used with a sense of a strong warning. So, people can be those who issue the warning as well as the one who receives it (Gen 43:3; Exod 19:21; 1 Sam 8:9; Neh 13:15). YHWH is also frequently described as the one who extends a warning to Israel (2 Kgs 17:13–15; Ps 50:7; 81:9; Jer 11:7). Often, he uses prophets as the channels through which he extends his solemn exhortations: Moses (Exod 19:21; Deut 8:19; 32:46) and others (2 Chron 24:19; Neh 9:26; Jer 42:19; Amos 3:13).[8]

According to Simian-Yofre,[9] *ʿûḏ* (עוּד) has two large semantic fields: in connection with *ʿēḏ* (עֵד), and in connection with *ʿēḏûṯ* (עֵדוּת) / *ʿēḏôṯ* (עֵדֹות). As the denominative verb of *ʿēḏ* (עֵד), *ʿûḏ* (עוּד) appears in juridical or legal contexts, or a religious setting in which a court situation is imitated, and it describes two activities: summoning or presenting witnesses, and their activity of testifying or witnessing. Occasionally, the verb *ʿûḏ* (עוּד) is used without connection to the noun *ʿēḏ* (עֵד), but from the text it is clear that personal and impersonal entities who engage in actions expressed by the verb *ʿûḏ* (עוּד) function as *ʿēḏ* (עֵד) or *ʿēḏîm* (עֵדִים). The use in Deuteronomy 4:26 and 30:19 of an expression: *haʿîdōtî ʾet-haššāmayim wᵊʾet-hāʾāreṣ* (הַעִידֹ־ תִי אֶת־הַשָּׁמַיִם וְאֶת־הָאָרֶץ) "I call the heavens and the earth," and in Deuteronomy 31:28 of the similar expression *wᵊʾāʿîḏāh bām ʾet-haššāmayim wᵊʾet-hāʾāreṣ* (וְאָעִידָה בָם אֶת־הַשָּׁמַיִם וְאֶת־הָאָרֶץ) include such instances. These formulae are probably inspired with the mention of deities and natural elements serving as judges in Hittite and Aramaic. In Deuteronomy heaven and earth are witnesses for Moses' certainty regarding the punishment that YHWH will impose on Israelites for breach of the covenant (Deut 31:28). Similarly, in Psalms 50:7 we have a picture of a court setting where YHWH invites heaven

---

7. Luke, 56–57.
8. Schultz, *"1576 עוּד."*, *TWOT* 649.
9. Simian-Yofre, *TDOT* 10:510–512.

and earth (v. 4), probably as his witnesses, and he also gathers his people to speak and testify against them, so he acts simultaneously both as a judge (v. 4) and as a witness (v. 7).[10]

The second semantic field of *ʿûḏ* (עוּד) is in connection with *ʿēḏûṯ* (עֵדוּת) / *ʿēḏôṯ* (עֵדְוֹת). The usual translation of this construction is "witness, attested, testify," but also more neutral expressions such as "point out, refer." The texts in this group involve a figure of authority such as YHWH's prophet or a public authority, and depending on the context, a proper translation can be "order, command" (Exod 19:23; Deut 32:46; 1 Sam 8:9; 2 Kgs 17:7–18 (v.15); Neh 9:32–34), "forbid" (Exod 19:21; Jer 42:19), or "admonish." In the latter case, YHWH himself admonishes (Neh 9:29; Ps 81:9[8]; Jer 6:10; 11:7; 42:19), or he does that through his prophets (2 Kgs 17:13; 2 Chron 24:19: Neh 9:26, 30), through his Spirit (Neh 9:30), or his messenger, angel (Zech 3:6)). The verb can also mean "threaten" (Gen 43:3; 1 Kgs 2:42; Neh 13:21); "reproach" (Neh 13:15).

The third but minor semantic field is *ʿûḏ* (עוּד) in the Hophal, which appears in Exod 21:29 and has a meaning similar to "proclaim/announce the law" in a sense that "if one has notified" or "if one has called this to his attention."[11]

1.2.2 ʿēḏ (עֵד) (sg.), ʿēḏîm (עֵדִים) (pl.)

The noun *ʿēḏ* (עֵד) "witness" deriving from the root *ʿûḏ* (עוּד), implies that a witness is someone, who by reiteration, emphatically affirms his testimony. On a basic level, this word primarily signifies a) persons or objects who were present at some situation or event and they passively record what was said or done (Gen 31:44, 48, 50; 1 Sam 12:5, etc.), b) the activity of witness in giving or providing a testimony – witnessing (Exod 20:16; 23:1; Deut 5:20;

10. Such usage of the expression "the heavens and the earth" is also known as "merism" which Jože Krašovec ("Poetic and Narrative Shape", 25–39) defines as "the way of expressing a totality by mentioning only parts, usually two extremes, and 'polar expression,' juxtaposing two polarized notions in order to convey the idea of totality of a given idea, quality or quantity . . . Merism is a substitution for abstract words like 'all,' 'every,' 'always,' etc." But merism should not be confused with antithesis, because while both uses opposite concepts such as the opposing word-pairs: day//night, good//evil, heaven//earth, in merism two opposing elements express totality, while in antithesis exclude each other in relation to a common idea.

11. According to Simian-Yofre (*TDOT* 10:498) *ʿûḏ* (עוּד) appears thirty-nine times in the OT. K. Luke ("Biblical Idea of Marturia", 56) says that this verb appears forty-six times in the OT, and Strong (*New Strong's Dictionary*) says that this verb appears forty-five times.

31:19, 21, etc.). Hence, the main idea is that a witness is someone who was present at some situation or event, and who can later in another situation report, confirm or provide evidence. Depending on the source, it is claimed that this word occurs sixty-nine times in the OT (forty-five sing., twenty-four pl.).[12] It appears in different contexts of witnessing such as legal (juridical) or religious, and it is associated with different subjects such as individual, group, YHWH, and impersonal entities.

In the Hebrew Bible *ʿēḏ* (עֵד) belongs primarily in a legal or judicial sphere where, for example, a witness is a person who is present at a legal transaction and can confirm it either orally (Ruth 4:7–9) or by signing or sealing a document or deed of purchase. Thus "witness" is a person who affirms the truth of a transaction by affixing their seals (Jer 32:12).[13] In the legal context the accused person had a right to be faced by his/her accuser and give evidence of his/her innocence, since usually the accused person was faced with someone who either saw or heard of the person's guilt. However, in such judicial procedure, one witness was not adequate for personal testimony against anyone (Deut 17:6; 19:15). This principle was incorporated into Jewish Law and reiterated in the New Testament (see: Matt 18:16; 2 Cor 13:1). Such a practice served as a form of safeguard from false testimonies and false witnesses, and if the testimony of an accuser was found to be false, that person was subjected to the punishment he had sought to have executed on the defendant (Deut 19:16–21).[14]

Various impersonal entities in the legal or social context function as witnesses. In Genesis 31:43–32:1 the heap of stones functions as a witness of a covenant between Jacob and Laban. The agreement also invokes YHWH as a "watchman" (v. 49), "witness" (v. 50) and "judge" (v. 53) between them as an assurance that both parties would obey their agreement. In Exodus 22:12–13, "witness" functions as "evidence" in the case where the owner lends a domestic animal to another person and that animal is mangled by beasts. Hence, the remains of a killed animal functions as "evidence" before the tribunal.

12. Simian-Yofre, *TDOT* 10:498. Other sources claim that it appears some sixty-seven times in the OT (e.g. Schultz, "1576 עוּד," *TWOT* 648).

13. Vine, Unger and White, *Vine's Complete Expository Dictionary*, 292.

14. Vine, Unger and White, 292.

Religious context is primarily concerned with YHWH and his relationship with people or nations. Although it differs from the legal context, it can also have legal or juridical overtones such as in Isaiah where lawsuit metaphors are strongly present (e.g. Isa 1:18 where YHWH is portrayed as putting Israel on trial, and Isa 40–55 where this lawsuit has a more cosmic dimension). Although this context in the OT is not dominant as legal, in this context YHWH as witness appears more than in a legal context. But given the nature of this context, this is expected. As in a legal context, personal and impersonal entities can serve as a witness in different modes of witnessing. In Job 16:19 Job declares that YHWH, who is in heaven, is a witness *for* him, and in the similar fashion Samuel in 1 Samuel 12:5 invokes YHWH as his witness. In Jeremiah 42:5 Israelites invoke YHWH as a witness *against* them if they will not obey him. The common denominator in all these cases is that YHWH is in a more passive role due to the fact that he is present. In Jeremiah 29:23, Malachi 3:5 and Micah 1:2 for example, YHWH takes a more active role of testifying against people and nations based on the fact that "he knows" (Jer 29:23), "he has heard" and "seen" (Mal 3:16). People can also serve as a witness in a religious context. In Joshua 24:21–22, the people's confession that they will serve YHWH becomes a witness *against* them. Deutero-Isaiah contains several statements that fall into this religious context: Isaiah 43:8–13, 44:6–9 and 55:4 are such examples. In Isaiah 55:4 it seems that YHWH proclaims the Davidic royal line to be a witness to the nations by taking YHWH's word to the nations.[15]

Impersonal entities also function as witnesses in the religious context. In Deuteronomy 31:19, YHWH commanded Moses to write "the song" and teach Israelites what will happen to them when they break the covenant with YHWH. In Joshua 24:27, Joshua erects "an altar" that serves as a witness *against* the people because it has heard everything that YHWH told his people. Isaiah 19:19–22 also mentions "an altar" and "a pillar" in the middle of Egypt, and these two elements serve as a sign and witness to YHWH. Psalm 89:37–38 seems to mention "the sun and the moon" as witnesses, yet this cannot be identified with certainty. However, the presence of these two witnesses in heaven serves as security that the promise given to king will be upheld. "Job's pain" is mentioned as a witness in Job 16:7–8. Job suffers, and

15. Smith, *Isaiah 40–66*, 503.

since his pain cannot be justified by any theological explanation, it changes into a witness of the persecution against Job.[16]

1.2.3 ʿēḏûṯ, ʿēḏuṯ (עֵדוּת, עֵדֻת) (sg.), ʿēḏôṯ (עֵדְוֹת) (pl.)

The word *ʿēḏûṯ* (עֵדוּת) occurs forty-six times in the OT. It has a meaning of a "testimony, reminder, warning sign," and is always used in reference to the testimony of YHWH. Since *ʿēḏûṯ* (עֵדוּת) derives from the verb *ʿûḏ* (עוּד) "to repeat" or "to do again," the idea of witness as an act which brings something back or makes something present for the second time as in verbally repeating or rehearsing an event is also present with *ʿēḏûṯ* (עֵדוּת).[17] According to Carl Schultz,[18] *ʿēḏûṯ* (עֵדוּת) is most frequently connected with the tabernacle (Exod 38:21; Num 1:50, 53), resulting in the expression "the tabernacle of the Testimony," and with the ark (Exod 25:22; 26:33, 34; 30:6, 26), resulting in the phrase "the ark of the Testimony." In fact, in several instances this word stands alone to indicate "the ark" (Exod 16:34; 27:21; 30:36; Lev 16:13). Also, Moses was instructed to put the testimony in (or before) (Exod 16:34; 27:21) "the ark" (Exod 25:21), but "Testimony" in these instances was a designation for "the two tablets of stone" upon which the Ten Commandments were written (Exod 24:12; 31:18; 32:15; 34:29), they are also called "the tablets of the covenant" (Deut 9:9, 11, 15). Furthermore, the Law of God itself is called "the Testimony" because it reveals YHWH's person and his purposes. This is nicely seen in Psalms 19:7 where "the Testimony of YHWH" is said to be "trustworthy." In the coronation ceremony of king Joash, the new king received with his crown "the Testimony" (2 Kgs 11:12; 2 Chron 23:11). In this case "the Testimony" is the book of the Law and this occurrence may be an example of the procedure prescribed in Deuteronomy 17:18–20.

ʿēḏôṯ (עֵדְוֹת) as plural form of *ʿēḏûṯ* (עֵדוּת) appears fifteen times only in texts exhibiting Deuteronomic/Deuteronomistic influence. *ʿēḏôṯ* (עֵדְוֹת) always refers to God's Law (Torah), and its usage can occur in the context of specific personal admonitions (1 Kgs 2:3), in decisions (2 Kgs 23:3 par. 2 Chron 34:31), in discourses (1 Chron 29:19), accusations against people (Neh 9:34; Jer 44:23), etc. Also, this word is used eight times in Psalms 119

16. Simian-Yofre, *TDOT* 10:507–508.
17. Lioy, *Decalogue in Sermon*, 14.
18. Schultz, "1576 עוּד", *TWOT* 649–650.

(verses 14, 31, 36, 99, 111, 129, 144, and 157) where the psalmist reflects his great delight in, and his great respect for, the Law of the Lord.[19]

1.2.4 ʿēḏāh (עֵדָה) (sg.), ʿēḏōṯ (עֵדֹת) (pl.)

The feminine noun *ʿēḏāh* (עֵדָה) occurs in the OT both separate from and in connection with the concept of witness. When it appears outside of the concept of witness, it can mean "appointed meeting" or "assembly" especially the congregation of Israelites (Exod 12:3; 16:1, 2, 9); "a private, domestic meeting," "a family" (Job 16:7; 15:34); "crowd" (in a bad sense) (Num 16:5; Ps 22:17); or "a swarm (of bees)" (Judg 14:8). These meanings come from the verb *yāʿad* (יָעַד). Another group of meaning comes from the root *ʿûḏ* (עוּד), and then this word takes the meaning of a "testimony." The singular noun *ʿēḏāh* (עֵדָה) is used only four times in the OT and designates an object which is given as a memorial or remembrance of an agreement and has a meaning of something that testifies or of a testimony (Gen 21:30; 31:52; Josh 24:27 2x).

ʿēḏōṯ (עֵדֹת) as the plural form of *ʿēḏāh* (עֵדָה) appears twenty-two times in the OT, and it always refer to God's Law (Torah). As we have seen, *ʿēḏōṯ* (עֵדֹת) exhibits the same meaning as *ʿēḏôṯ* (עֵדְוֹת). Accordingly, scholars are not sure about precise relationship between *ʿēḏûṯ* (עֵדוּת) and *ʿēḏāh* (עֵדָה), and consequently *ʿēḏôṯ* (עֵדְוֹת) and *ʿēḏōṯ* (עֵדֹת). It seems that *ʿēḏāh* (עֵדָה) is a variant pointing of *ʿēḏûṯ* (עֵדוּת).[20] Similarly, Brown, Driver and Briggs[21] says that in Masoretic text *ʿēḏāh* (עֵדָה) points to artificial derivation probably from *ʿēḏûṯ* (עֵדוּת), reading *ʿēḏuṯ* (עֵדֻת, which is sg. noun) for *ʿēḏōṯ* (עֵדֹת) (pl. noun) or regarding *ʿēḏōṯ* (עֵדֹת) as contraction from *ʿēḏôṯ* (עֵדְוֹת) – which is plural form of *ʿēḏûṯ* (עֵדוּת). For that reason, it seems that it is hard to decide whether plural form *ʿēḏōṯ* (עֵדֹת) should be connected with sg. *ʿēḏāh* (עֵדָה) or sg. *ʿēḏûṯ* (עֵדוּת). But in this work, we will treat *ʿēḏôṯ* (עֵדְוֹת) as plural form of *ʿēḏûṯ* (עֵדוּת), and *ʿēḏōṯ* (עֵדֹת) as plural form of *ʿēḏāh* (עֵדָה).

---

19. Schultz, "1576 עוּד.", *TWOT* 649–650.

20. Strong, *New Strong's Dictionary.*

21. *BDB,* 730.

2. Antonyms in the Old Testament

The OT contains several words that occur in the context of witness that are antonyms to the idea of witness that the OT demands and requires, and we will briefly introduce each of them.

2.1 šeqer (שֶׁקֶר)

The term *šeqer* (שֶׁקֶר) can refer to various kinds of lies, deceptions, or falsehoods. According to James Swanson[22] it can describe a) deception or misleading falseness which results in mistaken belief (Exod 20:16), b) a lie or verbal communication which is false (Job 13:4), c) a person who is a liar (Prov 17:4), or d) vanity or uselessness (1 Sam 25:21). *šeqer* (שֶׁקֶר) can be used for deception in word (Exod 20:16; Lev 5:24; Jer 5:31) or deed (2 Sam 8:13; Jer 23:14; Hos 7:1), or a more general idea of what is wrong, false, pretended, unreal (Isa 9:14; Jer 10:14).[23]

When it is used for false witness before the court, it is used with noun *ʿēḏ* (עֵד) "witness." Hence, *ʿēḏ šāqer* (עֵד שָׁקֶר) appears in Exodus 20:16; Deuteronomy 19:18; Psalms 27:12 (pl.); Proverbs 6:19; 12:17; 14:5; 19:5, 9; 25:18. Since *ʿēḏ šāqer* (עֵד שָׁקֶר) can be described as *ʿēḏ ḥāmās* (עֵד־חָמָס) (Deut 19:16) and produces *ḥāmās* (חָמָס) (Ps 27:12), "it becomes clear that *šeqer* (שֶׁקֶר) describes the witness as one who aggressively injures the other and as a violator of the Law who 'acts against the other contrary to the Law' (Deut 19:18; similarly Prov 25:18)."[24]

2.2 šāwʾ (שָׁוְא)

Biblical Hebrew usually uses *šāwʾ* (שָׁוְא) in the rather general sense of "deceit" or "wickedness, falseness" which can occur in the context of the administration of justice (Exod 23:1 "false report;" Deut 5:20 "false witness;" Isa 59:4; Hos 10:4; cf. Ps 144:8, 11; Prov 30:8), of idol worship (Ps 31:7; Is 1:13; Jer 18:15; Hos 12:12; Jonah 2:9), and of false prophecy (Lam 2:14; Ezek 12:24; 13:6–9, 23; 21:28, 34; 22:28; Zech 10:2).[25] Hence, *šāwʾ* (שָׁוְא) can describe: a) emptiness, vanity – such as the vanity of human deliverance

---

22. Swanson, *DBLH.*
23. Holladay, *Concise Hebrew and Aramaic*, 383.
24. Klopfenstein, "שֶׁקֶר šqr to deceive", *TLOT* 1401–1402.
25. Sawyer, "שָׁוְא šāwʾ deceit", *TLOT* 1310–1311.

(Ps 108:13), idols (Jonah 2:9), ineffective offering (Isa 1:13) or becoming nothing (Hos 12:12), b) emptiness of speech (Ps 12:3; 41:7; 144:8, 11; Prov 30:8; Isa 59:4; Ezek 13:8; Hos 10:4, Job 31:5), witnessing (Exod 23:1, Deut 5:20), or prophecy (Ezek 12:24, Lam 2:14), or c) worthlessness in conduct (Ps 26:4; Job 11:11; Isa 5:18; 30:28).[26] From all that we can see that *šāwʾ* (שָׁוְא) is used to designate that which is unsubstantial, unreal, worthless, either materially or morally,[27] which helps us to understand deceit, deception, falsehood as something that does not exist. Accordingly, "to lie" is to say something that is not existing and unreal in basis or fact, and the result of that is a deception.

2.3 ḥāmās (חָמָס)

A noun *ḥāmās* (חָמָס) usually refers to physical violence (e.g. Judg 9:24; 2 Sam 22:3; Jer 51:35; Obad 1:10; Hab 1:9), but more broadly it can refer to a wrong committed against another, such as injurious language or harsh treatment (e.g. Gen 16:5; Job 19:7).[28] According to Harris, *ḥāmās* (חָמָס) usually has a meaning "violence," and in the OT it is used almost always in connection with sinful violence.[29] It does not refer to the violence of natural catastrophes, and it is often a name for extreme wickedness. Hence, *ḥāmās* (חָמָס) was a cause of the flood (Gen 6:11, 13, parallel to "corrupt"). Such violence is understood as a destructive force resulting in acts that destroy and kill, often implying a lawlessness, terror, and lack of moral restraint (Gen 49:5; Prov 3:31).[30] Destruction may refer to the ruining of things, lands, or people, with a focus on the violence that accompanies these acts (Hab 2:8, 17). The second meaning of *ḥāmās* (חָמָס) is "wrong" or "unjust" such as violation of some standard, possibly implying a grievous or severe injustice (Gen 16:5; Job 19:7).

When *ḥāmās* (חָמָס) appears in the expression *ʿēḏ ḥāmās* (עֵד־חָמָס) "malicious witness," it refers to a malicious false witness who lies in a juridical setting (Exod 23:1; Deut 19:16; Ps 35:11).[31] Such a witness can be understood

26. *BDB*, 996.
27. Hamilton, "2338 שׁוא", *TWOT* 908.
28. Redding, *LTW.*
29. Harris, "678 חָמַס", *TWOT* 297.
30. Swanson, *DBLH.*
31. Swanson, *DBLH.*

either as a witness who practices and promotes violence and wrongdoing, or as the one who is a witness of wrong, that is, a false witness.[32] *ʿēḏ ḥāmās* (עֵד־חָמָס) originally probably indicated the plaintiff in a case of *ḥāmās* (חָמָס) and not the witness who perverts justice, since in Deuteronomy 19:18 we have a situation where the witness is a proven liar only after subsequent investigation. But then in a shift of meaning it generally became used for the "violent, law-breaking witness."[33]

2.4 kāzāḇ (כָּזָב)

According to Swanson[34], the noun *kāzāḇ* (כָּזָב) usually means: a) lie or falsehood – i.e. what is spoken as contrary to reality (Judg 16:10, 13), b) a false god as an entity to be worshiped by a deluded person, with a particular focus on the falseness of the god (Ps 4:3; 40:5; Amos 2:4), or c) deception, delusion, i.e. that which causes a wrong opinion about something (Prov 23:3). Francesco Bianchi[35] adds that this term refers to a lie or falsehood in a generic sense. It defines both liars and the activity of lying (e.g. Prov 14:5; 19:5; 21:28), and throughout the OT, the term is associated with false prophets (Ezek 13:19), idolatry (Amos 2:4), and the wicked (Ps 5:6; 58:3).

Klopfenstein[36] says that the chief meaning of the root כזב is "to lie," that is, "to pronounce verbal lies, speak untruth, maintain something that does not suit the facts." And although *kāzāḇ* (כָּזָב) often belongs in the legal context and as such often describes lying in the court, the *Sitz im Leben* of this term is probably the daily intercourse of people, one with another, where there is always an abundance of tempting opportunities for the misuse of speech. In this context, *kāzāḇ* (כָּזָב) denotes the discrepancy between statement and actuality or between promise and fulfilment. However, *kāzāḇ* (כָּזָב) is used in the context of witnessing in Proverbs 6:19; 14:5; 14:25; 19:5; 19:9; 21:28. There, in some instances, *kāzāḇ* (כָּזָב) occurs together with *ʿēḏ* (עֵד) (Prov 14:5; 21:28), in some instances laying/false witness is additionally described as the one who "utters lies" (Prov 6:19; 19:5, 9), but in some instances the

32. Gesenius and Tregelles, *GHCLOT*, 288.
33. Stoebe, "חָמָס ḥāmās violence", *TOLT* 438.
34. Swanson, *DBLH.*
35. Bianchi, "Deception", *LTW.*
36. Klopfenstein, "כזב *kzb* to lie", *TLOT* 607.

context (parallelisms) tells us that the person in view is (lying) witness (Prov 14:25).

2.5 pûaḥ (פּוּחַ)

According to Hamilton, the primary meaning of the verb *pûaḥ* (פּוּחַ) "to breathe/blow" when used in a negative sense is of uttering lies, being utterly deceitful.[37] The verb appears fifteen times in the OT, and six times in the context of witnessing. Five times the object of *pûaḥ* (פּוּחַ) is *kᵊzāḇîm* (כְּזָבִים) "lies" (Prov 6:19; 14:5, 25; 19:5, 9), but in Proverbs 12:17 the object of *pûaḥ* (פּוּחַ) is "truth." However, the reason why *pûaḥ* (פּוּחַ) is on the list of antonyms is Proverbs 14:25, where due to antithetical parallelism, the person opposite from the *ʿēḏ ʾĕmeṯ* (עֵד אֱמֶת) "truthful witness" is described as *wᵊyāp̄iaḥ kᵊzāḇîm* (וְיָפִחַ כְּזָבִים) "he who utters lies." Accordingly, *wᵊyāp̄iaḥ kᵊzāḇîm* (וְיָפִחַ כְּזָבִים) can be a synonym for being a "false witness."

2.6 bᵊliyyaʿal (בְּלִיַּעַל) and rāšāʿ (רָשָׁע)

The noun *bᵊliyyaʿal* (בְּלִיַּעַל) can mean: a) wickedness, namely, what does not conform to a right standard, so of no worth (Deut 15:9; Nah 1:11), b) an evil person, troublemaker, namely, a person who does evil, so is of little worth (1 Sam 30:22; 2 Sam 23:6; Nah 2:1), c) vile thing, namely, a thing abhorred or detested (Ps 101:3), d) wicked persons (Deut 13:14), e) troublemakers, that is, one who is a lawbreaker and unruly, and so rebellious (1 Sam 10:27), f) wicked person (1 Sam 25:25; 2 Sam 20:1; 1 Kgs 21:13b), g) a scoundrel (2 Sam 16:7; Prov 6:12; 16:27), or h) a wicked woman (1 Sam 1:16).[38]

In Prov 19:28 the noun *ʿēḏ* (עֵד) appears together with noun *bᵊliyyaʿal* (בְּלִיַּעַל) thus creating the expression "corrupt" or "worthless witness." Due to parallelism, *ʿēḏ bᵊliyyaʿal* (עֵד בְּלִיַּעַל) is additionally described with the adjective *rāšāʿ* (רָשָׁע) in the context of the expression *ûp̄î rᵊšāʿîm* (וּפִי רְשָׁעִים) "the mouth of the wicked." The adjective *rāšāʿ* (רָשָׁע) describes a person or activity indicating that the person's guilt is certain, or that the behaviour in question has unquestionably been established as wrong. Also, it describes people who resist obeying the laws (civil or religious) or who oppose

37. Hamilton, "1741 פּוּחַ", *TWOT* 718–719.

38. Swanson, *DBLH.*

YHWH's standard for righteous or good behaviour (Deut 25:2; Prov 17:23; Ezek 3:18; Mal 3:18).[39]

3. Preliminary Remarks

Before we analyze in detail the concept of witness in the OT, we have to take into consideration some preliminary remarks about particular aspects of witnessing that will help us navigate through the textual analysis. Hence, we will consider the following aspects: a) the spatial dimension of the concept of witness, b) contexts in which witnessing occurs, and, c) ontological categories of witnesses.

3.1 Spatial dimension of the concept of witness

Witness in the OT occurs in two spatial dimensions: vertical, from YHWH (or occasionally from some other entities) to human beings, and horizontal, from various entities to other entities. The primary context in which the vertical dimension of witnessing occurs in the OT is the Mosaic covenant. Covenant conveys revelation, revelation produces community (relationship), and community as the recipient of revelation receives mission. Because Israel had witnessed (*rā'āh* [רָאָה] "seen") YHWH's salvation work (Exod 19:4), if they will *šāma'* (שָׁמַע) "obey" YHWH's voice and keep his covenant, they will be "a priestly kingdom and a holy nation" (Exod 19:6). This furthermore implies the role of Israel as a witness to other nations on the horizontal level about YHWH's wisdom, power etc. (Deut 4:6–8). But the vertical dimension does not include only reception of the Torah and the covenant, but also the Tabernacle and accompanying elements. All this is a form of YHWH's witness to his people because they are a replica of heavenly realities. Furthermore, witness from above occurs also when YHWH speaks for or against someone (notably through his prophets), but also in his actions in the course of history, through which he executes his punishments.

While the majority of witnessing on the vertical level occurs from YHWH to human beings, in some instances this dynamic can be seen as reversed. In other words, people express their devotion and dedication, and even testify for YHWH, but such witness is never solely directed to YHWH, since

39. Gleaves, "Evil", *LTW*.

testimony is offered to the people as well. So, we can talk about the overlapping of these two dimensions. Example of such testimony we have in Joshua 22 where making the altar was the people's way of expressing their devotion to YHWH (v. 29), but also a form of testimony to other people (vv. 24–28). Furthermore, in Isaiah 19:20 the building of the altar and pillar is a sign and witness *layhwā* (לַיהוָה) "to the Lord." Even though altar and pillar are defined as witness "to the Lord," undoubtedly this testimony is given to other people about YHWH or in his favour. Also, Isaiah 43:9–10, 12 and 44:8–9 are examples of when people testify for YHWH but to other people as well.

The horizontal level of witnessing occurs when one entity testifies to another entity. However, due to the theocratic nature of OT Israel, every aspect of their lives was defined and ordained by YHWH. Laws were given by YHWH to be implemented into Israel's society, so while witnessing between entities occurs in legal or covenantal contexts, we must be aware that the foundation for this is in this vertical dimension. The only exception to this rule is the social context in Genesis where witnessing occurs between human beings without being grounded first and foremost in the revelation of YHWH.

3.2 Contexts of witnessing

Since OT Israel is a theocracy, the concept of witness in the OT appears in three different yet complementary or mutually connected contexts: social, covenantal (religious) and legal. The social context is the context where individuals or groups are free to resolve their disputes by way of agreement or covenant as they see fit, solutions that are then supported by some form of witnesses. YHWH or gods can be invoked as witnesses, but the way individuals or groups will handle their relationship (rules of conduct) is not prescribed or defined by YHWH or gods. The social context appears primarily in Genesis (23:30; 31:44, 48, 50, 52; 43:3), and possibly 1 Kings 2:42. As we can see, social context appears primarily prior to the giving of the Torah.

The covenantal or religious context is a context where the relationship between YHWH and Israelites is defined. Israel as a nation is a primary recipient of YHWH's testimony, and for that matter, she is now responsible to implement the standards of behavior established by the covenant with YHWH into every aspect of life and relationships. In one sense, the covenantal context encompasses: a) relationships between Israelites and YHWH, b) Israel's social life customs and manners, and c) Israel's legislation. However, the primary emphasis in this context is on relationships between Israelites and YHWH, that is, Israel's responsibility to obey YHWH's commandments. Accordingly, YHWH's dealing with Israelites in the OT is often presented as a lawsuit in which YHWH puts Israel on trial to establish her guilt or innocence. Furthermore, elements connected with the Israelite cult (Torah, ark, tabernacle, veil) are part of the covenantal context.

The legal context in the OT is first and foremost defined by the covenantal context or the relationship between YHWH and Israelites. YHWH prescribes standards of relationships and behaviors between people, and when those standards are violated or there is a suspicion of their violation, people are summoned to trial to establish their guilt or innocence. Although the legal context is based upon the covenantal context, the primary emphasis in this context is relationship between people in accordance with the Torah.

To summarize: when two entities define their relationship outside the spectrum of the Torah, we are dealing with the social context; when the guilt or innocence of person/s toward YHWH is at stake, we are dealing with the covenantal context; and when the guilt or innocence of one person toward another is at stake, we are dealing with the legal context. However, occasionally, the contexts are not easy to define because they overlap. For example, marriage is a social institution belonging to a legal context, but it is also a divine institution.[40] So, the question is which context will we take as the primary one? The same dilemma is present in some other cases, such as in Ruth[41] and Jeremiah 32.[42]

---

40. Marsman, *Women in Ugarit and Israel*, 112.

41. Bob Becking and Anne-Mareike Wetter ("Wetter Boaz in Gate", 89) argue that the scene at the gate should be seen as the description of a ritual with both religious and legal dimensions (265). They also cite authors who argue for either legal or religious contexts of this event. That is all to say that sometimes due to theonomic nature of OT Israel, it is difficult to separate the religious sphere from legal or social spheres of life.

42. As in the case of Ruth, the issue of whether purchase of the field is legal or covenantal/religious context, or both, is not simple. Philip J. King (*Jeremiah: Archaeological Companion*, 89) views the purchase of the field in Jeremiah 32 as a religious act. Jeremiah's cousin Hanamael was forced to sell his field, and Jeremiah as next of kin (*go'el*) was obligated to buy back the land as prescribed in Leviticus 25:25–32, so that the estate would not be alienated from the family. So, King concludes: "The institution of *go'el* was at the center of family solidarity in biblical times; the tradition of the *go'el* lies behind this property transaction involving Jeremiah. Basic to *go'el* in this context is that real property is a religious concept."

3.3 Ontological categories of witnesses

As Bruce Wells[43] notices, in the Hebrew Bible, people, animals, divine beings, and inanimate objects are all referred to as witnesses. For that matter it is important to grasp the ontological category of witnesses, and the distinction must be made between personal and impersonal entities. Personal entities are YHWH or gods, angels and people, and impersonal entities can be animals, heavens and earth, various material objects, covenants, or agreements between people, etc. Torah and various elements in connection with it are also in this work considered as impersonal entities.

In the OT, the primary personal entities that function as witnesses are humans. In several instances YHWH functions as a witness, and once the angel of the Lord is witness to the people. When we combine all together, personal witnesses in the OT testify in the following way:

a) *people to people*: Genesis 43:3; Exodus 19:23; 20:16; 21:29; 23:1; Leviticus 5:1; Numbers 5:13; 35:30; Deuteronomy 5:20; 8:19; 17:6, 7; 19:15, 16, 18; Joshua 24:22; Ruth 4:9, 10, 11; 1 Samuel 8:9; 12:5; 1 Kings 2:42; 21:10, 13; 2 Chronicles 24:19; Nehemiah 9:26; 13:15, 21; Job 29:11; Psalms 27:12; 35:11; Proverbs 6:19; 12:17; 14:5, 25; 19:5, 9, 28; 21:28; 24:28; 25:18; Isaiah 8:2; 43:9, 10, 12; 44:8, 9; 55:4; Jeremiah 6:10; 32:10, 12, 25, 44; 42:19; Lamentations 2:13; Amos 3:13,

b) *YHWH*: Genesis 31:50; 1 Samuel 12:5; 1 Kings 17:15; Nehemiah 9:29; Job 16:19; Psalms 50:7; 81:8; Jeremiah 11:7, 29:23; 42:5; Micah 1:2; Malachi 2:14; 3:5,

c) *YHWH through people*: Exodus 19:21; 2 Kings 17:13,

d) *YHWH's Spirit through people*: Nehemiah 9:30, and

e) *Angel of the Lord*: Zechariah 3:6.

Occasionally, people function as witnesses for YHWH: Isaiah 43:9–10, 12; 44:8–9. Probably Isaiah 43:9 and 44:9 refers to people who should function as witnesses for false gods. Amos 3:13 is somewhat in the middle, since YHWH invites people to witness to his charge against the "house of Jacob," but not to witness for him directly.

In the OT, the majority of impersonal entities that function as witnesses are connected with the Torah, that is, with witness occurs from YHWH toward people. For example, Exodus 31:18 explicitly defines the Ten

43. Wells, *Law of Testimony*, 21.

Commandments as "testimony," and this idea is furthermore confirmed in Deuteronomy 4:45; 6:17 and 6:20. Hence, God's Law – Torah – is a form of testimony.[44] However, not only is the Torah "testimony," but this characteristic is also imparted to the ark, tabernacle and veil, so these elements become the "ark of the Testimony" (Exod 25:22), "veil of testimony" (Lev 24:3) and the "tabernacle of the Testimony" (Num 1:50). But in what way does the Law function as a testimony? According to Osborn and Hatton, the word "testimony" generally refers to something spoken or written that serves as a witness or reminder of what YHWH has done or what YHWH requires.[45] The Law falls in this category, and consequently, objects like the ark or tabernacle are also the extension of that purpose: they serve as a reminder or witness of the terms of the covenant established at Mount Sinai.

In the context of witnessing among and between people, several entities appear. As material objects in Genesis 21:30 seven lambs serve as a witness between Abraham and Abimelech, and in the story of Laban and Jacob in Genesis 31:43–32:1 it seems that the contract between Laban and Jacob is a witness (v. 44), but so is a stone pillar and a stone heap (vv. 45, 52). Stone also appears as witness in Joshua 24:27 and so does a pillar in Isaiah 19:20. An altar as witness also appears in Joshua 22:27, 28, 34; Isaiah 19:20. In Exodus 22:12 the remains of the animal is a witness that this animal was not stolen but truly killed by the beast, and in Ruth 4:7 the giving of the sandal is

44. Clarification: the OT contains several words to describe written record of God's words: *ʿēḏûṯ* (עֵדוּת), *ʿēḏōṯ* (עֵדֹת), and *ʿēḏôṯ* (עֵדְוֹת). In one example Torah is even described as *ʿēḏ* (עֵד) (Deut 31:26). Accordingly, *ʿēḏûṯ* (עֵדוּת), *ʿēḏōṯ* (עֵדֹת), and *ʿēḏôṯ* (עֵדְוֹת) can refer to Decalogue, particular command from the Torah, some parts of the Torah, or the entire first five books of the OT (Pentateuch). Nowhere do these words for Torah refer to the prophetic speech, or the entire TNK - what we would call "the Old Testament." In 2 Kings 17:15, we have an example of both mentioning the Torah and YHWH's warnings he gave through prophets. But Torah is designated with *ʿēḏôṯ* (עֵדְוֹת) and prophetic speech with *ʿûḏ* (עוּד). Similar situation is in Nehemiah 9:34. The point is the following: we will not use the word *Torah* as form of YHWH's testimony as reference to Writings or Prophets. Torah will be used only as a description for Pentateuch and/or some parts of it. In two instances, prophetic (written) message is labelled as *təʿûḏāh* (תְּעוּדָה) (Isa 8:16, 20), and Isaiah 30:8 as *ʿēḏ* (עֵד). However, *təʿûḏāh* (תְּעוּדָה) is probably not used in these verses with reference to the Torah, so the distinction between *Torah as testimony* and prophetic message (spoken and/or written) still stands. Although, in the Bible Writings and Prophets are also form of YHWH's testimony, it is significant that nowhere in the OT these parts of the Scripture are labeled as *ʿēḏûṯ* (עֵדוּת), *ʿēḏōṯ* (עֵדֹת), or *ʿēḏôṯ* (עֵדְוֹת). As though the Pentateuch is, in some special way, a unique form of YHWH's witness – not that it only contains testimonies, but in its entirety, it can be described as such.

45. Osborn and Hatton, *Exodus*, 408.

a form of witness. Heaven and the earth appear as witnesses in Deuteronomy 4:26; 30:19 and 31:28, where they are witness to Moses's certainty that YHWH will punish the Israelites for breaching the covenant. Finally, the last group of witnesses begin as verbal testimony that is eventually written down on a scroll or in some other form. In Deuteronomy 31:19, 21 and 32:46 we have the song that Moses must write down which serves as a witness against Israel, and represents prophecy for the future, since YHWH knows them and what they will do in the future. In Isaiah 8:16, 20 the situation is puzzling since it is not clear whether prophecy remained in verbal form or was eventually written down. On the contrary, in Isaiah 30:8 we know that YHWH instructs Isaiah to write down the prophecy. In summary, impersonal witnesses in the OT are: a) Torah;[46] b) tabernacle,[47] c) ark of the covenant,[48] d) veil,[49] e) seven lambs,[50] f) covenant,[51] g) heap,[52] h) pillar,[53] i) remains of the animal,[54] j) Heaven and Earth,[55] k) song,[56] l) altar,[57] m) stone,[58] n) sandal,[59] and o) written scroll.[60]

46. Exodus 25:16, 21; 30:6, 36; 31:18; 32:15; 34:29; 40:20; Leviticus 16:13; Numbers 17:4, 10; Deuteronomy 4:45; 6:17, 20; 31:26; 1 Kings 2:3; 2 Kings 11:12; 17:15; 23:3; 1 Chronicles 29:19; 2 Chronicles 23:11; 34:31; Nehemiah 9:34; Psalms 19:7; 25:10; 78:5, 56; 81:5; 93:5; 99:7; 119:2, 14, 22, 24, 31, 36, 46, 59, 79, 88, 95, 99, 111, 119, 125, 129, 138, 144, 146, 152, 157, 167, 168; 122:4; 132:12; Jeremiah 44:23.

47. Exodus 38:21; Numbers 1:50, 53; 9:15; 10:11; 17:7, 8; 18:2; 2 Chronicles 24:6.

48. Exodus 16:34; 25:22; 26:33, 34; 27:21; 30, 6, 26; 31:7; 39:35; 40:3, 5, 21; Numbers 4:5; 7:89; Joshua 4:16.

49. Leviticus 24:3.

50. Genesis 21:30.

51. Genesis 31:44.

52. Genesis 31:48, 52.

53. Genesis 31:52; Isaiah 19:20.

54. Exodus 22:13.

55. Deuteronomy 4:26; 30:19; 31:28.

56. Deuteronomy 31:19, 21; 32:46.

57. Joshua 22:27, 28, 34; Isaiah 19:20.

58. Joshua 24:27.

59. Ruth 4:7.

60. Isaiah 8:16, 20; 30:8.

CHAPTER 3

The Concept of Witness in the Old Testament – Passage Analysis

To analyze the concept of witness in the OT, we will conduct analysis of every passage which contains the Hebrew words for witness/testimony. We will do this by combining all verses that contain particular words. Then we will analyze all these texts and compare them with the LXX. Analysis will be done primarily according to the aspects we have identified in preliminary remarks.

1. The concept of witness in the Pentateuch – passage analysis

1.1 Usage of ʿēḏ (עֵד) and ʿēḏîm (עֵדִים) in Pentateuch

The noun *ʿēḏ* (עֵד) and its plural form *ʿēḏîm* (עֵדִים) appear twenty-five times in the Pentateuch, and they are used for both personal and impersonal witnesses appearing in different contexts.

1.1.1 Impersonal witnesses

In Genesis 31:44, 48, 50, and 52 the concept of witness appears in the social context as part of the story of the covenant between Jacob and Laban. The first witness appears in Genesis 31:44 as *lᵊʿēḏ* (לְעֵד) conveying the meaning "as" or "for a witness." Commentators usually notice two problems: the first problem is the discrepancy in gender between the feminine noun *bᵊrîṯ* (בְּרִית) "covenant" and the Qal perfect (qātal) form of verb *hāyāh* (הָיָה) "and let it be" which is in this case a masculine verb. The second problem or suggestion is to take Hebrew *ʿē* for Aramaic *ʿā* to get *ʿād* ("pact, treaty") which would read "Let us make a covenant . . . let there be a pact."[1] Possible candidates for *ʿēḏ* עֵד)) are covenant, pile of stone or God, and whoever or whatever it is, it serves as a witness *lᵊʿēḏ* (לְעֵד) *bênî ûḇênekā* (בֵּינִי וּבֵינֶךָ) "between me and you."

In addition to the witness from Genesis 31:44 (probably covenant), a stone heap (Gen 31:48, 52) also functions as witness. The text provides names given to the heap by the two parties in their languages (Gen 31:47): "[t]he first naming is given in two languages, because Laban is an Aramaic speaker. Both the Aramaic version of the name, *yᵊgar śāhădûtāʾ* 'The heap of witness,' and the underlying Hebrew name, *gal ʿēḏ* 'The heap of witness,' are *hapax legomena* in the Hebrew Bible."[2] Hence, in Genesis 31:48 *haggal* (הַגַּל) "heap" functions as *ʿēḏ* (עֵד) or "witness" *bênî ûḇênᵊkā* (בֵּינִי וּבֵינֶךָ) "between me and you." There is no verb to modify the activity of *ʿēḏ* (עֵד), but the noun *hayyôm* (הַיּוֹם) "today" implies that a "heap" is today a witness between Jacob and Laban. Unlike in the previous case, *ʿēḏ* (עֵד) does not have the prepositions *lᵊ* (לְ) or *bᵊ* (בְּ) that could define the possible mode of witness. In Genesis 31:52 that *haggal* (הַגַּל) "heap" is once more labelled as *ēḏ* (עֵד) "witness"[3] together with *maṣṣēḇā* (מַצֵּבָה) "pillar," which is modified by *ʿēḏāh* (עֵדָה) "witness," "testimony."

In Exodus 22:12 (13) in the legal context *ʿēḏ* (עֵד) assumes the meaning of an "evidence."[4] In a trial, conflicted parties had a responsibility *bôʾ* (בוֹא) "to bring" witnesses before the court, and objects could also serve as physical evidence or witness. In the case of Exodus 22:12 a herdsman who was keeping a neighbour's domestic animal that was killed by a wild animal, must bring as evidence the remains of the carcass, which is then considered as *ʿēḏ* (עֵד) "witness", or even better, "a piece of evidence."[5]

1. Hamilton, *Book of Genesis*, 311.

2. Krašovec, *Transformation of Biblical Proper Names,* 23.

3. Again, the verb in this part of the sentence is missing, but the most probable way is to use the verb "is." Hence stone "is a witness" and heap "is a witness" (so NRSV and NIV).

4. In some Bible translations, this text is a part of verse 12, and in some translations part of verse 13.

5. Westbrook and Wells, *Everyday Law in Biblical Israel*, 42.

As part of the religious context, in Deuteronomy 31:19, 21, *šîrāh* (שִׁירָה) "song" appears as *lᵊʿēḏ* (לְעֵד) "for witness" *biḇnê yiśrāʾēl* (בִּבְנֵי יִשְׂרָאֵל) "against the sons of Israel." The verb that modifies the song in Deuteronomy 31:19 comes in the expression *tihyeh-llî* (תִּהְיֶה־לִּי). Hence, the song will be *for* YHWH *for a* witness *against* Israel, or as NASB correctly translates "so that this song may be a witness for me against the sons of Israel." An imperfect (yiqtōl) form of a verb *hāyāh* (הָיָה) implies future role of the song as witness. The song's function is furthermore described in Deuteronomy 31:21 where the future function of the song as a witness is confirmed with the verb *ʿānāh* (עָנָה) "to answer" in its future form, and expression *lᵊpānâw* (לְפָנָיו). Together with song as *lᵊʿēḏ* (לְעֵד) "for witness," we get an idea that the song will "answer" or "testify" "for" or "as witness" "to their faces," and certainly *lᵊ* (לְ) in the expression *lᵊpānâw* (לְפָנָיו) "to their faces" in this context does not have positive meaning. Finally, *sēp̄er hattôrāh* (סֵפֶר הַתּוֹרָה) "the Book of the Law" in Deuteronomy 31:26 serves as *lᵊʿēḏ* (לְעֵד) "as a witness" *bᵊḵā* (בְּךָ) "against you." The verb *hāyāh* (הָיָה) "to be" in weqātal (waw+perfect) form here probably serves as a waw conversive signifying the future role of the Book of the Law as witness.

1.1.2 Personal witnesses

In the story of the covenant between Jacob and Laban, YHWH also appear as a witness in Genesis 31:50. An interesting overlap occurs in Genesis 31:49 where Laban calls "the heap" a *miṣpâ* (מִצְפָּה) or "watchtower" (cf. 2 Chron 20:24 and Isa 21:8), and invokes YHWH as the one who will *yiṣep̄* (יִצֶף) "watch" (from the root *ṣāp̄āh* (צָפָה) "to keep watch, guard") between "me and you." In Genesis 31:50 YHWH is[6] a *ʿēḏ* (עֵד) "witness" *bênî ûḇêneḵā* (בֵּינִי וּבֵינֶךָ) "between me and you," the same expression as in Genesis 31:44 and 31:48, because Jacob and Laban cannot oversee the implementation of an arrangement. Invoking YHWH as a witness is possible because YHWH is present everywhere and can perform the function of a "watcher." Additionally, in Genesis 31:53, Laban emphasizes the role of God by declaring that God will not only watch, but also *yišpᵊṭû* (יִשְׁפְּטוּ) "judge" (plural) between them. Although in Genesis 31:49–50 Laban refers to God in singular, Genesis 31:53

6. Genesis 31:50 does not have a verb in connection with the noun "witness." Hence, the most probable meaning is to say that God "is" witness (so NRSV and NIV).

implies a plurality of deities. Mentioning "the God of Abraham and the God of Nahor" together with plural verb *yišpᵊṭû* (יִשְׁפְּטוּ) "to judge" stresses this conclusion. But in any case, the role of God(s) is double: to be a witness and a judge in this covenant.

In the following examples people appear as witnesses in the legal context. The first two examples (Exod 20:16; 23:1) deal with prohibition against giving a false testimony. Exodus 20:16: "You shall not bear false witness against your neighbour" (NRSV), and Exodus 23:1–3: "You shall not spread a false report. You shall not join hands with the wicked to act as a malicious witness. You shall not follow a majority in wrongdoing; when you bear witness in a lawsuit, you shall not side with the majority so as to pervert justice; nor shall you be partial to the poor in a lawsuit" (NRSV). In Exodus 20:16 the text describes a person who *ʿānāh* (עָנָה) "testifies, answers" *ḇᵊrēăḵā* (בְרֵעֲךָ) "against his neighbour" as *ʿēḏ šāqer* (עֵד שָׁקֶר) "false witness." Although the usual meaning of *ʿānāh* (עָנָה) is "to reply, answer," in this context the meaning of *ʿānāh* (עָנָה) is "testify."[7] The noun *rēaʿ* (רֵעַ) "neighbour," according to John I. Durham, in the OT refers always to a person with whom one stands in a reciprocal relationship, but in this legal context, it refers to a fellow member of the covenant community.[8] The false witness is described as *ʿēḏ šāqer* (עֵד שָׁקֶר), since the emphasis is not on a person who speaks lies, but on a description of a person as a lying person who speaks.[9] A literal translation would be: "Do not answer/testify as a false witness against your neighbour."[10]

Exodus 23:1a begins with the expression *lōʾ ṯiśśāʾ šēmaʿ šāwʾ*

7. Hamilton (*Book of Genesis*, 326) explains that the phrase *ʿānāh* + *bə* (עָנָה+ בְּ) ("testify against") without *bə* would mean "to respond, answer," but with this preposition it means "to respond as a witness," that is, "testify." Although on some occasions *ʿānāh* + *bə* (עָנָה+ בְּ) means "testify for" (Gen 30:33), more often it means "testify against" (1 Sam 12:3; 2 Sam 1:16; Job 15:6; Isa 3:9; 59:12; Jer 14:7; Mic 6:3).

8. Durham, *Exodus*, 296.

9. In Exodus 20:16 both translations miss the point that *šeqer* (שֶׁקֶר) modifies a person, and not the speech of the person. Hence, NRSV has "bear false witness" and NIV "give false testimony."

10. Dozeman (Dozeman, *Exodus*, 495) draws a parallel between Exodus 20:16 and Deuteronomy 5:20 which describe a witness as *ʿēḏ šāwʾ* (עֵד שָׁוְא) "deceitful witness." Wells (*Law of Testimony*, 135) thinks that Deuteronomy makes a law more restricting since the prohibition is applied to any testimony that is designed to deceive rather than just a testimony that contains manifest lies, and Doezman argues that the definition is broader because it forbids any evasive (double meaning) speech in court as well as lying.

(לֹא תִשָּׂא שֵׁמַע שָׁוְא) "You will not spread a false report" with the verb *nāśā'* (נָשָׂא) "lift up, to raise" in the imperfect (yiqtōl) form *tiśśā'* (תִשָּׂא). *šēma' šāw'* (שֵׁמַע שָׁוְא) can be translated as "vain report"[11] or "baseless rumour," since this text speaks not only about "unjustified comments or criticism, but a positive accusation that a crime has been committed which has no foundation in known fact."[12] Hence, "falsehood" is defined as presenting something as truth and real when in actuality it did not happen or does not exist. In using the verb *nāśā'* (נָשָׂא) "to lift up" and not the usual *'ānāh* (עָנָה) + *bᵊ* (בְּ) "testify against,"[13] sees the desire to incorporate other types of false testimony and not only false accusation. *nāśā'* (נָשָׂא) literally means "to lift up," but it can be translated as "do not start, do not pass," or "do not give." Stuart notices that the translation "do not spread" can be misleading because it could be misunderstood to refer only to an elaborate attempt to make a false accusation repeatedly and systematically.[14]

Exodus 23:1b continues with *'al-tāšeṯ yāḏᵊḵā 'im-rāšā'* (אַל־תָּשֶׁת יָדְךָ עִם־רָשָׁע) with the verb *šîṯ* (שִׁית) "to put, to place" in its imperfect (yiqtōl) form *tāšeṯ* (תָּשֶׁת), which can be translated as "you will not place your hand with a wicked person." In this instance, the expression *'al-tāšeṯ yāḏᵊḵā* (אַל־תָּשֶׁת יָדְךָ) "do not join hand" is an idiom for "cooperate with" or "give aid to, help," implying the possibility of two or more people in collaboration making a false accusation against someone, or falsely denying an accusation that was correct. Since the Israelite legal system highly valued the testimony of two or three witnesses, if two or three people would agree to falsify their testimony, more than likely, their testimony would be accepted as valid, and an innocent person would be punished.[15] The precise meaning of "placing hand with a wicked . . ." is explained by the expression *lihyōṯ 'ēḏ ḥāmās* (לִהְיֹת עֵד חָמָס) "to be a witness of violence," which refers to a false accusation where such a witness is trying to do violence to another by means of the justice system.[16]

11. Bailey, *Exodus*, 254.
12. Clements, *Exodus*, 148.
13. Wells, *Law of Testimony*, 137.
14. Stuart, *Exodus*, 523.
15. Stuart, *Exodus*, 524.
16. Wells, *Law of Testimony*, 137.

Third, similarly to Exodus 20:16 and 23:1, a command from Deuteronomy 5:20 says: "You shall not testify against your neighbour as a lying witness",[17] where the verb *ʿānāh* (עָנָה) "to reply" is once again used in the context of witness. While in Exodus 20:16 the testimony is described as *šāqer* (שָׁקֶר) "false, deceptive," here it is described as *šāwʾ* (שָׁוְא) "empty, worthless, in vain." But *šāwʾ* (שָׁוְא) modifies the noun *ʿēḏ* (עֵד) and not the verb *ʿānāh* (עָנָה). Hence, a better translation is "lying witness" referring to the person, instead of "false testimony" referring to the content of speech. *šāwʾ* (שָׁוְא) signifies that the accuser has no valid or substantial grounds for his claims, and therefore, the accused person is accused falsely.[18] So in this instance we have a mode of witness that is *witness against* as seen in the expression *ḇᵊrēʿăḵā* (בְרֵעֲךָ), "against your neighbour." The seriousness of false accusations is huge because, as Craigie reminds us, the evidence given against the defendant in a case will determine his future, so potentially the future of some person could be determined based on "nothing."[19] The other problem for accused was that the burden of proof in a legal process was placed to a large extent on the accused.[20]

The fourth example comes from Leviticus 5:1, where we have the most precise identification of what it means to be *ʿēḏ* (עֵד) "witness" in the legal context. The precise meaning of the expression *qôl ʾālāh* (קוֹל אָלָה) "public charge" or "voice of cursing" is debatable. It probably refers to a person who sins by failing to respond to a public oath, a calling for any witness to the event in question to come forth and testify.[21] This oath is made with an appeal to the divine realm to punish everyone who has important information regarding a particular case but does not reveal it. In doing so, that person becomes guilty of an offense and is subjected to punishment for refusing to testify.[22] Accordingly, Leviticus 5:1 probably deals with a witness who has an obligation to testify, and that obligation is imposed by means of a

17. Miller, *Deuteronomy*, 93.

18. Merrill, *Deuteronomy Vol. 4,* 155.

19. Craigie, *Book of Deuteronomy*, 162.

20. von Rad, *Deuteronomy*, 59.

21. Hartley, *Leviticus*, 68.

22. Wells, *Law of Testimony*, 56–57. Additionally, *qôl ʾālāh* (אָלָה קוֹל) can also be understood as blasphemous utterance against YHWH, or a lying oath in which someone claims something to be truth that is not (Wells 2004, 56–57).

conditional curse, but for some reason the witness refuses to perform his duty. A "public charge" or "voice of cursing" is not necessarily the curse that the victim utters against the perpetrator, but rather the public summons by the legal authorities. This text then describes witness that is obligated to testify because of the summons.[23]

A witness in this verse is described with two verbs in perfect form: *rāʾāh* (רָאָה) "to see" and *yāḏaʿ* (יָדַע) "to know." These two verbs are descriptions of requirements for being a witness who can then speak *for* or *against* someone or something. Interestingly, there is no verb in connection with the noun *ʿēḏ* (עֵד) , but it is apparent that this person as witness is required to speak verbally, otherwise he or she would be guilty of not doing *nāḡaḏ* (נָגַד) "to report, to tell." Wells makes a difference between these two types of witness claiming that a witness described in terms of the root *r'h* "to see" is an eyewitness – one who has seen an event and can speak to that event based on personal observation.[24] A witness described in terms of *yādaʿ* has acquired the knowledge of the event through some secondary or second-hand means, and Wells defines him as a "hearsay witness." If that is correct, this means that such a witness is considered as someone who either has first or second-hand experience about a certain event.[25] But as Wells[26] notices, the text is not clear whether whenever a crime was committed a kind of automatic subpoena fell on anyone who had some knowledge about the crime and such a person or persons are automatically subjected to punishment, or whether instead a person is obligated to testify only because a curse has been uttered that places him or her under such an obligation.

23. Simian-Yofre, *TDOT* 10:500.

24. Wells, *Law of Testimony*, 59.

25. "There are various ways in which a person may become a witness to an activity. One may see the wrongful act taking place. Or if one has not seen the act, one may come to know about it (ידע). It is not said how that one comes to know about it. Hoffmann (1:197) suggests that one learns about it from the guilty party. Another possibility is that the guilty party implicates the witness in the act, e.g., a thief shares some of the stolen loot with another, and that person thereby eventually comes to realize who has committed the robbery. The interpretation that a person fails to testify when called upon by a general oath coincides best with the wording that he sins. The issue in this case is the well-being of the community. In ancient Israel, a close-knit society without a police force, the security of the community depended on each citizen's informing the leaders of any wrongdoing or clandestine activity. Failure to report any aberrant activity would endanger the community's safety and solidarity" (Hartley, *Leviticus*, 68).

26. Wells, *Law of Testimony*, 62.

The next two examples come from Numbers 5:13 and 35:30. Numbers 5:13 deals with a peculiar case where a jealous husband suspects that his wife has committed adultery, but there is an absence of witnesses *wᵊ ʿēḏ ʾên* (וְעֵד אֵין) "no witness" *bāh* (בָּהּ) "against her." Accordingly, we can speak about so-called divine judgment which "was envisaged for those cases in which the question of guilt or innocence could not be clarified by human means."[27] Since it was forbidden to make a judgment without more than one witness, guilt or innocence of an accused wife will be determined by divine judgment through a specific ritually performed test. The purpose of such a test is not to administer a sentence but to establish the guilt or innocence of a woman and her husband.[28] However, the sentence is in the hands of YHWH (Num 5:16–31) which implies that YHWH has a proper witness knowledge, and accordingly can prove her innocence or punish her for her guilt.

Numbers 35:30 deals with the establishment of a sufficient number of witnesses for conviction,[29] and it is found in the context of handling murders and allegations of murder (Num 35:10–34). In the text we have two words for witness. First, the text says that a person is to be put to death by *lᵊpî ʿēḏîm* (לְפִי עֵדִים) "at/by the mouth of witnesses" which implies minimum of two "mouths." Secondly, in the text *wᵊ ʿēḏ ʾeḥāḏ lōʾ-yaʿăneh ḇᵊnep̄eš* (וְעֵד אֶחָד לֹא־יַעֲנֶה בְנֶפֶשׁ) "one witness will not answer/testify against a person" we again have a verb *ʿānāh* (עָנָה) "to reply, answer." Wells[30] emphasizes that Numbers 35:30 does not define the minimum number of witnesses. Rather it states that a plurality of witnesses is required and there is a broad consensus among scholars that in line with Deuteronomy 17:2–7 that means two witnesses are sufficient. The whole assembly was called to judge the case (v. 24), and in that step, the role of witnesses was crucial because only based on two or three witnesses was possible to establish whether the murder was intentional or not. Only then a person could be condemned to death.[31]

Furthermore, the story of a sufficient number of witnesses for conviction continues in Deuteronomy 17:6–7 with the legislation about the

27. Noth, *Numbers*, 48–49.
28. Czander, "You are my Witnesses", 109.
29. Czander, 91.
30. Wells, *Law of Testimony*, 105.
31. Czander, "You are my Witnesses", 91–92.

minimum number of witnesses required for enforcing the death penalty, and Deuteronomy 19:15–18 with the legislation for making a verdict regarding any accusation. Deuteronomy 17:2–7 deals with a person who has done *ʾeṯ-hāraʿ* (אֶת־הָרַע) "what is evil" which is defined as violation of the first commandment not to worship other gods. Deuteronomy 17:3 reveals that the accused party had broken covenant by *ʿāḇaḏ* (עָבַד) "serving" and *ḥāwāh* (חָוָה) "worshiping" other gods such as the sun, moon, and stars. Merrill observes that the responsibility for investigating rumors of such disloyalty to the covenant rested upon the community which is seen from the fact that throughout the passage the singular pronoun "you" is used.[32] In Deuteronomy 17:6 noun *ʿēḏîm* (עֵדִים) "witnesses" appears twice in the expression "two witnesses or three witnesses" and noun *ʿēḏ* (עֵד) "witness" once. The activity of witnesses is described with expression *ʿal-pî* (עַל־פִּי) "on the mouth," which imply that their testimony is primarily verbal. But in order to safeguard against injustice on the part of dishonest or mistaken witnesses, at a minimum the testimony of two witnesses was required. Also, public officials were charged to investigate thoroughly the accusation (v. 4), since "the person shall not be put to death on the testimony of a single witness."[33] If the community determined that an abomination had occurred in Israel, witnesses are primarily responsible for the execution of the sentence (it is not mentioned who is responsible for reaching the verdict), and this time other parts of the human body come into play: *yāḏ* (יָד) "hand." *ʿēḏîm* (עֵדִים) must by their "hand" (singular) put the guilty person to death (Deuteronomy 17:7). So, we have this connection between "mouth" and "hand."

In Deuteronomy 19:15 the noun *ʿēḏ* (עֵד) appears once, and *ʿēḏîm* (עֵדִים) twice. The verse begins with the prohibition, "One witness will not rise," where the activity of *ʿēḏ* (עֵד) is described with a verb *qûm* (קוּם) "to rise" in its imperfect (yiqtōl) form *lōʾ-yāqûm* (לֹא־יָקוּם) with negation *lōʾ* (לֹא) "no, not." Furthermore, a noun *ʿēḏîm* (עֵדִים) "witnesses" appears twice in the same expression as in Deuteronomy 17:6 ("two witnesses or three witnesses"), but with one difference: in Deuteronomy 17:6 a sufficient number of witnesses were needed in order to execute proper punishment, but in Deuteronomy 19:15, a sufficient number of witnesses were needed in order

32. Merrill, *Deuteronomy Vol. 4*, 260–261.
33. Christensen, *Deuteronomy 1:1–21:9*, 369–370.

to reach *dāḇār* (דָּבָר) "word" or in this case "verdict." As in Deuteronomy 17:6, the expression *ʿal-pî* (עַל־פִּי) "on the mouth" appears, emphasizing the verbal activity of witnesses.

Deuteronomy 19:16 discusses the situation when a false witness appears in the court. Such a witness *ʿēḏ* (עֵד) is described with the noun *ḥāmās* (חָמָס) "violence, wrong," and the activities of such witness are described with two verbs *qûm* (קוּם) "to rise" and *ʿānāh* (עָנָה) "to answer." And that such activities are pointed toward accusation or witnessing *against* is supported by the presence of expression *bᵊʾîš* (בְּאִישׁ) "against man." In Deuteronomy 19:18 "If the witness is a false witness" noun *ʿēḏ* (עֵד) appears twice. The first time it is modified with a noun *šeqer* (שֶׁקֶר) "deception, lie, falsehood," creating the expression "false" or "lying" witness. Second time *ʿēḏ* (עֵד) is brought in connection with the activity of speaking *ʿānāh* (עָנָה) "to answer," but such speech is qualified again with *šeqer* (שֶׁקֶר) thus creating an expression "answered/testified falsely" *ḇᵊʾāḥîw* (בְּאָחִיו) "against his brother."

The fact that false witness in Deuteronomy 19:16 is described as *ḥāmās* (חָמָס) and in Deuteronomy 19:18 as *šeqer* (שֶׁקֶר) for Wells means that such a person is not just a person who gives a testimony "against" someone, in order to confirm the accuser's accusation, but the accuser himself. The person described as a "false" or "malicious witness" (Person A) in v. 16 is the one who testifies falsely against another person (Person B) and 19:18–19 says that the court has determined that Person A is a false witness. Accordingly, Person A must be punished with the same punishment that he was attempting to impose upon Person B. From here Wells argues that Person A is someone who has an agenda to see Person B punished with a particular punishment and is not some merely disinterested third party in the case.[34] If Wells is correct, that means that "witness" in this case stands for "accuser."

From these few examples, we can see that the instruction for a sufficient number of witnesses (Num 35; Deut 17 and 19) was crucial for reaching the verdict and execution of the punishment because, particularly in life-and-death issues, one would want to rest a case on sound evidence and reliable testimony.[35] According to von Rad, since the burden of proof in the Israelite legal system was largely on the accused man, the influence of witnesses

34. Wells, *Law of Testimony*, 46.

35. Merrill, *Deuteronomy Vol. 4*, 279.

potentially could have a great impact on the verdict.[36] In order to minimize the influence of false witnesses who could be motivated by various reasons to show partiality or act on the basis of an evil agenda, this ordinance ensured "that only evidence corroborated by at least two persons shall be accepted against the accused." Also, this command ensures that the prohibition against false witness proscribed in the ninth commandment is obeyed even if this could not guarantee in every instance justice and fairness.

1.2 Usage of ʿēḏûṯ (עֵדוּת) in the Pentateuch

The concept of testimony in the Pentateuch is primarily vertical because it comes from YHWH to the people of Israel in the form of Mosaic covenant. All elements of the Mosaic covenant are connected with the noun *ʿēḏûṯ* (עֵדוּת), and they are present in the form of:

a) the Decalogue: Exodus 25:16, 21; 30:6, 36; 31:18; 32:15; 34:29; 40:20; Leviticus 16:13; Numbers 17:4, 10; Deuteronomy 4:45; 6:17, 20; 31:26,
b) the ark of the covenant: Exodus 16:34; 25:22; 26:33, 34; 27:21; 30:6, 26; 31:7; 39:35; 40:3, 5, 21; Numbers 4:5; 7:89,
c) the tabernacle: Exodus 38:21; Numbers 1:50, 53; 9:15; 10:11; 17:7, 8; 18:2, and
d) the veil: Leviticus 24:3.

The foundational idea is that the Decalogue or the "Ten Words" itself are a form of testimony, and other cultic elements in connection with it, receive this attribute of testimony. Accordingly, the Decalogue but also the tent, the ark, and the veil are "testimonies that speak of God and his desire to have a people unto himself, his election of his people in Egypt, and his covenant at Sinai."[37]

1.2.1 Decalogue

The primary element of such vertical testimony is "the two tablets of the Testimony" which in Exodus 16:34 and 25:16 is simply called *hā ʿēḏuṯ* (הָעֵדֻת) "the Testimony." In Exodus 31:18 they are additionally described

36. von Rad, *Deuteronomy*, 129.
37. Ashley, *Book of Numbers*, 67–68.

as *šᵊnê luḥōṯ hā ʿēḏuṯ* (שְׁנֵי לֻחֹת הָעֵדֻת) "two tablets of Testimony" and *luḥōṯ ʾeḇen* (לֻחֹת אֶבֶן) "tablets of stone," and in Exodus 34:28 "tablets" are understood as *diḇrê habbᵊrîṯ* (דִּבְרֵי הַבְּרִית) "the words of the covenant" and *ʿăśereṯ haddᵊḇārîm* (עֲשֶׂרֶת הַדְּבָרִים) "ten Words" or "Ten Commandments." So, there is an interesting dynamic and interplay between the Decalogue as testimony, covenant, and commandments.

Today what is commonly known as the "Ten Commandments" are also defined as "the Testimony." While the "Ten Words" as "commandments" imply a prescribed and obligatory way of behaviour that YHWH expects, if we understand them as "testimony," according to its foundational meaning of "repetition" or "doing something again," this draws a different and somewhat puzzling picture, and raises the question: in what way do the Ten Commandments function as testimony and to what exactly they are testifying?

First, eight out of the Ten Commandments are given in the imperfect (yiqtōl); the commandment about honoring your father and mother (Exod 20:12) is given in the imperative, and the commandment about remembering and keeping Sabbath (Exod 20:8) is given in the infinitive absolute. However, the following verbs in the same commandment "you shall labor and do" (Exod 20:9) is combination of imperfect (yiqtōl) and weqātal (waw+perfect), and in "you shall not do any work" (Exod 20:10) the verb is again in imperfect (yiqtōl). These eight commandments are formed with negation *lōʾ* (לֹא) which with imperfect (yiqtōl) is used almost exclusively for expressing commands, or commandments. Additionally, *lōʾ* (לֹא) with imperfect (yiqtōl) expresses a categorical prohibition of binding validity both for the present and the future.[38] Accordingly, the better translation is not the one which emphasizes present "do not," but the future aspect "you shall/will not." Probably in this present/future aspect of commandments we can find the place for the idea of testimony.

Second, these commandments serve as a witness of YHWH's will and the permanent standard or testimony for their lives, and this present/future aspect reveals their repetitive nature: YHWH does not have to repeat these commandments; since they are permanent (present and future) expression of his will, they stand as a witness of YHWH's will to every new generation

38. Hamilton, *Exodus: Exegetical Commentary*, 317.

of Israelites. Their repetitiveness lies in their permanency, which makes them testimony.

The two tablets of the Testimony are also described as "the words of the covenant" (Exod 34:28; cf. Exod 16:34). First, in Exodus 16:34 *hā ʿēḏuṯ* (הָעֵדֻת) semantically could be translated as "covenant" as it is in NEB and NRSV versions, but this word can also mean "treaty" and/or "testimony." Second, in Exodus 34:28 the Ten Words are brought in connection with the words of the covenant. This implies probably that the *Mosaic covenant* itself is a form of YHWH's testimony to the people of Israel. But this does not mean that the Ten Words equals covenant, because, as Exodus 34:27 says, they serve as conditions, requirements and foundation upon which YHWH made the Mosaic covenant with Israel.[39]

Based on all this we can see that in Exodus there is a semantic and theological overlap between "testimony," "words/commandments" and "covenant." This opens up an interesting perspective about the concept of witness, because the witness which YHWH provides is both verbal (YHWH spoke these words) and visible through particular object – "the two tablets." Semantically, if we understand the "Ten Commandments" as "Ten Words" or as the "two tablets of the Testimony," we have a diverse and rich description of YHWH's speech which resulted in the Ten Commandments: it is

---

39. When we compare in Exodus translations of *ʿēḏûṯ* (עֵדוּת) in the NRVS and NIV, we can see that the NRSV uses the expression "the covenant" and the NIV "covenant law." Hence, when *ʿēḏûṯ* (עֵדוּת) refers to the Decalogue, the NRSV uses the word "the covenant" (Exod 25:16, 21; 30:6, 36; 40:20) or the expression "the two tablets of the covenant" (Exod 31:18; 32:15; 34:29), while the NIV always uses the phrase "tablets of the covenant law" or "the two tablets of the covenant law." In Exodus 30:36 where the meaning of *ʿēḏûṯ* (עֵדוּת) is somewhat ambiguous, the NRSV translates as "the covenant" referring to the Decalogue, while the NIV says, "the ark of the covenant law." When *ʿēḏûṯ* (עֵדוּת) refers to the ark (Exod 16:34; 25:22; 26:33, 34; 27:21; 30:6, 26; 31:7; 39:35; 40:3, 5, 21), the NRSV uses the expression "the ark of the covenant," while the NIV uses "the ark of the covenant law." In Exodus 16:34 where the meaning of *ʿēḏûṯ* (עֵדוּת) is ambiguous (it can refer to the Decalogue or the ark), the NRSV translates as "the covenant," and the NIV as "the tablets of the covenant law." In Exodus 27:21 where *ʿēḏûṯ* (עֵדוּת) again stands alone, the NRSV uses "the covenant" while the NIV understands it as "the ark of the covenant law." And finally, when *ʿēḏûṯ* (עֵדוּת) is brought in the connection with tabernacle (Exod 38:21), the NRSV uses the expression "the tabernacle of the covenant" and the NIV "the tabernacle of the covenant law." It is noticeable that the NIV in its translation combines together the ideas of "covenant" and "law" creating the expression "covenant law" where the emphasis is on the "law," and "covenant" functions more as an adjective, the NRSV puts much more emphasis on the covenant. Thus, tablets, ark and tabernacle are defined by the idea of "covenant." However, for the sake of theological correctness, we must say that "covenant" is not the same as "Law." Keeping of the "Law" is the condition for continuation of the "covenant."

testimony, it produces YHWH's words/commandments and it can be even understood as covenant.

1.2.2 Ark, Tabernacle, Veil

The Decalogue which served as continuous testimony of YHWH's covenant with Israel, transfers or imparts its "testimony" to other objects (ark, tabernacle, and veil). What is the possible significance of such transfer?

The "two tablets of the Testimony" in Exodus are also called "the two tablets of stone," and some commentators see the presence of different traditions in this change. So, F. M. Cross notes that *ʿēḏûṯ* (עֵדוּת) is frequently the designation of cultic law in the P literature (Exod 25:16, 21, 22; 26:33, 34; 27:21; 30:6, 36), and it is also used to describe the worshiping congregation in the tabernacle (i.e. Num 1:2–3). In this way the content of the revelation from the Decalogue in the Non-P History (the two tablets of stone) is changed in the P history to the revelation of the tabernacle and its cult in Exodus 25:1–31:17.[40] The significance of this change is this:

> The "tablets of stone" limit the divine words to the Decalogue, thus emphasizing the presence of God as speech. The 'tablets of testimony', by contrast, contain the entire architectural plans of the tabernacle and its instructions for cultic rituals. . . . The Non-P History idealizes the presence of God as speech. The tent of meeting, the tablets of stone, and the setting of Mount Horeb conform to the account of theophany in the Non-P history, when God speaks directly to the people in issuing the Decalogue (19:9, 19; 20:1–20). The P history[41] emphasizes

40. Dozeman, *Exodus*, 679.

41. The "P history" refers to the JEDP Documentary Hypothesis which asserts that behind the Pentateuch are four source documents, called J (Yahwist), E (Elohist), D (Deuteronomist), and P (Priestly Code). However, in recent scholarship the classical version of the Documentary Hypothesis has undergone many revisions and adaptations. According to Jean-Louis Ska (*Pentateuch*, 161), new methods of research contribute to the study of Pentateuch, and there are so many schools of thought that he feels it is impossible to present them all in the scope of his book on introduction to the Pentateuch. Discussing the current emphasis on synchronic study of the Pentateuch (such as "canonical reading" of Scripture, structuralism, semiotics, and narratology), he observes that "The best method is the one that succeeds in explaining the text of the Pentateuch with the greatest clarity and without ignoring the complexity that the preceding chapters have attempted to underline. 'Losing' time by walking down the paths that have been opened by research during the past centuries is actually to gain time; one does not need to do the work that has already been done and may be able to avoid repeating past

> more the visual presence of God. The tabernacle, the tablets of testimony, and the setting on Mount Sinai provide location and structure for the fiery Glory of Yahweh to reside on earth.[42]

Accordingly, in Exodus, the tablets of the Testimony that will be put in the ark (Exod 25:21), will turn this ark into "the ark of the Testimony."[43] Similarly, the tabernacle becomes also "the tabernacle of the Testimony" (Exod 38:21). It is unclear whether this means that the ark and the tabernacle itself become one form of testimony, or they just receive this attribute due to the fact that they contain (as a container) the testimony of YHWH written in two tablets. Whatever the case, we observe the dynamic nature of testimony: things that receive or accept the testimony become involved and included in the testimony.

The element of the tabernacle in Leviticus 16:13 described as *ʿal- hā ʿēḏûṯ* (עַל־הָעֵדוּת) "above the Testimony" is an abbreviation for the phrase "ark of the Testimony" (see Exod 16:34; 27:21; 30:6, 36; Num 17:4, 10), and in Leviticus 24:3 *lᵉpārōḵeṯ hā ʿēḏuṯ* (לְפָרֹכֶת הָעֵדֻת) "the curtain of the Testimony," and expression that is unique in the OT.

In the book of Numbers, the cultic aspect of testimony is present in expressions such as *miškan hā ʿēḏuṯ* (מִשְׁכַּן הָעֵדֻת) "the tabernacle of the Testimony" in Numbers 1:50; 1:53; 10:11; *ʾōhel hā ʿēḏuṯ* (אֹהֶל הָעֵדֻת) "the tent of the

---

mistakes" (Ska, *Pentateuch*, 164). Jonathan Huddleston ("*Recent Scholarship on Pentateuch*", 194–195) observes that "Recent work on the Pentateuch has struggled with the methodological question of whether to use 'diachronic' (historical) or 'synchronic' (literary) analysis and to determine how these two perspectives do or do not fit together." He continues that the current scholarly consensus is that the Pentateuch is a composite work, and even those who speak of a single Pentateuchal "author" leave room for earlier source-material and later editing (Huddleston, "*Recent Scholarship on Pentateuch*", 196). However, contrary to Documentary hypothesis, many now think that the Pentateuch is already thoroughly exilic in character – even if it relies on earlier oral and written material. The focus is no longer on the earliest traditions attested in the Pentateuch, a "quest for the oldest sources," but on investigating the latest passages added at the end of the Pentateuch's growth – post-P material tying earlier traditions or sources together. The outlook is not that various sources have been combined mechanically together, but Pentateuch is viewed more and more as "rolling corpus" (in a sense that small piece of pre-existing text triggered exegesis or commentary. This corpus rolled over a long period of time and continued to roll in the post-exilic period) (Huddleston, "Recent Scholarship on Pentateuch," 200).

42. Dozeman, *Exodus*, 578.

43. Exodus 16:34; 25:22; 26:33, 34; 27:21; 30:6, 26; 31:7; 39:35; 40:3, 5, 21.

Testimony" in Numbers 9:15; 17:7–8 (Matt 17:22–23);[44] 18:2; *ʾărōn hā ʿēḏuṯ* (אֲרֹן הָעֵדֻת) "the ark of the Testimony" in Numbers 4:5; 7:89 and; *hā ʿēḏûṯ* (הָעֵדֻת) "Testimony" in Numbers 17:4 (Matt 17:19); 17:10 (Matt 17:25). An interesting overlap occurs in Numbers 9:15 where we have two synonymous expressions *miškān* (מִשְׁכָּן) "tabernacle" and *ʾōhel hā ʿēḏuṯ* (אֹהֶל הָעֵדֻת) "the tent of the Testimony." Two interpretations are possible. Either a) "tabernacle" describes the whole tabernacle, while "tent" is a specific narrower location in the tabernacle where the testimony was kept, or b) this genitive construction "the tabernacle (or dwelling-place) of the tent of the Testimony" describes the whole tabernacle.[45] Furthermore, in Numbers 17:4 (Matt 17:19) and Numbers 17:10 (Matt 17:25) the expression *hā ʿēḏuṯ* (הָעֵדֻת) appears, but to what does it refer? In some contexts, it refers to the Decalogue (Exod 25:16, 21; Exod 40:20), but in others it could refer to the "ark of the covenant" (cf. Lev 16:13).

An interesting question is whether the Israelites who accepted these two tablets become the people of testimony or not. Although Exodus does not explicitly attribute this characteristic to the people, Thomas Dozeman ties *hā ʿēḏuṯ* (הָעֵדֻת) in Exodus 16:34 to the description of the people as a "congregation" in Exodus 16:2 with the expression *kol- ʿăḏaṯ bᵊnê-yiśrāʾēl* (כָּל־עֲדַת בְּנֵי־יִשְׂרָאֵל).[46] As previously noted, *ʿăḏaṯ* (עֲדַת) derived from *ʿēḏāh* (עֵדָה) can signify congregation, or testimony and something that testifies.

On this basis, we can conclude that the idea of testimony or witness in connection with the "two tablets" is connected with both YHWH's speech (YHWH spoke these words and gave them to be written), and his visible presence (ark, tabernacle).

1.3 Usage of ʿēḏāh (עֵדָה) and ʿēḏōṯ (עֵדֹת) in the Pentateuch

In the Pentateuch *ʿēḏāh* (עֵדָה) appears in Genesis 21:30 and 31:52 for impersonal witnesses in the social context, and three times in its plural form *ʿēḏōṯ* (עֵדֹת) in the legal context as description for the Torah (Deut 4:45; 6:17, 20).

44. Beginning with Numbers 16:36, the verse numbers in the English Bible differ from the verse numbers in the Hebrew text (BHS). With Numbers 18:1 the verse numbers are again the same. Hence, Numbers 17:7–8 in English Bible is Numbers 17:22–23 in MT and so on. Verse numbers in LXX are the same as in English Bible.

45. Spence-Jones, *Numbers*, 79; Lange, *Numbers*, 54.

46. Dozeman, *Exodus*, 377.

1.3.1 Genesis

In the relationship between Abraham and Abimelech (Gen 21:22–34) which ends up with establishment of the covenant (Gen 21:32) the dispute is the question of who dug a well. Although this is a legal matter, we can notice that Abraham and Abimelech did not take this matter to the court. Instead, they made an agreement with each other: "No sacrificial activity is involved, nor is there any covenant meal. The parties swear to the pact simply in words. In accepting the lambs Abimelech releases rights over the well and concedes ownership to the patriarch. In other words, Abimelech is challenged to accept the reliability of Abraham's word."[47] Similarly, to Hamilton, Kenneth A. Mathews observes that by accepting the animals as a "witness," Abimelech would be accepting the version of Abraham's account of events, and commonly agreement such as this included witnesses such as heaven and earth (e.g. Deut 4:26), or an erected pillar (Gen 31:52) which served as memorials to which parties can make appeal.[48]

Seven lambs as *lᵊ ʿēḏāh* (לְעֵדָה) "for witness" or "to witness" (Gen 21:30) serve as explicit witness. The action verb *tihyeh-llî* (תִּהְיֶה־לִּי) "to be for me" signifies that these seven lambs are *witness for* Abraham. They testify to his claim that he dug this particular well. The imperfect (yiqtōl) form of the verb *hāyāh* (הָיָה) "to be" implies that the seven lambs confirm Abraham's claim from this point on. Although the lambs cannot speak nor do they have any past relationship with this well of water (such as knowing, hearing or being present when Abraham dig that well), they are presented as witnesses.

Since we have already analyzed the covenantal agreement between Laban and Jacob in Genesis 31, it is sufficient to say that in Genesis 31:52 stone pillar is identified as *ʿēḏāh* (עֵדָה) witness of this covenant as well. As in Genesis 31:48, the verb in this part of the sentence is missing, but the most probable reading is to supply the verb "is." Hence the stone (NIV "heap") "is a witness" and heap "is a witness" (so NRSV and NIV).

1.3.2 Deuteronomy

In presenting the Law as a testimony, Deuteronomy continues in the same vein as Exodus, Numbers and Leviticus. Deuteronomy 4:44 mentions *tôrāh*

47. Hamilton, *Book of Genesis*, 92.

48. Mathews, *Genesis 11*, 281.

(תּוֹרָה) "Law," and Deuteronomy 4:45 uses expressions such as *mišpāṭîm* (מִשְׁפָּטִים) "judgments," *ḥuqqîm* (חֻקִּים) "statutes" and *ʿēḏōṯ* (עֵדֹת) "the testimonies." By this construction Deuteronomy 4:45 further defines the Law by adding these three stipulations,[49] or summarizes the content of the Law as testimonies, statutes, and ordinances.[50] *ʿēḏōṯ* (עֵדֹת) "the testimonies" appears again together with *ḥuqqîm* (חֻקִּים) "statutes," *miṣwōt* (מִצְוֹת) "commandments" and *mišpāṭîm* (מִשְׁפָּטִים) "judgments" in Deuteronomy 6:17 and Deuteronomy 6:20.

1.4 Usage of ʿûḏ (עוּד) in the Pentateuch

In Pentateuch *ʿûḏ* (עוּד) is used in all three contexts (social, legal and religious), with two primary meanings: to describe the activity of witnessing and calling or summoning witnesses to witness.

1.4.1 ʿûḏ (עוּד) as the activity of witnessing

As part of the social context, in Genesis 43:3 Judah son of Jacob repeats Joseph's words from their meeting in Egypt: "The man solemnly warned us, saying, 'You shall not see my face unless your brother is with you'" (NRSV). Verb *ʿûḏ* (עוּד) is used as the Hiphil infinitive absolute *hāʿēḏ* (הָעֵד) and the Hiphil perfect (qātal) *hēʿiḏ* (הֵעִד).[51] The infinitive absolute is used to emphasize verbal meaning, so the perfect (qātal) "warned" prefaced with infinitive "solemnly" stands for a warning or threat that is not empty. It defines a warning as severe, clear, or certain.[52] This warning was given as *bānû* (בָּנוּ) "against us." Judah repeats this warning to his father Jacob, but this time the verb *ʾāmar* (אָמַר) "to say" is used twice: first time as the imperfect (yiqtōl) *wayyōʾmer* (וַיֹּאמֶר) and second time as the Qal infinitive construct *lēʾmōr* (לֵאמֹר) with preposition *lᵊ* (לְ) "to, for, etc."

The only example of testifying in the legal context comes from Exodus 21:29, which uses the Hophal weqātal (waw+perfect) *wᵊhûʿaḏ* (וְהוּעַד) in the expression *wᵊhûʿaḏ biḇʿālâw* (וְהוּעַד בִּבְעָלָיו) "testified to his owner." This denotes a judicial, formal (passive) warning. The owner has received a

49. Hall, *Deuteronomy*, 111.

50. O'Brien, *Deuteronomistic History Hypothesis*, 61.

51. The same construction occurs in 1 Samuel 8:9 and Jeremiah 11:7.

52. Reyburn and Fry, *Genesis*, 966.

"warning" about his ox's behavior from some third party. But since the owner did not control his ox and the beast gored and killed a man or a woman, both the ox and its owner should be brought before the court and executed. We could say that the ox who was first the object of the message has become a messenger or witness against his owner. According to Benno Jacob, the ox's "presence served as a constant warning that he was a declared gorer and his master should be cautious. The owner and the ox had to appear before the judiciary at the same time and were confronted there."[53] Once brought before the court, an ox becomes evidence that witnesses against his owner. Osborn and Hatton add that the expression "and the owner has been warned" does not reveal by whom its owner had been warned," nor whether we can know the owner was confronted with some material evidences, or if it was only a verbal report.[54]

Moses appears as witness in the religious context in Exodus 19:21, 23, and Deuteronomy 8:19 and 32:46. In Exodus 19 Moses is in YHWH's presence, and YHWH instructs him to go down and warn Israelites not to cross the boundary that YHWH has established. The fact that he was present when YHWH declared these words of warning qualifies Moses to act as a witness to the people, and to repeat the warning. Further, since Moses is the only one who had permission to cross the boundary, he held a unique mediatory position. Here, repetition of the warning is a result of his position as witness and serves to enforce his mediatory position. In Exodus 19:21 YHWH charges Moses with the verb *ʿûḏ* (עוּד) in the Hiphil imperative form *hāʿēḏ* (הָעֵד), to warn" *bāʿām* (בָּעָם) "people, nation." The same verb *ʿûḏ* (עוּד) is repeated in 19:23, but this time as Hiphil perfect *haʿēḏōṯāh* (הַעֵדֹתָה) "you warned," and the object of warning is *bānû* (בָּנוּ) "us." In addition to verb *ʿûḏ* (עוּד), in Exodus 19:23 we also have the Qal infinitive construct of the verb *ʾāmar* (אָמַר) "to say" which points out that "warning" was given verbally through "saying." According to Hamilton,[55] *ʿûḏ* (עוּד) can describe someone who is called to be a witness by repeating certain significant information to a given audience, and this is exactly what we have in Exodus 19:21–23.

53. Jacob, *Exodus*, 666.

54. Osborn and Hatton, *Exodus*, 511.

55. Hamilton, *Exodus: Exegetical Commentary,* 297.

Deuteronomy 8:19 also has *ʿûḏ* (עוּד) in perfect (qātal) form, but here Moses performs the activity of witnessing by giving specific warning. There are no other witnesses like in Deuteronomy 31:28. This verb can be translated with present tense "I testify" or with past tense "I have testified." Whichever translation is better, his testimony which consists of consequences that Israelites will suffer was given *hayyôm* (הַיּוֹם) "today." However, conjunction *ʾim* (אִם) "if" speaks about conditional situation where consequences will be experienced "if you do forget the LORD your God and follow other gods. . . ." Accordingly, we will argue later that Moses is presented as *witness about* – although *ḇāḵem* (בָּכֶם) "against you," carries the connotation of witnessing *against*.

In Deuteronomy 32:46, as in Deuteronomy 8:19,[56] Moses is the one who speaks, but this time *lᵉḵōl-haddᵉḇārîm* (לְכָל־הַדְּבָרִים) "all the words" are defined as testimony. The main verb is imperative of a verb *śîm* (שִׂים) "to place, to set, to put," and Israelites need to "take" *lᵉḵōl-haddᵉḇārîm* (לְכָל־הַדְּבָרִים) "all the words." Taken together with Hiphil participle absolute of *ʿûḏ* (עוּד) which governs this expression, "all the words," and with expressions *hayyôm* (הַיּוֹם) "today" and *bāḵem* (בָּכֶם) "against you," Deuteronomy 32:46 can be translated as "all the words that I am giving in witness against you"[57] or "all the words" through which I lay down my testimony".[58]

1.4.2 ʿûḏ (עוּד) as calling to witness

Examples where *ʿûḏ* (עוּד) means "call to witness" come from Deuteronomy, and there as witnesses in religious context refer to both personal and impersonal witnesses. In Deuteronomy 4:26 and 30:19 Moses "calls to witness" *ʾet-haššāmayim wᵊ ʾet-hā ʾāreṣ* (אֶת־הַשָּׁמַיִם וְאֶת־הָאָרֶץ) "the heavens and the earth"

56. It is interesting to notice that besides verb *ʿûḏ* (עוּד), the common denominator is expression *ḇāḵem* (בָּכֶם) which in the context of witness in Deuteronomy appears in Deuteronomy 4:26; 8:19; 30:19 and 32:46. Similar expression *bām* (בָּם) "against them" appears in Deuteronomy 31:28, and *hayyôm* (הַיּוֹם) which appears in Deuteronomy 4:26; 8:19; 30:19 and 32:46. *hayyôm* (הַיּוֹם) does not appear in Deuteronomy 31:28, but an idea of "today" can be seen in a noun *ʾōzen* (אֹזֶן) "ear, hearing" – ". . . that I may recite these words in their hearing. . . ."

57. Christensen, *Deuteronomy 21:10–34:12*, 823.

58. But to what exactly "all the words" refers to? It could refer to: the words of the song that Moses has just recited, or some or all of the earlier part of the book of Deuteronomy (Bratcher and Hatton, *Deuteronomy*, 566); the whole book of Deuteronomy, including the Song of Moses (Christensen, *Deuteronomy 21:10–34:12*, 823); or pre-eminently to the song which should help to faithfulness to the law (Schröeder, *Deuteronomy*, 218).

ḇāḵem (בָּכֶם) "against you." Both texts emphasize that "the heavens and the earth" are established as witnesses from that day on, since verb *ʿûḏ* (עוּד) is in qatal (perfect) and accompanied by expression *hayyôm* (הַיּוֹם) "today." In Deuteronomy 31:28 Moses *dāḇar* (דִּבֵּר) "speaks" to Israel *haddᵊḇārîm hāʾēlleh* (הַדְּבָרִים הָאֵלֶּה) "these words," and in doing so, he uses *ʿûḏ* (עוּד) to call *ʾet-haššāmayim wᵊʾet-hāʾāreṣ* (אֶת־הַשָּׁמַיִם וְאֶת־הָאָרֶץ) "the heavens and the earth," as witnesses, but this time *bām* (בָּם) "against them." Although "the heavens and the earth" are called as witness, they are invited as witnesses to the words that Moses speaks. Hence, their observing role here is emphasized.

2. The concept of witness in the Writings – passage analysis

Since the Writings are divided into two main sections: Historical Books, Wisdom, and Poetry, we will analyze the concept of witness in accordance with that division.[59]

2.1 Usage of ʿēḏ (עֵד), ʿēḏîm (עֵדִים), ʿēḏêḵā (עֵדֶיךָ) and ʿēḏêy (עֵדַי) in the Writings

Noun *ʿēḏ* (עֵד) and its plural forms *ʿēḏîm* (עֵדִים), *ʿēḏêḵā* (עֵדֶיךָ) and *ʿēḏêy* (עֵדַי) appear twenty-eight times in the Writings, and they are used for both impersonal and personal witnesses. While impersonal witnesses appear only in religious context, personal witnesses appear in both religious and legal contexts.

59. In the context of the Hebrew Bible "Writings" includes poetical books (Psalms, Proverbs, and Job), the Scrolls (Song of Solomon, Ruth, Lamentations of Jeremiah, Ecclesiastes, and Esther), prophecy (Daniel), and history (Ezra, Nehemiah, and I and II Chronicles). In Christian Bibles, books that belong to the category of "Writings" are put in different categories such as Historical Books, Wisdom, and Poetry. During the writing of my dissertation, I was advised to use label "Writings" for historical, wisdom and poetry books, so in this book "Writings" includes the following books: Joshua, Judges, Ruth, 1–2 Samuel, 1–2 Kings, 1–2 Chronicles, Ezra, Nehemiah, Esther, Psalms, Job, Proverbs, Ecclesiastes, Song of Solomon.

2.1.1 Usage of ʿēḏ (עֵד) ʿēḏîm (עֵדִים), ʿēḏêḵā (עֵדֶיךָ) and ʿēḏêy (עֵדַי) in the Historical Books

2.1.1.1 Impersonal witnesses

The only example of impersonal witness is the altar in Joshua 22:27, 28, 34 which was built by tribes of Reuben, Gad and the half-tribe of Manasseh. This altar is explicitly limited to function as a witness and is not used for sacrifice (Josh 22:26–27). But what was the scope of its witness? Probably, the altar functioned as a witness to both groups in that it testified to national unity, it testified to the fact that the unifying factor is YHWH, and it testified about his divinity.[60] However, to grasp the true nature of altar's witness, one has to be familiar with the story that surrounds the building of the altar. In Joshua 22:27 there is no verb that modifies the noun ʿēḏ (עֵד), and the purpose of this altar is described as *bênênû ûḇênêḵem ûḇên dōrôṯênû ʾaḥărênû* (בֵּינֵינוּ וּבֵינֵיכֶם וּבֵין דֹּרוֹתֵינוּ אַחֲרֵינוּ) "between us and between you, and between our generations after us." In Joshua 22:28 where ʿēḏ (עֵד) appears, again we do not have a verb that modifies it. However, we have repetition of the expression *bênênû ûḇênêḵem* (בֵּינֵינוּ וּבֵינֵיכֶם) "between us and between you" from the previous verse.

In Joshua 22:34 the use of ʿēḏ (עֵד) is ambiguous, due to textual variations.[61] It can be translated: a) as part of the lengthy name for the altar (NIV)[62] or, b) as the name of the altar, followed by the description of its function (NASB, REB, NRSV, NLT).[63] In any case, this altar is erected as a testimony that YHWH is God, but as an inanimate object it requires living voices who will explain the story behind its building. As in the previous case, there is no verb that modifies the noun ʿēḏ (עֵד), and we have seen that the function of this altar is to be a witness *bênōṯênû* (בֵּינֹתֵינוּ) "between us."

2.1.1.2 Personal witnesses

Israelites mentioned in Joshua 24:2 appear as witnesses *ʿēḏîm* (עֵדִים) in a religious context. To ensure the fidelity of Israel toward YHWH, Joshua does

60. Butler, *Joshua*, 249.

61. Bratcher and Newman, *Translator's Handbook*, 288.

62. "And the Reubenites and the Gadites gave the altar this name: A Witness Between Us that the Lord is God."

63. ". . . and the Reubenites and the Gadites called the altar 'Witness,' for it is a witness between us that the Lord is God."

two things: first, he puts Israelites under solemn oath that they will serve YHWH alone (Josh 24:19–24), and second, he establishes the covenant between Israelites and YHWH (Josh 24:25–28). In both instances witnesses are present. For the oath of Israelites, the people themselves in Josh 24:22 are *ʿēḏîm* (עֵדִים) "witnesses," and for the establishment of the covenant, a stone in Josh 24:27 functions as *ʿēḏāh* (עֵדָה) "witness." Even though YHWH is not a witness in this case, Joshua, holds people as witnesses to their confession (Josh 24:22), since their oath will serve as testimony that will condemn them if they forsake YHWH in the future. Accordingly, in Josh 24:22 where people confirm their oath to serve YHWH, we do not have a verb that modifies the noun *ʿēḏîm* (עֵדִים). But in the context of expression *ʿēḏîm ʾattem bāḵem* (עֵדִים אַתֶּם בָּכֶם) "witnesses you [are] against yourselves," it seems obvious to understand people's role as witnesses in present sense "you are" (NRSV and NIV). *bāḵem* (בָּכֶם) "against yourselves" implies a negative witness, as though people are already condemning themselves since their failure to obey YHWH seems sure. After Joshua's declaration that people are witnesses, the people themselves confirm their role by repeating the word *ʿēḏîm* (עֵדִים) "witnesses."

In the Writings, the first example of witness in a legal context comes from Ruth 4:9, 10, 11 where the noun *ʿēḏîm* (עֵדִים) is used. Since the noun *tᵊʿûḏāh* (תְּעוּדָה) appears as part of the same story in Ruth 4:7, and it appears only here in the Writings, we will analyze both nouns together. Unlike other examples (except 1 Sam 12:5, below) *ʿēḏîm* (עֵדִים) here performs the role of an *observing witness*. Because he wanted to marry Ruth, Boaz challenged a man who had a right to be kinsman-redeemer before him to transfer his right to Boaz. This legal action needed to be confirmed by witnesses. The meaning of the word *tᵊʿûḏāh* (תְּעוּדָה) in Ruth 4:7 can be connected with the act of taking off and handing over the sandal, thus bearing the meaning of "ratification" or "validation." It can also refer to the formal act of witnessing by the elders and the people in the gate. In any case, the gathered assembly performed the role of witness since three times in Ruth 4:9, 10, 11 they are described as *ʿēḏîm* (עֵדִים) or "witnesses." Who are the witnesses and what is their function? As verse 2 indicates, Boaz intentionally selected ten of the elders of the town to serve as witnesses, but also in verse 4 "those who are sitting here" are also defined as *ʿēḏîm* (עֵדִים). Hence, witnesses were intentionally selected, but those who unintentionally happened to be there were also included in this group. The function of the gathered group or legal forum was not only to settle and resolve disputes of various kinds, but also to perform a notarial function. Here they served to ratify the agreement that Boaz made with Naomi's relative. Accordingly, twice (4:9, 10) Boaz declared *ʿēḏîm ʾattem hayyôm* (עֵדִים אַתֶּם הַיּוֹם) "witnesses you [are] today." In Ruth 4:11 (cf. Josh 24:22), the people respond simply by repeating Boaz's last word *ʿēḏîm* (עֵדִים) as the sign of their affirmation and acceptance of their role as witnesses.

The second example is in 1 Samuel 12:5, which closes the story about transfer of leadership from Samuel to Saul which began in chapter eight. Withdrawing from his duty as judge and prophet, Samuel wanted to receive affirmation of his just leadership up to this point. The declaration of his innocence is presented as a legal matter. The context is not strictly legal but also religious. Here we have a legal process involving three parts: a) listing the witnesses before whom the process took place (v. 3), b) an appeal to the witnesses and the naming of the legal material which they were to attest (vv. 3–5), c) a response by the witnesses declaring their willingness to attest (v. 5).[64] The main question for us is to define who the witnesses are in this case. We must address this issue on two levels.

On the first level, it is obvious from 1 Samuel 12:3 that YHWH and his *māšîaḥ* (מְשִׁיחַ) "anointed" (i.e. king), are the primary witnesses, because they are the third party which observe and testify to this legal process. We should note that YHWH and the king are not witnesses for Samuel's innocence *per se*. They can only witness to the verdict that people would pronounce regarding Samuel's lifestyle. YHWH and his anointed one are affirmed as witnesses here:

ʿēḏ yhwh bāḵem wᵊ ʿēḏ mᵊšîḥô hayyôm hazzeh

(עֵד יְהוָה בָּכֶם וְעֵד מְשִׁיחוֹ הַיּוֹם הַזֶּה)

"YHWH [is] witness against you [plural], and his anointed [is] witness this day." There is a note of ambiguity at the end of 1 Samuel 12:5 where the text says *wayyōʾmer ʿēḏ* (וַיֹּאמֶר עֵד) "And he said, 'witness.'" So, we have a singular "someone" who affirms that "someone else" (a masculine singular noun) is a witness. This singularity is puzzling because in 1 Samuel 12:3 and 12:5 two witnesses are defined (YHWH and the anointed one), and it would

64. Klein, *1 Samuel*, 115.

be expected that gathered people affirm both these witnesses. However, instead of plurality, at the end of 1 Samuel 12:5 we have singularity. It seems that people affirm only YHWH's role as witness, and the text leaves unclear why the anointed king did not affirm his own role as witness.[65] Anyhow, in 1 Samuel 12:5 they are presented as witnesses, but with a difference that YHWH is witness *bāḵem* (בָּכֶם) "against them" (which probably implies that he is a witness for Samuel), while the king is witness *hayyôm hazzeh* (הַיּוֹם הַזֶּה) "this day."

On the second level, people themselves function as witnesses. Their function is not confirmatory, since they must establish the verdict (they must take sides, "for" or "against"). In 1 Samuel 12:3 Samuel invites them to *ʿănû ḇi* (עֲנוּ בִי) "reply [testify] against me." Although the most frequent meaning of *ʿānāh* (עָנָה) is "to reply, answer," it also has meanings such as "to speak" or "to testify." Used together with *ḇi* (בִי), *ʿānāh* (עָנָה) in this context means "testify against me." Hence, people are invited as in a court of justice to provide an answer to the posed question since they are the one who observed Samuel's life and conduct.

2.1.2 Usage of ʿēḏ (עֵד), ʿēḏîm (עֵדִים), ʿēḏêḵā (עֵדֶיךָ) and ʿēḏêy (עֵדַי) in the Wisdom and Poetic Books

2.1.2.1 Impersonal witnesses

Impersonal witnesses in Wisdom and Poetic Books appear only in reference to Job's sufferings in Job 16:8 and 10:17. Clines[66] notices that in Job 16:8[67] despite some uncertainties in the Hebrew text, YHWH is responsible for Job's condition, and that serves as proof – to everyone but Job – that Job is a dreadful sinner.[68] *Wattiqmᵊṭēnî* (וַתִּקְמְטֵנִי) in the Qal wayyiqtōl (waw-consecutive + imperfect) form of the verb *qāmaṭ* (קָמַט), which primarily means "to bound, to seize, to grasp,"[69] supported by the verb *hāyāh* (הָיָה) "to

65. Klein, *1 Samuel*, 115.

66. Clines, *Job 1–20*, 381.

67. *wattiqməṭēnî lə ʿēḏ hāyāh* (וַתִּקְמְטֵנִי לְעֵד הָיָה) "You have shriveled me up and it became for a witness. . . ."

68. Clines, *Job 1–20*, 382.

69. Instead of translating *wattiqməṭēnî* (וַתִּקְמְטֵנִי) as "shriveled me up" Robert L. Alden (*Job*, 184) argues that the proper translation is "to bound" which also makes a good parallel with the word "gauntness" in verse 8b. If that is correct, then the emphasis is not so much on his afflictions per se (wrinkles or shriveling), but his afflictions are marks of a deeper problem

be" in its perfect (qātal) form, functions as *lᵊ ʿēḏ* (לְעֵד) "for witness." Notice that noun *ʿēḏ* (עֵד) comes with preposition *lᵊ* (לְ) and not *bᵊ* (בְּ). The second part of v. 8[70] is somewhat parallel to the previous one, because Job speaks about *ḵaḥăšî* (כַּחֲשִׁי) "my leanness" which *wayyāqom* (וַיָּקָם) "has risen up" *bî* (בִּי) "against me" to *yaʿăneh* (יַעֲנֶה) "testifies" *bᵊpānay* (בְּפָנַי) "against my face." *ḵaḥăšî* (כַּחֲשִׁי) comes from a noun *kaḥaš* (כַּחַשׁ) which can signify "lie, fraud" and "deception," but also physical conditions such as emaciation and chronic sickliness. This part of verse 8 clearly indicates that "witness" in this verse functions as *witness against*. Two prepositions *bᵊ* (בְּ) together with two verbs *qûm* (קוּם) and once *ʿānāh* (עָנָה) that appear in the context of witness in the OT, prove that point. Finally, although the precise identity of witnesses in Job 10:17 is debatable,[71] it seems that Job's suffering appears one more time as a *witness against* him. The text says that YHWH is the one who *tᵊḥaddēš* (תְּחַדֵּשׁ) "renews" or "brings new"[72] *ʿēḏêḵā* (עֵדֶיךָ) "your witnesses" *negdî* (נֶגְדִּי) "against me [Job]."

2.1.2.2 Personal witnesses

We will analyze personal witnesses according to the contexts in which they appear. In religious context the first personal witness comes in Job 16:19. Two words for witness occur: in line A *ʿēḏî* (עֵדִי) "my witness," and in line B *wᵊśāhădî* (וְשָׂהֲדִי) whose root *śāhēḏ* (שָׂהֵד) is an Aramaic word for "witness." This word occurs only here and in Genesis 31:47 incorporated into the Aramaic name of Galeed, "Jegar Sahadutha"[73]. Who is this *ʿēḏî* (עֵדִי) and *wᵊśāhădî* (וְשָׂהֲדִי) to whom Job appeals? Reyburn notices that Job does not name YHWH as his witness, although many interpreters assume this

---

which is his condition of captivity. His afflictions are not merely his afflictions, but a state of captivity, and such state of captivity is a *witness against* Job.

70. . . . *wayyāqom bî ḵaḥăšî bəpānay yaʿăneh* (וַיָּקָם בִּי כַחֲשִׁי בְּפָנַי יַעֲנֶה) "my leanness has risen up against me and replies to me [against] my face."

71. Witnesses can be YHWH's anger (Clines, *Job 1–20, 250*), YHWH himself (Reyburn, *Job*, 210), or Job's suffering (Keil and Delitzsch, *K&D*, 4:337).

72. In Job 10:17 there is a slight difference between the NRSV and NIV. The NRSV reads "You renew your witnesses against me," while the NIV "You bring new witnesses against me." The difference here is that witnesses according to the NRSV are renewed – which means that they can be the same witnesses all over again, while for the NIV the idea is of bringing new witnesses.

73. Alden, *Job*, 187.

identification.[74] Some argue that Job's oriental logic allows him to see YHWH as both judge and witness at the same time. Although YHWH has caused Job's suffering, Job still trusts in the YHWH of righteousness and love. Others argue that the witness in heaven is some third party, a counterpart to the Satan of Job 2:3, who would act as a lawyer to defend Job in the heavenly council. Clines suggests that the best reading is that there is no personal "witness" in heaven.[75] Instead, Job's own protestation of innocence and his formal deposition are now recorded in the heavenly court and remains as perpetual witness to his character. Keil and Delitzsch, on the other hand, retain the idea that YHWH is Job's witness in heaven who will at the end function as witness to his innocence, even though that same YHWH now appears to be an enemy in pursuit of him.[76]

The second example from religious context comes from Psalms 89:37. This witness is described as *wᵊ ʿēḏ ne ʾĕmān* (וְעֵד נֶאֱמָן) "faithful" or "enduring witness," or alternatively, the translation can be "and a witness in the clouds shall be faithful."[77] From the text it is obvious that YHWH promised to David that his throne would stand forever just like the sun and the moon. However, it is unclear who that witness is, and interpretations differ: it could allude to the rainbow,[78] YHWH,[79] the sun and moon,[80] or David's throne or dynasty.[81]

As one might expect, we find far more references to witnesses in legal context. Several maxims from Proverbs reflect the concept. First are those proverbs that refer to false witnesses. Witnesses mentioned in Proverbs 6:19; 12:17; 19:5; 19:9; 25:18 are defined as *ʿēḏ šeqer* (עֵד שֶׁקֶר) "false" or "lying witness." In Proverbs 6:19 such witnesses are described as those who *yāp̄îaḥ*

74. Reyburn, *Job*, 318–319.
75. Clines, *Job 1–20*, 389–390.
76. Keil and Delitzsch, *K&D*, 4:402.
77. Tate, *Psalms 51–100*, 425.
78. Keil and Delitzsch, *K&D*, 5:589.
79. Spence-Jones, *Psalms*, 2:241.
80. Goldingay, *Psalms, Vol. 2*, 683.
81. Wells, *Law of Testimony*, 40; Zorn, *Psalms, Vol. 2.*, 160–161.

kᵊzāḇîm (יָפִיחַ כְּזָבִים) "pours out lies."[82] This appears to refer specifically to the person who seeks to subvert justice through false testimony in court.[83]

Proverbs 12:17 contrasts between true and false witness (antithetical parallelism). True witness is described as *yāp̄îaḥ ʾĕmûnāh yaggîḏ ṣeḏeq* (יָפִיחַ אֱמוּנָה יַגִּיד צֶדֶק) which can be literally translated as "[Whoever] breathes out faithfulness, reports righteousness."[84] Verb *pûaḥ* (פּוּחַ) can mean "to breath, to blow,"[85] the noun *ʾĕmûnāh* (אֱמוּנָה)[86] can mean "steadfastness, trustworthiness, faithfulness," and verb *yaggîḏ* (יַגִּיד) "to announce, to give evidence" or "make known." Such person is contrasted with *wᵊ ʿēḏ šeqārîm* (וְעֵד שְׁקָרִים) or literally "witness of falsehoods." The noun, in this case *šeqārîm* (שְׁקָרִים), functions attributively and creates the idea of "false witness." Its plural form may stand for the habitual actions of such a person.

Proverbs 19:5 and Proverbs 19:9 are almost identical texts. Unlike texts mentioned above, they do not contrast between two different persons (antithetical parallelism). Instead, line B of each verse describes the same person as line A (synonymous parallelism). Hence, in Proverbs 19:5 and 19:9 *ʿēḏ šᵊqārîm* (עֵד שְׁקָרִים) "a false witness" is additionally described as *wᵊyāp̄îaḥ kᵊzāḇîm* (וְיָפִיחַ כְּזָבִים) "one who breathes out lies."

Proverbs 25:18 is a statement of comparison. Here, in the first part of the verse we have a person who is described as "a hammer" or "club," "a sword" and "a sharp arrow." These are all weapons that can injure or kill people. Such person is further described as *ʾîš ʿōneh ḇᵊrēʿēhû ʿēḏ šāqer*

---

82. In Proverbs 6:19 *yāp̄îaḥ kəzāḇîm* (יָפִיחַ כְּזָבִים), the NIV translates this as "who pours out lies," while the NRSV translates this as "who testifies falsely." Accordingly, the activity of "pouring" can stand for "testifying."

83. Garrett, *Proverbs, Ecclesiastes, Song of Songs*, 98.

84. In Proverbs 12:17 *yāp̄îaḥ ʾĕmûnāh yaggîḏ ṣeḏeq* (יָפִיחַ אֱמוּנָה יַגִּיד צֶדֶק) the NRSV reads as "Whoever speaks the truth gives honest evidence," and the NIV as "An honest witness tells the truth." The NRSV follows more closely Hebrew syntax by translating verb and noun *yāp̄îaḥ ʾĕmûnāh* as verb (well, more as participial construction) and noun "Whoever speaks the truth," while for the NIV they become an adjective and noun "honest witness."

85. It is significant that a display of a person's character is connected with something as natural as breathing.

86. "The text has 'he pours out faithfully'; the word rendered 'faithfully' or 'reliably' (אֱמוּנָה, *ʾĕmûnāh*) is used frequently for giving testimony in court, and so here the subject matter is the reliable witness" (NET Bible). According to Fox (*Proverbs 10–31*, 555), "Hebrew *ʾĕmunah*, usually translated 'faith,' 'loyalty,' also means 'truth.' It is often paired with its synonym *ʾĕmet* 'truth,' which too means 'faith,' 'loyalty.' The antonym of 'faithful witness' is *yapiaḥ kᵉzabim*, 'a witness of deceit' or 'one who breathes out deceit' (in testimony); see 6:19; 14:5, 25; 19:5, 9."

(אִישׁ עֹנֶה בְרֵעֵהוּ עֵד שָׁקֶר) "the man who gives false witness against his neighbor." This description (18b) uses an expression similar to Exodus 20:16:

- Proverbs 25:18 *b̲ᵊrē ʿēhû ʿēd̲ šāqer* (בְּרֵעֵהוּ עֵד שָׁקֶר) "false witness against his neighbour"
- Exodus 20:16 *b̲ᵊrē ʿăk̲ā ʿēd̲ šāqĕr* (בְרֵעֲךָ עֵד שָׁקֶר) "false witness against your neighbour"

Both texts use the verb and the same verb *ʿānāh* (עָנָה) "to reply, to answer": Proverbs 25:18 as the participle *ʿōneh* (עֹנֶה), and Exodus 20:16 as the imperfect (yiqtōl) *t̲aʿăneh* (תַעֲנֶה).

Another group of references to false witness in Proverbs use a different vocabulary. In Proverbs 19:28 a false witness is described as *ʿēd̲ bᵊliyyaʿal* (עֵד בְּלִיַּעַל) "a witness who is worthless and wicked," and a person who *yālîṣ mišpāṭ* (יָלִיץ מִשְׁפָּט) "mocks at justice." Line b repeats the same idea by describing this person as *ûpî rᵊšāʿîm* (וּפִי רְשָׁעִים) "the mouth of the wicked" thus pointing out that worthlessness and wickedness are connected with a person's speech. Such a mouth *yᵊb̲allaʿ-ʾāwen* (יְבַלַּע־אָוֶן) "swallows evil" conveying the idea that what a person (metaphorically) swallows will come out through their mouth.[87]

In Proverbs 21:28 false witness is described as *ʿēd̲-kᵊzāb̲îm* (עֵד־כְּזָבִים) "a witness of lies," and contrasted with *wᵊʾîš šômēaʿ* (וְאִישׁ שׁוֹמֵעַ) "a man who hears." "A person who hears" refers to a person who reports only what he has heard and is careful not to report anything that he did not hear.

Finally, in Proverbs 24:28 the phrase *ʾăl-tᵊhî* (אַל־תְּהִי) "you will not be" is a command[88] that people should not be *ʿēd̲-ḥinnām bᵊrēʿek̲ā* (עֵד־חִנָּם בְּרֵעֶךָ) "witness for nothing" or "causeless" or "groundless witness" "against your neighbour." The idea of a witness "without cause," according to Murphy,[89] "is that the person concerned has no reason to give witness." The verse continues to explain that to be "witness without cause" means *biśpāt̲êk̲ā* (בִּשְׂפָתֶיךָ) "using your lips" to *wahăpittît̲ā* (וַהֲפִתִּיתָ) "deceive" or "mislead." Thus, the text forbids giving false testimony.

87. Fox, *Proverbs 10–31*, 662.

88. Although the first verb *hāyāh* (הָיָה) is in the jussive form, the jussive is also used in Hebrew to express a negative command in the second person (Heiser and Setterholm, *Glossary of Morpho-Syntactic Database*).

89. Murphy, *Proverbs*, 186.

Two examples from Proverbs describe witnesses positively. In Proverbs 14:5 *ʿēḏ* (עֵד) appears twice because the text describes *ʿēḏ ʾĕmûnîm* (עֵד אֱמוּנִים), literally "a witness of faithfulness," and notes that such a person *lōʾ yeḵazzēḇ* (לֹא יְכַזֵּב) "will not lie." The proverb then compares this person with *ʿēḏ šāqer* (עֵד שָׁקֶר), "a witness of falsehood," who (as in Proverbs 6:19a) *wᵊyāpîaḥ*[90] *kᵊzāḇîm* (וְיָפִיחַ כְּזָבִים) "breathes out" (NRSV) or "pours out" (NIV) lies.

In Proverbs 14:25 the emphasis is put on the *result* of truthful and false witness: salvation and deceit. Accordingly, *ʿēḏ ʾĕmeṯ*, (עֵד אֱמֶת) literally "a witness of truth" accomplishes *maṣṣîl nᵊpāšôṯ* (מַצִּיל נְפָשׁוֹת) "saves souls." Conversely, a person who *wᵊyāpîaḥ kᵊzāḇîm* (וְיָפִחַ כְּזָבִים) "breathes out lies" is *mirmāh* (מִרְמָה) "deceitful."

The book of Psalms also describes witnesses. In Psalms 27:12 and 35:11 the noun *ʿēḏîm* (עֵדִים) is likely used in the context of a lawsuit.[91] The psalmist is confronted with people who, in Psalms 27:11, are the psalmist's *šôrēr* (שׁוֹרֵר) "enemies," and in v. 12 *ṣāray* (צָרָי) "adversaries" or "oppressors" and *ʿēḏê-šeqer* (עֵדֵי־שֶׁקֶר) "lying witnesses." These false witnesses are doing two things. First, they *qāmû-ḇî* (קָמוּ־בִי), "rise up" against the psalmist. Second, they *wîpēaḥ ḥāmās* (וִיפֵחַ חָמָס) "breathe out violence." They breathe out words, but their words are lies, which will bring about death. Their testimony that will result in lawless violence.[92] Whatever was their identity, the psalmist uses these three terms (enemy, adversary, witnesses) to describe the same group of people.

Psalms 35 describes the persecution of a righteous person. The precise identity of the person or situation is unclear.[93] Psalms 35:11 describes the witnesses as *ʿēḏê ḥāmās* (עֵדֵי חָמָס) "malicious" (NRSV) or "ruthless witnesses" (NIV). As in Psalms 27:12, they also *qûm* (קוּם) "rise" (they stand to speak) and *yišʾālûnî* (יִשְׁאָלוּנִי) "asks questions to me." This again reflects the language of a legal context in a form of hearing before the court.

---

90. So thus far, the NRSV has used three different words to translate verb *pûaḥ* (פּוּחַ): in Proverbs 6:19 as "testifying" in Proverbs 12:17 as "speaking" and in Proverbs 14:5 as "breathing." The NIV is more consistent since in Proverbs 6:19 and 14:5 *pûaḥ* (פּוּחַ) is understood as "pouring," but in Proverbs 12:17 *pûaḥ* (פּוּחַ) is lost in translation.

91. Baan, *Necessity of Witness*, 70.

92. Goldingay and Payne, *Isaiah 40–55*, 399.

93. Craigie, *Psalms 1–50*, 285; Goldingay, *Psalms, Vol. 1*, 489–490; Bratcher and Reyburn, *Psalms*, 328.

2.2 Usage of ʿēḏûṯ (עֵדוּת) and ʿēḏôṯ (עֵדְוֹת) in the Writings

In the Writings the noun *ʿēḏûṯ* (עֵדוּת) appears nine times, and its plural form *ʿēḏôṯ* (עֵדְוֹת) fourteen times. All texts refer to the Torah and various cultic elements of the Mosaic covenant. First, we will analyze its usage in the Historical Books, and then in Wisdom and Poetic Books.

2.2.1 Usage of ʿēḏûṯ (עֵדוּת) and ʿēḏôṯ (עֵדְוֹת) in the Historical Books

In Josh 4:16 the ark is described as *ʾărôn hāʿēḏûṯ* (אֲרוֹן הָעֵדוּת) "the ark of the Testimony." As we have encountered in the Pentateuch, *ʿēḏûṯ* (עֵדוּת) "testimony" can refer to testimony or covenant. The description of the ark in Joshua 4:18 as *ʾărôn bᵊrîṯ-yᵊhwāh* (אֲרוֹן בְּרִית־יְהוָה) "the ark of the covenant of the Lord" confirms this.

In 2 Kings 11:12 we find *ʿēḏûṯ* (עֵדוּת) used as a description for the Torah (or at least some essential part of it, such as Decalogue, or maybe only Deuteronomy 17:14–20). During Joash's coronation ceremony, the priest Jehoiada gave him, among other items, *wᵊʾeṯ-hāʿēḏûṯ* (וְאֶת־הָעֵדוּת) "copy of the covenant" (NIV) or "covenant" (NRSV). The same event is described in 2 Chronicles 23:11, which says that Jehoiada gave Joash the *ʿēḏûṯ* (עֵדוּת) "testimony." Furthermore, 2 Chronicles 24:6 describes the tabernacle as *lᵊʾōhel hāʿēḏûṯ* (לְאֹהֶל הָעֵדוּת) "for tent of the Testimony" – an expression we have previously encountered in the Pentateuch (Num 9:15; 17:7–8; 18:2).

In 2 Kings 2:3, the plural form *ʿēḏôṯ* (עֵדְוֹת) likely refers to obedience to the Torah, although other interpretations are also possible.[94] In 2 Kings 17:15, *ʿēḏôṯ* (עֵדְוֹת) is in the form *ʿēḏôṯāw ʾăšer hēʿîḏ bām* (עֵדְוֹתָיו אֲשֶׁר הֵעִיד בָּם) "the statutes he had warned them" (NIV). Here, *ʿēḏôṯ* (עֵדְוֹת) could include rejection of prophetic warnings and the Law and statutes of Yahweh,[95] or YHWH's commandments which testify about him and his nature.[96]

In 2 Kings 23:3 King Josiah is determined to keep YHWH's "commandments, statutes [*ʿēḏôṯ* (עֵדְוֹת)] and decrees." In context, Josiah pledges to keep the entire Law, thus defining "statutes" as part of the written Law of YHWH. In 1 Chronicles 29:19, *ʿēḏôṯêḵā* (עֵדְוֹתֶיךָ) "your testimonies" refers

94. DeVries, *1 Kings*, 34–35; House, *1, 2 Kings*, 96.

95. Hobbs, *2 Kings*, 234.

96. Spence–Jones, *2 Kings*, 334.

to the written Law of God. This is also the case in 2 Chronicles 34:31, where *ʿēḏôṯ* (עֵדְוֹת) is used again alongside *miṣwāh* (מִצְוָה) "command" and *ḥōq* (חק) "statute, decree." In Nehemiah 9:34 *ʿēḏôṯ* (עֵדְוֹת) is used with *miṣwāh* (מִצְוָה) thus making the expression "commands and statutes" (NIV), referring to the words of the Torah.

2.2.2 Usage of ʿēḏûṯ (עֵדוּת) and ʿēḏôṯ (עֵדְוֹת) in the Wisdom and Poetic Books

In the next group of texts, *ʿēḏûṯ* (עֵדוּת) refers to the Torah. In Psalms 19:7 (8) the word appears when the psalmist specifies six aspects of the Torah: law, testimony, precepts, commandment, fear, and judgments. Psalms 78:5 uses *ʿēḏûṯ* (עֵדוּת) in the expression *wayyāqem ʿēḏûṯ* (וַיָּקֶם עֵדוּת) "established a decree or testimony." The second line says that YHWH *wᵊṯôrāh śām* (וְתוֹרָה שָׂם) "appointed a Law." This "establishment" and "appointing" was given *bᵊyaʿăqōḇ* (בְּיַעֲקֹב) "in Jacob" and *bᵊyiśrāʾēl* (בְּיִשְׂרָאֵל) "in Israel." The preposition *bᵊ* (בְּ), can indicate that such activities are positive ("in, among") or negative ("against"). In Psalms 81:5 *ʿēḏûṯ* (עֵדוּת) appears alongside *ḥōq* (חק) and *mišpāṭ* (מִשְׁפָּט) (v. 4) creating the familiar expression "statute, ordinance, decree" (NRSV) or "decree, ordinance, statute" (NIV). Here, *ʿēḏûṯ* (עֵדוּת) likely refers to the festival of tabernacles. The recipient of this *ʿēḏûṯ* (עֵדוּת) is Joseph, but the expression *bîhôsēp̄* (בִּיהוֹסֵף) like in the Psalms 78:5 due to preposition *bᵊ* (בְּ), can be positive or negative. In Psalms 119:88 we find *ʿēḏûṯ pîḵā* (עֵדוּת פִּיךָ) "testimony of your mouth." The noun *ʿēḏûṯ* (עֵדוּת) is in singular, and this expression is similar to Psalms 119:72 where the psalmist speaks about *tôraṯ-pîḵā* (תוֹרַת־פִּיךָ) "law of/from your mouth." Hence, it is justifiable to conclude that *ʿēḏûṯ* (עֵדוּת) here in singular refers to the totality of the Torah. And finally, *ʿēḏûṯ* (עֵדוּת) appears in Psalms 122:4 in the context of another festival, although which festival it refers to is unclear. Regardless, the psalm describes a pilgrim arriving in Jerusalem for one of the major annual festivals in the Temple.[97] Accordingly, *ʿēḏûṯ* (עֵדוּת) here refers to the command about the particular festival, and not the entire Torah.

Finally, in Psalms 119: 14, 31, 36, 99, 111, 129, 138, 144, 157, *ʿēḏôṯ* (עֵדְוֹת) is found in the context of other words that are synonyms for the Torah: *dāḇār* (דָּבָר) "word," *miṣwāh* (מִצְוָה) "command," *ʾimrāh* (אִמְרָה) "word," *ḥōq*

97. Bratcher and Reyburn, *Psalms*, 1055.

(חק) "law," "prescription," *mišpāṭ* (מִשְׁפָּט) "judgment," "decision," *piqqûḏîm* (פִּקּוּדִים) "instructions," *tôrāh* (תּוֹרָה) "law."

2.3 Usage of ʿēḏāh (עֵדָה) and ʿēḏōṯ (עֵדֹת) in the Writings

In the Writings the noun *ʿēḏāh* (עֵדָה) appears once in Joshua 24:27, and its plural form *ʿēḏōṯ* (עֵדֹת) nineteen times. First, we will analyze its usage in the Historical Books, and then in Wisdom and Poetic Books.

2.3.1 Usage of ʿēḏāh (עֵדָה) and ʿēḏōṯ (עֵדֹת) in the Historical Books

We saw previously how Joshua put Israelites under solemn oath that they will serve YHWH alone (Josh 24:19–24) and established the covenant between Israelites and YHWH (Josh 24:25–28). In that story the stone functions as *ʿēḏāh* (עֵדָה) "witness" (Josh 24:27). The stone is twice designated as *lᵊ ʿēḏāh* (לְעֵדָה) "for a witness." In the first instance, the stone is described with the verb *hāyāh* (הָיָה) "to be" in its Qal imperfect (yiqtōl) form *tihyeh* (תִּהְיֶה), further modified by *bānû* (בָּנוּ) "against us." In the second instance, the same verb is in its weqātal (waw+perfect) form *wᵊhāyṯāh* (וְהָיְתָה) in combination with *bāḵem* (בָּכֶם) "against you." The stone is portrayed as a living being because "it has heard." Although *ʾeṯ-haddᵊḇārîm hāʾēlleh* (אֶת־הַדְּבָרִים הָאֵלֶּה) "these words" from verse 26 probably refers to the words spoken by one side or the other (or the whole ceremony of renewing the covenant), it seems that the stone functions only as a witness to the words spoken by YHWH in verses 2–13. But as we have encountered in Joshua 22:27, 28, 34, the stone as object cannot play its role as witness unless those who hear its witness are familiar with the story.

2.3.2 Usage of ʿēḏāh (עֵדָה) and ʿēḏōṯ (עֵדֹת) in the Wisdom and Poetic Books

The plural form *ʿēḏōṯ* (עֵדֹת) appears nineteen times in the following Psalms: 25:10; 78:56; 93:5; 99:7; 119:2, 22, 24, 46, 59, 79, 95, 119, 125, 138, 146, 152, 167, 168 and 132:12. In Psalms 25:10 *ʿēḏōṯ* (עֵדֹת) occurs in the context of expression *bᵊrîṯô wᵊ ʿēḏōṯâw* (בְּרִיתוֹ וְעֵדֹתָיו) which can be translated as "covenant and his decrees" (NRSV). In Psalms 78:56 *ʿēḏōṯ* (עֵדֹת) also refers to the Torah; likewise, Psalms 93:5. In Psalms 99:7 *ʿēḏōṯ* (עֵדֹת) refers to the Torah together with the noun *ḥōq* (חק) "statute."

Psalms 119 contains thirteen references to *ʿēḏōṯ* (עֵדֹת). In verses 1–2 *ʿēḏōṯ* (עֵדֹת) affirms the same idea: an overlap between "testimony" and "Torah." In both verses the word *ʾašrê* (אַשְׁרֵי) "happy, blessed" appears. In 119:1 this describes blessing over those who *hālaḵ* (הָלַךְ) "walk" according to the *tôrāh* (תּוֹרָה). In 119:2 blessed are those who *nāṣar* (נָצַר) "keep" his *ʿēḏōṯâw* (עֵדֹתָיו) "statutes." Thus *ʿēḏōṯ* (עֵדֹת) of verse 2 is synonymous with *tôrāh* (תּוֹרָה) of verse 1. For the rest of the Psalm, *ʿēḏōṯ* (עֵדֹת) appears together with other synonyms of Torah: *dāḇār* (דָּבָר) "word," *tôrāh* (תּוֹרָה) "law," *miṣwāh* (מִצְוָה) "commandment," *mišpāṭ* (מִשְׁפָּט) "judgment," "decision," *ḥōq* (חֹק) "law," *ʾimrāh* (אִמְרָה) "word," *piqqûḏîm* (פִּקּוּדִים) "instructions," *ḥōq* (חֹק) "law."

Finally, in Psalms 132:12 *ʿēḏōṯ* (עֵדֹת) appears together with the expression *bᵉrîṯî* (בְּרִיתִי) thus signifying "my covenant and the statutes" (NIV) or "my covenant and my decrees" (NRSV). Here as in the previous cases, *ʿēḏōṯ* (עֵדֹת) thus refers to "the rules and laws the people of Israel must follow."[98]

2.4 Usage of ʿûḏ (עוּד) in the Writings

In the Writings, *ʿûḏ* (עוּד) appears twenty-one times. First, we will analyze its usage in the Historical Books, and then in Wisdom and Poetic Books.

2.4.1 Usage of ʿûḏ (עוּד) in the Historical Books

In 1 Samuel 8:9, YHWH tells Samuel to warn the people about the king's authority over them. Here, *ʿûḏ* (עוּד) appears twice in the expression *kî-hāʿēḏ tāʿîḏ* (כִּי־הָעֵד תָּעִיד) "but warn solemnly." The first verb *hāʿēḏ* (הָעֵד) the Hiphil infinitive absolute is followed by the imperfect (yiqtōl) *tāʿîḏ* (תָּעִיד). While the Hiphil imperative often implies causative action ("to take as" or "call someone to witness"), the infinitive absolute serves as intensifier of the action.[99] The syntax emphasizes the seriousness of the task which Samuel had, and of his warning to Israel. The elders' request for a king is not pleasing to YHWH, so Samuel is in the position to serve as a witness *bāhem* (בָּהֶם) "against them." His witness is verbal and pointed toward the future.

In 1 Kings 2:42 the verb *ʿûḏ* (עוּד) in its Hiphil wayyiqtōl (waw-consecutive + imperfect) form *wāʾāʿiḏ* (וָאָעִד) together with *bᵉḵā lēmōr* (בְּךָ לֵאמֹר)

98. Bratcher and Reyburn, *Psalms*, 1093.

99. Similar situation we had in Genesis 43:3 where infinitive absolute of the same root as verb was used to emphasize verbal meaning.

is used in the sense of warning, here about what will happen in the future if certain conditions will not be kept. This testimony is a warning because of the presence of conditions and consequences. Furthermore, *bᵊḵā* (בְּךָ) which can be translated as "against you" implies that the witnessing falls into the category of being a witness against. Finally, the presence of the verb *ʾāmar* (אָמַר) "to say" in its Qal infinitive construct form *lēmōr* (לֵאמֹר) reveals that this warning was given "by saying."

In 1 Kings 21:10 and 21:13 *ʿûḏ* (עוּד) appears in the context of a legal case. The underlying story is the refusal of Naboth to give his vineyard to the king Ahab. His refusal was connected with the ancestral law (cf. Lev 25) where family name and status were connected with the inherited land. Since the only way to get the land was to eliminate Naboth, queen Jezebel organized a plot which included two false witnesses who sat opposite Naboth and brought charges against him in a judicial process. This did not take place in court, but among the people in the public arena, and two witnesses were secured in order to fulfil legal requirements of the Torah (Num 35:30; Deut 17:6, 7; 19:5). These men's activity is described with the verb *ʿûḏ* (עוּד): in 1 Kings 21:10 as *wîʿiḏuhû* (וִיעִדֻהוּ), and in 1 Kings 21:13 as *wayʿiḏuhû* (וַיְעִדֻהוּ). However, they themselves are described as *bᵊnê-ḇᵊliyyaʿal* (בְּנֵי־בְלִיַּעַל) or "sons of Belial" (1 Kgs 21:10, 13; cf. Prov 19:28). The verbal nature of their witness against Naboth was shown by the verb *ʾāmar* (אָמַר) "to say" (1 Kgs 21:10, 13).

In 2 Kings 17:13 and 17:15 the verb *ʿûḏ* (עוּד) refers to the activity of warning. In 2 Kings 17:13 YHWH's prophets and seers verbally announce his testimonies as a warning to the northern tribe of Israel, warnings which contained conditions and consequences (vv. 13–18). Two things are interesting in 2 Kings 17:13. First, YHWH sends his warning by using *bᵊyaḏ* (בְּיַד) or "the hand" of prophets and seers. The connection of a "verbal warning" and "hand" is puzzling; we would think it more natural to say that YHWH warned Israelites through "the mouth" as the organ of speech. Second, in expression *wayyāʿaḏ yhwh bᵊyiśrāʾēl ûḇîhûḏāh bᵊyaḏ* (וַיָּעַד יְהוָה בְּיִשְׂרָאֵל וּבִיהוּדָה בְּיַד) "YHWH warned Israel and Judah by the hand," the preposition *bᵊ* (בְּ) occurs before words *yiśrāʾēl* (יִשְׂרָאֵל) "Israel," *yᵊhûḏāh* (יְהוּדָה) "Judah," and *yāḏ* (יָד) "hand." When used with "hand" as its object, the preposition *bᵊ* (בְּ) is usually translated as "by" or "through." This would make the prophets and seers mediums or agents of YHWH's testimony. But *bᵊ* (בְּ) can also serve as a designation for place or position; they testified "in Israel" "in Judah." It can also mean that Israel and Judah are objects of his warning. It can also mean that the activity of warning is not only for Israel and Judah, but also "against": "the Lord testified against Israel, and against Judah" (KJV). In 2 Kings 17:15 we find the expression *ʿēḏôṯâw ʾăšer hēʿîḏ bām* (עֵדְוֹתָיו אֲשֶׁר הֵעִיד בָּם) "the statutes he had warned them" (NIV), which contains the verb *ʿûḏ* (עוּד) in its perfect (qātal) form *hēʿîḏ* (הֵעִיד) and the noun *ʿēḏôṯ* (עֵדְוֹת).[100] We have previously seen that *ʿēḏôṯ* (עֵדְוֹת) can stand for the Torah, or Torah plus prophetic warnings. This ambiguity is also reflected in translations of the passage, since some translations uses "warnings" in a sense of verbal declarations made by prophets (NASB95, NRSV) and some "statutes" in a sense of written record (NIV). Whatever is the precise meaning of *ʿēḏôṯ* (עֵדְוֹת) these warnings were given *bām* (בָּם) "against them." The preposition *bᵊ* (בְּ) here carries a negative connotation.

Prophetic warnings are also the subject of 2 Chronicles 24:19. YHWH used prophets to *ʿûḏ* (עוּד) "warn" his people. These warnings contained conditions (*šûḇ* [שׁוּב] "to turn" and *ʾāzan* [אָזַן] "to listen") and consequences (YHWH will *ʿāzaḇ* (עָזַב) "forsake" them (v. 20)). *ʿûḏ* (עוּד) is here part of the expression *wayyāʿîḏû ḇām* (וַיָּעִידוּ בָם) "they testified against them."

In the book of Nehemiah *ʿûḏ* (עוּד) appears six times with the meaning of "warning." In Nehemiah 9 *ʿûḏ* (עוּד) is used in penitent prayer (9:26, 29, 30, 34)[101] with consistent meaning: prophets *warned* the people of Israel to return to YHWH by obeying his Law, but they refused to do so. They rejected YHWH, his Law, and all prophetic warnings and that is why they were punished. Customarily, the verb *ʿûḏ* (עוּד) appears in the context of conditions and consequences. Prophetic testimony is a warning because it contains conditions which must be fulfilled, and the primary condition is usually for them *šûb* (שׁוּב) "to return" to YHWH (Nehemiah 9:26, 29). If they do not obey these warnings, they will suffer consequences, which are primarily "being given into the hands of their enemies" (Nehemiah 9:27,

100. For NRSV *ʿēḏôṯ* (עֵדְוֹת) is translated as "warnings," yet literal translation of *ʿûḏ* (עוּד) is completely missing. Instead NRSV uses verb "gave them," so we have "the warnings that he gave them."

101. Nehemiah 9:26 *hēʿîḏû* (הֵעִידוּ) in qātal (perfect) form, Nehemiah 9:34 *haʿiḏōṯā* (הַעִידֹתָ) in qātal (perfect) form, and in Nehemiah 9:29, 30 as *wattāʿaḏ* (וַתָּעַד) in wayyiqtōl (waw-consecutive + imperfect) form.

28, 30). In verse 30 we have for the first time the clear idea that prophetic testimony has its origin in the activity of "God's Spirit" – *bᵊrûḥăḵā* (בְּרוּחֲךָ) "by your Spirit."[102]

Two additional things are interesting in Nehemiah 9 with regards to the verb *ʿûḏ* (עוּד). First, the usage of preposition *bᵊ* (בְּ) shows that this preposition can have both affirmative and condemning modes. In the expression *bām* (בָּם) the condemning mode is present (Neh 9:26, 30). Likewise, in the expression *bāhem* (בָּהֶם) in verse 29 where the activity of warning was given "against them." But the preposition *bᵊ* (בְּ) has an affirmative mode in the phrases *bᵊrûḥăḵā* (בְּרוּחֲךָ) "by your Spirit" and *bᵊyaḏ-nᵊḇîʾeḵā* (בְּיַד־נְבִיאֶיךָ) "by the hand of your prophets" in verse 30, since "the Spirit" and "prophets" are the media through which YHWH gave his warnings. Second, like in 2 Kings 17:13, we read that YHWH used *bᵊyaḏ* (בְּיַד) "the hand" of the prophets in this process of warning.

In verse 34 we have seen that *ʿûḏ* (עוּד) is used together with *ʿēḏôṯ* (עֵדְוֹת). And while it is obvious that *ʿēḏôṯ* (עֵדְוֹת) refers to the words of the Torah, the precise meaning of *ʿûḏ* (עוּד) is more complex. The object of *ʿûḏ* (עוּד) is likely *ʿēḏôṯ* (עֵדְוֹת) "testimonies" that is, the Torah. Accordingly, people were "warned" and admonished toward Torah obedience. However, some English translations blend *ʿûḏ* (עוּד) with *ʿēḏôṯ* (עֵדְוֹת) so *ʿēḏôṯ* (עֵדְוֹת) is understood as the content of speech – verbal warnings.[103] This is even more complicated with the fact that *haʿîḏōṯā* (הַעִידֹתָ) is followed by expression *bāhem* (בָּהֶם), which more naturally refers to verbal speech given by YHWH (presumably through prophets) "against them," rather than to say that the commandments of Torah were "against them."

In Nehemiah 13:15 and Nehemiah 13:21 *ʿûḏ* (עוּד) is again defined as a warning and appears in wayyiqtōl (waw - conversive + imperfect) form: in verse 15 as *wāʾāʿîḏ* (וָאָעִיד), and in verse 21 as *wāʾāʿîḏāh* (וָאָעִידָה). As in Nehemiah 9, Nehemiah's warnings here are supported by the preposition *bᵊ* (בְּ) which can have either an affirming or a condemning mode. In verse 15

---

102. In Numbers 11:24–30 we have a situation where the Spirit of God is connected with the activity of prophecy. However, in Nehemiah we have a clear connection between the Spirit, prophecy, and testimony / witness.

103. The NRSV reads "our kings, our officials, our priests, and our ancestors have not kept your law or heeded the commandments and *the warnings that you gave them*." (Emphasis added.)

the preposition *bᵊ* (בְּ) appears twice in the expression *bᵊyôm* (בְּיוֹם) – once in connection with "Sabbath" *bᵊyôm haššăbbāṯ* (בְּיוֹם הַשַּׁבָּת), and once in connection with "warning" *wāʾāʿîḏ bᵊyôm* (וָאָעִיד בְּיוֹם). Again, *bᵊyôm* (בְּיוֹם) can be translated as "at that time" (NRSV), "on the day" (NASB95, ESV), or in connection with *ʿûḏ* (עוּד), it can have negative connotation "I testified against them in the day," or "I testified against them in respect of the day."[104] Nehemiah 13:15, unlike verse 21, does not have an object of warning, and the notion that "warning" *ʿûḏ* (עוּד) is given "against them" must be supplemented from the context. Also, the verb *mikrām* (מִכְרָם) gives a sense that a warning was given about "their selling" food, that is, regarding the fact that "they sold" food. In verse 21 Nehemiah *wāʾāʿîḏāh* (וָאָעִידָה) "warned" *ḇāhem* (בָּהֶם), "them" or "against them."[105] As we have seen, *ʿûḏ* (עוּד) in itself does not carry the meaning "against," but in in conjunction with the preposition *bᵊ* (בְּ) in the expression *bāhem* (בָּהֶם), it can be understood as activity of "witnessing against." Furthermore, the text continues and explains that the warning is given verbally due to the verb *ʾāmar* (אָמַר) "to say" in its wayyiqtōl (waw-consecutive + imperfect) form *wāʾōmrāh* (וָאֹמְרָה) which was directed *ʾălêhem* (אֲלֵיהֶם) "to them."

2.4.2 Usage of ʿûḏ (עוּד) in the Wisdom and Poetic Books

In Job 29, Job recalls the time when God was with him, and how blessed he was in everything. As part of that speech, Job 29:11 uses the verb *ʿûḏ* (עוּד) to describe how Job received testimony from other people. As Alden says, verse 11 describes what oral witnesses said and what visual witnesses spoke, and he offers his translation: "When an ear heard, it pronounced me happy, [and when] an eye saw, it commended me."[106] "Commended" in his translation is actually the verb *ʿûḏ* (עוּד) which in this text is found in wayyiqtōl (waw-conversive + imperfect) form *wattᵊʿîḏēnî* (וַתְּעִידֵנִי). With its meaning "to be a witness" or "to witness something regarding someone, *ʿûḏ* (עוּד) here clearly refers to speaking in favor of someone.

104. Spence–Jones, *Nehemiah*, 141.

105. *wāʾāʿîḏāh ḇāhem wāʾōmrāh ʾălêhem* (וָאָעִידָה בָּהֶם וָאֹמְרָה אֲלֵיהֶם) "And I warned them and said to them."

106. Alden, *Job*, 283.

In Psalms, the verb *ʿûḏ* (עוּד) appears six times. Psalm 50 is organized as a divine trial, although the issue is religious in its nature. Here YHWH is the judge of the people of Israel, and the nature of Israel's worship is the question under dispute. In order to judge his people, YHWH first summons the court. The entire world (v. 1) is summoned to observe the proceedings. Then "heaven" and "earth" (v. 4) are summoned, as witnesses of the event (cf. Deut 32:1). And finally, the people themselves (v. 5) who are described as *ḥăsîḏāy* (חֲסִידָי) "pious" or "godly," and *kōrṯê ḇᵊrîṯî* (כֹּרְתֵי בְרִיתִי)[107] the one who "made a covenant with YHWH." When all parties are present in the court, YHWH steps into the scene, not only as a judge, but also as a witness. In verse 7, he is the one who *waʾăḏabbērāh* (וַאֲדַבֵּרָה) "I will speak" and *wᵊʾāʿîḏāh* (וְאָעִידָה) "I will testify" *bāḵ* (בָּךְ) "against you" (m.s.).[108]

We know that the content of YHWH's testimony is found in verses 7 to 21, but the question remains against whom YHWH is testifying? In 50:7–15 YHWH speaks to *ʿammî* (עַמִּי) "my people" and *yiśrāʾēl* (יִשְׂרָאֵל) "Israel," but in verse 16 the objects of the speech have apparently changed since YHWH is there speaking to *wᵊlārāšāʿ* (וְלָרָשָׁע) "wicked person." Commentaries differ as to whether these verses refer to the same group of people, two different groups (such as Israelites and gentiles), particular individuals of these groups. Perhaps the nation of Israel as a whole is addressed twice? Although the singulars "my people" in verse 7 and "wicked person" in verse 16 support the idea that YHWH is addressing the people as a whole, it is more likely that YHWH is addressing two different groups inside of his covenant people. The testimony against the first group of Israelites (described in 50:7–15) is explained in verse 14. The second group is also part of the covenant people, but their guilt is more serious. They proclaim the covenantal statutes which

107. "The words 'those about to make a covenant with me' (כרתי בריתי) are critical to the understanding of the text as a whole. RSV translates: 'who made a covenant with me . . .' (cf. NIV, NEB, et al.), but these translations fail to recognize the force of the participle כרתי. In this context, the participle functions as the 'participle of the immediate future,' as is commonly the case in covenant contexts. . . .Thus the covenant members are summoned by God; later in the day, they will be making, or renewing, the covenant, but first they must go through the searching preparatory ritual of divine scrutiny, to ensure that they are ready for the ceremony itself, in which the covenant 'sacrifice' (v 5b) would be offered" (Craigie, *Psalms 1–50*, 365).

108. Richard D. Patterson (*Nahum, Habakkuk, Zephaniah*, 325–326) observes that the text presents a courtroom scene in which God rises first as witness (Deut 8:19; 1 Sam 12:5; Job 16:19; Ps 50:7; Jer 29:23; Mic 1:2; Mal 3:5; Heb 6:13) on His own behalf and before the assemblage, and then presides as judge to deliver His sentence.

they in actuality ignore,[109] and the specifics are described in 50:17–21. In conclusion, *ʿûḏ* (עוּד) in verse 7 carries a meaning of "testifying against."

In Psalms 81:8 (v. 9) *ʿûḏ* (עוּד) is again used in a sense of warning. Lines a and b reflect parallelism since verb *šᵊmaʿ* (שְׁמַע) "to hear" and expression *ʿammî* (עַמִּי) "my people" in 8a are parallel to the verb *šᵊmaʿ* (שְׁמַע) "to hear" and noun *yiśrāʾēl* (יִשְׂרָאֵל) "Israel" of 8b. In the midst of that parallelism, we have Hiphil cohortative wᵊyiqtōl (waw-conjunctive + imperfect) form of *ʿûḏ* (עוּד) *wᵊʾāʿîḏāh* (וְאָעִידָה), and this verb is addressed toward *bāḵ* (בָּךְ) "against you" (m.s.). The way one translates *ʿûḏ* (עוּד) depends on how the context is understood. Clearly, 81:5–7 describes the deliverance of Israelites from Egypt. YHWH *heard* them (v. 5) and *delivered* them from slavery (past event), and now they have to *listen* to him in the present (v. 13) if they want to enjoy his favour and *deliverance* of verses14–16 (as something future). However, the immediate context of *ʿûḏ* (עוּד) in verse 8 refers to the testing at the waters of Meribah.[110] Goldingay[111] opts for the idea that in the text "Hear me, my people, and I will warn [*wᵊʾāʿîḏāh*] you—if you would only listen to me, Israel!", *wᵊʾāʿîḏāh* (וְאָעִידָה) should be translated as "declaration." I presume that Goldingay bases his argument on the fact that at the waters YHWH did not "testify against" them, the Israelites did not sin, and speech does not contain conditions and consequences. Instead, YHWH tested the people by laying down a declaration which essentially restates the first of the Ten Words from Sinai "You shall have no foreign god among you; you shall not worship any god other than me" (v. 9).

In last four examples, *ʿûḏ* (עוּד) appears outside its usual semantic range. First, in Psalms 20:9 (v.8) two lines of this verse makes a contrasting parallelism, yet each line has two verbs which are more or less synonymous in meaning. Verse 9a has two verbs: *kārʿû* (כָּרְעוּ) "to bow" or "break down," and *wᵊnāp̄ālû* (וְנָפָלוּ) "to fall, collapse," and verse 9b has *qamnû* (קַמְנוּ) "to rise, to get up," and *wannit̲ʿôḏāḏ* (וַנִּתְעוֹדָד) which is a form of *ʿûḏ* (עוּד) verb. Hence,

109. Goldingay, *Psalms*, 2: 117.

110. "The name *'Waters of Merîbah,'* which properly is borne only by *Merîbath Kadesh,* the place of the giving of water in the fortieth year (Num. 20:13; 27:14, Deut. 32:51; 33:8), is here transferred to the place of the giving of water in the first year, which was named *Massah u-Merîbah* (Ex. 17:7), as the remembrances of these two miracles, which took place under similar circumstances, in general blend together (vid., on 95:8f.)" (Keil and Delitzsch, *K&D*, 5:546).

111. Goldingay, *Psalms, Vol. 2*, 552.

ʿûḏ (עוּד) here has a meaning of "standing." Second, in Psalms 119:61 ʿûḏ (עוּד) reflects its etymological meaning of "repetition, doing something again, to go around." In this case, psalmist uses a figure of hunting when people are trying to trap animals with their nets. In the similar way, the psalmist's enemies are rᵊšāʿîm (רְשָׁעִים) "wicked persons" who are trying to "ensnare" (NRSV) or "bind" him (NIV). Since the verb ʿûḏ (עוּד) here is found in Piel ʿiwwᵊḏunî (עִוְּדֻנִי), it is not surprising that the idea of surrounding in attempt to confine it is expressed in translations. Finally, a Polel[112] form of the verb ʿûḏ (עוּד) in Psalms 146:9 yᵊʿôḏēḏ (יְעוֹדֵד) "he sustains," and in Psalms 147:6 mᵊʿôḏēḏ (מְעוֹדֵד) "sustaining" which has the same function as Piel, speaks about the intensity of action. Thus, the idea of "doing something again," "returning" and "repeating" expresses restoration, relieving, offering help and support.[113] Speaking about Psalms 146:9, Goldingay[114] notices that verbs yᵊʿôḏēḏ (יְעוֹדֵד) and yᵊʿawwēṯ (יְעַוֵּת) "to bend, to suppress" bears the idea of reversal: one is positive (for the orphan and widow) one is negative (for the wicked). This idea is also present in Psalms 147 where "casting the wicked to the ground" is also part of the restoration of the weak. All this underlines the idea that ʿûḏ (עוּד) is basically a verb of motion. Whether action is repeating, returning, turning back, or surrounding, etc., this indicates that the activity of testifying is temporally dynamic: a warning can be brought from the past into the present, or it can be sent from the present into the future.

3. The concept of witness in the Prophets – passage analysis

3.1 Usage of ʿēḏ (עֵד), ʿēḏîm (עֵדִים), ʿēday (עֵדַי), and ʿēḏêhem (עֵדֵיהֶם) in the Prophets

The noun ʿēḏ (עֵד) and its plural forms ʿēḏîm (עֵדִים), ʿēday (עֵדַי), and ʿēḏêhem (עֵדֵיהֶם) appear seventeen times in the Prophets. We will analyze their usage according to the distinction between impersonal and personal witnesses.

---

112. Polel is a rare Hebrew stem for middle waw/yoḏ weak verbs. GHCLOT defines ʿûḏ in 146:9 and 147:6 as Pilel, BDB and CHALOT as Polel, DBLH as Pilpel.

113. In Psalms 146:9 the NRSV translates ʿûḏ (עוּד) as "upholding" and in Psalms 147:6 as "lifting," and the NIV in Psalms 146:9 and Psalms 147:6 as "sustains."

114. Goldingay, *Psalms, Vol. 2*, 712, 721.

3.1.1 Impersonal witnesses

In two examples, *ʿēḏ* (עֵד) designates impersonal witnesses. The first example is found in Isaiah 19:20 where altar and pillar are defined as *ʿēḏ* (עֵד). The text *wehāyāh lᵊʾôṯ ûlᵊʿēḏ layhwāh* (וְהָיָה לְאוֹת וּלְעֵד לַיהוָה) "It will be a for a sign and for a witness to the Lord," refers to an *mizbēaḥ* (מִזְבֵּחַ) "altar" "in the center of the land of Egypt" (NRSV), and a *maṣṣēḇāh* (מַצֵּבָה) "pillar" "at its border" (NRSV). But what is the significance of these witnesses? Since an altar as a public symbol implies sacrifice and a priesthood, and pillars were often used to designate publicly "high places" in Canaan, the point is that the worship of YHWH in Egypt will be open and official.[115] Accordingly, these together are a sign and a witness *layhwāh* (לַיהוָה) "to the Lord." In another sense, they will be a witness of Egyptians – their faith, dedication, and convictions "about" YHWH or in his favor.

The second example of impersonal witness is in Isaiah 30:8. There Isaiah is instructed to write down something as a testimony. Two things are debatable here. First, it is not clear whether YHWH commands Isaiah to write down something,[116] or Isaiah is the one who "gives his own commentary, rooted in the language of the word in 30:1–5."[117] Second, what is the connection between *lûaḥ* (לוּחַ) "tablet" (NRSV, NIV) and *sēp̄er* (סֵפֶר) "book" (NRSV) or "scroll" (NIV)? Some argue that "tablet" could contain a brief form of the prophecy, set up in public to be read by all. "Book" then contains the prophecy in full, for the use of distant posterity.[118] Others claim that the terms could be used interchangeably because of the usage of *sēp̄er* (סֵפֶר) in Exodus 17:14. There a single leaf, including the contents written thereon, was called *sēp̄er*. Hence, "Isaiah was to write the oracle upon a table, a separate leaf of durable material."[119]

But what is the purpose and function of presenting the testimony in a written form? This text belongs to the conventional judgment pattern where in the first stage the charge is brought against the accused (vv. 9–11), and in the next stage the sentence is pronounced (vv. 12–14). Accordingly, Isaiah's

115. Watts, *Isaiah 1–33*, 258.

116. Young, *Book of Isaiah Vol. 2*, 343.

117. Friesen, *Isaiah*, 185.

118. Jamieson, Fausset and Brown, *CCEB* 1:463.

119. Keil and Delitzsch, *K&D*, 7:319.

document from verse 8 has the force of a legal document to be used as evidence in the future.[120] This testimony is not only valid for the future but has also a permanent or continuous character. The prepositional phrase *ʾittām* (אִתָּם) probably means that Isaiah had to write down this prophecy "with them," that is, before the eyes of the present people. Hence, people were acting as *observing witnesses*. But if we presume that Isaiah wrote two versions of the same prophecy, it is possible that the shorter version written on a tablet "might be kept so that it would always be before the people's eyes, that they might be warned and admonished thereby."[121]

Furthermore, the text is clear that this prophecy is written for *lᵉyôm ʾaḥărôn* (לְיוֹם אַחֲרוֹן) "latter day" ("time to come" (NRSV), "days to come" (NIV)), which implies that this testimony will in the future serve as an evidence that YHWH warned his people about their guilt and coming judgment.[122] This prophecy is also considered as *lāʿaḏ ʿaḏ-ʿôlām* (לָעַד עַד־עוֹלָם) "a witness forever." While used in the future, a written record of this prophecy in the form of a "book" would ensure that this prophecy would acquire characteristics of permanency or perpetuity. Interestingly, in MT "for a witness" reads as *lāʿaḏ* (לָעַד) "forever," and not as *lᵉʿēḏ* (לְעֵד) "for a witness." However, "with the exception of LXX, the versions (Th, Aq, Sym, Vg, Syr, Tg) do not read לעד as 'forever', but as 'as witness'. Literary-historical exegesis has almost universally adopted this reading."[123]

3.1.2 Personal witnesses

When personal witness is in view in the Prophets, the witness can either be YHWH himself, or more commonly people. The first place where YHWH is described as witness is in Jeremiah 29:23. YHWH first enumerates sins of particular people and is described as *hayyôḏēaʿ* (הַיּוֹדֵעַ) "one who knows" (cf. Lev 5:1), and as one who is *wāʿēḏ* (וָעֵד) "witness." Also, the context implies that YHWH is not trying to prove anyone's guilt, which is obvious. Not only is guilt assumed; future punishment is already declared.

120. Sawyer, *Isaiah: Vol. 1*, 248.

121. Young, *Book of Isaiah Vol. 2*, 343.

122. NET Bible.

123. Beuken, *Isaiah II*, 135.

In Jeremiah 42, the remnant of Israelites who stayed in their land after the Babylonian conquest came to Jeremiah requesting him to pray for them so that YHWH may tell them where they will go and what they will do. In Jeremiah 42:5 they demand the following: *yᵊhî yᵊhwāh bānû lᵊ ʿēḏ ʾĕmeṯ wᵊne ʾĕmān* (יְהִי יְהוָה בָּנוּ לְעֵד אֱמֶת וְנֶאֱמָן) "May YHWH be a true and faithful witness against us." The people's request for YHWH as witness was *if* they did not obey YHWH's instruction through Jeremiah. Being a witness who is *ʾĕmeṯ wᵊne ʾĕmān* (אֱמֶת וְנֶאֱמָן) "true and faithful/reliable" probably means that they are not calling YHWH to witness to the truthfulness of their statements. He is rather a faithful witness because he will surely punish them if they do not obey.[124]

A third example comes from Micah 1:2. There YHWH's witness is introduced with a lawsuit motif:
šimʿû ʿammîm kullām haqšîḇî ʾereṣ ûmᵊlōʾāh wîhî ʾăḏōnāy yᵊhwih bāḵem lᵊ ʿēḏ (שִׁמְעוּ עַמִּים כֻּלָּם הַקְשִׁיבִי אֶרֶץ וּמְלֹאָהּ וִיהִי אֲדֹנָי יְהוִה בָּכֶם לְעֵד) "Hear, you peoples, all of you; pay attention, O earth, and all that is in it, and let the Lord GOD be a witness against you" (NRSV). YHWH is presented as *bāḵem lᵊ ʿēḏ* (בָּכֶם לְעֵד) witness against, but the text is not clear about whom YHWH is to witness against. Without going into detailed textual analysis on that issue,[125] it is sufficient to say that the activity of YHWH as witness is described in verse 2b with the jussive wᵊyiqtōl (waw-conjunctive + imperfect) *wîhî* (וִיהִי) "will be." Waltke argues that the report in verse 2b seems to give basis for the summons in verse 2a,[126] and translates verse 2b as "for I AM will become a witness."[127] While jussive normally conveys a volitional sense of an urgent request or prayer ("may he testify!"), some hold that the jussive here functions as an ordinary imperfect.[128] Some translations render this usage in a traditional jussive sense of an urgent request with a temporal consequence: ". . . and let my Lord God be your accuser"

124. Keil and Delitzsch, *K&D,* 8:346.

125. For the debate about referents of YHWH's speech, see Waltke, *Commentary on Micah*, 45; Smith, *Micah–Malachi*, 15; Clark and Mundhenk, *Translator's Micah*, 128; Keil and Delitzsch, *K&D*, 10:290.

126. "When two volitional forms occur together, as here (imperative followed by jussive), the second signifies purpose or result" (Barker, *Micah, Nahum, Habakkuk, Zephaniah*, 49).

127. Waltke, *Commentary on Micah*, 46.

128. NET Bible; *Gesenius*, *GKC* 323.

(NJPS), ". . . and let the Lord God be a witness against you" (NRSV), or a dependent purpose/result: ". . . that the Sovereign Lord may witness against you" (NIV).[129]

The best reading seems to be that while YHWH acts as *bāḵem lᵊ ʿēḏ*[130] (בָּכֶם לְעֵד) "witness against you," against the nations, yet he will accuse Samaria and Jerusalem (v. 5) and sentence Samaria (vv. 6–7). Some have suggested that *lᵊ ʿēḏ bāḵem* (לְעֵד בָּכֶם) should be translated as "witness among" (instead of "witness against") in accordance with LXX, which uses the expression *en hymin* "in you" or "among you." However, in the expression *lᵊ ʿēḏ . . . be* (בְּ) (Exod 20:16; Deut 31:26; Prov 25:13; Jer 42:5) and its related form *ʿēḏ . . . bᵊ* (בְּ) (Num 5:13; Deut 31:19; Josh 24:22; 1 Sam 12:5; Prov 24:28; Mal 3:5), *bᵊ* (בְּ) always means "against." Furthermore, reading the phrase "among you" grants the role of judge to the earth, where YHWH limits himself only to the role of a witness – accuser. But context makes it clear that YHWH assumes the role of both judge (v. 6) and witness or accuser who presents evidence (v. 5).[131] Accordingly, "peoples" and "earth" are this lawsuit's "guilty parties",[132] and God's dealings with Israel and Judah are a witness to all nations. Judgments upon Israel and Judah should also warn nations far more guilty that they too must soon face the wrath of heaven's holy Judge.[133]

The final appearance of YHWH as a witness is found in Malachi 3:5 where we find another dispute between YHWH and the people. The argument begins in Malachi 2:17 with Malachi's accusation that people have wearied the Lord with their words. People ask the prophet "How have we wearied him?" requiring evidence for the accusation. The evidence that Malachi gives to support his accusation are people's own words that "All who do evil are good in the sight of the Lord, and he delights in them," and their questioning "Where is the God of justice?" The people's words here are a kind of accusation against YHWH (he is unjust and absent), so we see the two sides mutually accusing each other.

129. NET Bible.

130. *lə ʿēḏ* (לְעֵד) the NRSV reads as "be a witness" in a sense of witness as a person, and the NIV as "bear witness" emphasizing the activity of witness.

131. Waltke, *Commentary on Micah, 46–47.*

132. Jenson, *Obadiah, Jonah, Micah, Vol. 496*, 106.

133. Smith, *Minor Prophets*; Mic 1:2.

YHWH replies to the people's accusation verses 1–5. In verse 1 and 5 YHWH is the speaker, and in verses 2–4 the prophet.[134] As Smith notes, the language of verse 5 "draw near," "judgment," and "witness" (NIV), along with the presentation of evidence, suggests a court scene in the context of the covenant lawsuit form.[135] If YHWH had been accused that he is "distant," now he will "draw near"; if YHWH had been accused of being "unjust," now he will bring his "justice/judgment."[136]

Verse 5 begins with the idea that YHWH will *wᵊqārabtî* (וְקָרַבְתִּי) "draw near," but his presence will bring *lammišpāṭ* (לַמִּשְׁפָּט) "judgment." Since *mišpāṭ* (מִשְׁפָּט) can mean, among other things, judgment in the sense of an act that decides a legal dispute or case (judging),[137] various translations use different words. So, the NRSV uses the word "judgment"; NIV "trial," and Croatian translation in edition from Kršćanska sadašnjost uses the word "sud" or "court."[138] In that context YHWH *wᵊhāyîṯî ʿēḏ mᵊmahēr* (וְהָיִיתִי עֵד מְמַהֵר) "will be a swift witness." The verb *hāyāh* (הָיָה) "to be" is in as wᵊqātal (waw + perfect) form has an imperfective meaning. The expression *ʿēḏ mᵊmahēr* (עֵד מְמַהֵר) consists of the noun *ʿēḏ* (עֵד) "witness" and participle *māhar* (מָהַר) "hurry, quickly," which can function as a verb, adjective or substantive. Probably it is best read here as an adjective modifying the noun *ʿēḏ* (עֵד),[139] with meaning of "hurrying" or "swift witness." YHWH's witnessing is clearly described as "witnessing against" because the list of five types of sins in verse 5, all except the last are preceded by the preposition *bᵊ* (בְּ).[140] Note that in this verse we have a combination of noun *ʿēḏ* (עֵד) and preposition *bᵊ* (בְּ).

The picture that emerges from this example is that YHWH fulfils multiple roles: he is a witness, judge, and executioner. YHWH comes as witness

---

134. Smith, *Micah–Malachi*, 326–327.

135. Smith, 327.

136. The same word *mišpāṭ* (מִשְׁפָּט) is used in 2:17 when people ask, "Where is the God of justice?" and in 3:5 for "judgment" (NRSV) or "trial" (NIV).

137. Swanson, *DBLH*

138. While "trial" presumes legal process, "judgment" implies a verdict, and from the context it is clear that this will be a condemning verdict.

139. Petterson, *Haggai, Zechariah & Malachi*, 359.

140. Here we have four participles: *bamḵăššəp̄îm* (בַּמְכַשְּׁפִים) "sorcerers," *ûḇamnā ʾăp̄îm* (וּבַמְנָאֲפִים) "adulterers," *ûḇannišbā ʿîm* (וּבַנִּשְׁבָּעִים) "those who swear," and *ûḇə ʿōšqê* (וּבְעֹשְׁקֵי) "those who oppress."

against, and this presumes that as an eyewitness, he possesses knowledge about people's behavior. YHWH witnessed the crimes he will judge, and there will be no need to hear any other witness statements.[141] In that case, we would have a judgment that is based on just one witness. But he not only testifies to the truth but also vindicates wronged parties and judges wrongdoers.[142] However, as we have seen, one can also argue that YHWH performs the role of executioner, because "God comes as a practical witness against the wicked, convicting them of their guilt by punishing them,"[143] and in the covenant lawsuit, YHWH also executes the judgment.[144] This is supported by the way that witnesses sometimes participated in the execution of the verdict (e.g. Deut 17:7), and the fact that "judgment" sometimes includes the execution of the punishment.

In the following examples, men appear as witnesses. Isaiah 55:4 reads *hēn ʿēḏ lᵊʾûmmîm nᵊṯattîw* (הֵן עֵד לְאוּמִּים נְתַתִּיו) "See, I made him a witness to the peoples." Here it is unclear who has been set as witness, or what the object of the verb *nᵊṯattîw* (נְתַתִּיו) "to give him, to set him" is. It could refer to the historical David.[145] It could refer to Israel. Although the promise was originally given to the historical David (2 Sam 7:12–16), David is now dead and he cannot anymore impact the present or future status of the nation.[146] Hence, the glory of redeemed Israel draws the nations to YHWH (e.g. Isa 60:1–3; although no other text says that Israel calls the nations).[147] It could refer to the wider human family. While the David's dynasty ended, YHWH's everlasting covenant with David extends beyond David's house, and embraces the entire community of those obedient to God's word.[148] Or it could refer to the future Davidic messiah. This future messiah would witness to

141. Petterson, *Haggai, Zechariah & Malachi*, 365.

142. Taylor and Clendenen, *Haggai, Malachi*, 391–392.

143. Keil and Delitzsch, *K&D*, 10:658.

144. "The vocabulary here is reminiscent of a covenant lawsuit (*rîb*). This is a serious situation since in such lawsuits between covenant parties God fulfils the multiple roles of prosecuting attorney, witness, judge, and executioner." (Baker, *Joel, Obadiah, Malachi*, 274)

145. Oswalt, *Book of Isaiah*, Kindle Locations 7373–7374; Goldingay and Payne, *Isaiah 40–55*, 1:373; Westermann, *Isaiah 40–66*, 285.

146. Smith, *Isaiah 40–66*, 500.

147. Oswalt, *Book of Isaiah*, Kindle Locations 7370–7373; Westermann, *Isaiah 40–66*, 283; von Rad, *Old Testament Theology Vol. II*, 240.

148. Hanson, *Isaiah 40–66*, 179.

others about his life. Smith importantly notes: "In order for the Servant to function in the role of a light to the nations and a covenant to the people (42:6; 49:8), the nations would need to witness his life and hear of his life of suffering for their sins."[149]

In the following examples plural forms of noun *ʿēḏ* (עֵד) appear in the texts, yet men are those who perform the role of witnesses. Although in some of the texts, other words for the concept of witness appear, we will treat them separately. The first example comes from Isaiah 8:2. In Isaiah 8:1 YHWH instructs Isaiah to write the message "Maher-Shalal-Hash-Baz," and in Isaiah 8:2 Isaiah calls two witnesses. The reason for their calling is apparently to confirm the date of the prophecy since months or even years would pass before its completion. Hence, when prophecy is fulfilled, these two witnesses could confirm that Isaiah truly had written and prophetically announced this event long before the prophecy's fulfilment.[150] These two individuals are described as *ʿēḏîm neʾĕmānîm* (עֵדִים נֶאֱמָנִים) "reliable witnesses" – ones who support or sustain. However, the true nature of their witness is unclear. Either they could be trusted by the public as well as by Isaiah[151] and "their testimony would weigh with the people,"[152] or they were hostile toward Isaiah, thus witnesses that even Isaiah's enemies would believe.[153]

The next two examples are particularly significant for the concept of witness in Isaiah: Isaiah 43:8–12[154] and Isaiah 44:8–9.[155] These verses are part of the section Isaiah 43:8–44:22, which contains one of Isaiah's trial scenes,

149. Smith, *Isaiah 40–66*, 503.

150. Watts, *Isaiah 1–33*, 113; Jamieson, Fausset and Brown, *CCEB* 1: 438.

151. Watts, 113.

152. Keil and Delitzsch, *K&D*, 7:148.

153. Smith, *Isaiah 1–39*, 221.

154. "Bring forth the people who are blind, yet have eyes, who are deaf, yet have ears! [9] Let all the nations gather together, and let the peoples assemble. Who among them declared this, and foretold to us the former things? Let them bring their witnesses to justify them, and let them hear and say, "It is true."[10] You are my witnesses, says the Lord, and my servant whom I have chosen, so that you may know and believe me and understand that I am he. Before me no god was formed, nor shall there be any after me.[11] I, I am the Lord, and besides me there is no saviour.[12] I declared and saved and proclaimed, when there was no strange god among you; and you are my witnesses, says the Lord" (NRSV).

155. "Do not fear, or be afraid; have I not told you from of old and declared it? You are my witnesses! Is there any god besides me? There is no other rock; I know not one. [9] All who make idols are nothing, and the things they delight in do not profit; their witnesses neither see nor know. And so, they will be put to shame" (NRSV).

here a trial between YHWH and pagan gods. Israel and the pagan nations appear as witnesses, each for their God/gods. Each side is free to summon witnesses to support their arguments, yet it is YHWH who commands to Israel, the pagan nations, and their gods to assemble for a trial (Isa 43:8–9). Pagan gods cannot assemble their witnesses because they do not exist (Isa 43:10), let alone can they speak (Isa 43:9, 12) or know or do something (Isa 43:12). The irony is obvious.

Isaiah 43:8 speaks about *ʿam* (עַם) "[one] nation" which is blind and deaf. Who is this nation and what is their connection with witnesses from Isaiah 43:10 and 43:12? Some argue that this nation is Israel, figuratively described as deaf and blind in its lack of understanding.[156] Therefore, they also need to be convinced by YHWH just like other nations. However, there is a hope for these disabled witnesses because, in spite of their conduct, they possess ears and eyes so that their current state need not be their final state.[157] Others argue that these witnesses called by YHWH in Isaiah 43:8–9 are "witness for alternative gods, witnesses who are taken to be blind, deaf, and ineffectual. That is, the allegedly pitiful quality of the gods is, in this imaginative scenario, expressed in terms of the disability of the witnesses."[158] Note that the poem changes in verse 10, so that YHWH addresses Israel as his witness, and they are able to testify that YHWH is the only God and there are no other gods beside Him, and He alone declares and accomplishes salvation.

Smith's solution, which uses a "both/and" (instead of "either/or") approach, is perhaps the most appropriate. He claims that the legal language in this message is unusual because it addresses both Israel and (indirectly) the nations. The main audience is Israel, but invitation also brings the nations on board to verify who really is the superior supernatural power. Thus, if we take "nation" from 43:8 to refer to Israel, in 43:8–10 we have a chiastic structure:

- 43:8 – Israel
    - 43:9a – pagan nations
        - 43:9b – pagan gods
    - 43:9c – pagan nations as witnesses
- 43:10 – Israel as YHWH's witness

156. Delcor, "חרשׁ" *ḥrš to be silent*, 477.
157. Goldingay, *Message of Isaiah 40–55*, 197.
158. Brueggemann, *Theology of Old Testament*, 749.

The role of Israel as YHWH's witness is furthermore confirmed in Isaiah 43:12. Since Israel experienced and witnessed with their own eyes YHWH's great acts of salvation history (43:12b; 43:10), the telling of their story will only confirm YHWH's real divine qualities.[159]

The idea that Israel is YHWH's witness is furthermore confirmed by the statement "You are my witnesses" in Isaiah 43:10 as *ʾattem ʿēḏay* (אַתֶּם עֵדַי) and Isaiah 43:12 as *wᵊʾattem ʿēḏay* (וְאַתֶּם עֵדַי). Israel is here defined as *wᵊʿaḇdî* (וְעַבְדִּי) "my servant" (Is 43:10) and *bāḥārtî* (בָּחָרְתִּי) the one whom YHWH "chose" (Isa 43:10). Interestingly, Israel as a collective is a witness for YHWH, although YHWH addresses Israel with the plural "witnesses." This use is probably alluding to the Torah, where plurality of witnesses is needed to ensure the proper judgment about someone's guilt. Likewise, in Isaiah 44:8, Israel is defined one more time as YHWH's witness *wᵊʾattem ʿēḏāy* (וְאַתֶּם עֵדַי) "You are my witnesses."

In Isaiah 43:9 YHWH summons another party as well. This party is described as *kol-haggôyim* (כָל־הַגּוֹיִם) "all people, nations" and *lᵊʾummîm* (לְאֻמִּים) "peoples, nations." In 43:9b another entity is possibly introduced into the story as *mî ḇāhem* (מִי בָהֶם) or "who among them." It is not clear whether this refers to pagan gods or their nations, but whomever it is, YHWH invites them to *yittᵊnû ʿēḏêhem* (יִתְּנוּ עֵדֵיהֶם) "let them bring their witnesses."[160] The identity of the subjects of the verb *wᵊyišmᵊʿû* (וְיִשְׁמְעוּ) "let them hear" in Isaiah 43:9 is difficult to define. Perhaps a) the subjects are nations/peoples. Alternatively, b), if the conjunction *wᵊ* (וְ) in *wᵊyišmᵊʿû* (וְיִשְׁמְעוּ) is translated as "or," the meaning is "or must listen." Following this option, the nations/kings either speak via their witnesses or listen. This is an intriguing reading, but

159. Smith, *Isaiah 40–66*, 204.

160. Isaiah 43:9 *yittᵊnû ʿēḏêhem* (יִתְּנוּ עֵדֵיהֶם) the NRSV translates as "Let them bring their witnesses," and the NIV "Let them bring in their witnesses." The identity of witnesses is debatable, and this reflects in translations. The NRSV reads "Let all the nations gather together, and let the peoples assemble. *Who among them* [emphasis mine] declared this, and foretold to us the former things? Let them bring their witnesses to justify them, and let them hear and say, 'It is true.'" The NIV reads "All the nations gather together, and the peoples assemble. *Which of their gods foretold* [emphasis mine] this and proclaimed to us the former things? Let them bring in their witnesses to prove they were right, so that others may hear and say, "It is true.'" Both translations understand this reference to speak about pagan gods not pagan nations. Perhaps, John N. Oswalt (*Book of Isaiah*, Kindle Locations 2472–2473) is on the right track when he says: "Each of the nations and peoples has its god, but *Who among them* (the gods) *can declare* (foretell) a future like *this?*" (Emphasis orginal.)

"or" is a rare meaning for Hebrew *wᵊ* (וְ). It is also possible that c) witnesses are the subject in the sense that their task was to listen (cf. Isa 42:13–20), and to testify in due course to what they had heard. But the problem with this reading is that "listening" comes after "bringing forth," which suggests that witnesses speak and someone else is listening, not that witnesses have to do the listening. Or d) the court is the one who listens to the witnesses' testimony and acknowledges its truth.[161]

Accordingly, we can conclude that YHWH's invitation to pagan gods to summon witnesses and present their case is ironic because those gods do not exist. If they do not exist, they cannot do or say anything. Hence, they cannot have witnesses because there is nothing to witness to. And if witnesses appear, they are surely false witnesses because they do not have basis for their claims. But this is not the case with YHWH's witnesses (Isa 43:10–13) who have plenty of evidence to support YHWH's claim for superiority. They can witness that YHWH has in the past announced and accomplished something, but they can also witness to what will happen.[162]

In Isaiah 44:6–8[163] YHWH once again extends his challenge to pagan gods to present their case. YHWH's rhetorical questions (vv. 7–8) imply negative answers from the other side. Also, the text strongly emphasizes the contrast between YHWH's witnesses and witnesses of pagan gods. In the sentence: "have I not told you from of old and declared it? You are my witnesses!" (Isa 44:8) (NRSV), the verb "declared" is linked with the pronoun *ʾattem* (אַתֶּם) "you are," thus *wᵊhiggaḏtî wᵊ ʾattem ʿēḏāy* (וְהִגַּדְתִּי וְאַתֶּם עֵדָי) ". . . and declared it and you are my witnesses." According to Goldingay and Payne[164] these words "invite us to read this line as asking 'Did I not in time past inform you and announce [it]? And you are my witnesses'. The declaration 'You are my witnesses' thus gains in prominence." The other option is to adopt the structure 3–3 and read "You as my witnesses" as circumstantial noun

161. Goldingay and Payne, *Isaiah 40–55*, 1:284.

162. Oswalt, *Book of Isaiah*, Kindle Locations 2916–2917.

163. "Thus says the LORD, the King of Israel, and his Redeemer, the LORD of hosts: I am the first and I am the last; besides me there is no god. [7] Who is like me? Let them proclaim it, let them declare and set it forth before me. Who has announced from of old the things to come? Let them tell us what is yet to be. [8] Do not fear, or be afraid; have I not told you from of old and declared it? You are my witnesses! Is there any god besides me? There is no other rock; I know not one" (NRSV).

164. Goldingay and Payne, *Isaiah 40–55*, 1: 343.

clause[165] "Did I not in time past inform you and announce *with you as my witnesses*?"[166] Contrary to YHWH's witnesses, the witnesses for the pagan gods in Isaiah 44:9[167] are false witnesses. First, idol makers are described as *tōhû* (תֹהוּ) "empty," which means that if they speak up or testify for their idols, their testimony is empty. Second, the second part of the verse says that "their witnesses neither see [*rāʾāh* (רָאָה)] nor know [*yāḏaʿ* (יָדַע)]. And so, they will be put to shame" is somewhat problematic because the expression *wᵊʿēḏêhem* (וְעֵדֵיהֶם) "their witnesses" is followed by the pronoun *hēmmāh* (הֵמָּה) "they."[168] The line then literally reads "Their [own] witnesses they are." If this reading is correct, it could mean that the idols are blind and ignorant, and that the witnesses testify to this blindness to the idols' shame. Alternatively, the entities who are not seeing and not knowing must be the witnesses. By choosing to follow their gods, they have blinded themselves and will one day be ashamed by the failure of their gods.[169]

The next group of verses (Jer 32:10, 12, 25, 44) are the part of the same story. Although Jerusalem was sieged by the Babylonian king, YHWH commands Jeremiah to purchase the field in Anathoth. This purchase was a symbolic pledge that such activity would take place in the future (Jer 32:15). In order to purchase the field, Jeremiah needed witnesses to the purchase. In

165. The statement of the particular circumstances under which a subject appears as performing some action, or under which an action (or an occurrence) is accomplished.

166. In 2–2–2 structure, "You are my witnesses" thus gains the prominent emphasis.
6a Reason for confidence
6b Declaration of YHWH's uniqueness
7a Challenge to disprove that uniqueness
7b Challenge to announce events
8a Exhortation to confidence
8b Declaration of YHWH's uniqueness

In the structure 3–3, according to Goldingay and Payne, preferred reading of "You are my witnesses" is as circumstantial noun clause.
6a Reason for confidence
6b Declaration of YHWH's uniqueness
7a Challenge to disprove that uniqueness
7b Challenge to announce events
8a Exhortation to confidence
8b Declaration of YHWH's uniqueness

167. "All who make idols are nothing, and the things they delight in do not profit; their witnesses neither see nor know. And so, they will be put to shame" (NRSV).

168. Dots over each letter of the word in the MT, probably suggests that in the Masoretes' opinion the word should be omitted.

169. Oswalt, *Book of Isaiah*, Kindle Locations 3014–3020.

all four uses in Jeremiah 32, *ʿēḏîm* (עֵדִים) appears together with *ʿûd* (עוּד). Since the role of these witnesses depends on the meaning of *ʿûd* (עוּד), and we will analyze its meaning below, for now it is sufficient to say that these witnesses serve as witnesses who guarantee the legality of purchase.

3.2 Usage of ʿēḏûṯ (עֵדוּת) and ʿēḏôṯ (עֵדֹות) in the Prophets

The noun *ʿēḏûṯ* (עֵדוּת) is only used in the plural form *ûḇᵊʿēḏôṯâw* (וּבְעֵדְוֹתָיו) once in the prophets, Jeremiah 44:23. There it describes the Torah. We saw earlier that *ʿēḏûṯ* (עֵדוּת) is used to describe the Torah in the Pentateuch and Writings. Also, as in Psalms, *ûḇᵊʿēḏôṯâw* (וּבְעֵדְוֹתָיו) is here found together with other synonyms for the Torah: *ûḇᵊṯōrāṯô* (וּבְתֹרָתוֹ) "and in his Law" and *ûḇᵊḥuqqōṯâw* (וּבְחֻקֹּתָיו) "and in his statutes."

3.3 Usage of tᵊʿûḏāh (תְּעוּדָה) in the Prophets

In the Prophets, *tᵊʿûḏāh* (תְּעוּדָה) is used in Isaiah 8:16, 20, which is part of the story we encountered when discussing Isaiah 8:2. From Isaiah 8:5 to 8:15 Isaiah offers prophecy, and in Isaiah 8:16 the text says *ṣôr tᵊʿûḏāh ḥăṯôm tôrāh bᵊlimmuḏây* (צוֹר תְּעוּדָה חֲתוֹם תּוֹרָה בְּלִמֻּדָי) "Bind up the testimony, seal the teaching among my disciples" (NRSV). The precise meaning of *tᵊʿûḏāh* (תְּעוּדָה) "testimony" and *tôrāh* (תּוֹרָה) "law, instruction" is unclear.[170] Although *tᵊʿûḏāh* (תְּעוּדָה) generally refers to the message that someone has spoken and *tôrāh* (תּוֹרָה) to written words of YHWH (the first five books of the Bible), these two words can be understood as synonyms.[171] Watts[172] explains that *tôrāh* (תּוֹרָה) is a fitting term for the teaching activity of the prophet since in the OT the word is also used for description of the priestly teaching of tradition. Accordingly, *tᵊʿûḏāh* (תְּעוּדָה) probably refers to the prophetic messages YHWH has given Isaiah, and *tôrāh* (תּוֹרָה) probably refers to the prophet's exhortations and warnings (NET Bible). Or *tᵊʿûḏāh* (תְּעוּדָה) can be the words that YHWH spoke to Isaiah, and *tôrāh* (תּוֹרָה) can

---

170. Isaiah 8:16 *ṣôr təʿûḏāh ḥăṯôm tôrāh bəlimmuḏāy* (צוֹר תְּעוּדָה חֲתוֹם תּוֹרָה בְּלִמֻּדָי) the NRSV understands as "Bind up the testimony, seal the teaching among my disciples," and the NIV as "Bind up this testimony of warning and seal up God's instruction among my disciples." The NIV specifies *təʿûḏāh* (תְּעוּדָה) as "testimony of warning" and *tôrāh* (תּוֹרָה) as God's instruction, while the NRSV allows that *tôrāh* (תּוֹרָה) can refer to Isaiah's teaching as well.

171. Smith, *Isaiah 1–39*, 228–229.

172. Watts, *Isaiah 1–33*, 122.

be advice given in verses 12–15.[173] Another approach is that *təʿûḏāh* (תְּעוּדָה) deals with attesting the name "Maher-Shalal-Hash-Baz" (Isa 8:1–4) and the name's reference to the dissolution of the Damascus-Samaria alliance, and *tôrāh* (תּוֹרָה) refers in this context to the prophetic teaching of Isaiah.[174]

Finally, in Isaiah 8:20 again we have the appearance of *təʿûḏāh* (תְּעוּדָה) and *tôrāh* (תּוֹרָה).[175] The precise meaning of these words depends on how we understood them in Isaiah 8:16. It is also unclear to whom Isaiah speaks in this verse. Some take that Isaiah speaks about necromancers (v. 19), so the meaning of the passage becomes "They who are in the dark night of trial, without a dawn of hope, shall surely say so, do not seek, as we did, to necromancy, but to the law."[176] Others understand verses 19–20 as declarations regarding two different groups of people. The first group of people consults mediums and spiritists, the second consults God's Law and instruction. By this reading, testimony and Law is the source of true revelation about YHWH's will for the second group. Because of their reliance on that source, they can test and judge all prophetic statements. The other group turns to the spiritual world for their guidance. For such people, there is no true access to the divine light.[177]

3.4 Usage of ʿûḏ (עוּד) in the Prophets

In the Prophets *ʿûḏ* (עוּד) appears eleven times. The first example we encountered above in our discussion of Isaiah 8:2, where Isaiah called two witnesses to testify regarding what he wrote. The text describes their calling as *wəʾāʿîḏāh lî ʿēḏîm* (וְאָעִידָה לִּי עֵדִים) "So I called for me witnesses." The verb *ʿûḏ* (עוּד) in its Hiphil cohortative wəyiqtōl (waw-conjunctive + imperfect) form does not refer to "replying" or "testifying." It is the main verb in the sentence. It is unclear whether *ʿûḏ* (עוּד) describes the activity of YHWH or Isaiah, and commentators are divided. Accordingly, the verbal form ואעידה can be understood: a) as cohortative imperfect with prefixed *waw* (ו), suggesting that the Lord is announcing what he will do, b) as an imperative

173. Spence-Jones, *Isaiah*, 148.

174. Friesen, *Isaiah*, 77.

175. Both words in MT as prefix have proposition *lə* (לְ), so *lətôrāh wəliṯʿûḏāh* (לְתוֹרָה וְלִתְעוּדָה) lit. reads as "For the law and for the testimony."

176. Jamieson, Fausset and Brown, *CCEB* 1:439.

177. Smith, *Isaiah 1–39*, 231.

"and summon as witnesses," where YHWH commands Isaiah to carry out that task, c) the prefixed conjunction can be taken as a *waw conversive* (or consecutive), causing the imperfect to be translated as perfect, "So I summoned as witnesses," meaning that Isaiah is recalling his response to the Lord's commission (NET Bible). These differences are noticeable in some English translations (NIV,[178] NRSV,[179] NASB[180]).[181] The most likely meaning of *ʿûḏ* (עוּד) here is that it refers to the invitation of two witnesses who passively witness what Isaiah will write.

The second example comes from Jeremiah 6:10. Although in verse 9 the speaker is YHWH; it seems that from verse 10 to 12a Jeremiah is now the speaker. On this reading, verse 10 is part of a conversation between YHWH and Jeremiah. In the first part of the verse, two verbs appear: *ʾăḏabbᵊrāh* (אֲדַבְּרָה) "to speak," and the verb *ʿûḏ* (עוּד) in its Hiphil wᵊyiqtōl (waw-conjunctive + imperfect) form *wᵊʾāʿîḏāh* (וְאָעִידָה) "to warn." These verbs describe complementary (not contrasting) activities. Warning[182] is or will be given by Jeremiah verbally through speaking, and the content of this testimony will expose people's sins and announce the punishment.[183] In this verse *ʿûḏ* (עוּד) clearly refers to a *warning*, because YHWH's speech through Jeremiah contains conditions and consequences.

In Jeremiah 11:7 the verb *ʿûḏ* (עוּד) appears three times describing the history of YHWH with his people as a time of constant warning: *kî hāʿēḏ haʿiḏōṯî* (כִּי הָעֵד הַעִדֹתִי). This is a construction made of the Hiphil infinitive absolute *hāʿēḏ* (הָעֵד) and the Hiphil perfect (qātal) *haʿiḏōṯî* (הַעִדֹתִי), in which the infinitives emphasize the main verb. Thus, the phrase can be translated

178. "So, I called in Uriah the priest and Zechariah son of Jeberechiah as reliable witnesses for me."

179. "and have it attested for me by reliable witnesses, the priest Uriah and Zechariah son of Jeberechiah."

180. "And I will take to Myself faithful witnesses for testimony, Uriah the priest and Zechariah the son of Jeberechiah."

181. Additionally, Isaiah 8:2 *wᵊʾāʿîḏāh lî ʿēḏîm neʾĕmānîm* (וְאָעִידָה לִּי עֵדִים נֶאֱמָנִים) the NRSV translates as "and have it attested for me by reliable witnesses," and the NIV as "I called in Uriah the priest and Zechariah son of Jeberechiah as reliable witnesses for me." The NIV translations understand calling the witnesses as something Isaiah does for himself, and the NRSV as an activity which is only instrumentally done through Isaiah. But the invitation comes from God, and also witnessing is for him.

182. Jeremiah in the same verse mentions *ḏᵊḇar-yəhwāh* (דְּבַר־יְהוָה) "word of the Lord." It seems that Jeremiah considers his speech as "word of the Lord."

183. Keil and Delitzsch, *K&D*, 8:88.

as "warning I warned," or as NRSV translates "I solemnly warned," with the repetition accentuating the seriousness of the warning.[184] The recipients of these warnings were *ba'ăḇôṯêḵem* (בַּאֲבוֹתֵיכֶם) "your fathers." The third *'ûd* (עוּד) refers to Jeremiah contemporary situation. This occurrence appears as Hiphil infinitive absolute *wᵊhā'ēḏ* (וְהָעֵד) together with another Hiphil infinitive absolute *haškēm* (הַשְׁכֵּם), translated "repetition," alongside the infinitive construct *lē'mōr* (לֵאמֹר) "saying," thus creating the expression ". . . warning persistently saying. . . ."

The next examples come from Jeremiah 32:10, 25 and 44. In discussing this passage above, we noted the combination of *'ēḏîm* (עֵדִים) and *'ûḏ* (עוּד) and said that the meaning of *'ēḏîm* (עֵדִים) depends on the meaning of *'ûḏ* (עוּד). In verse 10 we find the expression *wā'ā'ēḏ 'ēḏîm* (וָאָעֵד עֵדִים), which consists of the verb *'ûd* (עוּד) in the Hiphil wayyiqtōl (imperfect) form *wā'ā'ēḏ* (וָאָעֵד), and the noun *'ēḏîm* (עֵדִים). This expression can be translated in various ways: "had it witnessed" (NIV) focusing on the final result which is a confirmation of transaction," "got witnesses" (NRSV) where focus is on the aspect of bringing the witnesses to the spot; "called in witnesses" (NASB95) which is one of the meanings of *'ûd* (עוּד).[185] In verse 25, Jeremiah repeats YHWH's command *wᵊhā'ēḏ 'ēḏîm* (וְהָעֵד עֵדִים). Here the verb *'ûd* (עוּד) is in Hiphil imperative. As in Jeremiah verse 10, the meaning is not completely clear.[186] One possible translation is "I had witnesses to witness," if we take *'ûd* (עוּד) to speak not about "calling" to witness, but of the specific act of witnessing itself.

In Jeremiah 32:44 we find the expression *wᵊhā'ēḏ 'ēḏîm* (וְהָעֵד עֵדִים). Here the verb *'ûd* (עוּד) takes the form of Hiphil infinitive absolute, and in verse 44 it is found together with other infinitives: *kāṯaḇ* (כָּתַב) "signed" and *ḥāṯam* (חָתַם) "sealed." Interestingly, both NRSV and NIV use passive voice[187]

184. Kršćanska sadašnjost translates as "ozbiljno opominjao."

185. We have seen that *'ûḏ* (עוּד) can be understood as "calling someone to witness" or as some "act of witnessing."

186. So, the NIV has "and have the transaction witnessed" and NRSV uses an expression "and get witnesses." In the NASB 95 "getting" is understood as "call in witnesses," but once again we can translate the combination of Hiphil imperative with *'ēḏîm* (עֵדִים) as "cause witnesses to testify" (YLT) or "call in witnesses to witness" (NET Bible).

187. "Fields shall be bought for money, and deeds shall be signed and sealed and witnessed" (NRSV), "Fields will be bought for silver, and deeds will be signed, sealed and witnessed" (NIV).

and translate the construction *wəhā ʿēḏ ʿēḏîm* (וְהָעֵד עֵדִים) with "will/shall be witnessed," while NASB 95 uses active voice,[188] "call in witnesses." YLT keeps the Hiphil stem in translation "cause witnesses to testify" and John A. Thompson[189] translates as "and witnesses shall witness."

Jeremiah 42:19 is a continuation of the story from Jeremiah 42:5. Here Jeremiah repeats YHWH's admonition not to go to Egypt. This time, however, Jeremiah does not use an "if-then" clause but rather declarative speech.[190] Here, Jeremiah is the witness who has testified *kî-ha ʿîḏōṯî* (כִּי־הַעִידֹתִי) about the future things, and his testimony is presented in the form of "warning" or "admonishment." Although the expression *kî-ha ʿîḏōṯî* (כִּי־הַעִידֹתִי) is accompanied by expression *ḇāḵem* (בָכֶם), "in you," the proper meaning could also be "against you." Hence, Jeremiah's testimony was "testimony against them" in a sense of conditional warning.

The verb *ʿûḏ* (עוּד) in Jeremiah 42:19 refers to giving testimony about future events, usually warning or admonishment. Such testimony requires prophetic insight. For Jeremiah, this insight came through the "coming of the word of the Lord" (v. 7). When prophet testifies about the things that YHWH will do, he does it not on the basis of what he saw and heard, but on the basis of knowing the will of YHWH. Here, Jeremiah serves as a witness against. Notice three things here. First, the testimony against Israel is conditional – if the remnant chooses to stay in Judaea and not to go in Egypt, they will receive YHWH's favor in Judea, and the witness against will not be fulfilled. Second, Jeremiah's warning about future damnation has a force of repetitive activity, which is one of the meanings of *ʿûd* (עוּד). In Jeremiah 42:18 YHWH said, "As my anger and wrath have been poured out on those who lived in Jerusalem, so will my wrath be poured out on you when you go to Egypt." Third, words of doom against the nations can at the same time be words of salvation to Israel. However, "in chapters 42–43, we have one of the examples where a word against another nations functions also as a word of doom against the people of Israel, as these sojourn in the country in question."[191]

188. "Men will buy fields for money, sign and seal deeds and call in witnesses" (NASB95).

189. Thompson, *Jeremiah*, 595.

190. Stulman, *Jeremiah, AOTC*, 336.

191. Barstad, "Prophecy in Book of Jeremiah," 91.

In Lamentations, we find the concept of witness in Lamentations 2:13, with the verb *ʿûḏ* (עוּד) in the form *māh-ʾăʿîḏēḵ* (מָה־אֲעִידֵךְ). The verbal form אעידך is very difficult to translate.[192] According to Robert B. Salters[193] "although LXX, P and T appear to derive (אֲעִידֵךְ) from the verb *ʿûḏ* (עוּד), 'to testify', the sense that emerges is far from satisfactory in the context: 'What shall I testify to/for you?'" *ʿûḏ* (עוּד) normally means "to testify" as in the story of Naboth in 1 Kings 21, thus some translations will understand the word more broadly as "saying," since testifying is one aspect of speaking.[194] Some translations agree with the Vulgate *comparabo te* "I will compare you." This requires an emendation where *ʾăʿîḏēḵ* (אֲעִידֵךְ) is changed into *ʾeʿĕr āk* (אֶעֱרָךְ), from the verb *ʿārak* (עָרַךְ) "to liken."[195] The verb *ʿārak* (עָרַךְ) normally means "to lay out, set in rows; to get ready, set in order; to line up for battle," but it also may denote "to compare (as a result of arranging in order), to make equal" (e.g. Ps 40:6; 89:6 [HT 7]; Job 28:17, 19; Isa 40:18; 44:7) (NET Bible). If that reading is accepted, then the translation would be something like "To what can I liken you?" instead of "What can I testify/say for you?" Commentators are divided on which reading is best. If we follow the Vulgate then all three verbs in verse 13, *ʿārak* (עָרַךְ), *dāmāh* (דָּמָה) "be like" and *šāwāh* (שָׁוָה) "compare," have the sense of "compare." This is rare in Hebrew poetry.[196] On the other hand, the MT reading: "How can I testify for you?" makes little sense in the context (NET Bible).[197] However, most English versions follow the MT reading: KJV, RSV, NRSV, NASB, NIV, TEV, CEV, with the remark that NASB 1995 uses the word "admonish," and NKJV "console."[198]

Regarding the content of the testimony, in this verse *ʿûḏ* (עוּד) does not function as *witness against* nor as a prophetic warning about future events, but as instruction and comfort. The writer identifies with the pain of "the

192. Garrett, *Song of Songs/Lamentations*, 387.

193. Salters, *Lamentations*, 152.

194. Reyburn and Fry, *Lamentations*, 60.

195. Garrett, *Song of Songs/Lamentations*, 371.

196. Reyburn and Fry, *Lamentations*, 60.

197. The LXX reads as Τί *μαρτυρήσω σοι* "What shall I testify to you," and in this way retains the MT's idea of witnessing.

198. For additional options of reading *ʿûḏ* (עוּד) in Lamentations 2:13 see Salters, *Lamentations*, 151–153.

daughter of Jerusalem," but he is unable to help and console her. Three times verse 13 uses the interrogative pronoun *māh* (מָה) "what" to ask questions: *māh-ʾăʿîḏēḵ* (מָה־אֲעִידֵךְ) "what can I say," *ʾăḏammeh-llāḵ* (אֲדַמֶּה־לָּךְ) "to what compare you," *ʾašweh-llāḵ* (אַשְׁוֶה־לָּךְ), "to what can I liken you." The verse further uses the interrogative pronoun *mî* (מִי) "who" one time, to ask *yirpāʾ-lāḵ* (יִרְפָּא־לָךְ) "who can heal you?" These communicate the writer's helplessness and inability to say anything that would bring comfort to his people.

In Amos 3:13 verb *ʿûḏ* (עוּד) is used in the covenant lawsuit where YHWH speaks against his nation. Our understanding of *šimʿû wᵊhāʿîḏû bᵊḇêṯ yaʿăqōḇ* (שִׁמְעוּ וְהָעִידוּ בְּבֵית יַעֲקֹב) depends upon several things. First, the subjects of the plural imperatives *šimʿû* (שִׁמְעוּ) "listen" and *wᵊhāʿîḏû* (וְהָעִידוּ) "testify" can refer to the prophets in general, the foreign national leaders of Amos 3:9, Amos alone, the citizenry of Israel, or it can be a rhetorical device intended to bring the hearers or readers to an awareness of the covenant lawsuit motif in this prophetic message. Second, the purpose of gathering of these witnesses can be: a) to consider the evidence against Israel, and hear YHWH's verdict,[199] b) to witness with their own eyes Samaria's corruptions above described, so that none may be able to deny the justice of Samaria's punishment[200] or, c) to hear YHWH's threat of punishment for sins associated with Israel's worship at Bethel and with their lifestyle, and testify to the verdict.[201] Hence, witnesses are invited in verse 13 either to observe the evidence (even "with their own eyes") and hear and testify to the verdict, or just to be witnesses to YHWH's verdict presumably "so that none may be able to deny the justice of Samaria's punishment."[202] Third, the verb *wᵊhāʿîḏû* (וְהָעִידוּ) in combination with the preposition *bᵊ* (בְּ) in the expression *bᵊḇêṯ* (בְּבֵית) "against the house" can mean that the "house of Jacob" is the entity against whom the witnesses were to testify.[203] In this case, witnesses would be summoned to witness (in a passive, observant way) either to the verdict that YHWH pronounces against the house of Jacob, or to her sins as well. However, Jorg Jeremias argues that *wᵊhāʿîḏû* (וְהָעִידוּ) does not have its usual meaning "testify" but rather a more

199. Stuart, *Hosea–Jonah*, 331.

200. Jamieson, Fausset and Brown, *CCEB* 1:672.

201. Smith and Page, *Amos, Obadiah, Jonah*, 81.

202. Jamieson, Fausset and Brown, *CCEB* 1:672.

203. Smith and Page, *Amos, Obadiah, Jonah*, 81.

active meaning, such as "enjoin, inculcate, admonish or warn (in a threatening fashion)." This meaning is present in Deuteronomistic theology where "warning" is usually the "manner in which Yahweh – primarily through his prophets – tries to bring his sinful people to its senses in the face of imminent punishment." In this instance, the people of YHWH expect "hearing" and "warning": "every individual member of the people of God whose eyes were opened to Israel's guilt through Amos' words and through the experience of the destruction of both Northern and Southern Kingdoms, is called upon to assume the prophet's office of watchman (v. 6a) in summoning their own contemporaries to repentance."[204]

We have seen that many things in Amos 3:13 are hard to define, and this lack of clarity impacts the way we interpret the text. For us, accompanying details are not as important as the overall character of these witnesses. Based on the context the best reading is that witnesses in this text have a passive role. Against this, note that the meaning of *wᵊhā ʿîḏû* (וְהָעִידוּ) is usually in active voice where witnesses verbally declare their messages. If we accept the first option, then we must conclude that the verb *ʿûḏ* (עוּד) is used in an unusual way in this verse. If we accept the second reading, the meaning of the *ʿûḏ* (עוּד) is more natural, but we must explain how these witnesses function as testifying witnesses when the context seems to imply their passive, observant role.

Zechariah 3:6 presents fewer interpretative difficulties. This verse is a part of a vision (Zech 3:1–5) in which the prophet Zechariah saw the symbolic re-clothing of the high priest Joshua. This action signified both the confirmation of Joshua into the office of high priest, and the continued existence and significance of this office. This vision is accompanied by the prophetic message given to the high priest Joshua in verse 6: *wayyā ʿaḏ mal ʾaḵ yᵊhwāh bîhôšua ʿ lē ʾmōr* (וַיָּעַד מַלְאַךְ יְהוָה בִּיהוֹשֻׁעַ לֵאמֹר) "And the angel of YHWH admonished (charged) Joshua, saying."[205] The message is information regarding

204. Jeremias, *Book of Amos*, 62.

205. The NIV does not translate the expression *lē ʾmōr* (לֵאמֹר) "saying," but more interestingly, for the idiom *ʿûḏ* (עוּד) . . . *bə* (בְּ), the NRSV uses the less "threatening" word "assured," while the NIV reads it as "charge." "Assurance" is perhaps not the best translation because *ʿûḏ* (עוּד) is usually connected with a strong *warning* or *admonishment* to fulfil certain duties, commands, or take some course of action in the *future*, and *negative consequences* in case of disobedience.

the future, it is conditional,[206] and it is introduced with the verb *ʿûḏ* (עוּד) in its Hiphil wayyiqtōl (waw-consecutive + imperfect) form *wayyāʿaḏ* (וַיָּעַד). The idiom *ʿûḏ* (עוּד) . . . *bᵊ* (בְּ) can mean "testify against" (Deut 4:26; 30:19; 31:28), but it can also have a more general meaning such as "admonish, warn or enjoin."[207] Translation of this passage must consider how *ʿûḏ* (עוּד) is usually connected with a strong warning or admonishment to fulfil certain duties, commands, or to take some course of action in the future, and negative consequences in case of disobedience. The same pattern is present also in Zechariah 3:1–10 because here we see "a transition from a positive disposition in the interpretation in Zechariah 3:4, which declared God's removal of guilt, to a darker nuance, reminding the priest that this new status cannot be taken for granted."[208]

The last example from the Hebrew Bible comes from Malachi 2:14 where *ʿûḏ* (עוּד) appears in the context of the speech about the covenant of marriage. The pattern of dispute between YHWH and his people follows this schema: Malachi accuses the people, here by asserting that YHWH does not accept their sacrifice. The people respond by asking "Why?" requiring evidence for the accusation. The prophet gives evidence to support the charge, here pointing to the people's unfaithfulness to the marriage covenant. Verse 14 starts with plural *waʾămartem* (וַאֲמַרְתֶּם) "And you ask," but the charge is against "you" in singular ("between *you* and the wife of *your* youth"). The offence that Malachi criticizes here is probably the practice of his day where men of Judah divorced their Jewish wives only to marry pagan women. So, Malachi is condemning the practice of divorce and mixed marriages. Accordingly, marrying "the daughter of a foreign god" from verse 11 refers

---

206. "The charge to Joshua embodied two conditions and three results of divine blessing. To walk in God's ways describes the personal attitude of the priests (and ultimately the nation) toward God and keeping God's requirements (cf. 1 Kgs 2:3) refers to the faithful performance of priestly duties. If Joshua met these conditions he would enjoy three things: (a) govern My house – have continued service in the temple, (b) have charge of My courts – guard the temple from idolatry and other religious defilement, and (c) receive a place among these standing here – perhaps referring to Joshua's free access to God (cf. Zech. 3:1) comparable to that of the angels (those who are 'standing' are distinguished from Joshua's fellow priests who are 'seated,' v. 8)" (Lindsey, "Zechariah", *Bible Knowledge Commentary* 1:1554).

207. Petersen, *Haggai and Zechariah 1–8*, 203.

208. Boda, *Haggai, Zechariah*, 254.

to this practice.[209] YHWH appears as witness in that context of marriage as covenant.[210] Malachi describes YHWH's activity as a witness with the perfect (qātal) *hē ʿîḏ* (הֵעִיד) in the context of the sentence: *kî-yᵊhwāh hē ʿîḏ bênᵊḵā ûḇên ʾēšeṯ nᵊ ʿûreḵā* (כִּי־יְהוָה הֵעִיד בֵּינְךָ וּבֵין אֵשֶׁת נְעוּרֶיךָ) "Because YHWH has witnessed between you and between the wife of your youth." So once again we have a combination of the verb *ʿûḏ* (עוּד) and preposition *bayin* (בַּיִן) "between."

The expression "Because YHWH has witnessed between you and between the wife of your youth," does not necessarily mean that YHWH is described as an avenging witness, because in this case *hē ʿîḏ* (הֵעִיד) would necessarily be construed with *bᵊ* (בְּ).[211] This puts YHWH primarily but not exclusively in the passive observing position, since marriage occurs before YHWH or looking up to YHWH.[212] However, the text implies that YHWH also assumes the role of witness against in cases where the covenant is violated. Although his role is primarily observing, he also watches over it, acting as a guarantor of the covenant or judge.[213] This implies that YHWH continues the activity of witnessing. Accordingly, YHWH not only witnessed their marriage vows, but he also witnessed how these same wives were being treated treacherously by their husbands.[214] Likewise, Petterson[215] says that "YHWH is a witness to the covenant and has testified and now testifies (the sense of the verb in the qatal) to the faithless action of the husband." Additionally, David W. Baker[216] points to the fact that YHWH performs the role of a witness in this lawsuit. Hence, Malachi 2:14 reveals the dynamic passive observing and active testifying role of a witness. An observing witness can also, if need be, function as a testifying witness.

209. Lujić, *Starozavjetni proroci*, 322.

210. The word "marriage" is not present in the MT, but from the context it can be assumed that the covenant of marriage" is in view.

211. Keil and Delitzsch, *K&D*, 10:652.

212. Keil and Delitzsch, 10:652.

213. We have a good parallel for this in Genesis 31:50 where YHWH is described as a witness. He also assumes the role of a judge (Gen 31:53), so that he can punish the offender in case the covenant would be violated.

214. Smith, *Minor Prophets; Malachi* 2:14

215. Petterson, *Haggai, Zechariah & Malachi*, 351–352.

216. Baker, *Joel, Obadiah, Malachi*, 255.

CHAPTER 4

LXX Textual Analysis

In this chapter we will analyze how the Hebrew words relating to the concept of witness are translated in the LXX. We will follow the same pattern which we used for the analysis of the MT. In the Pentateuch, Writings and Prophets in succession we will group texts by their Hebrew vocabulary and observe how the LXX translates them.

1. Pentateuch – passage analysis of the LXX

1.1 ʿēḏ (עֵד) and ʿēḏîm (עֵדִים) in the Pentateuch

Genesis 31:44–52 exhibits some textual variations between the MT and LXX. In Genesis 31:44 after *wᵊhāyāh lᵊʿēḏ bênî ûḇênekā* (וְהָיָה לְעֵד בֵּינִי וּבֵינֶךָ), the LXX adds: Ἰδού οὐθεὶς μεθ' ἡμῶν ἐστίν; ἴδε ὁ θεὸς μάρτυς ἀνὰ μέσον ἐμοῦ καὶσοῦ "Behold, there is no one with us; behold, God is witness between me and you."[1] For the LXX the "covenant" is clearly identified as μαρτύριον, but the LXX adds God as μάρτυς. In Genesis 31:46 (48),[2] the LXX adds Ὁ βουνὸς οὗτος μαρτυρεῖ ἀνὰ μέσον ἐμοῦ καὶ σοῦ σήμερον "This heap witnesses between me and you today" (with verb μαρτυρέω) to the MT. In Genesis 31:47 the LXX is consistent in its translation of all names. The compound phrase *yᵊḡar śāhăḏûṯāʾ* (יְגַר שָׂהֲדוּתָא) "Jegar Sahadutha" is correctly translated as Βουνὸς τῆς μαρτυρίας "Heap of witness," and the Hebrew nominal clause *galʿēḏ* (גַּלְעֵד) "Galeed" is again translated literally: Βουνὸς μάρτυς

1. Hamilton, *Book of Genesis*, 310.
2. In the LXX Swete's edition, this text is designated as part of verse 48 in brackets.

"Heap of witness"[3]. In Genesis 31:48 in the MT, only "heap" is described as *ʿēḏ* (עֵד), but in the LXX the "pillar" and the "heap" are twice described with the verb *μαρτυρέω*. In Genesis 31:50 the MT mentions God as *ʿēḏ* (עֵד) "witness", but the LXX lacks this expression. Finally, in Genesis 31:52 in the MT "heap" is defined as *ʿēḏ* (עֵד), but the LXX does not mention the heap's role as a witness.

In Exodus 20:16 the LXX says Οὐ *ψευδομαρτυρήσεις κατὰ τοῦ πλησίον σου μαρτυρίαν ψευδῆ*, but the MT reads "You will not answer as a lying witness against your neighbour." The LXX here is redundant: the Hebrew *ʿānāh* (עָנָה) "answer" or "reply" is translated with Greek verb *ψευδομαρτυρήσεις* "falsely testify," which is followed by *μαρτυρίαν ψευδῆ* "false testimony." Hence, the LXX reads, "You will not falsely testify a false testimony against your neighbour." Furthermore, for *ʿēḏ šāqer* (עֵד שָׁקֶר) "false witness" the LXX has *μαρτυρίαν ψευδῆ*, which refers to the content of witness that is, "false testimony." If the Hebrew followed the LXX it would read *ʿēḏûṯ šāqer* (שָׁקֶר עֵדוּת), "false testimony", rather than *ʿēḏ šāqer* (עֵד שָׁקֶר), "false witness."[4]

In Exodus 22:12 (LXX v. 13)[5] the LXX reads *yᵉbiʾēhû ʿēḏ* (יְבִאֵהוּ עֵד) as "he shall bring it as evidence" as "he shall take him to the prey." The LXX reads the noun *ʿēḏ* (עֵד) as *ʿad* "to," that is, as *ἐπί*. The support for this is that the "it" in "he shall bring it" *yᵉbiʾēhû* (יְבִאֵהוּ) is a masculine suffix, but the antecedent[6] of *hû* (הוּא) "it" is the feminine noun *haṭṭᵉrēpāh* (הַטְּרֵפָה) "what was torn."[7]

In Exodus 23:1–2[8] the verb in the MT is *nāśāʾ* (נָשָׂא) "lift up, raise," which the LXX reads as *παραδέχομαι* "to receive." Apparently, this shifts the emphasis from those who bring charges to those who are responsible for accepting

3. In the LXX Swete's edition, Βουνὸς *τῆς μαρτυρίας* is translated as Βουνὸς *μάρτυς* and Βουνὸς *μάρτυς* as Βουνὸς *μαρτυρεῖ*. (Krašovec, *Transformation of Biblical Proper Names*, 23)

4. Hamilton, *Exodus: Exegetical Commentary*, 326.

5. *ἐὰν δὲ θηριάλωτον γένηται, ἄξει αὐτὸν ἐπὶ τὴν θήραν, καὶ οὐκ ἀποτίσει*. "But if it was mauled by wild beasts, he will bring him to the prey, and the other will not make payment."

6. An antecedent is the word (or words) that a pronoun refers to. The word antecedent means "to go before" in Latin. It gets its name from the idea that a pronoun refers to something previously mentioned in the sentence.

7. Hamilton, *Exodus: Exegetical Commentary*, 400.

8. *Οὐ παραδέξῃ ἀκοὴν ματαίαν· οὐ συνκαταθήσῃ μετὰ τοῦ ἀδίκου γενέσθαι μάρτυς ἄδικος*. "You will not receive a groundless report; you will not agree with the person in the wrong *so that* you become an unjust witness."

and initiating proceedings since they receive false report. What is in the MT *ʿēḏ šāqer* (עֵד שָׁקֶר), in the LXX is *μάρτυς ἄδικος* "unrighteous witness."

Just like in the MT, in Leviticus 5:1[9] the LXX translates "seeing" and "knowing" as verbs, and *μάρτυς* "witness" is not accompanied by any verb.

In Numbers 5:13 the MT and LXX are parallel. In Numbers 35:30 the MT contains the Hebrew verb *ʿānāh* (עָנָה) "to reply, answer," but the LXX uses Greek verb *μαρτυρέω* "testify, bear witness."

While in Deuteronomy 5:20 the MT reads "You shall not 'answer' as laying witness against your neighbour," the LXX translates the Hebrew verb *ʿānāh* (עָנָה) "to answer" with *ψευδομαρτυρέω* "give false witness." The MT's *ʿēḏ šāwʾ* (עֵד שָׁוְא) is translated as *μαρτυρίαν ψευδῆ* "false testimony" – *ψευδής* an adjective meaning "false, lying." Hence, the LXX says *Οὐ ψευδομαρτυρήσεις κατὰ τοῦ πλησίον σου μαρτυρίαν ψευδῆ* "You will not falsely witness against your neighbour with a false testimony." This is like the redundancy we saw in Exodus 20:16.

In Deuteronomy 17:6–7 the LXX translates *ʿēḏ* (עֵד) and *ʿēḏîm* (עֵדִים) with *μάρτυς*. While the MT in Deuteronomy 17:6 uses a noun *peh* (פֶּה) "mouth" for the activity of witnessing, the LXX does not translate the word, nor does it have any verb to describe the activity. The LXX simply says: *ἐπὶ δυσὶν μάρτυσιν ἢ ἐπὶ τρισὶν μάρτυσιν ἀποθανεῖται ὁ ἀποθνήσκων, οὐκ ἀποθανεῖται ἐφ' ἑνὶ μάρτυρι* "On two witnesses or on three witnesses one who is to die shall die; he shall not die on one witness."

In Deuteronomy 19:15[10] the LXX translates *ʿēḏ* (עֵד) and *ʿēḏîm* (עֵדִים) with the noun *μάρτυς*. In the first part of Deuteronomy 19:15 the LXX supplies the verb *μαρτυρέω*, while in the second part it literally translates the MT's *peh* (פֶּה) "mouth," with *στόμα* "mouth." In Deuteronomy 19:16[11]

9. *Ἐὰν δὲ ψυχὴ ἁμάρτῃ καὶ ἀκούσῃ φωνὴν ὁρκισμοῦ, καὶ οὗτος μάρτυς ἢ ἑώρακεν ἢ σύνοιδεν, ἐὰν μὴ ἀπαγγείλῃ, λήμψεται τὴν ἁμαρτίαν* "And if someone sins and hears a swearing of an oath, and this witness either has seen or is aware of *it*, if he does not speak out, he will incur guilt."

10. *Οὐκ ἐμμενεῖ μάρτυς εἷς μαρτυρῆσαι κατὰ ἀνθρώπου κατὰ πᾶσαν ἀδικίαν καὶ κατὰ πᾶν ἁμάρτημα καὶ κατὰ πᾶσαν ἁμαρτίαν ἣν ἂν ἁμάρτῃ· ἐπὶ στόματος δύο μαρτύρων καὶ ἐπὶ στόματος τριῶν μαρτύρων στήσεται πᾶν ῥῆμα* "One witness shall not stand to be a witness against a man as regards any injustice and as regards any offence and according to any sin that he may have sinned; on the mouth of two witnesses and upon the mouth of three witnesses any word shall stand."

11. *ἐὰν δὲ καταστῇ μάρτυς ἄδικος κατὰ ἀνθρώπου καταλέγων αὐτοῦ ἀσέβειαν* "But if an unjust witness is set against a man, accusing him of impiety."

for *ʿēḏ ḥāmās* (עֵד־חָמָס) the LXX uses *μάρτυς ἄδικος* "unjust witness." For *ʿānāh* (עָנָה) "to answer," unlike in Deuteronomy 5:20, the LXX uses a verb *καταλέγω* "accuse of, tell, recount." For *qûm* (קום) "to rise" the LXX uses a verb *καθίστημι* "set down, appoint, establish." Furthermore, while the MT in Deuteronomy 19:18 twice uses the noun *ʿēḏ* (עֵד), the LXX translates a noun *ʿēḏ* (עֵד) with *μάρτυς* the first time and the second time with the verb *μαρτυρέω* "bear witness." For *šeqer* (שֶׁקֶר) "deception, lie, falsehood," the LXX uses an adjective *ἄδικος* "unjust," and for *ʿānāh* (עָנָה) "to answer" the verb *ἀνθίστημι* "set against, oppose, resist."

In Deuteronomy 31:19[12] for the imperfect form of *hāyāh* (הָיָה) "to be," the LXX (Rahlfs) uses aorist subjunctive verb *γίνομαι* "be, come to exist." Since the aorist subjunctive in Greek describes not the time of action but its aspect, in this case the LXX only shows finished action. The LXX translates *lᵊʿēḏ* (לְעֵד) "for witness" as *εἰς μαρτύριον* "for testimony."[13] Finally, "witness against" in the phrase *biḇnê yiśrāʾēl* (בִּבְנֵי יִשְׂרָאֵל) "against the sons of Israel," in the LXX is translated as *ἐν υἱοῖς Ισραηλ* lit. "in the sons of Israel."[14]

In Deuteronomy 31:21[15] the verb *ʿānāh* (עָנָה) "to answer" in the LXX is translated with the future form of a verb *ἀντικαθίστημι* "oppose, resist," and *lᵊpānâw* (לְפָנָיו) "against their faces" is translated with *κατὰ πρόσωπον* "toward/against face." Unlike in the MT of this text, where "faces" is in plural, the noun in the LXX is singular. *lᵊʿēḏ* (לְעֵד) "for witness," in the LXX is translated with the present active participle of the verb *μαρτυρέω*.

---

12. *καὶ γράψατε τὰ ῥήματα τῆς ᾠδῆς ταύτης, καὶ διδάξετε αὐτὴν τοὺς υἱοὺς Ἰσραήλ, καὶ ἐμβαλεῖτε αὐτὴν εἰς τὸ στόμα αὐτῶν, ἵνα μοι γένηται ἡ ᾠδὴ αὕτη κατὰ πρόσωπον, μαρτυροῦσα ἐν υἱοῖς Ἰσραήλ* "And write the words of this song and teach it to the children of Israel and put it in their mouth, in order that this song may be to me a witness among the children of Israel, toward *their* face."

13. In the LXX Swete's edition, *ləʿēḏ* (לְעֵד) "for witness" is translated with present active participle of the verb *μαρτυρέω* which probably resemble adverbial function for the main verb *γίνομαι*. However, literal translation is impossible, and the best way is to translate this participle with a noun "may be to me a witness."

14. However, in the LXX Swete's edition, *biḇnê* (בִּבְנֵי) "against the sons" is present in expression *κατὰ πρόσωπον . . . ἐν υἱοῖς Ἰσραήλ* "toward/against face [singular] among the children of Israel."

15. *καὶ ἀντικαταστήσεται ἡ ᾠδὴ αὕτη ⌜ κατὰ πρόσωπον ⌝ μαρτυροῦσα· οὐ γὰρ μὴ ἐπιλησθῇ ἀπὸ στόματος τοῦ σπέρματος αὐτῶν· ἐγὼ γὰρ οἶδα τὴν πονηρίαν αὐτῶν, ὅσα ποιοῦσιν ὧδε σήμερον πρὸ τοῦ εἰσαγαγεῖν με αὐτοὺς εἰς τὴν γῆν τὴν ἀγαθὴν ἣν ὤμοσα τοῖς πατράσιν αὐτῶν.* "And this song will confront ⸤them⸥ as a witness for it shall not be forgotten from the mouth of their descendants. For I know their evil, all that they are doing here today before my leading them into the good land that I swore to their fathers."

In Deuteronomy 31:26,[16] the LXX translates the verb *hāyāh* (הָיָה) "to be" with the future form of εἰμί "be." The LXX here translates *lᵊ ʿēḏ* (לְעֵד) with εἰς μαρτύριον "for a witness." However, the LXX is missing the expression *bᵊḵā* (בְךָ) "against you," and instead has ἐν σοὶ, which can be translated "among you," "to you" or "with you." Hence, while the MT presents the role of the book of the Law as a *witness against*, in the LXX its role is presented in a neutral or positive light.

1.2 ʿēḏûṯ (עֵדוּת) in the Pentateuch

In verses that use *ʿēḏûṯ* (עֵדוּת) in connection with Decalogue, ark of the covenant or tabernacle, the LXX uses the noun μαρτύριον. However, in the expression *ûšnê luḥōṯ hā ʿēḏuṯ* (וּשְׁנֵי לֻחֹת הָעֵדֻת) "two tablets of the Testimony" in Exodus 34:29, the LXX lacks the word for "testimony," and only has δύο πλάκες "two tablets." In Exodus 39:35 (LXX 39:14)[17] the MT has the expression *ʾeṯ- ʾārōn hā ʿēḏuṯ* (אֶת־אֲרֹן הָעֵדֻת), while the LXX translates *ʿēḏûṯ* (עֵדוּת) with διαθήκης "covenant," creating the expression κιβωτὸν τῆς διαθήκης "the ark of the covenant." Thus, while "covenant" is one semantic possibility for *ʿēḏûṯ* (עֵדוּת), the LXX uses διαθήκης to stress the idea of covenant and not testimony.

For the singular noun *ʿēḏûṯ* (עֵדוּת) in Leviticus 16:13, the LXX uses the plural noun μαρτυρίων "testimonies." While in the MT "veil" in Leviticus 24:3 receives the attribute of testimony, in the LXX that attribute is attached to the noun τῇ σκηνῇ "tabernacle": τοῦ καταπετάσματος ἐν τῇ σκηνῇ τοῦ μαρτυρίου "the veil in the tabernacle of witness."

For the Hebrew word *miškān* (מִשְׁכָּן) "tabernacle" in Numbers 1:50, 53 and 10:11, the LXX uses σκηνή "tent, tabernacle," and for *hā ʿēḏuṯ* (הָעֵדֻת) μαρτύριον "testimony, witness." In Numbers 9:15, for the Hebrew word *miškān* (מִשְׁכָּן) "tabernacle" the LXX uses σκηνή, and for *ʾōhel* (אֹהֶל) "tent" uses οἶκος "house, temple." While Numbers 17:19 (LXX Num 17:4) in the MT has only *hā ʿēḏuṯ* (הָעֵדֻת), the LXX has ἐν τῇ σκηνῇ τοῦ μαρτυρίου κατέναντι τοῦ μαρτυρίου "in the tent of witness opposite/before the testimony."

16. Λαβόντες τὸ βιβλίον τοῦ νόμου τούτου θήσετε αὐτὸ ἐκ πλαγίων τῆς κιβωτοῦ τῆς διαθήκης Κυρίου τοῦ θεοῦ ὑμῶν, καὶ ἔσται ἐκεῖ ἐν σοὶ εἰς μαρτύριον. "Having taken the book of this law, put it beside the ark of the covenant of the Lord your God, and it shall be there with you *as* a testimony."

17. In the LXX Swete's edition, Numbers 39:14 is designated as Numbers 39:15.

hāʿēḏuṯ (הָעֵדֻת) is translated as μαρτύριον but the expression "the tent of meeting" *bᵊʾōhel môʿēḏ* (בְּאֹהֶל מוֹעֵד) in the LXX is qualified as τῇ σκηνῇ τοῦ μαρτυρίου "tent of witness." Thus, the LXX substitutes "tent of testimony" for "tent of meeting." In Numbers 17:7–8 (Matt 17:22–23) and 18:2 the same Greek word σκηνή is used for the Hebrew word *ʾōhel* (אֹהֶל) "tent."

1.3 ʿēḏāh (עֵדָה) and ʿēḏōṯ (עֵדֹת) in the Pentateuch

In Genesis 21:30 the LXX uses the noun μαρτύριον for *ʿēḏāh* (עֵדָה). In Deuteronomy 4:45; 6:17, 20, the LXX translates the plural noun *ʿēḏōṯ* (עֵדֹת) with the plural noun μαρτύριον.

1.4 ʿûḏ (עוּד) in the Pentateuch

In Genesis 43:3 the LXX uses the noun διαμαρτυρίᾳ for the Hiphil infinitive absolute *hāʿēḏ* (הָעֵד). For the Hiphil perfect (qātal) verb *hēʿiḏ* (הֵעִד) the LXX uses the perfect verb διαμεμαρτύρηται, with the same meaning. Instead of the imperfect of *ʾāmar* (אָמַר) "to say," the LXX uses the aorist of λέγω "say, speak," and instead of the infinitive of *ʾāmar* (אָמַר) the present participle of λέγω.

In Exodus 19:21, 23 and 21:29 the LXX translates *ʿûḏ* (עוּד) with διαμαρτύρομαι. In all three examples of objects of warning, the Hebrew uses the preposition *bᵊ* (בְּ): in Exodus 19:21 *bāʿām* (בָּעָם) "the people" (LXX τῷ λαῷ), in Exodus 19:23 *bānû* (בָּנוּ) "us" (LXX ἡμῖν "us"), and in Exodus 21:29 *biḇʿālâw* (בִּבְעָלָיו) "to his owner" (LXX τῷ κυρίῳ αὐτοῦ "to his owner").

In Deuteronomy 4:26; 8:19; 30:19; 31:28 and 32:46, the LXX translates *ʿûḏ* (עוּד) with the verb διαμαρτύρομαι "testify, warn." The LXX translates the expression *ḇāḵem* (בָכֶם) / *bām* (בָּם) with the second person plural personal pronoun ὑμῖν "you."[18] The pronoun ὑμῖν "you," unlike *ḇāḵem* (בָכֶם) / *bām* (בָּם), does not carry the more precise idea of speaking or witnessing *against*. Where in the MT in Deuteronomy 4:26; 8:19; 30:19 and 31:28, *ʿûḏ* (עוּד) is in perfect form, and in Deuteronomy 32:46 it is a participle, the LXX translates all these occurrences with διαμαρτύρομαι (present indicative[19] first person singular).

18. In Deuteronomy 31:28 personal pronoun is not ὑμῖν but αὐτοῖς (3rd m.pl.).

19. In Deuteronomy 31:28 the LXX Rahlfs' edition, the verb is in subjunctive form διαμαρτύρωμαι. Swete's edition has all in present indicative form.

2. Writings – passage analysis of the LXX

2.1 ʿēḏ (עֵד) and ʿēḏîm (עֵדִים), ʿēḏệḵā (עֵדֶיךָ) and ʿēḏêy (עֵדֵי) in the Writings

2.1.1 ʿēḏ (עֵד) and ʿēḏîm (עֵדִים), ʿēḏệḵā (עֵדֶיךָ) and ʿēḏêy (עֵדֵי) in the Historical Books

In Joshua 22:27 and Joshua 22:28 the LXX uses the noun *μαρτύριον* "testimony" to translate *ʿēḏ* (עֵד). A missing verb from the MT in Joshua 22:27[20] is supplied by the LXX with *εἰμί* "be" in its present subjunctive mode *ᾖ*, and in Joshua 22:28[21] with the same verb in its present indicative form *ἐστιν*. Also, the expression *bênênû ûḇênêḵem* (בֵּינֵינוּ וּבֵינֵיכֶם) "between us and between you" in Joshua 22:28, the LXX translates *ἀνὰ μέσον ὑμῶν καὶ ἀνὰ μέσον ἡμῶν* "between you and between us," and also adds *καὶ ἀνὰ μέσον τῶν υἱῶν ἡμῶν* "and between our sons."

The LXX uses *μαρτύριον* for *ʿēḏ* (עֵד) in Joshua 22:34,[22] and again supplies a missing verb in the MT with *εἰμί*, this time in its present indicative form *ἐστιν*. While in the MT *ʿēḏ* (עֵד) probably refers to a part of the altar, the LXX treats *ēḏ* (עֵד) as a description of the altar's function. While the MT understands the function of the altar as witness *bênōṯênû* (בֵּינֹתֵינוּ) "between us," the LXX renders it as *ἀνὰ μέσον αὐτῶν* "among them" or "in the midst of them." While the pronoun "our" in the MT is inclusive, probably referring to all the tribes of Israel, the LXX usage of the personal pronoun *αὐτῶν* "them" (with possessive function) probably included only the tribes of Reuben, Gad and the half-tribe of Manasseh. This difference may be motivated by the fact that in the MT the tribes are the ones speaking – hence, their speech is inclusive. But in the LXX it is Joshua who speaks on the tribes' behalf. Also, while in the MT their statement is "YHWH is God" (direct), in the LXX this statement reads as *ὅτι κύριος ὁ θεὸς αὐτῶν ἐστιν* "that the Lord is their God" (indirect). So, the LXX adds the pronoun *αὐτῶν*, and uses *κύριος* "Lord" for the name YHWH.

---

20. *ἀλλ' ἵνα ᾖ τοῦτο μαρτύριον ἀνὰ μέσον ἡμῶν καὶ ὑμῶν* "but that this would be a testimony between us and you."

21. *ἀλλὰ μαρτύριόν ἐστιν* "but it is a testimony."

22. *καὶ ἐπωνόμασεν Ἰησοῦς τὸν βωμὸν τῶν Ρουβην καὶ τῶν Γαδ καὶ τοῦ ἡμίσους φυλῆς Μανασση καὶ εἶπεν ὅτι Μαρτύριόν ἐστιν ἀνὰ μέσον αὐτῶν ὅτι κύριος ὁ θεὸς αὐτῶν ἐστιν* "And Joshua named the altar of the Reubenites and the Gadites and the half tribe of Manasseh and said, 'It is a witness [among them] that the Lord is their God.'"

In 1 Samuel 12:5 the LXX uses the word *μάρτυς* for *ʿēḏ* (עֵד) three times. Here the MT and LXX differ at the end of verse 5, where the MT reads *wayyōʾmer ʿēḏ* (וַיֹּאמֶר עֵד) "and *he* said, 'witness,'" while the LXX reads καὶ εἶπαν Μάρτυς "And *they* said, 'witness.'" Εἶπαν is a third person plural verb, and thus refers to the gathered people as a collective. But that fact still does not clarify the reason for the singular *ʿēḏ* (עֵד) "witness." Finally, in 1 Samuel 12:6 the MT and LXX differ in their descriptions of "the Lord." The MT says: "The Lord who appointed Moses and Aaron. . . ," while the LXX defines the Lord as witness: Μάρτυς κύριος ὁ ποιήσας τὸν Μωυσῆν καὶ τὸν Ααρων "The Lord *is* witness, who appointed Moses and Aaron."

Joshua 24:22 also uses plural forms of *ʿēḏ* (עֵד), *ʿēḏîm ʾattem bāḵem* (עֵדִים אַתֶּם בָּכֶם) "witnesses you [are] against yourselves." The LXX faithfully follows the MT with Μάρτυρες ὑμεῖς καθ' ὑμῶν "You *are* witnesses against yourselves." As in the MT, the LXX has no verb to support the activity of witnesses. However, while in the MT the people confirm Joshua's claim that they are witnesses by repeating *ʿēḏîm* (עֵדִים), the LXX lacks any such repetition.

In Ruth 4:9, 10 and 11, the LXX uses *μάρτυρες* for *ʿēḏîm* (עֵדִים). In Ruth 4:9 and 10 the LXX translates the expression *ʿēḏîm ʾattem hayyôm* (עֵדִים אַתֶּם הַיּוֹם) "witnesses you [are] today" as Μάρτυρες ὑμεῖς σήμερον "Witnesses you [are] today."

2.1.2 ʿēḏ (עֵד), and ʿēḏîm (עֵדִים), ʿēḏêḵā (עֵדֶיךָ) and ʿēḏêy (עֵדַי) in the Wisdom and Poetic Books

In Job 16:8 (LXX Job 16:8–9)[23] the LXX closely resembles the MT, translating *wattiqmᵊṭēnî lᵊʿēḏ hāyāh* (וַתִּקְמְטֵנִי לְעֵד הָיָה) "You have shrivelled me up and it became for a witness" as καὶ ἐπελάβου μου, εἰς μαρτύριον ἐγενήθη "And you seized me, it became for a testimony." The LXX uses εἰς μαρτύριον for *lᵊʿēḏ* (לְעֵד) and translates the verb *hāyāh* (הָיָה) "to be" with γίνομαι. In the continuation of the verse, the LXX translates *wayyāqom bî ḵaḥăšî bᵊpānay yaʿăneh* (וַיָּקָם בִּי כַחֲשִׁי בְּפָנַי יַעֲנֶה) "my leanness has risen up against me and replies to me [against] my face," as καὶ ἀνέστη ἐν ἐμοὶ τὸ ψεῦδός μου, κατὰ

23. καὶ ἐπελάβου μου, εἰς μαρτύριον ἐγενήθη, καὶ ἀνέστη ἐν ἐμοὶ τὸ ψεῦδός μου, κατὰ πρόσωπόν μου ἀνταπεκρίθη "And you seized me, it became for a testimony, and it rose in me my falsehood, it answered back toward my face."

πρόσωπόν μου ἀνταπεκρίθη. This differs from the MT in that *kaḥaš* (כַּחַשׁ) "leanness, gauntness" becomes τὸ ψεῦδός μου "my lie" in the LXX. Likewise, *bî* (בִּי) "against me" is rendered as ἐν ἐμοὶ (literally "in me"), and the verb *ʿānāh* (עָנָה) "to answer, to reply" is translated with verb ἀνταποκρίνομαι "answer back, make a reply."

In 16:19 (LXX Job 16:20), the MT uses two words for witness: *ʿēḏî* (עֵדִי) "my witness," and *wᵊśāhădî* (וְשָׂהֲדִי) "my advocate/witness." For *ʿēḏî* (עֵדִי) the LXX uses ὁ μάρτυς μου "my witness," but for *wᵊśāhădî* (וְשָׂהֲדִי) "my advocate/witness," the LXX uses an adjective, συνίστωρ "one who knows." This choice is interesting because we saw in Leviticus 5:1 that one of the requirements for serving as a witness is knowledge.

For the expression *wᵊ ʿēḏ neʾĕmān* (וְעֵד נֶאֱמָן) "faithful" or "enduring witness" in Psalms 89:37 (LXX Ps 88:38), the LXX uses the equivalent ὁ μάρτυς . . . πιστός "faithful witness." In the MT this witness is located *baššaḥaq* (בַּשַּׁחַק) "in the cloud"; in the LXX, it is located ἐν οὐρανῷ "in heaven." Once again, we see the preposition *bᵊ* (בְּ) translated with the preposition ἐν, but here without its negative meaning "against."

The next few verses from Proverbs describe a person as *šeqer* (שֶׁקֶר). In Proverbs 6:19 the LXX translates *ʿēḏ šāqer* (עֵד שָׁקֶר) "false witness" as μάρτυς ἄδικος "unjust witness" and *yāpîaḥ kᵊzāḇîm* (יָפִיחַ כְּזָבִים) "pours out lies" (NIV) as ἐκκαίει ψεύδη "kindles lies." Here again the LXX translates the noun *šeqer* (שֶׁקֶר) with the adjective ἄδικος "unjust." The MT of Proverbs 12:17 has the phrase *yāpîaḥ ʾĕmûnāh yaggîḏ ṣeḏeq* (יָפִיחַ אֱמוּנָה יַגִּיד צֶדֶק) "[Whoever] breathes out faithfulness, reports righteousness." The LXX translates this as ἐπιδεικνυμένην πίστιν ἀπαγγέλλει δίκαιος. [24] The participle ἐπιδεικνυμένην is without definite article, and hence is adverbial (modifying the main verb). But the adjective δίκαιος without definite article should be predicative ("is just"), not adjectival ("just"). The second part of the same verse in Hebrew *wᵊ ʿēḏ šᵊqārîm mirmāh* (וְעֵד שְׁקָרִים מִרְמָה) "but a false witness deceit," the LXX translates as ὁ δὲ μάρτυς τῶν ἀδίκων δόλιος "but the unjust witness deceit."[25] The LXX literally translates the MT text in Proverbs 19:5

24. "A righteous man declares the open truth . . ." (Brenton, *Septuagint Version of OT*) or "A righteous person reports with demonstrable faithfulness."

25. This part of the verse Brannan (*LES*) translates as "but the witness of the unjust is deceitful," and Brenton's LXX English translation as "but an unjust witness is deceitful" (*LES*).

(LXX Prov 19:2); hence, *ʿēḏ šᵉqārîm lōʾ yinnāqeh* (עֵד שְׁקָרִים לֹא יִנָּקֶה) "witness of lies will not go unpunished" is μάρτυς ψευδὴς οὐκ ἀτιμώρητος ἔσται "False witness will not go unpunished." In the LXX *wᵊyāpîaḥ kᵊzāḇîm lōʾ yimmālēṭ* (וְיָפִיחַ כְּזָבִים לֹא יִמָּלֵט) "and who breathes out lies will not escape" is translated ὁ δὲ ἐγκαλῶν ἀδίκως οὐ διαφεύξεται "and the one who accuses unjustly will not escape." The only semantic difference is in the second part of the verse where Hebrew *wᵊyāpîaḥ* (וְיָפִיחַ) "the one who breathes" in Greek is ἐγκαλῶν "the one who accuses." So, we have an overlap between "breathing" and "accusing" as though one is using his/her own breath for accusation. Furthermore, the LXX considers *kᵊzāḇîm* (כְּזָבִים) "lies" as ἀδίκως "unjust," and hence, classifies "lies" as "injustice." Similarly, in Proverbs 19:9 (LXX Prov 19:6) the LXX translates *ʿēḏ šᵉqārîm lōʾ yinnāqeh* (עֵד שְׁקָרִים לֹא יִנָּקֶה) "witness of lies will not go unpunished" as μάρτυς ψευδὴς οὐκ ἀτιμώρητος ἔσται "A false witness will not go unpunished." But for *wᵊyāpîaḥ kᵊzāḇîm yōʾḇēḏ* (וְיָפִיחַ כְּזָבִים יֹאבֵד) "person who breathes out lies will perish" the LXX reads as ὃς δ' ἂν ἐκκαύσῃ κακίαν, ἀπολεῖται ὑπ' αὐτῆς "and whoever kindles wickedness will be destroyed by it." The LXX paraphrases the MT by translating "breathes out lies" as "whoever kindles wickedness" (another overlap is between *kᵊzāḇîm* (כְּזָבִים) which is understood this time as κακίαν "evil") and adding the idea that one will be destroyed ὑπ' αὐτῆς "by it" – meaning that false witness will be destroyed "by this wickedness." In the first part of Proverbs 25:18 both the MT and LXX use the words "club," "sword" and "sharp arrow" to describe false witness. In the second part of the verse the MT reads *ʾîš ʿōneh ḇᵊrēʿēhû ʿēḏ šāqer* (אִישׁ עֹנֶה בְרֵעֵהוּ עֵד שָׁקֶר) "is the man who responds against his neighbour as false witness"; the LXX reads as οὕτως καὶ ἀνὴρ ὁ καταμαρτυρῶν τοῦ φίλου αὐτοῦ μαρτυρίαν ψευδῆ "so is a man who bears witness against his friend with false testimony." So here the LXX translates the generic *ʿānāh* (עָנָה) "to reply, to answer" more specifically as καταμαρτυρέω "testify against." Further, the idea of "witnessing against" from *ḇᵊrēʿēhû* (בְרֵעֵהוּ) is not found in τοῦ φίλου αὐτοῦ "his friend" but in preposition κατά "against" in καταμαρτυρέω.

In the next three verses, false witnesses are described with different words. In Proverbs 19:28 (LXX Prov 19:25) the LXX significantly deviates from the MT. For *ʿēḏ bᵊliyyaʿal yālîṣ mišpāṭ* (עֵד בְּלִיַּעַל יָלִיץ מִשְׁפָּט) "A witness who is worthless and wicked mocks at justice," the LXX has ὁ ἐγγυώμενος παῖδα ἄφρονα καθυβρίζει δικαίωμα "The one who gives surety for a foolish child despises a commandment." Apparently, the idea of *ʿēḏ* (עֵד) in the LXX is missing, and as an equivalent for *bᵊliyyaʿal* (בְּלִיַּעַל) the LXX uses the adjective ἄφρων[26] "foolish" or "ignorant." Furthermore, *ûpî rᵊšāʿîm yᵊḇallaʿ-ʾāwen* (וּפִי רְשָׁעִים יְבַלַּע־אָוֶן) "the mouth of the wicked swallows evil," the LXX renders as *στόμα δὲ ἀσεβῶν καταπίεται κρίσεις* "the mouth of the ungodly will devour [swallow up] judgments." While in the MT the connection between "swallowing evil" and "mocking" is obvious and meaningful, the LXX obscures the point. Where the MT connects cause (swallowing) and effect (mocking), the LXX appears to use synonymous/synthetic parallelism, connecting "despising the commandment" and "devouring judgments."

The LXX translates the first half of Proverbs 21:28 *ʿēḏ-kᵊzāḇîm yōʾḇēḏ* (עֵד־כְּזָבִים יֹאבֵד) "A witness of lies will perish" literally: *μάρτυς ψευδὴς ἀπολεῖται*. But the second part of the verse is different: *wᵊʾîš šômēaʿ lāneṣaḥ yᵊḏabbēr* (וְאִישׁ שׁוֹמֵעַ לָנֶצַח יְדַבֵּר) "a man who hears will testify successfully [forever]" in the LXX becomes *ἀνὴρ δὲ ὑπήκοος φυλασσόμενος λαλήσει* ". . . but an obedient man will speak cautiously." So, the MT in the second part of the verse focuses on the result of hearing: "a man who hears" (hearing in order to discern what is true) speaks "victoriously" (result is in the focus). But the LXX's focuses on how a person should speak (process): the "obedient man" (obedient to what or whom? It is not specified) will "[speak] cautiously." In Proverbs 24:28 (LXX Prov 24:43) the MT has *ʾăl-tᵊhî ʿēḏ-ḥinnām bᵊrēʿeḵā* (אַל־תְּהִי עֵד־חִנָּם בְּרֵעֶךָ) "you will not be groundless witness against your neighbour." The LXX translates this as *μὴ ἴσθι ψευδὴς μάρτυς ἐπὶ σὸν πολίτην* "Do not be a false witness against your countryman [citizen]." Everything is the same except that the Greek word *πολίτην* probably implies the context of the Greek city states: your neighbour is a person from the same city. In the second part of the verse the MT has *wahăpittîṯā biśpāṯêḵā* (וַהֲפִתִּיתָ בִּשְׂפָתֶיךָ) "and use your lips to deceive." The LXX reads this as *μηδὲ πλατύνου σοῖς χείλεσιν* "or enlarge [exaggerate] with your lips." When we combine the MT and LXX, it is obvious that "deception" in the LXX consists of "exaggeration" or adding to something. Interestingly, Hebrew expression

---

26. According to Johann Cook (*Septuagint of Proverbs*, 173) "The Hebrew noun בְּלִיַּעַל occurs three times in the book of Proverbs: Chapters 6:12; 16:27 and 19:28. In all three cases the lexeme ἄφρων is used as equivalent in the LXX. This does imply a certain interpretation, for it acts as equivalent for nuances of 'foolishness' in many contexts."

wahăpittîṯā (וְהֲפִתִּיתָ) can have the meaning "to be open" in the sense of "opening wide," which corresponds to the LXX translation.

The next two examples describe an honest witness. In Proverbs 14:5 the LXX very closely follows the MT. The first part of the verse *ʿēḏ ʾĕmûnîm lōʾ yeḵazzēḇ* (עֵד אֱמוּנִים לֹא יְכַזֵּב) "faithful witness will not lie," the LXX translates as *μάρτυς πιστὸς οὐ ψεύδεται* "faithful witness will not lie." In the second part of the verse *ʿēḏ šāqer* (עֵד שָׁקֶר) "a witness of falsehood" is understood as *μάρτυς ἄδικος* and once more we have a situation where "falsehood" in LXX is understood as "injustice." The MT describes the result of such false witness as *wᵉyāpîaḥ kᵉzāḇîm* (וְיָפִיחַ כְּזָבִים) "breathes out lies," while the LXX reads *ἐκκαίει δὲ ψεύδη* "kindles lies." An interesting overlap occurs between *pûaḥ* (פּוּחַ) "breathing" and *ἐκκαίω* "kindling," because breathing can also be used to kindle the fire. The MT focuses more on the action (breathing), where the LXX focuses more on the result of the action. In Proverbs 14:25 the MT has *maṣṣîl nᵉpāšôṯ ʿēḏ ʾĕmeṯ* (מַצִּיל נְפָשׁוֹת עֵד אֱמֶת) "a witness of truth saves souls," which the LXX modifies to read *ῥύσεται ἐκ κακῶν ψυχὴν μάρτυς πιστός* "faithful witness will save soul from evil." In the second part of the verse, the MT describes the false witness as *wᵉyāpîaḥ kᵉzāḇîm mirmāh* (וְיָפִחַ כְּזָבִים מִרְמָה) "who breathes out lies is deceitful." The LXX describes this witness as *ἐκκαίει δὲ ψεύδη δόλιος* "but deceitful kindles lies." Once again, we see the interplay between "breathing" and "kindling."

Continuing with plural forms of *ʿēḏ* (עֵד), the MT of Job 10:17[27] reads *tᵉḥaddēš ʿēḏêḵā neḡdî* (תְּחַדֵּשׁ עֵדֶיךָ נֶגְדִּי) "bring new witnesses against me." The LXX reads this as *ἐπανακαινίζων ἐπ' ἐμὲ* "renewing upon me." However, what is been renewed is not *ʿēḏêḵā* (עֵדֶיךָ) "your witnesses" as in the MT, but *ἔτασίν μου* "my affliction." Hence, the LXX equates Job's affliction (sg.) with YHWH's witnesses (pl.).

The LXX reads the expression *ʿēḏê-šeqer* (עֵדֵי־שֶׁקֶר) "laying" or "false witnesses" in the MT of Psalms 27:12 (LXX Ps 26:12) as *μάρτυρες ἄδικοι* "unjust witnesses," where *šeqer* (שֶׁקֶר) is translated as *ἄδικος* "unjust." Similarly, in Psalms 35:11 (LXX Ps 34:11), the MT's *ʿēḏê ḥāmās* (עֵדֵי חָמָס) "malicious witnesses" are rendered in the LXX as *μάρτυρες ἄδικοι*. Hence, the term *ἄδικος* "unjust" combines the meanings of "falsehood or lie" and

27. ἐπανακαινίζων ἐπ' ἐμὲ τὴν ἔτασίν μου "Renewing upon me my affliction."

"malice." Although the MT focuses more on individual activity, the LXX is more concerned with the results of such activities.

2.2 ʿēḏûṯ (עֵדוּת) and ʿēḏôṯ (עֵדְוֹת) in the Writings

2.2.1 ʿēḏûṯ (עֵדוּת) and ʿēḏôṯ (עֵדְוֹת) in the Historical Books

In Joshua 4:16, the LXX renders the "ark of the Testimony" as τὴν κιβωτὸν τῆς διαθήκης "the ark of the covenant." Further, the LXX adds a descriptive phrase to "the ark of the covenant" with τοῦ μαρτυρίου κυρίου "of the testimony of the Lord." So, the full expression is "the ark of the covenant of the testimony of the Lord," with the LXX additions of τῆς διαθήκης "the covenant," and κυρίου "Lord." In 2 Kings 11:12 the LXX renders *ʿēḏûṯ* (עֵדוּת) with the noun μαρτύριον "testimony." In 2 Chronicles 23:11 the LXX uses μαρτύρια, a plural form of μαρτύριον, for the singular noun *ʿēḏûṯ* (עֵדוּת). Hence, the MT here can be read as "testimony" and the LXX as "testimonies." Finally, the expression *lᵊʾōhel hāʿēḏûṯ* (לְאֹהֶל הָעֵדוּת) "for tent of the Testimony" in 2 Chronicles 24:6 is translated literally in the LXX, εἰς τὴν σκηνὴν τοῦ μαρτυρίου.

In 1 Kings 2:3 the LXX leaves the plural *ʿēḏôṯ* (עֵדְוֹת) untranslated. But in 2 Kings 17:15[28] the LXX does translate the MT's plural noun *ʿēḏôṯâw* (עֵדְוֹתָיו) with the corresponding expression μαρτύρια αὐτοῦ "his testimonies." Likewise, 2 Kings 23:3, where the MT's *ʿēḏôṯ* (עֵדְוֹת) is translated in the LXX with the plural μαρτύρια. Μαρτύρια is also used to translate *ʿēḏôṯ* (עֵדְוֹת) in 1 Chronicles 29:19, and in 2 Chronicles 34:31. In Nehemiah 9:34[29] (Esdras B 19:34) the LXX again uses μαρτύρια (plural) for *ʿēḏôṯ* (עֵדְוֹת) (plural) and translates the verb *ʿûḏ* (עוּד) with διεμαρτύρω (plural of διαμαρτύρομαι). Here again, the LXX does not have an exact equivalent for *bāhem* (בָּהֶם) "against them," rather simply using the plural pronoun αὐτοῖς "them." Finally, for the word *ʿēḏôṯ* (עֵדְוֹת) in Psalms,[30] the LXX always uses different plural forms of the noun μαρτύριον.

---

28. καὶ τὰ μαρτύρια αὐτοῦ, ὅσα διεμαρτύρατο αὐτοῖς lit. "and his testimonies which he witnesses them."

29. καὶ τὰ μαρτύριά σου, ἃ διεμαρτύρω αὐτοῖς "and your testimonies which you testified to them."

30. Psalms 119:14 (LXX 118:14), 31, 36, 99, 111, 129, 144, 157.

2.2.2 ʿēḏûṯ (עֵדוּת) and ʿēḏôṯ (עֵדְוֹת) in the Wisdom and Poetic Books

For the word *ʿēḏûṯ* (עֵדוּת) in Psalms, the LXX uses word μαρτύριον for every occurrence except one: Psalms 78:5 (LXX 77:5); 81:5 (LXX 80:6); 119:88 (LXX 118:88);[31] 122:4 (LXX 121:4). The exception is in Psalms 19:7 (LXX 18:8), where the LXX uses the feminine μαρτυρία for *ʿēḏûṯ* (עֵדוּת).

2.3 ʿēḏāh (עֵדָה) and ʿēḏōṯ (עֵדֹת) in the Writings

2.3.1 ʿēḏāh (עֵדָה) and ʿēḏōṯ (עֵדֹת) in the Historical Books

In Joshua 24:27, the LXX translates *tihyeh-bānû lᵊ ʿēḏāh* (תִּהְיֶה־בָּנוּ לְעֵדָה) "will be for a witness against us," as ἔσται ἐν ὑμῖν εἰς μαρτύριον "will be among you [lit. "in you"] for a witness." The MT has Joshua including himself by saying that witness is "against us" (first person plural), but the LXX changes this, asserting that the witness is against the people (second person plural). In the continuation of the verse, where the LXX translates the MT's *wᵊhāyṯāh bāḵem lᵊ ʿēḏāh* (וְהָיְתָה בָכֶם לְעֵדָה) "will be for a witness against you" as ἔσται ἐν ὑμῖν εἰς μαρτύριον "will be among you for a witness."

2.3.2 ʿēḏāh (עֵדָה) and ʿēḏōṯ (עֵדֹת) in the Wisdom and Poetic Books

For *ʿēḏōṯ* (עֵדֹת) in the Psalms,[32] the LXX uses differing plural forms of noun μαρτύριον.

2.4 tᵊʿûḏāh (תְּעוּדָה) in the Writings

In Ruth 4:7, the LXX uses μαρτύριον "testimony, witness" for *tᵊʿûḏāh* (תְּעוּדָה). Where the MT has no verb, the LXX supplies εἰμί "be" in the imperfect tense ἦν. Thus, the giving of one's shoe was formerly understood as τοῦτο ἦν μαρτύριον ἐν Ισραηλ "this was a testimony in Israel."

2.5 ʿûḏ (עוּד) in the Writings

2.5.1 ʿûḏ (עוּד) in the Historical Books

The LXX uses the verb διαμαρτύρομαι once as participle and once as finite verb to translate the verb *ʿûḏ* (עוּד) in 1 Samuel 8:9. The LXX reads

31. *ʿēḏûṯ pîḵā* (עֵדוּת פִּיךָ) "testimony of your mouth," the LXX faithfully translates as τὰ μαρτύρια τοῦ στόματός σου.

32. Psalms 25:10 (LXX 24:10); 78:56 (LXX 77:56); 93:5 (LXX 92:5); 99:7 (LXX 98:7); 119:2 (LXX 118:2), 22, 24, 46, 59, 79, 95, 119, 125, 138, 146, 152, 167, 168; 132:12 (LXX 131:12).

διαμαρτυρόμενος διαμαρτύρῃ αὐτοῖς "by warning you might warn them" or "solemnly testify to them."

In 1 Kings 2:42, the LXX translates *wāʾāʿiḏ bᵊḵā lēʾmōr* (וָאָעִד בְּךָ לֵאמֹר) "and I warn you saying" as *ἐπεμαρτυράμην σοι λέγων* "gave witness to you saying." The LXX translates the expression *bᵊḵā* (בְּךָ), which clearly has a negative connotation "against you," with the more neutral *σοι* "you."

1 Kings 21:10 in the LXX has a complicated series of textual variants. In Brenton's and Rahlfs's editions, 1 Kings 21:10 is placed as 3 Kingdoms 20:10. Swete also has LXX 21:10 at 3 Kingdoms 20:10 and is abbreviated, containing only "And seat two men, sons of lawlessness," omitting the rest of the verse. For the MT's *wîʿiḏuhû lēʾmōr* (וִיעִדֻהוּ לֵאמֹר) "and have them testify against him saying" Rahlfs's LXX has *καταμαρτυρησάτωσαν αὐτοῦ λέγοντες* "let them testify against him saying," which matches the MT.

In Rahlfs' and Swete's edition, 1 Kings 21:13 is found at 3 Kingdoms 20:13. The Greek text there follows the MT (1 Kgs 21:13) with *καὶ κατεμαρτύρησαν αὐτοῦ λέγοντες* "bore witness against him saying."

In 2 Kings 17:13, the LXX uses *διαμαρτύρομαι* "give solemn testimony, warn" for *ʿûḏ* (עוּד). The Hebrew preposition *bᵊ* (בְּ) is translated with the more neutral *ἐν* "in," which removes the negative implications of witnessing carried by *bᵊ* (בְּ): *καὶ διεμαρτύρατο κύριος ἐν τῷ* Ισραηλ *καὶ ἐν τῷ* Ιουδα *ἐν χειρὶ* "And the Lord testified in Israel and in Judah by the hand." However, the LXX closely follows the MT by translating *yāḏ* (יָד) "hand" with Greek equivalent *χείρ* "hand." In 2 Kings 17:15[33] the LXX translates the plural noun *ʿēḏôṯâw* (עֵדְוֹתָיו) with *μαρτύρια αὐτοῦ* "his testimonies." This corresponds to the MT. But the LXX rendering again does not clearly say that YHWH testifies "against": the LXX uses *αὐτοῖς* "them" to translate *bām* (בָּם) in *hēʿîḏ bām* (הֵעִיד בָּם) "he warned [against] them." The LXX translates *ʿûḏ* (עוּד) with *διαμαρτύρομαι*.

In 2 Chronicles 24:19 the LXX translates the verb *ʿûḏ* (עוּד) in the expression *wayyāʿîḏû ḇām* (וַיָּעִידוּ בָם) "they testified against them" as *καὶ διεμαρτύραντο αὐτοῖς*.

33. *καὶ τὰ μαρτύρια αὐτοῦ, ὅσα διεμαρτύρατο αὐτοῖς* lit. "and his testimonies which he witnesses them."

In Nehemiah 9:26[34] (Esdras B 19:26) the LXX translates *ʿûḏ* (עוּד) with διεμαρτύραντο, and the expression *ḇām* (בָם) "against them" with ἐν αὐτοῖς "in them." In Nehemiah 9:29[35] (Esdras B 19:29) the verb *ʿûḏ* (עוּד) is translated with ἐπεμαρτύρω, a plural form of ἐπιμαρτύρομαι, and expression *bāhem* (בָּהֶם) "against them" with αὐτοῖς "them." In Nehemiah 9:30[36] (Esdras B 19:30) the LXX translates *ʿûḏ* (עוּד) with ἐπεμαρτύρω, *bām* (בָּם) "against them" with αὐτοῖς "them," *bᵊrûḥăḵā* (בְּרוּחֲךָ) "by your Spirit" with ἐν πνεύματί σου "in your Spirit," and *bᵊyaḏ-nᵊḇîʾeḵā* (בְּיַד־נְבִיאֶיךָ) as ἐν χειρὶ προφητῶν σου "by the hand of your prophets." In Nehemiah 9:34[37] (Esdras B 19:34) the LXX uses διεμαρτύρω for the verb *ʿûḏ* (עוּד). Once again, the LXX does not use an equivalent for *bāhem* (בָּהֶם) "against them." It rather uses the plural pronoun αὐτοῖς "them."

In Nehemiah 13:15[38] (Esdras B 23:15) the verb *ʿûḏ* (עוּד) is translated with ἐπεμαρτυράμην "testify that, bear witness about." The expression *bᵊyôm* (בְּיוֹם) appears twice, once in connection with "Sabbath" and once in connection with "warning." The LXX translates this expression as ἐν ἡμέρᾳ "in/on the day." Hence, the first phrase has the meaning "on the Sabbath day" and second "I warned [them] on the day of their sale." In Nehemiah 13:21[39] (Esdras B 23:21) the LXX translates *wāʾāʿîḏāh bāhem* (וָאָעִידָה בָהֶם) "warned against them" as καὶ διεμαρτυράμην ἐν αὐτοῖς which corresponds to the MT, although again the translators of the LXX did not translate the Hebrew preposition *bᵊ* (בְּ), here in the expression *bāhem* (בָּהֶם). When the translators do translate *bᵊ* (בְּ), as here, they often do so with the preposition *en* (ἐν), which generally corresponds to *bᵊ* (בְּ), but without the explicit implication of "against."

34. καὶ τοὺς προφήτας σου ἀπέκτειναν, οἳ διεμαρτύραντο ἐν αὐτοῖς ἐπιστρέψαι αὐτοὺς πρὸς σέ. ". . . and they killed your prophets who warn them to turn to you."

35. καὶ ἐπεμαρτύρω αὐτοῖς ἐπιστρέψαι αὐτοὺς εἰς τὸν νόμον σου. "And you warned them to return them to your law."

36. καὶ ἐπεμαρτύρω αὐτοῖς ἐν πνεύματί σου ἐν χειρὶ προφητῶν σου. "And you warned them in your Spirit (by the Spirit), by the hand of your prophets."

37. καὶ τὰ μαρτύριά σου, ἃ διεμαρτύρω αὐτοῖς. ". . . and your testimonies which you testified to them."

38. ἐν ἡμέρᾳ τοῦ σαββάτου, καὶ ἐπεμαρτυράμην ἐν ἡμέρᾳ πράσεως αὐτῶν. ". . . on the Sabbath day, and I warned them on the day of their sale."

39. καὶ διεμαρτυράμην ἐν αὐτοῖς καὶ εἶπα πρὸς αὐτούς . . . "And I warned them and said to them. . . ."

2.5.2 ʿûḏ (עוּד) in the Wisdom and Poetic Books

In Job 29:11, the LXX translates *wăttᵉʿîḏēnî* (וַתְּעִידֵנִי) "he witnesses in support of me" with με ἐξέκλινεν "turn," "keep away from me." This is a significant difference. In context, the MT presumes a positive witness on Job's behalf, but the LXX rendering is puzzling. The first clause is positive ("For the ear heard and blessed me") but the second indicates that the witness is turning away ("and the eye, seeing me, [με ἐξέκλινεν] turned away").

For *ʿûḏ* (עוּד) in Psalms 20:9 (LXX 19:9), the LXX uses ἀνορθόω "build up again," "restore," "rebuild." In Psalms 50:7 (LXX 49:7), the LXX uses διαμαρτύρομαι, but the idea that this testimony is against someone, clear in the MT due to *bāḵ* (בָּךְ) "against you" (m.s.), is not adequately represented with σοι "you" (sg.) in the LXX. We have an identical pairing in Psalms 81:8 (v. 9) (LXX 80:9), where *ʿûḏ* (עוּד) is translated διαμαρτύρομαι, and *bāḵ* (בָּךְ) with σοι. The MT of Psalms 119:61 (LXX 118:61) uses *ʿûḏ* (עוּד) outside its *usual* semantic range; here it is best understood as "surrounding in attempt to confine." The LXX follows this understanding with περιπλέκω "bind up, embrace (metaph.)." In Psalms 146:9 (LXX Ps 145:9), the LXX uses verb ἀναλαμβάνω "lift up and carry, take/bring along" to translate *ʿûḏ* (עוּד) with the meaning of "sustaining." In Psalms 147:6 (LXX Ps 146:6) the LXX also uses ἀναλαμβάνω to translate *ʿûḏ* (עוּד) outside its usual semantic meaning.

3. Prophets – passage analysis of the LXX

3.1 ʿēḏ (עֵד) and ʿēḏîm (עֵדִים), ʿēḏay (עֵדַי) and ʿēḏêhem (עֵדֵיהֶם) in the Prophets

In Isaiah 19:20 the MT reads *wᵉhāyāh lᵉʾôṯ ûlᵉʿēḏ layhwāh* (וְהָיָה לְאוֹת וּלְעֵד לַיהוָה) "It will be a for a sign and for a witness to the Lord. . . ." The LXX translates this as καὶ ἔσται εἰς σημεῖον εἰς τὸν αἰῶνα κυρίῳ "And it will be a sign for eternity to the Lord." The LXX reads *ûlᵉʿēḏ* (וּלְעֵד) "for testimony" as εἰς τὸν αἰῶνα "for eternity"; there may be confusion here with the consonants לעד read not as *lᵉʿēḏ* (לְעֵד) "for a witness" but as *lāʿaḏ* (לָעַד) "forever." We find a similar phenomenon in Isaiah 30:8 where the LXX chooses *lāʿaḏ* (לָעַד) "forever" over *lᵉʿēḏ* (לְעֵד) "for a witness," and translates the phrase καὶ ἕως εἰς τὸν αἰῶνα "and as long as for eternity" or "and even forever." As Ronald L.

Troxel[40] notes that the pleonasm ἕως εἰς might be due to the repetition of עד לעד in the MT. Hence, with preposition ἕως "until, as long as," the LXX follows the meaning of adverb *ʿaḏ* (עַד) "forever, continual." In Isaiah 55:4 the LXX translates the expression *hēn ʿēḏ lᵊʾûmmîm nᵊṯattîw* (הֵן עֵד לְאוּמִּים נְתַתִּיו) "See, I made him a witness to the peoples . . ." as *ἰδοὺ μαρτύριον ἐν ἔθνεσιν ἔδωκα αὐτόν* "Look! I gave him as a testimony among the nations."

In Jeremiah 29:23 (LXX 36:23) the MT reads *hayyôḏēaʿ wāʿēḏ* (הַיּוֹדֵעַ וָעֵד) "one who knows and is witness." Here the LXX omits "one who knows" and has only *καὶ ἐγὼ μάρτυς* ". . . and I am a witness. . . ." In Jeremiah 42:5 (49:5 LXX) the LXX renders *yᵊhî yᵊhwāh bānû lᵊʿēḏ ʾĕmeṯ wᵊneʾĕmān* (יְהִי יְהוָה בָּנוּ לְעֵד אֱמֶת וְנֶאֱמָן) "May YHWH be a true and faithful witness against us . . ." as Ἔστω Κύριος ἐν ἡμῖν εἰς μάρτυρα δίκαιον καὶ πιστόν "Let the Lord be among us as a just and faithful witness." The MT and LXX differ in a) the mode of verb "to be": the MT has jussive mode of *hāyāh* (הָיָה), and LXX imperative mode of εἰμί, b) the LXX translates *bānû* (בָּנוּ) "against us" as ἐν ἡμῖν "in us," but can be read also as "among us", c) the LXX translates *ʾĕmeṯ* (אֱמֶת) "true" as *dikaios* "righteous."

The LXX reads Micah 1:2:

šimʿû ʿammîm kullām haqšîḇî ʾereṣ ûmᵊlōʾāh wîhî ʾăḏōnāy yᵊhwih bāḵem lᵊʿēḏ (שִׁמְעוּ עַמִּים כֻּלָּם הַקְשִׁיבִי אֶרֶץ וּמְלֹאָהּ וִיהִי אֲדֹנָי יְהוִה בָּכֶם לְעֵד), as Ἀκούσατε, λαοί, λόγους, καὶ προσεχέτω ἡ γῆ καὶ πάντες οἱ ἐν αὐτῇ, καὶ ἔσται κύριος Κύριος ἐν ὑμῖν εἰς μαρτύριον "Hear *these* words, you peoples, and let the earth pay attention and all those in it; and the Lord God will be among you for a witness",[41] or "Hear the words, O people, and let the earth and all those in it pay attention, and the Lord God will be among you for a testimony."[42] According to W. Edward Glenny

> The LXX apparently renders "all of them [you]" (כלם) in the address in the MT "you people, all of you," as "words" (λόγους), perhaps influenced in this rendering by 4:1 where 'peoples' has no modifier or perhaps confused by the third-person pl. pronominal suffix. . . . the resemblance of כ and מ in both the paleo-Hebrew and early Aramaic square scripts could have

40. Troxel, *LXX–Isaiah*, 186.

41. Glenny, *Micah: Commentary*, 19 (emphasis original).

42. Brannan et al., *LES*

influenced the LXX translator to read the Hebrew "all of them [you]" (כלם) as "words" (מלים).[43]

Hence, instead of *kullām* (כֻּלָּם) "all of them," the LXX has λόγους "words," and *kullām* (כֻּלָּם) is syntactically added to the next clause καὶ προσεχέτω ἡ γῆ καὶ πάντες οἱ ἐν αὐτῇ "and let the earth and all those in her [it] pay attention.[44] Furthermore, the LXX renders the jussive *wîhiy* (וִיהִי) "for . . . will become," with the future indicative ἔσται "will be," and *bāḵem* (בָּכֶם) "against you" (m. pl.) is read in the LXX as ἐν ὑμῖν "among [in] you" (sg.); the MT referent is plural and the LXX referent is singular. The LXX reads *lᵊ ʿēḏ* (לְעֵד) lit. "for a witness" as εἰς μαρτύριον "for a testimony," where *ʿēḏ* (עֵד) refers to a person who is a witness, and εἰς μαρτύριον to the content of what the witness says.

In Malachi 3:5, the LXX reads *wᵊhāyîṯî ʿēḏ mᵊmahēr* (וְהָיִיתִי עֵד מְמַהֵר) literally, as καὶ ἔσομαι μάρτυς ταχὺς "and I will become a swift witness." The LXX translates the verb *hāyāh* (הָיָה), which has an imperfect meaning, with the future form of verb εἰμί "will be." The LXX uses μάρτυς to translate *ʿēḏ* (עֵד), and for the preposition *bᵊ* (בְּ), prefixed in the MT to four participles which describe different sins, the LXX uses preposition ἐπί, which has various meanings, and one of which is "against."

Continuing with plural forms of *ʿēḏ* (עֵד): in Isaiah 8:2, the LXX translates *ʿēḏîm* (עֵדִים) with μάρτυράς, and two witnesses described in the MT as *neʾĕmānîm ʿēḏîm* (נֶאֱמָנִים עֵדִים) "reliable witnesses" are in the LXX presented as πιστοὺς ἀνθρώπους "faithful men."

In Isaiah 43:9, *yittᵊnû ʿēḏêhem* (יִתְּנוּ עֵדֵיהֶם) "Let them bring their witnesses . . . ," the LXX translates this literally as ἀγαγέτωσαν τοὺς μάρτυρας αὐτῶν "Let them bring their witnesses." In Isaiah 43:10 the LXX inserts καὶ ἐγὼ μάρτυς "and I am a witness" to the MT's *ʾattem ʿēḏay nᵊʾum-yᵊhwāh* (אַתֶּם עֵדַי נְאֻם־יְהוָה) "You are my witnesses, says the Lord." Hence, the LXX reads γένεσθέ μοι μάρτυρες, καὶ ἐγὼ μάρτυς, λέγει Κύριος ὁ θεός "Be witnesses to me, and I am a witness, says the Lord God." Thus, YHWH himself also assumes the role of witness. In Isaiah 43:12 the LXX reads ὑμεῖς ἐμοὶ μάρτυρες κἀγὼ μάρτυς, λέγει κύριος ὁ θεός "You are my witnesses, and I am a witness, says the Lord God" for *wᵊʾattem ʿēḏay nᵊʾum-yᵊhwāh* (וְאַתֶּם עֵדַי נְאֻם־יְהוָה) "You are my witnesses, says the Lord." In Isaiah 44:8, the MT

43. Glenny, *Micah: Commentary*, 42.

44. Waltke, *Commentary on Micah*, 45.

reads *wᵊʾattem ʿēḏāy* (וְאַתֶּם עֵדָי) "you are my witnesses," but the LXX reads as *μάρτυρες ὑμεῖς ἐστε* "You are witnesses," lacking the possessive pronoun "my." In Isaiah 44:9 the LXX omits *wᵊʿēḏêhem hēmmāh bal-yirʾû ûḇal-yēḏʿû* (וְעֵדֵיהֶם הֵמָּה בַּל־יִרְאוּ וּבַל־יֵדְעוּ) "and their witnesses neither see nor know" (NRSV). Instead, the LXX reads *οἱ πλάσσοντες καὶ γλύφοντες πάντες μάταιοι οἱ ποιοῦντες τὰ καταθύμια αὐτῶν, ἃ οὐκ ὠφελήσει αὐτούς, ἀλλὰ αἰσχυνθήσονται* "Those who formed and carved *idols*, all useless, exercising their desires, which will not benefit them, but they will be put to shame."

In Jeremiah 32:10 (39:10 LXX), Jeremiah 32:25 (39:25 LXX) and Jeremiah 32:44 (39:44 LXX) LXX translates *ʿēḏîm* (עֵדִים) with *μάρτυρας*, and the LXX omits *ʿēḏîm* (עֵדִים) from Jeremiah 32:12 (39:12 LXX). Since in these verses (except Jer 32:12 [39:12 LXX]) have *ʿēḏîm* (עֵדִים) appearing together with *ʿûd* (עוּד), we will address them at greater length below.

3.2 ʿēḏûṯ (עֵדוּת) and ʿēḏôṯ (עֵדְוֹת) in the Prophets.

In Jeremiah 44:23 (51:23 LXX), the LXX translates *ûḇᵊʿēḏôṯâw* (וּבְעֵדְוֹתָיו) "and in his decrees" as *καὶ ἐν τοῖς μαρτυρίοις αὐτοῦ* "and in his testimonies," using the plural form of the noun *μαρτύριον* for *ʿēḏôṯ* (עֵדְוֹת).

3.3 tᵊʿûḏāh (תְּעוּדָה) in the Prophets

In Isaiah 8:16, where *tᵊʿûḏāh* (תְּעוּדָה) and *tôrāh* (תּוֹרָה) appear in the MT, the LXX reads Τότε φανεροὶ ἔσονται οἱ σφραγιζόμενοι τὸν νόμον τοῦ μὴ μαθεῖν "Then those who seal the Law not to learn will be evident" (LES). As J. Ross Wagner explains, in LXX

> The prophet predicts the exposure to God's judgment of those who "seal up the *νόμος* so as not to learn it" (*οἱ σφραγιζόμενοι τὸν νόμον τοῦ μὴ μαθεῖν*). In contrast to the Hebrew text, in which it is Isaiah's "testimony" (תעודה) and "teaching" (תורה) that are being sealed up among his disciples, in the LXX this *νόμος* is none other than God's Law, and those who seal it up do so out of rebellion against God.[45]

In Isaiah 8:20, the LXX renders *lᵊṯôrāh wᵊliṯʿûḏāh* (לְתוֹרָה וְלִתְעוּדָה) "For the Law and for the Testimony" as *νόμον γὰρ εἰς βοήθειαν ἔδωκεν* "For he gave

45. Wagner, *Isaiah and Paul in Romans*, 148.

a law *to be* a help" Accordingly, the LXX reads *wᵊliṯ ʿûḏāh* (וְלִתְעוּדָה) "for the Testimony" as εἰς βοήθειαν "for the help."

3.4 *ʿûḏ* (עוּד) in the Prophets

In Isaiah 8:2 the LXX translates *ʿûḏ* (עוּד) with the verb ποιέω "make, do," to convey the meaning καὶ μάρτυράς μοι ποίησον "make witnesses for me." In Jeremiah 6:10, the MT's *ʿal-·mî ʾăḏabbᵊrāh wᵊ ʾā ʿîḏoh* (עַל־מִי אֲדַבְּרָה וְאָעִידָה) "To whom shall I speak and testify," the LXX follows by translating it as πρὸς τίνα λαλήσω καὶ διαμαρτύρωμαι, using the verb διαμαρτύρομαι for *ʿûḏ* (עוּד).

A handful of verses contain both *ʿēḏîm* (עֵדִים) and *ʿûd* (עוּד).[46] In Jeremiah 32:10 (39:10 LXX), the LXX translates *wāʾāʿēḏ ʿēḏîm* (וָאָעֵד עֵדִים) as καὶ διεμαρτυράμην μάρτυρας. We encounter the same problem here which we encountered in the MT, regarding whether *ʿûd* (עוּד) should be understood as calling or as some specific form of witnessing, as we have in the LXX. The LES translates the LXX's καὶ διεμαρτυράμην μάρτυρας as "and affirmed a witness",[47] and Brenton as "and took the testimony of witnesses."[48] Strathmann explains that the first meaning of διαμαρτύρομαι is to "invoke someone (gods or men) as witness with reference to something."[49] His second meaning is "declare emphatically," whether with reference to facts or truths or in the sense of a summons, admonition, or warning. Accordingly, in Jeremiah 39:10 διαμαρτύρεσθαι μάρτυρας refers "to the part of witnesses at the signing of agreements."[50] Again, this leaves us with the option of translating διαμαρτύρεσθαι μάρτυρας as "invoking" or "calling someone" as a witness. Or we can follow Brenton, "took the testimony of witnesses."[51]

46. Jeremiah 11:7 is omitted from the LXX.

47. Brannan et al., *LES*

48. Brenton, *Septuagint Version of OT*

49. Strathmann, *"Martus", TDNT 4: 511–512.*

50. "Elsewhere it means 'to declare emphatically,' whether with ref. to statutes to be followed (Exod 18:20; 19:10, 21; 1 Βασ. 8:9), to representations made to someone (Exod 21:29; 2 Εσδρ. 23:21), occasionally to a promise given (Zech. 3:6), or commonly to prophetic warnings to repent (4 Βασ. 17:13; 2 Παρ. 24:19; 2 Εσδρ. 19:26, 34; ψ 49:7; 80:8; Ιερ. 6:10; Ezek. 16:2; 20:4 in these two passages with the obj. τὰς ἀνομίας). With these meanings we often find the dat of person, e.g., Deuteronomy 32:46; Exodus 19:21. There is a special use in Malachi 2:14: ὅτι Κύριος διεμαρτύρατο ἀνὰ μέσον σοῦ καὶ ἀνὰ μέσον γυναικός νεότητός σου, 'He was present as a witness'" (Strathmann, *4: 512*).

51. Brenton, *Septuagint Version of OT*

In Jeremiah 32:12 (39:12 LXX), the LXX does not translate *ʿēḏîm* (עֵדִים). Instead, the "LXX [Rahlfs' version] has τῶν ἑστηκότων,[52] 'the ones standing,' suggesting an original Hebrew העמדים, 'the ones standing,' which differs by only one letter from MT העדים, 'the witnesses.'"[53] Similarly, the LXX reads *wᵊhāʿēḏ ʿēḏîm* (וְהָעֵד עֵדִים) at Jeremiah 32:25 (39:25 LXX) as ἐπεμαρτυράμην μάρτυρας. This resembles Jeremiah 32:10, where ἐπιμαρτύρομαι could either be understood as "to call someone as one's witness",[54] or as Brannan, "took the testimony of witnesses."[55] This alternative implies that these witnesses performed some form of witnessing. Likewise, in Jeremiah 32:44 (39:44 LXX) the LXX translates *wᵊhāʿēḏ ʿēḏîm* (וְהָעֵד עֵדִים) as διαμαρτυρῇ μάρτυρας, and the translator faces the same challenge as we saw in Jeremiah 32:10 and 32:25. Brannan read these words as "and affirm *it* by witnesses,"[56] and Brenton as "and shalt take the testimony of witnesses."[57]

In Jeremiah 42:19–20 (49:19–20 LXX), the LXX reads ἃ ἐλάλησεν κύριος ἐφ' ὑμᾶς τοὺς καταλοίπους Ιουδα Μὴ εἰσέλθητε εἰς Αἴγυπτον. καὶ νῦν γνόντες γνώσεσθε ὅτι ἐπονηρεύσασθε. "The Lord has spoken these things against you who remain in Judah. Do not enter into Egypt! And now you will surely know that you have acted wickedly,"[58] lacking the expression *kî-haʿîḏōṯî ḇāḵem hayyôm* (כִּי־הַעִידֹתִי בָכֶם הַיּוֹם) "that I have warned against you today" from verse 19.

In Lamentations 2:13, the LXX reads *māh-ʾăʿîḏēḵ* (מָה־אֲעִידֵךְ) as Τί μαρτυρήσω σοι "What shall I testify to you," and in this way retains the MT's idea of witnessing. Although σοι is sometimes used for translating the idea of "witnessing against" (1 Kgs 2:42; Ps 50:7 and 81:8), in all those instances σοι translates personal pronouns with the preposition *bᵊ* (בְּ). We have seen that this carries the idea of "witnessing against." Here, however, *ʿûḏ* (עוּד) likely means "comforting," and the lack of the preposition *bᵊ* (בְּ) in the MT supports this reading.

52. In Swete's edition of LXX it says τῶν ἀνδρῶν τῶν παρεστηκότων ". . . the people who stood by. . . ."

53. Keown, *Jeremiah 26–52*, 143.

54. Liddell, *LSJ*, 296.

55. Brannan et al., *LES*

56. Brannan et al., *LES*

57. Brenton, *Septuagint Version of OT*

58. Brannan et al., *LES*

The LXX translates *šim ʿû wᵊhā ʿîḏû bᵊḇêṯ yaʿăqōḇ* (שִׁמְעוּ וְהָעִידוּ בְּבֵית יַעֲקֹב) "Hear and testify against the house of Jacob" (NRSV) in Amos 3:13 as ἀκούσατε καὶ ἐπιμαρτύρασθε τῷ οἴκῳ Ἰακώβ "Hear and bear witness to the house of Jacob." This corresponds to the MT. Both Swete and Rahlfs end verse 12 with the word ἱερεῖς "priests," but in Codex Vaticanus this is the first word in verse 13. Accordingly, if the subjects of *šim ʿû* (שִׁמְעוּ) "listen" and *wᵊhā ʿîḏû* (וְהָעִידוּ) "testify" in the MT are unclear, Codex Vaticanus identifies the subjects of these two verbs (priests). But Swete and Rahlfs make no such identification.

The LXX follows Zecheriah 3:6 strictly, rendering *wayyāʿaḏ malʾaḵ yᵊhwāh bîhôšuaʿ lēʾmōr* (וַיָּעַד מַלְאַךְ יְהוָה בִּיהוֹשֻׁעַ לֵאמֹר) as καὶ διεμαρτύρατο ὁ ἄγγελος Κυρίου πρὸς Ἰησοῦν λέγων. The LXX uses the verb διαμαρτύρομαι to translate *ʿûḏ* (עוּד), and translates the expression *bîhôšuaʿ* (בִּיהוֹשֻׁעַ), which contains the preposition *bᵊ* (בְּ), as πρὸς[59] Ἰησοῦν. Accordingly, Brannan translate this verse as "And the angel of the Lord warned Joshua, saying,"[60] and Brenton renders it, "And the angel of the Lord testified to Jesus, saying."[61]

kî-yᵊhwāh hēʿîḏ bênᵊḵā ûḇên ʾēšeṯ nᵊʿûreḵā (כִּי־יְהוָה הֵעִיד בֵּינְךָ וּבֵין אֵשֶׁת נְעוּרֶיךָ) in Malachi 2:14, LXX reads as ὅτι Κύριος διεμαρτύρατο ἀνὰ μέσον σοῦ καὶ ἀνὰ μέσον γυναικὸς νεότητός σου "Because the Lord has testified between you and between the wife of your youth." For *hēʿîḏ* (הֵעִיד), the LXX uses διαμαρτύρομαι, and for *bênᵊḵā* (בֵּינְךָ) and *ûḇên* (וּבֵין) the idiom ἀνὰ μέσον [*anà* – preposition; *meson* – adjective], which can be translated as "in the midst of,"[62] or "among something."[63]

59. Preposition πρός has variety of meanings: 1. to, extension toward a goal, 2. against, extension that will have contact and reaction, 3. at, by alongside a location, 4. among, with; in a location, 5. to, with; a marker of an experience of an event, 6. about, a marker of content, 7. with, a marker of association and interrelationships, 8. for, a marker of purpose, 9. according to, a marker of correspondence, implying reciprocity, 10. toward, a marker of a period of time, 11. at the time, 12. to the point of , 13. with regard to, between (Swanson, *DBLG*).

60. Brannan et al., *LES*

61. Brenton, *Septuagint Version of OT; Zechariah 3:7*

62. Stevens, *NT Greek Intermediate*, 118.

63. Mounce, *Biblical Greek*, 66.

4. Summary of the results

Here are the results of our comparison of the MT and LXX. We will focus on how the LXX translates particular Hebrew words and their semantic range, with some selected grammatical notes. Concretely, we will address nouns, verbs, prepositions, and antonyms.

Regarding nouns, in the MT *ʿēḏāh* (עֵדָה) is used only for impersonal entities (Gen 21:30; 31:52; Josh 24:27). The LXX translates *ʿēḏāh* (עֵדָה) as μαρτύριον (Gen 21:30; Josh 24:27). The noun *ʿēḏ* (עֵד) is rarely used for testimony from impersonal entities, but when it is so used the LXX translates it with the noun μαρτύριον: Genesis 31:44 (covenant), Deuteronomy 31:19 (song), Deuteronomy 31:26 (Torah), Joshua 22:27, 28, 34 (altar), Job 16:8 (Job's sufferings). In Genesis 31:48 (heap) and Deuteronomy 31:21 (song), the LXX uses the verb μαρτυρέω. In Exodus 22:12(13) (remains of an animal), the LXX uses the preposition *epí* (ἐπί) "to." The MT occasionally uses *ʿēḏ* (עֵד) to refer to impersonal witnesses: Isaiah 19:20 (altar and/or pillar) and 30:8 (written prophecy), but the LXX does not identify these things as witnesses. Conversely, for the testimony of personal witnesses, the MT usually uses *ʿēḏ* (עֵד) and *ʿēḏîm* (עֵדִים), which the LXX predominantly translates with μάρτυς. There are a few exceptions: in Exodus 20:16 and Proverbs 25:18, where *ʿēḏ* (עֵד) refers to human witness, it is translated with μαρτυρία. In Isaiah 55:4 *ʿēḏ* (עֵד) again refers to personal witness/witnesses, it is translated with μαρτύριον; likewise with YHWH in Micah 1:2. Furthermore, in the LXX μαρτυρία (Exod 20:16; Prov 25:18) and διαμαρτυρία (Gen 43:3) always refer to the content of the testimony of personal witnesses. Finally, in the MT *ʿēḏûṯ* (עֵדוּת) and its plural form *ʿēḏôṯ* (עֵדְוֹת) and *ʿēḏāh* (עֵדָה) and its plural form *ʿēḏōṯ* (עֵדֹת) always refer to impersonal entities as witnesses. Specifically, they refer to the Torah, ark, veil, and the tabernacle. The LXX always uses μαρτύριον to translate these words, except in Exodus 39:35 and Josh 4:16; there the LXX translates *ʿēḏûṯ* (עֵדוּת) as διαθήκη "covenant," thus identifying "testimony" as "covenant."

Sometimes, Hebrew verbs that in their semantic range can signify witness, are clearly designated as such in the LXX:

ʿānāh (עָנָה) as:

a) καταμαρτυρέω: Deuteronomy 5:20; Proverbs 25:18,

b) ψευδομαρτυρήσεις: Exodus 20:16,

c) μαρτυρέω: Numbers 35:30;

ʿûḏ (עוּד) as:

a) διαμαρτύρομαι: Genesis 43:3; Exodus 19:21, 23; 21:29; Deuteronomy 30:19; 31:28; 32:46; 1 Samuel 8:9; 2 Kings 17:13, 15; 2 Chronicles 24:19; Nehemiah 9:26, 34; 13:21; Psalms 50:7; 81:8; 119:61; Jeremiah 6:10; 32:10; Zecheriah 3:6; Malachi 2:14,

b) ἐπιμαρτύρομαι: 1 Kings 2:42; Nehemiah 9:29, 30; Jeremiah 32:25,

c) καταμαρτυρέω: 1 Kings 21:10, 13,

d) ἐπιμαρτυρέω: Nehemiah 13:15; Amos 3:13,

e) διαμαρτυρέω: Jeremiah 32:44,

f) μαρτυρέω: Lamentations 2:13.

Finally, we need to observe the usage of prepositions and antonyms. The preposition *lᵊ* (לְ) may signify direction (physical movement or of personal attention or attitudes); the direction or result of a transformation or change; location in space and time; possession, etc. Likewise, the preposition *bᵊ* (בְּ) also has a wide range of meanings, such as "in" (location), "at" (position in proximity to another object), "because" (cause or reason), "with" (accompaniment or of instrument), etc., but also "against" signifying opposition. Note that these prepositions convey both affirmative and adversarial meanings, and readings of them are dependent on the context. Here are few examples:

a) In Deuteronomy 31:19, the LXX translates *lᵊ ʿēḏ* (לְעֵד) as εἰς μαρτύριον "for witness," in the context of *biḇnê yiśrāʾēl* (בִּבְנֵי יִשְׂרָאֵל) "against the sons of Israel," which the LXX reads as ἐν υἱοῖς Ισραηλ lit. "in the sons of Israel",

b) in Deuteronomy 31:21, the LXX translates *lᵊpānâw* (לְפָנָיו) "toward their faces" as κατὰ πρόσωπον "toward/against face." Additionally, when the preposition κατά is used with different verbs (for example, ψευδομαρτυρήσεις in Exodus 20:16 and Deuteronomy 5:20) it clearly carries the meaning of "against" (cf. Prov 25:18; Job 16:8),

c) in Deuteronomy 31:26, the LXX translates *lᵊ ʿēḏ* (לְעֵד) as εἰς μαρτύριον; again, this occurrence appears in the context of *bᵊḵā* (בְּךָ) which the LXX renders as ἐν σοὶ "among you," "to you" or "with you",

d) in Deuteronomy 4:26; 8:19; 30:19; 32:46 the LXX uses personal pronoun ὑμῖν "you" for *ḇāḵem* (בָכֶם) "against you," and uses αὐτοῖς "them" for *bām* (בָּם) "against them" in Deuteronomy 31:28.

Lastly, we looked at antonyms, which describe the *character* of a person. We saw examples from the MT, such as Exodus 20:16 *ʿēḏ šāqer* (עֵד שָׁקֶר) "false witness" and Deuteronomy 5:20 *ʿēḏ šāwʾ* (עֵד שָׁוְא) "false witness."

The LXX translates these to describe the *activity* of a person; both of those examples the LXX reads as *μαρτυρίαν ψευδῆ* "false testimony." On the other hand, what the MT describes as *ḥāmās* (חָמָס) "violence" (Exod 23:1; Deut 19:16; Ps 35:11), and *šeqer* (שֶׁקֶר) "deception" or "lie" (Deut 19:18; Prov 6:19; 14:5), the LXX translates as *ἄδικος* "injustice." This leaves no room to view such activities as justifiable, e.g. noble acts of lying (cf. Exod 1:15–21) or violence.

CHAPTER 5

Major Aspects of the Concept of Witness in the Old Testament

To this point, we have offered a basic explanation of the concept of witness and analyzed individual texts from the OT. Here we will synthesize the results of the analysis, which will deepen our understanding of the biblical concept of witness and open some new perspectives. Here we continue to follow the categorization of witnesses used above. We will here introduce two additional categories, namely a temporal aspect, and the mode of witnessing. After showing how these categories revise our understanding of the concept of witness, we will end this chapter by discussing additional aspects of the concept of witness. These include: the function of witnesses in a given text, the definition of witness and witnessing/testifying, the importance of the concept in the OT, authority, and validation (valorization) of witness, and the dynamics of witnessing.

1. Types of witnesses

Building on the ontological categories introduced at the beginning of this study, witnesses can be further divided by their type into two categories, observing witnesses and testifying witnesses. We observed this division in our analysis of OT texts, and here we will elaborate it.

1.1 Observing witnesses

For someone to be a *testifying* witness, in some cases the person must first be an *observing* witness, the witness of someone or something. If a witness is "one who helps establish the truthfulness of a matter by testifying firsthand about what was seen or heard,"[1] or "one who tells what he or she has seen or personally experienced, often in a court of law",[2] the condition of being present at an event,[3] knowing, seeing and hearing, that is, being first of all witness of, is almost always necessary and foundational for further activity as a witness.

Observing witnesses can be impersonal or personal entities. Their role is primarily passive; they serve to record something that has been said or happened. Due to their passive role, the most common verbs which signify the actions of observing witnesses are: *šāma* ' (שָׁמַע) "to hear," *yāḏa* ' (יָדַע) "to know," *rā'āh* (רָאָה) "to see."[4] Furthermore, they often bear some of the following characteristics: a) they are designated as witnesses by someone else: Joshua 24:22; Ruth 4:9, 10; 1 Samuel 12:5; Jeremiah 42:5,[5] b) verbless clauses with Predicate-Subject word order such as we have in Joshua 24:22; Ruth 4:9, 10 and 1 Samuel 12:5 can signify observing witnesses,[6] c) they are object of the verb *'ûḏ* (עוּד) such as in Isaiah 8:2; Jeremiah 32:10, 25, 44.[7]

Wells divides observing witnesses into four subcategories. The first subcategory is transaction observers. Such witnesses perform the act of recording at formal legal events outside of a trial setting, such as sales, adoptions, the division of inheritance. Witnesses in the second subcategory are trial observers, who act as observing witnesses in court during an actual trial. Those in the third subcategory are accidental observers, who find themselves recording or observing an event without prior knowledge of it. Witnesses in the fourth subcategory are furtive observers, who are partially prearranged and partially coincidental. Their presence is prearranged but the event they observe may not be.[8]

1. Leschert, "Witness", *EDB* 1384.
2. Elwell and Comfort, eds., "Witness", *Tyndale Bible Dictionary* 1306.
3. Present in the sense of "one who is in contact" (Bovati, *Re-Establishing Justice*, 265).
4. Wells, *Law of Testimony*, 27–28.
5. Wells, 27.
6. The exception is Isaiah 44:9 where the Predicate-Subject word order seems to refer to testifying witness (Wells, 33).
7. Wells, 27.
8. As an example of *transaction observers*, Wells brings Jeremiah's purchase of the land in Jeremiah 32; Wells (*Law of Testimony*, 22–25) claims that the OT does not have examples of *trial observers* although a number of other Near Eastern documents mention the presence

1.2 Testifying witnesses

Witnesses in the second major type are testifying witnesses. Their function is to report what they have seen, heard or known. Hence, in most cases, testifying witnesses are those who in the past have been observing witnesses, and their testimony serves as evidence. As with observing witnesses, testifying witnesses can be either impersonal or personal. Their role is active, and their activity is described with active verbs such as: *qûm* (קוּם) "to arise" (Deut 19:15, 16; Ps 27:12; 35:11; Job 16:8), *ḥāḏaš* (חָדַשׁ) "to renew" (Job 10:17), *nāṯan* (נָתַן) "to give" (Isa 43:9; 55:4), *hāyāh* (הָיָה) "to be" (Exod 23:1; Prov 24:28; Job 16:8; Mic 1:2; Mal 3:5), and others. Testifying witnesses are connected with the activity of speaking: *nāḡaḏ* (נָגַד) "to declare" (Lev 5:1; Prov 12:17), *dāḇar* (דָּבַר) "to speak" (Ps 50:7; Prov 21:28), *ʿānāh* (עָנָה) "to reply" (Exod 23:2; Num 35:30; Deut 19:16, 18; 31:21; Job 16:8; 29:11; Prov 25:18).[9] Furthermore, testifying witnesses can be detected by the following characteristics: a) they are the subject of the verb *ʿûḏ* (עוּד), which in this case can be translated as "testify" (1 Kgs 21:10, 13; Job 29:11; Ps 50:7; Mal 2:14),[10] b) verbless clauses with word order Subject-Predicate often point to testifying witnesses (Gen 31:50; Isa 43:10, 12; 44:8; Jer 29:23).[11]

2. Revision of categorization: temporal aspect and mode of witnessing (of, for or against, and about)

Distinguishing between observing and testifying witnesses is helpful, because it demonstrates the complexity of roles that witnesses had in the OT. Our grasp of the role becomes even more nuanced if we distinguish witnesses by, a) the temporal aspect of observing and testifying and their subjects, and consequently, b) the mode of their witness.

Witnesses function in various temporal directions. In general, they can:

- in the present, observe something and be just passive recipients
- in the present, speak about the past

---

of such witnesses at trials. As an example of *accidental observers*, Wells mentions Numbers 5:13 where there are no witnesses to woman's supposed adultery. As an example of *furtive observers*, Wells points to Psalm 35.

9. Wells, *Law of Testimony*, 26–27.

10. Wells, 24.

11. Wells, 33.

- in the present, speak about the future
- in the present, speak about the past, present or future

This division attends to the temporal dynamics of witnessing. We must add a further, connected category, the mode of witness – that is, for what purpose and with what outcome these witnesses testify.

Based on textual analysis, we suggest that there are three different modes of witnessing: witnessing of, witnessing for or against, and witnessing about. Accordingly, the mode of an observing witness is always witness of because they passively receive information. Because they report what they have observed, the mode of testifying witnesses is active, and can constitute witnessing for or against,[12] or witnessing about.[13] When we add to that temporal spectrum of witnesses' activities and different modes of their witnessing to our consideration of the ontological categories and different types of witnesses, a complex picture emerges. Determining the temporal aspect and mode of witness will help us to define more precisely the *type* of witness and its functions.

Two examples will illustrate the usefulness of these divisions. First, we can look at Genesis 31:50. Wells says that the witness in this verse is difficult to classify, yet he classifies it as testifying witness.[14] However, he sees this witness as becoming a testifying witness in the future. In actuality, YHWH is at that point an observing witness. This illustrates why attention to the temporal aspect of witnesses helps us to define more precisely the type of witness. Genesis 31:50 does not have a verb to modify the activity of *ʿēḏ* (עֵד), and the expression *bênî ûḇênеḵā* (בֵּינִי וּבֵינֶךָ) "between me and you" (cf. Gen 31:44, 48) indicates witness in a passive role (observing witness) rather than an active role. Since YHWH is invoked as witness at the beginning of the covenant between Jacob and Laban (there is no reference to the past, just from present forward), we must classify YHWH here as an observing witness, a witness of the covenant. Malachi 2:14 provides an instructive parallel to Genesis 31:50. There the verb *ʿûḏ* (עוּד) occurs alongside

12. According to Bovati (*Re-Establishing Justice*, 264–65), only the context can tell us whether a witness is for or against someone.

13. Introducing the category "mode of witness" affects only testifying witnesses, since observing witnesses always function as witnesses of.

14. Wells, *Law of Testimony*, 43.

the expression *bênᵊkā ûḇên* (בֵּינְךָ וּבֵין) "between you [m.s.] and between," a similar expression to Genesis 31:50. That expression indicates that the witness is an observing witness. Yet, the Hiphil form of *ʿûḏ* (עוּד), which can be translated as "cause to witness," indicates that the witness is a testifying witness. YHWH was an observing witness of the marriage covenant in the past, so that in the present he can perform the function of a testifying witness. He testifies about the infidelity of husbands toward their wives, but he also acts as witness-enforcer. That YHWH testifies post factum is clear from the context (cf. Mal 2:13). So, the temporal aspect of witness (in the present about the past) supports our conclusion that YHWH here is testifying witness.

The second example comes from Joshua 22:27, which we included in the category of impersonal testifying witnesses. Wells classifies the altar from this verse as an observing witness, which serves as a symbolic (constant) reminder.[15] Pietro Bovati argues that the altar has "an indisputable juridical function as the sign of the pledge . . . but . . . do not enter into area of trial witness."[16] Trites sees it "as evidence of the reported arrangement."[17] By introducing the categories of temporal aspect and mode of witness, we can better understand this altar's role as witness. First, this altar is a visible expression of a particular testimony, here the people's determination to serve YHWH. This means that this altar is constructed sometime after the people's decision and not simultaneously with it, which then excludes the altar from the notarial role of observing witness. This altar is thus a testifying witness. But what kind of testifying witness? Bovati and Trites together claim that the altar communicates something: as sign and evidence. Therefore, we should consider it as *testifying witness*, but as a *witness about*. Consider the more detailed explanation offered below.

15. Wells, *Law of Testimony*, 41.

16. Bovati, *Re-Establishing Justice*, 264.

17. Trites, *NT Concept of Witness*, 18.

Table 1: Categorization of witnesses according to suggested revision – OT

Ontological category and type	Mode	Temporal aspect	Function	Specific Purpose	Qualification	Means
Person. Observing Witness	Witness of	In the present for the future	To record	To ensure confirmation	Being present, seeing, hearing, knowing	Seeing, hearing, or knowing.
Imperson. Observing Witness					Ascribed or imposed on	
Person. Testifying Witness	Witness for or against	In the present about the past	To report	To establish subject's guilt or innocence	Observing witness in the past	Verbal
	Witness about	(1) In the present what will/can happen in the future	To report	To warn, admonish	Position of power	Verbal
		(2) In the present what will /can / must happen in the future based on the past or present		To urge to change, to warn	God's revelation, designation or assumed role based on previous knowledge	Verbal
		(3) In the present about more than one dimension of time		To establish truth	God's election / appointment	Difficult to identify

Ontological category and type	Mode	Temporal aspect	Function	Specific Purpose	Qualification	Means
Imperson. Testifying Witness	Witness for or against	In the present about the past	To report	To establish truth regarding subject's guilt or innocence	Being recognized and affirmed as such by others	Material evidence; physical condition
	Witness about	(1) In the present what will happen in the future based on the past or present	To report	To warn, admonish, urge to change	God's revelation / inspiration	Material evidence
		(2) In the present about the past		To constantly remind	Being designated as such by others	Object itself as means of testimony
		(3) In the present about more than one dimension of time		To serve as visual reminder, and to confirm certain truths	God's revelation / inspiration	Object itself as means of testimony
		(4) In the present about the past		To confirm verbal report	Accepted as such by parties	Material evidence
		(5) In the present what will happen in the future		To declare intention	None	Symbolic action confirming verbal statement

2.1 Definitions according to the suggested revision

When we combine categories of ontology and type with mode and temporal *aspect* of witness, the following picture emerges.

2.1.1 Observing witnesses (personal and impersonal)

Observing witnesses receive the testimony, so their mode is always witnessing of something. But when we analyze observing witnesses through their temporal range, we can see that both impersonal and personal observing witnesses function in the present, with the potential of becoming testifying witnesses in the future if needed. Their function is to record and if necessary to confirm. Personal observing witnesses are qualified by the fact that they were present on the particular occasion and saw or heard something. Hence, they possess unique (eyewitness) knowledge that no one else has. Impersonal observing witnesses intrinsically do not possess attributes of hearing, seeing, and knowing, but these attributes are ascribed to them by others (personification).

2.1.2 Testifying witnesses: for or against, and about

Regarding testifying witnesses, the situation is far more complex. Their common feature is that their function is to report. This reporting comes in two modes of testifying: a) witnessing for or against and, b) witnessing about.

2.1.2.1 Personal and impersonal testifying witnesses for or against

The role of personal testifying witnesses for or against is active, and their function is to report what has been said or done. Temporally, they always speak in the present about the past; this temporal aspect is characteristic of them. The specific purpose of their testimony is to provide evidence with the goal of establishing the truth regarding the subject's guilt or innocence.[18] Guilt can be legal (toward men) or religious (toward God) in nature. What qualifies them to be testifying witnesses is having been observing witnesses in the past, and in the present offering their testimony in a legal or quasi-legal context. When such witnesses appear in covenantal context,

18. The rationale is to make distinction between *witnesses for* or *against*, and witnesses *about* precisely on the point of innocence and guilt. If witness is testifying in order to prove someone's innocence or guilt in relation to men or YHWH, such testifying witness is *witness for* or *against*. All other outcomes of *testifying witnesses* fall into the category of witnessing *about*.

the courtroom setting is emulated in order to provide a setting for establishing a subject's guilt or innocence. Occasionally, impersonal entities assume the role of witnesses for or against (impersonal testifying witnesses). In that case, the characteristics of personal testifying witnesses are ascribed to them through personification, although they do not intrinsically possess these characteristics. In other words, they cannot offer verbal testimony, but they speak through material evidence.[19] They function in the same way as personal testifying witnesses; their function is to report, with the specific purpose of establishing the truth regarding a subject's guilt or innocence. They are qualified for this rule by the fact that others recognize and affirm them as such witnesses.[20]

2.1.2.2 Personal and impersonal testifying witnesses about

Personal testifying witnesses about also have to report as their function. However, their temporal aspect, specific purpose, and qualifications differ from those of personal testifying witnesses for or against. In this category we have three groups. The first group of personal testifying witnesses about have the temporal aspect of announcing in advance what will or can happen, with specific purpose of warning or admonishing people. Such speech is usually accompanied by conditions and consequences ("if" . . . "then"). It describes the future. This description is given prior to any deeds done by the subject.[21] Thus the witness gives warnings and admonishments without any direct reference to the subject's past. Those who give such warnings/admonishments are qualified for this activity by their position of power, which enables them to execute consequences based on the future actions of hearers.

Sometimes the role of personal testifying witnesses about overlaps with witnesses for or against.[22] The temporal aspect of that second group is to announce in the present what will, can or must happen in the future, based

19. Speaking of Exodus 22:12 (13), Westbrook and Wells (*Everyday Law in Biblical Israel, 42*) say that "the object, even when called a witness, had only limited power to speak for itself. A human witness was required to put the object in context, and ultimately it was the testimony of the latter that the court had to believe."

20. In Exodus 22:13 the remains of an animal; in Job 10:17; 16:8 Job's physical condition.

21. More precisely, *warnings* can be recognized by the presence of conditions and consequences, and *admonishments* only stipulate conditions.

22. By overlapping we mean that it is difficult to distinguish between them due to many similarities.

on a subject's past or present actions. The specific purpose is to urge people to change through warnings and admonishments. These witnesses cover both parts of the temporal spectrum, past-present and future, and often mention a subject's guilt. Hence, the guilt speech is often included in their testimony and presumed as fact.[23] The qualification for being such a witness is: a) being inspired by YHWH to prophetically announce future events or receiving such knowledge from YHWH, b) possessing previous knowledge. In the second case, the witness is convinced that something will happen (or repeat) because of a similar event in the past.[24]

The temporal aspect of the third group of personal testifying witnesses about is transtemporal. They testify in the present, but the content of their testimony cannot be limited to only one temporal dimension. Hence, we say that they testify about more than one dimension of time. The specific purpose of their testimony is to testify about certain truths. They are qualified for this role by God's election and appointment.

Impersonal testifying witnesses about have the same function as the personal testifying witnesses about, yet other details are complementary or different. Based on the analysis, we can also divide these witnesses into five groups.

The first group's temporal aspect is to declare in the present what will happen in the future. Their testimony contains prophecy as evidence for the purpose of warning, admonishing and urging people to change. In such instances, these impersonal entities are qualified for their role because they are products of YHWH's inspiration or revelation. Once materially produced, they contain the prophetic message, and are means of witness. Some witnesses from this group are clearly described as witnesses containing messages about the future (Deut 31:19, 21, 26; 32:46), and/or are given in written form

23. Such witnesses do not testify in order to prove a subject's guilt or innocence. That is not an issue. The guilt of the subject is a given. The witnesses point to the guilt and then warn of the coming consequences, or at least tell what the person must do. Because of this complexity, I chose to treat these witnesses not simply as witnesses against (although fundamentally that is what they are), but as witnesses about, since they work in both temporal spectrums: past or present, and future. Witnesses for or against refer only to the subject's past.

24. Nehemiah 9:30 specifically says that YHWH's warnings were given by YHWH's Spirit through his prophets. This is example of the first type of qualification. But when Nehemiah in Nehemiah 13:15 rebukes his countryman, he warns them not to sin against God because such behaviour will invoke similar punishment as happened in the past. That is an example of the second type of qualification.

as prophetic messages (Deut 31:19, 26; Isa 8:16, 20; 30:8). These objects "speak" about their subjects' past, in the sense that their past guilt is the cause for future events. It is not always clear how the subjects' past determines what will happen in the future. For example, the prophecies from Isaiah 8:16, 20; 30:8 directly speak of the results of their subjects' past actions. Deuteronomy 31:19, 21, 26; 32:46, on the other hand, speak more in terms of a pattern: Israel has sinned in the past, and will do so again in the future.

The second group of impersonal testifying witnesses about has a present temporal aspect, to serve as a (constant) reminder of some testimony from the past. When considering this group, we must recognize that these entities are produced or designated as witnesses after the occurrence of testimony they reflect. Their function is also to report, but they perform this function by being visible signs of a particular testimony. Hence, the specific purpose of their testimony is to reveal and remind people of something. Their qualification for this task is that they are recognized as witnesses by others. Their very existence is the means of their testimony. Joshua 22:27, 28, 34 and Isaiah 19:20 are examples of such witnesses.

The third group of impersonal testifying witnesses about has the temporal aspect of reporting in the present about more than one dimension of time. Their specific purpose is to act in a visible manner to remind people of and confirm certain truths. They are qualified for this task because their existence is the result of YHWH's revelation/inspiration/command. Hence, the Torah,[25] veil, tabernacle and ark are visible expression of YHWH's speech and revelation.

The fourth group of impersonal testifying witnesses about has the temporal aspect of reporting in the present what happened in the past. Their specific purpose is to confirm a verbal report so that the truth of something under question may be established. The OT's only example of such witness is in Genesis 21:30 where Abimelech accepts seven lambs given to him by Abraham. This signifies that he accepts Abraham's claim to have dug the well. From that point on, Abraham's claim becomes the official story, truth or (created) reality. Although the lambs do not have any connection with the

25. In a sense, the Torah is given to shape Israel's present and future. It came into existence as a result of YHWH's revelation and speech, but with a purpose to communicate conditions of the Mosaic covenant and be permanent guide for Israel's life.

digging of the well, Abraham's willingness to support his claim with this symbolic act and Abimelech's willingness to accept it qualifies these lambs as evidence for Abraham's claim.

The fifth group of impersonal testifying witnesses about has the opposite temporal aspect to the fourth group, and their specific purpose is to declare regarding something in the future. There are no specific qualifications for this category of witnesses. The only example of such a witness is Ruth 4:7, where Boaz's act of giving his sandal to another visibly and tangibly confirmed his intention to marry Ruth.

2.2 Explanation of the concept's revision on concrete selected examples

After giving our rationale for expanding our model for analysis, and offering support for the suggested expansion, here we give additional concrete examples that illustrate and confirm the expansion. We will give examples according to the type of witnesses.

2.2.1 Observing witnesses

Four texts in this category of witness require additional examination. In Deuteronomy 4:26; 30:19 and 31:28, the impersonal entities of heavens and earth serve as observing witnesses. They are called or invited to witness to the message of Moses given to Israelites. Yet Moses also announces them as testifying witnesses against in the future, due to the use of Hiphil of *ʿûḏ* (עוּד) + *bᵊ* (בְּ). Moses prophetically announces Israel's apostasy by speaking about conditions ("if you do this") and consequences ("then this will happen").

In 1 Samuel 12:5, we find the combination *ʿēḏ* (עֵד) + *bᵊ* (בְּ), which could refer to a testifying witness. However, the context reveals that YHWH and Saul play the role of observing witnesses. In 1 Samuel 12:3 Samuel invites the gathered people to "testify against him" *ʿānāh* (עָנָה) + *bᵊ* (בְּ), and in 1 Samuel 12:4 they testify in Samuel's favor. So, in 1 Samuel 12:5, Samuel invokes both YHWH and Saul as witnesses, but their role was to observe and remember the witness brought by the people on that occasion. Hence, they are observing witnesses.

Furthermore, Jeremiah 42:5 clearly demonstrates the transition between observing and testifying witness. The people ask for YHWH to be a witness against them if they do not obey what YHWH tells them through Jeremiah.

ʾim (אִם) "if" points to the conditional role of YHWH. He is primarily an observing witness but—if the Israelites are not faithful to their commitment to follow YHWH's instruction—YHWH will become a witness against them. Hence, we must pay attention to the temporal dimension in order to classify the type and mode of witness properly.

Finally, above we said several factors show that the witnesses in Amos 3:13 are observing witnesses. First, these witnesses are invited to "hear," a characteristic activity of observing witnesses. Second, the summoning of witnesses uses a rhetorical device which creates the atmosphere of legal proceedings.[26] Third, these witnesses are likely summoned to testify to the verdict of YHWH.[27] In verses 14–15 YHWH announces the future punishment of Israel, and these witnesses observe YHWH's declaration. All this makes these summoned witnesses observing witnesses.

2.2.2 Testifying witnesses

2.2.2.1 Personal testifying witnesses

We also have several texts requiring additional explanation in this category. Let us first observe witnesses for or against. First, the witness in Job 16:19 is apparently a witness who defends Job and affirms his innocence (Hubbard[28]; likewise Wells[29]). As Alison Lo says, Job cries for heavenly witness who can testify to his integrity in the presence of YHWH.[30] Accordingly, we will treat this witness as witness for. Second, Isaiah 43:9, 10, 12; and 44:8, 9 use courtroom settings, because YHWH is bringing a lawsuit against false gods. According to Wells, Isaiah 43:9 and 44:9 refer to witnesses supporting the false gods, serving as defence witnesses.[31] Isaiah 43:10, 12 and 44:8 refer to witnesses for YHWH, which take the side of prosecution witnesses. In that emulated courtroom setting, YHWH's witnesses would be witnesses against, and the witnesses of the pagan gods witnesses for. But if we set the courtroom setting aside, we can view witnesses on both sides as witnesses for their side and against the other side. According to Giovanna Raengo Czander,

26. Mays, *Amos: Commentary*, 68.
27. Smith and Page, *Amos, Obadiah, Jonah*, 81.
28. Hubbard, *"Kinsman-Redeemer and Levirate"*, *DOTWPW* 328.
29. Wells, *Law of Testimony*, 47.
30. Lo, *Job 28*, 145.
31. Wells, *Law of Testimony*, 47.

witnesses for YHWH's side are first introduced as observing witnesses, using the terminology of "seeing," "hearing" and "knowing" (Isa 40:28; 41:20; 42:18–20).[32] Because they also see, hear, and know, Israel can now step into the role of testifying witness.[33] Third, the invitation of peoples to *šim ʿû* (שִׁמְעוּ) "hear" (pl.) and *haqšîḇî* (הַקְשִׁיבִי) "listen" in Micah 1:2 falls into line with the role of observing witnesses. Although in Jeremiah 42:5 construction of *ʿēḏ* (עֵד) + *lə* (לְ) + *bə* (בְּ) falls in the category of observing witness, that instance assumes a different situation: "On the basis of 2b, most commentators understand the peoples/earth not to be witnesses or judges in a lawsuit, but as those who stand indicted, although it is Israel's judgment that is announced. This judgment stands as an example for, or witness against, the nations."[34]

In the category of witnesses about, we will consider two texts. First, the type and mode of witness in Jeremiah 29:23 is difficult to determine. The facts that YHWH first enumerates the sins of particular people, and that YHWY is described as *hayyôḏēa ʿ* (הַיּוֹדֵעַ) "one who knows" (cf. Lev 5:1), and as one who is *wā ʿēḏ* (וָעֵד) "witness" both argue YHWH is an observing witness.[35] The fact that verbless clauses with word order Subject-Predicate are used in the OT to refer to testifying witnesses (Gen 31:50; Isa 43:10, 12; 44:8; Jer 29:23) argues that YHWH is here a testifying witnesses.[36] Also, the context implies that YHWH is not trying to prove the people's guilt; it is a given fact, and the future punishment is already declared. Accordingly, Juan Cruz observes that "[u]sually when the deity appears as a witness in prophetic literature, he is seen testifying against specific people for specific offences," and he uses Jeremiah 29 as an example of YHWH testifying against

32. Czander, "You are my Witnesses," 156.

33. Czander ("You are my Witnesses," 161) rightly argues that YHWH calls Israel to testify "because she has observed Yahweh at work in her own history and she has heard the message of the prophets, who announced what was going to happen *before* it occurred. As previously mentioned, Israel is called not as a witness (observing witness) of a crime, but a witness of YHWH's mighty acts. Israel is called as both a trial observer (of the *rîbs* against the gods and against nation) and as 'direct observer' type of witness (of YHWH's work in history). The purpose of making Israel observe YHWH's secondary trials against the nations and their gods is to bring awareness to Israel that she is YHWH's witness ('so that you may see and know' 40:21, 28, 41:20)."

34. Mathews, *Defending Zion*, 44.

35. Newman and Stine, *Matthew, 598*; Holladay, *Concise Hebrew and Aramaic, 109*; Ahn, *Exile as Forced Migrations, 132.*

36. Wells, *Law of Testimony*, 33.

Zedekiah and Ahab, charging them with perjury and adultery.[37] Hence, the arguments can cut both ways. But if we accept that YHWH here functions as a testifying witness, we still must define the mode of witness. Due to the assumption of the subject's guilt in Jeremiah 29:21–23 and the fact that the punishment is already defined, the best conclusion is to define this as an example of witness about.

Isaiah 55:4 deserves special attention. It seems to represent a rare type of witness in the OT,[38] because the witness in this verse is positive – witness for due to combination of *ʿēḏ* (עֵד) + *lᵊ* (לְ), and (unidentifiable) peoples are recipients of this testimony. However, witnessing for in this case does not have the normal temporal aspect for such a mode of witness, and the purpose is not to establish truth regarding the subject's guilt or innocence but rather to establish some religious truth. Hence, this witness we label as personal witness about, group 4.

2.2.2.2 Impersonal testifying witnesses

Several verses require additional explanation here. We will first observe two examples of witnesses for or against, and then discuss examples of the witnesses about category. The usage of *ʿēḏ* (עֵד) together with *neḡdî* (נֶגְדִּי) "against me" in Job 10:17 probably implies that Job's bad physical condition is itself a witness against Job. Job 16:8 makes the same implication. Accordingly, these texts reflect the personification of sufferings as witnesses, and Job interprets them as witnesses against him. This combination is unique to these texts.

Under the category of witnesses about, the first example is the Song of Moses (Deut 32), mentioned in Deuteronomy 31:19, 21; 32:46. The song functions as testifying witness against the Israelites. But unlike witnesses against who testify in the present about the past, this song functions as a prophecy about the future of the Israelites (imperfect of *hāyāh* (הָיָה) "to be" in Deut 31:19 and weqātal (waw + perfect) of *ʿānāh* (עָנָה) "to answer" in Deut 31:21). In the narrative context, it functions as witness about, prophetically announcing what can/will happen in the future. Yet the text clearly defines the

37. Cruz, *"Who is like Yahweh?"*, 82.

38. When we analyze semantic range of the concept of witness in the OT, we will see that due to the covenant with YHWH, Israel's role also includes witness to the world. But still, this aspect is not so prominent in the texts that contain specific Hebrew word for witness/testimony.

song's future role as witness for and against. Deuteronomy 31:19 says that the song is *lᵊʿēḏ* (לְעֵד) "for witness": for one party is it witness *llî* (לִי) "for me," and for the other it is witness *biḇnê yiśrāʾēl* (בִּבְנֵי יִשְׂרָאֵל) "against the sons of Israel." Similarly, in Deuteronomy 31:21 the song is again *lᵊʿēḏ* (לְעֵד), but this time it witnesses against the Israelites *lᵊpānâw* (לְפָנָיו) "to their faces."

Second, the book of the Law in Deuteronomy 31:26 also shows this overlap between witness about and witness against. In the narrative context, the book of Law serves as a witness about, because it speaks about future things. It cannot immediately function as a witness against because the Israelites' apostasy has not yet occurred. Yet, the text clearly indicates that the book of the Law will be a witness against in the future, due to the verb *hāyāh* (הָיָה) "to be" in weqatal (waw+perfect) where the Book of the Law is *lᵊʿēḏ* (לְעֵד) "for witness," but *bᵊḵā* (בְּךָ) "against you" (m.s.).

Third, the relationship between Genesis 31:44, 48 and Joshua 22:27, 28, 34 is interesting. These texts describe witnessing that occurs "between" two parties. But the witnesses in Genesis 31:44, 48 fall in the category of observing witnesses, and in Joshua 22:27, 28, 34 in the category of testifying witnesses. The distinction is that the altar of Joshua 22 is made after the testimony which it reflects, so it cannot play a role of an observing but testifying witness. The covenant and heap from Genesis 31 are made simultaneously with the event, so their role belongs in the category of observing witnesses. This illustrates how paying attention to the temporal aspect of witnessing can help us to determine the type of witnesses more clearly.

Fourth, Isaiah 8:16 and 20 probably refer to testifying witnessing about. Whether *tᵊʿûḏāh* (תְּעוּדָה) refers to verbal or written records,[39] the message refers to the future and not the past. Hence, we cannot consider this to be witnessing against, but witnessing about. Similarly, in Isaiah 30:8 we have a situation where the text becomes a form of testimony, since YHWH instructed Isaiah to write the Israelites' punishment upon the tablet.[40]

Fifth, Isaiah 19:20 has a situation very similar to Joshua 22, where material objects are created in order to convey a particular message. As Csaba Balogh

39. "Although some scholars have thought that the testimony in this passage is not the text but, as before, the authenticating testimony of the disciples, it seems to me that here the testimony is textual and the disciples are charged with its preservation" (Najman, "Symbolic Significance of Writing", 149–150).

40. Najman, *Perfection in Jewish Antiquity*, 15.

notices: "(a) The altar and the stone are a sign 'to/for YHWH' prepared by (?) the Egyptians. (b) These objects can be signs 'concerning YHWH', i.e. a testimony to the Egyptians and others. It is more likely that the stele and the altar are signs and markers aimed at the Egyptians and others indicating the extent of YHWH's power."[41] Hence, we can label this altar and pillar as *witnesses about* because they convey or express certain testimony.

Sixth, we have seen that the Torah was presented as a form of testimony, as were the accompanying elements (tabernacle, ark, . . .). We also defined these as witnesses about, due to their trans-temporal nature. However, in few instances, the Torah apparently could signify a mode of witnessing other than just witness about. In Psalms 119:31 we find the combination of *ʿēḏôṯ* (עֵדְוֹת) + *bᵊ* (בְּ) in the form of *ḇᵊ ʿēḏᵊwôṯêḵā* (בְעֵדְוֹתֶיךָ); in Psalms 119:46 *ʿēḏōṯ* (עֵדֹת) + *bᵊ* (בְּ) in the form of *ḇᵊ ʿēḏōṯêḵā* (בְעֵדֹתֶיךָ); and in Jeremiah 44:23 *ʿēḏōṯ* (עֵדֹת) + *bᵊ* (בְּ) in the form of *ûḇᵊ ʿēḏôṯāw* (וּבְעֵדְוֹתָיו). But based on the contexts, we cannot conclude that the Torah functioned as a witness against someone. Furthermore, in Psalms 78:5 the preposition *bᵊ* (בְּ) was not connected with the Torah but with the recipient, *bᵊyaʿăqōḇ* (בְּיַעֲקֹב) "Jacob" and *bᵊyiśrāʾēl* (בְּיִשְׂרָאֵל) "Israel." Also, the Hebrew verb translated "established" in "For He established a testimony in Jacob" (NASB) is verb *qûm* (קוּם) "to rise," which is occasionally found in the context of witness against (Deut 19:15, 16; Ps 27:12; 35:11; Job 16:8). Together these factors could give the impression that YHWH established a witness "against Jacob" and "against Israel." However, the text (Ps 78:5) depicts the establishing of the testimony positively, so the witness is not against.[42] Likewise, in Psalms 81:5, the preposition *bᵊ* (בְּ) is used positively with the recipient *bîhôsēp̄* (בִּיהוֹסֵף) "in / for Joseph." The only place in the OT where Torah is represented as a future *witness against* is in Deuteronomy 31:26, as we have seen above.[43]

41. Balogh, *Prophecies Concerning Egypt and Kush*, 260.

42. Speaking of Psalms 78:5, Wendy L. Widder (*"To Teach" in Ancient Israel*, 150) says: "Finally, a text in Psalms activates the aspect of ידע-H's meaning potential described in definition 2a. In Psalms 78:5, parents were to make known (ידע-H) YHWH's testimony and Torah to their children so they would know and recount them to their children and so on. The knowledge in Psalms 78:5 is indeed sourced in the divine realm (the testimony and the Torah), but its mediation from the divine realm happened at an earlier time – namely, when YHWH gave his testimony and Torah to Israel."

43. "In Deuteronomy 31:9–13 the written document received the positive *telos* of catalyzing the people's faithfulness to the covenant in their future in the land. In 31:26 the same document, now supplemented with the Song, is turned into a "witness against" (עד ב)

Based on these revisions to our categories, we can see which biblical texts belong to which category in the following table.

Table 2: Biblical texts according to the suggested revision – OT

Ontological category and type	Mode	Temporal aspect	Examples
Personal Observing Witnesses	*Witness of*	In the present for the future	Gen 31:50; Josh 24:22; Ruth 4:9, 10, 11; 1 Sam 12:5; Isa 8:2; Jer 32:10, 12, 25, 44; 42:5; Amos 3:13.
Impersonal Observing Witnesses			Gen 31:44, 48, 52; Deut 4:26; 30:19; 31:28; Josh 24:27.
Personal Testifying Witnesses[44]	*Witness for*	In the present about the past	Job 16:19; 29:11; Prov 14:5, 25; Isa 43:9; 44:9; 55:4.
	Witness against		Exod 20:16; 21:29; 23:1; Lev 5:1; Num 5:13; 35:30; Deut 5:20; 17:6, 7; 19:15, 16, 18; 1 Kgs 21:10, 13; Ps 27:12; 35:11; 50:7; Prov 6:19; 12:17; 14:5; 19:5, 9, 28; 21:28; 24:28; 25:18; Isa 43:10, 12; 44:8; Mic 1:2; Mal 2:14; 3:5.
	Witness about	(1) In the present what will/can happen in the future	Gen 43:3; Exod 19:21, 23; Deut 8:19; 1 Sam 8:9; 1 Kgs 2:42; Jer 42:19; Zech 3:6.
		(2) In the present what will / can / must happen in the future based on the past or present	2 Kgs 17:13, 15; 2 Chron 24:19; Neh 9:26, 29, 30, 34; 13:15, 21; Ps 81:8; Jer 6:10; 11:7; 29:23.
		(3) In the present about more than one dimension of time	Isa 55:4.

the same people 'for I know,' Moses states, 'how rebellious and stubborn you are' (31:27). The status of the written record is thus fundamentally transformed by the dramatic revelation – epitomized in the Song – of Israel's imminent breaking of the covenant. Moses transfers the (illocutionary) value attached by God to the Song (31:19, 'that this Song may be a witness for me against [לעד ב] the people of Israel') to the now completed 'book' (31:26, 'that it may be thee for a witness against you [בך לעד]'). The contagion is, so to speak, spatial. The embedded Song communicates its value of 'witnessing against' to the Torah 'book' to which it is attached" (Sonnet, *Book within Book, 166*).

44. Since the identity of witness in Psalms 89 is so debatable, I will not try to define the details.

Ontological category and type	Mode	Temporal aspect	Examples
Impersonal Testifying Witnesses	*Witness for*	In the present about the past	Exod 22:13.
	Witness against		Job 10:17; 16:8.
	Witness about	(1) In the present what will/can happen in the future based on the past or present	Deut 31:19, 21, 26; 32:46; Isa 8:16, 20; 30:8.
		(2) In the present about the past (constant reminder)	Josh 22:27, 28, 34; Isa 19:20.
		(3) In the present about more than one dimension of time	Torah,[45] ark,[46] veil,[47] tabernacle.[48]
		(4) In the present about the past	Gen 21:30.
		(5) In the present what will happen in the future	Ruth 4:7.

3. Other aspects of the concept of witness

The concept of witness in the OT is dynamic and has different aspects which contribute to its dynamism. We have sought to demonstrate how introducing the temporal aspect of witness and mode of witness redefines and expands our understanding of what witness and witnessing is in the OT. Here we will summarize the results of our research by discussing additional aspects of the concept of witness. These include: the function of witnesses; a further

45. Exodus 25:16, 21; 30:6, 36; 31:18; 32:15; 34:29; 40:20; Leviticus 16:13; Numbers 17:4, 10; Deuteronomy 4:45; 6:17, 20; 31:26; 1 Kings 2:3; 2 Kings 11:12; 17:15; 23:3; 1 Chronicles 29:19; 2 Chronicles 23:11; 34:31; Nehemiah 9:34; Psalms 19:7; 25:10; 78:5, 56; 81:5; 93:5; 99:7; 119:2, 14, 22, 24, 31, 36, 46, 59, 79, 88, 95, 99, 111, 119, 125, 129, 138, 144, 146, 152, 157, 167, 168; 122:4; 132:12; Jeremiah 44:23.

46. Exodus 16:34; 25:22; 26:33, 34; 27:21; 30:6, 26; 31:7; 39:35; 40:3, 5, 21; Numbers 4:5; 7:89; Joshua 4:16.

47. Leviticus 24:3.

48. Exodus 38:21; Numbers 1:50, 53; 9:15; 10:11; 17:7, 8; 18:2; 2 Chronicles 24:6.

expanded definition of witness and witnessing/testifying; the importance of the concept of witness in the OT; the authorizing and validation (valorization) of witnesses; and the dynamics of witnessing.

3.1 The function of witnesses

The two major categories of witnesses – observing and testifying – correspond to the two major functions of witnessing: to record (passive) what has been said and/or done, or to report (active). Usually, a witness must be an observing witness before they become a testifying witness. In the present they observe what is being said or done, with the potential of being called to testify in the future if needed. Since they always function from the present forward, this category of witnesses is easily recognizable. Furthermore, impersonal observing witnesses sometimes are personified inanimate objects, such as the stone in Joshua 24:27 or "heavens and earth" in Deuteronomy 4:26; 30:19; 31:28. These things "can hear" but cannot speak or do anything. Yet they too can also become testifying witnesses; as part of nature, "heavens and earth" by extension may be used by YHWH as a vehicle for the punishment of covenant breakers (cf. Mal 2:14). This personification points to the fact that such witnesses take that position simply because they are recognized and agreed upon as such by others. By introducing the temporal categories, we have shown that it is sometimes difficult to distinguish between observing and testifying witnesses. This is especially the case with combination of *ûḏ* (עוּד) + *bᵊ* (בְּ) (Deut 4:26; 30:19; 31:28; Amos 3:13) when witnesses are already in advance declared as witnesses against (Deut 4:26; 30:19; 31:28). Also, it is difficult to determine whether an observing witness has already stepped into the role of a testifying witness or not (Amos 3:13).

Within the category of testifying witnesses, we have encountered several nuances of reporting, especially when we connected them with temporal aspect of witnessing. This study has also shown that testifying witnesses – both personal and impersonal – can be divided according to their mode of witnessing. The picture that emerges is a complex one, but a textual analysis of biblical verses supports such categories. As a result, we have a more precise and accurate picture of the concept of witness. Testifying witnesses whose modes of witness is for or against are easy to recognize, because they always speak in the present about the past. They do so in order to establish truth regarding the subject's guilt or innocence. Hence, when we combine these two aspects (temporal aspect and guilt/innocence focus), we have a clear picture of testifying witness for or against.[49] Such witness may or may not come with combinations of *ʿēḏ* (עֵד) / *ûḏ* (עוּד) + *bᵊ* (בְּ); this word combination is not always a sign of witnesses for or against. Sometimes antonyms without the preposition *bᵊ* (בְּ) indicate that a text speaks about witness against,[50] but sometimes the context itself determines the mode of witness.[51] The majority of testifying witnesses, for or against, belong to the against category. But when the OT speaks about witnesses for, in these rare instances (Job 16:19; 29:11; Prov 14:5, 25, Isa 43:9; 44:9; 55:4), in two instances (Isa 43:9; 44:9) the witnesses for probably refer to witnesses for false gods. In only one instance do we find an impersonal witness for, and that is in Exodus 22:13, where the remains of an animal serve as evidence. Yet such impersonal witness/evidence must be accompanied with a story to provide context, otherwise their witnessing is incomprehensible.

By introducing the category of testifying witness about, the attempt was made to categorize all those testifying witnesses who were not obviously observing witnesses whose function does not focus on guilt/innocence. The picture that emerged was again complex. But by clearly defining their temporal aspect, specific purpose and outcome of witnessing, we were able to categorize different groups of personal and impersonal testifying witnesses about. The biggest challenge was to differentiate between the second group of personal witnesses about and witnesses against, because both groups of witnesses include guilt speech against subjects. Yet, as we have also seen, the group of witnesses about operates in the slightly different timeline. For them, guilt of the subjects is a given fact, and they cover multiple temporal foci: they warn the subjects about their future based on the subject's past or present actions. Hence, they are witnesses against, yet more than that.

49. If we focus only on the grammatical constructions *ʿēḏ* (עֵד) / *ûḏ* (עוּד) + *bə* (בְּ) and ignore the temporal aspect, it would seem that certain texts have a witness against mode of witness. However, for texts such as Deuteronomy 4:26; 30:19; 31:26, 28; Joshua 24:27; 1 Samuel 8:9; 12:5; 1 Kings 2:42; Nehemiah 9:26, 29, 30; 13:15, 21; Psalms 81:8; Jeremiah 11:7; 42:5 and Zecheriah 3:6 that is not the case. In spite of such grammatical construction, they are either observing witness, or have some other mode of witness than witness against mode.

50. Example: *ḥāmās* (חָמָס) without *bə* (בְּ) in Exodus 23:3; Psalms 35:11; *šeqer* (שֶׁקֶר) without *bə* (בְּ) in Proverbs 6:19; 14:5.

51. Leviticus 5:1 and Deuteronomy 17:6, 7, are examples where we do not have preposition *bə* (בְּ) or antonyms.

Furthermore, we have seen that some personal witnesses about (first group) function without being observing witnesses in the past. This group only speaks about what might/can happen in the future. Such speech is not strictly speaking prophecy, yet it talks about the future in the form of warning or admonishment. But when we come to the second group of personal witnesses about, speech about the future is usually in the form of a prophecy.

3.2 Definition of witness and witnessing/testifying

Based on these functions of witnesses, we can list key elements that will help us to observe the complexity of and define who is a witness according to the OT:

- Who: personal and impersonal entities
- Context: social, religious or legal context
- Role: passive or active role
- Temporal aspect: all three temporal aspects: past, present and future
- Mode of witness: of, about, for or against
- Purpose: to ensure confirmation, to establish subject's guilt or innocence, to warn or admonish or declare intention, etc.
- Qualifications: various
- Means of testimony: various

In addition to these key elements, we must also observe what witness/es do. Since a witness is the one who offers testimony or testifies, based on previous analysis, we can identify major activities that witnesses usually perform. First, seeing and hearing can be considered as activities of witnesses. Usually those who are passive observing witnesses use seeing and hearing as their means of witness. This also qualifies them or gives them authority to be observing witnesses, and in the future to step into the role of testifying witnesses if needed. Second, knowledge or remembrances is another faculty that describes observing witnesses. This faculty is the result of either seeing, hearing or both. Based on these two factors, a person gains knowledge which qualifies him for the position of observing witness and enables him to testify to that end in the future if needed. Third, while activities discussed previously describe observing witnesses, activities associated with testifying witnesses generally fall into the category of *speech*. Hence, even if some texts we do not use Hebrew technical terms for the concept of witness, activities such as "speaking," "replying," "answering," "telling," "warning," "admonishing," "urging," "testifying," "prophesying," etc. are all candidates for describing the activity of witnesses.

With impersonal entities the situation is a bit complex. First, when impersonal entities are labelled as witnesses, they are usually used by other personal entities as witnesses and defined as such. For example, in Genesis 31:44, 48, 52 a covenant agreement between two persons and a heap of stones made to mark the agreement are defined as witnesses by others. Exodus 22:13 envisions a scenario where the owner of an animal has given it to a neighbour for safekeeping, and the animal has been killed by wild predators. In this case, the one who kept the animal for safekeeping must *bring* the remains as evidence that the animal was truly killed (rather than stolen, etc.). In one instance Boaz uses *symbolic actions* to confirm verbal testimony (Ruth 4:7). Also, in one instance Abraham *gives* seven lambs as the way to confirm his verbal statement (Gen 21:30).

Second, even though impersonal witnesses are defined as "witnesses," it is not quite clear whether witnessing activity is ascribed to a personal entity, an impersonal entity, or both. In Deuteronomy 31, YHWH commands Moses to write down and teach to the Israelites the song that will become a witness against them (Deut 31:19) and will reply against them (Deut 31:21). In Deuteronomy 31:46 Moses uses "words" (which probably refers to the song), but in this part of the story the words of the song are not labelled as "witnesses." Instead, Moses is the one who testifies these words. In Joshua 22:27–28, 34, an altar is defined as a "witness," but this witness is also accompanied by an additional story which explains its purpose, and the stone from Joshua 24:27 is also defined as witness with ascribed ability to hear words that are spoken by people. The same complexity is present in Isaiah 19:20, which mentions an altar and monument; likewise, a tablet/scroll in Isaiah 30:8.

Third, sometimes impersonal entities are defined as witnesses not because they are used by someone else as witnesses, but due to their own activity of testifying. For example, in Deuteronomy 4:26; 30:19; 31:28, the heavens and earth will "testify against." Job's poor physical condition in Job 10:17 and 16:8 is also designated a witness. Although Job believes that YHWH is the author of this condition, he understands the condition itself as "witness."

Based on all this data we conclude that witness (whether as personal or impersonal entity) can be a) defined explicitly, b) defined as such based on its actions. In most cases *ʿēḏ* (עֵד) or *ʿēḏîm* (עֵדִים) modify personal entities. Exceptionally, *ʿēḏ* (עֵד) modifies impersonal entities.[52] Similarly, one can be defined as "witness" not only by usage of the noun *ʿēḏ* (עֵד) or *ʿēḏîm* (עֵדִים) but also by the presence of the verb *ʿûḏ* (עוּד); this applies to both personal and impersonal entities.[53] But we must also take into consideration the distinction between "testimony" and "witness." "Witness" is the one who gives "testimony," but "testimony" (the content which someone or something gives) is the "product" and not the "producer." Hence, when we talk about the concept of witness, we talk about two complementary but not identical things. When the OT uses words such as *ʿēḏāh* (עֵדָה), *tᵉʿûḏāh* (תְּעוּדָה), *ʿēḏûṯ* (עֵדוּת), *ʿēḏōṯ* (עֵדֹת) or *ʿēḏôṯ* (עֵדְוֹת), it is better to say that in these instances the OT speaks about "testimony" although, as we have seen, this distinction is not always clear. For example, in Deuteronomy 31:26 Torah is defined as *ʿēḏ* (עֵד) but in all other instances it is defined as *ʿēḏûṯ* (עֵדוּת), *ʿēḏōṯ* (עֵדֹת) or *ʿēḏôṯ* (עֵדְוֹת). Similarly, the song from Deuteronomy 31:19, 21; 32:46 or the altar from Joshua 22:27, 28, 34 are the product of someone's testimonial activity, yet they themselves are designated as "witnesses." For that matter on some occasions, we can even speak about transition from "testimony" to "witness" – that is, the product of someone's testimony can in some cases become "witness." This opens another interesting perspective: witness (person) is the one who gives witness (content) or testimony. But does the giving of the "testimony" automatically make or qualify someone as a "witness" (person)? The answer is no because, as we have seen, the testimony of a false witness cannot be qualified as a testimony.

Given these facts, our definition of "a witness" must: a) make a distinction between "witness" and "testimony" because testimony is a "product" which the witness produces, b) recognize that not every entity which gives "testimony" can be designated a "witness", c) include activities which witnesses perform and d) take into consideration the different functions of witnesses.

---

52. Genesis 31:44, 48, 52; Ex 22:13; Deuteronomy 31:19, 21, 26; Joshua 22:27, 28, 34; Job 10:17; 16:8; Isaiah 19:20; 30:8.

53. Since examples for personal entities are numerous, here we will identify only such examples for impersonal entities: heavens and earth – Deuteronomy 4:26; 30:19; 31:28; song – Deuteronomy 32:46.

Attempting to define witness, we can say the following: "a witness is a personal or impersonal entity who, based on particular qualifications and mode of witness in reference to specific temporal aspect, offers testimony with a specific purpose by using various means." This definition is general because it is impossible to include all possible details in it, yet it is specific enough to include all major aspects which make someone or something into a witness. On the other hand, "testimony is a product produced by personal or impersonal witnesses." This might include speaking particular messages, performing symbolic actions, or the writing or making of some testimonial object, etc.

3.3 The importance of the concept of witness in the Old Testament

The complexity of the concept of witness is also reflected in the question about the importance of that concept in the OT. In that regard, we can single out three things. First, we have observed that in the social context (primarily Genesis) witnesses are part of the agreement between individuals. From Exodus forward, the concept of witness becomes part of that theocratic society where the distinction between religious and legal contexts does not exist, and its importance is elevated to another level.

Second, the one who is a witness often has a unique position, opportunity and access to particular events, Walter Brueggemann argues that if a witness had access to some event, he or she was qualified to give testimony.[54] This would mean that a court would not have access to the actual event other than by the testimony of such witness, and it would be futile for the court to speculate beyond the testimony. Accordingly, a witness is someone who also has the role of a mediator between. So, when a witness utters testimony, the testimony becomes a public presentation that shapes and constitutes reality. In this way, the witness argues for his version of reality and causes this reality to recur, return and become alive once again. As Brueggemann says, "the utterance leads reality in the courtroom."[55] If and when the court accepted some version of reality, the testimony that is accepted as true became an official version of reality. This implies that testimony has a *creative force*, a

54. Brueggemann, *Theology of Old Testament*, 120–121.

55. Brueggemann, 121.

power to create reality and public truth, and it is imperative that testimony should be based on facts and reality.

Implications of this imperative can be seen in both legal and religious contexts. In the legal context, a witness is someone who determines the fate of the accused by virtue of his unique position, opportunity and access to particular events. He is assumed to be able to provide evidence that no one else can. Based on that evidence, the accused will be convicted or set free. In the religious context, the situation is more complex. The Sinai covenant is an important aspect of that religious context because, as we have already seen, this covenant is an example of a group of people (Israelites) witnessing to the revelation of YHWH. Based on that revelation they entered into a relationship with him. This relationship created a community – a community with a mission, which because of its unique position, opportunity and access to particular events, had an obligation to be faithful to that revelation and proclaim that revelation/testimony to others. For that matter, witnesses that appear in this context proclaim certain religious truths to outsiders and also remind insiders of those truths and invite them to faithful living.

Third, in the OT we did not encounter many explicit examples of witnessing in an attempt to establish some religious truth. Texts such as Isaiah 55:4 and Isaiah 43–44 fall into this category, but these are the only texts that contain specific Hebrew words for witness and speak in this direction. On the other hand, the foundational element for the concept of witness in the OT was Israel's covenant with YHWH (religious truth), and this covenantal relationship shaped the concept of witness on both vertical and horizontal axes. Since Israel had witnessed and experienced YHWH's activity in her history, Israel became the recipient of YHWH's testimonies in various ways: the event of Exodus, giving of the Law and establishing of the covenant at Sinai, the tablets of the Law, the tabernacle and various elements connected with it, etc. All these elements express that vertical dimension of testimony which came from YHWH to Israel. The standards of this vertical dimension of testimony also needed to be horizontally implemented and incorporated in Israel's everyday life and their mutual human relationships, in religious, legal and social contexts. Consequences for breaching of these standards would be harsh. For the individual, the acceptance of false testimony could lead to injustice and evil. The uncovering of false witness could lead to the death penalty for the witness. However, the fate of the entire nation, and not just individuals, depended on faithful observation of the testimony of YHWH – the Torah.

3.4 Authority and validation (valorization) of witnesses

In this section we discuss two related questions. First, who or what gives someone the right to be a witness? Second, what determines that someone's testimony is valid? Although we addressed these questions in the revision section under the qualifications for certain groups of witnesses, here we will elaborate further. In the most basic terms, a witness's authority comes from his unique access to an event, which in turn gives him a unique knowledge about that event, about which he can then testify. This basic definition works well when we deal with the dynamics around personal observing and testifying witnesses, and in cases when witnesses in the present address what happened in the past, especially in legal contexts. In that case, unique access provides unique knowledge which enables the court to determine what really happened. But we have seen that the role of witnesses in the OT is more complex than that. For that matter, the issue of authority is complex as well.

If we continue with personal witnesses, we notice that such witnesses may ground the authority of their testimony on their position of power when they speak (or warn) about possible future events. They warn others what will happen if such and such happens, and because they have power, they can execute such warning. But when personal witnesses talk what will, can or must happen in the future based on past or present, or they testify about more than one dimension of time, in that case the authority for such testimony may come from YHWH's revelation. Witnesses may be designated/elected by others (including God) to such positions, or they can simply exercise knowledge of previous events (not necessarily first-hand knowledge).

The authority attributed to the testimony of impersonal witnesses is also diverse. Qualifications of observing witnesses such as seeing, hearing or knowing are ascribed to such witnesses by others. When the issue is guilt or innocence in a legal context, the authority of such witnesses comes from their recognition and affirmation as witnesses by others. When such witnesses testify about what will happen in the future based on the past or present, in such cases we are talking about material objects (a song from Deut 31; 32, testimony from Isa 8:16, 20, a tablet/scroll from Isa 30:8) which are the result of YHWH's revelation/inspiration, and as such are authoritative. Some impersonal witnesses in the present serve as a constant reminder of some testimony from the past. In those cases, authority comes from the fact that they are recognized as witnesses by others. Impersonal witnesses such as Torah, the ark, the veil, the tabernacle, which in the present testify about more than one dimension of time draw their authority from the fact that they are a result of YHWH's revelation/inspiration. Finally, when impersonal witnesses are used in the present to confirm verbal report from the past, authority is based on the acceptance of such witnesses by others.

Addressing the second question: what determines that someone's testimony is valid? This question is most applicable to personal witnesses. Impersonal witnesses are either the result of YHWH's revelation or accepted as such by others. In those cases, the ability of seeing or hearing is ascribed to them. Occasionally, when such witnesses require acceptance from others as witnesses, we can say that their validity as witnesses is granted to them by others. We can even speak about the "acceptance by faith" of such witnesses. For example, some impersonal entities require context, verbal explanation or personal knowledge of the story, to grasp the nature of their witness. So, understanding the altar from Joshua 22 requires familiarity with the story of why this altar was built (Josh 22:27). Otherwise, one can pass it by and recognize that this altar represents something important without precisely knowing exactly what it represents. We see a similar situation in Genesis 31, although the context there was narrower since the story deals with the agreement between two individuals and their families. Some impersonal entities, such as the Book of the Law and accompanying elements (ark, veil, etc.), are themselves part of revelation and convey certain testimony. As part of the Mosaic covenant these entities permanently convey their message to those who are recipients of such revelation and party to that covenant.

With personal witnesses, the situation is more complex and dynamic, and we can trace several ways in which their testimony gains validity. First, most of the time a testifying witness must also have been an observing witness. Their observations give authority and validity to their testimonies. Second, witnessing in the Old Testament is usually verbal in nature, and speech is the most prominent form of witnessing and evidence. Witnesses' words are highly valued, and often they are not accompanied by any physical evidences. A defendant's fate can be sealed with nothing but words and a sufficient number of witnesses (Deut 17:6–7). In that case, where there is no material evidence, the validity of the witness's testimony depends greatly on the witness's character. Jonathan Burnside observes that witnesses had a high degree of responsibility because, unlike in modern systems of law where witnesses are seen as suppliers of neutral information, biblical witnesses took sides because they testified for or against, and they took personal responsibility for their testimony.[56] Hence, a witness could be a genuine witness or a false and violent witness who spoke lies and deception, whose testimony was empty and invalid. Such testimony would not be considered as testimony but as lie, and such false witnesses were subject to the punishments prescribed by the Torah. Third, although verbal witnesses are the dominant mode, there are also examples where verbal testimony receives additional demonstration, confirmation, or support through various visible evidences. In Genesis 21:30 we have a unique example where a verbal statement is confirmed with material evidence unrelated to the verbal claim. Lambs are not in any way connected with the digging of the well except that they maybe drink from it. Abraham's willingness to support his claim with material evidence seems to add weight to his claim. This verbal claim, once accepted, becomes an official truth. Also, in Exodus 22:13 we have an example where verbal claims can be supported with physical facts/evidence. In that case, no additional witnesses are needed. Ruth 4:7 is another example where verbal statement is additionally confirmed with symbolic act. Finally, one way to secure the validity of someone's testimony was the requirement of having two or three witnesses. This Old Testament stipulation is found in legal contexts and the purpose of it was to secure just verdicts. The testimony of a single witness was not enough to convict the accused. Practice, however, showed that even this rule could be manipulated (cf. 1 Kgs 21). Hence, this rule was not always able to produce and secure justice, even though it was one of the ways to secure the validity of a witness's testimony.

3.5 Dynamic of witnessing

The concept of witness is an incredibly dynamic concept in the OT. To begin with, it appears in all three contexts[57], both personal and impersonal entities

---

56. Burnside, *God, Justice, and Society*, 118.

57. See section 3.2.

are defined as witnesses, and the scope of their activities is broad and rich. Let us consider several aspects of this dynamic.

First, there is a dynamic tension between serving as observing and testifying witnesses. We have seen that testifying witnesses generally must be observing witness before they testify. In other words, one can testify only if he has first seen, heard or experienced something. From that (experiential) knowledge, the witness can testify. This implies that one can become a witness even "by accident," and that such a person is obliged to testify if needed. Also, consider the importance of experiential knowledge. On the one hand, a witness need not be personally detached from what he is testifying about, so subjectivity is something that can be assumed. We can even speak about a witness's passion. On the other hand, witnessing is not a theoretical or abstract discipline. On the contrary, it is very concrete and specific. And because of that tension between observing and testifying witnesses, sometimes it is difficult to categorize witnesses precisely.

Second, there is a dynamic tension between "witness" (the person or thing), and "testimony" (the product of a witness's testimony). Someone or something is designated as witness either by declaration or through some activity he, she or it performs, and these activities can either describe observing (seeing, hearing, etc.) or testifying witnesses (speaking, warning, etc.). However, the question remains: when can a particular activity, such as "hearing," "knowing" or "speaking," be automatically categorized as belonging to the concept of witness or not? We cannot address this issue more extensively here, so such research would have to be a subject of some future study. Furthermore, we have noticed that a "witness" produces "testimony," yet occasionally that "testimony" can in turn become a "witness" as well.[58] This dynamic is also interesting because it only happens in connection with impersonal witnesses. Personal witnesses are always defined as "witnesses" and never as "testimony."

Third, the dynamic of the concept of witness is particularly noticeable in the temporal aspects in which witnesses act. To be a witness you can be either active or passive. Passivity is acceptable when a particular entity is on the "receiving side," observing what is being said or done. But, when a

58. Torah (Deut 31:26); song (Deut 31:19, 21; 32:46); altar (Josh 22:27, 28); sandal (Ruth 4:7), etc.

particular entity is on the "giving side," he can be used in many different ways for many different purposes: to witness what happened in the past in order to establish someone's guilt or innocence; to declare what will happen in the future for the purpose of warning and admonishing or declaring intention; to declare what will happen in the future because of the past, and in this way establish a "cause – consequence relationship"; to offer witness about past, present or the future in order to establish particular truth, etc.

Fourth, the dynamic of the concept of witness is present in the overlapping with two significant OT topics: covenant and prophecy. The theophany of YHWH in establishing the Sinai covenant (Exod 19–24) was a testimonial event, and because of that, Israel was put in the position of a witness. But there is an additional dimension of the concept of witness that is present in this event: not only that the covenant itself is a form of testimony, but there is an overlap between "testimony," "words/commandments" and "covenant" in connection with various cultic elements. Hence, the tablets of the Law can be "tablets of the covenant" (Deut 9:9, 11, 15) or "testimony" (Exod 31:18; Deut 4:45; 6:17, 20), and ark can be "ark of the covenant" (Josh 4:18) or "testimony" (Exod 25:22; 26:33, etc.). From that we concluded that covenant stands as one form of testimony, as well as various cultic elements connected with it, but this does not mean that covenant can be reduced to testimony.

Since the concept of witness in this temporal aspect is far from being one-dimensional, we noticed that it overlaps with another significant OT concept – the concept of prophecy. On the basic level, the prophet's role is similar to that of a witness. Both have the role of a mediator between: the prophet stands between YHWH and men, and the witness stands between men, but also between YHWH and men. For example, Moses is a prophet (Deut 18:15), and Moses as a witness repeats Israel's history, as we saw in Deuteronomy 1–4. Also, at the end of Deuteronomy (31:19, 21; 32:46), Moses is charged to write down the song that is prophecy for the future, which will serve as a witness against Israel, since YHWH knows them and what they will do in the future. Similarly, in Isaiah 8 the prophet Isaiah is charged by YHWH to write down a prophecy which is a "testimony of warning" (NIV). As we already noticed, in Isaiah 8:16, 20 the situation is puzzling because the text does not make clear whether the prophecy remained in verbal form or was eventually written down. On the contrary, in Isaiah 30:8 we know that YHWH instructs Isaiah to write down the prophecy that serves as an "everlasting witness" (NIV). In some of these examples, we already noticed that personal witnesses give testimony, yet the product of their witness ("testimony") is sometimes classified as "witness" (Deut 31:19, 21; 32:46; Isa 30:8). Although witnesses sometimes produce "testimony," at other times they produce another "witness." In examples such as 2 Kings 17:15; Nehemiah 9:26, 29, 30, 34, prophetic activity is connected with the concept of witness in the form of "warnings." We have also seen that Nehemiah 9:30 is the first text to explicitly connect prophetic testimony and the activity of "God's Spirit" – *bᵊrûḥăḵā* (בְּרוּחֲךָ). This link is particularly important for the book of Acts, where a crucial element in the church's witnessing is the activity of the Holy Spirit. Additionally, in the same way we can classify the "warning" (Jer 42:19) which Jeremiah gives at the end of his prophecy (Jer 42:9–18) as a prophetic warning/testimony. Similarly, the warning which the Angel of the Lord gives to Joshua in Zechariah 3:6 is also part of prophetic speech. Hence, we could say that prophets can use a form of a testimony as a means to communicate their message, but that does not mean that everything that the prophets say or do belongs in the category of witness/testimony, or that we should automatically treat testimonies as prophecies.

Fifth, in connection with the third point, our analysis has shown that a witness is not just someone who speaks for, against or about, in the modern sense of a disinterested third party in a case, but the witness may assume additional juridical roles. In Deuteronomy 19:16–18, the witness who testifies may not only be a "witness" in this case but also the "accuser."[59] Furthermore, in Malachi 3:5 YHWH is himself the one who functions as witness, but the scope of his witnessing activity encompasses many things. He is a witness because it is implied that he possesses knowledge of people's sins, but he also seems to function as the "judge" who will pronounce the verdict, and the "executioner." This last point is in keeping with Deuteronomy 17.[60]

Finally, the dynamic of witness is also noticeable in the fact that the attribute of testimony can be imparted or transferred from one entity to another. Hence, the two tablets, due to their testimonial nature, transfer this attribute

59. Wells, *Law of Testimony*, 46.

60. Although in the NT we do not have examples where Christian witnesses perform role of "judges" or "executioners," we do have an idea that "testimony" is a form of "judgment," especially if it is rejected (cf. Matt 10:11–15; 23:37–39; Mark 6:7–13).

to other entities that are connected with them. Although this refers to material objects, this principle (that when receiving testimony, one becomes identified with it) will be important for the concept of witness in Luke/Acts.

4. Conclusion

We began this research with a literary analysis of Acts 1:8, with the intention of exploring the significance and impact of πνεῦμα ἅγιος on the concept of witness in Luke's theology. Then we explored the concept of witness in the biblical context. Our first step was to see how this concept was defined and developed in the OT. To that end we analyzed selected OT texts. Based on that analysis, we were able to offer a synthesis of results which showed the following.

The basic underlying idea of the concept of witness or testimony in various different and complementary ways reflects the idea of "repetition" and "recurrence" which originates from the etymology of words with the *'d*. root. The means of repetition are diverse (material evidence, verbal report, evidence and warning, or the combination of verbal announcement and actual fulfilment), and in some instances past events could serve as a paradigm for some future events that will occur. For example, in Jeremiah (Jer 42:18–19) a warning about future damnation has a force of repetitive activity which is one of the meanings of *'ûd* (עוד). In Micah 1:2 YHWH's punishment of his people serves as a model for YHWH's future punishment of other nations. Hence, this idea of repetition confirms the general definition of a witness who must either be present in order to see and hear something which makes him an eyewitness, or he or she must at least hear something to which he or she can testify. Based on these requirements, one is able to fulfil the role of witness and repeat what he/she saw, heard and knows. But we have also seen that this idea is not sufficient to describe all cases of testifying witnesses, since some of them speak about the future without any reference to the past. Also, even though it is basic, the idea of repetition does not summarize everything that witnesses do.

Witnesses appear in three different yet complementary contexts, they can be personal or impersonal entities, and can have passive or active roles. Furthermore, they may be defined explicitly or based on the activity they perform, and this is one additional reason why the semantic range of the concept of witness must be studied more fully in the next chapter. Taking seriously the underlying idea of the concept of witness or testimony as repetition, we paid attention to the temporal aspect of the concept of witness. This led us to distinguish between the three modes of witness (of, for or against, and about). We also summarized functions that witnesses perform, which gave us a basis for defining what is witness and what is testimony. We also observed the importance of the concept of witness in the OT, what gives authority and validation (valorization) to the witnesses. We further identified different ways in which the dynamic of the concept of witness manifests in the OT. In our analysis of this dynamic, special attention was given to the concept of witness in connection with the concept of covenant and prophecy.

These results will serve as our foundation for analyzing the concept of witness in the New Testament. There we will conduct a similar analysis for the purpose of gaining an overall picture of the witness in the Bible, then comparing this larger picture with the concept of witness in the Lukan writings and determining specific emphases of the concept of witness which are present in Lukan writings in the light of our research question. But before we step into the world of the NT, we must research the semantic range of the concept of witness in the OT.

CHAPTER 6

The Semantic Range of the Concept of Witness in the Old Testament – Selected Texts

Thus far we have observed that, strictly speaking, a witness is someone who has seen, heard and has knowledge about something, and on that basis speaks about the past or the future. However, the concept of witness in the OT is not confined to the phenomenological level, where concrete Hebrew terms referring to witness appear in the text. Other words, due to their semantical range, can likewise contain or reflect the concept of witness. We have seen that the most common verbs which signify the actions of observing witnesses are: *šāmaʿ* (שָׁמַע) "to hear," *yāḏaʿ* (יָדַע) "to know," *rāʾāh* (רָאָה) "to see." Testifying witnesses are the subject of *active verbs* such as: *qûm* (קוּם) "to arise," *ḥāḏaš* (חָדַשׁ) "to renew," *nāṯan* (נָתַן) "to give," *hāyāh* (הָיָה) "to be," and others, but also verbs that are connected with the activity of *speaking*: *nāḡaḏ* (נָגַד) "to declare," *dāḇar* (דָּבַר) "to speak," *ʿānāh* עָנָה)) "to reply," and others. Also, particular events can be loaded with the idea or carry the meanings of witness because they involve repetition or some other witnessing activity. For that reason, in this chapter we will study the dynamic of witnessing in the OT by analyzing the semantic range of selected words and events.[1] This will enrich our understanding of the concept of witness

1. I will not extensively focus on all possible words or combination of words that reflects the concept of witness. First, that would take a significant space to do that, and secondly, Bovati has done this partially in his book *Re-Establishing Justice: Legal Terms, Concepts and Procedures in the Hebrew Bible* (pp. 278–343). Also, the witness motif in the book of Psalms

in the OT and demonstrate how semantic range analysis can complement our phenomenological analysis.

1. Moses's call

The first example of this dynamic is Moses's call and mission described in Exodus 3:7–22. In this event, YHWH is presented as a witness of the suffering of his people, and he invites Moses to participate in the future deliverance. According to Ehlke, this story (Exod 3:1–15), illustrates YHWH's ever-present love for the Israelites since YHWH hears the cries of his people and assumes an active role in their liberation.[2] And the first step is "God's decision to descend from the heavenly realm and allow Moses to bear witness in the theophany of the burning bush." Hence, this invitation puts Moses into the role of a witness. First, Moses is a witness because he receives YHWH's testimony regarding his plans for the future. Now that Moses has seen, heard and knows what YHWH will do, he must deliver this testimony to the Israelites, and convince them of the certainty of deliverance (Exod 4:31). It is interesting that Moses is sent as a man with the message, but also with a promise that his message/testimony will be confirmed with *pālā*ʾ (פָּלָא) "wonders" (Exod 3:20), and *ʾôṯ* (אוֹת) "signs" (Exod 4:8, 30). Moses' verbal message/testimony will be accompanied with signs and wonders so that people can believe in the message. We will see this pattern (that YHWH's testimony requires an additional visible expression or manifestation for others, through signs and wonders or through community for example) again in the New Testament, in the Gospels and the book of Acts.[3]

---

was researched by Czander in her doctoral dissertation "You are my Witnesses": A Theological Approach to the Laws of Testimony (pp. 113–144).

2. Ehlke, *Crossroads of Agony*, 116.

3. This theme (that verbal testimony requires confirmation) can also be seen in the fascinating relationship between *peh* (פֶּה) "mouth" and *yāḏ* (יָד) "hand" in some texts. The first example comes from Deuteronomy 17:6–7, where in 17:6 a witnesses' "mouth" brings charges against someone, and after guilt is established, the witnesses' "hand" executes the judgment. A second example is connected with the activity of prophets (2 Kgs 17:13; Neh 9:30) where we observe that YHWH warned people through the *yāḏ* (יָד) "hand" of his prophets. This connection between "mouth" and "hand" will be important for us, because in the Lukan writings, witness includes *verbal* but also *visible* expression. As part of that *visible* expression, miracles are connected with the hand of God (cf. Luke 11:20).

2. Exodus

The event of the exodus itself is represented as a testimony first and foremost for the people of Israel, and then for other nations. In Exodus 4:30–31 Aaron and Moses are those who offer testimony to the people: they *dābar* (דָּבַר) "speak" (Exod 4:30) and the people *šāma'* (שָׁמַע) "listen" (Exod 4:31); Moses and Aaron also perform *'ôt* (אוֹת) "signs" before people's *'ayin* (עַיִן) "eyes" or "sight." The people's response was that they *'āman* (אָמַן) "believed," *qādad* (קָדַד) "bowed down" and *ḥāwāh* (חָוָה) "worshiped" (Exod 4:31). The story continues in Exodus 6, which is permeated with witnessing language. In Exodus 6:1 YHWH promises to Moses that he will *rā'āh* (רָאָה) "see" what YHWH will *'āśāh* (עָשָׂה) "do" to Pharaoh, which puts Moses and consequently Israel in the position of observing witnesses. YHWH says that his covenant with Israel is the reason why YHWH *šāma'* (שָׁמַע) "heard" Israel's cry for freedom (Exod 6:5). Now YHWH is presented as an observing witness who will act accordingly. As a result, the people will *yāda'* (יָדַע) "know" that YHWH is "Lord their God."

The exodus event also provides testimony about YHWH to the other nations. In Exodus 14:4 YHWH promises that because of the Exodus, pharaoh, his army and Egyptians will *yāda'* (יָדַע) "know" that YHWH is "YHWH." This idea is repeated in Exodus 14:18, and after YHWH destroys the Egyptian army, Exodus 14:18 says that Israelites *rā'āh* (רָאָה) "saw" (cf. Exod 14:13) what YHWH has done, and the result was that they *yārē'* (יָרֵא) "feared" the Lord and *'āman* (אָמַן) "believed" in YHWH (cf. Exod 4:31). All this shows that YHWH's activity in the course of human history brings the knowledge of YHWH to people, through observing YHWH's work and/or hearing his words. In the case of Israelites, this becomes a foundation for their role as witnesses for YHWH – an example we have in Deutero-Isaiah. On the micro level, in Exodus 18:8 Moses *sāpar* (סָפַר) "retells" the story of the exodus to Jethro. In this way, as an eyewitness to this event, he testifies to others about it.[4]

4. In the context of the Biblical narrative, we could say that the exodus is a repetitive event, a model of, or continuous testimony, of YHWH's salvific work. Even though Israel's concept of salvation was rooted in the historical experience of the exodus when they witnessed "the salvation of the Lord" (Exod 14:13) first-hand (Spender, "Salvation", 1884), Hughes and Laney (*TCBC*, 256) argue that "Neither creation nor exodus were simply onetime events. They were continuous models of God's ability to bring freedom out of bondage and order out of chaos."

In Exodus 19:4 YHWH again reminds Israelites on their role of witnesses who had *rāʾāh* (רָאָה) "seen" what he did to the Egyptians. This function is additionally supported by the fact that Israel was in the position to *šāmaʿ* (שָׁמַע) "listen" (Exod 19:9; 20:19; 24:27), and *rāʾāh* (רָאָה) "see" (Exod 20:18; 20:22; 24:10). Additionally, when YHWH re-establishes his covenant with the Israelites, Israel is once again put into the position of witnesses because Israelites will observe what YHWH will do for them (Exod 34:10). Again, this position of witnesses requires a response: an obedience to his commandments.

3. Mosaic covenant

Without doubt, the Mosaic covenant is one of the central elements in the OT theology. And as we already observed, in terms of contexts, until this point in Exodus, the concept of witness appears only in the social context. But, when the Mosaic covenant comes into place, the covenantal or religious context becomes prominent. Within that context, we also encounter the legal or juridical context as a subset of that religious context. The theophany of YHWH at Sinai (Exod 19–24) was a testimonial event, and Israel was portrayed as an observing witness due to the fact that she had an opportunity to *šāmaʿ* (שָׁמַע) "listen" (Exod 19:9; 20:19; 24:27), and *rāʾāh* (רָאָה) "see" (Exod 20:18; 20:22; 24:10). When YHWH re-established his covenant with Israelites in Exodus 34, Israelites were once again put into the position of witness, because they would observe the things that YHWH would do for them (Exod 34:10).

The result of all of the Sinai event was that Israel entered into the covenantal relationship with YHWH. Israel must keep the covenant (condition), and the result will be community – *hāyāh* (הָיָה) "you will be" (Exod 19:5) (consequence). Based on this result, we concluded that in this instance, covenant conveyed revelation, revelation produced the community (relationship), and the community as recipient of revelation received mission. From that point on, we can speak of a group of people called Israel as "collective witness." Israel saw what YHWH did for them in Egypt, they witnessed his mighty hand, and they were put in the position of observing witnesses. Now, in accordance with the dynamic of witness, Israel should be a community which is faithful to YHWH's revelation and implements that revelation into every aspect of their existence. Thereby, they have the mission of making YHWH's revelation known to others. Hence, Israel as a community must also be a testifying witness.

4. Building of the Tabernacle

The building of the tabernacle (Exod 25:1–6) is another testimonial event. We have seen that the tabernacle was called the "tabernacle of the Testimony" because the two tablets of the Testimony were placed in it. But tabernacle was also a form of testimony because it was built according to the pattern which was shown to Moses on the mountain (Exod 25:9, 40; 26:30; 27:8) and commanded (Exod 31:11; 36:1; 39:7, 29, 43; 40:16). Bailey notices that *tabnîṯ* (תַּבְנִית) "the pattern" may be a heavenly pattern or it may refer to a concrete image. Hence, some would argue that the tabernacle reflects an actual, visible, celestial temple of which the earthly structure is a replica, or that this refers to some ideal, invisible archetypal form that is present in YHWH's mind and manifested to Moses.[5] In any case the tabernacle is designed as a repetition of something (an actual celestial temple or an ideal that is present in YHWH's mind), and the repetition of this prototype indicates the presence of the concept of witness.

5. Spying of the Promised Land

In the book of Numbers, the spying of the Promised Land was another event where we can see the dynamic presence of the concept of witness, although explicit words for witness are not present. Basically, spies are sent to *tûr* (תּוּר) "explore" (Num 13:2, 25), *rāʾāh* (רָאָה) "see" (Num 13:18), *dāḇār* (דָּבָר) "submit report" and *rāʾāh* (רָאָה) "show" the fruit of the land (Num 13:26). All twelve spies as eyewitnesses return to the camp, all have the same report, yet they differ on the course of action: whether to enter the Promised Land or not. Interestingly, in Numbers 14:10–14 Israel is presented as one who *nāʾaṣ* (נָאַץ) "disrespects" and does not *ʾāman* (אָמַן) "believe" YHWH, while unbelieving nations have *šāmaʿ* (שָׁמַע) "heard" (Num 14:13–14) that YHWH

5. Bailey, *Exodus*, 277–278.

is among Israelites, obviously a reference to the Egyptians.[6] Accordingly, YHWH will punish his people, for although they *rāʾāh* (רָאָה) "saw" YHWH's miracles they refused to *šāmaʿ* (שָׁמַע) "hear/obey" his *qôl* (קוֹל) "voice." The consequences will not be limited to those who were disobedient, but will also affect their children, since they all will have to wander in the desert.[7]

6. Book of Deuteronomy

The book of Deuteronomy is permeated with the concept of witness. Moses is a witness who recapitulates and repeats Israel's history to this new generation. Israel is presented as witness of YHWH's work because she *rāʾāh* (רָאָה) "saw" how YHWH guided them (Deut 1:31). However, since they did not have *ʾāman* (אָמַן) "confidence" in YHWH (Deut 1:32), their punishment will be that they will not *rāʾāh* (רָאָה) "see" the Promised Land (Deut 1:35). Accordingly, Israel is repeatedly portrayed as someone who:

- *rāʾāh* (רָאָה) "saw" YHWH's deeds: Deuteronomy 1:31; 3:21; 4:3, 9, 35; 5:24; 7:19; 10:21; 11:2; 29:2. Some of YHWH deeds will be repeated in the future (Deut 3:21; 4:3; 7:19), so they serve as a model for his work. *rāʾāh* (רָאָה) of YHWH's deeds should result in not "forgetting" (*šāḵaḥ* [שָׁכַח]) with their eyes, not "slipping away" (sûr [סוּר]) from their "hearth" (*lēḇāḇ* [לֵבָב]) but making them "known" (yāḏaʿ [יָדַע]) to their offspring (Deut 4:9); and "knowledge" (*yāḏaʿ* [יָדַע]) that YHWH is God. Accordingly, Deuteronomy refers often to people's *ʿayin* (עַיִן) "eyes": Deuteronomy 1:30; 3:21; 4:3, 6, 9, 34; 6:8, 22; 7:19; 10:21; 11:7.

---

6. Speaking of the Numbers 14:13 "But Moses said to Yahweh, 'If the Egyptians hear of it, for you did bring up this people in your might from among them, then they will tell the inhabitants of this land,'" Budd (*Numbers*, 150) says that this verse is best taken as the protasis (clause which expresses condition).

7. Karlberg (*EDBT*) says that the false report brought by the ten spies is a denial, because they know what is true, yet confessed a falsehood. Accordingly, "denial may take the form of deception, lying, or rejection of the truth on evidence to the contrary, as when the spies reported falsely about the land of Canaan." Leithart (*House for My Name, 100*) even connects the death of ten spies with their punishment for being false witnesses: "When God punishes Israel, His punishments are always just. They always fit the crime. The false spies accuse the land of murder (Num. 13:32), and they are killed as false witnesses against the land (Num. 14:36–37; cf. Deut 19:16–19)."

- *šāma*ʿ (שָׁמַע) "heard" his voice: Deuteronomy 4:10, 12, 36; 5:23, 24, 25, 26, 27. Because of everything, Israel is admonished to continue to *šāma*ʿ (שָׁמַע) YHWH's words (Deut 5:1; 6:3–4), but also these words must *hāyāh* (הָיָה) "be" in their hearts; they must be *šānan* (שָׁנַן) "impressed" (through repetition) on their children and *dāḇar* (דָּבַר) "spoken" to them; and *qāšar* (קָשַׁר) "tied" on their hands and foreheads (Deut 6:6–8).[8] Accordingly, Deuteronomy occasionally refers to people's "ears" *ʾōzen* (אֹזֶן): Deuteronomy 5:1; 29:4.
- possesses *yāḏa*ʿ (יָדַע) "knowledge" of YHWH: Deuteronomy 4:35, 39, 7:9; 8:5; 9:3, 6; 11:2; 29:3. Because of this knowledge, Israel must be careful not to *šāḵaḥ* (שָׁכַח) "forget":
  a) events: Deuteronomy 4:9,
  b) covenant: 4:23,
  c) YHWH: 6:12; 8:11, 14, 19,
  d) the rebellion in the wilderness: Deuteronomy 9:7,
  e) to destroy the name of Amalek: Deuteronomy 25:19.
  On the other hand, Israel must also *zāḵar* (זָכַר) "remember":
  a) slavery in Egypt: Deuteronomy 5:15; 15:15,
  b) what YHWH did to Pharaoh: Deuteronomy 7:18,
  c) how YHWH led them in the wilderness: Deuteronomy 8:2,
  d) YHWH: Deuteronomy 8:18,
  e) their rebellion in the wilderness: Deuteronomy 9:7
  and, f) what the Amalekites did: Deuteronomy 25:17.

Based on these duties of Israel, we conclude that Deuteronomy describes Israel as a recipient of YHWH's revelation, and hence, his witness. We see Moses who acts as a *mediator*, and through his speech repeats events from Israel's history. He is a *mediator* because he as an eyewitness addresses a new generation of Israelites (cf. Deut 2:14). The assumption is that most of the people who are present while Moses gives these introductory remarks (Deut 1–4) were not alive during most of the events that Moses addresses. Yet, throughout his speech, Moses says that they themselves "saw" and "heard"

8. Deuteronomy 6:20–24 combines both "seeing" and "hearing" as prerequisite for teaching children. Repetition of the stories and Israel's history in the context of teaching children is also present in Deuteronomy 26:5.

all these things – that is, they are eyewitnesses. The reason for this could be that some of them truly witnessed all these events; part of the reason could be ascribed to the collective identity that Jewish thought nurtures;[9] and part of the reason could be that Moses as a mediator through his testimony (that is, repetition of events) creates the witnessing community anew. So even those who were not eyewitnesses themselves are labelled as "witnesses" in the fullest sense of this word. But what is the importance of their position? Deuteronomy 2:25 speaks about other nations who will *šāma*ʿ (שָׁמַע) "hear" about Israel and fear them (something negative); Deuteronomy 4:6 tells that other nations will *šāma*ʿ (שָׁמַע) "hear" and see with their "eyes" (*ʿayin* [עַיִן]) the wisdom of YHWH in Israelites – hence, Israel is a model for other nations (something positive); and in Deuteronomy 28:10 nations will *rāʾāh* (רָאָה) "see" and fear them. Additionally, in Deuteronomy 4:32–44 YHWH invites Israel to conduct an investigation into the deeds of other gods and search for witnesses who will confirm that some other god did similar things as YHWH did for Israelites – again something very similar we have encountered in Isaiah 43–44.

As we follow from Exodus the story of Israel as a "collective witness," the book of Deuteronomy is highly important, because it provides additional confirmation of what will become explicit in Isaiah 43–44, that Israel is YHWH's "witness" (Isa 43:10, 12; 44:8). This observation is important for us because as we will deal with Acts 1:8, we will see that Jesus uses the same idea to address his community as witnesses.

7. Different examples of seeing, hearing, knowing and/or proclaiming

The text of Judges 11:10 speaks of YHWH as witness even though the specific technical term is not used. However, the construction *yhwh yihyeh šōmēa*ʿ *bênôṯênû* (יְהוָה יִהְיֶה שֹׁמֵעַ בֵּינוֹתֵינוּ) "YHWH will be the one who hears between us" is another way of saying that he will be the witness, since *šāma*ʿ (שָׁמַע) "hearing" is one qualification for a witness (cf. Lev 5:1). Likewise, Isaiah 16:6 also uses *šāma*ʿ (שָׁמַע) in reference to hearing

9. Even today Jewish rabbis speak in the first person saying: "When *we* were brought out of Egypt . . ." "When *we* were disobedient in the desert . . . ," etc.

about someone or something. Hence, we can consider this verse also as an example of witnessing.

In the 2 Kings we have a story of Elijah's ascension to heaven, and Elisha who was a witness of that event.[10] The story is interesting because Elijah promises that Elisha will receive a double portion of Elijah's spirit if he *rāʾāh* (רָאָה) "sees" Elijah's ascension (2 Kgs 2:10). Previously, we read that Elisha was aware that Elijah would be taken from the earth, because Elisha is the one who *yāḏaʿ* (יָדַע) "knows" that will happen (2 Kgs 2:3, 5). Likewise, the company of the prophets also possessed this "knowledge" (2 Kgs 2:3, 5). So "knowledge" of something in this case comes prior to "seeing." And in 2 Kings 2:12 this is exactly what happens: Elisha *rāʾāh* (רָאָה) "sees" Elijah's ascension, and now Elijah's spirit rests on Elisha.[11] The company of the prophets, on the other hand, became aware that Elijah's spirit is resting on Elisha when they *rāʾāh* (רָאָה) "saw" how the water of Jordan was divided (2 Kgs 2:15), yet they were not sure that Elijah truly ascended to heaven because they went to *bāqaš* (בָּקַשׁ) "seek" or "search" for him. So, the dynamic of the concept of witnessing is fascinating: we have knowledge

10. Speaking about the story of Elijah and Elisha in 2 Kings 2:1–18, Palmisano ("La testimonianza", *BV* 79 (2019): 1, 91) says the following: "Il passo costituisce anche un esempio di quanto alcuni testi biblici, pur non presentando il vocabolario lessicografico fondamentale della testimonianza, ne possa rivelare tratti significativi." ("The passage also provides an example of how some biblical texts, while lacking the basic lexicographic vocabulary of witnessing, can reveal significant traits of it.").

11. Speaking about the importance of the verb "to see" for Elisha's role of a witness, Palmisano ("Palmisano, "La testimonianza," *BV 79* (2019): 1,87*)* says the following: "Il vocabolario utilizzato per descrivere il passaggio di Elia nel primo passo (ai vv. 2.3.5) a mo' di anticipazione come 'portare via' (in hebr. √לקח, *lqh*) (usato anche per descrivere il rapimento al cielo di Enoc in Genesi 5,24 dove ha come soggetto Dio) viene espresso ora il 'salire' di Elia nel carro di fuoco. In questo contesto assume un ruolo particolare l'esperienza di Eliseo che è presente e 'vede' il passaggio di Elia, 'vede ilsuo scomparire' (Walsh 1992, 465): egli è quindi l'unico testimone di questo momento particolare. Il verbo chiave che ricorre in questo passo è infatti il verbo 'vedere' (in hebr. √ראה, *r'h*) (ricorrente tre volte tra i vv. 10 e 12) avente come oggetto sempre Elia. La presenza di Eliseo, quando Elia sale verso il mondo di Dio, fa di lui un particolare testimone della sua 'morte.'" ("The vocabulary used to describe Elijah's transition in the first passage (in vv. 2, 3, 5) by way of anticipation as 'to take away' (in hebr. √לקח, lqh) (also used to describe Enoch's rapture to heaven in Genesis 5:24 where the subject is God) is now expressed as Elijah's 'ascending' in the chariot of fire. In this context the experience of Elisha, who is present and 'sees' Elijah's passage, 'sees his disappearance' (Walsh 1992, 465) takes on a special role: he is thus the only witness to this particular moment. The key verb that recurs in this passage is in fact the verb 'to see' (in hebr. √ראה, r'h) (recurring three times between vv. 10 and 12) always having Elijah as its object. Elisha's presence as Elijah ascends to the world of God makes him a particular witness to his 'death.'").

prior to seeing (Elisha, the company of the prophets). Yet, some who see believe (Elisha), but some do not (the company of the prophets). But there is one difference between Elisha and the company of the prophets: Elisha is an eyewitness of the event of Elijah's ascension, the company of the prophets are not. They have seen the evidence of Elijah's spirit of Elisha, but they still did not believe that Elijah was gone to heaven.

Isaiah 41:20–21 is yet another example of witnessing, since YHWH's activity in verse 19 is done with the purpose that "all may see [*rā ʾāh* (רָאָה)] and know [*yāḏa ʿ* (יָדַע)], all may consider [*śîm* (שִׂים)] and understand [*śāḵal* (שָׂכַל)], that the hand of the LORD has done this, the Holy One of Israel has created it" (NRSV).

Several examples come from the book of Jeremiah. First, Jeremiah 4:16 *hazkîrû laggôyim hinēh hašmî ʿû ʿal-yᵊrûšālaim* (הַזְכִּירוּ לַגּוֹיִם הִנֵּה הַשְׁמִיעוּ עַל־יְרוּשָׁלִַם) "Tell the nations, "Here they are!" Proclaim against Jerusalem" (NRSV), contains two verbs connected with speech: *zāḵar* (זָכַר) "to name, to mention," and *šāma ʿ* (שָׁמַע) "to hear, to listen," and two referents: *laggôyim* (לַגּוֹיִם) "to the nations" and *ʿăl-yerûšālaim* (עַל־יְרוּשָׁלִַם) "to Jerusalem." Given the proximity between prophecy and witnessing, and the fact that two speech verbs are used in announcing future events, this text can be also counted as a form of witnessing. Second, in Jeremiah 7:12–15, YHWH invites people of Judah to go and *rā ʾāh* (רָאָה) "see" what he has done to Shiloh (v. 12). Then in verse 13, YHWH is presented as someone who *dāḇar* (דָּבַר) "spoke" and *qārā ʾ* (קָרָא) "called" repeatedly. In verses14–15, YHWH announces that he will repeat with Jerusalem what he did with Shiloh. Although these verses use no word for witness, the invitation to "see," the repeated mentions of speaking, and the announcement that YHWH will "repeat" his actions, reveals the presence of the concept of witness. In Jeremiah 12:3, YHWH is presented as one who *yāḏa ʿ* (יָדַע) "knows" and *rā ʾāh* (רָאָה) "sees" Jeremiah, which obviously presents YHWH as a witness. Third, in Jeremiah 44:2 YHWH addresses Jews living in Egypt, saying to them *ʾattem rᵊ ʾîṯem* (אַתֶּם רְאִיתֶם) "You saw." Usage of the verb *rā ʾāh* (רָאָה) "see" in this context implies that they were witnesses to YHWH's punishment. At the end of this speech in verses 29–30, YHWH announces in advance their punishment that he will give them *ʾôṯ* (אוֹת) "sign." The sign will be the repetition of a punishment from the past; the text uses the preposition *ka ʾăšer* (כַּאֲשֶׁר) "just as" "I am going to give Pharaoh Hophra, King of Egypt, into the hands of his enemies, those who seek his life, just as I gave King Zedekiah of Judah into the hand of King Nebuchadnezzar of Babylon." The end result will be that they will *yāḏa'* (יָדַע) "know" that YHWH's threats will be accomplished. And finally, in Jeremiah 51:24, YHWH announces that he will do something *lᵊ'ênêḵem* (לְעֵינֵיכֶם) "before your eyes." This detail confirms that they (YHWH's people) will now observe or witness YHWH's punishment over Babylon.

In Ezekiel 3:17 Ezekiel is described as the one who performs a role of *ṣāpāh* (צָפָה) "watchman." But more than that, he must *šāma'* (שָׁמַע) "hear, listen" to what YHWH is saying, and then *zāhar* (זָהַר) "warn" them. Listening and speaking or repeating what one has heard belongs into the category of witnessing. In Ezekiel 8, the prophet now has a similar role, but this time it is more connected with the activity of seeing. In Ezekiel 8:5 we find *'ayin* (עַיִן) "eye," and the verb *rā'āh* (רָאָה) "to see" in Ezekiel 8:6, 7, 9, 10, 12, 13, 15 and 17, all relating to the prophet's observations of the sins of his people and speaking strongly for Ezekiel's role as a witness. In chap 12 Ezekiel's role as a witness changes one more time. This time he is himself a *môpēṯ* (מוֹפֵת) "sign" (Ezek 12:6, 11) to the Israelites. By his actions, he acts out a future refugee crisis. YHWH's charge against his people "who have eyes to see but do not see, who have ears to hear but do not hear" (Ezek 12:2) is heightened by the fact that Ezekiel as *môpēṯ* (מוֹפֵת) "sign" is the message for people's "eyes" (*'ayin* [עַיִן]) (12:3, 4, 5, 6, 7). Finally, in Ezekiel 40:4 Ezekiel is charged to use his *'ayin* (עַיִן) "eyes" to *rā'āh* (רָאָה) "see" and his *'ōzen* (אֹזֶן) "ears" to *šāma'* (שָׁמַע) "hear," in order to *nāḡaḏ* (נָגַד) "tell." Obviously, Ezekiel first has to observe and then tell what he has heard and seen.

Two final examples are connected with the verb *'ānāh* (עָנָה). In Isaiah 3:9, the phrase *hakkāraṯ pᵊnêhem 'ānṯāh bām* (הַכָּרַת פְּנֵיהֶם עָנְתָה בָּם) lit. "the look on their faces answers against them," contains a combination of the verb *'ānāh* (עָנָה) "to reply to answer" + *bām* (בָּם) "against them," which implies that the answer in this verse must be understood as a form of testimony. Hence, the NRSV translates *'ānāh* (עָנָה) as "bears witness" and the NIV as "testifies." Similarly, Jeremiah 14:7 contains the combination of the verb *'ānāh* (עָנָה) and expression *ḇānû* (בָנוּ) "against us," which both the NRSV and NIV translate as "testify against us." In Hosea 5:5 the verb *'ānāh* (עָנָה) "to reply, to answer" is used together with *bᵊpānāyw* (בְּפָנָיו) "against his face," again pointing to witnessing. Hence, the NRSV translation of "Israel's pride testifies against him" is a proper one.

8. Conclusion

This limited analysis of the semantic range has confirmed that different words (mostly verbs) and actions can be loaded with ideas or carry the concept of witness. Accordingly, we have confirmed that witnesses can be designated based on the activities they perform (such as "hearing," "knowing," "speaking," etc.). This means that our definition of witness must also include references to the concept of witness from the semantic domain which do not use the technical terms. The results of this semantic analysis do not change our definition of the concept of witness but supplement and confirm it.

Semantic analysis also confirmed the importance of the temporal aspect to understanding the concept of witness, and further confirmed the importance of the transition between observing and testifying witness. A notable example is Israel, whose experience with YHWH first put her into the position of an observing witnesses whose task was to convey the knowledge of YHWH to other nations; this implies the position of a testifying witness. Following that line, we tracked the development of the idea of Israel as a community of witnesses with a particular mission. The crucial point in that development was the establishing of the Mosaic covenant, which we defined as a testimonial event in itself. This additionally demonstrated the ground shared by the concept of witness and concept of covenant. Also, in Deuteronomy Moses is the mediator who addresses a new generation of Israelites as an eyewitness and by his speech repeats events from Israel's history. This role also confirms our observation of the overlap between the position of a witness and that of a prophet.

We also confirmed the importance of repetition for the concept of witness in several ways. First, some of YHWH's past deeds will be repeated in the future, and they serve as a model for his work. Second, the activity of repetition permeates examples such as Moses' repetition of Israel's history in the book of Deuteronomy to a new generation of Israelites or building of the tabernacle in Exodus according to a model. Third, repetition has the power to transform those who were not eyewitnesses so that they become witnesses. So, in the book of Deuteronomy, Moses through his testimony as an eyewitness retells the story of the exodus to those who were not there when those events happened, and thus *creates* out of them a community of witnesses. Through Moses' testimony, they have now become witnesses.

Accordingly, in this example we can speak about the attribute of witness being imparted or transferred from one entity to another.

Finally, the idea that verbal witness sometimes requires or is supported by some form of visible manifestation is also confirmed in semantic analysis. In the case of the Mosaic covenant, testimony was both verbal and visible. By giving them tablets containing the Ten Words and by the making of the tabernacle and accompanying elements, YHWH's speech and revelation were also visibly expressed or realized. When YHWH revealed to Moses his plan for deliverance in Exodus 4, Moses was sent as a man with both the *message* and the promise that his message/testimony would be confirmed with *pālāʾ* (פָּלָא) "wonders" (Exod 3:20), and *ʾôṯ* (אוֹת) "signs" (Exod 4:8, 30). Something similar, we will encounter in Luke/Acts.

CHAPTER 7

Introduction to the Concept of Witness in the New Testament

As we have analyzed the aspects of the concept of witness in the OT, a certain *model* of the concept of witness has emerged out of our analysis. In the OT, witnesses can be divided according to their ontological categories (impersonal and personal). The concept of witness in the OT: a) appears in three complementary contexts (social, legal and covenantal), b) has two primary types of activity, observing and testifying, c) has three different modes (of, for or against, and about), in accordance with its temporal aspect, and d) maintains a distinction between "witness" and "testimony." In order to see how the NT reflects or develops the concept of witness, from this chapter forward, we will compare the NT materials to this model. In this chapter our attention will be given to the etymology, occurrence, semantic range and usage of the particular Greek words that NT uses to refer to the concept of witness. In chapter eight we will analyze the concept of witness in various parts of the NT. In chapter nine we will analyze the dynamic of the concept of witness in the NT through the semantic range of key terms. In chapter ten, we will offer a synthesis of these results, and in chapter eleven, we will use these findings to study the concept of witness in the Lukan writings.

1. Etymology

The most important word for the NT concept of witness is μάρτυς. Μάρτυς with its cognates probably comes from the Indo-European root *smer* which means "to bear in mind, to remember, to be careful." Based on the etymology,

Strathmann[1] argues that witness is "probably 'one who remembers, who has knowledge of something by recollection, and who can thus tell about it,' i.e., the witness." Regarding the meaning of other cognates, the verb μαρτυρέω denotes a state or habitual activity, but can often take on trans, significance. Thus, it can mean "be a witness, come forward as a witness, bear witness to something." The noun μαρτυρία has in the first instance an abstract significance: "the bearing of witness," but it can then refer to the witness thus borne. Μαρτύριον is more concrete and denotes witness from the more objective standpoint as the proof of something. Any μαρτυρία can become a μαρτύριον, but the converse is not true.

2. Occurrence, semantic range and usage

2.1. Occurrence

The masculine noun μάρτυς occurs in the NT thirty-five times: five times in Synoptics (Matt 2, Mark 1, Luke 2), and most frequently in Acts: thirteen times. In Paul's writings it occurs nine times (six outside the Pastorals), in Hebrews twice, in 1 Peter once, and five times in Revelation. In the Gospel of John and 1–3 John, μάρτυς is absent even though the subject of witnessing is not absent.[2] The verb μαρτυρέω appears seventy-six times in the NT: sixty-three times in the active and thirteen times in the passive voice. It occurs most often in John (thirty-three times) and 1–3 John (ten times). Acts has eleven occurrences, Hebrews eight, Paul outside the Pastorals five, Revelation four, the Pastorals two, and in Matthew, Luke, and Colossians.[3] The feminine noun μαρτυρία appears thirty-seven times in the NT: four times in the Synoptics (three in Mark and one in Luke), fourteen in John, once in Acts, twice in Pastorals, seven times in 1 and 3 John, and nine times in Revelation. Hence, approximately a third of its uses in the NT are in the Gospel of John, and more than a third are in 1 John, 3 John, and Revelation.[4] The neuter noun μαρτύριον appears twenty times (nineteen times if we do not count 1 Cor

1. Strathmann, "Martus", *TDNT 4: 475.*
2. Beutler, "μαρτυς", *EDNT 2: 394.*
3. Beutler, "μαρτυρεω, διαμαρτύρομαι, μαρτύρομαι", *EDNT 2: 389.*
4. Beutler, "μαρτυρία", *EDNT 2: 392.*

2:1): nine times in the Synoptics, twice in Acts, six times in Pastorals, and once in Hebrews, James and Revelation.[5]

2.2 Semantic range and usage

The noun *μάρτυς* usually refers to a person (e.g. Acts 1:22; 22:15) or group (e.g. Acts 1:8) who provide testimony (e.g. Acts 1:22; 22:15).[6] Accordingly, *μάρτυς* "is not a mere eyewitness, simply present at a happening; he is active . . . called upon to tell what he has seen and heard, to proclaim what he knows."[7] In the original sense *μάρτυς* describes a person who is a witness to facts, i.e. the man who can speak about them from his own direct knowledge, especially in legal proceedings (e.g. Matt 26:65; Mark 14:63; Acts 6:13; 7:58).[8] References to a witness to facts can be found in general settings outside the judicial, for example when someone calls on God to be a witness to someone's processes and motives and no other factual witnesses are available to prove the veracity and authenticity of such claims (Rom 1:9; 2 Cor 1:23; Phil 1:8; 1 Thess 2:5, 10). There is also a sense where the activities of witnessing to facts and witnessing as evangelistic confession come together; the witness proclaims what he or she believes.[9] In summary, *μάρτυς* can signify (1) a witness to ascertainable facts: (a) legally (Matt 26:65), (b) generally, as one who testifies to something (Rom 1:9); (2) a witness who declares facts directly known to himself: (a) from first-hand knowledge (Acts 1:22) or, (b) from first-hand experience (Heb 12:1); (3) witness who tells what he believes (convictions), even though it results in his being killed for his *witness* (*martyr*) (Acts 1:8; Rev 17:6).[10] Speaking of the confessional aspect of witness, *μάρτυς* is also used to describe those who have suffered death in consequence of confessing Christ (of Stephen, Acts 22:20; of Antipas, Rev

---

5. Beutler, 2: 393.

6. Taylor, "testimony", *LTW*

7. Spicq and Ernest, *TLNT, 2:448.*

8. Strathmann, "Martus", *TDNT 4: 489.*

9. "These missionary-preachers are not content to tell about the deeds and words of Jesus—and this is where their testimony differs from a legal witness—they express their personal conviction and identify with the cause that they defend. In proclaiming of the Lordship of Jesus, they make public confession of their faith. It is not simply a matter of reporting facts—which need to be interpreted—but of speaking and vindicating the truth, of somehow insisting on doing it justice" (Spicq and Ernest, *TLNT 2:449*).

10. Friberg, Friberg and Miller, *BGNTL 254.*

2:13; see Rev 17:6), but this should not be understood as if their witness consisted only of their suffering death. Rather their witnessing about Jesus became the cause of their death. Furthermore, the plural μάρτυρες is used of those who announce the facts of the gospel and proclaim that gospel (Acts 2:32; 3:15; 10:39, 41; 13:31; Rev 11:3).[11]

The verb μαρτυρέω describes the activity of the μάρτυς. Accordingly, it is used for: (1) human declaration of ascertainable facts or events based on first-hand knowledge or experience: "bear witness to, declare, confirm." In that sense μαρτυρέω is not used for legal witness (cf. Matt 23:31; John 2:25; Acts 22:5; Rom 10:2; 1 Cor 15:15; 2 Cor 8:3; Gal 4:15; etc.). Furthermore, μαρτυρέω can refer to future events (cf. John 13:21) or to the general fact of experience (cf. John 4:44); (2) absolutely, of a good report - in an active ("give a good report, speak well (of)," "approve (of)" (Luke 4:22)) or passive sense ("receive a good report, be well-spoken of, be approved, have a good reputation" (Acts 6:3; 1 Tim 5:10)). The idea behind this use is that the person(s) can be vouched for on the basis of direct observation; (3) an emphatic declaration by an existing authority, such as God, the Spirit, Scripture with meanings such as: "testify, declare, witness (solemnly)." This special group of witnesses guarantees judgments or statements (cf. Acts 13:22; 14:3; Heb 7:8, 17; 11:2, etc.); (4) religious witness to truth and the factual content of the gospel as revealed truth from God: "be a witness, tell about, testify" (cf. Acts 23:11). In this sense, witnesses testify about divinely established facts and their witness is to revealed truth.[12]

If we observe how different NT writers use μαρτυρέω, we can see that:

a) in Matthew the word has a legal significance: the scribes witness against themselves that they are the sons of those who murdered the prophets (Matt 23:31);

b) Luke prefers a figurative meaning for the word (cf. Luke 4:22), and the same is true in Acts (God "spoke to David testifying" (13:22), "all the prophets bore witness" of Jesus (10:43), God "bore witness for the word of his grace with signs and wonders" (14:3)). Acts frequently uses the passive voice with meaning that someone "has received a good witness" or "has a

11. Zodhiates, *WSNTDICT*

12. Friberg, Friberg and Miller 2000, 4:253–254; Strathmann, "mártys", *TDNT 1:567–568.*

good reputation" (Acts 6:3 – the seven; 10:22 – Cornelius; 16:2 – Timothy; 22:12 – Ananias);[13]

c) In John witness is given not specifically to the facts of Jesus's history, but to the person of Jesus (John 1:15; 5:31ff.; 8:13ff.) as the eternal Son of God (John 1:15, 34). Accordingly, the Baptist has come to bear witness to the incarnate Logos as the light (John 1:8; cf. 8:12); witness to the truth is witness to him (John 3:26; 5:32–33); witness to Jesus is given by the Baptist (John 1:7–8), by Scripture (John 5:39), by God (John 5:32), by his works (John 5:36), by himself (John 8:13–14), and later by the Spirit (John 15:26) and by his disciples (John 15:27), etc. Since witness in John is equated with confession, the author of John and 1 John stress eyewitness (1 John 1:1–2). But witness in the Johannines is not limited to eyewitnesses and can be given by those who confess who Jesus was and what he signified. In the four occurrences in Revelation this term does not signify those who are put to death for their witness, but refers to bearing witness to the prophetic word (Rev 1:2; 22:20) or bearing witness to the threat which protects the prophecy (22:18);[14]

d) in Paul's writings we can find several usages of *μαρτυρέω*: a stronger forensic use is found in Paul's defence speeches in Acts 26:5 (all Jews know his conduct and can bear witness to it), and Acts 22:5 (he persecuted the Christian "way," as the high priest and the high council can attest). Possibly, Acts 23:11 has the same forensic note ("As you have testified of me, at Jerusalem, so you must also testify in Rome"); in an absolute sense for an assertion (2 Cor 8:3) or in the sense of "witness something to someone" (Rom 10:2; Gal 4:15; cf. Col 4:13); scriptural "witness" is familiar to Paul since the righteousness of God is "witnessed by the Law and the Prophets" (Rom 3:21);

e) in Hebrews witness involves various ways of a divine "attestation" or "confirmation": words of Scripture, in which *μαρτυρέω* is constructed in the passive either in a personal (e.g. Heb 7:8) or impersonal way (e.g. Heb 7:17); in Hebrew 10:15 the author refers to himself and credits the witness of Scripture to the Spirit; in chapter 11 the "witness" received by the forefathers and the faithful people of Israel is explicitly described as a witness of God (v. 4): the acceptable sacrifice of Abel (cf. Gen 4:4) was a "witness" that he

13. Beutler, "*μαρτυρεω, διαμαρτύρομαι, μαρτύρομαι*", *EDNT* 2: 389–390.

14. Strathmann, "mártys", *TDNT* 1: 567–568.

was just (Heb 11:4, nom. with inf.), and Enoch "received the witness [from Scripture] that he was pleasing to God" (Heb 11:5).[15]

In grammatical constructions, μαρτυρέω with the accusative of the thing means attest, testify, likewise with ὅτι (John 4:44, etc.); with the dative of the person and ὅτι, μαρτυρέω means "testify something to someone" (John 3:28, etc.); the dative can also be a dative of disadvantage, "against someone" (Matt 23:31); where μαρτυρέω stands with the true dative of the person (Luke 4:22), it means applaud a person, and where it stands with the dative of the thing, it means "bear witness for something" (only in John, 3 John, Acts 14:3). The passive voice can be used in a neutral sense, to say that something is "witnessed, testified," always in reference to Scripture (Rom 3:21; Heb 7:8, 17; 11:4), or in an evaluative sense, to say that someone "has received a good witness."[16]

The noun μαρτυρία describes either *someone* who gives testimony about something, or the *content* of the testimony. In John's writings where this noun appears predominantly, we can see these two usages: for example, John the Baptist in John 1:7 is identified as μαρτυρία, yet more often this noun applies to what such witnesses say: e.g. "the testimony (μαρτυρία) of John" (John 1:19). Outside of Johannine literature, μαρτυρία usually refers to the content of a testimony (e.g. Acts 22:18; Tit 1:13). Mark and Luke use it to refer to witnesses in court who testify to facts, i.e. the witness for the prosecution in the trial of Jesus (Mark 14:55–56, 59; Luke 22:71), and in 1 Timothy 3:7 it refers to a good report that overseer must have from outsiders.[17] Only in Acts 22:18 does the term have a specific religious and Christian reference, since μαρτυρία refers to evangelistic witness for the faith, and Christ is its content.[18] In the Johannine writings in John 8:17, and possible the first μαρτυρία in 1 John 5:9, signify human witness based on the principle of two or three witnesses (cf. Deut 17:6; 19:15). In 3 John 12 the word refers to the witness of a good Christian report regarding Demetrius. But in all other cases, μαρτυρία carries the specific religious and Christian meaning of an evangelistic witness to Christ's nature and significance which aims at faith.[19]

15. Beutler, "μαρτυρεω, διαμαρτύρομαι, μαρτύρομαι", *EDNT 2: 389–390.*

16. Beutler, 2: 389–390.

17. Taylor, "testimony", *LTW*

18. Strathmann, "*Martus*", *TDNT 4: 449.*

19. Strathmann, *TDNT 4: 449–502.*

The noun μαρτύριον can be used, first, for giving objective proof, and this may be seen in the phrase "for a testimony (or evidence) against" in James 5:3;[20] Mark 6:11, and cf. Mark 1:44–45.[21] Furthermore, we can say that witnessing against is present in Mark 13:9 as the disciples will bear testimony in the synagogues and before rulers, and in Matthew 24:14 preaching of the gospel will be a testimony to all nations - in the sense that a chance to believe may be offered, but it is also an evidence against someone in case of unbelief.[22] Second, it denotes "witness to something" with a genitive of subject[23] or object to which the statement relates.[24] In such instances μαρτύριον is equivalent to gospel, message, or teaching (cf. 1 Tim 2:6). Third, it has the active sense of attestation as in Hebrews 3:5 where Moses is described as a faithful servant who testified to what he received from God.[25]

There are other significant words for the concept of witness in the NT.

(1) The verb μαρτύρομαι appears five times in the NT. Three times comes with the dative of the person, and the meaning is "testify, attest." So, in Galatians 5:3, Paul "testifies" to everyone who is circumcised that he is bound to keep the whole Law (Gal 5:3), in Acts 20:26 Luke uses the same construction in relation to the elders of Ephesus, and in Acts 26:22 must "bear witness" before great and small. In Ephesians 4:17 and 1 Thessalonians 2:12 μαρτύρομαι carries the connotation of being emphatic in stating an opinion or desire – hence, "to insist" (NRSV, NIV).

---

20. "They would rather let their possessions rot than use them in works of mercy. Thus, the rust on their gold will be a witness for the prosecution against them on the day of judgment" (Strathmann, 4:503).

21. "If the cleansing is confirmed by the priest, this will be a severe indictment of the unbelief in which the people (αὐτοῖς) lingers still" (Strathmann, 4:503).

22. According to Strathmann (Strathmann, 4:503), in Mark 13:9 "the context the μαρτύριον, cannot be the evangelistic witness of missionary preaching, which offers the chance of conversion. The goal of this witness is to make opponents guilty," and for Matthew 24:14 "the reference is to the witness which makes the Gentiles guilty. Hence, we cannot translate: 'That they may be given a chance to believe.'"

23. 2 Corinthians 1:12 τὸ μαρτύριον τῆς συνειδήσεως ἡμῶν, "the testimony of our conscience"; 2 Thessalonians 1:10 τὸ μαρτύριον ἡμῶν "our testimony."

24. Acts 4:33 τὸ μαρτύριον . . . τῆς ἀναστάσεως "testimony . . . to the resurrection"; 1 Corinthians 1:6 τὸ μαρτύριον τοῦ Χριστοῦ "the testimony of Christ"; 1 Corinthians 2:1 τὸ μαρτύριον τοῦ θεοῦ "the testimony of God"; 2 Timothy 1:8 τὸ μαρτύριον τοῦ κυρίου "the testimony of the Lord."

25. Strathmann, "*mártys*", *TDNT* 1:569.

(2) διαμαρτύρομαι appears fifteen times in the NT, nine of which are in Acts. According to,[26] this verb describes "the act of making a declaration on the basis of personal knowledge." The usual meaning is "declare, assert, testify." Accordingly, in Acts, it refers to the apostles (including Paul) testifying about Jesus and the gospel (e.g. Acts 8:25; 10:42). Paul also says that the Holy Spirit "testifies" to him about the persecution that he will experience (Acts 20:23). In Hebrews 2:6 this verb refers to Scripture's testimony about Jesus. It can also mean "insist"[27] (Acts 2:40), "warn" (Luke 16:28) in a sense of testifying about negative consequences, and "charge" someone to do something (e.g. 1 Tim 5:21).[28]

(3) The verb συμμαρτυρέω appears three times in Romans (2:15; 8:16; 9:1) and has a meaning of "providing evidence by means of a testimony," that is, "bear witness with." Accordingly, it refers to confirming something by providing a supporting testimony, so Paul uses it of the following pairs: the Law and a person's conscience (Rom 2:15), the Spirit and the believer's spirit (Rom 8:16), and Paul's conscience and the Holy Spirit (Rom 9:1).[29]

(4) The verb συνεπιμαρτυρέω has a meaning of "testifying at the same time" or "adding further testimony, attest additionally."[30] This verb appears only in Hebrews 2:4.

(5) The verb καταμαρτυρέω describes the act of witnessing against someone, so it has a meaning of "testifying against." The verb appears three times in connection with Jesus's trials before the Sanhedrin and before Pilate: in Matthew 26:62 and Mark 14:60, the high priest asks Jesus whether he has an answer to what the false witnesses "testify against (καταμαρτυρέω)" him, and in Matthew 27:13, Pilate asks Jesus a similar question.[31]

(6) The verb ἐπιμαρτυρέω means "testify emphatically, appear as a witness decidedly for something."[32] This verb also appears only in 1 Peter 5:12 where it has a positive meaning of affirmation that something is true.

---

26. Taylor, "testimony", *LTW*.

27. "It is possible that διαμαρτύρομαι is somewhat stronger and more emphatic than μαρτύρομαι, but this cannot be shown from NT contexts" (Louw and Nida, *L&N* 1:412).

28. Swanson, *DBLG;* Taylor, "testimony", *LTW.*

29. Taylor, "testimony", *LTW*; Louw and Nida, *L&N* 1:417.

30. Newman, *Concise Greek-English Dictionary*, 173.

31. Taylor, "testimony", *LTW*

32. Zodhiates, *WSNTDICT*

(7) The verb προμαρτύρομαι describes the action of "stating with assurance what is to happen in the future - to predict, to foretell, hence it has a meaning "testify beforehand."[33] This verb occurs in 1 Peter 1:11 where Peter speaks about predicted sufferings of Christ.

The last three words fall into the category of antonyms to the concept of witness in the NT. As we have seen, Hebrews uses separate words that, when used in combination with words for witness, function as antonyms. In the Greek, the adjective ψευδής is added as a prefix to different root words thus creating antonyms.

(8) ψευδομαρτυρέω describes the act of providing a false witness, hence, it has a meaning "bear false witness."[34] In the NT, it occurs in Matthew 19:18; Mark 10:19; 14:56, 57; Luke 18:20 (and in some manuscripts of Rom 13:9) as a technical term for the act of bearing false witness.[35] Furthermore, such person may deceive in two aspects, "(1) in pretending to have been an eyewitness to an event and (2) in saying what is not true, but the focal element in ψευδομαρτυρέω is the fact that what is said is not true."[36]

(9) The noun ψευδόμαρτυς describes a person who testifies falsely – "false witness." It appears twice in the NT: Matthew 26:60 and 1 Corinthians 15:15, and according to Louw and Nida:

> The focal element in the evidence provided by "a false witness" is the fact that what is said is not true. It is also possible that such a person has pretended to have been present and thus an eyewitness of an event, but that is not the focus of the meaning. In fact, a false witness may have been present but at the same time may later provide false evidence as to what took place. It is possible to render ψευδόμαρτυς in some languages as "one who pretends to know about something but is really lying in what he says" or "one who lies about what he pretends to have seen.[37]

---

33. Louw and Nida, *L&N 1:420*.
34. Taylor, "testimony", *LTW*
35. Taylor, *LTW*
36. Louw and Nida, *L&N 1:417*.
37. Louw and Nida, 1:417.

(10) The noun ψευδομαρτυρία describes the content of what is testified falsely – "false testimony."[38] In the NT it appears twice: in Matthew 15:19 and 26:59.

3. Preliminary remarks

3.1 Spatial dimension of the concept of witness

As in the OT, the spatial dimension for the context of witnessing also appears in two directions: *vertical* (from YHWH to men) and *horizontal* (from men to men). First, the primary expression of the vertical dimension of witnessing in the OT was the Mosaic covenant. In the NT, however, especially in the light of the Gospel of John, the primary expression is the incarnation of Jesus. He was with God (John 1:1), he is "from above" (John 3:31), and he came to this earth to show us the Father (cf. John 14:8–11). In that sense, Jesus's person is the primary expression of the vertical dimension of witnessing. The book of Revelation continues in the same direction by showing Jesus who is now exalted in heaven yet continues to reveal to his servants what will happen in the future. In that sense, the angel of the Lord who mediates this revelation (Rev 1:1; 22:16) can also be put in this vertical dimension of witnessing.

Second, God himself acts as a witness in several ways. Occasionally, God can be invoked as a witness in the form of oath to confirm something (Rom 1:9; 2 Cor 1:23; Phil 1:8; 1 Thess 2:5, 10). In such instances, God is not a witness in a judicial sense (as part of judicial inquiry in the court of justice); this idea probably springs from the OT practice of calling on God as witness between parties (Josh 22:27; 1 Sam 12:5; Jer 42:5).[39] Furthermore, God can act as witness and his testimony can be given: a) in the Scripture (Acts 13:22; Heb 11:2, 4, 5, 39); b) through miracles (Acts 14:3; Heb 2:4); c) by giving of the Holy Spirit (Acts 15:8; Heb 2:4). In some instances, the specifics of God's testimony are not clearly stated or defined (John 5:32, 36, 37; 8:18; 1 John 5:9, 10, 11).

Third, the Holy Spirit is also designated as witness: a) he testifies about things that will happen in the future (Acts 20:23); b) together with other

38. Louw and Nida, 1:417.

39. Fee, *Philippians*, 94.

entities he provides testimony (in Rom 8:16 with human spirit and in Rom 9:1 together with human conscience); c) the Spirit's testimony can be found in the Scripture (Heb 10:15); d) his activity is sometimes described generically, in which case it is hard to define (Acts 5:32; 1 John 5:6, 7). In 3 John 1:12 "Truth" appears as a witness. Truth here is personified and can be identified with either God, Christ or the Spirit.[40]

Fourth, we have several entities that are rarely mentioned as witnesses. In the OT, the Scripture is many times referred to as a witness. In the NT, however, Scripture is referred to as witness only a few times (Acts 10:43; Rom 3:21; Heb 7:8, 17). The Scripture, especially in Hebrews, is the means through which testimony is given by God, Spirit or men. Furthermore, while the tabernacle in the OT is sometimes referred to as a form of testimony, in the NT it is only referred to in this way twice (Acts 7:44 and Rev 15:5. Acts 7:44 refers to tabernacle in the time of Moses; Rev 15.5 refers to the heavenly tabernacle.) Finally, the angel of the Lord who appears in Revelation 1:1 is explicitly designated in Revelation 22:16 as one who testifies to the revelation of Jesus Christ.

The *horizontal* dimension of witnessing (from men to men) in the NT is concerned primarily with religious truths. Disciples are the primarily subjects of witnessing:

a) they testify about historical facts concerning Jesus, but also interpret the meaning, significance and importance of these events, as well as his person,

b) sometimes their position of witnesses gives them an opportunity to warn or admonish other believers (1 Pet 5:1; 5:5),

c) testimony can be given to confirm a particular person, ministry, teaching, behaviour, etc. (1 Tim 6:12; 2 Tim 2:2; 3 John 1:3, 12),

d) sometimes their testimony appears in tandem with other entities: e.g. in 1 Thessalonians 2:10 the readers and God testify together for Paul and his team; in 3 John 1:12 the believers, John and his company, together with "truth" testify regarding another believer (Demetrius),

e) in Hebrews 12:1 we have a unique situation where deceased believers testify to living believers through the means of Scripture,

f) in Hebrews 2:6 the author introduces an OT quotation with the formula "someone said somewhere." It is unclear who "somebody" is, but the

40. Smalley, *1, 2, 3 John*, 361.

quotation is from the Scripture (Ps 8). The speaker could be any of three separate entities: the psalmist, Scripture, or God (since he is the one who speaks through Scripture),

g) finally, in 1 Peter 1:11 Peter introduces OT prophets as witnesses about Jesus.

The second largest group are "outsiders" who are not part of the believing community, yet they appear in multiple roles as witnesses:

a) those who are not designated as Jesus's disciples testify about Jesus (Matt 8:4; Mark 1:44; Luke 5:14; John 4:39),

b) false witnesses appears on Jesus's trial and testify falsely against him (Matt 26:59, 60, 62, 65; 27:13; Mark 14:55, 56, 57, 59, 60, 63; Luke 22:71; John 18:23),

c) false witnesses also appear at the disciples' trials: Acts 6:13; 7:58. In Acts 22:5 and 26:5 Paul refers to witnesses who can testify to Paul's past behaviour, and in this context they are not labelled as false witnesses,

d) a common OT quotation refers to establishing facts by the testimony of two or three witnesses (Matt 18:16; 2 Cor 13:1; 1 Tim 5:19; Heb 10:28),

e) an OT commandment against false witnessing is repeated several times (Matt 15:19; 19:18; Mark 10:19; Luke 18:20),

f) men can testify about the reputation of others (Acts 6:3; 10:22; 16:2; 22:12; 1 Tim 3:7; 5:10). Also Luke 4:22 can be put in this category although we are not sure whether the speaking about Jesus is positive or negative,

g) occasionally, people can testify against themselves (Matt 23:31; Luke 11:48),

h) we have one example where a pagan prophet is said to testify about his people (Titus 1:13) and,

i) in Luke 16:28 we have a parable testimony in the form of warning, when a dead man requests a warning for those still alive.

The NT refers to witness coming from unexpected entities. First, conscience functions as witness in Romans 2:15; 9:1 and 2 Corinthians 1:12. Determining whether conscience's witness in the NT is horizontal or vertical is not easy; in Romans 9:1, conscience is paired with the Holy Spirit. But since conscience is part of men, we will treat its testimony as horizontal witness. Second, Paul in Romans 8:16 seems to mention the human spirit as a witness. As with conscience, we will treat this testimony as horizontal witness. Third, the corrosion of wealth is portrayed in James 5:3 as form of testimony against rich people who are unjust. Lastly, water and blood from 1 John 5:7 probably refer to historical events from Jesus's life, and we will treat them as horizontal witnesses as well.

Finally, although we see men giving testimony to God in the OT, this type of testimony (vertical testimony from men to God) is not found in the NT, unless we consider for example, genitives like τὴν μαρτυρίαν Ἰησοῦ Χριστοῦ "testimony of Jesus Christ" from Revelation as objective genitives. Instead of the more common "testimony about Jesus" (although this is an objective genitive meaning), this can be read as "testimony given to Jesus."

3.2 Contexts of witnessing

We have seen in the OT that the majority of the texts that speak about witnessing appear in the context of Israel's theocracy, which was established with the Sinai covenant. Consequently, we have defined three contexts: social, covenantal (religious) and legal, which differ yet function in complementary ways. In the NT the concept of witness begins with Jesus in the Gospels among Israelites who, although under Roman occupation, were still people of the covenant, and for that matter still a theocratic nation. But Jesus creates a new community which consists of all those Jews and gentiles who accept him as Lord and Saviour. Accordingly, we do not talk about *one* separate "nation under God" where every aspect of life is under YHWH's rule (theocracy), but instead a new community which lives in the world as strangers, with ultimate allegiance to the God of Israel. For that matter, we can still detect three different contexts similar to those in the OT yet with minor differences.

First, in the OT we have defined the social context as a context in which people managed their affairs as they saw fit, with responsibility toward YHWH or other gods yet their actions were not strictly prescribed or defined by those deities (pre-theocratic period). In the OT this context primarily appears prior to the Sinai covenant. In the NT, however, it is difficult to see this social context standing alone. For example, texts such as Acts 6:3; 10:22; 16:2 and 22:12, mention individuals who have "good reputation." What "good reputation" means depends on the community's shared values. In these verses, however, the community's values are strongly embedded in religious values. Hence, the context in these cases is double: both social and religious. The situation in 1 Timothy 3:7 differs slightly, because those who offer their testimony about individuals are "outsiders," who do not belong to the same community of faith as those who are being testified for. The context in Luke 4:22 is difficult because it is not clear whether people offered positive or negative testimony regarding Jesus and what their testimony was based on.

Second, unlike in the OT, the covenantal context in the NT is better defined as *religious*. In the OT, the covenantal context operates in distinct nation which is based on a covenant relationship with YHWH. This covenant relationship continues in the NT with the establishment of the New Covenant and formation of new *ecclesia* containing both Jews and gentiles who believe in Jesus as Messiah. This new *ecclesia* lives in an environment which is hostile toward her and where outside standards of life are often not defined by YHWH. Although this *ecclesia* is ruled by YHWH, the societies in which this new community live (social life, customs, manners, legislative, etc.), are not ruled by YHWH and often hostile toward her. Hence, it is better to see the covenantal context as religious.

Still, the overlap between legal or juridical and religious/covenantal contexts which we encountered in the OT exists in the NT as well. First, believers are on trial in examples such as Matthew 10:18; Mark 13:9; Luke 21:13; Acts 22:20; 26:22. In John 18:37 Jesus himself is on trial. Hence, witnessing occurs in the legal context, although Jesus and the disciples are judged because of religious truths/claims. Accordingly, their testimony is primarily about, and not so much for or against, although in the legal context all such testimonies (no matter what is the charge) are considered as testimonies for or against. In the context of Jesus's trial and the trials of his disciples, we also have witnesses or testimonies for and against: Matthew 26:59, 60, 62, 65; 27:13; Mark 14:55, 56, 57, 59, 60, 63; Luke 22:71 are examples of such witnesses at Jesus's trial and Acts 6:13; 7:58 at disciples' trials. In John 18:23 Jesus requests that the court provide testimony against him, and twice in Acts 22:5 and 26:5, Paul declares that there are witnesses who can testify in his favor (that is, for him) about his conduct as a Jew. Secondly, texts such as Matthew 15:19; 19:18; Mark 10:19; Luke 18:20 repeat OT commands against false testimony. Since Israel's laws are also the product of Mosaic covenant, overlap is also present there. Similarly, texts such as John 8:17; 2 Corinthians 13:1; 1 Timothy 5:19 or Hebrews 10:28 repeat the OT stipulation for minimum two or three witnesses to establish a verdict.

3.3 Ontological categories of witnesses

The same ontological category that we saw in the OT, with a division between *personal* and *impersonal* entities, is present in the NT as well.

3.3.1 Personal entities as witnesses

In the NT as in the OT, the primary personal entities that function as witnesses are humans. God/Jesus/the Spirit appear more prominently as witnesses in the NT than in the OT: This is a logical effect of Jesus's incarnation. But numerically speaking, their testimony is in a minority.

- People: Matthew 8:4; 10:18; 15:19; 18:16; 19:18; 23:31; 24:14; 26:59, 60, 62, 65; 27:13; Mark 1:44; 6:11; 10:19; 13:9; 14:55, 56 (2x), 57, 59, 60, 63; Luke 4:22; 5:14; 9:5; 11:48; 16:28; 18:20; 21:13; 22:71; 24:48; John 1:7 (2x), 8, 15, 19, 32, 34; 2:25; 3:26, 28, 32 (2x), 33; 4:39; 5:33; 8:13, 17; 12:17; 15:27; 19:35 (2x); 21:24; Acts 1:8, 22; 2:32, 40; 3:15; 4:33; 5:32; 6:3, 13; 7:58; 8:25; 10:22, 39, 41, 42; 13:31; 16:2; 18:5; 20:21, 24, 26; 22:5, 12, 15, 18, 20; 23:11 (2x); 26:5, 16, 22; 28:23; Romans 10:2; 1 Corinthians 1:6; 2:1; 15:15 (2x); 2 Corinthians 8:3; 13:1; Galatians 4:15; 5:3; Ephesians 4:17; Colossians 4:13; 1 Thessalonians 2:10, 12; 4:6; 2 Thessalonians 1:10; 1 Timothy 2:6; 3:7, 10; 5:10, 19, 21; 6:12; 2 Timothy 1:8; 2:2, 14; 4:1; Titus 1:13; Hebrews 10:28; 12:1; 1 Peter 1:11; 5:1; 5:12; 1 John 1:2; 4:14; 5:9; 3 John 1:3, 6, 12 (3x); Revelation 1:2; 2:13; 6:9; 11:3, 7; 12:11, 17; 17:6; 19:10; 20:4
- Jesus: John 3:11; 4:44; 5:31 (2x); 5:34, 36, 39; 7:7; 8:14 (2x), 18; 10:25; 13:21; 15:26; 18:23, 37; 1 Timothy 2:6; Hebrews 2:6; 3:5; 3 John 1:12; Revelation 1:2, 5, 9; 3:14; 22:18, 20
- Father: John 5:32 (2x), 37; 8:18; Acts 13:22; 14:3; 15:8; Romans 1:9; 2 Corinthians 1:23; Philippians 1:8; 1 Thessalonians 2:5, 10; Hebrews 2:4; 11:2, 4, 5, 39; 1 John 5:9 (2x), 10 (2x), 11
- Holy Spirit: Acts 5:32; 20:23; Romans 9:1; Hebrews 10:15; 1 John 5:6, 7
- Angel: Revelation 22:16

3.3.2 Impersonal entities as witnesses

The list of impersonal witnesses in the NT is significantly shorter than that for the OT. The most prominent is Scripture, yet Scripture is not presented as witness nearly as often as it is in the OT. We have seen above that in some verses (Acts 13:22; Heb 10:15; 11:2, 4, 5, 39), Scripture is presented as the means or forum by which YHWH, or the Holy Spirit testify. Yet in other texts (Acts 10:43; Rom 3:21; Heb 7:8, 17), Scripture stands alone as a witness. When Peter mentions "prophets" in Acts 10:43, it is not clear whether he means the people, the collection of their writings, or both. In Romans 3:21 "Scripture" refers to the Law and prophets. But in all these verses we can argue for triple authorship because the Scriptures were given and inspired by God, inspired people declared them, and then their words were put in written form.

We also see two witnesses which come from the human inner being: the human conscience and spirit. It is difficult to classify them as personal or impersonal entities, yet here we will treat them as impersonal witnesses. Furthermore, a person's "works" as witness are difficult to define, because "works" might refer to miracles (cf. Acts 14:3; Heb 2:4; Rev 11:7) but can also refer to a person's entire life. But if we take "works" in the context of John 5:36, where Jesus refers to miracles, then although Jesus as personal witness is the one who is performing them, in this context they are detached from him to become independent witnesses for him and fall into the category of impersonal witness. Finally, in 1 John 5:8, if water and blood refer to Jesus's baptism and death, then although Jesus is the subject of these actions or events, the focus is on how these two historical events testify about Jesus. Hence, we will also consider them as impersonal witness. The complete list of impersonal entities as witnesses is as follows:

- Scripture: Acts 10:43; Romans 3:21 (Law and Prophets); Hebrews 7:8, 17
- Conscience: Romans 2:15; 9:1; 2 Corinthians 1:12
- Human spirit: Romans 8:16
- Tabernacle: Acts 7:44; Revelation 15:5
- Works: John 5:36
- Corrosion: James 5:3
- Water and blood: 1 John 5:8
- Miracles: Acts 14:3; Hebrews 2:4; Revelation 11:7

CHAPTER 8

The Concept of Witness in the New Testament – Passage Analysis

1. The concept of witness in Matthew and Mark – passage analysis

1.1 Μάρτυς in Matthew and Mark

In Matthew and Mark *μάρτυς* appears in Matthew 18:16; 26:65 and Mark 14:63. Matthew 18:16 deals with church discipline in a case when one believer (the offender) sins against another believer (the offended).[1] As part of the rebuke, the offended party is required to bring two or three witnesses with him. It is not clear whether these witnesses are witnesses to the rebuke or eyewitnesses to the transgression. If to the rebuke, then these witnesses are "invited to sit with two people who are seeking to settle a personal or private sin . . . that the witnesses did not themselves see. They become witnesses through this procedure."[2] The idea of taking two or three witnesses comes from Deuteronomy 19:15[3] which regulates evidence in a court of law. Here,

1. Leon Morris (*Gospel According to Matthew*, 466–467) says: "There is a difficult textual problem as to whether we should read *against you* or omit the words. If we accept them, Jesus is referring to what to do when another believer (*a brother;* see on 1:2) does something that we can only regard as sin against us, as wronging us in some way. If not, he is speaking of what we are to do when another believer sins in any way. In either case we are first to take the matter up with the sinner."

2. *Knight, Pastoral Epistles*, 235.

3. Speaking of Deuteronomy 19:15 in the LXX Hagner (*Matthew 14–28*, 532) says: "Matthew abbreviates the LXX by replacing the repeated *καὶ ἐπὶ στόματος τριῶν μαρτύρων*,

however, we have this same idea in a different context. Does this command (Deut 19:15) still carry the force of command in a different context, or is it just a principle which can be applied in different contexts? Regardless, it is interesting that the "mouths"[4] of the witnesses are prominent. Hence, *ἵνα ἐπὶ στόματος* or "on the mouth" of two witnesses or three, *πᾶν ῥῆμα* (which the NRSV reads as "every word," and the NIV as "every matter") must be established. Possible interpretations of *ῥῆμα* are a) the charge brought against the brother or b) the discussion (everything that is said) between parties. The second interpretation is probably correct because the witnesses' presence protects the sinner on one hand (the offended may well be wrong), and (on the other hand) the witnesses can confirm everything that was said.[5]

Μάρτυς occurs in Matthew 26:65 and Mark 14:63 in the context of Jesus's trial. After Jesus responded to the charges (Matt 26:64), the high priest tore his clothes and concluded that there was no need for more *μάρτυς* "witnesses" (Matt 26:65). Similarly, after Jesus declares himself to be the Son of Man in Mark 14:62, the high priest in verse 63 ironically concludes (from Mark's viewpoint) that there is no need for further *μάρτυς*, even though the witnesses against Jesus at his trial are from the beginning false witnesses, and their testimony is false testimony.

1.2 Μαρτύριον in Matthew and Mark

In Matthew and Mark *μαρτύριον* appears in Matthew 8:4; 10:18; 24:14; Mark 1:44; 6:11; 13:9. Matthew 8:4 and Mark 1:44 tell the story of Jesus healing a leper. After the healing, Jesus sends the man to a priest to examine and confirm his healing. As Nolland[6] explains, despite the elimination of the medical condition, the man would remain ritually unclean until the priestly examination and temple offering described in Leviticus 14:1–32. But what is the meaning of *εἰς μαρτύριον αὐτοῖς* "as a testimony to them" in these two verses? According to Hagner, this expression can be interpreted in several

'and by the mouth of three witnesses,' with *ἢ τριῶν*, 'or three,' and alters the verb *σταθήσεται*, 'shall stand,' to the subjunctive *σταθῇ*, 'may stand,' agreeing with the *ἵνα*, 'in order that.' Beyond these slight changes, the quotation is verbatim."

4. The NRSV translates *στόμα* "mouth" as "evidence," and the NIV as "testimony," which is another example where verbal testimony can be understood as "evidence."

5. *Newman and Stine, Matthew*, 571.

6. Nolland, *Matthew*, 350.

different ways: 1) as a witness to the priests or the people about Jesus's faithfulness to Torah, 2) as a witness against[7] the priests or the people (dative of disadvantage) that Jesus is indeed the Messiah, 3) as a testimony for the people (dative of advantage) concerning man's cleanness. Hagner rejects the first option, since in verse 3 Jesus commands this person to show himself to the "priest" (sg.) and in verse 4 this is a testimony to αὐτοῖς "them." Hagner also rejects the second option because it violates command to be silent about the healing. The third option is the most probable; the witness was necessary for this man's re-entry into society as fully clean and restored.[8]

On the other hand, Michael Green sees in this expression, "A testimony to what? To the fact that one greater than Moses had come; to the fact that what Judaism could not do, in cleansing from leprosy and from the disease of sin that it represented, the fulfiller of Judaism was doing. Here was no intrusion: it was the completion of all that Judaism pointed to. What a frontispiece for the book of miracles!"[9] France holds a similar view: "The command to *show yourself to the priest* . . . served as *a testimony to them* both of Jesus's respect for the Law and of his healing power as Messiah. But the balancing command *don't tell anyone* reminds us of the danger of attracting popular enthusiasm for the wrong reasons."[10] So, as we see, scholars are divided regarding the form and nature of testimony.

Several occurrences relate to witnessing for Christ. In Matthew 10:18 and Mark 13:9 Jesus talks about a future time when the disciples will be brought before the courts to bear witness for Christ. Matthew 24:14 and Mark 6:11 talk about witnessing for Christ in general. Matthew 10:18 and Mark 13:9 include the expression εἰς μαρτύριον αὐτοῖς "as a testimony to them." Nolland sees a comparison between Jewish and Roman justice systems behind this phrase.[11] He argues that submission to Jewish authority was a choice, but also necessary concomitant to membership in the Jewish community. Submission

7. The same expression occurs in Mark 6:11 in a hostile sense, and in Mark 13:9 in the context of opposition. Since priests later in the gospel are the one who take the lead in the opposition to Jesus, it is possible that the phrase εἰς μαρτύριον αὐτοῖς has a note of confrontation, with αὐτοί being the priestly establishment represented by the one ἱερεύς mentioned in verse 44 (France, *Mark*, NIGTC, 119–120).

8. Hagner, *Matthew 1–13*, 199–200.

9. Green, *Message of Matthew*, 115.

10. France, "Matthew", *New Bible Commentary*, 914–915 (emphasis original).

11. Nolland, *Matthew*, 424.

to the Roman authority was mandatory, and the Roman justice system was able to inflict more severe penalties than the Jewish authorities. However, in these cases the disciples would not be passive victims of the unjust use of the judicial system. Such trials, as part of the divine plan for mission, would give a perfect opportunity to offer witness. In any case, this expression signifies some purpose, even if the purpose is not explicitly stated. We can also take the phrase as referring to "testimony against them." Both texts say that εἰς μαρτύριον will happen ἕνεκεν ἐμοῦ "because of me [Jesus]," but this speaks only of the reason why they will be brought to trial. Their trials would be for the sake of Christ, and even their appearance in court serves as an act of witness.[12] Consequently, the content of their μαρτύριον would be the gospel of the kingdom mentioned in Matthew 10:10[13] (cf. Mark 13:10).[14]

In Matthew 24:14 εἰς μαρτύριον appears with πᾶσιν τοῖς ἔθνεσιν "as a testimony to all the nations" (NRSV). The text defines the content of the μαρτύριον as "the gospel of the kingdom," and indicates how this testimony would be shared (through the activity of κηρύσσω "preach, proclaim," which implies verbal testimony). The recipients of the testimony would be πᾶσιν τοῖς ἔθνεσιν "all the nations." Is the effect (mode) of this testimony positive ("for"), negative ("against"), or both at the same time? As Lenski[15] points out, the intention of testimony is to arouse faith. Hence, this testimony is positive because it provides opportunity to everyone to hear and believe. But, if people reject it, then it becomes a witness against those who refuse to believe.

In Matthew 6:11 εἰς μαρτύριον αὐτοῖς is connected with apostolic proclamation of the gospel, its rejection by its listeners, and symbolic action of the proclaimers shaking the dust off their feet. James A. Brooks explains that Jews returning to the Holy Land would remove foreign dust from their shoes and clothing in order not to defile the land.[16] In the same way, Jesus's instruction to his disciples was in line with the way the ancient prophets indicated first warning then judgment if the hearers persisted in their rejection

12. France, *Mark, NIGTC*, 515.

13. If Mark 13:10 defines the content of μαρτύριον from verse 9 as the gospel, this is not the case in Matthew 10:19. There Jesus says: ". . . do not worry about how you are to speak or what you are to say; for what you are to say will be given to you at that time."

14. Evans, *Mark 8:27–16:20*, 310.

15. Lenski, *Interpretation of St. Matthew's, 936.*

16. Brooks, *Mark, 102.*

of the message and messengers.[17] Brooks adds that this action may also symbolize that a town which rejected the message of the disciples was not a part of the true Israel. Later missionaries took this instruction literally (Acts 13:51; 18:6). While we have not always been sure if the expression *εἰς μαρτύριον αὐτοῖς* had a positive or negative meaning, there is no doubt that the meaning here is negative.[18]

1.3 Μαρτυρία in Matthew and Mark

Mark 14:55, 56, 59 use *μαρτυρία* in the context of Jesus's trial. R. T. France writes that *ἐζήτουν κατὰ τοῦ Ἰησοῦ μαρτυρίαν εἰς τὸ θανατῶσαι αὐτόν* "were seeking against Jesus's testimony to put him to death" in Mark 14:55 conveys two significant things about the nature of this hearing. Firstly, it was a hearing in search of a charge, not a trial based on an already formed accusation. This is the reason why they searched for some time for *μαρτυρία*. Secondly, although the charge may not have yet been decided, the verdict was decided from the outset. For France, this means that the trial was a "kangaroo" court, not an impartial judicial hearing.[19] The *μαρτυρία* they were looking for had to be the testimony of eyewitnesses, not simply circumstantial evidence, and the death penalty required the testimony of two or three witnesses to be properly established. The two imperfects *ἐζήτουν* "searching" and *οὐχ ηὕρισκον* "not finding" testimony *κατὰ τοῦ Ἰησοῦ* "against Jesus," imply significant effort on the part of the religious leaders to secure such testimony. Verse 56 reveals that many *ψευδομαρτυρέω* "falsely testified" (again an imperfect, *ἐψευδομαρτύρουν*) *κατ' αὐτοῦ* "against him," but their *μαρτυρία* was not in agreement.[20] In verse 58 for the first time Mark has witnesses bring

17. According to Guelich (*Mark 1–8:26, 322–323*), shaking the dust from feet could mean: a) that the place was declared "pagan", b) a gesture of judgment symbolizing the termination of any further contact and communication with the place, and denying any further opportunity to hear the message of salvation or experience the ministry of healing and deliverance, c) that the agents had done their job and were "washing their hands" of any further responsibility.

18. *εἰς μαρτύριον αὐτοῖς* could mean a) a witness to God's grace, b) a warning calling for repentance or, c) evidence against them in the final judgment. According to Guelich (*Mark 1–8:26, 323*), only the third option comes into play, since the locale has rejected them and their message and thus the disciples gesture testifies to that and against those who have spurned their only hope for pardon at the last judgment.

19. France, *Mark*, NIGTC, 604.

20. *ἴσος* 'equal,' 'alike': the adjective is in the feminine nominative plural form, agreeing with *hai marturiai* 'the testimonies.' In the context the adjective means 'consistent,' 'coherent':

concrete accusations against Jesus, but even then, he notes in verse 59 that their *μαρτυρία* "testimony" was not *ἴσος* "equal, alike" (v. 56).

1.4 Μαρτυρέω in Matthew and Mark

Since *μαρτυρέω* can refer to speaking or acting to confirm information about oneself or others, both in positive and negative (accusatory) ways, the context of a particular use defines its meaning. The only example of *μαρτυρέω* in the Synoptics is found in Matthew 23:31. It is followed by the pronoun *ἑαυτοῖς* "yourselves," in a dative of disadvantage, "against someone."[21] But what is the content of the witnessing here? Apparently, here we have the idea of repeated action, since the "sons of the prophets" (v. 31) (the teachers of the Law and Pharisees in Jesus's generation) build "the tombs of the prophets and decorate the graves of the righteous" (v. 29) whom their fathers killed (v. 30). By recognizing their "father's" deeds and claiming "father-son relationships" with them, Jesus's opponents provided the basis for *μαρτυρέω* against themselves. Jesus's exhortation *πληρώσατε τὸ μέτρον τῶν πατέρων ὑμῶν*, "fill up the measure of your fathers" is a prophetic announcement of what is going to happen through their coming rejection of Jesus. The sons will repeat the deeds of their fathers. Note: in this instance the teachers of the Law and Pharisees bear witness to something that they themselves did not personally see nor were they present when the killings of the prophets took place.

1.5 Καταμαρτυρέω in Matthew and Mark

In Matthew and Mark *καταμαρτυρέω* appears in the context of Jesus's trial in Matthew 26:62; 27:13 and Mark 14:60. The activity of two false witnesses in Matthew 26:62 is described as *τί οὗτοί σου καταμαρτυροῦσιν* "what things these are testifying against you." This implies that he was asking Jesus to refute what the witnesses said or to otherwise explain himself.[22] After Jesus responded in verse 64, the high priest tore his clothes and concluded that there is no need for further *μάρτυς* "witnesses" (v. 65). In the parallel in Mark

---

the accusations brought against Jesus by the witnesses were not consistent one with the other" (Bratcher and Nida, *Mark*, 462).

21. Beutler, "*μαρτυρεω, διαμαρτύρομαι, μαρτύρομαι*", *EDNT* 2, 389.

22. Newman and Stine, *Matthew*, 829.

14:60 the witnesses' activity is also described as *οὗτοί σου καταμαρτυροῦσιν* "these testify against you," which also indicates that they were witnesses *against* Jesus. In Matthew 27:13 Jesus appeared before Pilate. In this appearance, the chief priests and the elders were those who performed the activity of *σου καταμαρτυροῦσιν* "they testify against you." Thus, we see that the *testimony against* language from the Sanhedrin hearing is also used in the appearance before Pilate.

1.6 Ψευδομαρτυρέω in Matthew and Mark

In Matthew and Mark *ψευδομαρτυρέω* appears in two different contexts: as a command against false witnessing, and as a description of the witnesses in Jesus's trial. In Matthew 19:18 we have a repetition of the commandment against false witnessing: *οὐ ψευδομαρτυρήσεις* "you (sg.) will not testify falsely," and Matthew follows exactly tense, voice and mood of the verbs in LXX in Exodus 20:16 and Deuteronomy 5:20.[23] The context of the command is a courtroom setting, as implied by translations such as "false testimony" (NIV) or "false witness."[24] Mark 10:19 also repeats this command, but unlike Matthew (*οὐ* + indicative), Mark uses *μή* for negation + aorist subjunctive verbs.

In Mark 14:56, 57 we are once again at Jesus's trial. Verse 56 reveals that many *ψευδομαρτυρέω* "falsely testified" *κατ' αὐτοῦ* "against him," but (again) their *μαρτυρία* was not in agreement. In verse 57 we find *ψευδομαρτυρέω* together with *κατ' αὐτοῦ* "against him." Mark tells us that these witnesses' testimonies were only verbal; see the participle *λέγοντες* (from the verb *λέγω*) "speaking," which implies verbal accusations.

1.7 Ψευδόμαρτυς in Matthew and Mark

The noun *ψευδόμαρτυς* in Matthew and Mark appears only in Matthew 26:60. In Matthew 26:59 we read how the chief priests and the whole Sanhedrin were *ἐζήτουν ψευδομαρτυρίαν κατὰ τοῦ Ἰησοῦ* "looking for false evidence against Jesus." Craig L. Blomberg notes that the chief priests and the Sanhedrin

---

23. Although, this commandment is given in a reduced form without mentioning of "neighbour."

24. The question for discussion is does this prohibition cover lying in general, or is it restricted to lying in the courtroom.

were looking for spurious charges against Jesus, yet they wanted to keep the appearance of legality. However: regarding "false evidence," Blomberg says that the designation "false" stems from a Christian perspective, rather than reflecting a consciously illegal or unethical approach adopted by the Jewish authorities, because:

> They were genuinely convinced that Jesus was a blasphemer and worthy of death, so it was just a matter of time before the court could demonstrate it, even if all of the charges were not as seriously investigated as they might otherwise have been. As it turns out, it takes a while to find this testimony, probably surprisingly long from the authorities' standpoint. But, finally, two witnesses do agree, as verse 61 recounts a slightly garbled form of John 2:19 (Jesus did not originally say, "I am able to").[25]

Those who gave ψευδομαρτυρία in Matthew 26:60[26] are now described as ψευδόμαρτυς, although, as Hagner observes, Matthew avoids calling the final witnesses whose testimony agreed "false witnesses," "apparently regarding their evidence as true and not wanting to deny that Jesus had said what is reported by the witnesses."[27] The idea that the Sanhedrin "found none [witnesses] though many false witnesses came forward," indicates that some basic effort toward following the rules of evidence was made, and that the Sanhedrin did not prepare false witnesses with matching stories.[28] Also, the reluctance of the Sanhedrin to use many of the false witnesses sooner (since "many false witnesses came forward") was due to the fact that they either did not come up with testimonies that the Sanhedrin wanted to hear, or due to the lack of agreement between witnesses.

---

25. Blomberg, *Matthew: Exegetical and Theological Exposition*, 401–402.

26. Some early manuscripts have "many false witnesses came forward. And finally, two came forward," but other early manuscripts and related later witnesses have "many false witnesses came forward, they found none. But at last, two false witnesses came forward." Both options communicate essentially the same information, but the longer form provides more detail (Brannan and Loken, *Lexham Textual Notes*).

27. Hagner, *Matthew 14–28*, 798.

28. Nolland, *Matthew*, 1126.

1.8 Ψευδομαρτυρία in Matthew and Mark

The noun ψευδομαρτυρία appears twice in Matthew and Mark: in Matthew 15:19 and 26:59. In Matthew 15:19 we have an explicit connection between heart and mouth, and one of the things that comes through the mouth of people is ψευδομαρτυρία "false testimony." Morris[29] distinguishes between sworn (involving and appealing to the deity) and unsworn testimony, saying that in both instances testimony must be reliable for the sake of society and life in general. Morris seems to put this command into the category of unsworn testimonies. Ψευδομαρτυρία is followed by βλασφημία, which (since this term can be used for slander against people or offenses against God) can be connected with false testimony. Elsewhere (Matt 12:31; 26:65) βλασφημία is used of slander against God.[30]

Matthew 26:59 is another text which deals with Jesus's trial, and we read how the chief priests and the whole Sanhedrin were ἐζήτουν ψευδομαρτυρίαν κατὰ τοῦ Ἰησοῦ "looking false evidence against Jesus." Those who gave ψευδομαρτυρία, in Matthew 26:60 are also described as ψευδόμαρτυς "false witnesses."

2. The concept of witness in the Lukan writings – passage analysis

2.1 Μάρτυς in the Lukan writings

Μάρτυς appears fifteen times in the Lukan writings. Luke 11:48 refers to the same event as Matthew 23:31. Matthew used μαρτυρέω with the pronoun ἑαυτοῖς "yourselves" in a dative of disadvantage. In Luke, Jesus neutrally labels the religious leaders, μάρτυρές ἐστε "you are witnesses," but the context reveals that they are witness against themselves because they συνευδοκεῖτε τοῖς ἔργοις τῶν πατέρων ὑμῶν "approve of the deeds of your ancestors." Accordingly, these religious leaders did not witness these events themselves, but they bear witness in the sense of approving what their fathers did.

In Luke 24:48, unlike in Luke 11:48, ὑμεῖς μάρτυρες τούτων "you are witnesses of these things" (objective genitive) refers to the disciples as first-hand witnesses because of the pronoun *toútōn* (τούτων) "these." Nolland notes that

---

29. Morris, *Gospel According to Matthew*, 399.

30. Newman and Stine, *Matthew*, 490–491.

the scope of their testimony includes a) the pre-passion teaching of Jesus, b) the post-resurrection illumination of the Scriptures by the risen Lord, c) the passion events themselves, d) the reality of Jesus's resurrected state, e) the need for universal proclamation of the message of forgiveness in Jesus's name, and f) the need to begin this proclamation in Jerusalem.[31] Furthermore, if in Acts 1:8 the apostles are the ones labelled by Jesus as "my witnesses," then in Luke 24 the wider group of disciples is in view. This means that the role of the apostles, though central, in no way excludes or excuses the wider community of disciples from the witnessing task.

In Acts 1:8 Jesus uses the expression from Isaiah (43:10, 12; 44:8) to declare to his apostles, *ὑμᾶς καὶ ἔσεσθέ μου μάρτυρες* "and you will be my witnesses." Note several things. First, this apostolic witness was based on their place as eyewitnesses of the events of Jesus's life, death, and resurrection. Their position is unique because none of those events will ever be repeated again. Second, the content of their testimony can be understood as the gospel story with an emphasis on Jesus's passion and resurrection,[32] or as the speech about the resurrection which includes witness to all the other propositions of the Christian proclamation.[33] Third, the apostles shall not merely bear witness but be witnesses in their own persons.[34] The question is how to understand genitive *μου*? Peterson[35] argues for a combination of objective (bearing witness to the significance of Jesus and his ministry) and possessive genitive (they will do it as those who belong to him), with the emphasis on the first. Moessner also suggests a combination of objective and subjective genitive:

> the command to be "my witnesses" (*μου μάρτυρες*) in Acts 1:8 is pregnant with both objective and subjective referents of the genitive "my" (*μου*): the apostles are to *bear the presence* of the one concerning whom they bear testimony ('witnesses of/

31. Nolland, *Matthew*, 1220.
32. Keener, *Acts Vol. 2*, 696.
33. Barrett, *Acts 1–14*, 79.
34. Lange, et al., *Acts*, 13.
35. Peterson, *Acts*, 111.

to *me*') as well as *re-present the authority* of the one for whom their witness is given ("witnesses of *mine*").[36]

Probably the best solution is to say that distinction between objective and subjective genitive is unnecessary because those who bear witness have Jesus as the content of their witness and they serve as his envoys. Furthermore, their witness is not only concerned with facts from or of Jesus's life, but also with the significance of those facts.[37]

The issue of the content of the apostolic witness is further defined in Acts 1:22, where the necessary condition for selection as apostle is for the candidate to be *μάρτυρα τῆς ἀναστάσεως αὐτοῦ* "witness of his resurrection." As in the previous case, the meaning of this genitive expression is ambiguous, because it can describe Matthias as the one who is not only seen the Lord, but also that he must bear witness about it.[38]

In Acts 2:32 the apostles are once again designated witnesses to the fact of the resurrection. They are witnesses because they have seen the resurrected Jesus (first-hand experience), and for that matter they both attest (to the fact of his resurrection) and testify (in favour of his interpretation of the event). But verse 33 also reveals that the crowd gathered on Pentecost functioned as witnesses, because they both see and hear how Jesus poured out the Holy Spirit on the apostles. This meets the minimum of two witnesses required to establish facts. The text from Acts 2:32 *οὗ πάντες ἡμεῖς ἐσμεν μάρτυρες* "and of that all of us are witnesses" is repeated almost verbatim in Acts 3:15: *οὗ ἡμεῖς μάρτυρές ἐσμεν* "we are witnesses of this."

In Acts 5:32 Luke again presents the apostles as witnesses of *τῶν ῥημάτων τούτων* (lit. "these sayings"), which refers to the prophetic speech of David regarding the Messiah's resurrection. But then Luke adds another witness to the list: the Holy Spirit. This pairing of the witness of the Holy Spirit and of the apostles places the apostles' testimony on a higher level of divine inspiration, so that to disobey their message is equal to disobeying God.[39] Although Luke does not specify how the Holy Spirit functions as a witness, the very

36. Moessner, *"Gospel Acts" of Luke*, 192 (emphasis original).
37. Green, "Salvation to end of Earth", 84.
38. Witherington, *Acts of Apostles*, 125.
39. Keener, *Acts Vol. 2*, 302.

fact of the visible nature of the Holy Spirit's coming and the apostles' receiving (speaking in tongues) is itself a form of testimony to Jesus's resurrection.

In Acts 6:13 the noun *μάρτυς* is modified with adjective ψευδής "false," to describe the "false witnesses" in the trial against Stephen. Their testimony is verbal (λέγοντας), and they bring charges against Stephen based on what they had, allegedly, personally heard from Stephen. Joseph Shulam explains that the construction ἔστησάν . . . λέγοντας ("they set up false witnesses") is obscure because it can mean that the freedmen (v. 9) hired witnesses and told them what to say, or that they told the witnesses that they themselves had heard Stephen's blaspheming.[40] Accordingly, the witnesses' falsehood is in saying that they themselves had heard what Stephen said, when in actuality they did not. It is possible that freedmen heard Stephen, which makes the precise reconstruction of Stephen's teaching difficult. The story of Stephen's trial continues in Acts 7:58 where these witnesses are presented as the ones who carry out the sentence against Stephen by stoning him. The fact that they "laid their coats at the feet of a young man named Saul" speaks to that fact.

In Acts 10, Peter presents once again the scope of apostolic eyewitness testimony. In verse 39 he says: *καὶ ἡμεῖς μάρτυρες πάντων ὧν ἐποίησεν ἔν τε τῇ χώρᾳ τῶν 'Ιουδαίων καὶ [ἐν] 'Ιερουσαλήμ* "We are witnesses of everything he did in the country of the Jews and in Jerusalem," and in verse 41 the focus is on the Jesus's resurrection. That apostles are eyewitnesses of Jesus's resurrection is seen from the fact that they are the ones "who ate and drank with him after he rose from the dead."

In Acts 13:31 the apostle Paul as a speaker uses the word *μάρτυς* for the first time. He describes Jesus's post-resurrection appearances to those who came up with him from Galilee to Jerusalem; this includes the Twelve. He says that these companions *εἰσιν μάρτυρες αὐτοῦ πρὸς τὸν λαόν* "are his witnesses to the people." Here we again can observe how the same group of people can move from being observing witnesses to becoming testifying witnesses. According to criteria for being "his witnesses" previously stated, it seems that Paul is excluded from the role because he was not part of that "Galilee to Jerusalem" group.[41] Furthermore, the recipients of such testi-

40. Shulam and Le Cornu, *Jewish Roots of Acts*, 1:331–332.

41. Joseph Shulam (*Jewish Roots of Acts* 1:732) observes that Jesus appeared to a wider audience than the Twelve, and those who came up from Galilee to Jerusalem were presumably

mony are identified as witnesses πρὸς τὸν λαόν "to the people." Although λαός traditionally refers to Israel (cf. Acts 10:2, 42), Paul could here refer to both Jews and gentiles.[42]

In Acts 22:15 Paul is invited to be a witness ὅτι ἔσῃ μάρτυς αὐτῷ. μάρτυς αὐτῷ can be translated as "witness for him" or "to him." This is the first time in Acts that the task of witnessing is described with the word μάρτυς + a pronoun in dative instead of the genitive (such as in Acts 1:8 μου μάρτυρες; Acts 13:31 μάρτυρες αὐτοῦ; Acts 22:20 μάρτυρός σου), or that the object of the witnesses' observation is not in genitive (Acts 3:15 οὗ "this"; Acts 5:32 τῶν ῥημάτων "these sayings"; Acts 10:39 πάντων "everything"). Paul is a witness ὧν ἑώρακας καὶ ἤκουσας "of what you have seen and heard," but in a sense different from Acts 1:8. For that matter, Strathmann[43] distinguishes between witnesses to facts and confessional witness, whose witness proceeds from their beliefs. Accordingly, those who bear witness to these facts have lived through them (Luke 24:47; Acts 1:8), and those who have seen the risen Lord are in a special sense his witnesses (Acts 13:31). Paul fits somewhere in the middle of these groups. He is not a witness in the sense of Acts 1:8, but he has seen the risen Lord, and can testify to that fact. However, Paul "is a witness to the meaning of the facts, namely, as a witness for Jesus rather than to him (22:15). The confessional element is now stronger than the factual element, although naturally the confession itself embraces the historical facts of Christ's life, death, and resurrection."[44] Finally, the scope of Paul's witnessing is πρὸς πάντας ἀνθρώπους "to all people," which includes gentiles as well as Jews (cf. Acts 22:21).

---

not restricted to the Apostles. And while Paul agrees with Peter's testimony that the apostles were those whom Jesus called to be his witnesses, Paul also considered himself to be apostle, and it is unlikely that he clearly distinguishes between "they are now his witnesses to the people" (v. 31), and himself and his companions "we bring you . . ." (v. 32).

42. Shulam and Le Cornu, *Jewish Roots of Acts*, 1:732.

43. Strathmann, "mártys", *TDNT* 1:567.

44. Trites (*NT Concept of Witness*, 142) argues similarly: "Now it is true that there is a slight difference of emphasis between Paul and the Twelve; they had been earthly companions of Jesus throughout his public ministry while Paul had not (cf. 1:21–2; 10:39–41). Nevertheless, the important point surely is that Luke presents Paul as a witness to fact as well as a witness to convictions. Paul, like the Twelve, was pre-eminently a witness to the fact of the resurrection (25:19; cf. I Cor. 9:1; 15:8; Gal.1:15f); this point is underscored in the threefold telling of Paul's conversion story and encounter with the risen Christ."

In Acts 22:20, during his defence before the crowd in Jerusalem, Paul recalls his conversation with Jesus and calls Stephen τοῦ μάρτυρός σου "your witness." The genitive σου can be understood as objective or possessive genitive, but both meanings are fitting. On what basis does he regard Stephen as a witness? Peterson explains that Paul probably regards Stephen as a witness because he (Stephen) lost his life because of his testimony to Christ.[45] This could be a step in the direction of the later meaning of "martyr" (cf. Rev 2:13; 17:6).[46] Knowles adds that Stephen's testimony is not like that of the disciples who knew Jesus's earthly ministry or "ate and drank with him after he rose from the dead."[47] Stephen also does not mention the resurrection of Jesus. However, he *sees* the resurrected and ascended Jesus in a vision (Acts 7:56).

In Acts 26:16 Paul again recalls his calling/conversion and commissioning as a witness. Here he must also testify ὧν τε εἶδές [με] ὧν τε ὀφθήσομαί σοι "of what you have seen and will see of me [Jesus]." The relative pronoun is here in the genitive, ὧν "of what." Interestingly, Paul's basis here for being a witness consists only of seeing, not hearing as was the case in verse 15. He must be a witness of the things he "saw" (past tense) and the things he will "see" (future tense). These differences put Paul in a separate category than the witnesses of Acts 1:8, 10:41 and 13:31.

2.2 Μαρτυρέω in the Lukan writings

The verb μαρτυρέω appears only once in Luke's gospel (4:22). The subjects who perform the action of witnessing are πάντες "all," meaning all who were present is the synagogue in Nazareth. Here, as in Matthew 23:31, μαρτυρέω is accompanied by the pronoun αὐτῷ in dative. It is unclear here whether we have a dative of advantage, where μαρτυρέω can be taken as "praise," or disadvantage "bear witness against." An additional problem is that the verb that follows, ἐθαύμαζον "marvelled," can also be understood positively (Luke 7:9) or negatively (John 7:15, 21). If we take these verbs with a positive connotation, then the transition between this verse and the rest of the story is awkward. But most commentators understand the statement positively,

45. Peterson, *Acts*, 605.

46. Death is not a form of witness, but witness may result in or lead to death.

47. Knowles, *Of Seeds and People of God*, 166.

although a negative interpretation better fits the context.[48] If we accept the positive connotation, we can understand *μαρτυρέω* as "speaking well of" or speaking in an affirmative or positive manner about someone.[49]

In Acts *μαρτυρέω* appears eleven times. In Acts 6:3 the verb *μαρτυρέω* in the present participle passive form *μαρτυρουμένους* has the meaning of bearing witness, in the sense of having a good reputation with others, good character 'witnessed to' by others. The same form of *μαρτυρέω* is used with the same meaning in Acts 10:22. In Acts 16:2 *μαρτυρέω* has the same meaning, but the form is the imperfect passive *ἐμαρτυρεῖτο*. In Acts 22:5 Paul during his defence before the crowd appeals to witnesses who can testify to his zealous behaviour. So, the issue here is not so much his reputation (although it is included) but the fact that he arrested both men and women and threw them into prison for following Jesus. He does the same thing when on trial before Agrippa in Acts 26:5. Reputation or a person's character is once again the subject of people's witness in Acts 22:12.

In the next three cases, God is the subject who witnesses. In Acts 13:22 God verbally testifies concerning David about his character; in Acts 14:3 God testifies through signs and wonders on behalf of the message spoken by Paul and Barnabas (*τῷ μαρτυροῦντι ἐπὶ τῷ λόγῳ*); and in Acts 15:8 God's testifies by granting the Holy Spirit to gentile believers. Such charismatic experience was evidence that God accepted them into God's family. In the expression *ἐμαρτύρησεν αὐτοῖς* "testified to them," *αὐτοῖς* is probably a dative of indirect object.[50] The giving of the Spirit was testimony given not only to Cornelius and his company, but also to Peter and the circumcised believers. So, James Dunn writes that the outpouring of the Spirit was both God's testimony to Peter on behalf of Cornelius, and his dissolving of the differences between Peter and Cornelius, as though God bore witness to Cornelius's belief to Peter.[51]

In Acts 10:43 we see again the combination of *μαρτυρέω* and the dative pronoun *τούτῳ*, which in this case also functions as an indirect object. Barrett argues that if this verse ended with *μαρτυροῦσιν . . . τούτῳ*, *τούτῳ* would

48. Stein, *Luke*, 157.

49. According to Nadella (*Dialogue Not Dogma*, 36), *μαρτυρέω* with *αὐτῷ* in Luke is always used positive connotation, so it is logical to take it as dative of respect or advantage.

50. Trites, *NT Concept of Witness*, 73.

51. Dunn, *Baptism in Holy Spirit*, 81–82.

certainly be taken as masculine: "To him (this man) all the prophets bear witness."[52] Although the pronoun can be read as masculine, it can also be taken as neuter "to this," Barrett concludes that neuter is the more probable meaning, because elsewhere in Acts the prophets are not said to bear witness to Christ but rather to certain facts about him (2:16, 30; 3:18, 21, 24; 13:27, 40; 15:15; 24:14; 26:22, 27; 28:23, 25). Accordingly, the prophetic testimony contained in Scripture is that everyone who believes in Christ receives the forgiveness of sins through his name.

Acts 23:11 contains both *διαμαρτύρομαι* and *μαρτυρέω*. These two verbs hardly differ in meaning, and they are both in aorist. Paul's previous witness is described as *δεμαρτύρω τὰ περὶ ἐμοῦ* "testified about me," but his future witness in Rome is described with the aorist infinitive *μαρτυρῆσαι*, and verb *δεῖ* "must." So, Paul must accomplish this task of witnessing even in Rome, just like he did elsewhere in the past.

2.3 *Μαρτυρία* in the Lukan writings

Μαρτυρία appears twice in the Lukan writings. Luke 22:71 is a parallel passage with Matthew 26:65 and Mark 14:63. Both Matthew and Mark use the noun *μάρτυς*. Luke uses *μαρτυρία* instead of *μάρτυς* because in his record of Jesus's trial, there are no witnesses present at the Sanhedrin. In Acts 23:11, *μαρτυρία* refers to the content of the testimony, which in this instance is the same as in Acts 23:11 *περὶ ἐμοῦ* "about me."

2.4 *Μαρτύριον* in the Lukan writings

Μαρτύριον appears five times in the Lukan writings. Luke 5:14 is parallel to Matthew 8:4 and Mark 1:44. In this story Jesus heals a man with leprosy. All three use the expression *εἰς μαρτύριον αὐτοῖς* "for a testimony to them." Accordingly, the debate about what Jesus means by *εἰς μαρτύριον αὐτοῖς*, discussed above under Matthew and Mark, is also applicable here.

In Jesus's statement regarding shanking the dust off one's feet, Matthew (10:14) simply mentions the act without referring to that activity as *εἰς μαρτύριον αὐτοῖς* "as a testimony." In Mark's parallel (6:11), Mark adds that this action is *εἰς μαρτύριον αὐτοῖς* "as a testimony to or against them." Luke 9:5 adds the preposition *ἐπί* "upon" to make *εἰς μαρτύριον ἐπ' αὐτούς* lit. "for

52. Barrett, *Acts 1–14*, 528.

a witness upon them," and the pronoun referring to the recipients of such testimony is not in dative but accusative. While this does not change the meaning of their testimony, the spatial dimension of testimony that comes "from above" could be interesting.

Minor textual differences exist between Luke 21:13, Matthew 10:18, and Mark 13:9. All three use the expression εἰς μαρτύριον when Jesus talks about the disciples' testimony before legal authorities. Testimony here may refer to "testimony in the disciples' favour at the eschatological judgment," the majority of scholars think that Luke here essentially retains Markan meaning. Since ἀποβήσεται ὑμῖν εἰς μαρτύριον "this will give you an opportunity to testify" is a separate statement, it is unclear whether Luke places witness in the courtroom setting or thinks more narrowly of verbal witness to the Christian faith.[53]

In Acts 4:33 μαρτύριον refers to the content of the apostles' testimony. Notably, μαρτύριον is followed by the objective genitive τῆς ἀναστάσεως "resurrection," which is furthermore modified with τοῦ κυρίου Ἰησοῦ "of Jesus Christ." But further characterizes this testimony as δυνάμει μεγάλῃ "with great power." Δύναμις probably typifies not only the activity of the apostles but also the effect of their witness upon the people.[54] Larkin[55] seems to argue that δύναμις are not miracles or the new life of the believing community, but the effectiveness of their utterances, which force hearers to make decision either for or against the gospel.

Acts 7:44 is one of only two places in the NT where μαρτύριον refers to σκηνὴ τοῦ μαρτυρίου or "tent of witness" or "testimony" (see also Rev 15:5).

2.5 Διαμαρτύρομαι in the Lukan writings

The verb διαμαρτύρομαι appears once in Luke's gospel, in Luke 16:28, with the meaning of warning (cf. Exod 19:21; Deut 8:19; Neh 9:26; Jer 6:10). By "warning," the rich man here refers to the testimony of a person who has come back from dead, and who warns about the coming torment. The text points to the precedence of testimony from Scripture (Luke 16:31). Stein says that, although in all other instances where Luke uses διαμαρτύρομαι (Acts

53. Nolland, *Matthew*, 996.

54. Newman and Nida, *Acts*, 111.

55. Larkin, *Acts*, IVPNTC, 5

2:40; 8:25; 10:42; 18:5; 20:21, 23–24; 23:11; 28:23) the better translation is "to witness," the presence of conditions ("to repent" v. 30) and consequences ("coming to this place of torment" v. 28), justifies the translation of διαμαρτύρομαι here as a "warning."[56]

In Acts, διαμαρτύρομαι appears nine times. Acts 2:40 contains three verbs: διαμαρτύρομαι "testify to" in aorist, παρακαλέω "exhort" in imperfect, and λέγω "speak" in present. Commenting on the differences in tense between διαμαρτύρομαι and παρακαλέω, Bock says that "speech as a whole is a testimony that includes exhortation throughout. The testimony concerns the facts included in the preaching as well as the exhortation to the audience to respond."[57] Even though διαμαρτύρομαι usually means "testify to something"[58] or "call to witness",[59] in this instance the better translation would be "warning" because of the presence of conditions and consequences (Acts 2:38–41).

In Acts 8:25 διαμαρτύρομαι once again occurs in combination with other verbs: λαλέω "speak" in aorist participle form, and εὐαγγελίζω "tell the good news" in imperfect form. The combination of διαμαρτύρομαι and λαλέω indicates that testifying was done verbally. Viewed in combination with εὐαγγελίζω, these verbs show us the semantical overlap between these three words. According to Peterson, εὐαγγελίζω in verse 25 forms an inclusion with verse 4 (εὐαγγελιζόμενοι τὸν λόγον), which signifies that the apostles preached the same message as all the believers who had been scattered from Jerusalem.[60]

In Acts 10:42 διαμαρτύρομαι occurs together with κηρύσσω "proclaim." Again, the pair has significant semantical overlap. Here we are told the specific content of testimony: "that [Jesus] is the one ordained by God as judge of the living and the dead" (NRSV).

In Acts 18:5 διαμαρτύρομαι appears in participle form and refers specifically to the message about "Jesus being the Christ." The main verb of the sentence is συνέχομαι "hold together." The expression συνειχετο τῳ λογῳ "began devoting himself completely to the word" refers to Paul's focusing

56. Stein, *Luke*, 24.

57. Bock, *Acts*, BECNT, 145.

58. Bock, 145.

59. Robertson, *Word Pictures*

60. Peterson, *Acts*, 290.

his energies on sharing of the word once Silas and Timothy came to town.[61] Such devotion was manifested in testifying.

In Acts 20:21 διαμαρτύρομαι refers to "testifying" and the content of Paul's testimony to Jews and Greeks is "repentance toward God and faith toward our Lord Jesus."

In Acts 20:23 the Holy Spirit is the subject who testifies (διαμαρτύρομαι) to Paul, and the content is the future suffering that awaits Paul. The verb is present tense, but since this testimony prophetically speaks about future things, "warning" is a possible translation (NIV). Note though that διαμαρτύρομαι here is not accompanied with conditions and consequences.

In Acts 20:24 διαμαρτύρομαι has its usual meaning of "testifying," since Paul here refers to the message given to him. He testifies "to the good news of God's grace." Here we discover that Paul viewed this task of testifying as διακονία "ministry."

In Acts 28:23 the main verb ἐξετίθετο "explained" is modified by two participles: διαμαρτυρόμενος "testifying" and πείθων "convincing." Lenski[62] notes that expounding, testifying and persuading were Paul's methods of dealing with Jews, but his testimony was apostolic testimony, based on direct vision from and revelation by Jesus to him. The content of the testimony is also summarized as "the kingdom of God" and "Jesus."

2.6 Μαρτύρομαι in the Lukan writings

Μαρτύρομαι appears only twice in the Lukan writings. In Acts 20:26 μαρτύρομαι is used less in the sense of "bearing witness" and more to refer to "declaration" or "calling to witness." Trites observes that Paul in this speech twice "appeals to the knowledge of his hearers who can testify both to the faithful character of his ministry and the unstinting labour of his hands (Acts 20:18, 34)."[63] Likewise, Lenski notices that "Paul is not testifying (which would be μαρτυρέω) but is letting a great fact that no one can contradict, and question testify for him."[64] Paul here refers to his past work in Ephesus when he declared to them everything he was obligated by God to tell them.

61. Witherington, *Acts of Apostles*, 548.

62. Lenski, *Interpretation of Acts*, 1122–1123.

63. Trites, *NT Concept of Witness*, 72.

64. Lenski, *Interpretation of Acts*, 845.

Now in Acts 20:26, as with the watchman from Ezekiel 33:1–6, Paul "has sounded his warning, he is no longer responsible for the lives of those he is appointed to warn. Paul had preached the full gospel, the whole will of God. He had called people to repentance. Now the responsibility rested with them . . . This is the task of a Christian witness, to proclaim the full will of God. Witnesses can do no more. The response is not theirs but the hearer's responsibility."[65]

Acts 26:22 depicts Paul on trial. His defence does not focus on any crime he committed (he does not testify to his guilt or innocence) but instead on the facts of Jesus's life (v. 23) supported by or based on the Scripture. Paul was not a witness of Jesus's earthly life, yet he combines the testimony of Scriptures with the historical events from Jesus's life which served as fulfilment of these Scriptures. Neagoe[66] describes Paul's approach nicely: ". . . the account of Paul's trial before Festus and Agrippa provides ample evidence that the primary focus of the conflict in this part of Acts is not Paul's alleged guilt in relation to either Judaism or Rome, but his Christological assertions about Jesus. . . ."

2.7 Ψευδομαρτυρέω in the Lukan writings

In Luke 18:20 Luke repeats the commandment μὴ ψευδομαρτυρήσῃς "You shall not bear false witness." The mood of the verb is subjunctive; here Luke follows Mark (10:19). In the LXX the verb is indicative, which Matthew (19:18) follows.

3. The concept of witness in the Johannine writings – passage analysis

Speaking about the way John uses the word-group "witness" and the importance of it, Merrill C. Tenney says the following:

> Among the numerous terms that can be classed as specially Johannine, the word *witness*, whether a verb or a noun, is outstanding. The noun μαρτυρία occurs fourteen times in the Gospel, and the verb μαρτυρέω thirty-three times; in the

65. Polhill, *Acts*, NAC 26, 426.

66. Neagoe, *Luke's Trial Narratives*, 205.

Johannine Epistles μαρτυρία occurs seven times, and μαρτυρέω ten times; and in Revelation μαρτυρία is used nine times, and μαρτυρέω four times. The Johannine usages of these two terms outnumber their total usage in the rest of the New Testament. Obviously, John gave great importance to this concept in his presentation of the message about Christ.[67]

3.1 Μάρτυς in the Johannine writings

The noun μάρτυς appears five times in Johannine literature, but only in the book of Revelation. Of those appearances, two refer to Jesus: Revelation 1:5a and 3:14. The background of Revelation 1:5a comes from Psalm 89:38, 28 (LXX 88:38, 28). Here, Jesus is presented as ὁ μάρτυς, ὁ πιστός[68] "the faithful witness." Jesus's witness can be connected with:

a) the "witness which Jesus bore to God during his life on earth and to his faithfulness in maintaining his witness even at the cost of his life",[69]

b) his faithful witnessing in his life and death (cf. Ps 89:37; Prov 14:5, 25; Isa 8:2), and the designation of Jesus as "the firstborn from the dead" and "the ruler of the kings of the earth" (Rev 1:5), signifying that his witness is set against the background of his death,[70]

c) a reference to the exalted Jesus who guarantees the truth of the revelation transmitted through John. "The phrase 'faithful witness' is particularly applicable to Jesus Christ as the source of the revelation that John transmits to his audience, for it underlies its truth and reliability",[71]

d) to Jesus's role as mediator of revelation, but also to the larger purpose of his life as the one who bore witness to the truth from God (John 3:32–33; 18:37), with special emphasis on his death that followed as a result. In this

---

67. Tenney, "Topics from John", 229.

68. "ὁ μάρτυς ὁ πιστός ὁ πρωτότοκος 'the faithful witness, the firstborn' is nominative but should strictly be genitive (following ἀπὸ Ἰησοῦ Χριστοῦ). Like the solecism in 1:4 (also following ἀπό), the phrase here is kept in the nominative because it is part of an OT allusion that was nominative in its OT context . . ." (Beale, *Book of Revelation*, 192).

69. Bauckham, *Theology of Revelation*, 73.

70. Trites, *NT Concept of Witness*, 158.

71. Aune, *Revelation 1–5*, 37–38.

way, Jesus is presented as the faithful witness, and the model of how to stand firm and never compromise the truth of God.[72]

In Revelation 3:14 Jesus is presented not only as "faithful" but also as the "amen" and a "true" witness. As with Revelation 1:5, a major interpretive problem is whether Jesus Christ as *μάρτυς* refers to the historical Jesus (i.e. his faithfulness in completing his earthly ministry through his death) or to the exalted Jesus who guarantees the truth of the revelation transmitted through John.[73] If we accept the mediating position mentioned above as correct (both/and), we can then understand "amen" as a description for Christ, and what the title means is further expressed by the following appositional phrase, "the faithful and true witness." Interestingly, in Revelation 3:15 Jesus says, "I know (*οἶδα*) your deeds," which additionally confirms Jesus's role as a witness due to his faculty of knowledge.

The three other uses of *μάρτυς* describe believers. In Revelation 2:13 Antipas is described as *Ἀντιπᾶς ὁ μάρτυς μου ὁ πιστός μου* "Antipas my witness, my faithful one" (NRSV). The genitive *μου* is probably objective with a meaning "witness to me, faithful to me",[74] and the noun phrase *ὁ μάρτυς μου ὁ πιστός μου*, "my faithful witness," is a nominative of apposition modifying the noun "Antipas."[75] We should understand Antipas's witness not necessarily as witness given in a court, but in the sense of a faithful believer who bears witness to Christ by means of words and actions.[76] Although the text furthermore mentions Antipas's death, "most interpreters have seen the developing use of the word in this passage as coming to mean one whose witness for Christ led to his death."[77]

Revelation 11:3 mentions the two witnesses who will "prophesy for 1,260 days, clothed in sackcloth." In this text, the speaker is either God or Christ, due to the presence of the verb *δώσω*, "I will give," and the possessive pronoun *μου*, "my." There are a few interpretive questions here. First, we can understand the genitive *μου* in the expression *μάρτυσίν μου* as: possessive

72. Mounce, *Book of Revelation*, 48.

73. Aune, *Revelation 1–5*, 255.

74. Beale, *Book of Revelation*, 246.

75. Aune (p. 184) says that the noun Antipas is an indeclinable noun, and syntactically should be in the genitive case (for other examples see 1:5; 20:2).

76. Bratcher and Hatton, *Deuteronomy*, 52.

77. Patterson, *Revelation*, 102.

(witnesses *of* Jesus – they belong to him, they are his); subjective (Jesus's own witnesses") or objective (witnesses *to* or *about* Jesus). Second, the identity of these two witnesses is disputed. Third, we can view the witnesses' role negatively, as though the purpose of their witnessing was not to secure the world's repentance but rather to act as God's agents in judging the world. But Aune argues that "most of the inhabitants of the city were converted following the resurrection and ascension of the witnesses (v. 13) . . . The focus, therefore, is not on the character or the content of their message but rather on the fact that, whatever it is, it will surely be rejected as they themselves will be."[78]

Two more things are interesting about this verse. First, the fact that the text mentions "two witnesses" could imply the juridical character of the martyrs' testimony by honoring the OT requirement for two or three witnesses in legal cases.[79] Secondly, the connection between "witnessing" and "prophesying" is something we encountered in the OT. For the description of their activity, verse 3 uses the verb *προφητεύω*, in verse 6 the noun *προφητεία*, in verse 7 the noun *μαρτυρία*, and in verse 10 the two witnesses are called *δύο προφῆται* "two prophets." This connection will be also present in some other places in Revelation (cf. Rev 19:10).

Lastly, Revelation 17:6 mentions *τοῦ αἵματος τῶν μαρτύρων Ἰησοῦ* "the blood of the witnesses to Jesus" (NRSV). Again, the problem of the genitive arises, since *Ἰησοῦ* can be taken as a genitive of possession ("Jesus's witnesses") or an objective genitive (witness to Jesus). Beale notices that the genitive construction may be intentionally vague so that both objective and possessive notions are included. Like with 2:13 and 11:3, in this verse we also have a close connection between concepts of witness and martyrdom, since giving of their testimony results in their death.[80]

78. Aune, *Revelation 6–16*, 611–612.

79. "This legal atmosphere is enhanced by the use of *μαρτυρία* ("witness"), which we have seen refers to a legal witness (see on 1:9). This nuance is borne out by observing that in at least six of the nine uses of the word in the Apocalypse it refers to a witness that is rejected by the world's legal system and that results in penal consequences (so 1:9; 6:9; 12:11, 17; 20:4). This is clearly the case with *μάρτυς* in 11:3 and *μαρτυρία* in 11:7. In fact, rejection of the Christians' witness in the world court here becomes a basis for judgment of the persecutors in the heavenly court" (Beale, *Book of Revelation*, 575).

80. Beale, *Book of Revelation*, 860.

3.2 Μαρτυρέω in the Johannine writings

3.2.1 Μαρτυρέω in the Gospel of John

Μαρτυρέω describes the activity of a *μάρτυς*. This verb is not often used in the Gospel of John to refer to witnessing to the factuality of Jesus's history, though this is presupposed and even emphasized (John 15:27; 21:24; also 3:11, in so far as the address of Jesus here actually becomes the preaching of the Evangelist). The verb primarily is used to refer to witnessing about the nature and significance of his person.[81] The verb sometime occurs with no specific reference (cf. John 2:25; 3:28; 4:39, 44; 12:17; 13:21; 18:23).[82] Due to the great number of occurrences of *μαρτυρέω* in the Gospel of John, we will analyze this verb by focusing on the entities that bear witness.

First, John the Baptist appears as a witness in the Prologue (1:6).[83] He is described as a *μαρτυρία* (1:7) who came to *μαρτυρέω* "testify" *περὶ τοῦ φωτός* "for the light" (1:7, 8). Again, John is a prophet whose role is described primarily as being a witness. In John 1:15 John the Baptist testifies *περὶ αὐτοῦ* "concerning him," specifically about Jesus's pre-existence. Because of the verb λέγω "say," we see that his testimony is verbal. In John 1:32 John the Baptist offers witness concerning the historical event of the Spirit descending on Jesus. Again, the presence of the verb λέγω "say" signifies that his testimony is verbal, but he grounds his claim in what he had θεάομαι "seen." In John 1:34 John the Baptist again refers to his qualification of eyewitness with the verb ὁράω "see," but here he offers an interpretation of the event of the Spirit's descent on Jesus by speaking about Jesus's person: "this is the Son of God." Finally, in John 3:26 and 28 he summarizes his testimony by validating Jesus's ministry. In John 3:26 *μαρτυρέω* is in the perfect tense, which signifies permanence of John's testimony regarding Jesus (probably everything that he said thus far). In John 3:28 he reminds his listeners about

81. According to Parsenios (*Johannine Lawsuit Motif*, 2) "In the theological vision of the Fourth Gospel, therefore, the entire life of Jesus is a legal drama that begins and ends with the testimony of reliable witnesses."

82. "*μαρτυρεῖν περὶ αὐτοῦ*, 1:15; in the addresses of Jesus *περὶ ἐμοῦ* or *περὶ ἐμαυτοῦ*, 5:31–39; 8:13–18; 10:25; 15:26; but 3:26 *ᾧ σὺ μεμαρτύρηκας* (of the Baptist). The content of this witness is *ὅτι οὗτός ἐστιν ὁ υἱὸς τοῦ θεοῦ*, 1:34; hence His eternity, 1:15, or *ὅτι ὁ πατήρ με ἀπέσταλκεν*, 5:36f.; or *ὅτι ὁ πατὴρ ἀπέσταλκεν τὸν υἱὸν σωτῆρα τοῦ κόσμου*, 1 John. 4:14; or *ὅτι ζωὴν αἰώνιον ἔδωκεν ὁ θεὸς ἡμῖν καὶ αὕτη ἡ ζωὴ ἐν τῷ υἱῷ αὐτοῦ ἐστιν*, 1 John. 5:10 f" (Strathmann, "Martus", *TDNT* 4:497–498).

83. According to Tripp ("Ignorance and Intimidating Witnesses", 471), "In the Fourth Gospel, the Baptist is presented more as a witness than a baptizer (1:7–8, 15, 19, 34) . . ."

what he said about himself and Jesus. He then announces that his disciples are observing witnesses with αὐτοὶ ὑμεῖς μοι μαρτυρεῖτε "You yourselves testify to me" In John 5:33, Jesus speaks about John the Baptist and qualifies him as a witness with καὶ μεμαρτύρηκεν τῇ ἀληθείᾳ "and he testified to the truth" (NRSV). Here also John the Baptist is described as the one who testifies for the nature and significance of Jesus's person.

Second, in John 4:39 the speech of the unnamed Samaritan woman is qualified with μαρτυρέω. John 4:29 describes the content of her testimony, with the invitation δεῦτε ἴδετε ἄνθρωπον "come, see a man" (cf. John 1:39, 46). In this instance, a woman was able to invite others to see and experience Jesus the same way she did (repetition). In John 4:39 the phrase διὰ τὸν λόγον τῆς γυναικὸς μαρτυρούσης "because of the word of the woman who testified" reveals that woman's testimony was "in word(s)," and its result was that people ἐπίστευσαν εἰς αὐτὸν "believed in him." This time, the content of her testimony was ὅτι εἶπέν μοι πάντα ἃ ἐποίησα "He told me all that I ever did" which slightly differs from John 4:29.

Third, as the testimony of John the Baptist ends in John 3:30. In the section that follows, John 3:31–36 the author of the Gospel reflects on and summarizes the implications of chapter 3, by drawing together the messages from both the Nicodemus and John the Baptist stories.[84] Consequently, the author presents Jesus as the one who testifies. By saying in John 3:32 ὃ ἑώρακεν καὶ ἤκουσεν τοῦτο μαρτυρεῖ "He testifies to what he has seen and heard," we have a clear indication that the basis of Jesus's testimony is "seeing" and "hearing."[85] This text clearly justifies Jesus's position as a witness. It leaves open the question of whether his claims can be accepted as valid, because the acceptance of testimony requires a sufficient number of witnesses.

John 4:44 says αὐτὸς γὰρ Ἰησοῦς ἐμαρτύρησεν ὅτι προφήτης ἐν τῇ ἰδίᾳ πατρίδι τιμὴν οὐκ ἔχει "for Jesus himself had testified that a prophet has no honor in the prophet's own country" (NRSV). With this Jesus declares himself a prophet.

84. Borchert, *John 1–11*, 192–193.

85. Brown (*Gospel According to John*, 158) notices that "seen" is in perfect tense, while "heard" is aorist. Accordingly, emphasis is put on "seeing"; while parallel text 1 John 1:3 both "seeing", and "hearing" are both in perfect tense.

Confronted by accusations that he is guilty of blasphemy, a capital offense (5:18), Jesus in John 5 cites several who witness on his behalf. Currently, our focus is on 5:31, where the verb μαρτυρέω appears. Here the idea is not that Jesus does not testify about himself. He does so testify, but he has also other witnesses as well. The idea of an invalid single witness appears again in chapter 8. In John 8:13 the Pharisees rightly note that if Jesus testifies about himself (σὺ περὶ σεαυτοῦ μαρτυρεῖς lit. "you bear witness about yourself") his testimony would not be valid. Jesus replies in 8:14 that, even if he would testify about himself (κἂν ἐγὼ μαρτυρῶ περὶ ἐμαυτοῦ "Even if I testify on my own behalf . . ."), his testimony would be true.[86] The offered explanation is that "I know where I have come from and where I am going." Lenski says that there is no contradiction between John 8:14 and John 5:31:

> Why the notion of at least an apparent contradiction persists, is hard to understand. To be sure, a second witness is necessary, and Jesus Has that second witness. For that very reason the self-witness of Jesus must be accepted as being legally perfectly competent. While, if offered alone, it would amount to nothing before a court of law, corroborated by a second witness, it stands. So Jesus qualifies as a witness in his own case.[87]

In John 8:18, Jesus introduces his Father as the second witness beside himself (καὶ μαρτυρεῖ περὶ ἐμοῦ ὁ πέμψας με πατήρ "and the Father who sent me testifies on my behalf"). This points back to John 8:14, where Jesus is qualified as a witness by his knowledge of the facts.

In the next two examples, Jesus's testimony is focused on others. In John 7:7, Jesus refers to himself as someone who testifies against the world. The expression μαρτυρῶ περὶ αὐτοῦ "testify concerning it [world]," itself does not carry negative connotation, but the fact that the world hates Jesus and that Jesus testifies that "its works are evil," speaks to Jesus's witnessing against the world. In John 13:21, Jesus testifies regarding the coming betrayal: Ταῦτα εἰπὼν [ὁ] Ἰησοῦς ἐταράχθη τῷ πνεύματι καὶ ἐμαρτύρησεν καὶ εἶπεν· ἀμὴν ἀμὴν λέγω ὑμῖν ὅτι εἷς ἐξ ὑμῶν παραδώσει με "When Jesus had said these things, He was troubled in spirit, and testified and said, "Most assuredly, I say to

86. "Jesus means that his own witness concerning himself is true (ἀληθες [*alēthes*]) even if it contravenes their technical rules of evidence" (Robertson, *Word Pictures*).

87. Lenski, *Interpretation of St. John's*, 598.

you, one of you will betray Me" (NKJV). Even though Jesus speaks about future things, we see no conditions or consequences in the context, so we cannot classify this as a warning.

Finally, John 18:37 describes the purpose of Jesus's coming, which is similar to John the Baptist's purpose (John 5:33): *ἵνα μαρτυρήσω τῇ ἀληθείᾳ* "that I should bear witness to the truth" (NKJV). Truth here is not some general truth but specific; it is the truth which he saw and heard with his Father, the truth we need for our salvation.[88]

Fourth, John 5:32 introduces the Father as a witness on his behalf with *ἄλλος ἐστὶν ὁ μαρτυρῶν περὶ ἐμοῦ* "There is another who testifies on my behalf" (NRSV). Two other times, Jesus mentions his Father as a witness for him: in John 5:37, *μεμαρτύρηκεν περὶ ἐμοῦ* "testified on my behalf," and in John 8:18 *μαρτυρεῖ περὶ ἐμοῦ* "testifies on my behalf." The exact contents of the Father's witness are not specified in the text.[89]

Fifth, Jesus mentions his *ἔργον* "works" as another witness for him. In John 5:36 he says *αὐτὰ τὰ ἔργα ἃ ποιῶ μαρτυρεῖ περὶ ἐμοῦ ὅτι ὁ πατήρ με ἀπέσταλκεν* "the very works that I am doing, they testify that the Father has sent me" and John 10:25 *τὰ ἔργα ἃ ἐγὼ ποιῶ ἐν τῷ ὀνόματι τοῦ πατρός μου ταῦτα μαρτυρεῖ περὶ ἐμοῦ* "the very works that I am doing, testify on my behalf that the Father has sent me" (NRSV). But what does Jesus mean by "works"? He might be referring to his own activity as revealer. He might also be referring to the healing and salvation he brings. Or he might be referring to the signs, which include turning water into wine and to the whole range of

88. Lenski, *Interpretation of St. John's*, 1233.

89. "It is a question whether a new and different testimony from that of the works (v. 36) is here introduced. 1. This is the testimony of the works (Augustine, Grotius, Bauer, Neander, Stier, etc.). 2. The testimony of God at the baptism of Christ (Chrysostom, Bengel, Paulus). 3. The witness in the spirit of the believer, the drawing of the Father (De Wette [Alford], Baumgarten-Crusius, Tholuck; but wavering). 4. The testimony which God has given in His word, in the Scriptures of the Old Testament, to His Son (Cyril, Nonnus, etc., Bede, Calvin, Lücke, Meyer). Unquestionably this last interpretation is established by the perfect *μεμαρτύρηκε*, as well as by the ensuing discussion on the Holy Scriptures. Evidently, however, Christ combines the outward word with the inward word in the spirit; and He means not the abstract letter of the Scripture, but the concrete, living Old Testament revelation as a unity of word and spirit (see vv. 37, 38). The third and fourth interpretations, therefore, must be combined. This is the direct, strongly pronounced testimony of the Father" (Lange and Schaff, *John*, 194). Alternatively, Father's witness is not entirely external to Jesus but due to special relationship between Father and the Son, Father's testimony also happens through Jesus who speaks and does what his Father wishes" (Carson, *Gospel According to John*, 260).

the Creator's gifts.[90] While opinion differs, Morris provides a helpful survey of the use of ἔργον in John's gospel and concludes that ἔργον includes the entirety of Jesus's life, including his miraculous activities. With his every activity, with his whole life, Jesus points toward God since he does God's will and reveals God's glory.[91]

Sixth, in John 5:39, Jesus declares that the Scriptures are another witness for him: αἱ μαρτυροῦσαι περὶ ἐμοῦ "which testify of me." While Jesus confirms the idea that there is eternal life in the Scriptures, "he connects that reality with himself: 'they also bear witness about me.' In other words, . . . there is an implication that the Scriptures contain eternal life precisely because they speak of Jesus, or, more simply, that Jesus is the source of eternal life. And that, of course, is what the discourse is about."[92]

Seventh, Jesus presents the Holy Spirit (John 15:26) and disciples (John 15:27) as future witnesses.[93] As we talk about the need for future witnesses for Jesus, Billington's observation is very helpful:

> The trial with the world cannot cease, the witness cannot fall silent, for then his case will be lost by default. After Jesus's departure, the trial continues between the disciples and the hostile world (see e.g. 15:18–16:11). Throughout the Farewell Discourse, Jesus teaches them that his time of 'advocacy' is coming to an end; he is handing it over to them to continue the work. It will not be easy, they are warned; they will encounter intense opposition as Jesus did. How will they be able to face the daunting task?[94]

Precisely because the trial between Jesus and the world continues,[95] the need for witnesses likewise continues. In this context, Jesus mentions the Holy

90. Brodie, *Gospel According to John*, 253.

91. Morris, *Epistle to Romans*, 510–512.

92. Brodie, *Gospel According to John*, 254.

93. In one sense, disciples are already witnesses, since the verb μαρτυρέω is in the present tense (καὶ ὑμεῖς δὲ μαρτυρεῖτε "and you now bear witness"), but their future role as witnesses is also in view. Interestingly, in Acts 10:43 the verb μαρτυρέω is also in the present tense, yet it describes the past witness of the prophets.

94. Billington, "Paraclete and Mission", 100.

95. Billington says: "we maintain that the gospel can be analyzed as a presentation of Jesus' claims in the form of an extended trial, one which gives credence to witnesses, charges,

Spirit as one witness in John 15:26; his job will be to μαρτυρήσει περὶ ἐμοῦ "testify on my behalf." The specific way that the Spirit will testify for Jesus is not stated here.[96] Immediately in John 15:27 Jesus mentions disciples as the second future witness for Jesus: καὶ ὑμεῖς δὲ μαρτυρεῖτε, ὅτι ἀπ' ἀρχῆς μετ' ἐμοῦ ἐστε "You also are to testify because you have been with me from the beginning" (NRSV).[97] Two things are worth noticing: a) the witness of the Spirit and disciples is interconnected and united in the mission of the church, since the Spirit's witness is a witness through the believing community,[98] b) Trites argues that the Holy Spirit in the Gospel of John has a dual legal function and connects his function with the legal representatives in the OT lawsuit where a witness could be both witness and advocate.[99] Accordingly, "witness" is not always a judicial image, but in the Gospel of John it probably has forensic significance, just as the term often does in secular Greek and early Jewish literature.[100]

Eighth, people in general function as witnesses three times in the Gospel of John. John 2:25 says that Jesus did not need testimony of men about other men, because he knew what was in them. This statement presupposes that Jesus had supernatural knowledge which points to his deity. In John 12:17, John describes the multitude who witnessed Lazarus' resurrection with the imperfect verb ἐμαρτύρει "kept testifying." The idea is that those who saw this miracle continued testifying to what they had seen, thus magnifying the witness borne by the sign itself (cf. John 5:36; 10:38) and serving as models for all who bear witness to the truth.[101] John 18:23 shows Jesus on trial.

---

defence, prosecution, and verdict. The Paraclete takes his place, alongside the disciples, in this trial" ("Paraclete and Mission", 102).

96. From the wider biblical context, we can deduce two ways of the future witnessing of the Holy Spirit: a) toward disciples and, b) toward the world. Witness toward disciples would consist of facts about and further revelation of Jesus and miraculous aid and works that itself is a testimony to the continuing work of the Lord. Witness toward the world would exist out of conviction of men regarding sin, righteousness, and judgment (cf. John 16:8–11) (Tenney, "Topics from John", 239).

97. The NRSV's translation reads μαρτυρεῖτε as an action that belongs to the future. The NIV is on the same track ("And you also must testify, for you have been with me from the beginning."). Yet, we noticed that action verb is in the present tense, which implies that the disciples are presented as witnesses in both present and future.

98. Billington, "Paraclete and Mission", 109.

99. Trites, *NT Concept of Witness*, 120.

100. Keener, *John*, 1022–1023.

101. Carson, *Gospel According to John*, 435.

After a bystander slapped him in the face, Jesus said to the court: *εἰ κακῶς ἐλάλησα, μαρτύρησον περὶ τοῦ κακοῦ* "If I have spoken wrongly, testify to the wrong" (NRSV). With this statement, Jesus asked his accusers for a fair trial, insisting that they produce evidence for their charges.

Ninth, the author of the Gospel of John is himself presented as a witness for Jesus. In John 19:35a, he declares: *καὶ ὁ ἑωρακὼς μεμαρτύρηκεν* "And he who has seen has testified." More than likely, John here breaks the narrative to address his readers personally, and his purpose is to present himself as a witness. The perfect tense *μεμαρτύρηκεν* emphasizes the continuity of his testimony, which is grounded in the fact that "he has seen" something. John 21:24 repeats a similar idea, when John there writes about himself as the one *ὁ μαρτυρῶν περὶ τούτων* "who is testifying to these things."

3.2.2 Μαρτυρέω in John's epistles

In 1 John 1:1, the author claims eyewitness status for himself and his company through "hearing," "seeing," "looking" and "touching." In verse 2, the author bases their testimony on *ἑωράκαμεν* "seeing," and connects it with *ἀπαγγέλλομεν* "declaring." Hence, *καὶ ἑωράκαμεν καὶ μαρτυροῦμεν καὶ ἀπαγγέλλομεν* "and have seen and testify and declare" provides a link between incarnation, witnessing and declaration. The verb *ἀπαγγέλλω* "declare" has a semantic component in common with *μαρτυρέω*, namely that of reporting.[102] "Witness," on the other hand, can relate to both ends of the spectrum: "seeing," "hearing" and "knowing," but also "reporting" or "declaring." In other words, proclamation is an act of witness, but its emphasis is on the historical reality of that to which he bears witness.[103] The object of the author's eyewitnessing is "that which was from the beginning" and the "Word of life" (v. 1), although, as Brown notes, the focus is more on "life" than on "word."[104]

In 1 John 4:14 those who function as witnesses are again identified as *ἡμεῖς* "we." Here and in 1 John 1:2, the question is whether "we": a) refers to the original eyewitnesses of the ministry of Jesus, b) designates primarily the apostles themselves, and *includes* the church as represented by them,

102. Haas and Swellengrebel, *John*, 15.

103. Marshall, *Epistles of John*, 103.

104. Brown, *Gospel and Epistles of John*, 109.

or, c) refers to the church in solidarity with eyewitnesses.[105] The basis for their testifying is grounded in τεθεάμεθα "seeing," and the content of their μαρτυρέω is "that the Father has sent his Son as the Saviour of the world."

The next four occurrences (1 John 5:6, 7, 9, 10) are all found in the section that deals with the threefold witness of the Spirit, water and blood. In verse 6b the Spirit is presented as the one who τὸ μαρτυροῦν "one who testifies," and the content of his testimony is stated in verse 6a: "This is the one who came by water and blood, Jesus Christ, not with the water only but with the water and the blood." The present tense of μαρτυρέω indicates that the Spirit is testifying now, and Smalley[106] says that this happens "by means of preaching, inspired prophecy and the sacraments." However, the text is less clear on this point. Verse 7 introduces triple witness: ὅτι τρεῖς εἰσιν οἱ μαρτυροῦντες "For there are three that testify," which are then listed in verse 8. The use of three witnesses might be influenced by the OT requirement for "two or three witnesses" (Deut 17:6; 19:15). In verse 7 μαρτυρέω is also in a present participle form, which confirms the continuation of the testimony of these three witnesses. However, if "water and blood" refer to the historical facts of Jesus's life, which testify to his identity (that Jesus is Son of God and Messiah), we must ask how they continue to testify. John does not answer this question here.

Note two more things. First, John does not say that Jesus testified about something through "water and blood." Instead, "water and blood" are the subjects who testify. Second, this testimony continues, and according to Trites the continuation is sacramental: "[t]his concern for a continuing witness suggests that in addition to the historical attestation of Christ's baptism and crucifixion there is also a symbolic reference to the two great sacraments – a suggestion made more plausible by the fact that baptism and the Lord's Supper seem to be alluded to in John 3 and 6."[107]

After seeing the three witnesses in 1 John 5:9, we encounter the idea of a greater and lesser testimony, the testimony of men and God. By saying that God μεμαρτύρηκεν περὶ τοῦ υἱοῦ αὐτοῦ "has testified to his Son" with μαρτυρέω in the perfect tense, the author implies the continuing validity of

105. Smalley, *1, 2, 3 John*, 51.

106. Smalley, *1, 2, 3 John*, 280.

107. Trites, *NT Concept of Witness*, 127.

God's historical testimony to Christ.[108] Yarbrough explains that the perfect tense frequently connotes a solemn and lasting verdict, which makes God's testimony permanent and final, not to be set aside or altered by neglect or human tampering.[109] Finally, in verse 10 we see the same expression *μεμαρτύρηκεν . . . περὶ τοῦ υἱοῦ αὐτοῦ* appears as in verse 9. Again, the verb is in perfect tense and has the same object.

In 3 John *μαρτυρέω* appears in 1:3, 6 and twice in 1:12. In verse 3, John writes to and about Gaius, mentioning how he had received a testimony about Gaius from a group of unnamed brethren who came to John, who were *μαρτυρούντων σου τῇ ἀληθείᾳ* "testifying of your truth." By "testifying" we can understand that they made a report about what they had seen, heard, and experienced of Gaius.[110] The content of their testimony was *σου τῇ ἀληθείᾳ* that is, "the fact that Gaius was faithful to the truth of the Christian gospel as it was being preserved by the orthodox members of the Johannine community."[111] In verse 6 we find out that these brethren not only informed John about Gaius but also about Gaius's church. Here, the content of their *ἐμαρτύρησάν* "testifying" was *σου τῇ ἀγάπῃ* "your love." It is interesting that these brethren's witnessing activity is described with the present tense in verse 3, while their witnessing before the church in 1:6 is described with the aorist tense.

Finally, in 1:12, John recommends Demetrius to Gaius. In so doing, he names several witnesses. The verb *μαρτυρέω* appears twice. The first occurrence is in the perfect passive tense, *μεμαρτύρηται* "he has been testified to," which signifies that that the testimony to Demetrius had been given over a period of time and was still effective.[112] This testimony about Demetrius is given *ὑπὸ πάντων* "by all" and *ὑπὸ αὐτῆς τῆς ἀληθείας* "by the truth itself."[113]

---

108. Akin, *1, 2, 3 John*, 38.

109. Yarbrough, *1, 2, and 3 John*, 286.

110. Haas and Swellengrebel, *John*, 177.

111. Smalley, *1, 2, 3 John*, 346–347.

112. Smalley, 361.

113. "The phrase '(he is well spoken of) by the truth itself' is awkward . . . It is possible that the presbyter is personifying the 'truth,' and identifying it with God (although that is not a normal Johannine identification), Christ (cf. John 14:6) or the Spirit (cf. 1 John 5:6) . . . But in that case the divine witness of God (Father, Son or Holy Spirit) seems abrupt and out of place, occurring as it does between the entirely human testimony of 'everyone' on the one hand, and of the presbyter himself on the other. A more natural exegesis, therefore, is to understand the 'testimony of the truth' to Demetrius as an acknowledgment that his whole way of life

The second occurrence of μαρτυρέω is in the present tense, and this time the subject of the verb is ἡμεῖς "we." Without delving further into the identity of the witnesses "all," "truth" and "we," we can notice that John here offers threefold testimony concerning Demetrius.

3.2.3 Μαρτυρέω in the book of Revelation

Revelation 1:2 describes John's role in the production of the book of Revelation, and also describes the content of the book itself. Verse 1 indicates that the chain of communication is from God to Jesus to an angel to John, and finally to Christian "servants." Sometimes it is difficult to discern whether the speaker is God, Christ, or an angel, since John is receiving the message from all three.[114] But in verse 2, John is the subject of μαρτυρέω. Again, we encounter several interpretative questions. First, the genitive phrases τὸν λόγον τοῦ θεοῦ and τὴν μαρτυρίαν'Ιησοῦ Χριστοῦ can be taken as subjective ("God's word and "Jesus's testimony"), objective ("the word about God" and "the testimony about Jesus Christ"), or general genitives (including both subjective and objective aspects). Second, the expressions in 1:2 τὸν λόγον τοῦ θεοῦ "the word of God" and τὴν μαρτυρίαν 'Ιησοῦ Χριστοῦ "the testimony of Jesus Christ" do not refer to separate things but are complementary or parallel descriptions of these visions that John has received. Accordingly, the phrase "the testimony of Jesus Christ" clarifies the precise content of "the word of God." Finally, the final clause of the verse ὅσα εἶδεν "everything he [John] saw" is appositional and limits the scope of both. The message of God here attested to by Jesus consists of everything that John saw in his vision.[115] These factors clearly describe John first and foremost as an observing witness, who after the reception of revelation testifies to what he had seen.

In Revelation 22:16, Jesus's reference to sending the angel repeats language from Revelation 1:1–2. Here the angel (not John) is described as the one who μαρτυρῆσαι "testifies" ταῦτα "these things." As Stefanović notes, this angel functions in the role of Christ and speaks Christ's words, and it is often hard to distinguish his statements from the words of Christ.[116] Due to the

---

expressed a commitment to the truth of Christ which constantly resulted in 'good' (loving) conduct" (Smalley, 361).

114. Beale, *Book of Revelation*, 183.

115. Mounce, *Book of Revelation*, 42.

116. Stefanović, *Revelation*, 609.

combination of the threefold μαρτυρέω (Rev 22:16, 18, 20) with the penalty for disobeying the testimony (Rev 22:18), Bealeargues that "testify" here has a forensic sense.[117] In verse 18a Jesus continues as the speaker.[118] Here he is the one who issues testimony. Note not only that the book of Revelation is itself a testimony, but also that Jesus offers his testimony regarding this prophetic book in the form of a warning. He testifies to the validity of this book for the future and stipulates consequences for those who alter the message. These factors indicate that μαρτυρέω here should be read as "warning." Lastly, in verse 20 Jesus is again presented as the one who testify ταῦτα "these things" (cf. v. 16), which can refer to the book of Revelation or to warning given in verse 18. While the substantival participle of the verb μαρτυρέω "the one who testifies" refers to ταῦτα, the verb λέγω "he says" refers to the following statement: "Surely I am coming soon."

3.3 Μαρτυρία in the Johannine writings

3.3.1 Μαρτυρία in the Gospel of John

When we have studied the appearances of μαρτυρέω in the Gospel of John, the noun μαρτυρία also appeared in several verses. Hence, now we will look at these occurrences, together with other verses where μαρτυρία appears alone.

John 1:7 contains both the verb μαρτυρέω and the noun μαρτυρία. Here John describes the ministry of John the Baptist, who as a prophet came εἰς μαρτυρίαν "for testimony"[119] with a purpose ἵνα μαρτυρήσῃ "that he might testify" περὶ τοῦ φωτός "for the light," with desired outcome ἵνα πάντες πιστεύσωσιν δι' αὐτοῦ "that all through him might believe." The Baptist's story continues in verse 19, where John mentions ἡ μαρτυρία τοῦ 'Ιωάννου "testimony of John." Here τοῦ 'Ιωάννου is a subjective genitive since it refers to the content of John's testimony which is stated in the following verses.

117. Beale, *Book of Revelation*, 1143.

118. "Again, there is debate regarding the speaker, with some thinking it is Jesus (Swete, R. Charles, Schüssler Fiorenza, Mounce, Giesen, Michaels) but others believing it is John (Moffatt, Lohmeyer, Caird, Kraft, Roloff, Krodel)" (Osborne, *Revelation*, 794).

119. "The aorist ἦλθεν, while it is historical and reports the past fact, summarizes John's entire career" (Lenski, *Interpretation of St. John's*, 47).

In John 3:11, Jesus speaks: *καὶ τὴν μαρτυρίαν ἡμῶν οὐ λαμβάνετε* "yet you do not receive our testimony." The genitive *ἡμῶν* "our"[120] is a subjective genitive and refers to Jesus's testimony, which is based on what he "knows" and "[has] seen."

In John 3:32, the narrator connects the verb *μαρτυρέω* to what Jesus has seen and heard, but here the response to Jesus's witnessing is *καὶ τὴν μαρτυρίαν αὐτοῦ οὐδεὶς λαμβάνει* "yet no one accepts his testimony." As in the previous cases, the genitive *αὐτοῦ* "his" functions as a subjective genitive. In the following verse, the text reads: *ὁ λαβὼν αὐτοῦ τὴν μαρτυρίαν ἐσφράγισεν ὅτι ὁ θεὸς ἀληθής ἐστιν* "Whoever has accepted his testimony has certified this, that God is true." Since the participle *ὁ λαβὼν* "whoever has accepted" reveals that there are people who accepts Jesus's testimony, *οὐδεὶς* "no one" in verse 32 does not mean a total rejection of Jesus. The genitive *αὐτοῦ* "his" here also refers to subjective genitive. The idea behind the verb *σφραγίζω* "sealing" is that a seal certifies the approval of a legal document. This indicates that that those who receive him become witnesses who further attest to the veracity of his claim.[121] It also points to the relationship between Jesus's testimony and the Father's truth. 1 John 5:9–10 explains this relationship by saying that those who reject Jesus's testimony also make God a liar.[122]

The next group of verses using *μαρτυρία* are John 5:31, 32, 34, 36. With the exception of verse 34, these all pair *μαρτυρέω* with *μαρτυρία*. In these occurrences, the noun *μαρτυρία* refers to the specific content of testimony. In verse 31 Jesus testifies for himself, but he is not a single witness; in verse 32 he introduces his Father as witness for his cause, and again we see here the connection between "testimony" and "truth"; and in verse 36 John the Baptist and Jesus's works are presented as witnesses. Although the sufficient number of witnesses necessary to condemn a man is not an issue in John 5, Jesus alludes to this principle when discussing witnesses to confirm someone's testimony.[123] In verse 34, Jesus's statement, "Not that I accept such

120. Plurals in verse 11 can be explained in the following ways: a) historical Jesus identifies himself with his disciples, b) it reports what the church of John's day said to the synagogue, c) when Nicodemus first approached Jesus he said: "we know . . ." Jesus now uses "we" to respond back to him, d) they are editorial plurals or plurals of majesty (Carson, *Gospel According to John*, 198–199; Borchert, *John 1–11*, 178).

121. Keener, *Acts Vol. 2*, 582.

122. Brown, *Gospel According to John*, 161.

123. Brown, 223.

human testimony," indicates that he is not dependent on human testimony for the truth concerning himself.[124] However, he offered human corroboration for their sake ("so that you may be saved") because John the Baptist was recognized as a prophet and a man of God. However, as Lenski explains,

> Jesus can afford to dispense with the Baptist's testimony, great though it is, because he has "the testimony" that is far greater than his . . . Jesus, as the defendant facing these Jews as his accusers, does not call on the Baptist to bring in the decisive testimony (τὴν μαρτυρίαν, note the article). Jesus' great witness is God himself.[125]

Jesus acts as though further evidence (that of John the Baptist) is unnecessary, yet he provides it anyway.[126]

Our next group of verses come from John 8. John 8:13–14 also contain both the verb μαρτυρέω and the noun μαρτυρία, and John 8:17 contains only μαρτυρία. In verse 13, the Pharisees basically repeat what Jesus already confirmed in John 5:31, that the testimony of a single witness is not valid. Jesus's mention of ἡ μαρτυρία μου "my testimony" in verse 14 is a reference to his claim that if he testifies about himself, his testimony is "true" due to his knowledge of the facts. In verse 17 Jesus confirms again that, according to the standards of the Law, his testimony is valid because the Lawgiver (Father) testifies for Jesus also. We have to note here that the matter is not criminal case, where judgment must be established by minimum of two witnesses (cf. Num 35:30; Deut 17:6; 19:15, etc.). This depends rather on the general legal principle that a case could be settled on the basis of the congruent testimony of two persons.[127] Keener rightly notices that if Jesus is who he claims, his own claim is hardly restricted by the Law.[128] However, Jesus appeals to the highest possible witness alongside himself, namely his Father. Interestingly, Jesus says ὅτι δύο ἀνθρώπων ἡ μαρτυρία ἀληθής ἐστιν "that the testimony of two men [witnesses] is true." In addition to the fact that the text here mentions the testimony "of two men," (ἄνθρωποι), whereas

124. Ridderbos, *John*, 202.

125. Lenski, *Interpretation of St. John's*, 405.

126. Keener, *John*, 657.

127. Ridderbos, *John*, 296.

128. Keener, *John*, 741–742.

Deuteronomy reads "of two witnesses" (μάρτυρες),[129] and the fact that one of the two witnesses may be testifying in his own case,[130] the question is how to understand that the testimony of two men equals ἀληθής "truth"? We know, for example that, two false witnesses can agree to speak a lie (cf. 1 Kgs 21:10–13). This is obviously not stating universally that the witness of two witnesses in agreement guaranties truth. Rather the principle is that two witnesses are needed to uphold the validity of a claim, and that their testimony would be admitted as "true" or "fact."

Two last examples John 19:35 and 21:24 also contain both μαρτυρέω and μαρτυρία. In John 19:35 we have seen that John's testifying activity is based on what he has "seen." He was an eyewitness and thus trustworthy; eyewitness testimony was considered the most reliable. Hence, ἀληθινὴ αὐτοῦ ἐστιν ἡ μαρτυρία "his testimony is true." Similar wording between John 19:35 and 21:24 "This is the disciple who is testifying to these things . . . and we know that his testimony is true," suggests that the eyewitness of John 19:35 and the disciple referred to in John 21:24 are one and the same person.[131] We also see that John's testimony has been put in written form which makes this document "a testimony." Finally, in John 21:24b the phrase καὶ οἴδαμεν ὅτι ἀληθὴς αὐτοῦ ἡ μαρτυρία ἐστίν "and we know that his testimony is true" is puzzling, because it implies some additional confirmation and approval of John's testimony by others. Οἴδαμεν "we know" probably stands for communal approval of John's, yet we cannot be sure about identity of this community. The present tense of the verb μαρτυρέω in John 21:24, may mean that the author is still alive and still testifies, or he may be dead, but his testimony still continues in written form and inside of the community.

3.3.2 Μαρτυρία in John's Epistles

By saying in 1 John 5:9a εἰ τὴν μαρτυρίαν τῶν ἀνθρώπων λαμβάνομεν, ἡ μαρτυρία τοῦ θεοῦ μείζων ἐστίν "If we receive human testimony, the testimony of God is greater," John introduces the categories of lesser and greater testimony. Εἰ "if" stresses that if human witness is accepted as valuable, how

129. Which might be intentional change to point out the difference between testimonies of two people (witnesses), and, in this case, two divine persons: Jesus and his Father.

130. Lenski, *Interpretation of St. John's*, 605.

131. Ridderbos, *John*, 620.

much more can God's testimony about his Son be trusted. This is especially true, since it was given in a threefold manner which is the prescribed standard for the testimony. The genitives in the expressions *τὴν μαρτυρίαν τῶν ἀνθρώπων* and *ἡ μαρτυρία τοῦ θεοῦ* are subjective genitives, which means they speak about testimonies which are given by men and God. But what is the content of these testimonies? Kruse says that this can hardly refer to the threefold testimony of the Spirit, water, and blood.[132] Instead, John may be alluding to the witness of John the Baptist (John 5:33–36), or to the testimony of the eyewitnesses (1 John 1:1–2). The last option is to understand this as a general statement indicating that God's testimony is always more important than human testimony. The content of God's testimony is also debatable. It could be: a) the threefold witness of the Spirit, the water, and the blood, b) the Spirit/anointing which believers have received, through the baptizing and atoning work of Jesus, c) God's testimony which supplements the threefold witness that can be either God's voice which Jesus hears but not his opponents (cf. John 5:37), or the testimony of the eyewitnesses since God is speaking through them.

1 John 5:9b says *ὅτι αὕτη ἐστὶν ἡ μαρτυρία τοῦ θεοῦ ὅτι μεμαρτύρηκεν περὶ τοῦ υἱοῦ αὐτοῦ* "for this is the testimony of God that he has testified to his Son." The first *ὅτι* is a causal conjunction, meaning "for." The next word, *αὕτη* "this," might in some way point back to the threefold testimony of verses 7–8, but it certainly points forward to the *ὅτι* clause which follows: "that he has testified to his Son." 1 John 5:9b can be read in three ways: a) John records the fact that God gave testimony but does not say anything about its content, b) God's testimony is the testimony described in verses 6–8, or c) John is recapitulating the testimony already described but with emphasis on it value. In other words, it's worth consists in the fact that *God* has given it to his *Son*. No testimony could be more trustworthy.[133]

1 John 5:10 continues with the topic of testimony by using both *μαρτυρέω* and *μαρτυρία*. The new idea introduced here is that the one who believes in the Son of God *ἔχει τὴν μαρτυρίαν ἐν ἑαυτῷ* "has the witness in himself." Based on this effect, the "testimony" from verse 10 refers to the inward witness of the Spirit that believers receive. Having such inward witness "enables

132. Kruse, *John*, 180–181.

133. Smalley, *1, 2, 3 John*, 283–284.

the believer to render an effective outward testimony by keeping Jesus in the focus of his consciousness."[134] The repeated verb μαρτυρέω that refers to God's μαρτυρία is in the perfect tense in both verse 9 and verse 10. This probably indicates that those who believe in the Son of God accept and keep God's testimony,[135] whatever that might be.

Finally, in 1 John 5:11, John concludes his discussion of testimony by declaring: Καὶ αὕτη ἐστὶν ἡ μαρτυρία, ὅτι ζωὴν αἰώνιον ἔδωκεν ἡμῖν ὁ θεός, καὶ αὕτη ἡ ζωὴ ἐν τῷ υἱῷ αὐτοῦ ἐστιν "And this is the testimony: God gave us eternal life, and this life is in his Son" (NRSV). If John in the previous verses was describing God's witness concerning his Son, in verse 11 he stops discussing the content of God's testimony[136] and turns to the result of that testimony, which is nothing less than eternal life.[137]

3.3.3 Μαρτυρία in the book of Revelation

Μαρτυρία appears nine times in Revelation. Four times the accusative phrase τὴν μαρτυρίαν appears in connection with τὸν λόγον τοῦ θεοῦ "the word of God" (Rev 1:2, 9; 6:9; 20:4). In Revelation 11:7 μαρτυρία is modified with personal pronoun αὐτῶν. In Revelation 12:11 τὸν λόγον is followed by genitive phrase τῆς μαρτυρίας αὐτῶν. In Revelation 12:17 μαρτυρία is coupled with τὰς ἐντολὰς τοῦ θεοῦ "the commandments of God." Finally, in Revelation 19:10 μαρτυρία appears twice, once in the accusative τὴν μαρτυρίαν and then in the nominative ἡ . . . μαρτυρία, both times modified by genitive Ἰησοῦ "Jesus."

Commentators debate the function of the genitives in the verses that contain the expression "the testimony of Jesus." The phrase "the testimony of Jesus Christ" in Revelation 1:2 can refer either to the witness which Christ Himself imparts (subjective) or the witness of life which John gave to Him

134. Tenney, "Topics from John," 241.

135. Marshall, *Epistles of John*, 241.

136. Parsenios (*First, Second and Third John*, 123–124) argues differently. Commenting on verses 10–11 he says that the content of the testimony is described in the final line of verse 11, and the meaning of having testimony "in himself" is explained in verse 12: "Having the testimony is equivalent to having life, because the content of the testimony is that God gave eternal life through his Son (5:11). Thus to 'have' the testimony in verse 10 is to have eternal life."

137. Akin, *1, 2, 3 John*, 201–202.

(objective). There is a similar debate over Revelation 1:9 and 12:17.[138] We say that the genitives make more sense as subjective genitives. So, "the word of God and the testimony of Jesus" from Revelation 1:9 refer to "the word spoken by God and the testimony borne by Jesus," and "the commandments of God and the testimony of Jesus" from Revelation 12:17 are "the commandments given by God and the testimony borne by Jesus." Reading these all as subjective genitives receives further confirmation in Revelation 19:10, where "the testimony borne by Jesus is the spirit which inspires the prophets." In other words, Christian prophets speak words that are spoken by God, attested by Jesus and put by the Spirit into their mouths. Revelation 11:7 and 12:11 can also be understood as subjective genitives, since "their testimony" refers to the testimony that subjects in these verses give. The overall idea is that Jesus gave his testimony to the faithful and it is their task to maintain and "hold" it even in the face of hostility, persecution and death.[139]

The expression *ἡ μαρτυρία Ἰησοῦ* in Revelation 19:10 has been understood in three ways. First, some commentators favour the objective genitive, the "testimony about Jesus," asserting that the testimony in question has Jesus for its object. Second, some opt for the subjective genitive, thus "the testimony borne by Jesus." The most probable option for Bandy[140] is to regard this as a general genitive, which would read "the witness by and to Jesus," or "our testimony about Jesus in response to his testimony about God." In this way, both the objective and subjective senses are kept, so that the witness was first borne by Jesus and then transmitted to believers, and the witness they bear is about Jesus.

The two remaining passages, Revelation 6:9[141] and 20:4, can be also viewed as subjective genitives, since those who keep the word, that God

138. The construction *διὰ τὸν λόγον τοῦ θεοῦ καὶ τὴν μαρτυρίαν Ἰησοῦ* "because of the word of God and the testimony of Jesus" due to preposition *διὰ* can be understood differently. It can mean that John was on the Pathmos *because of* "the word of God and the testimony of Jesus" (cause), or that he was on the Pathmos *for* "the word of God and the testimony of Jesus" (purpose). In the first instance John would end up on Pathmos because he was already preaching "the word of God and the testimony of Jesus" which implies objective meaning of the genitive. In the second instance, he went to Patmos to receive "the word of God and the testimony of Jesus" which implies subjective meaning of the genitive.

139. Trites, *NT Concept of Witness*, 156–157.

140. Bandy, "Words and Witness," 18–20.

141. In essence, *martyría* refers to Jesus's testimony – his life and teaching, but believers are those who *ἔχω* "have it" or "keep it." Their keeping it, includes verbal testimony, but

uttered and the testimony that Jesus gave are doing so to the point of death. Accordingly, death might in some instances be the result of the believers' testimony, but testimony is never so strongly identified with martyrdom that μάρτυς becomes the equivalent of "martyr," or that μάρτυς is used absolutely to refer to martyrdom without reference to witness.[142]

3.4 Μαρτύριον in the Johannine writings

The single appearance of this noun is in Revelation 15:5. Here we have an interesting expression, ὁ ναὸς τῆς σκηνῆς τοῦ μαρτυρίου. τῆς σκηνῆς is probably an appositional genitive phrase with a meaning "the sanctuary [temple] which is the tabernacle" or "the temple, that is, the tent of witness." τοῦ μαρτυρίου, "of witness," is a descriptive genitive.[143] Beale explains that this sanctuary in heaven reminds us of the tabernacle that was with Israel in the wilderness which contained the testimony, or the Ten Commandments placed in the ark.[144] In a similar fashion,

> [t]he "testimony" in 15:5 includes not only the Law but "the testimony of Jesus," who sums up the OT 'commandments of God' in himself (see on 12:17). This is suggested by the use of the μαρτυρέω word-group elsewhere in the Apocalypse . . . exclusively for testimony about or from Jesus. The point is that God is about to reveal his just will from his heavenly dwelling place by sending forth judgments on the earth against those who reject his testimony.[145]

---

probably more than just that – even their entire life. The same situation is in Revelation 12:17 and 19:10 where different subjects who "have" or "keep" Jesus's testimony, and they are doing that verbally, but also in some other ways. Revelation 20:4 does not describe witnesses as those who "had" or "kept" Jesus's testimony, yet from the context it is obvious that they did the same thing.

142. Trites, "Μάρτυς and Martyrdom," 80.

143. Beale, *Book of Revelation*, 801; Aune, *Revelation 6–16*, 877.

144. Beale, 801–802. Osborne (*Revelation*, 569) claims that "[t]he purpose for this description is to insert the idea of covenant, with its attendant blessings and cursings. The nations have broken covenant with God and must face the consequences. In 11:19 the ark may have been a sign of mercy, but here it is a sign of judgment."

145. Beale, *Book of Revelation*, 802.

4. The concept of witness in the Pauline writings – passage analysis

4.1 Μάρτυς in the Pauline writings

In the Pauline writings, *μάρτυς* appears nine times. It describes: YHWH as witness (Rom 1:9; 2 Cor 1:23; Phil 1:8; 1 Thess 2:5, 10); it is found in references to the OT requirement of two or three witnesses (2 Cor 13:1; 1 Tim 5:19); and it is also used in reference to multiple witnesses (1 Tim 6:12; 2 Tim 2:2).

In several places, Paul invokes God as a witness. According to Dunn, this practice was common in both Greek and Jewish literature as a way of underlining a writer's concerns, something not to be understood lightly (cf. 2 Cor 11:31; Gal 1:20).[146] Dunn concludes: "If he knew Jesus's teaching on oaths (Matt 5:33–37; cf. Jas 5:12) he presumably did not regard it as necessarily relevant to such conversational conventions." To assert something and call upon God as witness is equivalent to speaking under oath.[147] An alternative to Dunn's view is that Paul's use of oath formulae "reflects the early church's understanding that Jesus's teaching was directed against inappropriate use of oaths rather constituting a blanket prohibition."[148]

In Romans 1:9 Paul invokes God as witness *μάρτυς γάρ μού ἐστιν ὁ θεός* "For God is my witness" to his bold claim that he prays for the church in Rome "without ceasing." Paul wants the readers to know that his statement of concern for them was not idle rhetoric, so he called God to be his witness that what he was saying was true.[149] Morris adds that truthfulness of such things that Paul said could only be known to God.[150] Accordingly, "[h]e cannot adduce earthly witnesses of the peculiarity of the facts which he has to assure; they are of heavenly origin, and he calls on God as their witness: that is, his whole knowledge of God, and his apostolic conscience, must be pledged."[151]

In 2 Corinthians 1:23, the subject of discussion is the changes Paul made to his traveling plans in regard to Corinth. In this context, Paul uses the following oath formula: Ἐγὼ δὲ μάρτυρα τὸν θεὸν ἐπικαλοῦμαι ἐπὶ τὴν ἐμὴν

146. Dunn, *Romans 1–8*, 28.

147. Kruse, *Romans*, 59.

148. Kruse, 59.

149. Mounce, *Romans*, 66–67.

150. Morris, *Epistle to Romans*, 57.

151. Lange, et al., *Romans*, 68.

ψυχήν "But I call God as witness upon my soul." With this statement, Paul invokes God as both his witness (μάρτυρα) and his judge (ἐπὶ τὴν ἐμὴν ψυχήν). Elsewhere Paul uses a different oath formula: "God is my witness," where ὁ θεός is nominative (Rom 1:9; Phil 1:8; 1 Thess 2:5; cf. 2:10), but here his invocation of God is in the accusative case. Hence, "[a]s a μάρτυς . . . God is the one who not only knows all human actions but also perceives all human motives. In the absence of human witnesses who could vouch for his motivation in making or changing his travel plans, Paul appeals to the irrefutable knowledge of God."[152] Regarding ἐπὶ τὴν ἐμὴν ψυχήν, the Greek is literally "to witness upon my soul (life)." Although some read it in a positive sense, "for my life",[153] this statement probably reflects Hebraism *ʿal-napšî* (על־נפשי) "on my soul" or "against my soul." With this invocation, a person literally says, "if I am lying, God will punish me for the perjury."[154]

Philippians 1:8 is similar to Romans 1:9 since Paul invokes God as witness to his love for the church in Philippi with μάρτυς γάρ μου ὁ θεὸς "For God is my witness." As in Romans 1:9, by this statement Paul reinforces the point about his deep affection for the Philippians.[155] God is witness "not in a judicial sense of witness to facts, but in a more general sense of his witnessing to the processes and motives in Paul's inner life or the reasons for his behavior under particular circumstances . . . since no other factual witnesses could be produced to prove the truthfulness and authenticity of what he affirmed."[156]

Speaking about his work and the work of his companions in Thessaloniki, in 1 Thessalonians 2 Paul invokes twice God as witness. First, in 1 Thessalonians 2:5, Paul's invocation is simple: θεὸς μάρτυς "God is witness." As in the previous cases, he uses the practice of appealing to God as a witness when his inner motivations are in question and can only be verified independently by God.[157] But unlike the previous cases, here Paul can also appeal to others since in the same verse he says that the believers in Thessaloniki also have knowledge: καθὼς οἴδατε "as you know." Hence, God is "witness"

152. Harris, *Second Epistle to Corinthians*, 212.

153. Lange, et al., *2 Corinthians*, 25.

154. Martin, *2 Corinthians*, 34.

155. O'Brien, *Epistle to Philippians*, 70.

156. O'Brien, 71.

157. Wanamaker, *Thessalonians*, 97–98.

and Thessalonians are the ones who "know." In 1 Thessalonians 2:10, Paul confirms the following: ὑμεῖς μάρτυρες καὶ ὁ θεός "You are witnesses and God." In previous examples, Paul did not include people as witnesses to his motives, but here he is referring to time which he spent with the readers. Accordingly, when he writes to the Romans, Corinthians and Philippians, he is absent from them. Here, in 1 Thessalonians 2, Paul invokes two witnesses in accordance with Deuteronomy 19:15, even though this situation is outside of juridical contexts, and deals with the character of a person.[158]

The next two examples deal with the principle of two or three witnesses. In 2 Corinthians 13:1, Paul introduces a citation from Deuteronomy 19:15 ἐπὶ στόματος δύο μαρτύρων καὶ τριῶν σταθήσεται πᾶν ῥῆμα, "on the mouth of two witnesses or three shall every saying be established" (YLT). [159] This stipulation is distinct from Roman and Greek law, since neither rejected the validity of a single witness.[160] The expression ἐπὶ στόματος, which literally means "on the mouth," should be read as "on the basis of (verbal) testimony or evidence." Such *evidence* must come from a minimum of two or three witnesses (there is likely no upper limit) in order that πᾶν ῥῆμα must be established. While ῥῆμα denotes spoken word, here it translates the Hebrew term *dāḇār* and refers to a subject spoken about (πρᾶγμα). Thus, ῥῆμα should be understood as "matter, issue," or in a specifically legal sense, "case, charge."[161] By ῥῆμα, Paul is probably referring to the matters he mentioned in 2 Corinthians 12:20–21. The identity of the two or three witnesses can be understood in various ways: (1) Paul speaks in general terms about legal procedures he would apply during his formal inquiry into the charges made against him or into the Corinthians' offenses (cf. 12:20–21) that required discipline. This view implies that Paul will hold court and, on the testimony of two or three witnesses, convict and punish the offenders. (2) "Two witnesses" are the two warnings (προείρηκα καὶ προλέγω) in 2 Corinthians 13:2 which Paul gave to the church. Now, when he comes for the third time, he

158. Green, *Thessalonians*, 132.

159. "Paul's citation is essentially the same as the LXX of Deuteronomy 19:15, the only differences being that the LXX repeats ἐπὶ στόματος between καί and τριῶν and repeats μαρτύρων after τριῶν" (Harris, *Second Epistle to Corinthians*, 906–907). Hence, LXX reads: ἐπὶ στόματος δύο μαρτύρων καὶ ἐπὶ στόματος τριῶν μαρτύρων στήσεται πᾶν ῥῆμα.

160. Harris, *Second Epistle to Corinthians*, 906.

161. Harris, 907.

will take action against those who continued in sin. Or the warnings could be 1 Corinthians 4:21, the second visit and the severe letter, and the third visit mentioned in 2 Corinthians 13:2. Accordingly, the warnings function as testimonies that would later be sufficient to indict the offenders. This would be something similar to Exodus 21:29, where a past warning or warnings serve as a basis for conviction. (3) The three witnesses are Paul's two previous and one future visit to Corinth. His next visit will be the third and decisive witness against the troublemakers. But that would mean that Paul is taking the Deuteronomic legal principle which speaks about people and applies it to visitations and accompanying warnings.[162]

1 Timothy 5:19 describes the bringing of accusations against a presbyter: *κατὰ πρεσβυτέρου κατηγορίαν μὴ παραδέχου, ἐκτὸς εἰ μὴ*[163] *ἐπὶ δύο ἢ τριῶν μαρτύρων* "Do not entertain an accusation against an elder unless it is brought by two or three witnesses" (NIV). As we have seen previously, *ἐπί* means "on the basis of," i.e. "on the evidence of," rather than "before" in the sense of "in the presence of," since such meaning is also present in similar passages like Matthew 18:16 and 2 Corinthians 13:1.[164] Unlike the parallel references to Deuteronomy 19:15 in Matthew 18:16 and 2 Corinthians 13:1, 1 Timothy 5:19 does not use *στόματος*, but this does not indicate that Paul is not thinking here about "spoken testimony." Once again, we see an application of Deuteronomy 19:15 in the context of church discipline, but unlike Matthew 18:16, in both 2 Corinthians 13:1 and here (1 Tim 5:19) we are not given any clear procedure, nor can we easily pinpoint the role and function of such witnesses. For example, a) are we dealing here (and in 2 Cor 13:1) with sin of one person against another, or just sin in general? b) do we need to follow the procedure of Matthew 18:16 or not? c) are the witnesses in 1 Timothy 5:19 witnesses of the offense who also bring the charge against presbyter, or are they just verifying an accusation that may come from only one individual? The answers to these questions affect the way we understand the concept of witness in this verse.

---

162. Harris, 906–908.

163. "*ἐκτὸς εἰ μή* (a combination of *ἐκτός* and *εἰ μή*; 1 Cor. 14:5; 15:2) is a double (pleonastic) form of negation in postclassical Greek (BAGD s.v. *ἐκτός*) and means 'unless' or 'except'" (Knight, *Pastoral Epistles*, 235).

164. Knight, 235.

The last two examples of *μάρτυς* in Paul's letters are connected with Timothy's confession in the presence of many witnesses. In 1 Timothy 6:12 Paul mentions *καὶ ὡμολόγησας τὴν καλὴν ὁμολογίαν ἐνώπιον πολλῶν μαρτύρων* "and have confessed the good confession in the presence of many witnesses" (NKJV). Knight believes that *καλὴ ὁμολογία* refers to a public acknowledgment of Jesus as the resurrected Lord.[165] Accordingly, Paul reminds Timothy of that historical moment when he made this confession in the presence of many witnesses, and that these witnesses would be able to testify to it and thus to Timothy's public commitment, the commitment to which Paul now calls him. The occasion of Timothy's confession could be Timothy's baptism, when he confessed his faith, or Timothy's ordination as a minister of the gospel. Also, confession could refer to a Christian testimony, given by him during some public persecution or severe conflict.[166] We cannot be sure to which occasion Paul refers here, but the witnesses here likely had a notarial function.

In 2 Timothy 2:2, Paul also refers to *πολλῶν μαρτύρων* "many witnesses," this time in the context of the things Timothy has *ἀκούω* "heard" Paul say. Hence, the first statement *καὶ ἃ ἤκουσας παρ' ἐμοῦ* "and what you heard from me" is qualified with *διὰ πολλῶν μαρτύρων* "through many witnesses." *διὰ* could mean that Timothy has received Paul's message "through" the teaching and ministry of others. Or it could mean that Timothy heard it "in the presence of" these witnesses, so that these witnesses testified to what was taught.[167] In that sense, these witnesses confirmed and guaranteed that what Paul was saying is truth which needs to be passed on. Hence, the issue here is the "content" of the doctrine which a) Paul taught, b) witnesses confirmed, c) Timothy heard, and now, d) Timothy needs to *παρατίθημι* "entrust" to others, so that, e) they can *διδάσκω* "teach" others.

4.2 Μαρτυρέω in the Pauline writings

In the Pauline writings, *μαρτυρέω* appears eight times. The first occurrence is Romans 3:21 where the subject is *δικαιοσύνη θεοῦ* "the righteousness of God." Paul says God's righteousness was *φανερόω* "revealed" or "manifested," and

165. Knight, *Pastoral Epistles*, 264.

166. cf. Lange, et al., *1 & 2 Timothy*, 73.

167. Knight, *Pastoral Epistles*, 390.

that it is μαρτυρουμένη ὑπὸ τοῦ νόμου καὶ τῶν προφητῶν "being witnessed by the Law and the Prophets." The participle μαρτυρουμένη is in the passive voice, which makes ὑπὸ τοῦ νόμου καὶ τῶν προφητῶν "the Law and the Prophets" two witnesses[168] for the righteousness of God. Dunn explains that the imagery of the law court (vv. 19–20) here influences Paul's language, since "the Law and the Prophets" are summoned as witnesses.[169] Based on the grammatical tenses of the verbs (πεφανέρωται is perfect, and μαρτυρουμένη is present), we can even say that the "manifestation" still continues, and the testimony of the Scriptures continually accompanies that manifestation.[170]

In Romans 10:2 Paul presents himself as a witness by saying: μαρτυρῶ γὰρ αὐτοῖς ὅτι ζῆλον θεοῦ ἔχουσιν ἀλλ' οὐ κατ' ἐπίγνωσιν "For I testify[171] about them that they have a zeal for God, but not in accordance with knowledge." In this Greek construction, the dative of the persons points to the ones about whom the testimony is given, and ὅτι indicates the content of the testimony.[172] Hence, Paul speaks about Jews, and his testimony is that they have a zeal for God but without proper knowledge. The expression μαρτυρῶ γὰρ αὐτοῖς ὅτι itself does not indicate whether the testimony which is given is favorable or unfavorable.[173] In this instance, favorable and unfavorable testimony are mixed: Paul commends the Jews for their zeal while criticizing their lack of proper knowledge.

In 1 Corinthians 15:15 εὑρισκόμεθα δὲ καὶ ψευδομάρτυρες τοῦ θεοῦ, ὅτι ἐμαρτυρήσαμεν κατὰ τοῦ θεοῦ ὅτι ἤγειρεν τὸν Χριστόν, "we also are found false witnesses of God, because we did testify of God that He raised up the Christ" (YLT), Paul uses two words for witnessing: the verb μαρτυρέω and the noun ψευδόμαρτυς. Speaking about the resurrection of Jesus and the Christian testimony regarding it, Paul refers to their past and present. Speaking about

168. Although, "the Law and the Prophets" is an expression that stands for the whole OT (cf. Matt 5:17; 22:40; Luke 24:27) (Morris, *Epistle to Romans*, 174).

169. Dunn, *Romans 1–8*, 165.

170. Lenski, *Interpretation of St. Paul's*, 246; Morris, *Epistle to Romans*, 174.

171. Although both the NRSV and NIV say, "I can testify . . .," Morris rightly observes that we should translate μαρτυρῶ as "I testify." Paul is actually giving his testimony, not affirming that he could do so if necessary (Morris, *Epistle to Romans*, 378).

172. Dunn, *Romans 9–16, 586.*

173. Dunn, 586.

the possibility of being ψευδόμαρτυς τοῦ θεοῦ "false witness of God,"[174] Paul ties this noun with present passive form of the verb εὑρίσκω "find." Thus currently, Paul and his companions are "exposed" or "discovered" (by others) as false witnesses if Jesus is not raised. They are found to be so "because" ὅτι they "gave testimony;" here Paul uses the aorist form of the verb μαρτυρέω. The expression κατὰ τοῦ θεοῦ in connection to ἐμαρτυρήσαμεν can be understood in various ways: a) the preposition κατά with the genitive retains its proper meaning "against" and cannot be reduced to περί "concerning",[175] or, b) the phrase can be translated "concerning God," with the preposition plus genitive implying not direct antagonism but indirect dishonor of God.[176] Whether κατὰ should be read as "concerning," "of" (NRSV), "about" (NIV), or "against" (NASB95), if anyone would say that God did something when he did not, their statement would be a lie and consequently *testimony against*.

In 2 Corinthians 8:3 Paul testifies to the generosity of the Macedonian believers by saying ὅτι κατὰ δύναμιν, μαρτυρῶ, καὶ παρὰ δύναμιν, αὐθαίρετοι which literally reads as "For according to power,[177] I testify, and beyond power, of their own accord." The two prepositional phrases κατὰ δύναμιν and παρὰ δύναμιν do not express a stark antithesis "according to . . . contrary to," but a mild contrast, "according to . . . beyond." Accordingly, Paul functions as a witness to the Corinthians from his personal knowledge about the Macedonian believers and testifies to their generosity toward believers in Jerusalem. His testimony includes a value judgment, because he claims that their actions were not reckless or unbalanced but were positive.[178]

In the polemical context of Paul's argument with the Galatian believers, Paul recalls his past relationship with his readers, saying: ποῦ οὖν ὁ μακαρισμὸς ὑμῶν; μαρτυρῶ γὰρ ὑμῖν ὅτι εἰ δυνατὸν τοὺς ὀφθαλμοὺς ὑμῶν ἐξορύξαντες ἐδώκατέ μοι "What has become of the goodwill you felt? For I testify that, had it been possible, you would have torn out your eyes and

174. ψευδομάρτυρες τοῦ θεοῦ can be translated as "false witnesses concerning God" (gen. obj.), or "false witnesses belonging to God" (gen. subj.) i.e. who pretend to be witnesses and are not (Lange et al., *1 Corinthians, 314*).

175. Thiselton, *First Corinthians, 1219*.

176. Jamieson, Fausset and Brown, *CCEB, 2:292*.

177. Δύναμιν refers to "resources/means" or "ability/capability" (Harris, *Second Epistle to Corinthians, 565*).

178. Harris, *Second Epistle to Corinthians*, 565.

given them to me" (Gal 4:15, NRSV). Paul begins with a rhetorical question "What has become of the goodwill you felt?" or "Where then is your blessedness?" which points to their good will toward Paul and willingness to be a blessing to him, and/or their willingness to receive the benefits of his ministry. Now that their attitudes toward Paul tend in the opposite direction, Paul confronts them with a form of a testimony. He says *μαρτυρῶ γὰρ ὑμῖν* "For I testify you." Bruce[179] says that this expression originates in a forensic context, which give them the effect of a solemn declaration. The dative plural pronoun *ὑμῖν* may be interpreted as an indirect object denoting the persons who receive the testimony ("I testify to you that") or as a dative of advantage denoting those to whose credit the testimony is borne ("I testify on your behalf that").[180] The content of such testimony is *ὁ μακαρισμὸς ὑμῶν* "your blessedness" toward Paul. He further characterizes their blessedness by nothing *ὅτι εἰ δυνατὸν τοὺς ὀφθαλμοὺς ὑμῶν ἐξορύξαντες ἐδώκατέ μοι* "had it been possible, you would have torn out your eyes and given them to me" (NRSV). So even as Paul testifies "on their behalf," he clearly does so to show the unjust change in their behavior toward him.

In Colossians 4:13 Paul says of his co-worker Epaphras, *μαρτυρῶ γὰρ αὐτῷ ὅτι ἔχει πολὺν πόνον ὑπὲρ ὑμῶν καὶ τῶν ἐν Λαοδικείᾳ καὶ τῶν ἐν Ἱεραπόλει* "For I testify for him that he has worked hard for you and for those in Laodicea and in Hierapolis." Here Paul asserts his first-hand knowledge and acts as an eyewitness on behalf of Epaphras. As in Galatians 4:15, *μαρτυρῶ γὰρ αὐτῷ* carries a degree of formality and note of solemnity.[181] The pronoun *αὐτῷ* is a dative of advantage.

1 Timothy 5:10 Paul speaks about qualifications for widows who may be put on the list of widows. One qualification is that they must be *ἐν ἔργοις καλοῖς μαρτυρουμένη* "in good works attested." Since the verb *μαρτυρέω* is in the passive voice, the idea is that these widows must receive a good report from others; others must speak well about them or in their favor. Obviously, such reports must be the product of first-hand knowledge. Otherwise, they would be false claims.

179. Bruce, *Epistle to Galatians*, 210.

180. Longenecker, *Galatians*, 192–193.

181. Dunn, *Epistles to Colossians*, 281.

Above we saw Timothy's example in 1 Timothy 6:12; he "made the good confession in the presence of many witnesses" (NRSV). In 1 Timothy 6:13 Paul mentions Jesus's confession: *καὶ Χριστοῦ Ἰησοῦ τοῦ μαρτυρήσαντος ἐπὶ Ποντίου Πιλάτου τὴν καλὴν ὁμολογίαν* "and of Christ Jesus, who while testifying before Pontius Pilate made the good confession" (NIV). This text confronts us with several interpretative decisions. First, since *μαρτυρέω* is in aorist, Paul could refer to a particular occasion in the past when Jesus stood before Pontius Pilate,[182] although *ἐπὶ* can have spatial meaning "before," or temporal "in the time of."[183] Secondly, verse 13 shares important vocabulary with the preceding verse: *ὡμολόγησας* "confessed," *μαρτυρήσαντος* "witnessed," and *τὴν καλὴν ὁμολογίαν* "good confession." This raises the question of the extent to which Jesus's (v. 13) and Timothy's (v. 12) confessions are parallel. As previously noted, it is unclear whether Paul here refers to something that Jesus said before Pontius Pilate, or this confession refers to the witness of his life and ministry, and particularly his suffering and eventual death.[184] Hence, we can either equate *μαρτυρέω* with *ὁμολογία*[185] or presume that Jesus's *μαρτυρέω* was not merely verbal, but also included his suffering and death.[186]

4.3 Μαρτυρία in the Pauline writings

Μαρτυρία appears only twice in the Pauline writings. The first occurrence is 1 Timothy 3:7 where Paul says that one of conditions to be a candidate to serve as overseer is *δεῖ δὲ καὶ μαρτυρίαν καλὴν ἔχειν ἀπὸ τῶν ἔξωθεν* "He must also have a good reputation with outsiders" (NIV). What the NIV translates as "have a good reputation" and the NRSV as "be well thought of" is literally "good witness/testimony." The preposition *ἀπό* indicates the originator of the action of the verb. It is combined with the infinitive *ἔχειν*, which here signifies receiving something from someone. Hence, *ἀπὸ τῶν ἔξωθεν* "from the outsiders" probably stands for unbelievers, or those who are not or are no longer members of the Christian body.[187] *Μαρτυρία* as testimony here has

182. Knight, *Pastoral Epistles*, 265.

183. Mounce, *Pastoral Epistles*, 358.

184. Arichea and Hatton, *Paul's Letter*, 156.

185. Lange, et al., *1 & 2 Timothy*, 73.

186. Lea and Griffin, *1, 2 Timothy, Titus*, 173.

187. Knight, *Pastoral Epistles*, 165.

the sense of judgment on religious or moral matters, passed by one person upon another.

The second example is Titus 1:13, where Paul instructs Titus regarding his work with Cretan believers. In verse 12 Paul uses a saying from a Cretan προφήτης "prophets" (Epimenides of Crete): "Cretans are always liars, vicious brutes, lazy gluttons" (NRSV). In verse 13, Paul qualifies this statement as μαρτυρία "testimony," saying ἡ μαρτυρία αὕτη ἐστὶν ἀληθής "that testimony is true" (NRSV). Several things are interesting here. First, here is yet another connection between a prophet and testimony. Moreover, here we are surprised that Paul would label a pagan as "prophet." Second, this statement is a generalization; not every single Cretan fits this description. Third, while Paul's value judgment about Cretan character obviously comes from his experience there, he uses the testimony from a Cretan prophet as a secondary witness to support his judgment. Here he gives his apostolic authority to something said by a non-Christian.[188] As Knight says, "'this testimony is true,' indicates more than mere agreement: It is Paul's certification that the evaluation is really true and not an extreme statement."[189]

4.4 Μαρτύριον in the Pauline writings

Μαρτύριον appears six times in the Pauline writings. In 1 Corinthians 1:6 Paul uses μαρτύριον in reference to Christ: καθὼς τὸ μαρτύριον τοῦ Χριστοῦ ἐβεβαιώθη ἐν ὑμῖν "just as the testimony of Christ has been strengthened among you" (NRSV). For proper understanding of this text, we must make several interpretative decisions. First, does καθώς denote the manner ("just as") or the cause of the impact of the gospel on the readers (in which case it should be translated as "for indeed"). Second, is Χριστοῦ a subjective genitive (Christ is doing the witnessing) or an objective genitive (Christ is the object of witness – it is a testimony about him). Third, in what way was μαρτύριον τοῦ Χριστοῦ being βεβαιόω "confirmed" "in" or "among" them? The passive form of the verb implies outside activity, but there are differences in interpretations regarding the idea of "confirmation."[190] Due to these com-

188. Mounce, *Pastoral Epistles*, 398.

189. Knight, *Pastoral Epistles*, 299.

190. Thiselton, *First Corinthians*, 94–95; Jamieson, Fausset and Brown, *CCEB*, 2:263; Lange et al., *1 Corinthians*, 24; Lenski, *Interpretation of St. Paul's*, 32–33; Pratt, Jr. *I & II Corinthians*, 7; Robertson, *Word Pictures*.

plexities, we cannot easily determine who is giving witness. The subjective genitive implies that Christ himself is doing the witnessing in some way. The objective genitive implies that someone else (Holy Spirit, God, Paul, . . .) is witnessing about Christ. If the first option is chosen, then the witnessing occurs in the present. If the second, then the testimony includes witnessing about historical facts (from the past) about Christ.

In 1 Corinthians 2:1 we find a usage of *μαρτύριον* that may help solve some of the difficulties from 1 Corinthians 1:6. Paul writes: *Κἀγὼ ἐλθὼν πρὸς ὑμᾶς, ἀδελφοί, ἦλθον οὐ καθ' ὑπεροχὴν λόγου ἢ σοφίας καταγγέλλων ὑμῖν τὸ μυστήριον τοῦ θεοῦ* "When I came to you, brothers and sisters, I did not come proclaiming the mystery of God to you in lofty words or wisdom." This verse has a textual problem: should we read *τὸ μυστήριον τοῦ θεοῦ* "the mystery of God" or *μαρτύριον τοῦ θεοῦ* "the testimony of God." Metzger explains, "[t]he reading *μαρτύριον* seems to be a recollection of 1:6, whereas *μυστήριον* here prepares for its usage in verse 7."[191] If we accept reading *μαρτύριον τοῦ θεοῦ*, then we must again decide whether the genitive *τοῦ θεοῦ* is subjective or objective. In that case, the connection Paul makes here between *μαρτύριον τοῦ θεοῦ* and the verb *καταγγέλλω* "proclaim," and the additional reference in 1 Corinthians 2:4 to *καὶ ὁ λόγος μου καὶ τὸ κήρυγμά μου* "my word and my preaching" indicate that the best solution is to understand *τοῦ θεοῦ* as objective genitive. Paul thus here speaks about his declaration of testimony about God.[192]

In 2 Corinthians 1:12, "conscience" acts as a witness: *Ἡ γὰρ καύχησις ἡμῶν αὕτη ἐστίν, τὸ μαρτύριον τῆς συνειδήσεως ἡμῶν* "Indeed, this is our boast, the testimony of our conscience" (NRSV). Granted, for Paul the judgment of his conscience is submitted to the judgment of God (1 Cor 4:4), which means that conscience is not the ultimate witness.[193] One can ap-

191. Metzger, *Commentary on Greek NT*, 480.

192. However, C. K. Barrett (*Second Epistle to Corinthians*, 63) observes: "If the reading *testimony* is accepted our problems are not at an end. Paul's words are literally *the testimony of God*; this could be taken (as in the translation) to mean *my testimony about God* (objective genitive), or *the testimony borne by God* (subjective genitive) or *initiated by God* (genitive of the author). As in 1:6 (the testimony of Christ), and for similar reasons, the first is the most probable construction, though Lightfoot contrasts the two genitives, taking 1:6 as objective, 2:1 as subjective: 'It is the testimony borne by God (τοῦ θεοῦ) to Christ (τοῦ Χριστοῦ).' "

193. Barrett (*Second Epistle to Corinthians*, 71) explains this nicely: "His conscience is not so much the bar at which his conduct is tried, as a major witness, who can be called on either side as the case may be."

peal to a witness that turns out to be a false witness. We should understand "conscience" here as the human capacity for critical self-evaluation, so as to approve or disapprove of one's own actions and those of others. In that context, Paul argued that the inner tribunal of his conscience has assessed that he conducted himself according to the norms of holiness and godly sincerity. Consequently, the judgment of our conscience is only right if it accords with God's norms.[194]

In 2 Thessalonians 1:10 Paul speaks about Parousia of Christ, which for some will be a time of punishment and for others a time of glorification. In this context, Paul explains that membership in each group depends upon the acceptance or rejection of "their [Paul and his companions] testimony": ὅτι ἐπιστεύθη τὸ μαρτύριον ἡμῶν ἐφ' ὑμᾶς "because our testimony was trusted with you." Μαρτύριον in this verse refers to the preaching and teaching activity of Paul and his colleagues, that is, their proclamation of the gospel. As Wanamaker notices, μαρτύριον is followed by genitive ἡμῶν "our," which he views as subjective genitive.[195] But the genitive does not mean that Paul is the subject of the gospel, because, as Bruce notes: "it is their testimony because they are the witnesses."[196] If τὸ μαρτύριον ἡμῶν "our testimony" is equivalent to the gospel message, this equivalency creates an interesting overlap between the concept of testimony and εὐαγγέλιον in the NT. Accordingly, expressions such as τὸ εὐαγγέλιον ἡμῶν "our gospel" (2 Cor 4:3; 1 Thess 1:5; 2 Thess 2:14), τὸ εὐαγγέλιόν μου "my gospel" (Rom 2:16; 16:25), and even τὸ κήρυγμα ἡμῶν "our proclamation" 1 Corinthians 15:14, can be connected with the concept of testimony. If in the OT we saw an overlap between "testimony" on the one side and "covenant"/ "commandments" on the other side, here we see the concept of testimony connected to the core and foundational NT doctrine of the gospel.

1 Timothy 2:6, the first part of the sentence is a doctrinal statement, which is in the second part referred to as testimony: ὁ δοὺς ἑαυτὸν ἀντίλυτρον ὑπὲρ πάντων, τὸ μαρτύριον καιροῖς ἰδίοις "who gave Himself as a ransom for all, the testimony given at the proper time" (NASB95). The phrase τὸ μαρτύριον has been understood in different ways. Either the giving of Christ himself

194. Garland, *2 Corinthians*, 88–89.

195. Wanamaker, *Thessalonians*, 232.

196. Bruce, *1 and 2 Thessalonians*, 153.

(the first half of the sentence) is the testimony (of Christ to God's desire for the salvation of all men), or someone (Paul and others) bear testimony to that event.[197] Knight argues for the following:

> The solution is probably to be found in a both-and rather than in an either-or understanding (in accord with the same correlation stated in Tit. 1:2, 3): The act of Jesus' self-giving for all bears witness to the desire of the one God that all be saved (cf. Jn. 3:16), and Paul was appointed to continue to bear testimony to this act. . . . On this understanding, the temporal dative *καιροῖς ἰδίοις* refers not only to the time of Christ's ministry but also to the time since, characterized as the era in which such a testimony can be borne.[198]

If we accept this "both-and" approach, we can notice the dual dimension of testimony: Christ's testimony is a historical fact, a testimony about God's saving purposes; and Paul and others function as witnesses to that testimony.

In 2 Timothy 1:8 Paul urges Timothy *μὴ οὖν ἐπαισχυνθῇς τὸ μαρτύριον τοῦ κυρίου ἡμῶν μηδὲ ἐμὲ τὸν δέσμιον αὐτοῦ* "Do not be ashamed, then, of the testimony about our Lord or of me his prisoner." *μὴ οὖν ἐπαισχυνθῇς* "Do not be ashamed" is in the subjunctive mood, and so presupposes that in face of opposition Timothy *might* become ashamed. Concretely, Paul charges him to not be ashamed of *τὸ μαρτύριον* "the testimony," which here stands for the gospel message or the preaching of it, and *τοῦ κυρίου* here is an objective genitive, with the meaning "about the Lord."[199] In addition, as Paul charges Timothy not to be ashamed of him, he surprisingly refers to himself as the prisoner of *αὐτοῦ*, "his," i.e. the prisoner of Christ.

4.5 Μαρτύρομαι in the Pauline writings

Μαρτύρομαι is used three times in the Pauline writings. The first is in Galatians 5:3 where Paul writes: *μαρτύρομαι δὲ πάλιν παντὶ ἀνθρώπῳ περιτεμνομένῳ ὅτι ὀφειλέτης ἐστὶν ὅλον τὸν νόμον ποιῆσαι* "Once again I testify to every man who lets himself be circumcised that he is obliged to obey the entire law"

---

197. Knight, *Pastoral Epistles*, 123.

198. Knight, 124.

199. Knight, 372.

(NRSV). Πάλιν "again" here signifies that Paul repeats the warning from verse 2: Obviously, Paul's *μαρτύρομαι* is essentially a "warning" regarding the future, because it contains conditions and consequences. The condition is *περιτεμνομένῳ* "being circumcised," and the consequence is *ὅτι ὀφειλέτης ἐστὶν ὅλον τὸν νόμον ποιῆσαι* "that he is obliged to obey the entire law." "Without an objective accusative, *μαρτύρομαι* is not a call for others to bear witness to something but a solemn declaration on the part of a speaker or writer as to what follows."[200] Accordingly, the sum of all these arguments is that *μαρτύρομαι* should be understood as referring to "warning."

The second use of *μαρτύρομαι* is in Ephesians 4:17: *Τοῦτο οὖν λέγω καὶ μαρτύρομαι ἐν κυρίῳ* "This, then, I solemnly declare in the Lord." Here we have two verbs for speech: *λέγω* "say" and *μαρτύρομαι* "testify." Lincoln explains that *μαρτύρομαι* here does not have the specific connotation of bearing witness or of speaking under oath, but the more general meaning of "I affirm, declare."[201] Together with *λέγω*, *μαρτύρομαι* serves to strengthen the importance and urgency of the exhortation. Furthermore, *ἐν κυρίῳ* "in the Lord" points to the source of authority from which Paul speaks. Even though Paul here speaks about conditions, but not consequences, we can understand *μαρτύρομαι* as "warning" or "admonishment."

The third use of *μαρτύρομαι* is found in 1 Thessalonians 2:12, as the participle *μαρτυρόμενοι* in series with two other participles: *παρακαλοῦντες* "urging" and *παραμυθούμενοι* "encouraging": *παρακαλοῦντες ὑμᾶς καὶ παραμυθούμενοι καὶ μαρτυρόμενοι εἰς τὸ περιπατεῖν ὑμᾶς ἀξίως τοῦ θεοῦ* "urging and encouraging you and pleading that you lead a life worthy of God." The first two participles can be viewed as closely related to one another or synonymous, since both of them can signify admonition and comfort. Wanamaker thinks that *παραμυθεῖσθαι* places a more pronounced emphasis on comfort, while *παρακαλεῖν* on exhortation or urging a person to follow a certain mode of conduct.[202] The third participle then, *μαρτυρόμενοι*, is much stronger than the two that precede it, because it indicates that the missionaries, with the authority of God, "insisted" on a certain standard of behavior from their converts. Accordingly, *μαρτύρομαι* has lost here its original

200. Longenecker, *Galatians*, 226.

201. Lincoln, *Ephesians*, 276.

202. Wanamaker, *Thessalonians*, 106–107.

force of invoking witnesses,[203] just as we saw in Ephesians 4:17. And as in Ephesians 4:17, Paul here speaks only about conditions but not consequences.

4.6 Διαμαρτύρομαι in the Pauline writings

Paul uses the verb *διαμαρτύρομαι* four times. The first is in 1 Thessalonians 4:6, where it appears in the second part of the verse: *καθὼς καὶ προείπαμεν ὑμῖν καὶ διεμαρτυράμεθα* "as we told you and warned you before" (NIV). In this context, *διαμαρτύρομαι* seems to have the more specific meaning of "warning" rather than the general meaning of "declaring" or "testifying." It appears together with the compound verb *προεῖπον* "tell before." Since both verbs are in the aorist, Paul here reminds them of something he told them before. Hence, we see the idea of repetition, or "telling again." But verses 3–6 contain conditions and consequences. Therefore, the understanding of *διαμαρτύρομαι* here as "warning" is strongly supported.

The second use is in 1 Timothy 5:21. In verse 19, Paul gave instructions to Timothy about how to deal with charges against elders. In verse 21 he urges Timothy to strive to follow these instructions.[204] *Διαμαρτύρομαι ἐνώπιον τοῦ θεοῦ καὶ Χριστοῦ Ἰησοῦ καὶ τῶν ἐκλεκτῶν ἀγγέλων, ἵνα ταῦτα φυλάξῃς χωρὶς προκρίματος, μηδὲν ποιῶν κατὰ πρόσκλισιν* "I charge [you] before God and Christ Jesus and the elect angels that you keep these ["things" or "instructions"] without prejudging, doing nothing with partiality." *Διαμαρτύρομαι* here refers to a "solemn charge," the authoritative declaration of an apostle. Paul gives the charge in the presence of God, Jesus Christ and selected angels. Mounce notices, "The atmosphere of the verse is the law court: *διαμαρτύρομαι* carries the nuance of testifying under oath; *φυλάξῃς*, 'keep,' conveys the idea of keeping a law from being broken; and *προκρίματος*, 'prejudging,' is a legal term for making up one's mind before hearing the facts."[205] Accordingly, we can view God, Christ and angels as witnesses to Paul's charge to Timothy.

Paul uses *διαμαρτύρομαι* in 2 Timothy 2:14 in the context of dealing with false teachers: *Ταῦτα ὑπομίμνῃσκε διαμαρτυρόμενος ἐνώπιον τοῦ θεοῦ μὴ*

---

203. Bruce, *1 and 2 Thessalonians*, 36.

204. Opinion differs whether Paul refers to the things he said in verses 19–20, or he also includes things from verses 17–19.

205. Mounce, *Pastoral Epistles*, 314–315.

λογομαχεῖν, ἐπ' οὐδὲν χρήσιμον, ἐπὶ καταστροφῇ τῶν ἀκουόντων "Remind them of these things, charging them before the Lord not to strive about words to no profit, to the ruin of the hearers" (NKJV). Ταῦτα "these things" marks the beginning of the new section and it is followed by the imperative ὑπομίμνησκε "remind." In the active voice, this imperative means "to remind others," and most translations supply the object "them." It is followed by participle of διαμαρτύρομαι, and since both are in the present tense, the action of the participle is concurrent with that of the imperative. Hence, the force of the imperative carries over so that the participle is in effect a second command.[206] Based on the grammar, διαμαρτύρομαι has the meaning of "charging" or "warning." The expression ἐνώπιον τοῦ θεοῦ "before God" implies that God functions as witness to these two activities.

The final use is in 2 Timothy 4:1, where Paul says: Διαμαρτύρομαι ἐνώπιον τοῦ θεοῦ καὶ Χριστοῦ Ἰησοῦ τοῦ μέλλοντος κρίνειν ζῶντας καὶ νεκρούς, καὶ τὴν ἐπιφάνειαν αὐτοῦ καὶ τὴν βασιλείαν αὐτοῦ "I solemnly charge you in the presence of God and of Christ Jesus, who is to judge the living and the dead, and by His appearing and His kingdom" (NASB95). Knight observes that with διαμαρτύρομαι, Paul here issues a charge that is made even more solemn by the (invisible) witnesses before whom it is made, God and Christ, and by the reminders of the comprehensive judgeship and return of Christ.[207] Accordingly, in 1 Timothy 5:21; 2 Timothy 2:14 and 4:1, Paul combines his declaration with the naming of witnesses in front which declarations are made. In 1 Thessalonians 4:6, Paul does not mention witnesses, but he does say that "The Lord will punish all those who commit such sins." This implies God's knowledge of such sins, which further implies the role of an observing witness.

4.7 Συμμαρτυρέω in the Pauline writings

Paul uses συμμαρτυρέω three times, and only in Romans: 2:15; 8:16 and 9:1. As we have seen, the basic meaning of this verb is to confirm something by providing supporting testimony. In the first part of Romans 2:15, Paul says

206. What is not clear is whether the activity of διαμαρτυρόμενος ἐνώπιον τοῦ κυρίου belongs with ὑπομίμνησκε "remind" or with μὴ λογομαχεῖν "not to strive about words." In other words, does Timothy need to διαμαρτύρομαι people not to strive about words or διαμαρτύρομαι people on what Paul charges him to remind people?

207. Knight, *Pastoral Epistles,* 451.

that the gentiles by their conduct ἐνδείκνυμαι "show" or "demonstrate" that what the Law requires is written on their hearts. In the second part of the verse, he adds an additional witness: συμμαρτυρούσης αὐτῶν τῆς συνειδήσεως, "their conscience also bearing witness." Here, it is the conscience that "testifies with." But according to Morris

> Paul does not add what it is with which conscience is in accord. It may well be the law of which he has just spoken (so Barrett), or the good life (Hodge), or the "heart" (Leenhardt). In general, it seems either that Paul is using the verb in the sense "witness" ("with" simply strengthening the idea), or that he is linking conscience with the act that shows that the work of the law is written on people's hearts.[208]

Schreiner observes that it is a mistake to view the Law and conscience together as sources of moral norms.[209] The Law provides the norms; conscience only passes judgment on whether or not one abides by those norms. Although the meaning of the prefix σύν "with" in συμμαρτυρούσης is debatable ("bear witness" or "bear witness with"), Schreiner argues that Paul's purpose is to show that gentiles, although without written Law, have twofold witness: a) the Law is written on their heart and, b) their conscience testifies to the validity of those moral norms in that it condemns or approves their behavior.

In Romans 8:16, we see the testimony of the Holy Spirit and believer's spirit: αὐτὸ τὸ πνεῦμα συμμαρτυρεῖ τῷ πνεύματι ἡμῶν ὅτι ἐσμὲν τέκνα θεοῦ "The Spirit himself testifies with our spirit that we are God's children" (NIV). The first πνεῦμα refers to the Spirit of God, and the second πνεῦμα to the human spirit. It is unclear how we should understand συμμαρτυρεῖ τῷ πνεύματι ἡμῶν: do we say that the Spirit bears witness "to" our spirit (notice the dative case), or that the Spirit bears witness "with" our spirit? The form of the verb σύν "together," "with" + μαρτυρέω "testify" seems to support the reading "with." However Strathmann, says:

> If we take συμμαρτυρεῖν strictly, it is implicitly said that the spiritual ego of the man in Christ already declares him to be a child of God. But it is hard to think that Paul could say this.

208. Morris, *Epistle to Romans*, 126–127.

209. Schreiner, *Romans*, 123.

> Hence, we are forced to give to συμμαρτυρεῖν here the simple sense of "bear witness."[210]

Morrisadds that we should focus on the role of our spirit in this matter: "Unaided, we cannot testify to the reality of our standing before God. But we are not unaided; the Spirit of God testifies to our Spirit and gives us the assurance of our membership in the heavenly family. There is a direct operation of the Holy Spirit on our spirit."[211] Perhaps we can offer an interpretation that is in line with the verbal form "testify with" but also retains the idea of "testifying to." As Morris says, our spirit cannot stand unaided alongside the Holy Spirit and give testimony. But if our spirit is made alive in Christ, then because of the work of the Holy Spirit in our lives, we are able to offer such testimony together with God's Spirit. With that argument, we can argue that in this case as well the prefix σύν retains its meaning. Accordingly, we have twofold testimony: that of the Holy Spirit and that of the human spirit.

In Romans 9:1 Paul combines "conscience" from Romans 2:15 and "the Holy Spirit" from Romans 8:16 in the following sentence: Ἀλήθειαν λέγω ἐν Χριστῷ, οὐ ψεύδομαι, συμμαρτυρούσης μοι τῆς συνειδήσεώς μου ἐν πνεύματι ἁγίῳ "I tell the truth in Christ, I am not lying, my conscience also bearing me witness in the Holy Spirit" (NKJV). This verse relates to verse 2, where Paul expresses his affection for his Jewish people. To prove his point, in verse 1 he mentions two witnesses: himself and his conscience. First, Paul makes himself a witness (although he is not explicitly identified as such in the text) when he says: Ἀλήθειαν λέγω ἐν Χριστῷ, οὐ ψεύδομαι "I tell the truth in Christ, I am not lying." He does not call God as a witness to his words in the form of an oath but asserts positively that he is speaking the truth "in Christ" and then reinforces it by asserting negatively, "I am not lying."[212] Second, his conscience is also a witness: συμμαρτυρούσης μοι τῆς συνειδήσεώς μου ἐν πνεύματι ἁγίῳ "my conscience also bearing me witness in the Holy Spirit." The expression συμμαρτυρούσης μοι "bearing me witness" (notice the dative case of μοι) implies that Paul is the recipient of the witness given by τῆς συνειδήσεώς μου "my conscience." Or, if we follow the etymological meaning of the verb more strictly, his conscience bears witness

210. Strathmann, "Martus", *TDNT*, 4:509.

211. Morris, *Epistle to Romans*, 317.

212. Kruse, *Romans*, 368.

with him for what he says. Dunn observes that with such speech, conscience is being perceived or experienced as a semi-autonomous faculty (not wholly autonomous because of "my conscience") whose independence of testimony can be trusted.[213] Paul knows that his conscience is not infallible, and thus adds "in the Holy Spirit," saying that his conscience's testimony is validated and affirmed by the Holy Spirit.[214] Accordingly, we see that Paul here is testifying to something, and that he has two supporting witnesses, or that three witnesses (counting Paul) testify for the same thing.

5. The concept of witness in the rest of the New Testament documents – passage analysis

5.1 Μάρτυς in the rest of the New Testament documents

In the rest of the NT documents *μάρτυς* appears three times. First, in Hebrews 10:28, the author discusses the severe punishment or fate of those who rejected the Mosaic law. Then in Hebrews 10:29 he compares that punishment with the punishment of those who reject Jesus. Hebrews 10:28 says: *ἀθετήσας τις νόμον Μωϋσέως χωρὶς οἰκτιρμῶν ἐπὶ δυσὶν ἢ τρισὶν μάρτυσιν ἀποθνῄσκει* "Anyone who has violated the Law of Moses dies without mercy 'on the testimony of two or three witnesses'" (NRSV). Our interest is in the mention of "two or three witnesses" here. The background for this usage is texts from Deuteronomy 17:6; 19:15 and Numbers 35:20. Deuteronomy 17:6 is the closest in wording to Hebrews, and also relevant due to its reference to apostasy (Deut 17:2-7). Deuteronomy 19:15 is also relevant to the argument of Hebrews, since it follows a passage distinguishing sins of ignorance (Deut 19:4) from deliberate sins (Deut 19:11) sins[215]. Lane explains that Hebrews 10:28 combines two texts.[216] The first is Deuteronomy 17:2–7, which prescribed the death penalty for idolatry provided that the offense could be proven by two or three witnesses. The second is Deuteronomy 13:8 which says that the offender must be put to death "without pity." The

213. Dunn, *Romans 9–16*, 523.

214. Barrett (*Epistle to Romans*, 165) observes the following: "He speaks the truth *in Christ*, and his conscience bears witness *in the Holy Spirit*. In comparison with these divine witnesses (8:26, 34) the verdict of his own conscience is unimportant (1 Cor. 4:4)."

215. Ellingworth, *Epistle to the Hebrews,* 537.

216. Lane, *Hebrews 9–13,* 293.

witnesses mentioned in Deuteronomy are, as we have seen, testifying *witnesses against.* In Hebrews, however, they are brought up only in the comparison of the severity of punishment. The death penalty for violations of the Law of Moses was possible on the testimony of witnesses. Yet, when the author in Hebrews 10:29 says that those who neglect or reject the salvation offered in the gospel deserve *so much worse* punishment, we only know that the punishment is χείρων "worse"; the witness motif is lost. But we may assume that the "worse punishment" requires witnesses as well.

Hebrews 12:1a says: Τοιγαροῦν καὶ ἡμεῖς τοσοῦτον ἔχοντες περικείμενον ἡμῖν νέφος μαρτύρων "Therefore, since we are surrounded by so great a cloud of witnesses . . ." For Allen, this refers to the heroes from chapter 11.[217] Their identification as witnesses has been interpreted in two ways: a) they were faithful witnesses in the past, and they now witness from heaven the lives of present believers, b) their lives have borne witness to their faith. He opts for the second interpretation because: "The author's focus is on the importance of current believers learning from those who have gone before, not on those who have gone before watching current believers." Hence, the best way to consider the function of the witnesses from Hebrews 12:1 is to reject the idea of them as spectators to our lives. These witnesses bear witness through the pages of Scriptures, and their lives of faith convey the message about the character and promises of God.

Finally, in 1 Peter 5:1, Peter declares himself as witness to Christ's sufferings: Πρεσβυτέρους οὖν ἐν ὑμῖν παρακαλῶ ὁ συμπρεσβύτερος καὶ μάρτυς τῶν τοῦ Χριστοῦ παθημάτων, ὁ καὶ τῆς μελλούσης ἀποκαλύπτεσθαι δόξης κοινωνός "To the elders among you, I appeal as a fellow elder and a witness of Christ's sufferings who also will share in the glory to be revealed" (NIV). Michaels notices that the word μάρτυς is governed by the same article as συμπρεσβύτερος, and for that matter is virtually equivalent to the rare word σύμμαρτυς "fellow witness."[218] Furthermore, the absence of an emphatic ἐγώ in Peter's self-reference (contrast Eph 3:1 and 4:1) confirms the impression that the author's primary interest is in the elders to whom he writes. Taken together, this means that the role of elder for them is the role of "witness to the sufferings of Christ" and "sharer as well in the glory to be revealed."

217. Allen, *Hebrews,* 572.

218. Michaels, *1 Peter, WBC 49,* 280–281.

With that logic, Michaels argues that *μάρτυς* here does not refer to an eyewitness, for the elders of Asia Minor did not share Peter's status as eyewitness to Jesus's sufferings. Also, the Gospels emphasize that Peter was not an eyewitness of the scourging or crucifixion of Jesus, but was an eyewitness of Jesus's majesty and glory, presumably at the Transfiguration.

It is true that Peter combines two nouns *συμπρεσβύτερος* and *μάρτυς* under one article (*ὁ*), and *μάρτυς* in this context can refer either to an eyewitness of Christ's sufferings or to the one who bears witness about Christ sufferings. Still, the idea that these elders also share in Christ's sufferings (by way of proclaiming Christ's sufferings and possibly suffering for their commitment to Christ) does not remove from Peter his unique status as an eyewitness and apostle, two positions that these elders do not share with Peter. As Clowney notes: "They are not fellow apostles, chosen, like Peter, to be eyewitnesses of Christ's resurrection. They are, nevertheless, fellow elders, called by the Lord to exercise oversight in his church. They have received the witness of the apostles, and with them they confess Jesus Christ."[219] Hence, one can be witness to Christ's sufferings without having been "an eyewitness" of these sufferings.

5.2 Μαρτυρέω in the rest of the New Testament documents

The verb *μαρτυρέω* appears eight times in the rest of the NT. All appearances are in the book of Hebrews: Hebrews 7:8, 17; 10:15; 11:2, 4 (2x), 5, 39. Ellingworth notes that *μαρτυρέω* always refers to the witness of the Scripture, which significantly simplifies our understanding of these verses.[220] In Hebrews 7:8 we find the story of Abraham who gave a tenth of his plunder not to Levitical priest but to Melchizedek. The contrast between these two is obvious: *καὶ ὧδε μὲν δεκάτας ἀποθνῄσκοντες ἄνθρωποι λαμβάνουσιν, ἐκεῖ δὲ μαρτυρούμενος ὅτι ζῇ* "Here mortal men receive tithes, but there he receives them, of whom it is witnessed that he lives" (NKJV). *Μαρτυρούμενος ὅτι ζῇ* "of whom it is witnessed that he lives" refers to Melchizedek. The idea that Melchizedek is living comes from the Scripture. The text does not simply say that Melchizedek is living, but that he is declared to be living. The author builds his typology from silence since Scripture lacks any

219. Clowney, *The Message of 1 Peter*, 197.

220. Ellingworth, *Epistle to the Hebrews*, 368.

historical information about his death. This argument is supported from Genesis 14:17–20 and Psalms 110:4.[221]

If the scriptural testimony in 7:8 was implicit, in verse 17 it is made explicit by a quotation of Psalms 110:4: *μαρτυρεῖται γὰρ ὅτι σὺ ἱερεὺς εἰς τὸν αἰῶνα κατὰ τὴν τάξιν Μελχισέδεκ.* "For it is witnessed of him, "You are a priest forever, after the order of Melchizedek" (ESV). Instead of *μαρτυρεῖται* "it is testified," which is supported by early manuscripts, some other manuscripts and related later witnesses have *μαρτυρεῖ* "he testifies," which implies that God is the subject who testifies. Accordingly, either Scripture or God is the witness in this text.

In Hebrews 10:15 the author also talks about the witness of the Holy Spirit through the Scripture: *Μαρτυρεῖ δὲ ἡμῖν καὶ τὸ πνεῦμα τὸ ἅγιον· μετὰ γὰρ τὸ εἰρηκέναι* "And the Holy Spirit also testifies to us, for after saying . . ." (NRSV). This verse contains two verbs: first *μαρτυρέω* in the present tense refers to the testifying activity of the Holy Spirit. We may conclude that present tense indicates that through the quotation of the prophetic oracle the Holy Spirit is speaking now.[222] The second verb is the perfect infinitive *τὸ εἰρηκέναι* in neuter gender, literally "to have said." Although the Holy Spirit is also in neuter gender, it is possible that the referent of this infinitive could be Scripture instead.

Hebrews 11:2 says: *ἐν ταύτῃ γὰρ ἐμαρτυρήθησαν οἱ πρεσβύτεροι*[223] "This is what the ancients were commended for" (NIV). The subject of the sentence is *οἱ πρεσβύτεροι* "the ancients," who received *μαρτυρέω* "commendation" *ἐν ταύτῃ* lit. "in this," and *ταύτῃ* refers to the quality of faith mentioned in verse 1. Again, they received "commendation" from God, but through the Scripture. As Trites says: ". . . the heroes of faith mentioned in chapter 11 who are cited in the pages of the OT . . . they who enjoy the approving testimony of Scripture, and consequently of God himself, who speaks by his Spirit through the written word."[224] What is not clear is this: since God gave witness through the *means* of the Scripture, does this make the Scripture a witness

221. Allen, *Hebrews*, 417.

222. Lane, *Hebrews 9–13*, 268.

223. "*Πρεσβύτεροι* is not used as a title but in the ordinary sense and should not be translated 'elders'; it is our 'ancients,' people who lived in olden times no matter how many years old each of them may have been" (Lenski, *Interpretation of Hebrews*, 378).

224. Trites, *NT Concept of Witness*, 221.

as well? Further, although *μαρτυρέω* primarily means giving testimony, in the passive voice the verb can also mean "give recognition to," in the sense of receiving (public) approval and bearing favorable testimony for someone (deeds and/or character).[225]

Hebrews 11:4 is the text that begins the list of "people of faith."[226] Here the verb *μαρτυρέω* appears twice, first as an aorist passive and then as a participle in a genitive absolute. Πίστει πλείονα θυσίαν Ἄβελ παρὰ Κάϊν προσήνεγκεν τῷ θεῷ, δι' ἧς ἐμαρτυρήθη εἶναι δίκαιος, μαρτυροῦντος ἐπὶ τοῖς δώροις αὐτοῦ τοῦ θεοῦ, καὶ δι' αὐτῆς ἀποθανὼν ἔτι λαλεῖ "By faith Abel offered to God a better sacrifice than Cain, through which he obtained the testimony that he was righteous, God testifying about his gifts, and through faith, though he is dead, he still speaks" (NASB95). Although nowhere else in the Scripture are we told that Abel received testimony, the author either appeals to tradition[227] or offers a new interpretation of Scripture (based on the fact that God "accepted" Abel's sacrifice). Μαρτυρέω in the passive form[228] refers to God's testimony in Scripture. The genitive absolute that follows, *μαρτυροῦντος . . . θεοῦ*, expands and gives emphasis to the preceding *ἐμαρτυρήθη*.[229]

Hebrews 11:5b says of Enoch, πρὸ γὰρ τῆς μεταθέσεως μεμαρτύρηται εὐαρεστηκέναι τῷ θεῷ "For before he was taken, he was commended as one who pleased God" (NIV). As in previous cases, *μαρτυρέω* here refers to the witness of Scripture, namely that Enoch received divine approval prior to his translation. That *μαρτυρέω* is in the perfect tense signifies that this testimony stands to this day and continues. Lenski[230] adds that, because of the phrase beginning with *πρό* "before," we should not think that God's testimony consisted of his miraculously translating Enoch. If that was the

---

225. de Silva, *Perseverance in Gratitude*, 385; O'Brien, *Hebrews*, 400.

226. Lane (*Hebrews 9–13*, 333) rightly notices: "Although there is rarely in Scripture an explicit warrant for categorizing them as exemplars of *πίστις*, 'faith,' they share in common that they acted within the scope of faith as set forth in verse 1 and thus demonstrated the effective power of faith."

227. According to Ellingworth (*Epistle to the Hebrews*, 572) "a Jewish tradition . . . taken up among others by Theodotion and Luther, holds that God answered by fire (cf. 1 Kgs. 18:1–40)."

228. Trites (*NT Concept of Witness*, 73) notices that sometimes the person concerned is approved in the pages of the OT by using *μαρτυρέω* followed by a nominative and infinitive construction, such as in Hebrews 11:4a, 5.

229. Ellingworth, *Epistle to the Hebrews*, 572–573.

230. Lenski, *Interpretation of Hebrews*, 368.

writer's view, we would expect the aorist tense of the verb μεμαρτύρηται instead of perfect tense. On the contrary ". . . the permanent testimony Enoch has received from God consists of what the Scriptures permanently record about his having lived for a long time in a way that was well-pleasing to God prior to his translation. The author therefore also uses the perfect infinitive [here Lenski refers to εὐαρεστηκέναι "to have pleased"] which expresses past duration." However, the passive form of μαρτυρέω implies that Enoch is a recipient as well. First, Enoch received testimony, and then this testimony was preserved in the Scripture.

Referring to the heroes of faith in Hebrew 11, Hebrews 11:39 says: Καὶ οὗτοι πάντες μαρτυρηθέντες διὰ τῆς πίστεως οὐκ ἐκομίσαντο τὴν ἐπαγγελίαν "Yet all these, though they were commended for their faith, did not receive what was promised" (NRSV). By using μαρτυρέω in verse 2 and 39, the author of Hebrews forms an *inclusio*. This indicates that all the people mentioned in the *inclusio* are heroes of faith, who because of their faith received μαρτυρέω. In this context, μαρτυρέω has a positive connotation. Due to μαρτυρέω being in the passive voice, we see that these heroes of faith are not presented as *being* witnesses themselves, but witness was given *about them* by someone else: God, Scripture, or God in/through Scripture. Two questions remain unresolved. First, we know that these heroes received favorable testimony from God. Was Scripture the only means by which these testimonies were given? Or could these heroes of faith somehow have received these testimonies prior to the testimony being recorded in Scripture? Second, since God gave witness through the *means* of Scripture, does this make the Scripture a witness as well, or not?

5.3 Μαρτύριον in the rest of the New Testament documents

The noun μαρτύριον appears twice in the rest of the NT. First, in Hebrews 3:5 καὶ Μωϋσῆς μὲν πιστὸς ἐν ὅλῳ τῷ οἴκῳ αὐτοῦ ὡς θεράπων εἰς μαρτύριον τῶν λαληθησομένων "Now Moses was faithful in all His house as a servant, for a testimony of those things which were to be spoken later" (NASB95). The problem in this verse lies in the meaning of the future passive participle τῶν λαληθησομένων. It is not clear whether the author thinks of Moses himself speaking in the future, or that Moses would speak indirectly through later figures such as the prophets, the apostles, or Christ himself. If Moses is himself the speaker, does τῶν λαληθησομένων refer to the things he would say in and about the near future, especially in giving the Law? Or does it refer to things he would prophesy about the more distant future, especially about the coming of Christ?[231] In any case, we find here a reference to Moses being God's mouthpiece whenever God desired to speak in the future about current or future things. Alternatively, Moses gave testimony "to what was to be spoken in the future by another and a greater than he."[232] Or as Ellingworth and Nida[233] say, Moses "pointed ahead to greater things which God was to *say in the future* through the Son."

The second occurrence of *μαρτύριον* is in James 5:3. Here James writes about unjust riches: *ὁ χρυσὸς ὑμῶν καὶ ὁ ἄργυρος κατίωται καὶ ὁ ἰὸς αὐτῶν εἰς μαρτύριον ὑμῖν ἔσται καὶ φάγεται τὰς σάρκας ὑμῶν ὡς πῦρ. ἐθησαυρίσατε ἐν ἐσχάταις ἡμέραις*. "Your gold and silver are corroded. Their corrosion will testify against you and eat your flesh like fire. You have hoarded wealth in the last days" (NIV). James mentions corrosion (*κατιόω* "rust"),[234] but then adds that *ὁ ἰὸς αὐτῶν* "their poison"[235] *εἰς μαρτύριον ὑμῖν ἔσται* "will be for a witness against you" (pl.). Obviously, *ὑμῖν* here is a dative of disadvantage, which means that the testimony is a testimony *against*. But the entity which testifies is "the rust" or "corrosion." Kurt A. Richardson explains:

> The "corrosion" (*ios*, "rust," translated "poison" in 3:8 and Rom 3:13) on their hoarded gold and silver would be made to "testify" against the rich oppressors in James's version of a covenant lawsuit. The rust is personified. The rich had willfully refused to listen to the voice of justice calling for fair wages; now the rust was given a voice declaring their guilt. Thus, instead of paying wages, the gold and silver would be paid to the rust. The hoarded wealth would help pay for the trial against them.[236]

---

231. Ellingworth, *Epistle to the Hebrews*, 207–208.

232. Vincent, *Word Studies in NT*, 4: 412–413.

233. Ellingworth, and Nida, *Hebrews*, 56.

234. "The word 'corroded' translates a Greek word *(katioō)* that means 'rust'; yet, of course, gold and silver are metals that cannot rust. A few commentators think that James, because of his lower-class origins, might simply be ignorant about the properties of gold and silver. But, in fact, 'rust' was already being attributed to silver and gold (see, e.g., Sir. 29:10; Ep. Jer. 10). The word seems to have taken on a general sense of 'decay' (see also Ezek. 24:6, 11, 12)" (Moo, *James*, 213).

235. *ἰός* "poison" here stands for "corrosion" (Moo, 213).

236. Richardson, *James*, 206–207.

Lenski adds that the "rust shall eventually speak most mightily as a witness whose testimony cannot be contradicted. The very presence of rust is a testimony. There is no need to say what the testimony declares."[237]

5.4 Διαμαρτύρομαι in the rest of the New Testament documents

In Hebrews 2:6a, the author introduces a quotation from Psalms 8 with διεμαρτύρατο δέ πού τις λέγων "But someone has testified somewhere" (NRSV). Διαμαρτύρομαι is here used to introduce a quotation from the OT, the only such occurrence in the NT. The vague expression πού τις "somewhere someone" is in accordance with the author's general practice of not identifying the source or author of his quotations. As Lane[238] observes, "[p] recisely because it is God who speaks in the OT, the identity of the person through whom he uttered his word is relatively unimportant."

5.5 Συνεπιμαρτυρέω in the rest of the New Testament documents

The verb συνεπιμαρτυρέω appears in Hebrews 2:4: συνεπιμαρτυροῦντος τοῦ θεοῦ σημείοις τε καὶ τέρασιν καὶ ποικίλαις δυνάμεσιν καὶ πνεύματος ἁγίου μερισμοῖς κατὰ τὴν αὐτοῦ θέλησιν "God also testified to it by signs, wonders and various miracles, and by gifts of the Holy Spirit distributed according to his will" (NIV). This verse is a part of one long sentence that starts in verse 2 and ends in verse 4. The author is concerned with σωτηρία "salvation," which was: a) first announced by the Lord, b) then confirmed "to us" by those who heard him, and c) then συνεπιμαρτυροῦντος by God in the way described in verse 4. Since the meaning of the present participle συνεπιμαρτυρέω is "bear witness at the same time,"[239] this illustrates how, in addition to the testimony of Christ and those who heard him, the author refers to the consentient divine testimony through signs, wonders, various miracles and gifts of the Holy Spirit.[240] Significantly, the description of the activity of the Lord in verse 3 with λαμβάνω "receive" (in the sense of received a

237. Lenski, *Interpretation of Hebrews*, 647.

238. Lane, *Hebrews 1–8*, 46.

239. Trites, *NT Concept of Witness*, 77.

240. Trites, 7.

start in "being spoken"), and those who heard him with βεβαιόω "confirm" both in aorist tense, in verse 4 changes into present tense. Thus Ellingworth writes that the present tense describes the events by which God continues to give additional confirmation of the oral testimony mentioned in verse 3.[241] However, he adds that "[t]he use of the present does not necessarily imply that the events mentioned have continued to the time at which Hebrews was written." Possibly, two things are unclear in verse 4, a) it is not clear whether *according to his will* (v. 4b) is linked only with *distributing the gifts of the Holy Spirit* or also with signs, wonder and various miracles, b) the text literally says, "distributions of the Holy Spirit" and does not necessarily refer to "gifts" of the Holy Spirit." Accordingly, one aspect of testimony is either a distribution of the Holy Spirit himself, or distribution of the gifts proceeding from the Holy Spirit.[242]

5.6 'Επιμαρτυρέω in the rest of the New Testament documents

The verb ἐπιμαρτυρέω in the NT appears only in 1 Peter 5:12 Διὰ Σιλουανοῦ ὑμῖν τοῦ πιστοῦ ἀδελφοῦ, ὡς λογίζομαι, δι' ὀλίγων ἔγραψα παρακαλῶν καὶ ἐπιμαρτυρῶν ταύτην εἶναι ἀληθῆ χάριν τοῦ θεοῦ εἰς ἣν στῆτε "Through Silvanus, whom I consider a faithful brother, I have written this short letter to encourage you and to testify that this is the true grace of God. Stand fast in it" (NRSV). Peter here mentions "the true grace of God," which probably refers to the contents of the letter as a whole.[243] Regarding this true grace of God, Peter ἔγραψα "writes" them, with two participles modifying ἔγραψα: παρακαλῶν "encouraging" and ἐπιμαρτυρῶν "testifying." Although "encouraging" refers to ethical exhortation and "testifying" to proclamation, these participles express the purpose of the epistle in terms of exhortation and testimony and are connected with the epistle. What he has written is a *testimony* in which he exhorts them to "stand fast."

241. Ellingworth, *Epistle to the Hebrews*, 141.

242. Ellingworth and Nida, *Hebrews*, 31.

243. Schreiner, *1, 2 Peter, Jude*, 249–250.

5.7 Προμαρτύρομαι in the rest of the New Testament documents

In the NT, *προμαρτύρομαι* appears only in 1 Peter 1:11 *ἐραυνῶντες εἰς τίνα ἢ ποῖον καιρὸν ἐδήλου τὸ ἐν αὐτοῖς πνεῦμα Χριστοῦ προμαρτυρόμενον τὰ εἰς Χριστὸν παθήματα καὶ τὰς μετὰ ταῦτα δόξας* "inquiring about the person or time that the Spirit of Christ within them indicated when it testified in advance to the sufferings destined for Christ and the subsequent glory" (NRSV). In verse 10 Peter mentions generally how prophets of the past spoke about future times and events. Then in verse 11 he mentions one specific topic of the prophets: they were *προμαρτύρομαι* "testifying in advance" about Christ's sufferings and glory. Προμαρτύρομαι consists of the preposition *πρό*, and verb *μαρτύρομαι*, and the prepositional prefix refers to foretelling or telling about something in advance before it happens.[244]

244. Speaking about technical terminology for divine foreknowledge in the NT, William L. Craig (*Only Wise God*, 31–32), mentions several words associated with it, which all have in common preposition *πρό*.

CHAPTER 9

Major Aspects of the Concept of Witness in the New Testament

In our study of the concept of witness in the NT we offered preliminary remarks regarding the concept of witness and analyzed individual texts. In this chapter we will offer a synthesis of the results of this analysis, which can confirm or revise our understanding of the concept as we established it in our parallel study of the OT. It can also demonstrate how the concept of witness continues to develop in the NT. Accordingly, in the following sections we will continue with the categorization of witnesses by defining types of witnesses and introduce the categories of *temporal aspect* and *mode of witness* into our model for the NT concept of witness. After we observe how these two categories revise our understanding of the concept of witness, we will end this chapter by discussing additional aspects of the concept of witness. These include: the function of witnesses, our definition of witness and witnessing/testifying, the importance of the concept of witness in the NT, the authority and validation (valorization) of witness, and the dynamic of witnessing, we will then summarize the results with a conclusion.

1. Types of witnesses

In the NT, we can also divide witnesses into two primary types of categories: a) ontological categories and b) the type of witness performed, that is, categorization by functional categories. Since we have already discussed ontological categories, and in the OT developed our model by establishing the categories mode of witness and temporal aspect of witness, we will discuss these categories here as well. First, we will address two primary functional categories of witnesses: observing and testifying witnesses. Then in the next section we will see how mode of witness and temporal aspect of witness further impact these categories.

1.1 Observing witnesses

First, we have seen that being an observing witness is foundational for most witnesses and witnessing activity in the NT. Unlike in the OT, in the NT we do not find impersonal observing witnesses (such as heap, covenant, heavens and the earth, stone, etc.), only personal observing witnesses. Second, in the OT the actions of observing witnesses were detected in the following ways: by the presence of particular verbs such as *šāmaʿ* (שָׁמַע) "to hear," *yāḏaʿ* (יָדַע) "to know," *rāʾāh* (רָאָה) "to see"; by being designated by others as such; by being the object of the verb *ʿûḏ* (עוּד); or by sentence construction that reflects the presence of observing witnesses. In the NT, however, the situation is more complicated. Here, observing witnesses are usually identified by the fact that such a function fits best in the context of particular passages. Hence, argumentation that a particular witness is an observing witness requires interpretation and speculation. We will demonstrate this problem below.

1.2 Testifying witnesses

Testifying witnesses in the NT have the same function as they have in the OT, yet their identification in the NT is largely based on the context of a particular verse. In this way, they are also like observing witnesses in the NT. However, the actions of testifying witnesses in the NT can sometimes be detected by the following grammatical constructions as well:

(1) The verb μαρτυρέω: with preposition περὶ "about, of, for"; or μαρτυρέω is followed by some object of testimony, "testify about": John 1:7, 8, 15; 2:25; 5:31, 32, 36, 37, 39; 7:7; 8:14, 18; 10:25; 15:26; 18:23; 21:24; 1 John 5:10. Μαρτυρέω can be used with the preposition ὑπό "by," then followed by some object of testimony: in Acts 10:22; 16:2 and 22:12 some people enjoy a good reputation with others; in Romans 3:21 and 3 John 1:12 something or someone is being witnessed by something or someone else. Μαρτυρέω can be used with the preposition διά "through," "because"; here μαρτυρέω signifies testimony obtained because or through something: Hebrews 11:39 "through faith." Μαρτυρέω can be used with the preposition ἐπί; here μαρτυρέω can

refer to testimony given "before" (in a location in front of) someone (1 Tim 6:13), or "about" something (Heb 11:4). And finally, when used with the conjunction ὅτι "that," μαρτυρέω sometimes introduces the particular content of testimony: Matthew 23:31; John 1:32, 34; 3:28; 4:39, 44; 5:36; 7:7; Acts 26:5; Romans 10:2; 1 Corinthians 15:15; 2 Corinthians 8:3; Galatians 4:15; Col 4:13; Hebrews 7:8, 17; 1 John 4:14. But sometimes ὅτι does not point to particular content, but rather has the meaning "because" or "for," and conveys the reason of basis for giving testimony (John 8:14; 15:27; 1 John 5:6).

(2) The verb μαρτύρομαι with the conjunction ὅτι "that" introduces the particular content of testimony (Gal 5:3). The same idea is present in 1 Thessalonians 2:12 with preposition εἰς "to."

(3) The verb διαμαρτύρομαι with the conjunction ὅτι "that" introduces the particular content of testimony (Acts 10:42; 20:26). When διαμαρτύρομαι is used with the preposition περὶ "about," it is followed by an object of testimony ("about me" Acts 23:11). And finally, when διαμαρτύρομαι is used with the preposition ἐνώπιον "before," it refers to giving testimony "before," "in front" or "in the presence" of someone (1 Tim 5:21; 2 Tim 2:14; 4:1).

(4) The verb ψευδομαρτυρέω is used with the preposition κατά in Mark 14:56, 57 to emphasize that false testimony is given "against" someone.

(5) The verb συμμαρτυρέω is used with the conjunction ὅτι "that" in Romans 8:16 to introduce the particular content of testimony.

These verbs are sometimes accompanied with other verbs that additionally expand, explain or modify the activity of testifying. Hence, μαρτυρέω is accompanied by: a) κράζω "shout, cry out" + λέγω "say, speak": John 1:15, b) λέγω "say, speak": John 1:32; Revelation 22:20 (εἶπον 3:28; 13:21), c) γράφω "write": John 21:24, d) ἀπαγγέλλω "announce, proclaim": 1 John 1:2, e) θεάομαι "behold, see": 1 John 4:14, f) ὁράω (εἶδον) "see": John 1:34; 19:35. The verb μαρτύρομαι is accompanied by: a) ἵστημι "make stand": Acts 26:22), b) λέγω "say, speak": Ephesians 4:17, c) παρακαλέω "exhort, urge" + παραμυθέομαι "comfort, encourage": 1 Thessalonians 2:12. The verb διαμαρτύρομαι is accompanied by: a) παρακαλέω "exhort, urge" + λέγω "say, speak": Acts 2:40, b) λαλέω "speak" + εὐαγγελίζω "proclaim the good news": Acts 8:25, c) κηρύσσω "announce, proclaim": Acts 10:42, d) λέγω "say, speak": Acts 20:23; Hebrews 2:6, e) πείθω "convince, persuade": Acts 28.23, f) προλέγω "tell beforehand, say in advance": 1 Thessalonians 4:6, g) ὑπομιμνήσκομαι "remind, remember": 2 Timothy 2:14.

We also find important grammatical constructions involving nouns:

(1) *μάρτυς* is used with the conjunction ὅτι "that" to introduce the particular content of testimony, for which Paul invokes God as witness (2 Cor 1:23). In Acts 26:16 the noun ὑπηρέτης "servant" is used together with *μάρτυς* to describe Paul's future ministry. Μάρτυς is also accompanied by various verbs:

a) εἰμί "be" (Luke 11:48 [pres.]; Acts 1:8 [fut.]; 2:32 [pres.]; 3:15 [pres.]; 5:32 [pres.]; 13:31 [pres.]; 22:15 [fut.]; Rom 1:9 [pres.]),

b) γίνομαι "become" (Acts 1:22),

c) ἵστημι "make stand" + λέγω "say, speak" (Acts 6:13),

d) ἐπικαλέω "call upon" (2 Cor 1:23),

e) ἵστημι "make stand" (2 Cor 13:1),

f) προφητεύω "prophesy" (Rev 11:3).

(2) *μαρτυρία* is used with the preposition περὶ "about" to introduce the object to which testimony refers (Acts 22:18). It is used with the conjunction ὅτι "that" to introduce the particular content of testimony (John 21:24; 1 John 5:11). Conjunction ὅτι appears also in 3 John 1:12, but there it precedes *μαρτυρία*, and does not refer to the content of the testimony but rather introduces a dependent clause. It provides the contents of what the readers οἶδας "know," and acts as direct object of οἶδας.[1] In Mark 14:55, *μαρτυρία* is used with the preposition εἰς "to, so that"; in Mark 14:55 εἰς follows the noun and introduces the desired outcome of the testimony. In John 1:7 εἰς precedes the noun and creates a prepositional phrase that modifies the verb ἦλθεν "came." Finally, in 1 John 5:10 *μαρτυρία* appears twice, the second time with εἰς, thus creating a prepositional phrase which modifies the verb πεπίστευκεν "have believed."

(3) *μαρτύριον* is used with the preposition εἰς "to, so that" to identify the person to whom testimony is given:

a) αὐτοῖς "to them": Matthew 8:4; Mark 1:44; 6:11; 13:9; Luke 5:14,

b) αὐτοῖς καὶ τοῖς ἔθνεσιν "to them and to the nations": Matthew 10:18,

c) πᾶσιν τοῖς ἔθνεσιν "to all the nations" Matthew 24:14,

d) ἐπ' αὐτούς "against them": Luke 9:5,

e) ὑμῖν "to you": James 5:3.

In Luke 21:13 after εἰς *μαρτύριον* there is no stated object to whom testimony is given, but this object is implied by verse 12. In Hebrews 3:5 εἰς *μαρτύριον*

1. Bateman IV, *Workbook for Intermediate Greek*, 80–81.

does not point to the person or persons to whom testimony is given, but instead the content which is *λαληθησομένων* "things that would be spoken later" (NRSV).

(4) *ψευδομαρτυρία* is used with the preposition *κατά* in Matthew 26:59 to emphasize that false testimony was given "against" Jesus.

We have also seen that, due to dynamic relationship between observing and testifying witnesses, it is not always easy to make a distinction between them. But on most occasions, to be a testifying witness one first must be an observing witness. This is confirmed by the way that testifying witnesses sometimes base their testimony on first-hand experiences. Note the following examples: *θεάομαι* "see" (John 1:32, 34; 19:35; 1 John 4:14); *ὁράω* "see" (1 John 1:2); *ὁράω* "see" + *οἶδα* "know" (John 3:11); *ὁράω* "see" + *ἀκούω* "hear" (John 3:32); *οἶδα* "know" (John 8:14; 21:24; Acts 15:8; 26:5); *γινώσκω* "know" (John 2:25); *συνεσθίω* "eat" + *συμπίνω* "drink" (Acts 10:41), but also verse 40 *ἐμφανής* "visible," and; *εἶδον* + *ὁράω* "see" (Acts 26:16).

2. Revision of categorization: temporal aspect and mode of witnessing (of, for or against, and about)

Based on the analysis of the OT texts, we have seen that division based only on ontological categories and types of witness is helpful yet insufficient. To those categories we added two more: a) the temporal aspect in which witnesses function and, b) the mode of the witness. When we apply these four categories to the NT treatment of the concept of witness, the following picture emerged. Detailed explanation follows below.

Table 3: Categorization of witnesses according to suggested revision – NT

Ontological category and type	Mode	Temporal aspect	Function	Specific Purpose	Qualification	Means
Person. Observ. Witnesses	*Witness of*	In the present for the future	To record	To ensure confirmation	Being present, seeing, hearing, knowing	Seeing, hearing or knowing.
Person. Testif. Witnesses	*Witness for or against*	In the present about the past	To report	To establish subject's guilt or innocence	Observing witness in the past	Verbal
	Witness about	(1) In the present what will / can happen in the future	To report or declare	To announce in advance or warn	Prophetic inspiration	Revelation; verbal and/or written form.
		(2) In the present what will /can / must happen in the future based on the past or present		To warn with intent to change (negat.), admonish (posit.) or announce future judgment.	The knowledge of God's will; God as the source of testimony	Verbal, symbolic action, written form
		(3) In the present about the past		To confirm / establish the truth	Observing witness in the past	Verbal, material evidence, written form
		(4) In the present about more than one dimension of time		To confirm / establish the truth	Eyewitness; recipient of revelation; divine testimony; mediator of revelation	Verbal; revelation/vision; Scripture; miracles, gifts of the Spirit

Ontological category and type	**Mode**	**Temporal aspect**	**Function**	**Specific Purpose**	**Qualification**	**Means**
Imperson. Testif. Witnesses	*Witness for or against*	In the present about the past	To report	To establish truth regarding subject's guilt or innocence	"Observing witness;" recognized and affirmed as such by others	Inner communication; material evidence
	Witness about	(1) In the present about more than one dimension of time	To report	Visible constant reminder of certain truths	God's revelation	Objects themselves as means of testimony
		(2) In the present about more than one dimension of time		To confirm / establish the truth	God's revelation / inspiration	Written form
		(3) In the present about more than one dimension of time		To be a constant reminder	God's revelation / inspiration	Events or symbolic actions as means of testimony

2.1 Observing witnesses

Observing witnesses are witnesses whose mode of witness is of something. In the NT we find only personal observing witnesses, and we have already established the way they function. All aspects of such witnesses are the same as in the OT. The only minor variation from our established pattern are examples such as Luke 24:48; John 3:28; 2 Corinthians 1:23 and 1 Thessalonians 2:5, 10 where, if we follow the timeline of action, *observing witnesses* testified to something in the past but did not step into the role of *testifying witness*. In texts such as Romans 1:9 and Philippians 1:8, we can say that the observing function of these witnesses still continues.

2.2 Testifying witnesses: for or against, and about

As in the OT, the common denominator for testifying witnesses in the NT is to report, and this report comes in two different modes of testifying: a) witnessing for or against and, b) witnessing about.

2.2.1 Personal and impersonal testifying witnesses for or against

As we have seen, the role of personal testifying witnesses for or against is active, and their function is to report what has been said or happened. They always speak in the present about the past with the specific purpose of establishing the truth regarding a subject's guilt or innocence. Such witnesses can appear in either legal or religious contexts. What qualifies them to be testifying witness is that they have been in some capacity an observing witness in the past. The means of their witness is primarily verbal, although on two occasions (Matt 23:31; Luke 11:48) subjects witness by means of their actions. On the two occasions when the Holy Spirit is designated as a witness (Rom 8:16; 9:1), the means of his witness cannot be identified beyond the general label "internal communication."

Impersonal testifying witnesses for or against have the same role and function as personal testifying witnesses. In the NT such witnesses are a) conscience (Rom 2:15; 9:1; 2 Cor 1:12), b) human spirit (Rom 8:16) and c) corrosion (Jas 5:3). Note that conscience and human spirit function as some "inner voice" or "moral compass" inside of a person. For that matter, being an observing witness is not the best way to define the qualifications of such witnesses, although we can say that human conscience and spirit, being permanently present inside of a person, possess intimate knowledge of person's past. We can metaphorically call them observing witnesses. When corrosion functions as a witness against, it can only be recognized as such by others, and accompanied with an explanatory story.

2.2.2 Personal and impersonal testifying witnesses about

The function of the personal testifying witnesses about is also to report, but these witnesses' specific purpose and qualifications differ from the personal testifying witnesses for or against. In this category, we have four groups of witnesses. The first group of personal testifying witnesses about announce in advance what will or can happen in the future. Unlike what we saw of these witnesses in the OT, in the NT these testimonies are usually not accompanied by conditions and consequences ("if" . . . "then"), and their specific purpose is to announce future events or issue future warnings. Accordingly, we can consider such testimonies in the NT as prophecies, and the future events are not always dependent on the subject's past. Some NT texts follow the OT pattern of conditions and consequences ("if" . . . "then"), however. Among these are Galatians 5:3, where Paul speaks about the future in a conditional way; likewise, Revelation 22:18 and 22:20. We can say that Paul is qualified to testify as he does in Galatians 5:3 because he acts based on YHWH's revelation. Similarly, the warnings in Revelation 22:18 and 22:20 are the result of prophetic inspiration. Consequently, the qualifications of such witnesses lie either in the prophetic inspiration, or those who testify are the source of prophecy (the Holy Spirit in Acts 20:23; Heb 10:15; and Jesus in Rev 22:18, 20). The means of witness is revelation, which is expressed in verbal and/or written form.

The second group of personal testifying witnesses about declare in the present what will/can/must happen in the future (consequences) based on the subject's past or present actions (condition). We already established in the OT that the function of such witnesses overlaps with witnesses for or against, because in these cases what will happen in the future is a result of the subject's past or present. Often the subject's guilt is presumed and does not need to be proven. The specific purpose of such witnesses is to announce future judgment as a sure fact, or to warn people in hopes of changing their course or turning them from something bad. Alternatively, sometimes the mention of future events serves as fuel to admonish recipients to continue something positive that they are already doing or to initiate something positive that they must do. In those cases, testifying has positive sense, and does not presume a subject's guilt. The qualifications for this group of witnesses lie in: a) a knowledge of God's will which is based on God's revelation (Acts 2:40; 20:21; Eph 4:17; 1 Thess 2:12; 4:6; 1 Tim 5:21; 2 Tim 2:14; 4:1; 1 Pet 5:12), b) personal experience (Luke 16:28) (although this example comes from the parable), c) or testimony received from Jesus or God (Mark 6:11; Luke 9:5; John 13:21; Acts 13:22). The means of witness may be verbal, symbolic action, or a written testimony, or some combination of these.

The third group of personal testifying witnesses about reports in the present what happened in the past, with the purpose to confirm or establish the truth regarding a past event. In some instances, the things which witnesses testify about the past still continue and are valid today.[2] The qualifications for such witnesses are either that they were an observing witness in the past or that they possess pertinent experience. In one example, this knowledge can be attributed to the revelation of prophetic knowledge (John 2:25). These witnesses usually testify verbally, but occasionally their verbal witness is accompanied by physical/material evidence (Matt 8:4; Mark 1:44; Luke 5:14). Also, the Bible itself appears as a means of testimony here (Heb 11:2, 4, 5, 39).

The fourth group of personal testifying witnesses about cannot be limited to only one specific time dimension. When we deal with events in the past, or something that will happen in the future, the timeframe of testimony is clear. But, when the content of the testimony is the message of the gospel, the coming of the kingdom of God, or Jesus's identity and personhood, etc., the timeframe of testimony is not always so clearly or easily defined. The message of the gospel is a matter of the past (historical events) and the present (Jesus's exalted position) and future reality (the Second coming). So, it is also with the message about the kingdom of God and Jesus's identity and personhood. Because these events operate in multiple times, we cannot simply select one-time dimension as correct. It is better to take an "all-inclusive" approach, since it is not possible to put such references to witness in the specific timeframe categories already defined. Accordingly, this group of

2. Romans 10:2: Jews are still zealous but without knowledge; Colossians 4:13: Epaphras is still working hard; Titus 1:13: Cretans are always liars, evil brutes, lazy gluttons, etc. (cf. Heb 2:6; 3 John 1:3, 6, 12).

personal testifying witnesses about also report, with the specific purpose of confirming and/or establishing some truth. Since in this category we find human, angelic, and divine (Father, Son, Spirit) witnesses, the qualifications for such witnesses differ. Humans can either be eyewitnesses, chosen[3] to be witnesses, or the recipients of revelation (e.g. John in the book of Revelation). Angelic witnesses in Revelation 19:10 and 22:16 are presented as mediators of Jesus's revelation. The divine witnesses (Father, Son and Spirit) are difficult to classify as eyewitness testimony, although elements of eyewitness testimony can be found (cf. John 5:37). The means used by such witnesses vary: a) sometimes the way testimony will be offered is not specified,[4] b) testimony is often given verbally, c) when angelic witnesses serve as a mediators for Jesus's testimony, the means of testimony is spoken revelation or vision, d) miracles, sign, wonders and gifts of the Holy Spirit also serve as the means of divine testimony (John 5:36; 10:25; Acts 14:3; Heb 12:4), e) the Scripture is also means of testimony (Heb 12:1).

In the category of impersonal testifying witnesses about, we find three groups of witnesses. These witnesses' general function is to report, but they perform this task with different specific purposes. The first group testifies in the present about more than one dimension of time, and their specific purpose is to serve as a visible reminder of certain truths. Such witnesses are a product of God's revelation, which is also their qualification for the task. Consequently, these visible material objects as witnesses convey their message through their very existence. The only such witness mentioned in the NT is the tabernacle (Acts 7:44).

The second group also testifies in the present about more than one dimension of time. Their specific purpose is to speak about the past but also future things and events that will take place. These witnesses are also a product of God's revelation, which qualifies them as witnesses, and they also contain in themselves the message they testify. The only example of such witnesses are the Scriptures themselves. The Scriptures speak about the past (Heb 7:8, 17)

3. John the Baptist is chosen by God to be Jesus's witness, and he testifies for some things that he did not see or experienced. Yet, occasionally, his testimony incudes specific historical events (John 1:34).

4. For example, in John 15:26 and Acts 5:32 it is not specified how Spirit will testify about Jesus.

but also about future things and events that will take place (John 5:39; Acts 10:43; Rom 3:21).

Finally, the third such group of impersonal witnesses also testifies in the present about more than one dimension of time; here their specific purpose is to speak about a historical event that is symbolically repeated. The only such example in the NT is 1 John 5:7 where John mentions "water and blood" as witnesses. We concluded that this expression refers to the historical events of Jesus's baptism and death, events that are unrepeatable which at the same time can be symbolically repeated through the sacraments of water baptism and Eucharist. On this basis we can also say that their specific purpose is to be a constant reminder of some truths, the same purpose as group one. But unlike the first group, their means of witness is through events and/or symbolic actions rather than material objects.

2.3 Explanation of the concept's revision on concrete selected examples

Now that we have given a rationale for revising the model and offered definitions in accordance with the suggested revision, here we will use selected additional examples to explain the revision and confirm the revised model's validity and conclusions. Examples will be given according to the type of witnesses.

2.3.1 Personal observing witnesses

Since NT does not contain impersonal observing witnesses, we will discuss only personal observing witnesses. We have classified the witnesses from Matthew 18:16 as observing witnesses on the basis of two things. First, the function of these witnesses is to testify to the reproof, which means they are (probably) not witnesses of the transgression. Second, the witnesses' function is described as *σταθῇ* "confirmation" of *πᾶν ῥῆμα* "every matter." Since *σταθῇ* from the verb *ἵστημι* is in passive form, this could imply that these witnesses take only a passive (observing) role.[5] Consequently, it seems that the witnesses in Matthew 18:16 cover the whole span of testifying activity, showing

5. However, Paul uses the same verb in the passive voice in 2 Corinthians 13:1 to refer to the activity of testifying witnesses against. With this logic, we could apply that same function to witnesses in Matthew 18:16 as well.

how observing witnesses can eventually become testifying witnesses, but the primary focus in that passage is on them being observing witnesses.

Regarding witnesses in Luke 24:48, the question is whether Jesus labels them as witnesses in an observing or testifying sense? The question is valid because Jesus here declares that they are already witnesses "of these things." Yet in Acts 1:8 the story is told with a slight difference, because there Jesus tells that same group that they "will be [fut.] his witnesses." A possible explanation for this difference is that Jesus in Luke addresses them as observing witnesses who will very soon step into the new role of testifying (Acts 1:8).

In John 3:28 John the Baptist says αὐτοὶ ὑμεῖς μοι μαρτυρεῖτε "You yourselves can testify to me." The verb μαρτυρέω does not necessarily make this people testifying witnesses, even though is in present tense and active form. The question of their role is answered by the context. Μοι "to me" stands in dative case, which means that John addresses some people as witnesses to him ("bear witness to me") who can verify his claims. Obviously, they can perform this function because they heard his speech (notice the aorist εἶπον "said"). Does this make them observing witnesses or testifying witnesses? Based on the context, they are probably still observing witnesses, and John the Baptist does not yet require them to verbally testify to and affirm his claim. John the Baptist's claims were made in the past. That is the time frame in which these witnesses heard John's claims. Even though what they have seen and heard is in the past, they are still observing witnesses. Further, they can step into the role of testifying witnesses if needed.[6] If this reading is correct, we find a similar thing happening as what we saw in Luke 24:48.

It is difficult to determine the category for μάρτυς in Acts 10:39, 41. Since διαμαρτύρομαι in verse 42 clearly defines the apostles as testifying witnesses, it seems that Peter in verse 39 and verse 41 designates the apostles as observing witnesses. This is emphasized by Peter's use of the adjective ἐμφανής "manifest, visible" (v. 40) and of his references to συνεσθίω + συμπίνω "eating and drinking with the risen Jesus" (v. 41). These activities are more consistent with the role of observing witnesses. In that case, Peter recollects and refers to their past role of observing witnesses. This past role

6. The same situation we have in Luke 24:48, but also 2 Corinthians 1:23 and 1 Thessalonians 2:5, 10.

then serves as the basis for their current role of testifying witnesses (v. 42), which is supported by Scripture (v. 43).

Acts 22:15 is a notable example of how observing witnesses can become testifying witnesses in the future. Paul is as an observing witness due to his ὧν ἑώρακας καὶ ἤκουσας "seeing and hearing," but in the future he will be a testifying witness and will testify about the things from the past (v. 15). The situation is even more complex in Acts 26:16 where Paul refers to Jesus's words to him on the road to Damascus. Here he adds something new: Paul is addressed as observing witness due to his εἶδές "having seen" (not hearing as in Acts 22:15), and his task is to be a testifying witness in the future. Yet, Jesus promises him future revelations as well with ὀφθήσομαί "and will see," so Paul will go from observing to testifying, then back to observing and again to testifying.

In instances where YHWH appears as witness (Rom 1:9; 2 Cor 1:23; Phil 1:8; 1 Thess 2:5, 10) it is also extremely difficult to define whether YHWH functions as an observing or a testifying witness. Even grammar here is not helpful to determine the type of witness. In Romans 1:9 verb εἰμί "be" is in the present active form. The other cases omit εἰμί (Phil 1:8; 2 Thess 2:5, 10), but the present active meaning can be assumed. Also, in all these uses ὁ θεός "God" is in nominative case: hence, we have meaning "God (is) witness." However, Paul's invocation of YHWH as witness to Paul's claims still does not mean that YHWH functions as a testifying witness. Trites[7] says that the idea of YHWH as witness is rooted in the fact that YHWH possesses knowledge of certain things and cites as an example Jeremiah 29:30. Paul here makes a general assertion about YHWH being a witness on Paul's behalf. He does not indicate the way in which YHWH testifies or any information about the content of YHWH's testimony. Hence, we think it best to conclude that YHWH functions as an observing witness who has not yet stepped into the role of testifying witness.

In 2 Corinthians 1:23 Paul ἐπικαλέω "invokes" YHWH as his witness, and here both ὁ θεός and μάρτυς are in accusative case. The imagery is that of a courtroom where the witness is invited to approach the bench to offer testimony. However, even that imagery speaks about transition from observing to testifying witness. So, our conclusion is that in all these instances YHWH

7. Trites, *NT Concept of Witness*, 64.

is pictured as an observing witness who possesses certain knowledge. If needed, he can step into the role of testifying witness.

Two factors in 1 Timothy 6:12 show that the witness should be classified as observing. First, Paul presents Timothy in the active role of a speaker who ὁμολογέω "professes" the καλὴ ὁμολογία "good confession." Secondly, due to the preposition ἐνώπιον "before" preceding πολλῶν μαρτύρων "many witnesses," it seems that πολλῶν μαρτύρων "many witnesses" have served a notarial or observing role to Timothy's confession.

2.3.2 Testifying witnesses

In this category we will first examine impersonal and then personal testifying witnesses.

2.3.2.1 Impersonal testifying witnesses

The first few witnesses in the category of impersonal testifying witnesses for or against are ontologically difficult to define. The first is conscience in Romans 2:15 and 2 Corinthians 1:12; conscience also appears in combination with the Holy Spirit in Romans 9:1. Should we consider the human conscience as personal or impersonal witness? Being internal to us, conscience is personal, yet by itself the conscience does not make up a whole person, in which case we could consider it as a person. The activity of conscience in Romans 2:15 is described with two participles: κατηγορέω "accusing" and ἀπολογέομαι "defending." In 2 Corinthians 1:12 Paul attributes positive function to the conscience: it confirms the behavior of Paul and his companion, so that they can boast καύχησις "boast" in their testimony. However, except for in Romans 2:15, where Paul mentions τῶν λογισμῶν "thoughts," we are not told what means conscience uses to testify. Finally, in Romans 9:1 the conscience appears as witness in tandem with the Holy Spirit, and together they seem to function as witnesses for Paul's claims. The fact that Paul mentions two witnesses (rather than one) and his insistence that he is "not lying" creates the setting for guilt/innocence language. Although the context is not legal, such language reveals that Paul's intention is to establish his blamelessness in the matter at hand, and not just establish truth regarding something. Since both conscience and the Holy Spirit testify to the same things, the witnesses in this verse will be counted as both impersonal and personal.

The second witness from the same category that is also difficult to define ontologically is the human spirit, which appears together with the Holy Spirit as a witness in Romans 8:16. As with the conscience, the human spirit is personal, yet by itself does not make up a whole person so as to be treated as a person. Also, as in Romans 9:1, having two witnesses could establish the expectation of guilt/innocence language, but the context here is not legal, and these witnesses do not seem to function to establish the subject's guilt or innocence. However, chapter 8 begins with "There is therefore now no condemnation for those who are in Christ Jesus" (Rom 8:1), which in the context of speech about justification makes the human spirit and the Holy Spirit function as defending witnesses or witnesses for.

Finally, in James 5:3 corrosion or rust is appealed to in a unique way as a witness. James's usage of such imagery makes rust a witness against the unjust rich. Even with a context that is not necessarily legal or judicial, James sees the guilt of these people primarily as guilt before YHWH, and rust as witness against such people.

In the category of impersonal testifying witness about we have three different groups. The NT twice refers to the tabernacle itself as testimony. In Acts 7:44 Stephen refers to the historic tabernacle from Moses's time. In Revelation 15:5 John refers to the "temple of the tabernacle of testimony" in heaven. The tabernacle in Revelation 15:5 seems to be YHWH's dwelling place in heaven. But unlike with the tabernacle from Acts 7:44, it is difficult to define content, timeline or the means of witness for this heavenly tabernacle.

The next group of impersonal testifying witness about is Scripture itself, which can function in different temporal aspects. For example, Hebrews 7:8, 17 refers to testimony given about Melchizedek. Timewise, Hebrews talks about Melchizedek by referring to past events. In other instances, in Hebrews, Scripture is the *means* through which some other subject or subjects offer witness or testimony (Heb 2:6; 3:5; 10:15; 11:2, 4, 5, 39; 12:1). But in these two examples (Heb 7:8, 17) it is Scripture itself that offers testimony, other than Scripture there are no specific subjects in mind who offer their testimony. In examples such as John 5:39; Acts 10:43 and Romans 3:21, Scripture testifies for things that will come in the future (from the perspective of when they were given; these things are all now in the past). In John 5:39 Jesus says that γραφάς "Scriptures" testifies about him. Likewise, Moses and his writings testify about Jesus in John 5:45–47. Jesus here is referring to the Torah, and this reference is in keeping with the OT's referring to the Torah as a form of YHWH's testimony. In Acts 10:43 the OT prophets offer witness, and by "prophets" we mean their speeches as part of the Scripture, the written record of their speeches.[8] This idea of the prophets as witnesses is also confirmed in Romans 3:21, where both Law and Prophets testify about God's righteousness.

The third group is the triple witness of "the Spirit, water and blood" in 1 John 5:7–8. It is difficult, however, to assess what "water" and "blood" refer to. If we take "water and blood" as references to historical events from Jesus's life, then "water and blood" are the subjects who testify, not Jesus. For that matter, as historically unrepeatable events (not material objects), we should consider them as impersonal testifying witnesses. But "water and blood" could also refer to the sacraments, which gives another dimension to their testimony, as Leonhard Goppelt[9] notes: "Christ is attested by the historical events of His way when they are proclaimed and the Spirit speaks through this proclamation (John 15:26; 16:7, 13) and specifically through its operation in baptism and the Eucharist." Accordingly, the testimony of "water and blood" is historically unrepeatable, yet it continues to live in apostolic preaching, and also through baptism and the Eucharist. Additionally, the Holy Spirit falls into the personal testifying witness category, because as ever-present witness, testifies about historical Jesus.

2.3.2.2 Personal testifying witnesses

Personal testifying witnesses for or against are easy to define because they appear predominantly in legal contexts. Some texts here refer to the command against giving false testimony (Matt 15:19; 19:18; Mark 10:19; Luke 18:20), or the need for multiple witnesses (John 8:17; Heb 10:28). Some speak about witnesses who offer their testimonies during a trial as witnesses against someone (against Jesus: Matt 26:59, 60, 62, 65; 27:13; Mark 14:55, 56 (2x), 57, 59, 60, 63; Luke 22:71; John 18:23; against Stephen: Acts 6:13; 7:58). We also have a few examples where witnesses during a trial can function as

8. Stegal, *Crossless Gospel*, 190.

9. Goppelt, *"ὕδωρ"*, *TDNT* 8: 330.

witnesses for. For example, Paul mentions witnesses who could testify in his favor about his past (Acts 22:5; 26:5).

It is not clear whether the description of Stephen in Acts 22:20 as *τοῦ μάρτυρός σου* "your witness" refers to Stephen's testimony in Acts 7 or to his witness about Jesus in general. Accordingly, should we consider his testimony as witness against or about? If we limit only to Stephen's trial, it seems preferable to consider his testimony as witnessing against, because the bulk of his testimony concerns Israel's past and her guilt in terms of her covenantal relationship with YHWH. It is Stephen who is on trial, yet he becomes a witness against his prosecutors.

But witnesses against are not always tied to legal contexts. They also appear in religious/covenantal contexts. We identify them primarily based on the context, but other indicators are occasionally present. So, in Matthew 23:31 Jesus said to the teachers of the Law and Pharisees *μαρτυρεῖτε ἑαυτοῖς* "you testify to yourselves." Here *ἑαυτοῖς* is taken as dative of disadvantage and this is confirmed by the rest of the sentence, where Jesus talks about the bad deeds of their fathers. Likewise, the parallel passage in Luke 11:48; again, *μάρτυρές ἐστε* "you are witnesses" can be either positive or negative, but the context reveals the negative content of their testimony. That Jesus in John 7:7 is a witness against is seen primarily from the context, since he testifies that "the works of the world are evil." This makes the expression *περὶ αὐτοῦ*, which again can be either positive or negative (cf. John 1:47) "about him [the world]" as something negative: "against him."

In the Pauline writings, we have two examples of witnesses against in a religious context. First, in 1 Timothy 5:19 it is obvious that the witnesses mentioned there function as witnesses against, due to the preposition *κατὰ*. Additional factors include the noun *κατηγορία* "accusation," and the mention of "two or three witnesses." Second, Paul's multiple visits to Corinth (2 Cor 13:1) are obviously witnesses against, yet again this trial occurs in the religious context and not in front of some tribunal.

Twice in Paul's writings, the Holy Spirit appears as a witness for or against: in Romans 8:16 in combination with the human spirit, and in Romans 9:1 with Paul's conscience. In both instances, the Holy Spirit functions in a positive way as a witness for. The context in Romans 8:16 is not legal, nor does it seem that these witnesses testify to establish the truth about the subject's guilt or innocence. Because the Spirit gives witness in the context of communication about the believer's justification (cf. Rom 8:1), he is a defending witness or a witnesses for. And in Romans 9:1 Holy Spirit functions as a witness for Paul's claims.

In the category of personal testifying witnesses about we have four groups. The first group announces in advance what will or can happen. So, in Acts 20:23 the Holy Spirit testifies and speaks (pres.) to Paul about future hardships. Hebrews 3:5 presents Moses as one who speaks of future things. Likewise, the Spirit's testimony in Hebrews 10:15 is about future things because of the content of verse 16, which focuses on future things that YHWH will do. Finally, 1 Peter 1:11 uses the participle προμαρτύρομαι "bear witness in advance," which shows that the content of the speech refers to future things. Galatians 5:3 deviates from this pattern because Paul there speaks about what Galatians will have to do *if* they are circumcised. The conjunction ὅτι "that" here has a conditional function because the consequences of their contemplated action follow. In Revelation 22:18, the conjunction ἐάν "if" has the same conditional function. Revelation 22:20 additionally confirms and testifies for things said in verses 18–19.

This second group of personal testifying witnesses about declare in the present what will / can / must happen in the future on the basis of or as a consequence of the subject's past or present actions (consequences). This group functions in three different ways. The first subgroup of texts presumes the subject's guilt and announces future judgment in advance. Here we can count texts such as Mark 6:11, where the symbolic action of "shaking off the dust from one's feet" makes αὐτοῖς in the expression εἰς μαρτύριον αὐτοῖς dative of disadvantage "as testimony against them." See also Luke 9:5 εἰς μαρτύριον ἐπ' αὐτούς, where ἐπί with the accusative has the meaning of "as a testimony against them." John 13:21 is problematic: here Jesus prophesies about Judas's future actions with no reference to Judas's past or future consequences (customarily seen with witness about group 1). But in the wider NT context, most notably Matthew 26:24 and Mark 14:21, we find statements about the future consequence of Judas's future action ("woe to . . .") (in accordance with witness about group 2). Based on that we can put John 13:21 in either witness about group 1 or 2. Ultimately, we treat the testimony in this verse as belonging to witness about group 2 and include it in this first subgroup of texts. The second subgroup of texts also presumes the subject's guilt, or at least presumes that the subjects might be guilty of something, and then gives a warning about future consequences (sometimes in its immediate context), in hopes that the subject changes behavior now to avoid these future consequences. In this subgroup belong following texts: Luke 16:28; Acts 2:40; 20:21; Ephesians 4:17; 1 Thessalonians 4:6; 2 Timothy 2:14. The third subgroup of texts also connects past or present with the future, but in a positive way. Here subjects are generally commended for past or present behavior, complemented, and then admonished to continue in this good way and receive future reward. In this subgroup belongs the following texts: Acts 13:22; 1 Thessalonians 2:12; 1 Timothy 5:21; 2 Timothy 4:1; 1 Peter 5:12.

The third group of personal testifying witnesses about reports in the present what happened in the past, in hopes of confirming or establishing the truth regarding something. So, texts like Matthew 8:4; Mark 1:44 or Luke 5:14 speak of the healing of a leper who then presents his cleansed body as a proof of the healing that Jesus performed. Furthermore, some texts focus on a subject's reputation: Luke 4:22; Acts 6:3; 10:22; 16:2; 22:12; 1 Timothy 3:7; 5:10; Titus 1:13). In these verses, testimony is offered regarding the past words, deeds and behavior of particular subjects. In general, in all these verses subjects testify about the past for the purpose of establishing truths, and they are able to offer that testimony based on their first-hand knowledge. Only in John 2:25 does it seem that Jesus's knowledge of people's hearts is the result of revelation or prophetic (divine) knowledge. Occasionally, we can assume that the thing which was testified about in the past still continues in the present. So, in Romans 10:2 the Jewish zeal for God without proper knowledge still continues. In Colossians 4:13 Epaphras' hard work for churches still continues. In Titus 1:13 the Cretans' bad reputation is still accurate, etc. (cf. Heb 2:6; 3 John 1:3, 6, 12).

In the fourth group of personal testifying witnesses about, the subject's testimony cannot be defined by or limited to only one specific time dimension. Accordingly, in the Synoptics, testifying about "this good news of the kingdom" (Matt 24:14, NRSV) is equally a matter of past, present and future reality of the Kingdom. Mark 13:9 and Luke 21:13 mention testimony about Jesus is general, yet such testimony can contain the past (Jesus's earthly life and ministry), present (his exalted position), and future (the second coming and the final judgment). In the Johannine writings, most of texts which contain the concept of testimony deal with Jesus's personhood. From the start of his gospel, John articulates Jesus's pre-existence, and John's primary focus is to offer witness regarding Jesus's identity and personhood. And speaking about Jesus's identity and personhood is not limited to only one temporal dimension. For example, John the Baptist precedes Jesus, and he speaks about him (in the present about the future). But when Jesus is revealed to Israel, John the Baptist continues to testify about Jesus. Testimony can be about a specific historical event from Jesus's earthly life (John 1:32, 34; 4:39, 44; 19:35; 21:24), his pre-existence (John 3:32, 33), or future events (John 13:21). But in most cases, it is not possible to pinpoint the specific timeframe of testimony, other than to say that witnessing about Jesus encompasses past, present and future (e.g. John 1:7, 8, 15, 19; 3:26; 5:31, 32, 33, 34, 36, etc.). In Acts 8:25 "testifying the word of the Lord" is also a general reference to testimony about Jesus; so also Acts 20:24 ("the good news of God's grace"), Acts 22:18 ("testimony about me"), and Acts 13:31 ("his witnesses" but without specific content of the testimony). Speaking about the kingdom of God (Acts 28:23) can also contain references to the past, present and future; so also Acts 14:3, where God testifies through miracles for "the message of his grace" (NIV). In Acts 26:22, Paul testifies about Jesus based on the Scriptures. His specific content is outlined in verse 23, where Paul refers both to past events from Jesus's life (suffering, death and resurrection) and to present events (the proclamation of the light both to the Jews and to the Gentiles). Testimony about Jesus can sometimes also focus primarily on future events (e.g. Acts 10:42, Jesus will judge people), or Jesus's present status (Acts 18:5, "Jesus is the Christ"). We see the same multiple timeframes in the Pauline epistles: 1 Corinthians 1:6 "testimony of Christ"; 2 Corinthians 2:1 "testimony of God"; 2 Thessalonians 1:10 "because our testimony to you was believed" (NRSV); 2 Timothy 1:8 "the testimony about our Lord," and in 2 Timothy 2:2 where Timothy hears something "through many witnesses."

Sometimes the content of witnessing about Christ is narrowly defined and specific. In the Johannine writings the message about Christ focuses on his transcendence. In Acts, on the other hand, testimony focuses more on specific events from Jesus's life, yet his transcendence is not absent. In Acts 2:32 Peter testifies about a specific historical fact (Jesus's resurrection). In the same breath, he refers to Jesus's current exalted position (vv. 33–36). We see the same pattern in Acts 3:15–16, where Peter testifies about Jesus's resurrection, and then immediately describes Jesus's current activities. So, we see that personal testifying witnesses about group 3 and 4 are occasionally

Table 4: Biblical texts according to the suggested revision – NT

Ontological category and type	Mode	Temporal aspect	Examples
Personal Observing Witnesses	Witness of	In the present for the future	Matt 18:16; Luke 24:48; John 3:28; Acts 10:39; 10:41; 22:15; 26:16; Rom 1:9; 2 Cor 1:23; Phil 1:8; 1 Thess 2:5; 2:10; 1 Tim 6:12.
Personal Testifying Witnesses[1]	Witness for or against	In the present about the past	Matt 15:19; 19:18; 23:31; 26:59, 60, 62, 65; 27:13; Mark 10:19; 14:55, 56 (2x), 59, 60, 63; Luke 11:48; 18:20; 22:71; John 7:7; 8:17; 18:23; Acts 6:13; 7:58; 22:5, 20; 26:5; Rom 8:16; 9:1; 1 Tim 5:19; Heb 10:28.
	Witness about	(1) In the present about what will/can happen in the future	Acts 20:23; Gal 5:3; Heb 3:5; 10:15; 1 Pet 1:11; Rev 22:18; 22:20.
		(2) In the present about what will / can / must happen in the future based on the past or present.	Mark 6:11; Luke 9:5; 16:28; John 13:21; Acts 2:40; 13:22; 20:21; Eph 4:17; 1 Thess 2:12; 4:6; 1 Tim 5:21; 2 Tim 2:14; 4:1; 1 Pet 5:12.
		(3) In the present about the past	Matt 8:4; Mark 1:44; Luke 4:22; 5:14; John 1:32; 2:25; 3:11 (2x), 32 (2x), 33; 4:39, 44; 12:17; 19:35 (2x); 21:24 (2x); Acts 1:22; 4:33; 6:3; 10:22; 15:8; 16:2; 20:26; 22:12; Rom 10:2; 2 Cor 8:3; Gal 4:15; Col 4:13; 1 Tim 3:7; 5:10; Tit 1:13; Heb 2:6; 11:2, 4, 5, 39; 1 Pet 5:1; 3 John 3, 6, 12(3x).
		(4) In the present about more than one dimension of time	Matt 10:18; 24:14; Mark 13:9; Luke 21:13; John 1:7 (2x), 8, 15, 19, 34; 3:26; 5:31 (2x), 32 (2x), 36 (2x), 37; 8:13 (2x), 14 (2x), 18; 10:25; 15:26, 27; 18:37; Acts 1:8; 2:32; 3:15; 5:32; 8:25; 10:42; 13:31; 14:3; 18:5; 20:24; 22:18; 23:11 (2x); 26:22; 28:23; 1 Cor 1:6; 2:1; 15:15 (2x); 2 Thess 1:10; 1 Tim 2:6; 6:13; 2 Tim 1:8; 2:2, Heb 2:4; 12:1; 1 John 1:2; 4:14; 5:6, 7, 9 (3x), 10 (2x), 11; Rev 1:2 (2x), 5, 9; 2:13; 3:14; 6:9; 12:11, 17; 17:6; 19:10; 20:4; 22:16.

1. The mode of witness in Revelation 11:3, 7 is difficult to determine, although they belong to the personal *testifying witness* category.

Ontological category and type	Mode	Temporal aspect	Examples
Impersonal Testifying Witnesses[2]	Witness for or against	In the present about the past	Rom 2:15; Rom 8:16; 9:1 2 Cor 1:12; Jas 5:3.
	Witness about	(1) In the present about more than one dimension of time	Acts 7:44.
		(2) In the present about more than one dimension of time	John 5:39; Acts 10:43; Rom 3:21; Heb 7:8, 17.
		(3) In the present about more than one dimension of time	1 John 5:7.

2. It is difficult to define any details regarding heavenly tabernacle from Revelation 15:5.

woven together, especially in the Johannine writings and Acts. The historical facts serve as the foundation for pronouncements concerning the present and/or future. So even when we find in some texts specific historical testimony about the gospel, the kingdom of God, or Jesus, we must remember that these subjects in biblical context are not limited to only one dimension in time. Although sometimes we can precisely label them as personal testifying witnesses about group 3, this label does not exclude their transcendent reality.

3. Other aspects of the concept of witness

As we did in the OT part, here we must discuss several additional aspects of the concept of witness. These include the function of witnesses, based on which we will offer a definition of witness and witnessing/testifying; the importance of the concept of witness in the NT; what gives authority and validation (valorization) to witnesses; and the dynamic of witnessing.

3.1 The function of witnesses

The NT also allows us to classify witnesses according to their type – observing and testifying witnesses – with their specific functions. Even though having played the role of an observing witness is usually foundational to witnessing, the picture that has emerged is more complex. Witnesses in the NT can sometimes function as witnesses without first having been observing witnesses. Due to the temporal category of witness, sometimes it is difficult to distinguish whether a particular witness has observing or testifying functions (i.e. Acts 10:39, 41). But unlike the OT, in the NT we do not have impersonal entities explicitly defined as observing witnesses.[10]

Furthermore, like OT witnesses, NT witnesses can be classified by their mode of witnessing and temporal aspect. Here also testifying witnesses for or against always speak in the present about the past in order to establish truth regarding a subject's guilt or innocence. They can perform this function in either a legal or a religious context. As in the OT, the majority of personal testifying witnesses for or against belong to the against category. In the category of impersonal testifying witnesses for or against, we have

10. By analogy we could, for example, define as witnesses "stones" from Luke 19:40 who will "cry out." But that does not change our conclusion.

some unique entities that appear as witnesses in the NT: "human spirit" and "conscience." Although they are part of the human person, we viewed them as impersonal witnesses and noted that they are not infallible witnesses. Some witnesses, such as "corrosion" from James 5:3, can only be recognized as such by others, and must be accompanied with an explanatory story, much like what we saw in Exodus 22:13.

In the category of testifying witness about, we also find a somewhat complex division of witnesses. The complexity is justified by the fact that we have testifying witnesses who are not necessarily observing witnesses, and do not function with the guilt/innocence focus. As in the OT, the biggest challenge in the NT is to differentiate between the second group of personal testifying witnesses about and witnesses for and against, because they presume the subject's guilt, yet the timeframe and specific purpose of witnessing differ from that of witnesses for or against. Furthermore, some witnesses from this category announce what will or could happen in the future, others report what happened in the past with the purpose of confirming or establishing the truth regarding something, and still other witnesses have testimony that cannot be defined by or limited to only one specific dimension of time.

3.2 Definition of witnesses and witnessing/testifying

In the OT, after we revised the categorization of witnesses and summarized their functions based on witnesses' activities, we offered a definition of "witness" and (based on that definition) a definition of "testimony." The key elements in the NT that help us to observe the complexity of witnessing and define who is a witness are much the same as in the OT:

- Who: personal and impersonal entities
- Context: social, religious or legal context
- Role: passive or active role
- Temporal aspect: all three temporal aspects: past, present and future
- Mode of witness: of, about, for or against
- Purpose: to ensure confirmation, to establish subject's guilt or innocence, to warn or admonish or declare intention, etc.
- Qualifications: various
- Means of testimony: various

In addition to these key elements, the major activities that witnesses perform to testify are similar to those in the OT. Observing witnesses use seeing and hearing as the means of their witness. This qualifies them or gives them authority to serve as observing witnesses, and, if needed in the future, to step into the role of testifying witnesses. Furthermore, knowledge or remembrance is another faculty that describes observing witnesses. This faculty is the result of seeing, hearing or both. Based on these actions, a person gains knowledge which qualifies him or her to serve as an observing witness and enables him or her to testify in the future if needed. However, we need to say that hearing, having knowledge or remembrance do not in themselves mean that this person has first-hand knowledge. These qualifications can be also a result of secondary knowledge (Matt 2:3; Luke 17:32; 2 Cor 8:1, etc.).

Activities associated with testifying witnesses in the NT also generally fall in the category of speech. Hence, even if we do not find explicit Greek words for the concept of witness in some texts, activities such as "speaking," "saying," "spreading news," "telling the good news," "proclaiming," etc., are all possible candidates for describing the activity of witnesses. In some cases, the activity of an impersonal testifying witness is challenging to define, particularly when we deal with conscience (Rom 2:15; 9:1; 2 Cor 1:12) or human spirit (Rom 8:16), because the communication occurs inside of men. Conscience (Rom 2:15; 9:1) or human spirit (Rom 8:16) are "co-testifying" (συμμαρτυρέω) but we cannot precisely describe how that happens. Or "conscience" in 2 Corinthians 1:12 produces *μαρτύριον* in Paul's life, but (again) it is difficult for us to grasp this process. Likewise, "water and blood" *μαρτυρέω* (1 John 5:7), but due to difficulty of defining what objects "water and blood" refer to, it is difficult to define how these two entities are doing *μαρτυρέω*.

Based on the data we have gathered, we conclude that in the NT (as we have already seen in the OT), "witness" can be referred to with specific terms denoting witness or inferred based on actions associated with witness. We likewise must consider the distinction, previously mentioned, between "witness" and "testimony," where "witness" is the person or thing who gives "testimony," and "testimony" is the content which witness produces. Consequently, the concept of witness includes two connected elements: witness and testimony. These two elements are complementary, not identical.

Further, since specific Greek words denote the concept of witness, and since their semantic range can contain or reflect the concept of witness, we can affirm the conclusion we drew from the OT material: our definition of "a witness": a) must separate "testimony" from "witness," because this is "a product" which witness produces, b) might not include every entity which gives "testimony," since not every such entity can be considered as "witness", c) include activities which witnesses perform and, d) must take into consideration the different functions of witnesses. For that matter, we can say that the NT definitions of "witness" and "testimony" are the same as in the OT: "witness is a personal or impersonal *entity* who, based on particular *qualifications* and *mode* of witness in reference to a specific *temporal aspect*, offers testimony with a *specific purpose* by using various *means*." Testimony, on the other hand, is "a product that personal or impersonal witness produces."

In this discussion about differences between "witness" and "testimony," it is worth noticing that the NT word μάρτυς, which is equivalent to *ʿēḏ* (עֵד) or *ʿēḏîm* (עֵדִים) in the OT, is always used for personal entities. So, in the NT we do not find any situations where impersonal entities are explicitly referred to as "witnesses," but impersonal entities may show that they are witnesses on the basis of their activities. This means, for example, that although the Scripture in the NT is never referred to as μάρτυς (unlike in the OT), Scripture can give μαρτυρέω (John 5:39; Acts 10:43; Rom 3:21; Heb 7:8, 17). For that matter, we should treat the Scriptures as "witness" as well. Accordingly, the dynamic between "witness" and "testimony" seen in the OT is present in the NT as well.

3.3 The importance of the concept of witness in the New Testament

In our discussion of the OT, we saw the theocratic nature of OT Israel, and the unique function of witnesses there. In that setting, witnesses were mediators who created public truths which, if accepted, created realities. That OT function is the basis for the importance of the concept of witness in the NT as well, and it continues both in legal and religious context.

Although Jesus's NT community is not a theocracy as OT Israel was, the NT repeats OT commands prohibiting false witnesses and affirms the need for "two or three witnesses" to establish the verdict. Also, as in the OT, we have seen in the NT that having multiple witnesses does not always guarantee a just and truthful verdict, but (as in the OT) this caution does not diminish the importance of "mouths" in witnesses' testimony. We can additionally say that the NT develops the command about the need for two or three witnesses. This norm was originally given for legal or juridical context, but in the NT, it is cited mostly in the context of conflict inside the church community, be it doctrinal or ethical (John 8:17; Matt 18:16; 2 Cor 13:1; 1 Tim 5:19; Heb 10:28). Since this command is also implicitly present in the NT (for example: Rom 9:1; 1 Thess 2:10; 1 John 5; Rev 11:3, etc.), the question is whether this OT command should continue to be viewed as a "command" in the NT, or has it become a "principle" that can be applied in various different ways and contexts.

In the OT we did not encounter many explicit examples of witnessing in attempt to establish religious truths. In the NT, however, the story is different. The Gospels are full of examples of witness where religious truth is at stake, especially the Gospel of John. But this phenomenon continues through the entire NT. Even when we find the disciples on trial (actual or future, cf. Matt 10:18; Mark 13:9), their testimony is or will be primarily about, rather than for or against. We most clearly see the role of witnesses in shaping reality and public truth in a religious context when we deal with testimony about Jesus's resurrection, the most important article of Christian faith (cf. 1 Cor 15:17). Although no witnesses saw the event of resurrection, a significant group of individuals saw the resurrected Jesus. Based on their testimony, Christians today believe that Jesus's resurrection was a historical event, and not the product of imagination or wishful thinking. Furthermore, the witnesses' testimony is often accompanied by interpretations. In other words, witnesses testify not only to what happened but also to the significance and meaning of the event. This is particularly important for testimony given in religious context.

Finally, in the OT the Sinai covenant is the testimonial event that created a missional community. In the NT, the incarnation of Jesus Christ is the paramount testimonial event, with an outcome of equal significance: it reveals God in a way that enables people to enter into a relationship with him, and this relationship creates a missional community. Because this community has a unique position, opportunity and access to particular events, it also has an obligation to proclaim that revelation/testimony faithfully to others, so that those who will accept it will continue to walk in the community's steps.

3.4 Authority and validation (valorization) of witness

To better define who or what gives someone the authority to be a witness and what determines someone's testimony as valid in the context of the NT, we will further examine the qualifications needed by particular groups of witnesses.

As in the OT, on the most basic level a witness's authority and validation come from his unique access to events, which in turn gives him unique knowledge about the events upon which basis he can then testify. We already noted that these qualifications are crucial for the dynamic between observing and testifying witnesses. But we have also seen that the *modus operandi* of various testifying witnesses makes the issue of authority and validation rather complex.

1. Personal testifying witnesses may declare in the present what will/can happen in the future, and their authority for doing so may come from either who they are (Holy Spirit: Acts 20:23; Heb 10:15; Jesus: Rev 22:18, 20) or because they are prophets (Heb 3:5; 1 Pet 1:11) who act on the basis of YHWH's revelation (Acts 20:23).

2. If these personal testifying witnesses declare in the present what will will/can/must happen in the future on the basis of the subjects' past or present, they draw their authority from: a) knowledge of God's will based on God's revelation (Acts 2:40; 20:21; Eph 4:17; 1 Thess 2:12; 4:6; 1 Tim 5:21; 2 Tim 2:14; 4:1; 1 Pet 5:12), b) personal experience (Luke 16:28), c) in four occasions Jesus and God are the source of testimony (Mark 6:11; Luke 9:5; John 13:21; Acts 13:22). Unlike the previously mentioned group of witness, here the witnesses' authority does not proceed so much from *who* they are (although this element is not excluded) but is based on their knowledge of God's will.

3. Personal testifying witnesses who in the present testify about the past usually do so on the basis of being observing witnesses in the past or having personal experience.

4. Finally, among personal testifying witnesses whose testimony cannot be limited to *only one* specific time dimension we have human, angelic and divine witnesses. As such the source of their authority is diverse: humans can either be eyewitnesses, chosen to be witnesses, or recipients of revelation; the angel from Revelation 19:10 and 22:16 is presented as mediator of

Jesus's revelation, and divine witness of Father, Son and the Spirit is based on who they are.

Since the NT does not often use impersonal testifying witnesses, the issue of these witnesses' authority is much simpler. Besides a reference to the "tabernacle of testimony" from the OT (Acts 7:44) and "water and blood" (1 John 5:7), the primary witness in this category is Scripture itself, which draws its authority from being the product of God's revelation (the same is true for the tabernacle).

Regarding the second question, asking what determines if someone's testimony is valid: as in the OT, this question is most applicable to personal witnesses. Impersonal witnesses are either result of YHWH's revelation (Scripture, tabernacle), unrepeatable historical events (water and blood), significance recognized by others (corrosion in Jas 5:3), or they are observing witnesses (conscience and human spirit). Accordingly, the testimony of impersonal witnesses contains its own validity.

The testimony of personal witnesses gains validity in the NT in a way similar to the OT. First, for the majority of testifying witnesses the prerequisite is to be an observing witness. Therefore, being an observing witness or having personal experiences of an event gives validity to their testimony. Second, as in the OT the most prominent aspect of testimony is that it is verbal, because there are often no other means of establishing the truth regarding something. For that matter, a witnesses' character is crucial, because, as we saw, testimony has the power to create reality and/or public truth. False witnesses can bring death (Jesus, Stephen), accuse another person wrongly (2 Cor 13:1; 1 Tim 5:19) or make people believe a lie (1 Cor 15:15). Hence, the witness's truthfulness is of paramount importance. Interestingly, the NT does not mention punishment for false witness(es). Third when witnesses' authority comes from who they are or the fact that they act on the basis of YHWH's revelation. This is particularly true when we consider divine testimony from the Father, Son and Holy Spirit, because the authority and validity of them comes from who they are. When a witness's authority comes not so much from who he is but from his knowledge of God's will, recipients of testimony who do not recognize the witness's knowledge of God's will have no reason to accept this testimony as valid or binding for them. If the messenger is not accepted, neither will his message be accepted. Fourth, the verbal testimony of witnesses can receive additional demonstration, confirmation, or support through other means. Although we must recognize the prominence of verbal testimony, with the coming of Jesus and the Spirit's activity in the early church, testimony is often accompanied by signs and wonders or various other manifestations. We can say that the verbal announcement (for those with ears to hear) is joined with physical manifestations (for those with eyes to see). Additionally, while the cultic element was a significant visible element to the concept of witness in the OT, in the NT the cultic element is virtually absent. Fifth, due to the prominence of verbal testimony, the NT repeats the OT commands about the prohibition of false witnesses and the need for "two or three witnesses" to establish verdicts. At the same time, we also see that having multiple witnesses does not always guarantee a just and truthful verdict, but this fact does not diminish the importance of "mouths" in testimony.

When we combine these all the data regarding the authority and validity of witnesses' testimony, we observe the following pattern: when witnesses testify about the past, their authority usually comes from having been an observing witness or having personal experience. This gives validity and reliability to their testimony. When witnesses speak about the future, their authority usually comes from knowledge of God's will. However, in that case, the recipients of this testimony must recognize and accept the witness. Hence, we can say that faith has a more prominent role in these cases. Occasionally, such testimony can be confirmed by other visible means. Of course, divine testimony constitutes a separate category of witnesses because the authority and validity of the divine witnesses comes from *who* they are.

3.5 Dynamic of witnessing

As we talk about the dynamic of the concept of witness in the NT, we see that the NT to a great extent follows the dynamic we already saw in the OT. First there is a dynamic between observing and testifying witnesses, and everything we wrote for the OT applies to the NT as well.

Second, with minor variations (because the NT does not use impersonal observing witnesses, and the cultic elements are virtually missing), the dynamic of the concept of witness is also present in the temporal aspects in which witnesses' function. We have noticed, for this reason, that the concept of witness overlaps with two significant OT concepts, namely "covenant" and "prophecy." In the NT, the overlap between "witness" and "prophecy" continues as in the OT, but we must also address the incarnation and the message of the gospel. The NT outdoes the OT in highlighting the overlap between witness and prophecy. A few examples:

a) John the Baptist is the prophet whose task is, among other things, to testify (John 1:6, 7, 15),

b) Jesus viewed himself as a prophet (John 4:4) with a task to testify for the truth (John 18:37). He was also considered as a prophet "mighty in word and deed" (Luke 24:19),

c) Revelation is full of examples of the connection between prophecy and testimony,

d) as noted in Mark 6:11, Jesus sends his disciples in the tradition of the ancient prophets to first indicate warning, and then judgment if the recipients persisted in rejection of message and messengers,

e) Paul in Titus 1:13 quotes a gentile "prophet" and labels the statement "testimony."

We will address this connection more extensively in Luke/Acts, when we argue that the disciples in Acts inherit and continue Jesus's prophetic ministry.

But the concept of witness in the NT overlaps with another core and foundational NT concept: the gospel itself. Apostles not only testify for the resurrection (cf. Acts 4:33 where resurrection is the content of their testimony), but their testimony can be equated with the gospel (cf. 1 Cor 1:6; 1 Cor 2:1; 2 Thess 1:10; 2 Tim 1:8). We also concluded that expressions such as *τὸ εὐαγγέλιον ἡμῶν* "our gospel" (2 Cor 4:3; 1 Thess 1:5; 2 Thess 2:14), *τὸ εὐαγγέλιόν μου* "my gospel" (Rom 2:16; 16:25), and even *τὸ κήρυγμα ἡμῶν* "our proclamation" (1 Cor 15:14) can be connected to the concept of testimony. Based on that connection, we say that the gospel as historical event is a form of "testimony," which has the power to and effect of creating new witnesses when it is proclaimed (facts + meaning of it). We encountered the same thing with Moses's retelling of the exodus story in Deuteronomy.

But as Sinai and the Mosaic covenant are central elements in OT theology, the incarnation of the Son of God is undoubtedly as central to the NT. Jesus is the eyewitness of heavenly realities who comes to the earth to speak about them (John 3:31–36) as he "tabernacles" (*σκηνόω* John 1:14) among us. In that sense, there is no witness to these things other than him. But through his ministry he revealed his identity. Those who were with him could become observing witnesses through "seeing," "hearing" and "touching" (cf. 1 John 1:1;

2 Pet 1:16: ἐπόπται "eyewitnesses") – similarly to the Israelites at Sinai (*šāmaʿ* [שָׁמַע] "listen" Exod 19:9; 20:19; 24:27, and *rāʾāh* [רָאָה] "see" Exod 20:18; 20:22; 24:10). Through that relationship they were able to grasp his identity, put their faith in him, and be eyewitnesses of his life and ministry. Admittedly, the disciples were not eyewitnesses of Jesus's pre-existence or the event of resurrection. This means that accepting some of the things about Jesus required faith on their part. But they were eyewitnesses of Jesus's life and ministry. As such, after his departure, they continued to testify to the facts of Jesus's life and ministry as well as their meaning and importance. The end result was similar to what we saw in Exodus 19–24: the creation of a community. As we said in our treatment of the OT: covenant conveyed revelation, revelation produced community (relationship), and community as the recipient of revelation received mission. Now this community must live faithfully to Jesus's revelation and implement that revelation into every aspect of their existence. Their faithfulness requires them to make this new revelation of Jesus known to others.

Third, unlike the OT, the NT does not have this dynamic between "witness" as a person and "testimony" as a product of the witness's testimony.[11] When impersonal witnesses appear in the NT, their activities are all already designated as "witnesses" (with the exception of the tabernacle in Acts 7:44), so this specific dynamic is not part of the NT. What we do have is an example from John 1:7 where John the Baptist surprisingly is not called μάρτυς "witness" but μαρτυρία "testimony," and as such, he performs the activity of μαρτυρέω. So, this is a unique case where "testimony" produces the activity of testifying. Furthermore, in the NT we do not have cases where the attribute of testimony is imparted or transferred from one impersonal witness to another. However, as we already said, although this does not happen in reference to material objects, we see this activity on another level where, similar to Moses in the book of Deuteronomy, the testimony of witnesses can create other witnesses, with Jesus and his disciples as the ultimate example. We will address this point specifically in our discussion of the unique contribution Luke/Acts makes to the concept of witness. Finally, in the OT we said that a witness is not just someone who speaks for, against or about, in the modern sense of a witness as disinterested third party. In the OT, the

11. By that we mean that "testimony" becomes "witness."

witness may assume additional juridical roles, such as "accuser," "judge" and "executioner." In the NT witnesses are likewise not disinterested third parties, but we do not find explicit references of them in the roles of "judge" or "executioner." Yes, the disciples' symbolic actions of shaking off the dust from their feet (Mark 6:11; Luke 9:5) announces future judgment. And yes, when the Son of Man returns his apostles will "sit on twelve thrones, judging the twelve tribes of Israel" (Matt 19:28 NIV). But other than those examples, in the NT human witnesses do not take on the role of "judges" or "executioners." (Although the role of executioner who is also a witness in the NT is attributed to Jesus in Rev 19).

4. Conclusion

In our study of the concept of witness in the NT, we first introduced the Greek word group that carries the explicit meaning of witness/testimony. Then we analyzed all texts containing these terms and synthesized the results. Based on this analysis, we conclude that the concept of witness in the NT builds upon the OT understanding of that same concept. Our study of the NT has demonstrated several other similarities with the OT.

First, the NT also supports the division of witnesses according to type, observing and testifying witnesses, with the same specific functions. Witnesses in the NT can also be divided according to their mode of witnessing and temporal aspect. Testifying witnesses for or against always speak in the present about the past in order to establish truth regarding subject's guilt or innocence, and they can do it in a legal or religious context. The category of testifying witness about is again somewhat complex; justification for the complexity comes from the fact that testifying witnesses are not necessarily required to be observing witnesses, and they do not function in that guilt/innocence focus. Furthermore, some witnesses from this category announce what will or can happen in the future, some report what happened in the past with the purpose of confirming or establishing the truth regarding something, and some witnesses' testimony cannot be defined by or limited to only one specific time dimension.

Second, the concept of witness in the NT differs across the NT in various complementary ways. Like the OT, it also reflects the idea of "repetition"; repetition does not summarize everything that witnesses do, but it is a consistent general characteristic of the concept of witness. Even though the etymology of μάρτυς emphasizes predominantly mental activity, especially verbal repetition, this repetition could also include a particular lifestyle, notably the lifestyle of a prophet. Jesus's style of ministry reflected the prophet's lifestyle (words + miraculous deeds), and the disciples also inherited this lifestyle. Occasionally, repetition is announced as a future event in a form of symbolic action (cf. Mark 6:11; Luke 9:5). Also, after the Holy Spirit initially being poured out on the day of Pentecost in Acts 2, this activity was repeated with the Spirit's coming in Acts 10 and 19.

Third, as in the OT, the verbal aspect of testimony is the most prominent aspect in the NT, often because there are no other means of establishing the truth regarding something. But while prominent, the verbal aspect is often accompanied with signs and wonders or various other manifestations in Jesus's and the disciples' ministry. In that sense, the role of the Holy Spirit is also significant. The OT does not explicitly connect the Spirit and the concept of witness, except in Nehemiah 9:30. In the NT the story is different, however. The Spirit can witness internally (Rom 8:16; 9:1), through the Scripture (Heb 10:15) or in some unidentifiable ways (John 15:26; Acts 5:32; 20:23; 1 John 5:6, 7). We have also initially seen that in Acts the Spirit's role is paramount for the concept of witness.

In some aspects, the concept of witness in the NT continues to develop and change. First, the biggest change from the OT is the change of context. In the OT the concept of witness was embedded in the context of Israelite theocracy. In the NT this concept shapes new *ecclesia* which contains both Jews and gentiles who believe in Jesus as Messiah. This *ecclesia* lives in an environment which is hostile toward her, and where outside standards of life are not defined by YHWH. One concrete expression of this change can be seen in the overlap between the legal or juridical and religious/covenantal contexts. In the following examples, Jesus's disciples are, or will, be brought to trial: Matthew 10:18; Mark 13:9; Luke 21:13; 22:20; John 18:37; Acts 26:2. Yet, at these trials disciples do not function as witnesses for or against, but as witnesses about, testifying primarily about something. They are on trial because of their religious convictions which ruling authorities oppose.

Second, in the NT the cultic elements as witnesses practically disappear. For this reason, in the NT we do not find cases where the attribute of testimony can be imparted or transferred from one element to another.

However, the NT introduces new entities as witnesses: human conscience and the human spirit. Although they are part of humans, we viewed them as impersonal entities, noting that they are not infallible witnesses. The fact that they are mentioned as witnesses speaks about the internalization of the concept of witness, and the reality and possibility of an individual's internal dialogue as one form of witness.

Third, we already noted that in the OT we did not encounter many explicit examples of witnessing in an attempt to establish some religious truth. Due to the incarnation of Jesus, the truth about Jesus Christ becomes the focal point of the concept of witness in the NT. Verbal testimonies, miracles, creation of a new community, Scripture, work of the Holy Spirit, etc., are all in the service of the proclamation of this particular religious truth, and faithful living to that revelation.

Our research thus far has given us a comprehensive picture of the concept of witness in the Bible. We have been able to identify various aspects of the concept, and to track its development. But before we turn to the concept of witness in the Lukan writings, with the goal of determining the significance and impact of *πνεῦμα ἅγιος* on the concept of witness in Luke's theology, we need to analyze the semantic range of other words that belong to or reflect the concept of witness in the NT.

CHAPTER 10

The Semantic Range of the Concept of Witness in the New Testament – Selected Texts

We have seen in the OT that the concept of witness is present not only at the phenomenological level, but also at the semantic. The same is true for the NT. Hence, in this chapter we will study words and events in selected parts of the NT which contain or reflect the concept of witness. We will analyze the dynamic of witnessing in the NT through the semantic range of particular words connected with the faculties of "speaking," "seeing," "hearing" or "knowing." Our analysis will not be extensive (that is, we will not analyze every usage of a particular word in the NT), but we will select examples that demonstrate the usage of particular words with the concept of witness. Also, we will study selected events which, we believe, represent a form of witness. This semantic study should enrich our understanding and give us a fuller picture of the aspects of the concept of witness in the Bible.

1. Events

As did the OT, the NT also contain events which represent a form of witness. We cannot treat any in detail. It will be sufficient to mention and briefly analyze them.

1.1 Incarnation

No doubt the most significant event which represents a form of witness is the event of incarnation, and this aspect is especially emphasized in the Gospel of John. Speaking of John 1:14 and the word σκηνόω "take up residence," Keener says: "Just as God 'tabernacled' with his people in the wilderness, God's Word tabernacled among the witnesses of the new exodus accomplished in Jesus . . . John may emphasize that Jesus, rather than the temple or tabernacle, is the true locus of God's activity among humanity."[1] Jesus's coming to the earth was not only an opportunity for people to see God's glory, but Jesus also revealed his Father. Astonishingly, he even declared to his disciples that "Anyone who has seen me has seen the Father" (John 14:9). All this demonstrates that incarnation is an event which gave people opportunity to see and experience another dimension of reality. This is further affirmed by John's dualism ("from above" vs. "from below"). Such language belongs to the context of witness. To that, we can add that the second coming of Christ is also an event which represents witness, because the phenomena as foretold include observation and seeing: "Then will appear the sign of the Son of Man in heaven. And then all the peoples of the earth will mourn when they see the Son of Man coming on the clouds of heaven, with power and great glory" (Matt 24:30 NIV).

1.2 Miracles

A logical extension of the incarnation is the way that Jesus brought his world with him and demonstrated its reality. His miracles are part of this demonstration. When John's disciples question Jesus in Matthew 11:1–6, Jesus points to what they have witnessed (including miracles) as manifestations of the kingdom: "Jesus replied, 'Go back and report to John what you hear and see: The blind receive sight, the lame walk, those who have leprosy are cleansed, the deaf hear, the dead are raised, and the good news is proclaimed to the poor. Blessed is anyone who does not stumble on account of me.' " The NT uses several words for miracles, and particularly important for our analysis is the noun σημειον, usually translated as "sign." According to Ladd, "A 'sign' is a mighty work wrought by Jesus that represents the revelatory

1. Keener, *John*, 408–410.

and redemptive event happening in him."[2] Ladd explains further: "Signs, like works, witness to the presence and power of God in the person of Jesus . . . Their meaning is in revealing of the redemptive action of God in Jesus that they represent."[3] As such, signs do not point to themselves but reveal and point to a greater reality. For this reason, we must recognize the presence of the concept of witness in Jesus's miracles as well.

1.3 Pentecost

We also see the concept of witness in the coming of the Spirit at Pentecost, for two reasons. First, the events themselves had observing witnesses. The apostles themselves ὁράω "saw" tongues of fire coming on themselves (Acts 2:3). Other people gathered in Jerusalem ἀκούω "heard" the φωνή "sound" of the apostles speaking in tongues (Acts 2:6, 8, 11). Thus, Pentecost was a visible and observable event; this was exactly Peter's point when he notes at the conclusion of his sermon (Acts 2:33) that people ἀκούω and βλέπω the Spirit being poured out.[4]

Second, we have seen that the underlying idea behind the concept of witness in the OT was "repetition." Thus, it is interesting that in the book of Acts we find three detailed accounts of the Spirit being poured out on believers: chapters 2, 10 and 19. Of course, we cannot say that Acts contains three Pentecosts, and only in Acts 2 is fire mentioned as a phenomenon accompanying the coming of the Spirit. Yet the repetition is nevertheless present. God has poured out his Spirit, and he is doing it again and again. Based on these two arguments, we can undoubtedly count the pouring out of the Spirit as an event which represent a form of testimony.

2. Ladd, *Theology of NT*, 309.

3. Ladd, 410.

4. Archer (*Gospel Revisited*, 53) describes Pentecost as God's disclosure and exposure: "The self-disclosure of God involves the act of self-exposure. God is revealed as liberator through Israel's exodus. Jesus is revealed as the messianic Lord through the resurrection. At Pentecost, God is revealed as the Spirit of Life. Pentecost is a definitive historic moment in the salvific journey of the people of God. Pentecost is an intimate yet 'tangible' revealing of the Holy Spirit who becomes a permanent sojourner with the pilgrim people of God in the absence of the resurrected Christ."

2. Words

2.1 Speaking

There are several words for speaking that we can take into consideration in our analysis. The general meaning of the verb ἀναγγέλλω is "report." Its usage with relation to the concept of witness is connected either with witnesses who report about what has happened through their immediate knowledge[5] (John 5:15; Acts 14:27; 15:4; 19:8; 2 Cor 7:7; 1 John 1:5), or with speech about the future and witnesses who will in the future give reports based on their immediate knowledge (John 16:13, 14, 15).

The verb ἀπαγγέλλω "tell, declare" is used in the context of witnessing to refer to eyewitnesses who either saw and/or heard something (function of observing witnesses), or did something and then gave report about that act (function of testifying witnesses). So, Herod in Matthew 2:8 requests that the Magi find the newborn king of Israel and ἀπαγγέλλω to him. In Matt 8:33, Mark 5:14 and Luke 8:34, the pig herdsmen, after witnessing the destruction of the pigs, went into the town to ἀπαγγέλλω to others what had happened. As a result, those who heard their report went to εἶδον "saw" (Mark 5:14; Luke 8:35) for themselves what happened. When they arrived, they give additional witness, since in Mark 5:16 the original witnesses describe what happened to the demon-possessed man and pigs. Luke 8:36 mentions only description of what happened to the demon-possessed man. In Mark 5:19, Jesus charges the now-delivered man to go home to his own people and ἀπαγγέλλω what the Lord has done for him. That same charge is repeated in Luke 8:39, but instead ἀπαγγέλλω, Luke uses the verb διηγέομαι "tell."

In Matthew11:4, Jesus tells the disciples of John the Baptist to inform their teacher about Jesus's ministry based on what they ἀκούω "hear" and βλέπω "see." The same event is described in Luke 7:22 but instead βλέπω Luke uses the verb εἶδον, which has the same meaning. Interestingly, Matthew says that John sent his disciples because of what John ἀκούω about Jesus. Luke 7:18 explains that John's "hearing" about Jesus comes from his disciples, themselves eyewitnesses who ἀπαγγέλλω to him about Jesus's ministry.

In Matthew 28:10 the women meet risen Jesus, who charged them to ἀπαγγέλλω the other disciples that he would meet them in Galilee. First, the women are *observing witness*, but because of the encounter with Jesus, they

---

5. Immediate knowledge as *eyewitness knowledge* or *first-hand knowledge*.

must become *testifying witness*. The same pattern awaits the disciples, who first must ὁράω "see" him.

All other examples of the usage of ἀπαγγέλλω follow this same pattern. In Mark 6:30 the apostles gathered around Jesus to report to him all they had done and taught. In Mark 16:10 Mary Magdalene wants to tell Jesus's disciples that he has risen from the dead. In Acts 4:33, upon their release from prison, Peter and John went back to their own people and reported all that the chief priests and the elders said to them. In Acts 5:22–23 the officers report that the apostles are no longer in jail. In Acts 11:33 Cornelius gave report about his vision of an angel. The servant girl in Acts 12:14, after seeing Peter, reports about his release from prison. Peter in Acts 12:17 charges those who were praying for his release to go and tell others about his freedom. In Acts 15:27 the Jerusalem council sends two representatives with the letter to verbally ἀπαγγέλλω the council's decision. In all these examples and others (such as Acts 16:36, 38; 1 Thess 1:9; 1 John 1:2, 3) reporting (testifying witness) is done based on eyewitnesses' knowledge (observing witness). In a few cases (e.g. Acts 23:16, 17, 19) we cannot be sure whether the report is based on eyewitness or second-hand knowledge. Similarly, in Acts 28:21, where we find ἀπαγγέλλω + λαλέω "speak," both could be based on first-and/or second-hand knowledge.

The verb λέγω "speak" or its aorist form εἶπον sometimes refer to "testifying." Not all speaking is testifying, but it can be on occasion. In Matt 17:9, Jesus forbids Peter, James and John to "speak" about what they had ὅραμα "seen." They have been observing witnesses to the event of Jesus's transfiguration yet must for a time remain silent. In Matthew 26:69, 71 the servant girls testify that Peter was a companion of Jesus. In Matthew 28:5 the angel of the Lord testifies about a past event (perhaps as an eyewitness) when Jesus declared that he would rise from the dead, and verse 6 contains the content of his testimony. Furthermore, by telling the women to εἶδον "see," he invites the women to perform the role of observing witnesses. Then in verse 7 he charges them to go and εἶπον "speak" to other disciples the message that Jesus is alive. In Mark 3:22 the teachers of the law give an interpretative conclusion about Jesus: based on their observing and hearing, they declare that Jesus is possessed by Beelzebul! Such speech we can qualify as testimony.

The verb διηγέομαι "tell" predominantly signifies speaking based on eyewitness knowledge or experience. In Mark 5:16 "telling" is based on εἶδον "seeing," and in Mark 9:9, just as in Matthew 17:9, Jesus forbids his disciples to speak about the transfiguration. In Luke 8:39; 9:10 and Acts 12:17, "telling" is also a result of being an eyewitness. Only in Acts 9:27, where Barnabas testifies about Paul's conversion experience, is διηγέομαι used when the subject was not an eyewitness of that which he testifies to.

The following group of words appear rarely, yet they also contribute to the dynamics of the concept of witness. On three occasions (Mark 1:45; 5:20; 7:36), the verb κηρύσσω "proclaim, tell" refers to speech as eyewitness testimony. In Mark 1:45, alongside κηρύσσω, the verb διαφημίζω "spread" also appears. The content of man's testimony is his healing presented as λόγος "word" or "news." The verb προσφωνέω "speak, address" is used in Acts 21:40 and 22:2 to introduce Paul's testimony in chapter 22. Finally, the verb κράζω "shout, cry out" is used in Mark 3:11 to describe the confession that evil spirits make when they θεωρέω "see" Jesus. In John 1:15 κράζω is used together with the verbs λέγω and μαρτυρέω to describe John the Baptist's testimony about Jesus. And in James 5:4, κράζω describes the cry of the wages that corrupt rich people failed to pay to their workers.

The verb λαλέω "speak" presents a more complex situation. In several examples, subjects "speak" about future things. So, those who speak do not have to be observing witness of the things they speak about. For example, in Luke 24:6 angels remind women who went to Jesus's tomb of something that Jesus previously said regarding future events, and the content of this testimony is in verse 7. Obviously, the women witnessed when Jesus spoke about his future, so angels appeal to their memory. However, we cannot be sure whether those angels were also present for Jesus's speech on the topic; perhaps their knowledge of this thing comes from some other source. In Luke 24:25 Jesus reminds his disciples of what the prophets spoke regarding the coming Messiah. The prophets' words did not come from immediate knowledge, nor were Jesus's disciples present when prophets spoke. Hence, here we have another example of the overlap between prophecy and testimony. Similarly, in Acts 2:31 David spoke about future things because he προοράω "foresaw" them and Acts 3:21 also refers to the prophets' predictions about future things (in this case overall restoration).

In a few examples the verb λαλέω appears alongside Greek words for testimony. In John 3:11 we see synonymous parallelism between ὃ οἴδαμεν λαλοῦμεν "we speak of what we know" and ὃ ἑωράκαμεν μαρτυροῦμεν "testify to what we have seen." Accordingly, "knowledge" is a basis for "speaking" just as "seeing" is a basis for "testifying." The fact that λαλέω here refers to testifying is further confirmed at the end of the verse, where such speaking and testifying is labelled as μαρτυρία "testimony." In Acts 8:25 λαλέω is connected with διαμαρτύρομαι in διαμαρτυράμενοι καὶ λαλήσαντες τὸν λόγον τοῦ κυρίου "having testified and spoken the word of the Lord." Finally, Paul in Acts 26:22 is described as the one who stands in order to μαρτυρόμενος "testify" and λέγων "speak." Thus, here is another example of speaking linked with testifying.

On a few occasions, λαλέω results from "hearing" or "seeing." In such instances, we view "speaking" as a form of testimony. In John 8:26 Jesus declares that he "speaks" what he has "heard" from his Father κἀγὼ ἃ ἤκουσα παρ' αὐτοῦ ταῦτα λαλῶ. In John 8:38, ἃ ἐγὼ ἑώρακα παρὰ τῷ πατρὶ λαλῶ, Jesus's "speaking" is grounded in "seeing." Finally, in Acts 4:20 Peter and John's λαλέω is grounded in both εἶδον "seeing" and ἀκούω "hearing." In those instances, the role of observing witnesses (through seeing and/or hearing) is the basis for their speech as testifying witnesses.

Finally, on a few occasions, we can deduce that speaking implies testimony solely from the context. Acts 16:32 connects λαλέω with speaking τὸν λόγον τοῦ κυρίου "the word of the Lord"; this expression stands for the gospel, which is a historical record of Jesus's life, passion, resurrection and second coming.[6] Similarly, Phil 1:14 connects λαλέω with λόγος, again referring to the gospel. In Acts 21:39 λαλέω introduces Paul's testimony in chapter 22. And Romans 15:18 connects λαλέω with speaking about "what Christ has accomplished through me in leading the Gentiles to obey God by what I have said and done" (NIV).

The verb καταγγέλλω "proclaim" appears in the context of witness in three different ways. First, it occurs in connection with proclamation of a particular message: τὸν λόγον τοῦ θεοῦ "the word of God" (Acts 13:5; 17:13); τὸν λόγον τοῦ κυρίου "the word of the Lord" (Acts 15:36); τὸ μυστήριον τοῦ θεοῦ "the mystery of God" or τὸ μαρτύριον τοῦ θεοῦ "the testimony of God"

6. In John, gospel also entails the story of Jesus's pre-existence.

(1 Cor 2:1);[7] *ὁ εὐαγγέλιον* "the gospel" (1 Cor 9:14). In these cases, those who testify can have full (the Twelve), partial (Paul) or non-existent (Barnabas) eyewitnesses experience of what they are talking about. Second, it occurs in connection with speaking about future things, since there is a strong link between prophecy and testimony, and speech about future sometimes can be classified as testimony. So, in Acts 3:24 Peter mentions how prophets *λαλέω* "spoke" and *καταγγέλλω* "proclaimed" future things. Both the NIV and NRSV translate *καταγγέλλω* in terms of speaking about future things, the NIV as "foretold," and the NRSV as "predicted." In Acts 4:2 the apostles *καταγγέλλω* about future things, here the resurrection of the dead. In these cases, those who testify were not observing witnesses, so their authority to speak about the future is grounded in other factors (such as revelation, or inspiration). Third, Romans 1:8 uses *καταγγέλλω* with the content of "the story of how they [believers in Rome] came to faith [which] was widely known throughout the world."[8] Hence, this report may include those who actually witnessed to that faith.

The verb *φημί* "say" is used in one of four ways. First, it refers to eyewitness testimony, regardless of whether the witnesses themselves experienced something or were present when something happened. Examples of such usage are: Mark 9:38; Luke 22:58; Acts 10:30; 16:37; 17:22; 22:2; 25:24. Second, it is used in Acts 7:2 to introduce Stephen's testimony. Stephen's testimony is not an eyewitness testimony, but he repeats the commonly known history of the Jewish people. Third, it is used in Matthew 26:61, in Jesus's trial, when false witnesses relate what Jesus allegedly said. Finally, it is used in Matthew 26:34 by Jesus to announce Peter's future betrayal.

The final word that we will consider is the verb *εὐαγγελίζω* "tell the good news." Although "the good news" can be many different things, in the NT the good news is primarily connected with Jesus. Since we already established that the gospel is a historical record of Jesus's life and ministry (plus

---

7. "From an exegetical point of view the reading *μαρτύριον τοῦ θεοῦ*, though well supported (ℵ^{c} B D G P Ψ 33 81 614 1739 *Byz* it^{d,} vg syr^{h} cop^{sa} arm eth Origen *al*), is inferior to *μυστήριον*, which has more limited but early support in P$^{46?}$ ℵ* A C 88 436 it$^{, 61}$ syr^{p} cop^{bo} Hippolytus Ambrosiaster Ephraem Ambrose Pelagius Augustine Antiochus. The reading *μαρτύριον* seems to be a recollection of 1:6, whereas *μυστήριον* here prepares for its usage in verse 7" (Metzger, *Commentary on Greek NT*, 480).

8. Mounce, *Romans, 66*.

his pre-existence and future events), speaking about those events is a form of testimony. Accordingly, εὐαγγελίζω can be connected with: news about Jesus's birth (Luke 2:10); "the kingdom of God" (Luke 4:43; 8:1; 16:16; Acts 8:12 [and the name of Jesus Christ]); the idea that Jesus is Messiah (Acts 5:42); λόγος "word" (Acts 8:4; 1 Cor 15:2; cf. Acts 8:25); Jesus (Acts 8:35); the message about "peace through Jesus Christ" (Acts 10:36) or "peace" (Eph 2:17); "the Lord Jesus" (Acts 11:20); "fulfilled promise given to the fathers" (Acts 13:32); "command to turn from idols to the living God" (Acts 14:15); "the word of the Lord" (Acts 15:35); "Jesus and the resurrection" (Acts 17:18); "the good news of God" (2 Cor 11:7), "the good news" (Gal 1:11) or "eternal gospel" (Rev 14:6); αὐτὸν "him" (Gal 1:16); τὴν πίστιν "faith" (Gal 1:23); "the boundless riches of Christ" (Eph 3:8); "entrance into the rest" Hebrews 4:2, 6; ῥῆμα κυρίου "word of the Lord" (1 Pet 1:25), etc. On two occasions, εὐαγγελίζω is not strictly connected with Jesus. It is used to refer to the news that the angel Gabriel brought to Zechariah about the future birth of John the Baptist (Luke 1:19), and it was used to refer to the good report that Timothy brought to Paul from the church in Thessaloniki (1 Thess 3:6). Finally, εὐαγγελίζω can stand alone in the text: Matthew 11:5; Luke 3:18; 4:18; 7:22; 9:6; 20:1; Acts 8:25;[9] 8:40; 14:7, 21; 16:10; Romans 1:15; 10:15; 15:20; 1 Corinthians 1:17; 9:16, 18; 15:1;[10] 2 Corinthians 10:16; Galatians 1:8, 9; 4:13; 1 Peter 1:12; 4:6; Revelation 10:7.

2.2 Hearing

The verb ἀκούω "hear" when used in the context of witness usually refers to those who hear something. On most occasions, those who speak are eyewitnesses (and for that matter function as testifying witnesses), and those who "hear" are recipients of these testimonies. As such, their hearing in these cases is indirect or second-hand knowledge, not eyewitness or first-hand. Since there are many examples of these, I will summarize the results.

For example, in Matthew 2:3 Herod hears the news about appearance of the star in connection with the birth of Messiah. He receives testimony

9. Although, from the context it is clear that εὐαγγελίζω is synonymous with proclamation of "the word [logos] of the Lord" and testifying "about Jesus."

10. From the context it is clear that εὐαγγελίζω stands for historical record of Jesus death, burial, resurrection, and post-resurrection appearances (1 Cor 15:3–8).

from those who had seen it, and his "hearing" is not eyewitness or direct knowledge. These same ideas are also present in Matthew 2:22; 4:12; 5:21, 27, 32, 38, 43; 11:2; 14:1, 13; 24:6 (+ ἀκοή "report"); 28:14; Mark 3:8, 21; 6:14, 16, 29, 55; 13:7; 16:11; Luke 1:58; 4:23; 7:3; 9:7, 9; 16:2; 21:9; 22:71; 23:8; John 1:40; 4:1, 47; 9:35; 11:4, 6, 20, 29; 12:12, 18; 19:8; Acts 2:37; 4:24; 5:5, 11, 24, 33; 7:12; 8:14; 9:13, 21, 38; 11:1; 15:24; 17:8; 21:20 (people received testimony through their hearing), 22; 28:15; Galatians 1:13, 23; Ephesians 1:15; 3:2; 4:21; Philippians 1:27; 2:26; Colossians 1:4, 9; 2 Thessalonians 3:11; Philemon 1:5; 1 John 2:7, 24; 3:11; 2 John 1:6; 3 John 1:4; Revelation 3:3.

Sometimes it is difficult to determine whether those who "hear," hear something because they are observing witnesses or because they are observing witnesses who also have received knowledge second-hand. Such examples are Acts 19:26 (+ θεωρέω "observe"); 23:16; Philippians 4:9 and 2 Timothy 1:13.

The verb ἀκούω is also used to describe the "hearing" of observing witnesses. Examples of such hearing can be found in: Matthew 9:12; 11:4; 13:13–15 (cf. Mark 4:12; Luke 8:9–10 + βλέπω "see");[11] 17:6; Mark 2:17; Luke 7:22; John 3:22; 8:26, 38, 40; 12:29; 14:28; 15:15; Acts 1:4; 2:22;[12] 2:33 (+ βλέπω "see"); 4:20; 7:34; 9:4, 7; 11:7; 14:11; 21:12; 22:7, 14 (+εἶδον "see"), 15 (+ὁράω "see"); 26:14; 2 Corinthians 12:4; 2 Timothy 2:2; 2 Peter 1:18; 1 John 1:1, 3. Also, throughout the book of Revelation, John is described as eyewitness because of what he hears: Revelation 1:10; 4:1; 5:11, 13; 6:1, 3, 5, 6, 7; 7:4; 8:13; 9:13; 10:4, 8; 12:10; 14:2, 13; 16:1, 5, 7; 18:4; 19:1, 6; 21:3; 22:8.

Finally, ἀκούω can be used to refer to hearing about future events, such as the coming of the antichrists (1 John 2:18) or the spirit of Antichrist (1 John 4:3). Also, in Mark 14:58 and Acts 6:14, the witnesses against Jesus and

11. Seeing and hearing in these verses refer primarily to Isaiah's generation, yet Jesus takes these lines and applies it to his generation. Paul does the same in Acts 28:26–27.

12. Acts 2:22 signifies hearing of observing witnesses, because Peter concludes that Jesus was "a man attested to you by God" (NRSV), and for "attested" Luke uses verb ἀποδείκνυμι which has a sense of being or becoming displayed in a manner accessible or observable by the public. For that matter, Peter just reminds them of what they themselves had already seen and heard.

Stephen base their testimonies on the false premise that they had "heard" them saying certain things about future events.

2.3 Seeing

There are several words that are used for seeing in the context of witnessing in the NT. The most significant word is the verb ὁράω "see" or its aorist form εἶδον. It is most often used to describe the "seeing" of observing witnesses who, as a consequence of their observation, may or may not be or become testifying witnesses. We can detect several ways ὁράω is used.

The first group of people "see" something that makes them observing witnesses. This can be seen from the following examples: Matthew 2:2, 9; 3:16; 13:17; 14:26; 17:3; 21:32; 24:15; 26:58; 28:10, 17; Mark 1:10; 2:12, 16; 16:5; Luke 1:12; 9:32; 10:24; Acts 7:31; 13:12; Philippians 1:27;[13] 1:30;[14] 4:9.[15]

The second group of people observe something and respond by becomes testifying witnesses. Examples of such usage are following texts: Matthew 9:8 (δοξάζω "praise"); 27:54 (λέγω "speak");[16] Mark 2:12; 14:67 (λέγω "speak"); 5:16; 9:9 (διηγέομαι "describe"); 9:38 (φημί "said"); 15:39 (εἶπον "said"); Luke 2:15 (v. 16 γνωρίζω); 5:8, 26 (λέγω "speak"); 9:49; 22:56 (εἶπον "said"); 23:47; 26:71 (λέγω "speak"); John 1:34 (μαρτυρέω "testify"); 6:14; 20:50 (λέγω "speak"); 12:41 (λαλέω "say"); 20:18 (ἀπαγγέλλω "announce"); Acts 7:34;[17] 7:44;[18] 14:11 (ἐπαίρω "raise voice");[19] 28:4 (λέγω "speak"); 1 John 1:1–3 (μαρτυρέω + ἀπαγγέλλω "testify" + "announce").

13. Probably εἶδον "seeing" refers to first-hand knowledge, and ἀκούω refers to second-hand knowledge.

14. Philippians saw Paul's struggle (first-hand experience), and now they ἀκούω about his struggle. Yet, their hearing is a second-hand experience.

15. "Hearing" and "seeing" include first-hand experiences, although "hearing" can be also second-hand experience.

16. In this example as well as in Mark 15:39 and Luke 23:47 Roman soldier is an *observing witness*, yet he also offers interpretation of event of Jesus's death.

17. This is quotation from the exodus story where YHWH had "seen" and "heard" Israel's groaning, so now he will act to ἐξαιρέω "deliver" them.

18. As in Acts 7:34, *observing witnesses* do not testify for what they seen, but acts upon it. In this case, the text speaks about ποιέω "making" of the tabernacle based on the patter Moses saw.

19. In this case, people interpreted miracle in a wrong way.

The third group observe something, and their response is to challenge or ask questions. For example, in Matthew 9:11 and Mark 2:16,[20] the Pharisees saw Jesus eat with tax collectors and sinners. They responded by asking questions, which is a form of challenge. In Matthew 12:2 the Pharisees are again the ones who saw Jesus's disciples do something unlawful on the Sabbath, so they protested.

Finally, the last group are people who are told that they will see certain things in the future. So, in Matthew 24:15; Mark 13:14; Luke 21:20 and 21:31, Jesus warns his disciples about future events. He tells them that when they "see" these things, they must respond in a certain way. John 8:56 is puzzling because Jesus says that Abraham εἶδον "saw" Jesus's day and that he (Abraham) was glad to see it. This could mean that Abraham experienced some preincarnate manifestation of Jesus, or that he had a vision which enabled him to see the future. Or "seeing" means that he metaphorically foresaw Messiah's coming through the eyes of faith. In any case, Abraham was able to see the future.

John in Revelation is in a special category. Throughout he is described as eyewitness, sometimes because of the faculty of "seeing." Sometimes John only observes, and other times he speaks: Revelation 1:2 (μαρτυρέω), 12, 17, 19 (γράφω "write"), 20; 4:1; 5:1, 2, 6, 11; 6:1, 2, 5, 8, 9, 12; 7:1, 2, 9; 8:2, 13; 9:1, 17; 10:1, 5; 13:1, 2, 11; 14:1, 6, 14; 15:1, 2, 5; 16:13; 17:3, 6, 8, 12, 15, 16, 18; 18:1; 19:11, 17, 19; 20:1, 4, 11, 12; 21:1, 2, 22.

The verb βλέπω "see, look at" in the context of witness points to observing witnesses. In Matthew 6:4, 6, 18 God is the one who sees what people do in secret. In Matthew 13:16 and Luke 10:24 Jesus claims that his disciples are blessed because they have an opportunity to βλέπω and ἀκούω him. A similar combination of βλέπω and ἀκούω appears in Mark 4:12, where Jesus repeats Isaiah's statement about "ever seeing but never perceiving, and ever hearing but never understanding," and in Acts 2:33 where people saw and heard the coming of the Spirit. Further, in Matthew 15:31 people were eyewitnesses to Jesus's miracles. In Luke 24:12 Peter sees an empty tomb and tries to interpret this event. In John 5:19 Jesus presents himself as the one who observes what the Father is doing and then repeats what he observes. In Acts 8:6 people observed the miracles that Philip performed. In Revelation

20. The same text is in Luke 5:27–31, yet there Luke does not use the verb ὁράω.

1:11, Jesus instructs John to write to the churches what he βλέπω. Seeing is a faculty of an observing witness, while writing is a faculty of testifying witness. His role as observing witness of different heavenly things is additionally confirmed in Revelation 1:12; 17:8; 22:8.

The verb θεωρέω "observe" in the context of witness also points to observing witnesses, who occasionally can also be testifying witnesses. We find θεωρέω used to describe observing witnesses in the following examples. In Mark 5:15; John 2:23; Acts 3:16 and 8:13, people observed miracles performed by Jesus and/or the apostles. In John 6:2 the crowd follows Jesus because they saw his signs. In Matthew 27:55 and Mark 15:40 a group of women observed Jesus on the cross. In Luke 23:48, when the people observed Jesus's death, they beat their breasts and went away. In John 20:6–7 Peter sees Jesus's clothes in the tomb. In John 20:12 Mary Magdalene saw two angels in Jesus's tomb. And in Luke 24:39 the disciples saw Jesus's resurrected body. We find other examples of *observing witnesses*. The disciples in Luke 21:6 who see the stones of the Temple, which would in the future be removed. The disciples in John 6:19 saw Jesus walking on water. Peter in Acts 10:10 saw a vision. In Acts 19:26, Demetrius the silversmith addresses the people of Ephesus as observers when he speaks against Paul. He appeals to the people's knowledge of Paul based on their θεωρέω and hearing ἀκούω. In 1 John 3:17, John instructs his readers to help other believers if they observe them in need. And in Revelation 11:11, 12, people who observe what happened with two witnesses.

Sometimes, observing witnesses who θεωρέω "observe" something step into the role of testifying witnesses. First, a few texts describe Jesus in these terms. In Mark 12:41–44, Jesus observes people put their money into the temple treasury, concluding with his testimony λέγω about the poor widow's offering (12:43). In Luke 10:18 Jesus εἶπον "said" that he "saw" Satan falling from heaven. Second, people who have been observing Jesus can become testifying witnesses about Jesus. The women in Mark 15:47 saw the tomb where Jesus was laid; in Mark 16:4 they witnessed that the stone was rolled away from the tomb; then in 16:7 the angel instructs them to εἶπον disciples about Jesus's resurrection. In Luke 23:35, people who observed Jesus on the cross mocked him by λέγω: "He saved others; let him save himself if he is God's Messiah, the Chosen One" (NIV). In John 4:19 the Samaritan woman observes Jesus then λέγω that he is a prophet. And in Acts 7:56,

Stephen sees heaven open and the exalted Jesus, then εἶπον to the religious leaders. Third, a few texts describe people's testimony about other people. In John 9:8 people saw the man born blind now healed and began to λέγω, "Isn't this the same man who used to sit and beg?" (NIV). In Acts 17:16, Paul observed the idols in Athens and then he φημί about their idolatry (v. 22). Finally, in Acts 28:6, after people saw that Paul was not killed by the poisonous snake's bite, they λέγω that he is a god.

We find three special uses of the verb θεωρέω, which do not fall into the categories defined above. In John 17:24, as part of his prayer, Jesus asks that his disciples might θεωρέω his glory in the future. In Acts 27:10, Paul uses θεωρέω in his prophetic statement about the near future shipwreck. In Hebrews 7:4, the author of Hebrews asks his readers to θεωρέω "see" Melchizedek's greatness in light of Abraham's tithe of the plunder to Melchizedek. Obviously, such examples of "seeing" are more in line with having proper understanding than the individual serving as an observing witness.

The verb θεάομαι "see" is predominantly used for an observing witness. So, Jesus warns not to do our righteousness in front of others to be seen by them (Matt 6:1). Likewise, he speaks against the teachers of the Law and the Pharisees in Matthew 23:5 because they do their deeds to be seen by others. Further, in Luke 23:55 the women observed the tomb where Jesus's body was laid; in John 1:32 John speaks of seeing the Spirit come from heaven and remain on Jesus; in Acts 1:11 the angels speak to the disciples about how they had seen Jesus ascending to into heaven; in Acts 22:9, Paul's companions saw the light but did not hear the voice that spoke to Paul (Acts 22:9).

On a few occasions, θεάομαι denotes the basis for performing the role of a testifying witness. In the long ending of Mark (16:11), Mary Magdalene is presented as an *observing witness* because she saw the resurrected Jesus alive. We also know that she spoke about what she had seen to the other disciples because they "heard" ἀκούω "that Jesus is alive" . . . but "they did not believe it" (NIV). In 1 John 1:1 θεάομαι is one of a list of verbs that serve as the basis for apostolic testimony (1:2); this is also the case in 4:14, where θεάομαι serves as the basis for μαρτυρέω.

Two other verbs are used in a significant way to refer to seeing in the context of witnessing. First, notice the noun βλέμμα "looking," "the act of seeing" (BDAG). This noun is used in 2 Peter 2:8 to describe Lot's soul's torment as he βλέμμα "saw" and ἀκούω "heard" the lawless deeds of his neighbours. Second, we include the noun ὅραμα "the thing seen," which in Matthew 17:9 refers to Peter, James and John's having been observing witnesses at the Mount of transfiguration.

2.4 Remembrance

We have already seen that the word μάρτυς and its cognates probably comes from the root *smer*, which refers to "bearing in mind, remembering, being careful of something." With that concept in mind, we find two Greek verbs that refer to the activity of remembrance as a form of witnessing. Generally, remembrance is an activity of going mentally into the past to recollect certain events, situations or sayings. This is possible for those who were eyewitnesses of particular events. Based on that memory, a witness may then testify in various ways.

The first verb is μνημονεύω "remember." In the following examples subjects are required to remember something which they had previously seen, heard or experienced: Matthew 16:9; Mark 8:18; John 16:21;[21] Acts 20:31; Ephesians 2:11; 1 Thessalonians 2:9; 2 Thessalonians 2:5; Hebrews 13:7; Revelation 2:5; 3:3; 18:5. In John 16:4, Jesus speaks about a time in the future when his disciples will remember his words.

In some instances, however, being an eyewitness or having a personal experience with some event or fact is not a prerequisite for remembrance. The question we must ask is whether we can consider such recollection as a form of witness or not? For example, as Jesus teaches his disciples about the coming of the Kingdom, he requires his disciples to remember Lot's wife (Luke 17:32). Likewise, Paul, who was not present to hear Jesus's statement, "It is more blessed to give than to receive," accepted them as trustworthy and repeats them to his listeners (Acts 20:35). Further, Paul in Colossians 4:18 asks his readers to remember his chains. Likewise, in 2 Timothy 2:8 he charges Timothy to remember Jesus Christ raised from the dead. What is common in all these examples is that testimony (about someone or something) is received through some mediator (Scripture, other eyewitness). Hence, the act of remembrance (remembering the past in order to inform the present) occurs only if a person accepts what is conveyed to him or her as trustworthy and true, and then act upon that basis.

21. Here Jesus speaks hypothetically about a woman who gives birth to her child.

The same dynamic is present in the verb *μιμνήσκομαι* "remember, recollect." Sometimes remembrance can spring from eyewitness accounts: Matthew 5:23; 26:75; Luke 16:25; 24:6, 8; John 2:22; 12:16; Acts 10:31; 11:16; 2 Timothy 1:4, Hebrews 13:3. The principle is the same in Luke 23:42, but request to remember refers to the future. Again, however, remembrance is not necessarily the result of personal experience. In John 2:17 Jesus's disciples remembered a particular text from the Scripture when they recognized its fulfilment in Jesus's life. We have a similar situation in 2 Peter 3:2, when Peter urges his readers to remember the words spoken in the past by the holy prophets. In Jude 17 we cannot be sure whether *μιμνήσκομαι* (of "the predictions of the apostles") is a result of direct or indirect knowledge of a particular event, or a combination of both. As with *μνημονεύω* we conclude that remembrance can occur if people accept what is conveyed to them as trustworthy and true, and then act upon that basis.

2.5 Knowledge

Since knowledge is one of the prerequisites for being a witness, we will analyze verb *γνωρίζω*. The basic meaning of this verb is to give information to someone, and hence "make known." In the context of the concept of witness, *γνωρίζω* refers to special knowledge that God made known to humans, which in turn may be proclaimed to other humans.

In Luke 2:15 angels *γνωρίζω* to the shepherd's information about Jesus's birth. After they see the event for themselves (Luke 2:16), we see the shepherds *γνωρίζω* these things to other people (Luke 2:17). In 1 Corinthians 15:1 *γνωρίζω* is connected with the *εὐαγγέλιον* in the sense that the content of *γνωρίζω* was *εὐαγγέλιον*. Interestingly, while NIV and NRSV translate *γνωρίζω* here as "remind" (since Paul is referring to his previous preaching to the Corinthians); the NKJV translates *γνωρίζω* here as "declare" and the NASB "made known." *Γνωρίζω* and *εὐαγγέλιον* are also brought together in Ephesians 6:19 where Paul talks about "making known the mystery of the gospel." The content of information can be also general things, like Paul informing Corinthians about a situation with Macedonian churches (2 Cor 8:1), or Paul's companions (Tychicus in Eph 6:21; Tychicus and Onesimus in Colossians 4:7, 9) informing others about Paul's circumstances. In 2 Peter 1:16 the content of *γνωρίζω* is future things ("the coming of the

Lord Jesus"), but this *γνωρίζω* is based on apostles being *ἐπόπτης* "eyewitnesses" of Jesus's majesty.

2.6 Other significant words

The noun *φήμη* appears twice in the NT, and both times it has a meaning of "a report, news." So, in Matthew 9:26 *φήμη* about Jesus raising a dead girl *ἐξέρχομαι* "spread" through all that region. Likewise, in Luke 4:14 *φήμη* about Jesus *ἐξέρχομαι* "spread" throughout the whole countryside. In both cases we can assume that spreading of news was done by both eyewitnesses and those who received a report from others and passed it on.

Sometimes the noun λόγος can assume the meaning of "news." In Mark 1:45 the *κηρύσσω* "announcing" and *διέρχομαι* "spreading" of λόγος refers to the "news" about healing a man with leprosy. In Luke 5:15 the λόγος about Jesus *διέρχομαι* "spread," and in Luke 7:17 the action of spreading the λόγος about Jesus is carried by the verb *ἐξέρχομαι*. In John 4:39 the λόγος about Jesus is a result of the woman's *μαρτυρέω* about him. In John 21:23 the subject λόγος "news" that *ἐξέρχομαι* "spreads" is that the disciple (the author of the John's gospel) would not die. In Acts 5:24 λόγος refers to the "report" from verse 23. And in Acts 11:22 λόγος refers to the news about the spread of the gospel and growth of the church. In these two instances, λόγος is received through *ἀκούω* "hearing."

Occasionally, λόγος is even more narrowly defined to specifically refer to the gospel. In Philippians 1:14 λόγος (in reference to the gospel) stands alone. Likewise, in 1 Thessalonians 1:6, but the mention of *εὐαγγέλιον* in verse 5 brings λόγος in connection with *εὐαγγέλιον*. In Colossians 3:16 Paul defines "gospel" as Ὁ λόγος τοῦ Χριστοῦ "the word of Christ." In Colossians 4:3, he further defines λόγος as the *μυστήριον* τοῦ Χριστοῦ "mystery of Christ."

The noun *ἀκοή*, "hearing" or "report," is also used in the context of witness. It is used in different, complementary ways. First, *ἀκοή* does not necessarily signify eyewitness testimony; it can also refer to rumors or talk among people about someone or something. Examples are Matthew 4:24; 14:1; 24:6; Mark 1:28; 13:7,[22] etc. Secondly, *ἀκοή* can reflect the messenger's

22. In Matthew 24:6 and Mark 13:7 *ἀκούω* "hear" signifies hearing about the facts (wars), and *ἀκοή* "report" signifies rumour about wars – that is possibilities that wars might happen (optional).

side of an exchange, where a report is "given" or proclaimed. It can also refer to the recipient's side, where a message is heard and accepted or rejected. Texts that reflect the messenger's side of ἀκοή can be recognized by the presence of verbs that describe the activity of messengers. In those cases, ἀκοή refers to the news or message which is proclaimed. Examples are Matthew 4:24 with ἀπέρχομαι "go away, depart"; Mark 1:28 with ἐξέρχομαι "spread"; John 12:38 and Romans 10:16[23] with πιστεύω "believe." Texts that reflect the recipient's side of ἀκοή use verbs that describe the activity of recipients. In those cases, ἀκοή has the meaning of "hearing" news or a message. Examples of this second use are more numerous: Matthew 13:14, 24:6; Mark 13:7; 14:1; Acts 28:26 with ἀκούω. In Luke 7:1 ἀκοή describes the activity of hearing. In Galatians 3:2 and 3:5 ἀκοή is part of the expression ἐξ ἀκοῆς πίστεως which can be translated as "hearing of faith." In 1 Thessalonians 2:13 we find the combination of λόγον ἀκοῆς "word of hearing" with verb παραλαμβάνω "receive." Hebrews 4:2 uses the expression ὁ λόγος τῆς ἀκοῆς "word of hearing." And 2 Peter 2:8 mentions Lot as distressed by his βλέμμα "observing" and ἀκοή "hearing" about lawless deeds, etc.

Other minor words that fit into the context of witness are the nouns ἐπόπτης "eyewitness" (2 Pet 1:16) and αὐτόπτης "eyewitness" (Luke 1:2). Lastly, the verb δοξάζω "praise" is also used in the context of witness because it is used as a response to what was seen or heard (Matt 9:8 εἶδον, and Luke 2:20 ἀκούω + εἶδον).

3. Conclusion

As with the OT, our analysis of the semantic range confirmed that different words (notably verbs) and events can be loaded with ideas or carry the concept of witness. Accordingly, we confirmed here as well that witnesses can be defined based on the activities they perform. That means that our definition of witness according to the NT must also include the semantic dynamic of the concept of witness. Results of this semantic analysis do not change our definition of witness but add confirmation to it.

23. It is debatable whether ἀκοή in Romans 10:17 means the activity of "hearing," or the particular content of the "message" or "report."

Semantic analysis confirmed the dynamics of the temporal aspect in the concept of witness, and also confirmed the separation or transition between observing and testifying modes of witness. This dynamic seems to be especially connected with the activity of speaking when it is done based on hearing, seeing, or experiencing something.

We previously noticed that witnesses can also be defined based on the activities they perform, but the question remains as to when particular activities, such as "hearing," "knowing" or "speaking," can be categorized as belonging to the concept of witness. We also said that this question requires future study. However, our semantic analysis took one step in this direction and gave us some answers.

First, we saw that various verbs such as δοξάζω, λέγω, φημί, λαλέω, ἀπαγγέλλω, etc., can be used to describe the work of testifying witnesses. Second, we saw that "hearing" does not always refer to first-hand experience. Instead, "hearing" can mean receiving testimony from other eyewitnesses. In these instances, those who receive this testimony will have indirect or second-hand knowledge. These examples enable us to see the presence of the concept of witness even when it is not necessarily connected with eyewitnesses and eye witnessing. Third, sometimes "seeing" describes the seeing of future events, but such seeing requires faith on the part of listeners. We saw examples where Jesus warns his disciples about future events by telling them that when they "see" these things, they must act upon what they see in a certain way. Another example is how Abraham was able to see Jesus's day. Also, the verb θεωρέω "to observe", "to see" can be used to refer to seeing future events, and in one instance (Heb 7:4) seeing has to do more with having proper understanding than with simply observing something. We have a similar situation with "hearing," because people can hear about future events such as the coming of the antichrists (1 John 2:18) or the spirit of the Antichrist (1 John 4:3). When the concept of witness is focused on future events, the concept may be connected with prophecy, since speech about the future can sometimes be classified as testimony. So, we saw that in examples such as Acts 3:24; 4:2 prophets speak about future events, and they do so not as observing witnesses but on the basis of revelation/inspiration.

The importance of repetition for the concept of witness is also confirmed in this analysis. Basically, all three selected events (incarnation, miracles, Pentecost), in the context of biblical story, reflect the idea of repetition.

From Genesis 1–2 to Revelation 21–22 and at all points between, YHWH's intention is to dwell among the people on the Earth. So, Jesus's incarnation is a continuation of that intention. Furthermore, even though miracles are signposts of a greater reality, in the NT they mark not only Jesus's ministry but also the ministry of his disciples. As an expression of the kingdom of God, we can expect miracles to be repeated because of the unchanging reality of the kingdom of God that came with Jesus. Finally, the Holy Spirit was poured out on the day of Pentecost in Acts 2, yet a similar repetition of Spirit's coming occurs in Acts 10 and 19. Even though Spirit's coming is one-time event, filling with the Holy Spirit in the Bible is repeated event.

Semantic analysis also additionally confirms the overlap we saw between the concept of witness and the gospel. Since speaking about that historical event is a form of testimony, in our semantic analysis we came across different words that describes the activity of testifying about that event. So, in Acts 16:32 and Philippians 1:14 *λαλέω* "to speak" is connected with *τὸν λόγον τοῦ κυρίου* "the word of the Lord" and *λόγος* "the gospel", and *καταγγέλλω* "to proclaim" appears in the context of witness about the gospel (Acts 13:5; 15:36; 17:13; 1 Cor 2:1; 9:14). We also observed different ways in which verb *εὐαγγελίζω* "to tell the good news" was used for the proclamation of the gospel.

Finally, since the word *μάρτυς* with its cognates probably comes from the root *smer* which means: "to bear in mind," "to remember," "to be careful," semantic analysis also demonstrated the role of remembrance in the concept of witness. Subjects can remember something which they have previously seen, heard or experienced, but sometimes subjects are required to remember something that they received through some mediator (Scripture, other eyewitness). We concluded that in these instances, the act of remembrance depends on whether person accepts what is conveyed to her as trustworthy and true. Hence, remembrance can be but does not have to be a result of personal experience.

CHAPTER 11

Unique Aspects of the Concept of Witness in Luke/Acts

The aim of this research is to explore the Lukan concept of witness in its wider biblical context. Specifically, we are exploring the significance and impact of *πνεῦμα ἅγιος* on the concept of witness in Luke's theology. For this reason, at the outset of this study we analyzed Acts 1:8 and the usage of *πνεῦμα* and *δύναμις* in Luke/Acts. This introductory step led us to study further the concept of witness in the OT and NT. In that study we analyzed numerous texts, defined various aspects, and compared similarities and differences between the OT and the NT presentations of the concept of witness.

Based on the preceding research, we enter now into the debate about the Lukan concept of witness by summarizing the major views and issues connected with them. Then we will offer our interpretation of the significance of the *πνεῦμα ἅγιος* for the concept of witness in Luke's theology. We will do this by analyzing the development of the concept of witness in Acts, evaluating the role of miracles alongside verbal proclamation, discussing why Luke portrays the apostles as the predominant witnesses in Acts, and establishing the significance of the Old Testament for the Lukan concept of witness. That interpretation will then enable us to compare the concept of witness in the Lukan writings with the wider biblical context and see similarities and differences between the Lukan writings and the rest of Scripture. Consequently, in the next chapter we will outline constructive theological implications and applications of the Lukan concept of witness for the witnessing of the church today.

1. The debate about the Lukan concept of witness

In the introduction we discussed the importance of Lukan pneumatology for his concept of witness. We defined areas of agreement. More importantly, we defined the areas of disagreement, such as *what*, *why* and *when*. Regarding *what*, the issue is whether the Spirit in Acts is Joel's "Spirit of prophecy" alone, or is it a gift that comprises more than just prophecy? Regarding *why*, is the purpose of the baptism of the Spirit: a) exclusively for the mission, b) primarily as empowering for mission, but also to benefit the church, c) for all the benefits mentioned under b), with the Spirit also playing a soteriological and transforming role in the life of the individual believer and the church. Regarding *when* the baptism of the Spirit is received, four possible answers are given. People receive the baptism of the Spirit: a) as *donum superadditum*, an additional gift received after salvation (usually through laying on of hands; b) in water baptism; or c) in the process of repentance, faith and water baptism; d) the book of Acts does not give us consistent answer regarding that question.

We also noticed that even when scholars argue for a particular view, they do not necessarily claim that the Lukan concept of witness is applicable or mandatory in the same way for the church today. In other words, the debate is whether all church members participate in the same way in Jesus's paradigm of witnessing, or was this participation only for selected individuals in the early church? We concluded that the debate is complex, and our understanding of the concept of witness in Luke/Acts will depend on our view of Lukan pneumatology. Consequently, our understanding of how to apply Luke's writings to today's church will also be guided by these assumptions.

2. The importance of the πνεῦμα ἅγιος for the Lukan concept of witness

While we cannot here go into depth in this debate, the unique contribution of Luke to the biblical concept of witness may help clarify some aspects of it. Note the following. First, in all of the Bible only Luke stipulates that one must receive πνεῦμα and consequently the δύναμις that πνεῦμα brings in order to be a witness. Although John's gospel discusses the coming of the "Comforter," Penney[1] rightly notes that "[t]he Spirit in John is never a power which falls upon people, but the 'Comforter' who comes from the Father (John 14.16) and Son (15.26; 16.7). His witness is primarily internal, declaring the things of Christ to the believer (John 16.13–14)." The Spirit in John will testify, and so will disciples, but there is no direct assertion that the reception of the Spirit is *conditio sine qua non* for being a witness.

Second, in Luke 24:48 Jesus declares to the group of his disciples that they are already witnesses of the things mentioned in verses 45–47. Although, in Luke's gospel the disciples were involved in proclamation of the kingdom of God, in verse 48 Jesus addresses them as observing witnesses. As such they are qualified after his departure to become testifying witnesses. Against that context Jesus in Acts 1:8 charges them with the task of witnessing, but they will only be able to perform this task after they receive πνεῦμα and his δύναμις. Crucial question: why does Jesus make this a condition for being his witness?

When we analyzed the usage of πνεῦμα and δύναμις in the context of witnessing in Luke/Acts at the beginning of this study, we saw that Luke uses πνεῦμα and δύναμις together when he introduces major characters and their ministries into the story. Jesus's ministry is introduced twice in this way (Luke 4:14; Acts 10:38), and in both instances Jesus is presented in imagery corresponding to a "prophet mighty in word and deed" (Luke 24:19). When we observed how Luke uses πνεῦμα and δύναμις, we saw that δύναμις is mostly used in the context of miracles and the miraculous, and that the most prominent activities of the Spirit in Acts are coming, the filling with the Spirit, and speaking. Instead of going deeper into pneumatological debate, we can observe how Luke builds and develops the concept of witness in Acts. Our thesis concerning the Lukan concept of witness is that the significance of πνεῦμα ἅγιος and δύναμις in the ministry of Jesus's disciples lies in the claim that for Luke, witnessing about Christ includes repetition of Jesus's ministry. And the whole church participates in this repetition.[2] Let us consider preliminary argumentation for such claim, which we will support with additional arguments below.

1. Penney, *Lukan Pneumatology*, 120.

2. The idea of "whole church participates" can be understood differently. Especially, the issue of participation is debatable.

Just as Jesus's ministry was the result of anointing with πνεῦμα ἅγιος and δύναμις (Luke 4:14; Acts 10:38), so also the disciples' ministry will demonstrate the same pattern (Acts 1:8). On the basis of the above research, we agree with Menzies and Menzies and Haya-Prats that both πνεῦμα ἅγιος and δύναμις modify and define the concept of witness. While πνεῦμα ἅγιος is the source for δύναμις, in Luke's theology each defines a distinct aspect of witnessing: πνεῦμα ἅγιος inspires and produces the verbal aspect of testimony while δύναμις provides a miraculous aspect of witnessing. The two belong together and complement each other. In other words, for Luke, being a witness is not just a matter of words, but also of miraculous deeds. Consequently, we can talk about two types or forms of witnessing: one given verbally by πνεῦμα ἅγιος, and the other given by δύναμις through the signs and wonders. We will call this first type of witness *kerygmatic*, and the second *charismatic*.

Accordingly, apostolic testimony does not only provide verbal testimony about Jesus, his message and deeds, but faithfully reflects and continues or repeats Jesus's ministry in the same way. Being filled with πνεῦμα ἅγιος enables disciples to testify about historical events from Jesus's life. Hence, πνεῦμα ἅγιος inspires repetition of the verbal testimony about Jesus. But the presence of δύναμις enables disciples to testify through the repetition of Jesus's deeds, signs and wonders. By taking these two aspects of testimony together, we have reasonable grounds to claim the following: Luke's emphasis on the πνεῦμα ἅγιος as the source of kerygmatic testimony, and δύναμις as the source for charismatic testimony, as *conditio sine qua non* for being his witnesses in Acts 1:8 is not accidental. For Luke these two aspects of witness go together, because the verbal aspect confirms and complements the miraculous, and vice versa.[3]

In this way, the Jesus event is being repeated in disciples' present, as a transtemporal replica. While the Jesus event is impossible to repeat except in verbal form, the signs and wonders represent present reality and are manifested in front of people's eyes and ears. Accordingly, witnessing in Acts is almost always done based on what Jesus is doing in the present, whether through baptism in the Spirit, miracles, or exorcisms. Of course, Luke does

---

3. In the Acts we can encounter the pattern where verbal announcement of Jesus's message is confirmed by signs and wonders, and vice versa where some miracles open the door for verbal announcement.

not present his theology in a systematic way, and therefore it is possible to encounter certain deviations from the above-mentioned pattern. But generally speaking, Acts gives us sufficient ground for claiming that witnessing is not just an announcement of the message about the historical Jesus, but also witnessing about Jesus based on what he is doing in the present. If this claim is correct, then we can say that Jesus offers a pattern of testimony according to which it is not enough to say who Jesus is and what he has done in the past, without demonstrating what Jesus is doing "here and now."

So: our thesis is that Luke offers a unique model of witness in which the whole church may participate equally. We will offer additional proofs for this thesis in the following ways: a) by considering the development of the concept of witness in Acts, b) by considering the role of miracles in verbal proclamation of the gospel, c) by addressing the reason why Luke focuses mostly on the apostles as the ones involved in the task of witnessing, d) by considering the OT background for Acts 1:8 and the role of the Spirit in Acts.

2.1 The development of the concept of witness in Acts

Even if we start from the premise that Acts 1:8 provides us with the most narrow view of the concept of witness, according to which: a) only the apostles are charged with the task of witnessing, b) being an eyewitness is a requirement for being a witness, and, c) all those who receive πνεῦμα ἅγιος and δύναμις do not become witnesses as the apostles do, the Lukan portrayal of witness in Acts remains complex. The way Luke presents and develops this concept in Acts can be interpreted in different ways. Here we will address this challenge.

One can argue that the concept of witness in Acts develops in three complementary stages. First, a witness is someone who is able to testify based on his or her personal experience and direct knowledge (observing witnesses). In this sense, the apostles are qualified to be witnesses because they meet this qualification. But the apostles do not present mere facts. Along with facts, they also offer interpretations and provide explanations of the meaning of these events. Second, a witness becomes someone who, like Paul, can testify to some things from his own personal experience, but not only on that basis. Paul has seen the risen Christ, but he depends on others who were eyewitnesses of the events for other facts from and about Jesus's life. Accordingly, Paul is a type of witness who, like the witnesses in the first stage, provides interpretations and explanations of the meaning of these events. He does this not only based on factual evidence but also as an expression of personal conviction, since witnesses also testify to the truth in which they believe. Regarding Paul, Strathmann notes that he is not a factual witness in the same sense as the older apostles because he cannot guarantee the story of Christ from first-hand knowledge.[4] However, he is a witness to truth who seeks to propagate the Christian faith by confession.[5] Third, a witness is someone who believes in the testimony of the apostles, sealed in his heart by the Holy Spirit, and testifies to a truth in which he believes.[6] As an example of such a third stage, de Dietrich points to Stephen. Stephen does not belong in the same category with either the Twelve or Paul. Hence, he is a third stage witness. Strathmann considers Stephen as a confessional witness, but the difference between Paul and Stephen is that Paul partly shares same qualifications with the Twelve.[7] For Stephen, this is not the case. The conclusion de Dietrich offers regarding this stage is that

> the testimony of the Spirit . . . allows the second generation of Christians and all following generations to this day to be true witnesses of Christ the Lord in spite of not having met him in the flesh; our witness rests on that of the prophets and apostles (Eph 2:20), sealed in our hearts by the Holy Spirit.[8]

Four additional factors support these three stages developmental view of the concept of witness in Acts. First, in the Lukan writings we find three occasions where Luke's reference to witness cannot refer to first-hand experience. In Luke 11:48, the Pharisees who built tombs for the prophets killed

---

4. Strathmann, "Martus", *TDNT*, 4: 493–494.

5. Ohers argue similarly like Strathmann. Do (*Lucan Journey*, 159–160) argues that in the case of Paul μάρτυς (22:15; 26:16) carries different meaning, since he was not an eyewitness of Jesus's life as disciples were. Because of that, μάρτυς loses its fundamental significance as witnessing to observable fact(s) and becomes the description for someone who profess the faith in the Risen Lord, following a call to conversion to that Lord (cf. 160). Kyaligonza ("You Will be My Witnesses", 120) would say the same thing in a different way: "Paul is not a factual witness in the same sense as the Twelve, but a witness to truth, one seeking to propagate the Christian faith by confession" (p. 120). For him this is also an argument that "[f]or Luke the concept of witnesses includes witness to facts as well as witness in the sense of evangelistic confession."

6. de Dietrich, "You Are My Witnesses", 274.

7. Strathmann, "Martus", *TDNT*, 4: 493–494.

8. de Dietrich, "You Are My Witnesses", 278.

by their ancestors' become witnesses of these ancestral deeds. The testimony of prophets in Acts 10:43 is another example. Further, Paul in Acts 20:26 testified that he is not responsible for the fate of Ephesians to whom he has declared the whole counsel of God. According to Penney, in these references "witness" refers to a speech based on inner conviction or knowledge that certain things are true.[9]

Second, commenting Peter's speech in Acts 10, Soards argues that in Acts 10:42 the simple witness motif becomes kerygmatic proclamation.[10] He also adds that Peter, after declaring the facts from Jesus's life, turns to the prophets and Scripture "in order to comprehend and communicate the meaning of Jesus and particularly of God's work in relation to him."[11] Hence, even though apostolic testimony is crucial, it does not stand alone in a vacuum.

Third, according to Keener, most scholars recognize that the activity of the Spirit primarily emphasized in Acts is the empowering of witnesses for mission.[12] Thus, it is possible to claim that the commission given to the Twelve becomes paradigmatic for other, later witnesses. So, Keener argues that even though "[t]he particular language of 'witness' is more often restricted to the apostles . . . it is paradigmatic for the entire church's cross-cultural evangelistic mission."[13] Paul (Acts 22:15, 18; 23:11; 26:16, 22; cf. 20:26) and Stephen (Acts 22:20) are considered as witnesses; others would "see and hear" dramatic events about which they could bear witness (Acts 2:33; 8:6; and esp. 22:15; for the original disciples, see Luke 10:24; Acts 4:20; for others before the disciples, Luke 2:20; 7:22); the prophets testified about Christ's coming (Acts 10:43; cf. 1 Pet 1:11–12); and also God himself is included among witnesses (13:22; 14:3; 15:8). Additionally, Trites argues that apostolic witness is not limited to the Twelve because both Barnabas and

9. Penney, *Lukan Pneumatology*, 60. Penny's argumentation deserves additional explanation. It is true that in these three instances witnesses speak about something they themselves did not personally observe. Yet, in Luke 11:48 testimony is offered *post factum*, and in Acts 10:43 testimony of prophets is given *ante factum*. Acts 20:26 is an example of speech which contains the element of inner conviction, yet this conviction is given as a result of Paul's first-hand knowledge.

10. Soards, *Speeches in Acts*, 75.

11. Soards, 202.

12. Keener, *Acts Vol. 1*, 689.

13. Keener, *Acts Vol. 1*, 696.

Paul are called "apostles" (14:4, 14).[14] Furthermore, in Luke 1:2 apostles were called ὑπηρέται "servants," just as Paul in Acts 26:16 is called both ὑπηρέτης "servant" and μάρτυς "witness."[15] This speaks to the fact that others beside the apostles can share in apostolic commission.

Fourth, the development of the concept of witness in Acts also impacts the requirements for being a witness. Denaux[16] addresses the question of how Christians today can be witnesses in this original sense of the word, having neither seen nor followed Jesus Christ while he was living on Earth, and certainly having not witnessed his resurrection. Denaux says that, after the first generation of disciples and apostles, the witness of the church went on in a different way. The requirement of having known Jesus Christ in the flesh was gradually given up, and the vision of the risen Lord became the essential qualification. However, in time the term "witness" came to be used for those who responded in faith to the testimony of the apostles under the guidance of the Holy Spirit. So today, being a witness implies faithfulness to the testimony of the apostles, and our witness rests on that of the prophets and apostles, sealed in our hearts by the Holy Spirit.

Criticizing the view that the role of the church is to conserve and transmit this apostolic witness, F. Durrwell says that

> if that were really the case, the church would not be the witness of Christ. For bearing witness is not simply conserving and reporting what certain human beings claim to have seen in the distant past. A witness testifies to what he or she has seen and heard; witnessing depends on personal experience and involves us in a personal commitment.[17]

Adding to Durrwell's view, Kelly argues that the book of Acts contains two witness theories: one is a Petrine theory, according to which only eyewitnesses can be witnesses. The other is the Lukan view, by which the Holy Spirit is the "democratizing element in Luke's witness theology," because the title of μάρτυς must be applied also to those to whom the Spirit gives

14. Trites, "Two Witness Motifs", 18.

15. Trites, 19.

16. Denaux, "You are Witnesses", 76–77.

17. Durrwell, "Christian Witness", 125–126.

utterance to speak in the name of Jesus.[18] Therefore, Kelly viewed Agabus (Acts 21:11) as a witness, along with those who warned Paul "through the Spirit" not to go to Jerusalem (Acts 21:4).[19] Accordingly, we must recognize the element of personal experience and/or the Spirit's speaking through the people as valid requirements for calling someone witness, even though this practice may not fully align with the original meaning of the word.

Speaking about the impact of the portrait of the Holy Spirit in Acts on the reader, Hur claims that the impact on the implied reader is to become a witness to Jesus.

> Moreover, this implied reader may be encouraged to become a witness to Jesus, expecting to be inspired to preach in powerful words and/or to perform miraculous deeds, and to be met with acceptance and rejection. Implied readers are encouraged to believe that the Holy Spirit would empower and guide them to fulfil the will of God or the desire of Jesus, in spite of difficulties and hardships ultimately caused by Satan. In this way, the implied reader might identify either with the charismatic witnesses of Jesus or with the ordinary members of local communities, confessing Jesus as the Lord and God's Messiah.[20]

In discussing the scope of apostolic testimony and the example of Paul's testimony as a paradigm for Christians' testimony today, Jean-Noël Aletti observes that the testimony about Jesus's public life and ministry is not exclusive, because the apostles were not the only ones to follow their teacher.[21] Even those who did not belong to their group participated in certain events. What is exclusive is the testimony about the resurrection, because Jesus appeared only to a select group of people. Hence, for the resurrection, the reference to apostolic witness is therefore essential. But even this, Aletti claims, is not exclusive, because the Scriptures testify for that same thing. Hence, Aletti concludes:

---

18. Kelly, "Development of Witness", 148–149, 153.

19. Kelly, 149.

20. Hur, *Dynamic Reading*, 284–285.

21. Aletti, "Evangelizzare e/o testimoniare?"

> prima gli apostoli, e, solo dopo, le Scritture. Così va stabilita la necessaria complementarità dei due momenti; le Scritture non bastono: senza l'incontro personale con il Risorto, esse rimangono profezie non compiute; ma, senza le profezie, l'annuncio degli Apostoli potrebbe essere ricevuto come quello di uomini stregati, squilibrati o creduli.[22]

Speaking about Paul's testimony in Acts 22 and 26, Aletti says that Paul does not speak much about the risen Lord. Instead speaking about the life of Jesus, he emphasizes the transformation brought by this encounter. Hence, for him to witness means telling the story of his conversion, of love received and proclaimed. By telling this story, Paul reveals the forgiveness and love of his Lord. On that basis, Aletti concludes:

> Così il narratore degli Atti fa capire al suo lettore il tipo di testimonianza richiesto da lui, lettore, che, come Paolo, non ha conosciuto Gesù sulle strade di Galilea e Giudea. Certo, la nostra testimonianza non si sostituisce a quella degli apostoli, ma la loro, pur rimanendo un punto di riferimento necessario, può avere la sua forza dimostrativa e attiva solo se i credenti di tutti i tempi possono testimoniare del loro incontro personale con Cristo e di ciò che quell'incontro ha cambiato nella loro vita.[23]

In conclusion, we can say with Lora Angeline B. Embudo that for Luke, witness is both apostolic and evangelistic: "If apostolic witness is eyewitness testimony to the facts of Jesus, evangelistic witness is a combination of proclamation of apostolic message and personal testimony. All these are superintended by the Holy Spirit, who empowers the witnesses."[24] On that

22. "First the apostles, and only later, the Scriptures. Thus, the necessary complementarity of the two moments must be established; the Scriptures are not enough: without the personal encounter with the Risen One, they remain unfulfilled prophecies; but, without the prophecies, the announcement of the Apostles it could be received like that of bewitched, deranged or credulous men." Aletti, "Evangelizzare e/o testimoniare?"

23. "Thus, the narrator of Acts makes his reader understand the type of testimony required by him, the reader, who, like Paul, did not know Jesus on the roads of Galilee and Judea. Of course, our testimony does not replace that of the apostles, but theirs, while remaining a necessary point of reference, can have its demonstrative and active force only if the believers of all time can testify of their personal encounter with Christ and of what that meeting has changed in their lives." Aletti, "Evangelizzare e/o testimoniare?"

24. Embudo, "Lukan Paradigm of Witness", *AJPS 20 (2017a): 15.*

basis, we conclude that "witness to Christ involves the witness of the wider community, not just of some individuals."[25]

2.2 The role of miracles in verbal proclamation

We have already established that πνεῦμα ἅγιος provides *kerygmatic* and δύναμις *charismatic* witness. Consequently, witnessing in Acts is almost always done based on what Jesus is doing in the present, whether it is baptism in the Spirit, miracles, or exorcisms. Now we will observe concrete examples of this phenomenon.

(1) The Coming of the Holy Spirit on the day of Pentecost – Acts 2

Although the coming of the Spirit on Pentecost cannot be considered as miracle in a narrow sense of the word, it is significant that this event joins together in itself testimony about Jesus from the past with assertions about what Jesus is doing in the present. Quoting from the prophet Joel, Peter explains that the outpouring of the Spirit itself testifies about Jesus's life, death, resurrection, and resurrection (vv. 22–36). But within that historical testimony, Peter points out the present dimension of this testimony when he declares in Acts 2:33: "Being therefore exalted at the right hand of God and having received from the Father the promise of the Holy Spirit, he has poured out this that you both see and hear" (NRSV)." This "seeing and "hearing" refers to what Jesus has just done, so Peter joins together these two dimensions of testimony in that one message.

(2) Healing the Lame Beggar – Acts 3 and 4

The healing the Lame Beggar from Acts 3–4 is another example that clearly shows how the reception of δύναμις results in miracles, so as to supplement the verbal message about the historical Jesus with what Jesus is doing in the present. After the healing, Peter's words in Acts 3:16 are significant: "And by faith in his name, his name itself has made this man strong, whom you see and know; and the faith that is through Jesus has given him this perfect health in the presence of all of you" (NRSV). Likewise Acts 4:7–12, where Peter responds to the Sanhedrin's question, "By what power [δύναμις], or by what name did you do this?" (Acts 4:7, NRSV) Peter replies: "this man is

25. Embudo, 15.

standing before you in good health by the name of Jesus Christ of Nazareth, whom you crucified, whom God raised from the dead" (Acts 4:10, NRSV). From these quotes, note how Peter's testimony about Jesus's resurrection is based on the fact that Jesus is alive. And because he is alive, he is able to heal this man. If he remained dead, he would not be able to heal this man, as he would not have been able to pour out the Holy Spirit in Acts 2.

(3) Prayer for God's extended hand Acts 4:23–35

In this example we find filling with the Spirit (v. 31), which resulted in bold speaking, combined with the apostles giving testimony with δυνάμει μεγάλῃ "great power." If we accept the claim that δύναμις here stands for miracles, then δυνάμει μεγάλῃ does not modify their verbal message or the way in which they spoke about Christ (with courage, great effectiveness, etc). Given the context of their prayer for "signs and wonders" (v. 30), this is yet another example where miracles speak about the fact that Jesus is alive. If he was not alive, he would be able to do nothing.

(4) Miracles through apostles – Acts 5:12–29

Although here we do not find explicit examples of miracles based upon which the apostles then proclaim the gospel, two quotations taken together again show us witnessing which includes testimony about what Jesus is doing now and what he has done before. In Acts 5:12–16, we read about miracles that lead to the apostles ending up in prison. Then we see God charge them to go again into the Temple and speak "the whole message about this life" (Acts 5:20, NRSV). Thus, Luke here again connects testimony about what Jesus is doing after the cross with what he did before the cross. It is significant that in Acts 5:32 Peter and other apostles point back to the event of Pentecost as an act of Jesus performed after his resurrection and ascension.

(5) Stephen – Acts 6 and 7

Stephen is described as a man full of δύναμις, who thereby did great wonders and signs (Acts 6:8). He is also described as full of πνεῦμα ἅγιος. In Stephen's case, we see the blending of the two dimensions of testimony about Jesus: what he did in the past, and what he is doing in the present. Luke says that Stephen did many wonders and he spoke overwhelmingly (Acts 6:8–10). The telling of Stephen's ministry is only an introduction to his arrest, which gave him the opportunity to explain the entire history of Israel's backsliding and disobedience, culminating in rejection of the Messiah. The peak of Stephen's speech is his vision of Christ standing at the right hand of God (Acts 7:56). Taken all together, we see that Stephen's testimony about Jesus's resurrection is based on the fact that Jesus is alive, and that the living Christ is acting in the present.

(6) Philip in Samaria – Acts 8:4–8

The description of Philip's work in Samaria also provides us with the pattern according to which testimony about Jesus is based on what Jesus is doing through signs, wonders and exorcisms. These serve as a confirmation that Jesus, who was rejected and killed, is alive and exalted. Interestingly, people accepted what Philip spoke based on *hearing* and *seeing* the signs that he did. This is another example where *speech* about Jesus encompasses *listening* (ears) to the message and *observing* (eyes) signs, and this faithfully reflects the pattern of Jesus's ministry. Luke in Acts 1:1–2 states that he is writing "about all that Jesus did and taught from the beginning until the day when he was taken up to heaven" (NRSV). Philip, like Jesus, does not separate message from the demonstration, because teaching about Jesus is incomplete without demonstration of what Jesus is doing.

(7) The Healing of Aeneas – Acts 9:32–35

This short record contains one important statement. While healing Aeneas, Peter declares "Jesus Christ heals you" (Acts 9:34, NRSV). By this, Peter testifies that Jesus is alive, for if he were not, he would not be able to heal this man. The result of this miracle was that "all the residents of Lydda and Sharon saw him and turned to the Lord" (Acts 9:35, NRSV).

(8) The church in Antioch – Acts 11:19–21

This brief record of disciples' activity in Antioch contains two important paragraphs. First, we see that the content of the gospel is the proclamation of Jesus as Lord. This is important because the proclamation of the gospel is the message about how Jesus of Nazareth was demonstrated to be κύριος "Lord." This means that the content of their message was Jesus's entire life and ministry. Second, the expression "the hand of the Lord" reminds us of Acts 4:30, where "the hand of the Lord" is likely synonymous with signs and wonders. If that conclusion is correct, we have here another example of the message about Jesus being accompanied by miracles that Jesus did at that point and time.

(9) Proconsul Sergius Paulus – Acts 13:4–12

In this example, the proconsul Sergius Paulus wanted to hear the word of God from Barnabas and Paul, but the magician Elymas opposed them and tried to turn the proconsul away from the faith. As a result, God through Paul blinded Elymas (blindness was the result of God's "hand"; cf. Acts 4.30; 11:21), and the outcome was that the proconsul "believed" (Acts 13:12). Two things are important here: first, Sergius Paulus heard the message, but he also saw God's hand in action. Second, the miracle that occurred resulted in proconsul being "astonished" not by the miracle itself but by their διδαχή "teaching." From this we deduce that miracles are not obstacles to the proclamation of the word. Consequently, the emphasis in proclamation of the gospel should not be on any miraculous aspects but on the doctrine.

(10) Preaching in Iconium – Acts 14:1–3

Here we have an explicit example of God testifying for "the word of his grace" by "signs and wonders," done "through the hands"[26] of Paul and Barnabas. Again, the testimony about the historical Jesus is accompanied by what the risen Lord is doing "here and now." Based on this example, we can also conclude that for Luke, verbal testimony about Christ without the charismatic aspect of testimony is incomplete.

(11) Healing of the paralyzed man in Lystra – Acts 14:8–21

The event in Lystra is a bit odd, because Luke does not explicitly say that Paul proclaimed the gospel before the miracle (cf. v. 9). After Paul healed the paralytic there, people declared that he and Barnabas were Hermes and Zeus. Therefore, Paul sought to show that they were not gods, and he delivered a short speech about monotheism. Luke does not explicitly connect the miracle with Paul's message, yet we find out from Acts 14:21 that they proclaimed the gospel in that city. Even though Luke does not explicitly

26. Again, we have the connection between hands and miracles, although this time, hand is not God's but human.

connect the miracle with the message, both aspects of testimony are still clearly present in this case as well.

(12) The church in Ephesus – Acts 19:8–20

The last example from Acts is Luke's description of Paul's activity in Ephesus. We see that Paul debated and tried to persuade people regarding the kingdom of God (Acts 19:8), but also that God through his hands did extraordinary miracles (cf. Acts 14:1–3). The result was that people converted to faith in Christ, and Luke in his conclusion says that all these factors led to the spread of the word and its growing influence (cf. Acts 19:20).

2.3 Lukan portrays of apostles as predominant witnesses in the Acts

Some claim that Luke does not represent "average" believers as witnesses, saving that description solely or mainly for the apostles. Contra this position, we noted above how Luke develops the concept of witness in Acts through three stages. We can here offer additional information to refute this claim. In the prologue of his first volume (the Gospel of Luke), Luke states the purpose of his two-volume work: so that Theophilus (and presumably others through him) "may know the certainty of the things you have been taught" (Luke 1:4, NRSV). Wrapped in that purpose statement is the reason why Luke writes that the Spirit is for all believers while also focusing his presentation mainly on the apostles as the ones anointed by the Spirit and the power to testify about Christ. O'Reilly outlines Luke's strategy to show the spreading of the Word.[27] When Luke shows the message of Christ spreading from Jerusalem, across Judea, then Samaria and further, in every new phase or geographical area, Luke focuses on one representative and portrays this representative as a prophet, anointed with the Spirit and performing miracles. In the first phase (Jerusalem), the apostles as a collective hold that prophetic ministry. Later, Stephen is presented as that representative to the Hellenists, and his death prompts the expansion of Christianity beyond Judaism. Later, Philip in Judea and Samaria, and finally Paul and his companions serve as representatives of the spreading of the Word to the ends of the earth. Accordingly, O'Reilly concludes:

27. O'Reilly, Leo. *Word and Sign in Acts*, 210–211.

> At the beginning of each of these missions Luke takes care to show that the prophetic missionary was, like Jesus, authenticated by signs and wonders which God caused to take place at his hands. Thus, the word of the missionary is attested from the start as the word of God. . . . Every geographical region has experienced the powerful saving message of the gospel both in word and deed in the prophetic ministries of the missionaries. Luke's own generation, his own readers, can be assured that everything that Jesus began to do and teach is still being done and taught (Acts 1:1).[28]

If O'Reilly is correct, then believers who received the Pentecostal gift of the Spirit, then and today, have their share in the proclamation of the gospel in the power of the Spirit. Luke's *silence* about whether average believers have a share in such prophetic ministry is motivated by his purpose for these two documents, since in them he portrays the apostles as guarantors of the accuracy of the message. The fact that all believers may receive this gift provides the basis for claiming that all believers can also proclaim the gospel by emulating or following Jesus's model of ministry (cf. Acts 10:38).

2.4 The significance of the Old Testament for Lukan concept of witness

Finally, as we look at the role of the Spirit in Acts, particularly in the light of Acts 1:8, we also must recognize that the OT plays a significant role in Luke's theology of witness. Our interest here is not to show all possible backgrounds and influences on the Lukan concept of witness. Rather, by remaining in the biblical context, we can trace certain OT characteristics of the concept of witness and point to particular OT passages that were important for Luke's development of the concept of witness.

First, as we studied the concept of witness in the OT, we noticed that the concept of witness is dynamic, and that a witness in the most basic sense is someone who testifies based on eyewitness's experience. However, in the temporal aspect, witness is not only restricted to testimony about the past or present. For that matter, we cannot say that those who are *not* eyewitnesses

28. O'Reilly, Leo. *Word and Sign in Acts*, 210–211.

are not witnesses in the true sense of this word. Further, the dynamic of the concept revealed that eyewitness testimony has the power to create other witnesses. We saw this dynamic in Deuteronomy, when Moses addressed the new generation of Israelites as though they themselves had "seen" and "heard" all the things that Moses was speaking about. Also, the dynamic was present in the fact that the attribute of testimony can be imparted or transferred from one impersonal entity to another. We cannot claim a direct link between these characteristics and the Lukan concept of witness, but we have seen that Luke develops his concept of witness in stages where he portrays as witnesses even those second-generation Christians who were not eyewitnesses of Christ.

Second, the OT considers Israel as a collective as YHWH's witness. Israel as a nation witnessed YHWH's revelation at Sinai and beyond, and because of that event, all Israelites share in that vocation. Accordingly, membership in the community that shares a common history and tradition qualifies members as witness. This is particularly noticeable in the book of Isaiah, which Luke uses to inform his concept of witness. Kuecker[29] asserts that, beginning with his use of Isaiah 49:6 in Acts 1:8, Luke utilizes Isaiah 40–55 for much of his imagery of witness. Accordingly, Isaiah 40–55 establishes theocentric identity marked by both Spirit and witness. Since in Isaiah 44:1–8 LXX, God promises to place his Spirit upon the seed and children of Jacob and Israel (44:3), causing them to spring up (44:4) and identify themselves as "'I am the Lord's' . . . and a different one will write 'I am the Lord's because of the name of Israel'" (Isaiah 44:5) "those who proclaim their God-centred identity are witnesses (μάρτυρες; Isaiah 44:8) of God's sovereignty." A similar link appears in Isaiah 43:4–13 LXX where "everyone who is called by my name" (v. 7) is described with "You are my witnesses." Penney[30] adds that, although Luke primarily uses the concept of witness in the sense of eyewitnesses, "the theological background for Luke's use is that of the Isaianic servant–true Israel–and participation in true Israel through the gospel thereby makes every Christian a witness." Alan J. Thompson[31] explains that Acts 1:8 contains three phrases that come from Isaiah: a) "When the Holy Spirit comes on

29. Kuecker, *Reconciliation in Luke-Acts*, 106–107.

30. Penney, *Lukan Pneumatology*, 59–60.

31. Thompson, *Acts of the Risen Jesus*, 106–107.

you" reflects Isaiah 32:15, and refers to the end of the desolation of Judah and the coming of the new age with the pouring out of the Holy Spirit (cf. also Isa 44:3–5), b) "You will be my witnesses" reflects the wording of Isaiah 43:12 where the people of God will be transformed and become witnesses to the salvation of God when the new age arrives (cf. also Isa 44:8), c) "To the ends of the earth" reflects the wording of Isaiah 49:6 where this figure of a Servant will restore Israel (49:5–6) and include Gentiles in this restoration. With the description in 1:8, Jesus affirms to his disciples that God's promises of restoration are about to be fulfilled. On this basis, we conclude with Keener[32] that Isaiah's speech about Israel or its remnant as being "witnesses" for YHWH (Isa 43:10; 44:8) applies here to witnesses for Jesus.

Third, the overlap between the concept of witness and prophecy is also significant for Luke for several reasons. We have seen that the position of a prophet is similar to that of a witness: both serve as mediators between different parties. Also, prophets can be witnesses pointing back to YHWH's revelation, declaring future events, and inviting people to repentance and obedience. Further, in the Lukan writings the image of Jesus as a prophet is strongly emphasized. Jesus refers to himself as a prophet (Luke 4:24), and this self-description comes immediately after Luke, using Isaiah 61:1–2, introduces Jesus as someone anointed by the Spirit to proclaim (verbal activity) and set people free (concretization of proclaimed realities). Other people recognized Jesus as a prophet due to the miracle of revivification (Luke 7:16). His disciples proclaimed him to be the prophet like Moses (Acts 3:22; 7:37), and it is interesting that both references to Jesus as the prophet like Moses are found in the context of miracles (Acts 3:1–16; 7:36). The connection between Jesus's prophetic role and the Spirit is also present in the scene of Jesus's ascension in Luke 24:49–51 and Acts 1:8–9 where, after Jesus announces the coming of the Spirit, he ascends to heaven. This scene reflects the story of Elijah and Elisha, where Elisha receives Elijah's spirit after Elijah's ascension to heaven. And just as Elisha continued in the footsteps of the Elijah after Elijah's ascension, so Jesus's disciples continued Jesus's ministry.[33] Accordingly, all these examples support seeing the early

32. Keener, "Power of Pentecost", 51.

33. "Nel contesto della successione profetica abbiamo potuto osservare il ruolo svolto dalla testimonianza oculare (»vedere«), ovvero dalla presenza di Eliseo nel momento del

church as the extension of Jesus's prophetic work, an additional element shaping the Lukan concept of witness.

Fourth, Acts 2 uses Joel 2 to show that the presence of signs and wonders in the life of the church testifies about the coming of the last days. The use of Joel 2 continues the demonstration of the importance of the Spirit for Luke's theology of witness. Luke shows this by altering Joel's text in Acts 2:19. To that point Menzies and Menzies say:

> In this passage Luke adds three words that are not in the LXX text of Joel: *anō* (above), *sēmeia* (signs) and *katō* (below). Joel's text is thus transformed so as to read: "I will show wonders in the heaven *above*, and *signs* on the earth *below*." The significance of these insertions, which form a collection of "wonders" and "signs," becomes apparent when one looks at the larger context of Luke–Acts. The Acts verse immediately following the Joel citation reads: "Jesus . . . was a man accredited by God to you by miracles, wonders and signs" (2:22). Then, throughout Acts we repeatedly read of the followers of Jesus working "wonders and signs."[34] Thus, through his alteration of Joel 2 in Acts 2:19, Luke links the miraculous events associated with Jesus (Acts 2:22) and his disciples (e.g. 2:43) together with the cosmic portents listed by Joel (see 2:19b-20) as "signs and wonders" that mark the end of the age. In other words, the miracles of Jesus and his disciples are precursors of those cosmic signs

passaggio di Elia alla vita di Dio che corrisponde alla sua morte e alla conclusione della sua esperienza terrena. L'analisi di alcuni passi neotestamentari in cui viene menzionato il profeta Elia ed il momento dell'ascensione di Gesù al cielo, al termine della sua vita terrena, possono essere accostati al passo considerato consentendoci di riconoscere come la testimonianza nell'AT e nel NT unisca fortemente il testimone alla realtà testimoniata e ne trasforma l'identità posta al servizio di Dio e della sua volontà di salvezza che continua a rivelarsi nei suoi testimoni" (Palmisano, "La testimonianza", 91). ("In the context of prophetic succession we have observed the role played by the eyewitness ('seeing'), that is, the presence of Elisha at the moment of Elijah's transition to the life of God, corresponding to his death and the conclusion of his earthly experience. The analysis of some New Testament passages mentioning the prophet Elijah and the moment of Jesus' ascension to heaven at the end of his earthly life can be compared to the passage discussed, allowing us to recognize how the witnessing in the Old and the New Testament strongly connects the witness to the testified reality and transforms his identity in the service to God and his salvific will, which continues to reveal itself through his witnesses" (Palmisano, "La testimonianza," 91).)

34. Acts 2:19, 22, 43; 4:30; 5:12; 6:8; 7:36; 14:3; 15:12.

> that signal the Day of the Lord. . . . Undoubtedly, Luke is conscious of the significant role that miracles have played in the growth of the early church and anticipates that these "signs and wonders" will continue to characterize the ministry of the church in these "last days."[35]

Apparently, Luke views the pouring of the Spirit as the beginning of the "last days" which are characterized, among other things, by *προφητεύω* "prophecy" (Acts 2:17, 18), and *τέρατα* "wonders" and *σημεῖα* "signs." The Lukan concept of witness in the "last days," which still continue today, shares the same characteristics.

3. The Lukan concept of witness within the biblical context

Our analysis of the concept of witness in the OT resulted in a synthesis that gave us a clear picture of the various aspects and characteristics of that concept. We provided a similar analysis for the NT with similar results, and also compared the ways in which the concept of witness in the NT is both similar to and a development of the concept in the OT. Then we analyzed the concept of witness in the Lukan writings, arguing that Luke brings unique elements to the concept of witness in the biblical context. Now we will compare Luke's concept of witness with the concept in the rest of the Bible.

When we combine the results of our study of the concept of witness in the Bible with the concept of witness in Lukan writings, the following picture emerges. On one hand, Luke's concept of witness follows the general pattern established in the rest of the Bible. First, in Luke/Acts we encounter two major types of witnesses, observing and testifying, and we can also categorize witnesses according to their mode of witnessing and temporal aspect.

Second, the verbal aspect of testimony is the most prominent form of witness, but verbal testimony is often accompanied with signs and wonders or various other manifestations.

Third, the overlap between the concepts of concepts of witness and prophecy is significant in Luke/Acts, and the Spirit plays a major role in both

35. Menzies and Menezis, *Spirit and Power*, 147.

witness and prophecy. All these characteristics reflect, to the various degrees, the concept of witness in the Bible.

Fourth, the idea of "repetition" permeates Lukan concept of witness, and the concept of witness is also highly valued because witnesses often have unique status or access to particular events or persons. Because of that access, their testimony shapes and constitutes reality. Furthermore, witnesses not only speak about facts, but explain significance and meaning and provide interpretation of the things they testify to. For that matter witnesses, in Luke/Acts often attempt to establish some religious truth. For this reason, a witness's personal character is crucial, due to the witness's power to create reality and/or public truth through his testimony.

Fifth, repetition also has the power to transform those who were not eyewitnesses so that they become witnesses. Just as Moses' retelling the story of the exodus to those who were not there when those events happened *creates* the witnessing community anew, so it is with Luke.

Sixth, as we studied the development of the concept of witness in Acts, we identified three stages of its development. A witness may be a person: a) who is an eyewitness and provides meaning and explanation, b) who is partially an eyewitness and partially depends on the testimony of others, and then testifies and provides meaning and explanation, c) who received testimony from trusted sources, and testifies to others on the basis of his convictions without being an actual eyewitness, and then provides meaning and explanation.[36] In this way, Luke enables Christians throughout history to be counted as "witnesses," even though they do not share the same qualifications as those who testified based on their eyewitness experience. Hence, Luke's

36. As we talk about being a *witness to conviction* or witness without being an eyewitness, we have to take into consideration the timeframe of witnessing activity. In some cases, witnesses testify about events *ante factum*. Speeches about future events or what might happen in the future fall into this category. In some cases, witnesses may speak about events *post factum* without themselves being eyewitnesses. Hence, their conviction is crucial. Special subcategory of *post-factum* witnesses may be all those testimonies that speak about facts of Christ's pre-existence. Such claims are not based on eyewitness observance (no one had seen Christ in his pre-existence glory), but ultimately springs from one's conviction. For our research *post factum* witness to conviction is of our interest due to importance of Acts 1:8 for Lukan concept of witness.

"all-inclusive" approach enables those who followed apostolic teaching to perform the role of witnesses.[37]

On the other hand, when we compared the concept of witness in Luke/Acts with the rest of the Bible, we argued the following. First, Acts 1:8 is the key Lukan text for understanding the concept of witness in Acts. In that verse we find Luke's unique condition for being a witness, receiving the Holy Spirit and power. Although the Holy Spirit has a minor role in witnessing in the OT, and a greater role in the NT, nowhere else in the Bible is the Spirit's role as central as in Acts. The closest parallel is in the Johannine writings, notably John 15:26, but (unlike in Acts) John never says that the disciples must receive the Spirit in order to be witnesses.

Second, although the fundamental idea of witness is "repetition," for Luke the unique element is not the act of repetition but the content of repetition. Just as with Jesus, witnessing for the disciples is both a matter of manifestation of *πνεῦμα ἅγιος* through speech, and *δύναμις* through miracles. In this way, the disciples in Acts repeat and continue Jesus's ministry. In the context of Luke/Acts, the witness mandate in Luke 24 and Acts 1 includes not only verbal repetition of the message about Jesus (which is in keeping with the Greek idea of *μάρτυς* as someone who "bears in mind" or "remembers" something) but also his charismatic ministry. In that way, Luke truly reflects both sides of the spectrum, since the Greek idea of witness puts more emphasis on mental activity while the Hebrew idea puts more emphasis on concrete, practical repetition or representation. So, here lies the importance of *πνεῦμα ἅγιος* and *δύναμις* for the Lukan concept of witness, and for that matter his uniqueness in the biblical context.

Finally, we must note that in comparison with the NT, and for that matter the whole Bible, the concept of witness probably takes its most prominent place in the Lukan writings. Luke uses *μάρτυς* more than any other NT writer (thirteen times). Granted, John uses *μαρτυρέω* and *μαρτυρία* more than any

37. Witness to conviction is not a unique element of the Lukan concept of witness, because this element is also significantly present in Johannine writings. When John labels people as *μάρτυς*, those people by default die because of their witness or their faith (Rev 2:13; 11:3; 17:6; cf. Acts 22:20). But with *μαρτυρέω* the situation is somewhat different. *Μαρτυρέω* describes those who confess evangelistically who Jesus was and what He signified but with the difference "that with the verb there is no discernible movement towards reserving the term for those witnesses who have suffered martyrdom as such" (Strathmann, "Martus", *TDNT*, 4:499).

other NT writer,[38] but Luke is emphasizing the witness as a person, while John is more interested in the activity of witnessing and its product, testimony. Furthermore, Luke begins and ends both of his documents with the concept of witness. At the beginning of his gospel, Luke presents his clear intention to write to Theophilus a document with a purpose ἵνα ἐπιγνῷς περὶ ὧν κατηχήθης λόγων τὴν ἀσφάλειαν "so that you may know the certainty of the things you have been taught" (Luke 1:4 NIV). To do that, Luke uses several written accounts (διήγησις, Luke 1:1), and the testimony of those who αὐτόπται καὶ ὑπηρέται γενόμενοι τοῦ λόγου "were eyewitnesses and servants of the word" (Luke 1:2, NRSV). In essence, what Luke does is give a testimony. As a second-generation Christian, he acts as a witness and testifies to Theophilus about the events concerning Christ. The gospel ends with a group of people identified by Jesus as "witnesses" (Luke 24:48). The book of Acts begins with that same group of people, once again identified by Jesus as "witnesses" (Acts 1:8) and ends with Paul in Rome doing that same thing, διαμαρτύρομαι about the kingdom of God and Jesus (Acts 28:23) (cf. Acts 28:31 κηρύσσω "proclaim" and διδάσκω "teach"). This *inclusio* confirms the importance of the concept of witness in Lukan writings.[39]

38. On the other hand, Luke uses the verb διαμαρτύρομαι more than other NT writers, and John does not use it at all. Luke also uses the noun μαρτύριον five times while John uses it only once.

39. Granted, John in his writings builds his *inclusio* also has *inclusio* of the concept of witness. In his Gospel, John begins (1:7–8) and ends (21:24) with the concept of witness. Likewise, 1 John begins (1:2) and ends (5:11–12) with it, and the book of Revelation also begins (1:2) and ends (22:16) with it. Nevertheless, it seems that Luke puts more emphasis than John on the *continuation* of the concept of witness and the inclusion of others in it, while John is more concerned with establishing the authority of existing witnesses and their testimonies.

CHAPTER 12

The Lukan Concept of Witness: Application

We began this research by asking why Jesus makes reception of πνεῦμα ἅγιος a necessary condition for his disciples to be his witnesses in Acts 1:8, and how πνεῦμα ἅγιος impacts their witness. Our study showed that the why refers to the repetition and continuation of Jesus's ministry, and the how refers to πνεῦμα ἅγιος providing *kerygmatic* and δύναμις *charismatic* types of witness. In other words, those who are witnesses continue Jesus's ministry by proclaiming specific content (the kingdom of God, the gospel message about Jesus, etc.) and performing various miracles, signs and wonders as part of their testimony. We also concluded that Luke is more interested than other biblical writers in witnesses as "persons," and thus the development of the concept of witness in Acts demonstrates that even those who were not eyewitnesses of Jesus's ministry are nonetheless considered witnesses in the full sense of the word. Hence, Jesus's condition from Acts 1:8 applies to them as well. Consequently, it applies to us today, and as such, it should inform the way church does its ministry.

According to Johnson the book of Acts provides a prophetic vision for the church today.[1] On that basis, he offers two claims. First, "as part of canonical Scripture, the voice and vision of Luke-Acts has a prophetic function for the church in every age. It does not simply report past events; it imagines a world that challenges the one that humans in every age construct on their own terms." Second, "if we in the church today choose to heed Luke's challenge,

1. Johnson, *Challenge of Luke–Acts,* VII.

we shall need to think of the church in more explicitly prophetic terms and find ways of embodying and enacting God's vision for humans." If Johnson's claims are correct, then our job is not so much to ask, "was the early church as Luke describes it?" but rather "how does Luke's portrayal of the early church challenge the church in every age?"[2] This naturally led Johnson to claim that the church must examine itself to guard against the tendency to dismiss the radical characterization of Jesus.[3] The church can be tempted to admire Jesus and neglect to emulate his radical manner of life. But if the church in Acts emulated and embodied Jesus's manner of life, then "[t]here is no real reason why the prophetic spirit that expressed itself in radical terms among the apostles might not also find such embodiment today."[4] On the basis of this outlook, we can draw several applications for the church today.

The first application is that, in keeping with the final quote from Johnson above, note that Jesus's charge in Acts 1:8 provides a specific model of witnessing. In other words, the disciples provided witness to Jews and Gentiles through miracles, not only through speech. Witnessing was both a manifestation of *πνεῦμα ἅγιος* through speech and of *δύναμις* through miracles. If we assume that Luke's model of witnessing is still valid for today, we can learn several lessons from him in regard to witnessing. The first lesson is that, for Luke, miracles are joined with the proclamation of the Word of God, and do not stand on their own. The apostles, like Jesus, preached, and God confirmed the message with miracles. The two go together. Care must be taken to avoid two extremes:

1. Miracles can become disassociated from kerygma and draw attention to themselves. This is counterproductive because people become attracted to miracles without any desire to hear and apply God's word to their lives. This situation, in our estimation, creates superficial believers.
2. A kind of Christianity can develop where it is normal to proclaim the gospel without any accompanying signs and wonders.
   This is also counterproductive because it potentially creates a

2. Johnson, 6.
3. Johnson, 108.
4. Johnson, 109.

Christianity that relies on human wisdom and strength, not God's (cf. 1 Cor 2:4–5).

The second lesson is that, while moral values are paramount in shaping Christian identity, πνεῦμα ἅγιος and δύναμις in Lukan writings are not disconnected from witnessing and reduced to the moral transformation of believers alone. In the case of such detachment, Christianity develops where the only manifestation of God's power that people expect and seek is in moral transformation. Moral transformation is to be expected but reducing δύναμις to that activity alone is against the testimony of Scripture. We see this notion in Ambrosiaster's commentary on 1 Corinthians 12:31, for example, where he claims that people in his time came to faith by noticing the good deeds of Christians and not through miracles.[5] His point was that the miracles were no longer necessary. Given that moral transformation is necessary, is it not better to expect both rather than to take an either/or approach?

The third lesson begins with the fact that some authors assert that the Christian church has historically been focused more on God's power in moral transformation than on miracles. However, in the West over the past 20 years or so, there has been a shift of focus from Paul to the Gospels among some branches of Protestantism,[6] so that Jesus's kingdom ministry (e.g. Matt 4:23; 10:7–8) becomes the model for church life and ministry. In the academic circles, this shift is seen with the so-called "New Perspective on Paul," most prominently represented by N. T. Wright. This shift is welcome because Jesus's model of ministry is presented not only in the NT but also can be traced in patristic texts as well. Hence, instead of choosing either the proclamation of the Word or miracles, the church is significantly better off when she keeps and nurtures both aspects of witnessing.

The second application is that the community as a whole plays an important part in the task of witness. We have already noticed in Acts what we called the "democratization" of the concept of witness. We can take that idea one step further and say that the very existence of the community of faith and mutual relationships between believers is a form of witness. According to Embudo, "the Christian community is a form of witness."[7] She bases this

5. Ambrosiaster, *Romans and 1–2 Corinthians*, 182.
6. More specifically, in "evangelical Christianity."
7. Embudo, "Lukan Paradigm of Witness Part I", 12.

claim on the fact that the wider community of believers in Acts was included in the task of witnessing. This new community had *κοινωνία* not only in their adherence to the apostolic teachings, but also in their practice of sharing goods.[8] Guder makes the same point from a different perspective:

> Our Lord intended, in preparing his disciples for their ministry, that they proclaim the message so that people might hear, and that they incarnate the reality and meaning of that message in their lives individually and corporately, so that their message will be visible and audible. Just as Jesus both said and did the Good News, his followers, as witnesses, are to be messengers whose message cannot be separated from their persons and their lives. Jesus did not equip the disciples and the church that was to form out of them, merely to be good communicators. Rather, he equipped them to be credible witnesses, people whose whole lives make their communication authentic and powerful. Whenever the Christian church has failed to grasp this incarnational necessity, that the message and the messengers cannot be divided in our understanding nor in our practice, a diluted gospel has resulted.[9]

Both Embudo and Guder are making the same point. Being a witness is not just a matter of performing some rhetorical activity or verbal task. Witnessing includes not only a verbal aspect but also an incarnational aspect: one has to be a witness and live the witness, and not merely talk witness. Hence, we should hear Johnson's words carefully:

> The church's reflection on what it can learn about witness from Luke–Acts should not begin by repudiating these understandings and practices, but by deepening and broadening them. It can broaden them by thinking about witness not simply in terms of individual speech – preaching, storytelling, apology – but also in terms of communal activity, how the church as church bears witness to the world. It can deepen its understanding by

8. Embudo, 12; Embudo, "Lukan Paradigm of Witness Part II", 22

9. Guder, *Be My Witnesses*, 27.

> thinking about witness first of all as embodiment and enactment of God's vision and secondarily as speaking about that vision.[10]

We can conclude that, just as we can say that in Isaiah 40–48 Israel is collectively addressed as "witness," the same singularity-plurality applies to the church in Luke/Acts. The very existence of the church is a form of witness, and the way the Christian church "walks" is just as important as the way it "talks." The incarnational aspect of witnessing cannot be neglected.

The third application concerns the inclusion of believers in the task of witnessing. We have seen that those who received πνεῦμα ἅγιος and δύναμις experienced various manifestations: some spoke in different tongues, some prophesied, some were involved in bold proclamation and performance of miracles, some manifested characteristics of wisdom and faith, etc. All these manifestations speak about the experiential side of the Christian faith. One cannot receive πνεῦμα ἅγιος and δύναμις and remain the same, bearing no fruit. This fruit should be manifested both internally and externally; that is why Jesus said to his disciples "you will be my witnesses." Jesus here speaks not just about doing something, but about being someone. "To be," comes before "to do." Witnessing is not just some activity that one does, witnessing is a result of one's identity. That is why Luke puts so much emphasis on witnesses as persons, and not on witnessing activities. Furthermore, if the whole community of believers shares in the vocation of witness, then even laity can participate in that ministry. Again, in churches where there is a division between clergy and laity, this is difficult to implement in comparison to those churches that put more emphasis on the "priesthood of all believers." Nevertheless, there should be a place for lay believers, those who do not have any official ecclesiastical position, to participate in some way or other with their gifts, talents and abilities, in the life and work of the church. Therefore, the responsibility of church ministers is to teach these truths, and train and guide the people toward these realities.

When we say that the ministers of the church are responsible "to teach these truths, and train and guide the people toward these realities," we are aware that different churches have different traditions and theological understandings of the work of the Holy Spirit. Accordingly, not all churches

10. Johnson, *Challenge of Luke–Acts*, 182.

or even theologians will understand Lukan pneumatology the same way, nor will all agree that the Lukan concept of witness is applicable or mandatory in the same way for the Christians today. Motivated by this lack of unanimity, we could enter into this complex debate trying to argue for a specific ecclesiastical position/tradition, but we will not do that here. Regardless of what our position regarding the reception of the Holy Spirit and its purpose is, we cannot deny the impact that πνεῦμα ἅγιος and δύναμις have on the concept of witness. Consequently, we call each church tradition to consider Luke's record and the theological, didactic, and practical applications of his concept of witness.

The fourth and final application concerns the ministry of the church toward outsiders or toward the world. This research showed that the witness is often in the position of a mediator, and as such speaks with the authority and determination. The witness does not merely suggest; he proclaims, argues, teaches, persuades, etc. The witness does not offer yet another version of reality or truth to the marketplace of ideas, he offers the truth and the version of reality. He possesses conviction (witness to conviction). His goal is to persuade others to buy into this truth so that those "others" can become part of the same community and share in the same vocation of witness. In terms of Christian faith, Christian testimony is based on historical realities, tradition, personal conviction and personal experience.

All that is to say is that the Christian faith was, is, and should remain a public truth which relates to all people and has importance for individuals and society in general.[11] But, as Johnson reminds us, being a witness is problematic and challenging.[12] Specifically, there is no "objective truth" about God, so subjectivity is at the very heart of religious confession. The flip side of this is the reality that no individual's truth is (or can be) everyone's version of the truth; we mean by this that witnesses speak from a distinctive and irreducible perspective. Johnson argues:

> Because witness is not simply opinion but involves serious personal commitment, furthermore, the clash of witness can easily escalate to other forms of conflict – the very sort of "acting out" that the strict rules of courtrooms seek to preclude. But

11. Budiselić, "Christian Witness for 21st Century," 411.

12. Johnson, *Challenge of Luke–Acts*, 167.

in the public forum, a contrary witness is not simply "another opinion," it is a personal challenge.[13]

On that basis we can say that Christianity has a message which is valid and binding for all people in all times in all places, but this claim does not mean that Christians have a right to impose their message onto others through any form of coercion or violence. Instead, our way of "spreading the word" must be through "witness," which (both the person and/or message) can be accepted or rejected. Christianity claims one God as creator of all that exists, and as such, everything there is belongs to him. And although this single story of the Bible (creation – fall – Israel – redemption in Christ – new creation) ends in destruction and God's triumph over all evil, the Christian witness must be coercion-free. Simultaneously, Christians must testify about the coming kingdom of God and the benefits of his rule. Because where God rules, there is no exploitation, greed, oppression, destruction, lie, falsehood, etc. But this benefit does not cancel out the fact that at the end God will cleanse his creation from all that is evil. Nor does it minimize the conflicting nature of the gospel message in the present time. On that final point, we can say with N. T. Wright: "if Jesus is Lord, then Caesar is not."[14] And to confess "Jesus as Lord," means that he is not only Lord of certain individuals or the church, but also the Lord of the entirety of creation.[15]

In conclusion, we can say that God wants to be known. As we tracked the concept of witness throughout the Bible, we observed that God's activity throughout the course of human history brought the knowledge of God to people, through observing his work (eyes) and/or hearing his words (ears). This naturally implies the connection between "words" and "deeds" which we encountered in the Lukan concept of witness. The knowledge of God also has a strong communal aspect. That is, from the outset of the biblical narrative, God has his chosen "seed" (Gen 3:15), and that seed in Abraham's case (Gen 12:1–3) receives the promise of becoming a nation.[16] To this nation

---

13. Johnson, 167.

14. Wright, *Surprised by Hope*, 50.

15. Budiselić, "Christian Witness for 21st Century," 411.

16. According to Heiser (*Unseen Realm*, chap. 14), Genesis 12 is important because here YHWH puts aside other nations and ties Himself to Israel in a special way: "Yahweh disinherited the nations, and in the very next chapter of Genesis, he calls Abram out of—you guessed it—Mesopotamia. Again, this is not accidental. Yahweh would take a man from the

of Israel God reveals himself, and as we already noticed, revelation enables relationship, and relationship creates the missional community. This community has been tasked with living lives faithful to that revelation of God, and to pass this revelation on to others, so that others will also be included into God's family. And this *modus operandi* (Abraham – Israel – Jesus's disciples – early church – church today) is still valid today.

As we think about the knowledge of God in connection with these two elements (God's activity in history and embodiment in community), we must realize how deeply embedded in this formulation is the concept of witness. With that in mind, to think about applications of the Lukan concept of witness is to think about how to make God known to others, how to manifest what has already been manifested or revealed. Arising from Judaism, Christianity is a religion of revelation that bears a specific content of revelation. This also means that Christianity is a religion of witness in which this specific content of revelation must be kept, preserved, passed on, and proclaimed to others. The Lukan concept of witness in the context of the wider biblical narrative, to use Johnson's words, is prophetic and challenging, and invites us to embodiment and enaction. We suggested a few possible ways in which the church today could carry out these tasks, but whatever we do and however we do it, we should bear in mind that at stake is the knowledge of God.

---

heart of the rebellion and make a new nation, Israel. But in his covenant with Abram, God said that all the nations of the earth would be blessed through Abram, through his descendants (Gen 12:1–3). The covenant language reveals that it was God's intention, right on the heels of his decision to punish the nations, that the Israelites would serve as a conduit for their return to the true God. This is one of the reasons Israel is later called 'a kingdom of priests' (Exod 19:6). Israel would be in covenant with 'the God of gods' and the 'Lord of lords' (Deut 10:17). Those disinherited would be in spiritual bondage to the corrupt sons of God. But Israel would be a conduit, a mediator. Yahweh would leave a spiritual bread-crumb trail back to himself. That path would wind through Israel and, ultimately, Israel's messiah. From the fateful decision at Babel onward, the story of the Old Testament is about Israel versus the disinherited nations, and Yahweh versus the corrupt, rebel *elohim* of those nations. The division of the nations and their allotment under other *elohim* is behind the scenes in all sorts of places in biblical history."

Conclusion

We began this work by asking why Jesus in Acts 1:8 makes the reception of the Holy Spirit a necessary condition for his disciples to be his witnesses, and how the Holy Spirit impacts their witness. In our exploration, we studied the Lukan concept of witness in relation to the Spirit within the wider biblical context of the concept of witness. We began with an introductory analysis of Acts 1:8 and the usage of *πνεῦμα* and *δύναμις* in Luke/Acts. Then we analyzed the concept of witness in the OT and synthetized the results of our findings. We conducted the same analysis and synthesis for the NT. On that basis we were able to compare the ways the concept of witness in the NT corresponds to the OT and in what ways it continues to develop. Then we returned to the Lukan writings, arguing that Luke offers a unique contribution to the biblical concept of witness. On that basis we offered certain applications for the life of Christians and the ministry of the church, always claiming that the concept of witness, particularly in the book of Acts, provides a prophetic vision for the church today.

Our study of the aspects of the concept of witness in the Bible, which included the entities who are defined as witnesses, witnessing activities and the product of witnessing/testimony, confirmed that the concept of witness in the Bible reflects the idea of "repetition." Repetition does not summarize everything that witnesses do, but it serves as an accurate general description of their activity. Even though the etymology of *μάρτυς* emphasizes predominantly mental activity and the etymology of the Hebrew verbal root *'d* is broad, the general idea of witnessing as "repetition" or "doing something again" is in most cases a common theme. Such repetitions might include presenting material evidence, offering verbal report, warning about the future, or some combination of verbal announcement and actual fulfilment. In some instances, past events could serve as a paradigm for future events that will occur. This observation about repetition led us to pay special attention to the temporal aspect of witness in our analysis of different aspects of the concept of witness. Hence, in each case we tried to identify whether witnesses in their present repeat something from the past, announce something about the future or just passively observe something in the present. Based on these parameters we further identified and classified witnesses according to different categories such as: mode of witness, function, specific purpose, qualifications and means of witness. The picture that emerged was rather complex, but we were able to show that witnesses can be categorized according to this pattern in both the OT and NT, with some minor differences. As a result, we were able to refine our understanding of the concept of witness, particularly in two ways:

(1) To the usual categories of observing and testifying witnesses, we added an additional distinction: witnesses for or against, and witnesses about. Witnesses for or against can be spotted easily because they always speak in the present about the past for the purpose of establishing truth regarding a subject's guilt or innocence. Witnesses about are those witnesses who are not observing witnesses and do not belong to the category of witnesses for or against someone or something. What distinguishes them from witnesses for or against is that they sometimes operate in a different timeline, and for a different purpose.

(2) We have demonstrated that having played the role of observing witness is not always necessary to serve in the role of testifying witness. This is especially true in cases when witnesses speak about what might/can happen in the future in a message of warning (negative) or admonishment (positive). Witness is usually defined as "a person who declares what has been seen or heard." In the light of this research, a more complete definition of witness includes not only the notarial function of witnesses (which some definitions occasionally include), but also note the witnesses' speech about future.

Furthermore, as we were studying the concept of witness in the Bible, we identified the concept's development as it unfolds on the pages of Scripture. For example, in the OT we defined three primary contexts in which the concept of witness appears: social, covenantal or religious, and legal or juridical. But in the NT, the legal context becomes less important and the religious gains prominence. Hence, witnesses as mediators are important not only because they help establish truth about someone's guilt or innocence, but also to establish religious truths. And if in the OT we had a *theonomy* and the overlap between legal and religious, as we stepped into the NT the religious context became primary, and the focus of the story moved to this new *ecclesia* which lives in the environment that is hostile toward her and where outside standards of life are not defined by God.

The summary of results for both the OT and the NT gave us a solid picture of various aspects of the concept of witness in the Bible. On that basis we were able to return to the Lukan writings and argue for a specific understanding of that concept in his writings. First, we established, that in the biblical context, Luke in Acts 1:8 brings a unique requirement for someone to be a witness: they must receive πνεῦμα ἅγιος and δύναμις. Although we had encountered other mentions in the Bible of πνεῦμα ἅγιος in the context of witness/testimony (Neh 9:30; John 15:26–27; 1 John 5:6–8; Rev 19:10), only in Lukan writings is reception of πνεῦμα ἅγιος prerequisite for being a witness.

Second, we demonstrated that πνεῦμα ἅγιος inspires and produces verbal witness while δύναμις produces the miraculous aspect of witnessing. On that basis, we were then able to describe two types or forms of witnessing: one given verbally by πνεῦμα ἅγιος, and the other given by δύναμις through signs and wonders. This first type of witness we identified as *kerygmatic*, and the second as *charismatic*. For Luke these two aspects of witness go together, so that witness in Acts is almost always done based on what Jesus is doing in the present, whether it is baptism in the Spirit, miracles or exorcisms. This led us to conclude that, although Luke follows the general fundamental idea of witness as "repetition," for Luke the prominent element in the concept of witness is not repetition *per se*, but the content of repetition: repetition of Jesus's ministry. Although we did not enter too extensively into debate about Lukan pneumatology, we believe this sheds some light on that debate.

Third, we argued that the whole church participates in this repetition of Jesus's ministry. We tried to prove this by considering the development of the concept of witness in Acts, the role of miracles in verbal proclamation of the gospel, by explaining why Luke mostly portrays the apostles as the ones involved in the task of witnessing, and by considering OT background for Acts 1:8 and the role of the Spirit in Acts.

What is the original contribution of this work? a) Methodologically, we argued for unique aspects of the concept of witness in Lukan writings based on analysis and synthesis of the concept in the context of the whole Bible. To our knowledge, no one has previously undertaken such an extensive project. b) Based on the idea that the foundational meaning of witness is repetition, we paid careful attention to the timeline of witnessing activity, which led us to revise the categories of witnesses and conclude that the usual definition of witness does not always adequately summarize the biblical depiction of witness;[1] c) We sought to ascertain why Jesus makes the reception of the Holy Spirit a necessary condition for his disciples to be his witnesses in Acts 1:8, and how the Holy Spirit impacts their witness. To this end, we demonstrated that in the biblical context, Luke has a unique condition for being a witness, and a unique content of repetition. Although we did not discuss all pneumatological issues in Lukan writings, we tried to contribute to that discussion from the perspective of the biblical concept of witness with the results that came as a result of this research. Although there are many different opinions regarding Lukan pneumatology, the Lukan view of witness in terms of our faithfulness in emulating Jesus's life and ministry undoubtedly poses significant challenge for us today.

The concept of witness is a foundational biblical theological concept. Christianity, with its Jewish roots, is a religion of revelation. Such revelation is often brought through witnesses, who because of their unique position and opportunity, serve as mediators and guarantors of that revelation. Their unique position gives them great responsibility because, as we have also seen, their testimony becomes the public presentation of certain claims. If they are accepted by others, these claims then shape and constitute reality and public truth. For that matter, witnessing inevitably produces conflicts, because witnesses either function based on their unique and exclusivist position, or on the basis of their firm conviction that something is true/fact. This aspect of conflict to witness/testimony is even more challenging in today's *zeitgeist*, which is marked by dominant values of tolerance, dialogue and political correctness. In the application, we suggested that, in line with Johnson's view, the book of Acts provides a prophetic vision for the church today, because the church is called to emulate Jesus's radical manner of life. Accordingly,

1. In other words, usually witness is defined as someone who speaks in the present about the past. Sometimes a passive role of a witness in the present is mentioned, but speaking about the future is also a form of witness. For this last aspect, one does not have to have a first-hand knowledge.

the church is not only challenged to keep, preserve and proclaim the content of that revelation, but also to preserve and emulate the prophetic lifestyle of Jesus and the early church.

This study has raised several questions that, due to limitation of this work, remain open and require additional work and research. First, we did not enter too deeply into debate about Lukan pneumatology (although we hope to have shed light on aspects of it). We did show the idea that πνεῦμα ἅγιος and δύναμις are responsible for different types of witness (in accordance with argumentation of Menzies and Menzies and Haya-Prats). This is in keeping with the underlying idea of witness as repetition; for Luke, this results in repetition of Jesus's ministry. Due to limitations of this work, we did not discuss other possible functions of πνεῦμα ἅγιος and δύναμις on Christian life or church.

Second, in our research we saw that in the OT the concept of "witness/testimony" overlaps with concepts of "covenant" and "prophecy." In the NT, this overlap with prophecy is even more emphatic. Furthermore, the concept of witness overlaps with another core NT concept, "the gospel." In fact, these overlap to such an extent that in some instances testimony is equivalent with the gospel. We did not explore these connections more deeply, and they could be the subject of further research.

Third, we will here mention two things we encountered as we studied the dynamic of the concept of witness. The first is the dynamic relationship between "witness" as a person, and "testimony" as a product of a witness' testimony. "Witness" produces "testimony," yet occasionally "testimony" can become "witness," or "witness" may even be considered as "testimony." The second is that, due to their semantic range, some words such as "hearing," "knowing" or "speaking" can sometimes be categorized as belonging to the concept of witness.

Finally, the command for "two or three witnesses" was originally given in a juridical context. This OT command is repeated in the NT a) in the context of resolving conflicts inside the church community or, b) as a principle or methodology used to support religious claims and convictions. Hence, we see here a development from command to principle, and the change in context from juridical to religious. This development should be more deeply explored in connection with the concept of witness.

Bibliography

1. Primary Sources

Ambrosiaster. "Commentary on 1 Corinthians." Pages 119–206 in *Commentaries on Romans and 1–2 Corinthians.* Edited by Gerald L. Bray. Downers Grove: InterVarsity Press, 2009.

Biblia Hebraica Stuttgartensia: With Westminster Hebrew Morphology. Electronic ed.; Stuttgart: German Bible Society; Glenside: Westminster Seminary, 1996.

Brannan, Rick, Ken M. Penner, Israel Loken, Michael Aubrey, and Isaiah Hoogendyk, eds. *The Lexham English Septuagint.* Bellingham: Lexham Press, 2012.

Lexham Hebrew Bible. Bellingham: Lexham Press, 2012.

Nestle, E., Aland, B., Aland, K., Karavidopoulos, J., Martini, C. M., and Metzger, B. M. *The Greek New Testament.* 27th ed.; Stuttgart: Deutsche Bibelgesellschaft, 1993.

NET Bible. Biblical Studies Press, 2006.

Swete, Henry Barclay, *The Old Testament in Greek: According to the Septuagint.* Cambridge: Cambridge University Press, 1909.

Tan, Randall K., David A. deSilva, and Isaiah Hoogendyk. *The Lexham Greek-English Interlinear Septuagint.* H.B. Swete Edition; Bellingham: Lexham Press, 2012.

2. Literature

Ahn, John J. *Exile as Forced Migrations: A Sociological, Literary, and Theological Approach on the Displacement and Resettlement of the Southern Kingdom of Judah.* Berlin & New York: Walter de Gruyter GmbH & Co., 2010.

Akin, Daniel L. *1, 2, 3 John*. NAC 38. Nashville: Broadman & Holman Publishers, 2001.

Alden, Robert. L. *Job*. NAC 11. Nashville: Broadman & Holman Publishers, 1993.

Aletti, Jean-Noël. "Evangelizzare e/o testimoniare? Il caso di Paolo nel libro degli Atti degli Apostoli." *Consolata* (2009). Cited 26 July 2015. Online : http://www.consolata.org/new/index.php/ mission/missioneoggiarchi/6240-evangelizzare-o-testimoniare-il-caso-di-paolo-negli-atti-degli-apostoli.

———. "Testimoni del Risorto: Spirito Santo e testimonianza negli Atti degli Apostoli." Rivista dell'Evangelizzazione 2 (1998): 287–298.

Allen, David. L. *Hebrews*. NAC 35. Nashville: Broadman & Holman Publishers, 2010.

Archer, Kenneth J. *The Gospel Revisited: Towards a Pentecostal Theology of Worship and Witness*. Eugene: Wipf & Stock Pub, 2011.

Arichea, Daniel C., and Howard Hatton. *A Paul's Letters to Timothy and to Titus*. UBS Handbook Series. New York: United Bible Societies, 1995.

Ash, Anthony, and Richard Oster Lee. *Djela Apostolska*. Dobra vest: Novi Sad, 1986.

Ashley, Timothy R. *The Book of Numbers*. NICOT. Grand Rapids: William B. Eerdmans, 1993.

Aune, David E. *Revelation 1–5*. WBC 52A. Dallas: Word, Incorporated, 1998a.

———. *Revelation 6–16*. WBC 52B. Dallas: Word, Incorporated, 1998b.

Baan, Ariaan. *The Necessity of Witness: Stanley Hauerwas's Contribution to Systematic Theology*. Eugene: Wipf and Stock Publishers, 2015.

Bailey, Randall C. *Exodus*. CPNIV. Joplin: College Press Publishing, 2007.

Baker, David W. 2006. *Joel, Obadiah, Malachi*. NIVAC. Grand Rapids: Zondervan, 2006.

Balogh, Csaba. *The Stele of YHWH in Egypt: The Prophecies of Isaiah 18–20 Concerning Egypt and Kush*. Leiden & Boston: Brill, 2011.

Bandy, Alan S. "Words and Witness: An Analysis of the Lawsuit Motif in Revelation Based on Witness Terminology." *GJCT* 6:1–34.

Barker, Kenneth L. *Micah, Nahum, Habakkuk, Zephaniah*. NAC 20. Nashville: Broadman & Holman Publishers, 1999.

Barrett, C. K. *The Second Epistle to the Corinthians*. BNTC. London & New York: Continuum, 2008.

———. *The Epistle to Romans*. BNTC. Peabody: Hendrickson Publishers, 1991.

———. *Acts 1–14*. ICC. Edinburgh: T&T Clark, 1994.

Barstad, Hans M. "Prophecy in the Book of Jeremiah and the Historical Prophet." Pages 87–100 in *Sense and Sensitivity: Essays on Reading the Bible in Memory of Robert Carroll.* Edited by Alastair G. Hunter and Philip R. Davies. London & New York: Sheffield Academic Press, 2002.

Bateman IV, Herbert W. *A Workbook for Intermediate Greek: Grammar, Exegesis, and Commentary on 1–3 John*. Grand Rapids: Kregel, 2008.

Bauckham, Richard. *The Theology of the Book of Revelation*. Cambridge: Cambridge University Press, 2003.

Beale, Gregory K. *The Book of Revelation: A Commentary on the Greek Text*. NIGTC. Grand Rapids: William B. Eerdmans; Carlisle: The Paternoster Press, 1999.

Becking, Bob, and Anne-Mareike, "Wetter Boaz in the Gate (Ruth 4, 1–12): Legal Transaction or Religious Ritual?" *ZAR* 19 (2013): 253–265.

Beuken, Willem A. M. *Isaiah II: Isaiah Chapters 28–39*. HCOT. Leuven: Pieters, 2000.

Beutler, Johannes. "μαρτυρεω, διαμαρτύρομαι, μαρτύρομαι." Pages 389–391 in vol. 2 of EDNT. Edited by Horst Robert Balz and Gerhard Schneider. Grand Rapids: Eerdmans, 1990a.

———. "μαρτυρία." Pages 391–393 in vol. 2 of *EDNT*. Edited by Horst Robert Balz and Gerhard Schneider. Grand Rapids: Eerdmans, 1990b.

———. "μαρτυς." Pages 393–395 in vol. 2 of *EDNT*. Edited by Horst Robert Balz and Gerhard Schneider. Grand Rapids: Eerdmans, 1990c.

Bianchi, Francesco. "Deception." In *Lexham Theological Wordbook.* Edited by Douglas Mangum, Derek R. Brown, Rachel Klippenstein, and Rebekah Hurst. Bellingham: Lexham Press, 2014.

Billington, Anthony. "The Paraclete and Mission in the Fourth Gospel." Pages 89–115 in *Mission and Meaning: Essays Presented to Peter Cotterell.* Edited by A. Billington, T. Lane and M.M.B. Turner. Carlisle: Paternoster, 1995.

Bloomberg, Craig L. *Matthew: An Exegetical and Theological Exposition of Holy Scripture*. NAC 22. Nashville: Broadman Press, 1992.

Bock, Darrell L. BECNT. Grand Rapids: Baker Academic. 2007.

Boda, Mark J. *Haggai, Zechariah*. NIVAC. Grand Rapids: Zondervan. 2004.

Borchert, Gerald L. *John 1–11*. NAC 25A. Nashville: Broadman & Holman Publishers, 1996.

Bovati, Pietro. *Re-Establishing Justice: Legal Terms, Concepts and* Procedures *in the Hebrew Bible*. Sheffield: Sheffield Academic Press, 1994.

Brannan, Rick, and Israel Loken. *The Lexham Textual Notes on the Bible. Lexham Bible Reference Series*. Bellingham: Lexham Press, 2014.

Bratcher, Robert G., and Barclay Moon. *A Translator's the Book of Joshua*. London & New York: United Bible Societies, 1983.

Bratcher, Robert G., and Eugene Albert Nida. *A Handbook on the Gospel of Mark* UBS Handbook Series. New York: United Bible Societies, 1993.

———. Robert G., and Howard A. Hatton. *A Deuteronomy*. New York: United Bible Societies, 2000.

Bratcher, Robert G., and Howard Hatton. *A Handbook on the Revelation to John.* UBS Handbook Series. New York: United Bible Societies, 1993.
Bratcher, Robert. G., and William David Reyburn. *A Translator's the Book of Psalms*. New York: United Bible Societies, 1991.
Brenton, Lancelot Charles Lee. *The Septuagint Version of the Old Testament: English Translation*. London: Samuel Bagster and Sons, 1870.
Brodie, Thomas L. *The Gospel According to John: A Literary and Theological Commentary*. New Your & Oxford: Oxford University Press, 1997.
Brooks, James A. *Mark*. NAC 23. Nashville: Broadman & Holman Publishers, 1991.
Brown, Francis, Samuel Rolles Driver and Charles Augustus Briggs. *Enhanced Brown-Driver-Briggs Hebrew and English Lexicon*. Oxford: Clarendon Press, 1977.
Brown, Raymond. *The Gospel According to John (I–XII)*. AB 29. New York: Doubleday & Company, Inc, 1966.
———. *The Gospel and Epistles of John: A Concise Commentary*. Collegeville: The Liturgical Press, 1988.
Bruce, Frederick F. *1 and 2 Thessalonians*. WBC 45. Dallas: Word, Incorporated, 1998.
———. *The Epistle to the Galatians: A Commentary on the Greek Text*. NIGTC. Grand Rapids: Eerdmans, 1982.
Brueggemann, Walter. *Theology of the Old Testament*. Minneapolis: Fortress Press, 1997.
Budd, Philip. J. *Numbers*. WBC 5. Dallas: Word Books Publisher, 1998.
Budiselić, Ervin. "Christian Witness for the 21st Century: Contemporary, yet Orthodox and Radical." *BV* 74 (2014): 399–412.
Burnside, Johnathan. *God, Justice, and Society: Aspects of Law and Legality in the Bible*. New York: Oxford University Press, 2011.
Butler, Trent C. *Joshua*. WBC 30. Dallas: Word, Incorporated, 1998.
Carson, Donald A. *The Gospel According to John*. PNTC. Leicester: Inter-Varsity Press; Grand Rapids: Eerdmans, 1991.
Christensen, Duane L. *Deuteronomy 1:1–21:9*. WBC 6A. Dallas: Word Books Publisher, 2001.
———. *Deuteronomy 21:10–34:12*. WBC 6B. Dallas: Word, Incorporated, 2002.
Clark, David J., and Norm Mundhenk. *A Translator's the Book of Micah*. London & New York: United Bible Societies, 1982.
Clements, Ronald E. *Exodus*. CBCOT. London: Cambridge University Press, 1972.
Clines, David. J. A. *Job 1–20*. WBC 17. Dallas: Word, Incorporated, 1998.
Clowney, Edmund P. *The Message of 1 Peter: The Way of the Cross*. BST. Leicester & Downers Grove: InterVarsity Press, 1988.

Cook, Johann. *The Septuagint of Proverbs–Jewish and/or Hellenistic Proverbs?* Leiden, New York & Köln: Brill, 1997.
Craig, William L. *The Only Wise God: The Compatibility of Divine Foreknowledge and Human Freedom*. Eugene: Wipf & Stock Publishers, 2000.
Craigie, Peter C. *The Book of Deuteronomy*. NCOT. Grand Rapids: Eerdmans, 1976.
———. *Psalms 1–50*. WBC 19. Dallas: Word, Incorporated, 1998.
Cruz, Juan. *"Who is like Yahweh?": A Study of Divine Metaphors in the Book of Micah*. Göttingen: Vandenhoeck & Ruprecht, 2016.
Czander, Giovanna Raengo. *"You are my Witnesses": A Theological Approach to the Laws of Testimony*. Ann Arbor: ProQuest LLC, 2009.
Delcor, Mathias. "חרשׁ" ḥrš to be silent. Pages 477–479 in *Theological Lexicon of the Old Testament*. Edited by Ernst Jenni and Claus Westermann. Peabody: Hendrickson Publishers, 1997.
Denaux, Albert. "You are Witnesses of these Things": Being a Witness of Jesus Christ in a Pluralist World. Pages 67–85 in *Living Today the Church of Tomorrow*. Edited by Kate Davson and Nagypál Szabolcs. Brussels, Rye, Budapest: International Ecumenical Fellowship (IEF), 2009.
de Dietrich, Suzanne. "You Are My Witnesses—A Study of the Church's Witness." *Interpretation* 8 (1954): 173–179.
de Silva, David A. *Perseverance in Gratitude: A Socio-Rhetorical Commentary on the Epistle to the Hebrews*. Grand Rapids: Eerdmans, 2000.
DeVries, Simon J. *1 Kings*. WBC 12. Dallas: Word, Incorporated, 2003.
Do, Maria Yen Thi. *The Lucan Journey: A Study of Luke 9:28–36 and Acts 1:6–11 as an Architectural Pair*. Bern & New York: Peter Lang AG, 2010.
Dozeman, Thomas B. *Exodus*. ECC. Grand Rapids: Eerdmans, 2009.
Dunn, James D. G. *Baptism in the Holy Spirit: A Re-examination of the New Testament Teaching on the Gift of the Spirit in Relation to Pentecostalism Today*. Philadelphia: The Westminster Press, 1970.
———. *The Epistles to the Colossians and to Philemon: A Commentary on the Greek Text*. NIGTC. Grand Rapids: Eerdmans; Carlisle: The Paternoster Press, 1996.
———. *Romans 1–8*. WBC 38A. Dallas: Word, Incorporated, 1998a.
———. *Romans 9–16*. WBC 38 B. Dallas: Word, Incorporated, 1998b.
———. *Jesus and the Spirit: A study of the religious and charismatic experience of Jesus and the first Christians as reflected in the New Testament*. Grand Rapids: Eerdmans, 1997.
Durham, John. I. *Exodus*. WBC 3. Dallas: Word Books Publishers, 1998.
Durrwell, François-Xavier. "Christian Witness: A Theological Study." *International Review of Mission* 69, no. 274 (1980): 121–134.

Ehlke, Troy D. *Crossroads of Agony: Suffering and Violence in the Christian Tradition*. Bloomington: Xlibris, 2008.

Ellingworth, Paul. *The Epistle to the Hebrews: A Commentary on the Greek Text*. NIGTC. Grand Rapids: Eerdmans & Carlisle: The Paternoster Press, 1993.

Ellingworth, Paul, and Eugene Albert Nida. *A Handbook on the Letter to the Hebrews*. UBS Handbook Series. New York: United Bible Societies, 1994.

Ellis, Earle E. "'The End of the Earth'(Acts 1:8)." Bulletin for Biblical Research 1 (1991): 123–132.

Elwell, Walter A., and Philip Wesley Comfort, eds. "Witness." *Tyndale Bible Dictionary* 1306–1307. Wheaton: Tyndale House Publishers, 2001.

Embudo, Lora Angeline B. "A Lukan Paradigm of Witness: Community as a Form of Witness, Part I." *AJPS* 20 (2017a): 1.7–18.

———. "A Lukan Paradigm of Witness: Community as a Form of Witness, Part I." *AJPS* 20 (2017b): 1,19–35.

Evans, Craig A. *Mark 8:27–16:20*. WBC 34B. Dallas: Word, Incorporated, 2001.

Fee, Gordon. *Paul's Letter to the Philippians*. NICNT. Grand Rapids: Eerdmans, 1995.

Fox, Michael V. *Proverbs 10–31*. AYB 18B. New Haven & London: Yale University Press, 2009.

France, R. T. *The Mark: A Commentary on the Greek Text*. NIGTC. Grand Rapids: Eerdmans; Carlisle: The Paternoster Press, 2002.

——— Pages 904–945 in *New Bible Commentary: 21st Century Edition* Edited by Donald A. Carson, Richard T. France, John A. Motyer, and Gordon J. Wenham. Leicester & Downers Grove: InterVarsity Press, 1994.

Friberg, Timothy, Barbara Friberg and Neva F. Miller. *Analytical Lexicon of the Greek New Testament*. BGNTL. Grand Rapids: Baker Books, 2000.

Friesen, Ivan D. *Isaiah*. BCBC. Scottdale & Waterloo: Herald Press, 2009.

Garland, David E. *2 Corinthians*. NAC 29. Nashville: Broadman & Holman Publishers, 1999.

Garrett, Duane A. *Song of Songs/Lamentations*. WBC 23B. Dallas: Word, Incorporated, 2004.

———. *Proverbs, Ecclesiastes, Song of Songs*. NAC 14. Nashville: Broadman & Holman Publishers, 1993.

Gaventa, Beverly Roberts. "You Will Be My Witnesses: Aspect of Mission in the Acts of the Apostles." *Missiology* 10 (1982): 413–425.

Gesenius, Friedrich Wilhelm, *Gesenius' Hebrew Grammar*. Edited by Emil Kautzsch and Sir Arthur Ernest Cowley. Oxford: Clarendon Press, 1910.

Gesenius, Friedrich Wilhelm, and Samuel Prideaux Tregelles. *Gesenius' Hebrew and Chaldee Lexicon to the Old Testament Scriptures*. Bellingham: Logos Bible Software, 2003.

Gleaves, G. Scott. "Evil." In *Lexham Theological Wordbook.* Edited by Douglas Mangum, Derek R. Brown, Rachel Klippenstein, and Rebekah Hurst. Bellingham: Lexham Press, 2014.

Glenny, W. Edward. *Micah: A Commentary Based on Micah in Codex Vaticanus.* Leiden and Boston: Brill, 2015.

Goldingay, John. *Psalms, Vol. 3: Psalms 90–150.* BCOTWP. Grand Rapids: Baker Academic, 2008.

Goldingay, John, and David Payne. *Isaiah 40–55: A Critical and Exegetical Commentary.* Vol 1. ICC. London & New York: T&T Clark, 2006.

Goldingay, John. *The Message of Isaiah 40–55: A Literary-Theological Commentary.* London & New York: T&T Clark, 2005.

———. *Psalms, Vol 1: Psalms 1–41.* BCOTWP. Grand Rapids: Baker Academic, 2006.

———. *Psalms, Vol 2: Psalms 42–89.* BCOTWP. Grand Rapids: Baker Academic, 2007.

Goppelt, Leonhard. "ὕδωρ." *Theological Dictionary of the New Testament* 8:314–33. Edited by Gerhard Kittel, Geoffrey W. Bromiley and Gerhard Friedrich. Grand Rapids, Eerdmans, 1964.

Green, Gene L. *The Letters to the Thessalonians.* PNTC. Grand Rapids: Eerdmans; Leicester: Apollos, 2002.

Green, Joel B. "Salvation to the end of the Earth: God as Saviour in the Acts of the Apostles." Pages 83–106 in *Witness to Gospel: the Theology of Acts.* Edited by Howard Marshall and David Peterson. Grand Rapids: Eerdmans. 1998.

Green, Michael. *The Message of Matthew: The Kingdom of Heaven.* BST. Leicester & Downers Grove: InterVarsity Press, 2001.

Guder, Darrell L. *Be My Witnesses.* Grand Rapids: Eerdmans, 1985.

Guelich, Robert A. *Mark 1–8:26.* WBC 34A. Dallas: Word, Incorporated, 1998.

Haas, C., Marinus de Jonge, and J. L. Swellengrebel. *A Handbook on the Letters of John.* UBS Handbook Series. New York: United Bible Societies, 1994.

Hagner, Donald A. *Matthew 1–13.* WBC 33A. Dallas: Word, Incorporated, 1998a.

———. 1998b. *Matthew 14–28.* WBC 33B. Dallas: Word, Incorporated, 1998b.

Hall, Gary Harlan. *Deuteronomy.* Joplin, MO: College Press, 2000.

Hamilton, Victor P. *The Book of Genesis: Chapters 18–50.* NICOT. Grand Rapids: Eerdmans, 1995.

———. *Exodus: An Exegetical Commentary.* Grand Rapids: Baker Academic, 2011.

———. "1741 פָּנֶה." Pages 718–719 in *Theological Wordbook of the Old Testament.* Edited by Robert. L. Harris, Gleason. L. Archer Jr., and Bruce. K. Waltke. Chicago: Moody Press, 1999a.

———. "2338 שׁוא." In: Robert. L. Harris, Gleason. L. Archer Jr., and Bruce. K. Waltke. *Theological Wordbook of the Old Testament*, 908. Chicago: Moody Press, 1999b.

Hanson, Paul D. *Isaiah 40–66*. IBCTP. Louisville: John Knox Press, 1995.

Harris, Murray J. *The Second Epistle to the Corinthians: A Commentary on the Greek Text*. NIGTC. Grand Rapids: Eerdmans; Milton Keynes: The Paternoster Press, 2005.

Harris, Robert. L. "678 חָמָס." *Theological Wordbook of the Old Testament* 297. Edited by Robert. L. Harris, Gleason. L. Archer Jr., and Bruce. K. Waltke. Chicago: Moody Press, 1999.

Hartley, John E. *Leviticus*. WBC 4. Dallas: Word Books Publishers, 1998.

Haya-Prats, Gonzalo. *Empowered Believers: The Holy Spirit in the Book of Acts*. Eugene: Cascade Books, 2011.

Heiser, Michael S., and Vincent M. Setterholm. *Glossary of Morpho-Syntactic Database Terminology*. Bellingham: Lexham Press, 2013.

———. *The Unseen Realm*. Bellingham: Lexham Press, 2015.

Hobbs, T. R. *2 Kings*. WBC 13. Dallas: Word, Incorporated, 1998.

Holladay, William Lee. *A Concise Hebrew and Aramaic Lexicon of the Old Testament*. Leiden: Brill, 2000.

———. *Jeremiah: A Fresh Reading*. New York: Pilgrim's Press, 1990.

House, Paul R. *1, 2 Kings*. NAC 8. Nashville: Broadman & Holman Publishers, 1995.

Hubbard Jr., Robert L. "Kinsman-Redeemer and Levirate." Pages 378–83 in *Dictionary of the Old Testament: Wisdom, Poetry & Writings*. Edited by Tremper Longman III and Peter Enns. Downers Grove: InterVarsity Press, 2008.

Huddleston, Jonathan. "Recent Scholarship on the Pentateuch: Historical, Literary, and Theological Reflections." *RQ* 55 (2013): 4,193–211.

Hughes, Robert. B., and J. Carl Laney. *TCBC*. Wheaton: Tyndale House Publishers, 2001.

Hur, Ju. *A Dynamic Reading of the Holy Spirit in Luke-Acts*. Sheffield: Sheffield Academic Press, 2001.

Jabini, Frank. "Witness to the End of the World: A Missional Reading of Acts" 8:26–40. *Conspectus* 13 (2012): 51–72.

Jacob, Benno. *The Second Book of the Bible: Exodus*. Transl. Walter Jacob. New Jersey: Ktav Publishing House, 1992.

Jamieson, Robert, A. R. Fausset, and David Brown. *Commentary Critical and Explanatory on the Whole Bible*. 2 vols. Oak Harbor: Logos Research Systems, Inc, 1997.

Jenson, Philip Peter. Obadiah, Jonah, Micah: A Theological Commentary. Vol. 496. Bloomsbury Publishing, 2008.

Jeremias, Jorg. *The Book of Amos: A Commentary*. OTL. Louisville: Westminster John Knox Press, 1998.

Johnson, Luke Timothy. *Prophetic Jesus, Prophetic Church: The Challenge of Luke-Acts to Contemporary Christians*. Grand Rapids: Eerdmans, 2011.

Karlberg, Mark W. Denial. In: Walter A. Elwell, ed. *EDBT*. Grand Rapids: Baker Book House, 1996.

Keener, Craig S. "Power of Pentecost: Luke's Missiology in Acts 1–2." *AJPS* 12 (2009): 1,47–73.

———. *Acts: An Exegetical Commentary. Introduction and 1:1–2:47*. Vol. 1. Grand Rapids: Baker Academic, 2012a.

———. *The John: A Commentary*. 2 vols. Grand Rapids: Baker Academic, 2012b.

———. *Acts: An Exegetical Commentary. 3:1–14:28*. Vol. 2. Grand Rapids: Baker Academic, 2013.

Keil, Carl Friedrich, and Franz Delitzsch. *Commentary on the Old Testament*. 10 Vols. Peabody: Hendrickson Publishers, Inc, 1996.

Kelly, David J. "The Development of the Witness Motif in Luke-Acts." Ph.D. diss., McGill University Montreal, 1972.

Keown, Gerald L. *Jeremiah 26–52*. WBC 27. Dallas: Word, Incorporated, 1998.

King, Philip J. *Jeremiah: An Archaeological Companion*. Louisville: Westminster/John Knox Press, 1993.

Klein, Ralph W. *1 Samuel*. WBC 10. Dallas: Word, Incorporated, 1998.

Klopfenstein, Martin A. "כזב kzb to lie." Pages 606–610 in *Theological Lexicon of the Old Testament.* Edited by Ernst Jenni and Claus Westermann. Peabody: Hendrickson Publishers, 1997.

Klopfenstein, Martin A. "שֶׁקֶר šqr to deceive." In: Ernst Jenni and Claus Westermann, eds. Theological Lexicon of the Old Testament, 1401–1402. Translated by M. E. Biddle. 3 vols. Peabody, Mass., 1997.

Knight, George W. *The Pastoral Epistles: A Commentary on the Greek Text*. NIGTC. Grand Rapids: Eerdmans; Carlisle: The Paternoster Press, 1992.

Knowles, Michael P. *Of Seeds and the People of God: Preaching as Parable, Crucifixion, and Testimony*. Eugene: Cascade Books, 2015.

Krašovec, Jože. *The Transformation of Biblical Proper Names*. New York & London: T&T Clark, 2010.

———. "The Poetic and Narrative Shape of the Hebrew Bible and Literary Forms of Antithesis." *Religious and Sacred Poetry: An International Quarterly of Religion, Culture and Education* 1 (2013): 23–39.

Krentz, Edgar. *The Historical-Critical Method*. Philadelphia: Fortress Press, 1977.

Kruse, Colin G. *The Letters of John*. PNTC. Grand Rapids: Eerdmans; Leicester: Apollos, 2000.

———. *Paul's Letter to the Romans*. PNTC. Cambridge & Grand Rapids: Eerdmans; Nottingham: Apollos, 2012.

Kuecker, J. Aaron. *The Spirit and the 'Other': Social Identity, Ethnicity and Intergroup Reconciliation in Luke-Acts*. Fife: St. Mary's College, 2008.

Kyaligonza, Francis. "You Will be My Witnesses Not Only in Jerusalem but Throughout Judaea and Samaria, and to the End of the Earth." In *An Exegetical-Theological Study of Acts 1:4–8*. Ph.D. diss., Pontificia Università Urbaniana Rome, 2004.

Ladd, George Eldon. *A Theology of the New Testament*. Grand Rapids: Eerdmans, 1993.

Lane, William L. *Hebrews 1–8*. WBC 47A. Dallas: Word, Incorporated, 1998a.

———. *Hebrews 9–13*. WBC 47B. Dallas: Word, Incorporated, 1998b.

Lange, John Peter, and Philip Schaff. *A Commentary on the Holy Scriptures: John*. Bellingham: Logos Bible Software, 2008.

Lange, John Peter, Philip Schaff, and J. J. van Oosterzee. *A Commentary on the Holy Scriptures: 1 & 2 Timothy*. Bellingham: Logos Bible Software, 2008.

Lange, John Peter, Philip Schaff, Christian Friedrich Kling and Conway P. Wing. *A Commentary on the Holy Scriptures: 2 Corinthians*. Bellingham: Logos Bible Software, 2008.

Lange, John Peter, Philip Schaff, Christian Friedrich Kling and Daniel W. Poor. *A Commentary on the Holy Scriptures: 1 Corinthians*. Bellingham: Logos Bible Software, 2008.

Lange, John Peter, Philip Schaff, F. R. Fay, J. F. Hurst and M. B. Riddle. *A Commentary on the Holy Scriptures: Romans*. Bellingham: Logos Bible Software, 2008.

Lange, John Peter, Philip Schaff, Victor Lechler Gotthard, Charles Gerok and Charles F. Schaeffer. *A Commentary on the Holy Scriptures: Acts*. Bellingham: Logos Bible Software, 2008.

Lange, John. Peter. *A Commentary on the Holy Scriptures: Numbers*. Bellingham: Logos Bible Software, 2008.

Larkin, William J., Jr. *Acts*. IVPNTC 5. Downers Grove: InterVarsity Press, 1995.

Lea, Thomas D., and Hayne P. Griffin. *1, 2 Timothy, Titus*. NAC 34. Nashville: Broadman & Holman Publishers, 1992.

Leithart, Peter J. *A House for My Name: A Survey of the Old Testament*. Moscow: Canon Press, 2000.

Lenski, R. C. H. *The Interpretation of St. Paul's Epistle to the Romans*. Columbus: Lutheran Book Concern, 1936.

———. *The Interpretation of the Epistle to the Hebrews and of the Epistle of James*. Columbus: Lutheran Book Concern, 1938.

———. *The Interpretation of St. John's Gospel*. Minneapolis: Augsburg Publishing House, 1961a.

———. *The Interpretation of St. Matthew's Gospel*. Minneapolis: Augsburg Publishing House, 1961b.

———. *The Interpretation of the Acts of the Apostles*. Minneapolis: Augsburg Publishing House, 1961c.

———. *The Interpretation of St. Paul's First and Second Epistle to the Corinthians*. Minneapolis: Augsburg Publishing House, 1963.

Leschert, Dale. F. "Witness." Page 1384 in *Eerdmans Dictionary of the Bible.* Edited by David Noel Freedman, Allen C. Myers, and Astrid B. Beck. Grand Rapids: Eerdmans, 2000.

Liddell, Henry G. *A Lexicon: Abridged from Liddell and Scott's Greek-English Lexicon*. Oak Harbor: Logos Research Systems, Inc, 1996.

Lincoln, Andrew T. *Ephesians*. WBC 42. Dallas: Word, Incorporated, 1990.

Lindsey, F. Duanne. "Zechariah." Pages 1:1545–1573 in *The Bible Knowledge Commentary: An Exposition of the Scriptures.* Edited by John F. Walvoord, and Roy B. Zuck. Wheaton: Victor Books, 1985.

Lioy, Dan. *The Decalogue in the Sermon on the Mount*. NY: Peter Lang Publishing, 2004.

Lo, Alison. *Job 28 as Rhetoric: An Analysis of Job 28 in the Context of Job 22–31*. Leiden & Boston: Brill, 2003.

Longenecker, Richard N. *Galatians*. WBC 41. Dallas: Word, Incorporated, 1998.

Louw, Johannes P., and Eugene Albert Nida. *Greek-English Lexicon of the New Testament: Based on Semantic Domains*. 2 vols. New York: United Bible Societies, 1996.

Lujić, Božo. *Starozavjetni proroci*. Zagreb: Kršćanska sadašnjost, 2004.

Luke, K. "The Biblical Idea of Marturia (Witness)." Pages 55–65 in *Evangelization, Dialogue and Development.* Edited by Mariasusai Dhawamony. Universita Gregoriana Editrice: Roma, 1972.

Marshall, Howard. *The Epistles of John*. NICNT. 2nd Revised Edition. Grand Rapids: Eerdmans, 1978.

Marsman, Hennie J. *Women in Ugarit and Israel: Their Social and Religious Position in the Context of the Ancient Near East*. Leiden & Boston: Brill, 2003.

Martin, Ralph P. *2 Corinthians*. WBC 40. Dallas: Word, Incorporated, 1998.

Mathews, Claire R. *Defending Zion: Edom's Desolation and Jacob's Restoration (Isaiah 34–35) in Context*. Berlin & New York: Walter de Gruyter, 1995.

Mathews, Kenneth A. *Genesis 11:27–50:26: An Exegetical and Theological Exposition of Holy Scripture*. NAC 1B. Nashville: Broadman & Holman Publishers, 2005.

Mays, James Luther. *Amos: A Commentary*. Philadelphia: The Westminster Press, 1969.

Melbourne, Bertram L. "Acts 1:8 Re-Examined: Is Acts 8 Its Fulfillment?" *JRT* 57/58 (2005): 2:1–18, 2005.

Menzies, Robert. *Empowered for Witness: The Spirit in Luke-Acts*. Sheffield: Sheffield Academic Press, 1994.

Menzies, William W., and Robert P. Menzies. *Spirit and Power: Foundations of Pentecostal Experience.* Grand Rapids: Zondervan, 2000.

Merrill, Eugene H. *Deuteronomy Vol. 4: An Exegetical and Theological Exposition of Holy Scripture*. NAC 4. Nashville: Broadman & Holman Publishers, 1994.

Metzger, Bruce Manning. *A Textual Commentary on the Greek New Testament*. Second edition. A companion Volume to the United Bible Societies' Greek New Testament (4th rev. ed.). London & New York: United Bible Societies, 1994.

Michaels, J. Ramsey. *1 Peter*. WBC 49. Dallas: Word, Incorporated, 1998.

Miller, Patrick D. *Deuteronomy*. IBC. Louisville: Westminster John Knox Press, 1990.

Moessner, David Paul. *Luke the Historian of Israel's Legacy, Theologian of Israel's 'Christ': A New Reading of the 'Gospel Acts' of Luke*. Berlin & Boston: Walter de Gruyter, 2016.

Moo, Douglas J. *The Letter of James*. PNTC. Grand Rapids: Eerdmans; Leicester: Apollos, 2000.

Moore, Thomas S. "'To the End of the Earth': the Geographical and Ethnic Universalism of Acts 1:8 in Light of Isaianic Influence on Luke." *JETS* 40 (1997): 3,389–399.

Morris, Leon. *The Epistle to the Romans*. PNTC. Grand Rapids: Eerdmans; Leicester: InterVarsity Press, 1988.

———. *The Gospel According to Matthew*. PNTC. Grand Rapids: Eerdmans; Leicester: InterVarsity Press, 1992.

Mounce, Robert H. *Romans*. NAC 27. Nashville: Broadman & Holman Publishers, 1995.

———. *The Book of Revelation*. NICNT. Grand Rapids & Cambridge: Eerdmans, 1997.

Mounce, William D. *Pastoral Epistles*. WBC 46. Dallas: Word, Incorporated, 2000.

———. *Biblical Greek: A Compact Guide*. Grand Rapids: Zondervan, 2011.

Murphy, Roland. E. *Proverbs*. WBC 22. Dallas: Word, Incorporated, 1998.

Nadella, Raj. *Dialogue Not Dogma: Many Voices in the Luke*. London & New York: T&T Clark, 2011.

Najman, Hindy. "The Symbolic Significance of Writing in Ancient Judaism." Pages 139–173 in *The Idea of Biblical Interpretation: Essays in Honor of*

James L. Kugel. Edited by Hindy Najman and Judith H. Newma. Leiden & Boston: Brill, 2004.
———. *Past Renewals: Interpretative Authority, Renewed Revelation, and the Quest for Perfection in Jewish Antiquity*. Leiden & Boston: Brill, 2010.
Neagoe, Alexandru. *The Trial of the Gospel: An Apologetic Reading of Luke's Trial Narratives*. Cambridge: Cambridge University Press, 2004.
Newman, Barclay M., Jr. *A Concise Greek-English Dictionary of the New Testament*. Stuttgart: Deutsche Bibelgesellschaft & United Bible Societies, 1993.
Newman, Barclay M., Jr., and Philip C. Stine. *A Jeremiah*. UBS Handbook Series. New York: United Bible Societies, 2003.
Newman, Barclay M., Jr., and Eugene Albert Nida. *A Handbook on the Acts of the Apostles*. UBS Handbook Series. New York: United Bible Societies, 1972.
Newman, Barclay M., Jr., and Philip C. Stine. *A Handbook on the Gospel of Matthew*. UBS Handbook Series. New York: United Bible Societies, 1992.
Nolland, John. *Luke 18:35–24:53*. WBC 35C. Dallas: Word, Incorporated, 1998.
———. *The Matthew: A Commentary on the Greek Text*. NIGTC. Grand Rapids: Eerdmans; Carlisle: The Paternoster Press, 2005.
Noth, Martin. *Numbers*. Philadelphia: The Westminster Press, 1968.
O'Brien, Peter T. *The Letter to the Hebrews*. PNTC. Grand Rapids & Nottingham: Eerdmans, 2010.
———. *The Epistle to the Philippians: A Commentary on the Greek Text*. NIGTC. Grand Rapids: Eerdmans, 1991.
O'Brien, Mark A. *The Deuteronomistic History Hypothesis: A Reassessment*. Göttingen: Vandenhoeck & Ruprecht, 1989.
O'Reilly, Leo. *Word and Sign in the Acts of the Apostles: A Study in Lucan Theology*. Rome: Editrice Pontificia Università Gregoriana, 1987.
Osborn, Noel. D., and Howard A. Hatton. *A Handbook on Exodus*. UBS Handbook Series. New York: United Bible Societies, 1999.
Osborne, Grant R. *Revelation*. BECNT. Grand Rapids: Baker Academic, 2002.
Oswalt, John N. *The Book of Isaiah, Chapters 40–66*. NICOT. Grand Rapids: Eerdmans Publishing Co. Kindle Edition, 1998.
Palmisano, Maria Carmela. "La testimonianza nella successione profetica in 2 Re 2, 1–18." *Bogoslovni vestnik* 79 (2019): 1,83–92.
Parsenios, George L. *First, Second and Third John*. PCNT. Grand Rapids: Baker Academic, 2014.
———. *Rhetoric and Drama in the Johannine Lawsuit Motif*. Tubingen: Mohr Siebeck, 2010.
Patterson, Paige. *Revelation: An Exegetical and Theological Exposition of Holy Scripture*. NAC 39. Nashville: B&H Publishing Group, 2012.

Patterson, Richard D. *Nahum, Habakkuk, Zephaniah: An Exegetical Commentary*. Peabody: Biblical Studies Press, 2003.

Penney, John Michael. *The Missionary Emphasis of Lukan Pneumatology*. London & New York: Sheffield Academic Press, 1997.

Petersen, David L. *Haggai and Zechariah 1–8: A Commentary*. Philadelphia: The Westminster Press, 1984.

Peterson, David G. *The Acts of the Apostles*. PNTC. Grand Rapids & Nottingham: Eerdmans, 2009.

Petterson, Anthony R. *Haggai, Zechariah & Malachi*. AOTC. Downers Grove: InterVarsity Press, 2015.

Polhill, John B. *Acts*. NAC 26. Nashville: Broadman & Holman Publishers, 1992.

Pratt, Richard L., Jr. *I & II Corinthians*. HNTC 7. Nashville: Broadman & Holman Publishers, 2000.

Redding, Jonathan. D. "Violence." In *Lexham Theological Wordbook.* Edited by Douglas Mangum, Derek R. Brown, Rachel Klippenstein, and Rebekah Hurst. Bellingham: Lexham Press, 2014.

Reyburn, W. David. *A Handbook on the Book of Job*. New York: United Bible Societies, 1992.

Reyburn, W. David, and Euan McGregor Fry. *A Handbook on Lamentations*. UBS Handbook Series. New York: United Bible Societies, 1992.

———. *Genesis*. UBS Handbook Series. New York: United Bible Societies, 1998.

Richardson, Kurt A. *James*. NAC 36. Nashville: Broadman & Holman Publishers, 1997.

Ridderbos, Herman. *The John: A Theological Commentary*. Grand Rapids & Cambridge: Eerdmans, 1997.

Robertson, Archibald. T. *Word Pictures in the New Testament*. Nashville: Broadman Press, 1933.

Russell, Walt. "The Anointing with the Holy Spirit in Luke-Acts." *Trinity Journal* 7 (1986): 1,47–63.

Salters, Robert B. *Lamentations: A Critical and Exegetical Commentary*. ICC. London & New York: T&T Clark, 2011.

Sawyer, John F. A. *Isaiah: Volume 1, Chapters 1–32*. DSB. Louisville: Westminster John Knox Press, 1984.

Sawyer, John F. A. "שָׁוְא šāw' deceit." In: Ernst Jenni and Claus Westermann, eds. Theological Lexicon of the Old Testament, 1310–1311. Translated by M. E. Biddle. 3 vols. Peabody, Mass., 1997.

Schreiner, Thomas R. *1, 2 Peter, Jude*. NAC 37. Nashville: Broadman & Holman Publishers, 2003.

———. *Romans*. BECNT. Grand Rapids: Baker Book House, 2006.

Schröeder, Wilhelm J. *A Commentary on the Holy Scriptures: Deuteronomy*. Bellingham: Logos Bible Software, 2008.

Schultz, Carl. "1576 עוּד" Pages 648–50 in *Theological Wordbook of the Old Testament.* Edited by Robert. L. Harris, Gleason. L. Archer Jr. and Bruce. K. Waltke. Chicago: Moody Press, 1999.

Schwartz, Daniel R. "The End of the ΓH (Acts 1:8): Beginning or End of the Christian Vision?" *JBL* 105 (1986): 4,669–676.

Shelton, James B. *Mighty in Word and Deed: The Role of the Holy Spirit in Luke–Acts*. Eugene: Wipf and Stock Publishers, 2000.

Shepherd, William H., Jr. *The Narrative Function of the Holy Spirit as a Character in Luke-Acts*. Atlanta: Scholars Press, 1994.

Shulam, Joseph, and Hilary Le Cornu. *A Commentary on the Jewish Roots of Acts*. 2 vols. Clarksville: Lederer Books, 2009.

Simian-Yofre, Horacio. "ʿēḏ (עֵד) witness." *Theological Dictionary of the Old Testament* 10:495–517. Edited by Johannes Botterweck, Helmer Ringgren, Heinz-Joseph Fabry. Grand Rapids: Eerdmans, 1999.

Ska, Jean-Louis. *Introduction to Reading the Pentateuch*. Winona Lake: Eisenbrauns, 2006.

Smalley, Stephen S. *1, 2, 3 John*. WBC 51. Dallas: Word, Incorporated, 1989.

Smith, Billy K., and Frank S. Page. *Amos, Obadiah, Jonah*. NAC 19B. Nashville: Broadman & Holman Publishers, 1995.

Smith, Gary V. *Isaiah 1–39: An Exegetical and Theological Exposition of Holy Scripture*. NAC 15A. Nashville: Broadman & Holman Publishers, 2007.

———. *Isaiah 40–66: An Exegetical and Theological Exposition of Holy Scripture*. NAC 15B. Nashville: B&H Publishing Group, 2009.

Smith, James E. *The Minor Prophets*. OTS. Joplin: College Press, 1994.

Smith, Ralph L. *Micah–Malachi*. WBC 32. Dallas: Word, Incorporated, 1998.

Soards, Martin L. *The Speeches in Acts: Their Content, Context, and Concerns*. Louisville: Westminster/John Knox Press, 1994.

Sonnet, Jean-Pierre. *The Book within the Book: Writing in Deuteronomy.* Leiden, New York & Köln: Brill, 1997.

Spence-Jones, H. D. M, ed. *2 Kings*. TPC. London & New York: Funk & Wagnalls Company, 1909a.

———. *Nehemiah*. TPC. London & New York: Funk & Wagnalls Company, 1909b.

———. *Psalms*. Vol. II. TPC. London & New York: Funk & Wagnalls Company, 1909c.

———. *Isaiah*. Vol. I. TPC. London and New York: Funk & Wagnalls Company, 1910a.

———. *Numbers*. TPC. London and New York: Funk & Wagnalls Company, 1910b.

Spender, Robert D. "Salvation." Pages 1884–1885 in vol. 2 *BEB*. Edited by Walter A. Elwell and Barry J. Beitzel. Grand Rapids: Baker Book House, 1988.

Spicq, Ceslas, and James D. *Theological Lexicon of the New Testament*. Peabody: Hendrickson Publishers, 1994.

Stefanović, Ranko. *Revelation of Jesus Christ: Commentary on the Book of Revelation*. Berrien Springs: Andrews University Press, 2002.

Stegal, Thomas Lewis. *The Gospel of the Christ: A Biblical Response to the Crossless Gospel Regarding the Contents of Saving Faith*. Milwaukee: Grace Gospel Press, 2009.

Stein, Robert H. *Luke*. NAC 24. Nashville: Broadman & Holman Publishers, 1992.

Stevens, Gerald L. *New Testament Greek Intermediate: From Morphology to Translation*. Eugene: Cascade Books, 2008.

Strathmann, Hermannn. "Martus." Pages 474–514 in vol. 4 *Theological Dictionary of the New Testament*. Edited by Gerhard Kittel, Geoffrey W. Bromiley and Gerhard Friedrich. Grand Rapids: Eerdmans, 1964.

———. "mártys, martyréō, martyría, martyrion." Pages 564–571 in *The Theological Dictionary of the New Testament, Abridged in One Volume*. Edited by Gerhard Kittel, Geoffrey W. Bromiley and Gerhard Friedrich. Grand Rapids: Eerdmans, 1985.

Strong, James. *The New Strong's Dictionary of Hebrew and Greek Words*. Nashville: Thomas Nelson, 1996.

———. *Enhanced Strong's Lexicon*. Bellingham: Logos Bible Software, 2001.

Stronstad, Roger. *The Charismatic Theology of St. Luke*. Peabody: Hendrickson Publishers, 1984.

———. *The Prophethood of all Believers: A Study in Luke's Charismatic Theology*. Sheffield: Sheffield Academic Press, 2004.

Stuart, Douglas K. *Hosea–Jonah*. WBC. 31. Dallas: Word, Incorporated, 2002.

———. *Exodus*. NAC 2. Nashville: Broadman & Holman Publishers, 2006.

Stulman, Louis. *Jeremiah*. AOTC. Nashville: Abingdon Press, 2005.

Stoebe, Hans Joachim. "חָמָס ḥāmās violence." In: Ernst Jenni and Claus Westermann, eds. Theological Lexicon of the Old Testament, 438. Translated by M. E. Biddle. 3 vols. Peabody, Mass., 1997.

Swanson, James A. *Dictionary of Biblical Languages with Semantic Domains: Hebrew (Old Testament)*. Oak Harbor: Logos Research Systems, Inc, 1997a.

———. *Dictionary of Biblical Languages with Semantic Domains: Greek (New Testament)*. Oak Harbor: Logos Research Systems, Inc, 1997b.

Tate, Marvin E. *Psalms 51–100*. WBC 20. Dallas: Word, Incorporated, 1998.

Taylor, G. D. "testimony." In *Lexham Theological Wordbook*. Edited by Douglas Mangum, Derek R. Brown, Rachel Klippenstein and Rebekah Hurst. Bellingham: Lexham Press, 2014.

Taylor, Richard A., and E. Ray Clendenen. *Haggai, Malachi*. NAC 21A. Nashville: Broadman & Holman Publishers, 2004.

Tenney, Merrill C. “Topics from the John Part III: The Meaning of ‘Witness’ in John.” *BSac* 132 (1975): 229–241.

Thiselton, Anthony C. 2000. *The First Epistle to the Corinthians: A Commentary on the Greek Text*. NIGTC. Grand Rapids: Eerdmans.

Thayil, Philip. “Witness Mandate of the Risen Jesus in Luke 24,48 and Acts 1,8.” Ph.D. diss., Roma: Facultate Theologiae Pontificiae Universitatis Gregorianae. 1993.

Thompson, Alan J. *The Acts of the Risen Lord Jesus: Luke's Account of God's Unfolding Plan*. Downers Grove: InterVarsity Press, 2011.

Thompson, John A. “Expansions of the עד Root.” JSSR 10 (1965): 222–240.

———. *The Book of Jeremiah*. Grand Rapids: Eerdmans Publishing Co, 1980.

Tiede, David L. “Acts 1:6–8 and the Theo-Political Claims of Christian Witness.” *Word & Word* 1 (1981): 41–51.

Tripp, Jeffrey M. “Claiming Ignorance and Intimidating Witnesses: Reading John 9 in Greco-Roman Forensic Context.” *The Catholic Biblical Quarterly* 80 (2018): 470–490.

Trites, Alison A. *The New Testament Concept of Witness*. Cambridge: Cambridge University Press, 2004.

———. “Two Witness Motifs in Acts 1:8 and the Book of Acts.” *Themelios* 7 (1970): 17–22.

———. “Μάρτυς and Martyrdom in the Apocalypse: A Semantic Study.” *Novum Testamentum* 15 (1973): 72–80,

Troxel, Ronald L. *LXX-Isaiah as Translation and Interpretation: The Strategies of the Translator of the Septuagint of Isaiah*. Boston & Leiden: Brill, 2008.

Turner, Max. *Power from on High: The Spirit in Israel's Restoration and Witness in Luke-Acts*. Sheffield: Sheffield Academic Press, 2000.

———. “The Spirit of Prophecy as the Power of Israel's Restoration and Witness.” Pages 327–348 in *Witness to the Gospel: The Theology of Acts*. Edited by I. Howard Marshall and David Peterson. Grand Rapids: Eerdmans, 1998.

Vincent, Marvin Richardson. *Word Studies in the New Testament*. New York: Charles Scribner's Sons, 1887.

Vine, W. E., Merril F. Unger, and William White Jr. eds. Vine's Complete Expository Dictionary of Old and New Testament Words. Nashville: Thomas Nelson, 1996.

von Rad, Gerhard. *Old Testament Theology Volume II: The Theology of Israel's Prophetic Traditions*. Louisville: Westminster John Knox Press, 1965.

———. *Deuteronomy*. Philadelphia: The Westminster Press, 1966.

Wagner, J. Ross. *Heralds of the Good News: Isaiah and Paul in the Concert in the Letter to the Romans*. Boston & Leiden: Brill Academic Publishers, 2003.

Waltke, Bruce K. *A Commentary on Micah*. Grand Rapids: Eerdmans, 2007.

Wanamaker, Charles A. *The Epistles to the Thessalonians: A Commentary on the Greek Text*. NIGTC. Grand Rapids: Eerdmans, 1990.

Watts, John. D. W. *Isaiah 1–33*. WBC 24. Dallas: Word, Incorporated, 1998.

Wells, Bruce. *The Law of Testimony in the Pentateuchal Codes*. Wiesbaden: Otto Harrassowitz, 2004.

Westbrook, Raymond, and Bruce Wells. *Everyday Law in Biblical Israel: An Introduction*. Louisville: Westminster John Knox Press, 2009.

Westermann, Claus. *Isaiah 40–66*. Philadelphia: The Westminster Press, 1969.

Widder, Wendy L. *"To Teach" in Ancient Israel: A Cognitive Linguistic Study of a Biblical Hebrew Lexical Set*. Berlin & Boston: Walter de Gruyter GmbH, 2014.

Witherington, Ben, III. *The Acts of the Apostles: A Socio-Rhetorical Commentary*. Grand Rapids: Eerdmans, 1998.

Wright, N. T. *Surprised by Hope*. New York: HarperCollins Publishers, 2008.

Yarbrough, Robert W. *1, 2, and 3 John*. BECNT. Grand Rapids: Baker Academic, 2008.

Young, Edward. *The Book of Isaiah: Volume 2, Chapters 19–39*. Grand Rapids: Eerdmans Publishing Co, 1969.

Zodhiates, Spiros. *The Complete Word Study Dictionary: New Testament*. Chattanooga: AMG Publishers, 2000.

Zorn, Walter D. *Psalms, Vol 2*. CPNIV. Joplin: College Press Publishing Company, 2004.

Appendix

Table 5. Personal observing witnesses – OT

Text	Grammar	Witness	Context
Gen 31:50	*ʿēḏ* (עֵד), no verb; *bênî ûḇêneḵā* (בֵּינִי וּבֵינֶךָ)	YHWH	Social
Josh 24:22	*ʿēḏîm* (עֵדִים) + *bᵊ* (בְּ)	People	Covenantal
Ruth 4:9	*ʿēḏîm* (עֵדִים), no verb	People	Legal/covenantal
Ruth 4:10	*ʿēḏîm* (עֵדִים), no verb	People	Legal/covenantal
Ruth 4:11	*ʿēḏîm* (עֵדִים), no verb	People	Legal/covenantal
1 Sam 12:5	*ʿēḏ* (עֵד) + *bᵊ* (בְּ)	YHWH and Saul	Legal
Isa 8:2	*ʿûḏ* (עוּד) + *ʿēḏîm* (עֵדִים)	People	Covenantal
Jer 32:10	*ʿûḏ* (עוּד) + *ʿēḏîm* (עֵדִים)	People	Legal/covenantal
Jer 32:12	*ʿēḏîm* (עֵדִים)	People	Legal/covenantal
Jer 32:25	*ʿûḏ* (עוּד) + *ʿēḏîm* (עֵדִים)	People	Legal/covenantal
Jer 32:44	*ʿûḏ* (עוּד) + *ʿēḏîm* (עֵדִים)	People	Legal/covenantal
Jer 42:5	*ʿēḏ* (עֵד) + *lᵊ* (לְ) + *bᵊ* (בְּ)	YHWH	Covenantal
Amos 3:13	*ʿûḏ* (עוּד) + *bᵊ* (בְּ)	People	Covenantal

Table 6. Impersonal observing witnesses – OT

Text	Grammar	Witness	Context
Gen 31:44	*ʿēḏ* (עֵד) + *bênî ûḇêneḵā* (בֵּינִי וּבֵינֶךָ)	Covenant	Social
Gen 31:48	no verb; *ʿēḏ* (עֵד) + *bênî ûḇêneḵā* (בֵּינִי וּבֵינֶךָ)	Heap	Social
Gen 31:52	no verb; *ʿēḏ* (עֵד) and *ʿēḏāh* (עֵדָה)	Heap and pillar	Social
Deut 4:26	*ʿûḏ* (עוּד) + *bᵊ* (בְּ)	Heavens and earth	Covenantal
Deut 30:19	*ʿûḏ* (עוּד) + *bᵊ* (בְּ)	Heavens and earth	Covenantal
Deut 31:28	*ʿûḏ* (עוּד) + *bᵊ* (בְּ)	Heavens and earth	Covenantal
Josh 24:27	*ʿēḏāh* (עֵדָה) + *bᵊ* (בְּ)	Stone	Religious

Table 7. Personal testifying witnesses – OT

Text	Grammar	Witness	Context	Mode of witness	Means	Purpose
Gen 43:3	*ʿûḏ* (עוּד) + *b*ᵊ (בְּ)	Joseph	Social	About 1	Verbal	Warning
Exod 19:21	*ʿûḏ* (עוּד) + *b*ᵊ (בְּ)	YHWH	Covenantal	About 1	Verbal	Warning
Exod 19:23	*ʿûḏ* (עוּד) + *b*ᵊ (בְּ)	Moses	Covenantal	About 1	Verbal	Warning
Exod 20:16	*ʿēḏ* (עֵד) + *b*ᵊ (בְּ)	People	Legal	Against	Verbal	Guilt or innocence
Exod 21:29	*ʿûḏ* (עוּד) + *b*ᵊ (בְּ)	People	Legal	Against	Verbal	Guilt or innocence
Exod 23:1	*ʿēḏ* (עֵד)	People	Legal	Against	Verbal	Guilt or innocence
Lev 5:1	*ʿēḏ* (עֵד), no verb	People	Legal	Against	Verbal	Guilt or innocence
Num 5:13	*ʿēḏ* (עֵד) + *b*ᵊ (בְּ)	People	Legal	Against	Verbal	Guilt or innocence
Num 35:30	*ʿēḏ* (עֵד); *ʿēḏîm* (עֵדִים) + *b*ᵊ (בְּ)	People	Legal	Against	Verbal	Guilt or innocence
Deut 5:20	*ʿēḏ* (עֵד) + *b*ᵊ (בְּ)	People	Legal	Against	Verbal	Guilt or innocence
Deut 8:19	*ʿûḏ* (עוּד) + *b*ᵊ (בְּ)	Moses	Covenantal	About 1	Verbal	Warning
Deut 17:6	*ʿēḏîm* (עֵדִים)	People	Legal	Against	Verbal	Guilt or innocence
Deut 17:7	*ʿēḏîm* (עֵדִים)	People	Legal	Against	Verbal	Guilt or innocence
Deut 19:15	*ʿēḏ* (עֵד) + *b*ᵊ (בְּ); *ʿēḏîm* (עֵדִים)	People	Legal	Against	Verbal	Guilt or innocence
Deut 19:16	*ʿēḏ* (עֵד) + *b*ᵊ (בְּ)	People	Legal	Against	Verbal	Guilt or innocence
Deut 19:18	*ʿēḏ* (עֵד) + *b*ᵊ (בְּ)	People	Legal	Against	Verbal	Guilt or innocence
1 Sam 8:9	*ʿûḏ* (עוּד) + *b*ᵊ (בְּ)	People	Legal	About 1	Verbal	Warning
1 Kgs 2:42	*ʿûḏ* (עוּד) + *b*ᵊ (בְּ)	People	Social	About 1	Verbal	Warning

Text	Grammar	Witness	Context	Mode of witness	Means	Purpose
1 Kgs 21:10	*'ûḏ* (עוּד); no *bᵊ* (בְּ)	People	Legal	Against	Verbal	Guilt or innocence
1 Kgs 21:13	*'ûḏ* (עוּד); no *bᵊ* (בְּ)	People	Legal	Against	Verbal	Guilt or innocence
2 Kgs 17:13	*'ûḏ* (עוּד) + *bᵊ* (בְּ)	YHWH through prophets	Covenantal	About 3	Verbal	Warning
2 Kgs 17:15	*'ûḏ* (עוּד) + *bᵊ* (בְּ)	YHWH	Covenantal	About 3	Verbal	Warning
2 Chron 24:19	*'ûḏ* (עוּד) + *bᵊ* (בְּ)	People	Covenantal	About 3	Verbal	Warning
Neh 9:26	*'ûḏ* (עוּד) + *bᵊ* (בְּ)	Prophets	Covenantal	About 3	Verbal	Warning
Neh 9:29	*'ûḏ* (עוּד) + *bᵊ* (בְּ)	YHWH	Covenantal	About 3	Verbal	Warning
Neh 9:30	*'ûḏ* (עוּד) + *bᵊ* (בְּ)	YHWH's Spirit through prophets	Covenantal	About 3	Verbal	Warning
Neh 9:34	*'ûḏ* (עוּד) + *bᵊ* (בְּ)	YHWH	Covenantal	About 3	Verbal	Warning
Neh 13:15	*'ûḏ* (עוּד) + *bᵊ* (בְּ)	Nehemiah	Covenantal	About 3	Verbal	Warning
Neh 13:21	*'ûḏ* (עוּד) + *bᵊ* (בְּ)	Nehemiah	Covenantal	About 3	Verbal	Warning
Job 16:19	*'ēḏ* (עֵד)	YHWH	Covenantal	For	Verbal	Guilt or innocence
Job 29:11	*'ûḏ* (עוּד)	People	Difficult to identify	For	Verbal	Guilt or innocence
Ps 27:12	*'ēḏêy* (עֵדֵי) + *bᵊ* (בְּ)	People	Legal	Against	Verbal	Guilt or innocence
Ps 35:11	*'ēḏêy* (עֵדֵי)	People	Legal	Against	Verbal	Guilt or innocence
Ps 50:7	*'ûḏ* (עוּד) + *bᵊ* (בְּ)	YHWH	Covenantal	Against	Verbal	Guilt or innocence
Ps 81:8	*ûḏ* (עוּד) + *bᵊ* (בְּ)	YHWH	Covenantal	About 3	Verbal	Warning
Ps 89:37	*'ēḏ* (עֵד)	Difficult to identify				

Text	Grammar	Witness	Context	Mode of witness	Means	Purpose
Prov 6:19	*ʿēḏ* (עֵד)	People	Legal	Against	Verbal	Guilt or innocence
Prov 12:17	*ʿēḏ* (עֵד)	People	Legal	Against	Verbal	Guilt or innocence
Prov 14:5	*ʿēḏ* (עֵד)	People	Legal	For and against	Verbal	Guilt or innocence
Prov 14:25	*ʿēḏ* (עֵד)	People	Legal	For	Verbal	Guilt or innocence
Prov 19:5	*ʿēḏ* (עֵד)	People	Legal	Against	Verbal	Guilt or innocence
Prov 19:9	*ʿēḏ* (עֵד)	People	Legal	Against	Verbal	Guilt or innocence
Prov 19:28	*ʿēḏ* (עֵד)	People	Legal	Against	Verbal	Guilt or innocence
Prov 21:28	*ʿēḏ* (עֵד)	People	Legal	Against	Verbal	Guilt or innocence
Prov 24:28	*ʿēḏ* (עֵד) + $b^{ə}$ (בְּ)	People	Legal	Against	Verbal	Guilt or innocence
Prov 25:18	*ʿēḏ* (עֵד) + $b^{ə}$ (בְּ)	People	Legal	Against	Verbal	Guilt or innocence
Isa 43:9	*ʿēḏêhem* (עֵדֵיהֶם)	People	Covenantal	For	Verbal	Guilt or innocence
Isa 43:10	*ʿēḏêy* (עֵדַי)	People	Covenantal	Against	Verbal	Guilt or innocence
Isa 43:12	*ʿēḏêy* (עֵדַי)	People	Covenantal	Against	Verbal	Guilt or innocence
Isa 44:8	*ʿēḏêy* (עֵדַי)	People	Covenantal	Against	Verbal	Guilt or innocence
Isa 44:9	*ʿēḏêhem* (עֵדֵיהֶם)	People	Covenantal	For	Verbal	Guilt or innocence
Isa 55:4	*ʿēḏ* (עֵד) + $l^{ə}$ (לְ)	One man, people, nation?	Covenantal	About 4	?	To establish truth
Jer 6:10	*ûḏ* (עוּד)	Jeremiah	Covenantal	About 3	Verbal	Warning
Jer 11:7	*ûḏ* (עוּד) + $b^{ə}$ (בְּ)	YHWH	Covenantal	About 3	Verbal	Warning

Text	Grammar	Witness	Context	Mode of witness	Means	Purpose
Jer 29:23	*ʿēḏ* (עֵד), no verb	YHWH	Covenantal	About 3	Verbal	Warning
Jer 42:19	*ûḏ* (עוּד) + *bᵊ* (בְּ)	Jeremiah	Covenantal	About 1	Verbal	Warning
Lam 2:13[1]	*ûḏ* (עוּד) + *lᵊ* (לְ)	Jeremiah	Covenantal	Difficult to identify		
Mic 1:2	*ʿēḏ* (עֵד) + *lᵊ* (לְ) + *bᵊ* (בְּ)	YHWH	Covenantal	Against	Verbal	Guilt or innocence
Zech 3:6	*ûḏ* (עוּד) + *bᵊ* (בְּ)	Angel	Covenantal	About 1	Verbal	Warning
Mal 2:14	*ûḏ* (עוּד) + *bᵊ* (בְּ)	YHWH	Legal	Against	Verbal	Guilt or innocence
Mal 3:5	*ûḏ* (עוּד) + *bᵊ* (בְּ)	YHWH	Covenantal	Against	Verbal	Guilt or innocence

1. It is difficult to determine type and mode of witnessing in this verse as Simian-Yofre (*"ʿēḏ (עֵד) witness", TDOT* 10: 510) says, since the meaning of verb *ûḏ* (עוּד) in this verse does not seem to fit any of the suggested semantic group for *ʿûḏ* Hiphil (order/command, forbid, admonish, threaten, reproach).

Table 8. Impersonal testifying witnesses – OT

Text	Grammar	Witness	Context	Mode of witness	Means	Purpose
Gen 21:30	*ʿēḏāh* (עֵדָה)	Seven lambs	Social	About 4	Seven lambs	To confirm
Exod 22:12 (13)	*ʿēḏ* (עֵד)	Remains of the animal	Legal	For	Material evidence	Guilt or innocence
Deut 31:19	*ʿēḏ* (עֵד) + *bᵊ* (בְּ)	Song	Covenantal	About 1	Verbal / material evidence	Warning
Deut 31:21	*ʿēḏ* (עֵד) + *lᵊpānâw* (לְפָנָיו)	Song	Covenantal	About 1	Verbal / material evidence	Warning
Deut 31:26	*ʿēḏ* (עֵד) + *bᵊ* (בְּ)	Book of Law (Torah)	Covenantal	About 1	Material evidence	Warning
Deut 32:46	*ʿûḏ* (עוּד) + *bᵊ* (בְּ)	Song	Covenantal	About 1	Verbal / material evidence	Warning
Josh 22:27	*ʿēḏ* (עֵד) + *bênênû ûḇênêḵem* (וּבֵינֵיכֶם בֵּינֵינוּ); no verb	Altar	Covenantal	About 2	Material evidence	Reminder
Josh 22:28	*ʿēḏ* (עֵד) + *bênênû ûḇênêḵem* (וּבֵינֵיכֶם בֵּינֵינוּ); no verb	Altar	Covenantal	About 2	Material evidence	Reminder
Josh 22:34	*ʿēḏ* (עֵד) + *bênōṯênû* (בֵּינֹתֵינוּ); no verb	Altar	Covenantal	About 2	Material evidence	Reminder
Ruth 4:7	*tᵊʿûḏāh* (תְּעוּדָה); no verb	Sandal	Legal	About 5	Material evidence	To confirm
Job 10:17	*ʿêḏêḵā* (עֵדֶיךָ)	Job's suffering	Covenantal	Against	Physical condition	Guilt or innocence
Job 16:8	*ʿēḏ* (עֵד) + *bᵊ* (בְּ)	Job's suffering	Covenantal	Against	Physical condition	Guilt or innocence

Text	Grammar	Witness	Context	Mode of witness	Means	Purpose
Ps 89:37[2]	*ʿēḏ* (עֵד)	Difficult to identify	Covenantal	Difficult to identify		
Isa 8:16	*tᵊʿûḏāh* (תְּעוּדָה)	Written prophetic message	Covenantal	About 1	Verbal or written evidence	Warning / admonishment
Isa 8:20	*tᵊʿûḏāh* (תְּעוּדָה)	Written prophetic message	Covenantal	About 1	Evidence in written form	Warning / admonishment
Isa 19:20	*ʿēḏ* (עֵד)	Altar and pillar	Covenantal	About 2	Material evidence	Reminder
Isa 30:8	*ʿēḏ* (עֵד)	Scroll	Covenantal	About 1	Evidence in written form	Warning
Witness about 3						

Object	Hebrew word	Text
Torah	*ʿēḏûṯ* (עֵדוּת)	Exod 25:16, 21; 30:6, 36; 31:18; 32:15; 34:29; 40:20; Lev 16:13; Num 17:4, 10
	ʿēḏōṯ (עֵדֹת)	Deut 4:45; 6:17, 20; 31:26; Ps 25:10; 78:56; 93:5; 99:7; 119:2, 22, 24, 46, 59, 79, 95, 119, 125, 138, 146, 152, 167, 168, 132:12
	ʿēḏôṯ (עֵדְוֹת)	1 Kgs 2:3; 2 Kgs 17:15; 23:3; 1 Chron 29:19; 2 Chron 34:31; Neh 9:34; Ps 119:14, 31, 36, 99, 111, 129, 144, 157; Jer 44:23
	ʿēḏûṯ (עֵדוּת)	2 Kgs 11:12; 2 Chron 23:11; Ps 19:7; 78:5; 81:5; 119:88; 122:4
Ark	*ʿēḏûṯ* (עֵדוּת)	Exod 16:34; 25:22; 26:33, 34; 27:21; 30:6, 26; 31:7; 39:35; 40:3, 5, 21; Num 4:5; 7:89; Josh 4:16
Veil	*ʿēḏûṯ* (עֵדוּת)	Lev 24:3
Tabernacle	*ʿēḏûṯ* (עֵדוּת)	Exod 38:21; Num 1:50, 53; 9:15; 10:11; 17:7, 8; 18:2; 2 Chron 24:6

2. Since the identity of witness in Psalms 89 is so debatable, I did not discuss it.

Table 9. Personal observing witnesses – NT

Text	Grammar	Witness	Context
Matt 18:16	mártys	People	Religious or legal?[3]
Luke 24:48	mártys	People	Religious
John 3:28	martyréō	John the Baptist	Religious
Acts 10:39	mártys	Apostles	Religious
Acts 10:41	mártys	Apostles	Religious
Acts 22:15	mártys	Paul	Religious
Acts 26:16	mártys	Paul	Religious
Rom 1:9	mártys	God	Religious
2 Cor 1:23	mártys	God	Religious
Phil 1:8	mártys	God	Religious
1 Thess 2:5	mártys	God	Religious
1 Thess 2:10	mártys	People and God	Religious
1 Tim 6:12	mártys	People	Religious

3. According to Darrell L. Bock (*BECNT, 64*), witnesses from Matthew 18:16 are witnesses in a legal sense, because they help establish facts objectively through verifiable observation. Witnesses who do the same in the context of the church (2 Cor 13:1 and 1 Tim 5:19) he also considers as witnesses in a legal sense. But here we make distinction between *context* in which testifying may appear (legal, religious, etc.), and sense in which witnesses' function. That means that witness in legal sense can function in both legal and religious context.

Table 10. Personal testifying witnesses – NT

Text	Grammar	Witness	Context	Mode of witness	Means	Purpose
Matt 8:4	*martýrion*	People	Covenantal	About 3	Physical evidence	To confirm / establish the truth
Matt 10:18	*martýrion*	Disciples	Legal	About 4	Verbal	To confirm / establish the truth
Matt 15:19	*pseudomartyría*	People	Legal	against	Verbal	Guilt or innocence
Matt 19:18	*pseudomartyréō*	People	Legal	against	Verbal	Guilt or innocence
Matt 23:31	*martyréō*	People	Covenantal	against	Verbal + making of the tombs	Guilt or innocence
Matt 24:14	*martýrion*	People	Covenantal	About 4	Verbal	To confirm / establish the truth
Matt 26:59	*pseudomartyría*	People	Legal	against	Verbal	Guilt or innocence
Matt 26:60	*pseudómartys*	People	Legal	against	Verbal	Guilt or innocence
Matt 26:62	*katamartyréō*	People	Legal	against	Verbal	Guilt or innocence
Matt 26:65	*mártys*	People	Legal	against	Verbal	Guilt or innocence
Matt 27:13	*katamartyréō*	People	Legal	against	Verbal	Guilt or innocence
Mark 1:44	*martýrion*	People	Covenantal	About 3	Physical evidence	To confirm / establish the truth
Mark 6:11	*martýrion*	Disciples	Covenantal	About 2	Symbolic act	Announcement of future judgment
Mark 10:19	*pseudomartyréō*	People	Legal	Against	Verbal	Guilt or innocence
Mark 13:9	*martýrion*	Disciples	Legal	About 4	Verbal	To confirm / establish the truth
Mark 14:55	*martyría*	Men	Legal	Against	Verbal	Guilt or innocence
Mark 14:56	*pseudomartyréō*	People	Legal	Against	Verbal	Guilt or innocence

Text	Grammar	Witness	Context	Mode of witness	Means	Purpose
Mark 14:56	*martyría*	People	Legal	Against	Verbal	Guilt or innocence
Mark 14:57	*pseudomartyréō*	People	Legal	Against	Verbal	Guilt or innocence
Mark 14:59	*martyría*	People	Legal	Against	Verbal	Guilt or innocence
Mark 14:60	*katamartyréō*	People	Legal	Against	Verbal	Guilt or innocence
Mark 14:63	*mártys*	People	Legal	Against	Verbal	Guilt or innocence
Luke 4:22	*martyréō*	People	Social? Or covenantal?	About 3	Verbal	To confirm / establish the truth
Luke 5:14	*martýrion*	People	Covenantal	About 3	Physical evidence	To confirm / establish the truth
Luke 9:5	*martýrion*	Disciples	Covenantal	About 2	Symbolic act	Announcement of future judgment
Luke 11:48	*mártys*	People	Covenantal	Against	Making of the tombs[4]	Guilt or innocence
Luke 16:28	*diamartýromai*	People	Covenantal	About 2	Difficult to identify	Warning to change
Luke 18:20	*pseudomartyréō*	People	Legal	Against	Verbal	Guilt or innocence
Luke 21:13	*martýrion*	Disciples	Legal	About 4	Verbal	To confirm / establish the truth
Luke 22:71	*martyría*	People	Legal	Against	Verbal	Guilt or innocence
John 1:7	*martyría*	John the Baptist	Religious	About 4	Verbal	To confirm / establish the truth
John 1:7	*martyréō*	John the Baptist	Religious	About 4	Verbal	To confirm / establish the truth
John 1:8	*martyréō*	John the Baptist	Religious	About 4	Verbal	To confirm / establish the truth

4. Unlike in Matthew 23:31, there is no verbal testimony.

Text	Grammar	Witness	Context	Mode of witness	Means	Purpose
John 1:15	*martyréō*	John the Baptist	Religious	About 4	Verbal	To confirm / establish the truth
John 1:19	*martyría*	John the Baptist	Religious	About 4	Verbal	To confirm / establish the truth
John 1:32	*martyréō*	John the Baptist	Religious	About 3	Verbal	To confirm / establish the truth
John 1:34	*martyréō*	John the Baptist	Religious	About 4	Verbal	To confirm / establish the truth
John 2:25	*martyréō*	About men	No specific reference	About 3	Revelation or prophetic knowledge	To confirm / establish the truth
John 3:11	*martyréō*	Jesus	Religious	About 3	Verbal	To confirm / establish the truth
John 3:11	*martyría*	Jesus	Religious	About 3	Verbal	To confirm / establish the truth
John 3:26	*martyréō*	John's disciples	Religious	About 4	Verbal	To confirm / establish the truth
John 3:32	*martyréō*	Author of John's gospel	Religious	About 3	Verbal	To confirm / establish the truth
John 3:32	*martyría*	Author of John's gospel	Religious	About 3	Verbal	To confirm / establish the truth
John 3:33	*martyría*	Author of John's gospel	Religious	About 3	Verbal	To confirm / establish the truth
John 4:39	*martyréō*	Woman	Religious	About 3	Verbal	To confirm / establish the truth
John 4:44	*martyréō*	Jesus	Religious	About 3	Verbal	To confirm / establish the truth
John 5:31	*martyréō*	Jesus	Religious	About 4	Various	To confirm / establish the truth
John 5:31	*martyría*	Jesus	Religious	About 4	Various	To confirm / establish the truth
John 5:32	*martyréō*	Father	Religious	About 4	Various	To confirm / establish the truth
John 5:32	*martyría*	Father	Religious	About 4	Various	To confirm / establish the truth

Text	Grammar	Witness	Context	Mode of witness	Means	Purpose
John 5:33	*martyréō*	John the Baptist	Religious	About 4	Verbal	To confirm / establish the truth
John 5:34	*martyría*	Jesus	Religious	About 4	Verbal	To confirm / establish the truth
John 5:36	*martyréō*	Jesus	Religious	About 4	Works	To confirm / establish the truth
John 5:36	*martyría*	Jesus	Religious	About 4	Works	To confirm / establish the truth
John 5:37	*martyréō*	Father	Religious	About 4	Various	To confirm / establish the truth
John 7:7	*martyréō*	Jesus	Religious	Against	Verbal	To confirm / establish the truth
John 8:13	*martyría*	Jesus	Religious	About 4	Verbal[5]	To confirm / establish the truth
John 8:13	*martyréō*	Jesus	Religious	About 4	Verbal	To confirm / establish the truth
John 8:14	*martyréō*	Jesus	Religious	About 4	Verbal	To confirm / establish the truth
John 8:14	*martyría*	Jesus	Religious	About 4	Verbal	To confirm / establish the truth
John 8:17	*martyría*	People	Legal	For or against	Verbal	Guilt or innocence
John 8:18	*martyréō*	Jesus and Father	Religious	About 4	Various	To confirm / establish the truth
John 10:25	*martyréō*	Jesus	Religious	About 4	Works	To confirm / establish the truth
John 12:17	*martyréō*	People	Religious	About 3	Verbal	To confirm / establish the truth
John 13:21	*martyréō*	Jesus	Religious	About 2	Verbal	Announcement of future judgment
John 15:26	*martyréō*	Holy Spirit	Religious	About 4	Various	To confirm / establish the truth

5. For John 8:13 and 14 verbally, but potential other means of testimony are included.

Text	Grammar	Witness	Context	Mode of witness	Means	Purpose
John 15:27	*martyréō*	Disciples	Religious	About 4	Various	To confirm / establish the truth
John 18:23	*martyréō*	Jesus	Legal	Against	Verbal	Guilt or innocence
John 18:37	*martyréō*	Jesus	Legal	About 4	Verbal	To confirm / establish the truth
John 19:35	*martyréō*	Author of the gospel	Religious	About 3	Verbal and / or in written form	To confirm / establish the truth
John 19:35	*martyría*	Author of the gospel	Religious	About 3	Verbal and / or in written form	To confirm / establish the truth
John 21:24	*martyréō*	Author of the gospel	Religious	About 3	Written form	To confirm / establish the truth
John 21:24	*martyría*	Disciples	Religious	About 3	Written form	To confirm / establish the truth
Acts 1:8	*mártys*	Disciples	Religious	About 4	Various	To confirm / establish the truth
Acts 1:22	*mártys*	Apostles	Religious	About 3	Various	To confirm / establish the truth
Acts 2:32	*mártys*	Apostles	Religious	About 4	Verbal	To confirm / establish the truth
Acts 2:40	*diamartýromai*	Peter	Religious	About 2	Verbal	Warning to change
Acts 3:15	*mártys*	Peter & John	Religious	About 4	Verbal	To confirm / establish the truth
Acts 4:33	*martýrion*	Apostles	Religious	About 3	Verbal + possible miracles	To confirm / establish the truth
Acts 5:32	*mártys*	Apostles and Holy Spirit	Religious	About 4	Verbal + difficult to identity for the HS	To confirm / establish the truth
Acts 6:3	*martyréō*	People	Social / Religious	About 3	Verbal	To confirm / establish the truth
Acts 6:13	*mártys*	People	Legal	Against	Verbal	Guilt or innocence

Text	Grammar	Witness	Context	Mode of witness	Means	Purpose
Acts 7:58	*mártys*	People	Legal	Against	Verbal	Guilt or innocence
Acts 8:25	*diamartýromai*	Peter & John	Religious	About 4	Verbal	To confirm / establish the truth
Acts 10:22	*martyréō*	People	Social / Religious	About 3	Verbal	To confirm / establish the truth
Acts 10:42	*diamartýromai*	Disciples	Religious	About 4	Verbal	To confirm / establish the truth
Acts 13:22	*martyréō*	God	Covenantal	About 2	Verbal	Admonishment
Acts 13:31	*mártys*	Apostles	Religious	About 4	Verbal	To confirm / establish the truth
Acts 14:3	*martyréō*	God	Religious	About 4	Miracles	To confirm / establish the truth
Acts 15:8	*martyréō*	God	Religious	About 3	Spirit's baptism	To confirm / establish the truth
Acts 16:2	*martyréō*	Men	Social / Religious	About 3	Verbal	To confirm / establish the truth
Acts 18:5	*diamartýromai*	Paul	Religious	About 4	Verbal	To confirm / establish the truth
Acts 20:21	*diamartýromai*	Paul	Religious	About 2	Verbal	Warning to change
Acts 20:23	*diamartýromai*	Holy Spirit	Religious	About 1	Difficult to identify	Announcing in advance
Acts 20:24	*diamartýromai*	Paul	Religious	About 4	Verbal	To confirm / establish the truth
Acts 20:26	*martýromai*	Paul	Religious	About 3	Verbal	To confirm / establish the truth
Acts 22:5	*martyréō*	High priest and elders	Legal	For	Verbal	Guilt or innocence
Acts 22:12	*martyréō*	Men	Social / Religious	About 3	Verbal	Reputation
Acts 22:18	*martyría*	Paul	Religious	About 4	Verbal	To confirm / establish the truth

Text	**Grammar**	**Witness**	**Context**	**Mode of witness**	**Means**	**Purpose**
Acts 22:20	*mártys*	Stephen	Legal	Against	Verbal	To confirm / establish the truth
Acts 23:11	*martyréō*	Paul	Religious	About 4	Verbal	To confirm / establish the truth
Acts 23:11	*diamartýromai*	Paul	Religious	About 4	Verbal	To confirm / establish the truth
Acts 26:5	*martyréō*	Jewish people	Legal	For	Verbal	To confirm / establish the truth
Acts 26:22	*martýromai*	Paul	Legal	About 4	Verbal	To confirm / establish the truth
Acts 28:23	*diamartýromai*	Paul	Religious	About 4	Verbal	To confirm / establish the truth
Rom 8:16	*symmartyréō*	Holy Spirit + human spirit	Religious	For	Difficult to identify	Guilt or innocence
Rom 9:1	*symmartyréō*	Holy Spirit + conscience	Religious	For	Difficult to identify	Guilt or innocence
Rom 10:2	*martyréō*	Paul	Religious	About 3	Written form (epistle)	To confirm / establish the truth
1 Cor 1:6	*martýrion*	Difficult to identify	Religious	About 4	Difficult to identify	To confirm / establish the truth
1 Cor 2:1	*martýrion*	Paul	Religious	About 4	Verbal	To confirm / establish the truth
1 Cor 15:15	*martyréō*	Paul and others	Religious	About 4	Verbal	To confirm / establish the truth
1 Cor 15:15	*pseudomartyréō*	Paul and others	Religious	About 4	Verbal	To confirm / establish the truth
2 Cor 8:3	*martyréō*	Paul	Religious	About 3	Written form (epistle)	To confirm / establish the truth
2 Cor 13:1	*mártys*	People	Religious	Against	Verbal	To confirm / establish the truth
Gal 4:15	*martyréō*	Paul	Religious	About 3	Written form (epistle)	To confirm / establish the truth
Gal 5:3	*martýromai*	Paul	Religious	About 1	Written form (epistle)	Future warning
Eph 4:17	*martýromai*	Paul	Religious	About 2	Written form (epistle)	Warning or admonishment

Text	**Grammar**	**Witness**	**Context**	**Mode of witness**	**Means**	**Purpose**
Col 4:13	*martyréō*	Paul	Religious	About 3	Written form (epistle)	To confirm / establish the truth
1 Thess 2:12	*martýromai*	Paul and his coworkers	Religious	About 2	Verbal	Admonishment
1 Thess 4:6	*diamartýromai*	Paul and his coworkers	Religious	About 2	Verbal	Warning
2 Thess 1:10	*martýrion*	Paul and his coworkers	Religious	About 4	Verbal	To confirm / establish the truth
1 Tim 2:6	*martýrion*	Jesus / People	Religious	About 4	Jesus's life / verbal	To confirm / establish the truth
1 Tim 3:7	*martyría*	People	Social	About 3	Verbal	To confirm / establish the truth
1 Tim 5:10	*martyréō*	People	Religious	About 3	Verbal	To confirm / establish the truth
1 Tim 5:19	*mártys*	People	Religious	Against	Verbal	To confirm / establish the truth
1 Tim 5:21	*diamartýromai*	Paul	Religious	About 2	Written form (epistle)	Admonishment
1 Tim 6:13	*martyréō*	Jesus	Religious	About 4	Jesus's life / verbal	To confirm / establish the truth
2 Tim 1:8	*martýrion*	Timothy	Religious	About 4	Verbal	To confirm / establish the truth
2 Tim 2:2	*mártys*	People	Religious	About 4	Probably verbally	To establish the truth
2 Tim 2:14	*diamartýromai*	Paul	Religious	About 2	Verbal	Warning to change
2 Tim 4:1	*diamartýromai*	Paul	Religious	About 2	Written form (epistle)	Admonishment
Tit 1:13	*martyría*	Crete's prophet	Social	About 3	Verbal / written form	To confirm / establish the truth
Heb 2:4	*synepimartyréō*	God	Religious	About 4	Signs, wonders, miracles, gifts of the Spirit	To confirm / establish the truth

Text	Grammar	Witness	Context	Mode of witness	Means	Purpose
Heb 2:6	*diamartýromai*	Someone (God or humans)	Religious	About 3	Scripture	To confirm / establish the truth
Heb 3:5	*martýrion*	Moses	Religious	About 1	Verbal / Scripture	Announcing in advance
Heb 10:15	*martyréō*	Holy Spirit	Religious	About 1	Scripture	Announcing in advance
Heb 10:28	*mártys*	People	Legal	Against	Verbal	To confirm / establish the truth
Heb 11:2	*martyréō*	God	Religious	About 3	Scripture	To confirm / establish the truth
Heb 11:4	*martyréō*	God	Religious	About 3	Scripture	To confirm / establish the truth
Heb 11:5	*martyréō*	God	Religious	About 3	Scripture	To confirm / establish the truth
Heb 11:39	*martyréō*	God	Religious	About 3	Scripture	To confirm / establish the truth
Heb 12:1	*mártys*	People from chap 11	Religious	About 4	Scripture	To confirm / establish the truth
1 Pet 1:11	*promartýromai*	Prophets	Covenantal	About 1	Verbal / Scripture	Announcing in advance
1 Pet 5:1	*mártys*	Peter	Religious	About 3	Verbal / written form	To confirm / establish the truth
1 Pet 5:12	*epimartyréō*	Peter	Religious	About 2	Written form	Admonishment
1 John 1:2	*martyréō*	John and others	Religious	About 4	Verbal / written form	To confirm / establish the truth
1 John 4:14	*martyréō*	John and others	Religious	About 4	Verbal / written form	To confirm / establish the truth
1 John 5:6	*martyréō*	Holy Spirit	Religious	About 4	Difficult to identify	To confirm / establish the truth
1 John 5:7	*martyréō*	Spirit, water and blood	Religious	About 4	Difficult to identify	To confirm / establish the truth
1 John 5:9	*martyría*	People	Religious	About 4	Probably verbal	To confirm / establish the truth
1 John 5:9	*martyría*	God	Religious	About 4	Difficult to identify	To confirm / establish the truth

Text	Grammar	Witness	Context	Mode of witness	Means	Purpose
1 John 5:9	*martyréō*	God	Religious	About 4	Difficult to identify	To confirm / establish the truth
1 John 5:10	*martyréō*	God	Religious	About 4	Difficult to identify	To confirm / establish the truth
1 John 5:10	*martyría*	God	Religious	About 4	Difficult to identify	To confirm / establish the truth
1 John 5:11	*martyría*	God	Religious	About 4	Difficult to identify	To confirm / establish the truth
3 John 1:3	*martyréō*	Believers	Religious	About 3	Verbal	To confirm / establish the truth
3 John 1:6	*martyréō*	Believers	Religious	About 3	Verbal	To confirm / establish the truth
3 John 1:12	*martyréō*	People and Truth	Religious	About 3	Verbal, but not specified	To confirm / establish the truth
3 John 1:12	*martyréō*	John and others	Religious	About 3	Verbal + epistle?	To confirm / establish the truth
3 John 1:12	*martyría*	John and others	Religious	About 3	Verbal + epistle?	To confirm / establish the truth
Rev 1:2	*martyréō*	John	Religious	About 4	The book of Revelation	To confirm / establish the truth
Rev 1:2	*martyría*	Jesus Christ	Religious	About 4	Jesus's life and teaching	To confirm / establish the truth
Rev 1:5	*mártys*	Jesus Christ	Religious	About 4	Jesus's life and teaching	To confirm / establish the truth
Rev 1:9	*martyría*	Jesus Christ	Religious	About 4	Jesus's life and teaching	To confirm / establish the truth
Rev 2:13	*mártys*	Antipas	Religious	About 4	Verbal + his life	To confirm / establish the truth
Rev 3:14	*mártys*	Jesus Christ	Religious	About 4	Jesus's life and teaching	To confirm / establish the truth
Rev 6:9	*martyría*	Believers	Religious	About 4	Difficult to identify[6]	To confirm / establish the truth

6. By difficult to identify in Revelation 6:9; 12:17; 19:10 and 20:4 we mean that testimony of these subjects is verbal, but probably includes some other aspects that are not explicitly identified, but we can presuppose them.

Text	Grammar	Witness	Context	Mode of witness	Means	Purpose
Rev 11:3	*mártys*	Two witnesses	Religious	Difficult to identify		
Rev 11:7	*martyría*	Two witnesses	Religious	Difficult to identify		
Rev 12:11	*martyría*	Believers	Religious	About 4	Verbal	To confirm / establish the truth
Rev 12:17	*martyría*	Believers	Religious	About 4	Difficult to identify	To confirm / establish the truth
Rev 17:6	*mártys*	People	Religious	About 4	Verbal + their life	To confirm / establish the truth
Rev 19:10	*martyría 2x*	Believers + angel	Religious	About 4	Difficult to identify	To confirm / establish the truth
Rev 20:4	*martyría*	Believers	Religious	About 4	Difficult to identify	To confirm / establish the truth
Rev 22:16	*martyréō*	Angel	Religious	About 4	The book of Revelation	To confirm / establish the truth
Rev 22:18	*martyréō*	Jesus	Religious	About 1	The book of Revelation	Future warning
Rev 22:20	*martyréō*	Jesus	Religious	About 1[7]	The book of Revelation	Announcing in advance

Table 11. Impersonal testifying witnesses – NT

Text	Grammar	Witness	Context	Mode of witness	Means	Purpose
John 5:39	*martyréō*	Scripture	Religious	About 2	Scripture	To confirm / establish the truth

7. If this *martyréō* refers to the book of Revelation, then it belongs into category about 4. If refers to the warning given in 22:18, then it belongs into category about 1.

Acts 7:44	*martýrion*	Tabernacle	Religious	About 1	Tabernacle	To be a visible constant reminder of certain truths
Acts 10:43	*martyréō*	Scripture	Religious	About 2	Scripture	To confirm / establish the truth
Rom 2:15	*symmartyréō*	Conscience	Religious	For / against	Difficult to identify	Guilt or innocence
Rom 3:21	*martyréō*	Law and Prophets / Scripture	Religious	About 2	Scripture	To confirm / establish the truth
Rom 8:16	*symmartyréō*	Human spirit	Religious	For / against	Difficult to identify	Guilt or innocence
Rom 9:1	*symmartyréō*	Paul's conscience	Religious	For / against	Difficult to identify	Guilt or innocence
2 Cor 1:12	*martýrion*	Conscience	Religious	For / against	Difficult to identify	Guilt or innocence
Heb 7:8	*martyréō*	Scripture	Religious	About 2	Scripture	To confirm / establish the truth
Heb 7:17	*martyréō*	Scripture	Religious	About 2	Scripture	To confirm / establish the truth
Jas 5:3	*martýrion*	Corrosion	Religious	For / against	Difficult to identify	Guilt or innocence
1 John 5:7	*martyréō*	Water and blood	Religious	About 3	Difficult to identify	To be a constant reminder
Rev 15:5	*martýrion*	Tabernacle	Religious	Difficult to identify	Difficult to identify	Difficult to identify

Langham Literature, with its publishing work, is a ministry of Langham Partnership.

Langham Partnership is a global fellowship working in pursuit of the vision God entrusted to its founder John Stott –

> ***to facilitate the growth of the church in maturity and Christ-likeness through raising the standards of biblical preaching and teaching.***

Our vision is to see churches in the Majority World equipped for mission and growing to maturity in Christ through the ministry of pastors and leaders who believe, teach and live by the word of God.

Our mission is to strengthen the ministry of the word of God through:

- nurturing national movements for biblical preaching
- fostering the creation and distribution of evangelical literature
- enhancing evangelical theological education

especially in countries where churches are under-resourced.

Our ministry

Langham Preaching partners with national leaders to nurture indigenous biblical preaching movements for pastors and lay preachers all around the world. With the support of a team of trainers from many countries, a multi-level programme of seminars provides practical training, and is followed by a programme for training local facilitators. Local preachers' groups and national and regional networks ensure continuity and ongoing development, seeking to build vigorous movements committed to Bible exposition.

Langham Literature provides Majority World preachers, scholars and seminary libraries with evangelical books and electronic resources through publishing and distribution, grants and discounts. The programme also fosters the creation of indigenous evangelical books in many languages, through writer's grants, strengthening local evangelical publishing houses, and investment in major regional literature projects, such as one volume Bible commentaries like the *Africa Bible Commentary* and the *South Asia Bible Commentary*.

Langham Scholars provides financial support for evangelical doctoral students from the Majority World so that, when they return home, they may train pastors and other Christian leaders with sound, biblical and theological teaching. This programme equips those who equip others. Langham Scholars also works in partnership with Majority World seminaries in strengthening evangelical theological education. A growing number of Langham Scholars study in high quality doctoral programmes in the Majority World itself. As well as teaching the next generation of pastors, graduated Langham Scholars exercise significant influence through their writing and leadership.

To learn more about Langham Partnership and the work we do visit **langham.org**

Milton Keynes UK
Ingram Content Group UK Ltd.
UKHW020653040424
440620UK00014B/628

9 781839 737916